Opportunities and Challenges of Business 5.0 in Emerging Markets

Sumesh Dadwal
Northumbria University, UK

Pawan Kumar
Lovely Professional University, India

Rajesh Verma
Lovely Professional University, India

Gursimranjit Singh
Lovely Professional University, India

IGI Global
PUBLISHER of TIMELY KNOWLEDGE

A volume in the Advances in Business Strategy and Competitive Advantage (ABSCA) Book Series

Published in the United States of America by
IGI Global
Business Science Reference (an imprint of IGI Global)
701 E. Chocolate Avenue
Hershey PA, USA 17033
Tel: 717-533-8845
Fax: 717-533-8661
E-mail: cust@igi-global.com
Web site: http://www.igi-global.com

Library of Congress Cataloging-in-Publication Data

Names: Dadwal, Sumesh, 1973- editor.
Title: Opportunities and challenges of business 5.0 in emerging markets / Sumesh Dadwal, Pawan Kumar, Rajesh Verma, and Gursimranjit Singh, editors.
Description: Hershey, PA : Business Science Reference, [2023] | Includes bibliographical references and index. | Summary: "This book provides insights on the impact of industrial revolution 5.0 offering various research perspectives on the implication of transformation of revolution from 1.0 to 5.0 for readers in both industry and academia to assist them in teaching and training the next generation leaders through universities and corporate training"-- Provided by publisher.
Identifiers: LCCN 2022039895 (print) | LCCN 2022039896 (ebook) | ISBN 9781668464038 (hardback) | ISBN 9781668464045 (paperback) | ISBN 9781668464052 (ebook)
Subjects: LCSH: Industries--Developing countries. | Economic development--Developing countries.
Classification: LCC HC59.7 .O52935 2023 (print) | LCC HC59.7 (ebook) | DDC 338.09172/4--dc23/eng/20220831
LC record available at https://lccn.loc.gov/2022039895
LC ebook record available at https://lccn.loc.gov/2022039896

This book is published in the IGI Global book series Advances in Business Strategy and Competitive Advantage (ABSCA) (ISSN: 2327-3429; eISSN: 2327-3437)

British Cataloguing in Publication Data
A Cataloguing in Publication record for this book is available from the British Library.

For electronic access to this publication, please contact: eresources@igi-global.com.

Advances in Business Strategy and Competitive Advantage (ABSCA) Book Series

Patricia Ordóñez de Pablos
Universidad de Oviedo, Spain

ISSN:2327-3429
EISSN:2327-3437

Mission

Business entities are constantly seeking new ways through which to gain advantage over their competitors and strengthen their position within the business environment. With competition at an all-time high due to technological advancements allowing for competition on a global scale, firms continue to seek new ways through which to improve and strengthen their business processes, procedures, and profitability.

The **Advances in Business Strategy and Competitive Advantage (ABSCA) Book Series** is a timely series responding to the high demand for state-of-the-art research on how business strategies are created, implemented and re-designed to meet the demands of globalized competitive markets. With a focus on local and global challenges, business opportunities and the needs of society, the **ABSCA** encourages scientific discourse on doing business and managing information technologies for the creation of sustainable competitive advantage.

Coverage

- Customer-Orientation Strategy
- Joint Ventures
- Entrepreneurship & Innovation
- Strategic Alliances
- Small and Medium Enterprises
- Economies of Scale
- Core Competencies
- Strategy Performance Management
- Resource-Based Competition
- Balanced Scorecard

IGI Global is currently accepting manuscripts for publication within this series. To submit a proposal for a volume in this series, please contact our Acquisition Editors at Acquisitions@igi-global.com or visit: http://www.igi-global.com/publish/.

The Advances in Business Strategy and Competitive Advantage (ABSCA) Book Series (ISSN 2327-3429) is published by IGI Global, 701 E. Chocolate Avenue, Hershey, PA 17033-1240, USA, www.igi-global.com. This series is composed of titles available for purchase individually; each title is edited to be contextually exclusive from any other title within the series. For pricing and ordering information please visit http://www.igi-global.com/book-series/advances-business-strategy-competitive-advantage/73672. Postmaster: Send all address changes to above address.

Titles in this Series

For a list of additional titles in this series, please visit: www.igi-global.com/book-series/advances-business-strategy-competitive-advantage/73672

Challenges and Opportunities for Aviation Stakeholders in a Post-Pandemic World
Salim Kurnaz (Suleyman Demirel University, Turkey & Kazimiero Simonaviciaus University, Lithuania) Antonio Rodrigues (Instituto Superior de Gestão, Portugal) and Dorothea Bowyer (Western Sydney University, Australia)
Business Science Reference • © 2023 • 314pp • H/C (ISBN: 9781668468357) • US $260.00

Handbook of Research on Business Model Innovation Through Disruption and Digitalization
Erik Stavnsager Rasmussen (University of Southern Denmark, Denmark) and Nicolaj Hannesbo Petersen (UCL University College, Denmark)
Business Science Reference • © 2023 • 425pp • H/C (ISBN: 9781668448953) • US $325.00

Strategic Management and International Business Policies for Maintaining Competitive Advantage
Ailson J. De Moraes (Royal Holloway University of London, UK)
Business Science Reference • © 2023 • 340pp • H/C (ISBN: 9781668468456) • US $250.00

Rapid Innovation and Development in the Global Cannabis Market
Pfano Mashau (University of KwaZulu-Natal, South Africa) and Jabulani Nyawo (University of KwaZulu-Natal, South Africa)
Business Science Reference • © 2023 • 352pp • H/C (ISBN: 9781668463468) • US $250.00

Analyzing International Business Operations in the Post-Pandemic Era
Bryan Christiansen (The Christiansen Foundation, USA) and John D. Branch (University of Michigan, USA)
Business Science Reference • © 2023 • 309pp • H/C (ISBN: 9781668437490) • US $250.00

Intellectual Capital as a Precursor to Sustainable Corporate Social Responsibility
Bartolomé Marco-Lajara (University of Alicante, Spain) Patrocinio Zaragoza-Sáez (University of Alicante, Spain) and Javier Martínez-Falcó (University of Alicante, Spain & Stellenbosch University, South Africa)
Business Science Reference • © 2023 • 291pp • H/C (ISBN: 9781668468159) • US $250.00

The Transformation of Global Trade in a New World
Bartolomé Marco-Lajara (University of Alicante, Spain) Ahu Coşkun Özer (Marmara University, Turkey) and Javier Martínez Falcó (University of Alicante, Spain)
Business Science Reference • © 2023 • 308pp • H/C (ISBN: 9781668459508) • US $250.00

IGI Global
PUBLISHER of TIMELY KNOWLEDGE

701 East Chocolate Avenue, Hershey, PA 17033, USA
Tel: 717-533-8845 x100 • Fax: 717-533-8661
E-Mail: cust@igi-global.com • www.igi-global.com

Editorial Advisory Board

Table of Contents

Detailed Table of Contents

In Industry 5.0, entrepreneurship, an entrepreneurial mindset, and entrepreneurial skills will be crucial for success. Entrepreneurs will be able to identify opportunities and innovate, adapting to changes in the market and leveraging new technologies to create value and drive growth. This will require a deep understanding of the industry, strong leadership, and the ability to work collaboratively with others to achieve shared goals. Ultimately, entrepreneurs who can excel in this environment will be well-positioned to thrive and succeed in the era of industry 5.0. The purpose of this chapter is to go through the major entrepreneurship theories that can potentially alter the growth and performances of start-ups and micro, small, and medium-sized enterprises (MSMEs). This chapter also proposed a framework that synthesizes all relevant entrepreneurial dimensions and theories including entrepreneurial mindset, entrepreneurial marketing, entrepreneurial orientation, entrepreneurial ecosystem, entrepreneurial intention and entrepreneurial education in the era of Industry 5.0

Technology is a science to solve a problem or to simplify the tasks carried out by humans. Technology in simple words is a way of doing things. There are various benefits associated, such as communication; technologies have not only helped in making the world a smaller place by bringing people closer together, but also widened the gap between people which has come to be known as 'virtual distance.' Since the first Industrial Revolution, manufacturing has seen advancements making manufacturing processes more sophisticated and sustainable to control effectively. Industry 5.0 enables people to transition from mass manufacturing to mass personalization as people now demand the human touch of mass personalization.

The research discusses several theoretical and practical aspects related to international business and the main tendencies the international business development in the post-pandemic period. Attention is paid to the main principles of international trade, activities of the Transnational Corporations, e-commerce, leading commercial companies in the world, cryptocurrency, and the future of international business based on industry 5.0. In this regard, there are discussed several aspects related to the possible impact of Industry 5.0 on international economic relations and business.

Industry 4.0 and Industry 5.0 are changing the ways business operations are carried out. The organisations across the sectors have been facing challenges in managing the supply chain and logistics across the UK and the world. Industrial Revolution 4.0 has led to the use of digital technologies to improve the efficiency and effectiveness of supply chain processes, such as demand forecasting, inventory management, transportation routing, and order fulfillment. Industry 5.0 is an attempt to humanise the use of potential new-age digital technologies that can for sustainable supply chain management and logistics in the FMCG and automotive sectors. The chapter also advises operation and strategic managers to follow the latest trends in these technologies and follow some short-, medium-, and long-term strategies to gain a competitive edge in the market.

Industry 5.0 may assist businesses to become more constructive and competitive in the global economy in the Fifith Industrial Revolution era. Therefore, a critical review of prior literature is presented in this paper to examine how industry 5.0 will impact supply chain operations within the agricultural sector. Additionally, it examines influencing factors, challenges, stakeholder roles, and recommendations identified from the literature. Industry 5.0 has multiple benefits for the agri-food sector such as improved agility, responsiveness, efficiency, productivity, precise decision-making, as well as cost-effectiveness.

Industry 5.0 requires an organisation to maintain supply chain sustainability by using environmental, social, and governance (ESG) initiatives, thus avoiding social, environmental, ethical, or other risks.

impact of India's trade share with the East and Southeast Asian countries on the economic growth rate. The results show that the India-ASEAN trade share has a significant positive impact on India's GDP growth rate in the long run, while the impact is found significantly negative in the short run. The results raise the need for greater regional trade openness, hence highlighting the policy lessons and potential challenges on the part of the Free Trade Agreement (FTA) with the ASEAN countries. India tends to gain in the short run if it extends the scope of FTA from trade in goods to trade in services.

This study aims to develop a scale to measure the readiness of export-oriented e-commerce for companies that will face the reality of moving from Industry 4.0 to Industry 5.0. This scale, which aims to determine companies' readiness level for e-export, is the first attempt in this sense in the literature. Several steps have been followed in the scale development process. First, a draft scale consisting of 69 items and different dimensions is created based on the literature review. Next, a focus group study is conducted, and expert opinions are collected. After testing the content validity and running the factor analysis, eight factors comprising 28 positive and negative statements were formed. Validity and reliability analyses of the pilot study, including 50 companies, show that the scale is applicable. These results show that human resources and management functions, whose essential element is human, at the Industry 5.0 level; it also demonstrates its compatibility with processes, most of which are machine and digital, and the importance of cooperation between them.

Viewed as entrepreneurship in financial solutions and based on blockchain technology, cryptocurrency is the most recent development in digital currency and is gaining substantial interest in recent years. The intersection of Industry 5.0 and cryptocurrency adoption could lead to new business models and revenue streams, with cryptocurrency potentially being used as a secure and efficient means of payment in Industry 5.0. This study aims to explore cryptocurrency adoption literature using a thorough literature review and bibliometric analysis. The study primarily used the Scopus database for the extraction of relevant literature. The literature review and bibliometric analysis have been done both quantitatively and qualitatively based on various techniques such as network analysis (keyword Co-occurrence analysis) and science mapping techniques. i.e., word cloud and word tree map with the help of tools such as VOSviewer, and R Studio Biblioshiny. The study reveals that the use of cryptocurrency in Industry 5.0 has the potential to improve efficiency, security, and transparency.

Foreword

Dear Readers,

Thank you for your decision to enter a new chapter of your life, which came with the first line of this book. Don´t look at it with fear, but joy and curiosity which will help you to find meaningfullness of your life the same I found on the shore of a blue ocean called Wasteless World that is being built with Industry 5.0.

My name is Michael Rada; I am a human.

At the same time, I am the Founder of Industry 5.0 which was launched on December 1, 2015, by an article named "Industry 5.0 From Virtual to Physical."

The authors who contribute to the creation of this book are members of the audience of the Lovely Professional University, who have learned about the existence of Industry 5.0, its origin, and principles from me, during one of the webinars that took place not only there, but already on more than 350 universities, colleges, high schools, and schools all over the globe.

It was not the money that attracts them, it was not the celebrity status, it was not the order to take part. No. It was their own will to know more and learn, the same WILL that attracts you to this book.

Industry 5.0 is the first industrial evolution ever led by man (human) and if anyone will call it the 5th industrial revolution, he does not speak the truth. Industry 5.0 recognizes and prevents five categories of waste: physical, social, urban, process waste, and wasting of time.

There is only one person responsible for your future. You meet the person every time when you stand in front of a mirror, or you look at the reflection of your face on a water surface.

Every single one of us was born as human. We will leave this world as human. It is our highest honor and obligation to live as human as well. I believe I will see you soon on the construction site of the Wasteless World that we build for all.

We are living in the waste age, and it is the only age in mankind's history that we can influence by our own actions. Calling for change is worthless if we do not change ourselves first.

Industry 5.0 was born just 75 km from the location where 93 years earlier the word "robot" sounds for the first time in the work of Karel Čapek in his screenplay R.U.R. Not to lose the humanity we should keep technology as a tool, but never let it to rule our lives.

Have a nice time free of waste and wasting in all its forms, stay safe and free.

Michael Rada
IBSCD Lab s.r.o., Czech Republic

Preface

Emerging technologies are changing the ways countries, industries, organisations and individuals are affected. The technologies such as artificial intelligence, robotics, drone technologies, 3-D technologies, blockchain technologies, big data analytics etc are offering a range of opportunities and challenges. The success of industries and organisation depends upon how well they can proactively embed and utilise those technologies to achieve efficiency, effectiveness and sustainability. Whereas the business 4.0 philosophy has an emphasis on the technologies aspects such as, the use of big data, the internet of things (IoT), artificial intelligence (AI) and has ignored, human, environmental societal and, and sustainability effects. Business 5.0 philosophy humanises, socialises and sustainablises the use of technologies in the business. This brings a holistic approach to an agile and human-centric, society and sustainability in business operations and practices.

This book aims to present the state and future outlook of Business 5.0 and it aims to achieve comprehensive insights on the implications of Business 5.0 in emerging markets. As the world of business has witnessed and experienced a huge transformation due to the growth of the industrial revolution. This book will provide insights to marketers, entrepreneurs, and practitioners to unravel the opportunities and mitigate the challenges in the competitive world. It seems that when we were finally understanding, implementing and getting used to industry 4.0, the term Industry or Business 5.0 started appearing on the horizon. Business or Industry 5.0 takes the human touch, innovation and efficiency a step further in creating turnaround strategies and practices in the organisations. This transformation has brought many questions to the minds of stakeholders like When did this happen? Why so fast? We may even think: "We have not even finished adapting to Industry 4.0! Are we ready to land our business landscapes fit in Industry 5.0?" This book deliberates a deep dive to explore the prospects and challenges of Industry 5.0.

While working as academicians, and researchers,s the editors of this book noticed the enlarging gap between traditional business practices and emerging methods and processes. This book is an attempt to bridge the gap.

AUDIENCE

This book is written from the perspective of learners, practitioners, educationist, researchers, and policymakers of organisations in a range of industries and national economies . The book would be more apt for the business management disciplines i.e., accounting; business and management history; corporate governance, responsibility and business ethics; critical management studies; entrepreneurship and small business management; human resource management; international business; leadership; management education; marketing; operations & information management; organizational studies; public &non-profit management; research methods; strategic management; technology and innovation management, MBA and Ph.D. programmes.

he readers will gain varied research perspectives on the implication of the transformation of revolution from 1.0 to 5.0. The book will provide sufficient literature to the researchers. Moreover, experts in the field of marketing, and management science have been always been interested the importance of revolution from 1.0 to 5.0 while taking into consideration the various challenges and opportunities in context to emerging markets, however, there is a dearth of literature available in this area so this book is an attempt to provide insights for both industry and academia to assist them in teaching and training the next generation leaders through universities and corporate training.

KEY FEATURES OF THE BOOK

The book brings in ideas from east and west in one place and is useful in light of UNO s Millennium Development Goals, in particular of least developed countries, developing countries and emerging markets. The book has scholarship blended with contemporary applications, examples and managerial orientation. The book has a focus to humanise technological applications in a green and sustainable way.

ORGANISATION OF THIS BOOK

The book has covered a range of functional areas of the organsations. An integrated approach is taken to organise this book from top to lower levers of organisations. The book sets the scene on Industry 5, followed by an entrepreneurial mindset, this further lead to operational action in various functional areas like HRM, Operations, Marketing, Supply chain management etc. Though each chapter on its own has independent standing and can be read for its relevance to relevant functional areas, however the coordinated approach for organising each chapter ensures smooth flow, coherence, depth of k knowledge and enjoyment in reading the book.

This book is organised into 15 chapters. A brief description of the chapter is given in the next sections.

Chapter 1. An Overview and Synthesis of Entrepreneurial Theories for Start-Ups and MSMEs in the Era of Industry 5.0

The rise of entrepreneurship as its own academic literature, separating themselves from management theories has led to countless new theories conceptualizing practical entrepreneurial activities, all for the sake of supporting the growth of entrepreneurs, which in turn promotes economic development and diversification. The purpose of this paper to go through the major entrepreneurship theories that can potentially alter the growth and performances of start-ups and Micro, Small and Medium-sized enterprises (MSMEs). This paper also proposed a framework that synthesizes all relevant entrepreneurial dimensions and theories including Entrepreneurial Mindset, Entrepreneurial Marketing, Entrepreneurial Orientation, Entrepreneurial Ecosystem, Entrepreneurial Intention and Entrepreneurial Education.

Chapter 2. Man, Mind, and Machine: A Vulnerable Symbiosis

Technology is a science to solve a problem or to simplify the tasks carried out by humans. Technology in simple words is a way of doing things. There are various benefits associated such as communication technologies have not only helped in making the world a smaller place by bringing people closer together but also widened the gap between people which has come to be known as 'virtual distance'. Since the first Industrial Revolution, manufacturing has seen advancements making manufacturing processes more sophisticated and sustainable to control effectively. Industry 5.0 enables people to transition from mass manufacturing to mass personalization as people now demand the human touch of mass personalization. Mass customization is becoming a reality, and needs fast-moving advancements in manufacturing processes, system digitization, and intelligence. This article addresses a few important dimensions of technology such as technology being treated as human extension, coevolution between humans and technology, human dependence on technology and vulnerability of mankind due to technology.

Chapter 3. Developing a Model for the Adoption of Industrial Revolution 4.0 Among Malaysian Manufacturing SMEs for Sustainable Growth

Industry 4.0 was introduced in Germany, pursuing the idea of creating smart factories so that emerging technologies such as the Internet of Things, cloud computing, robotics systems, virtual reality, big data analytics, and additive manufacturing could produce human–equipment interfaces and cyber-physical systems that generate environmental, economic, and socially sustainable manufacturing systems (Kamble et al., 2018). Therefore, this study effort to evolve a model for the adoption of the 4IR among Malaysian manufacturing SMEs for sustainable growth. This study proposed a research model based on the theory of innovation diffusion (DOI) and TOE. The result of this study can contribute to the realization of the Industry4WRD policy. The model itself can provide guidance to industry and policymakers to promote SME growth. The study is expected to benefit regulators and the business ecosystem in understanding the challenges of implementing 4IR in Malaysia and, most importantly, for them to formulate intervention processes and programs for successful adoption.

Chapter 4. Artificial Intelligence and Value Creation at the Crossroads of Industry 5.0: A Bibliometric and Content Analysis Discourse

Today, businesses are evolving in an extremely competitive market. As we enter Industry 5.0, modern firms' dynamic business processes need a technological boost to enable them to create and deliver superior value while keeping humans at the core of the business processes. One such technology is artificial intelligence, which is creating innovative options for businesses to further add consumers value by taking a dynamic approach, mitigating unpredictability, and augmenting cost-effectiveness. Development of AI as a business engine to generate value is advancing and is an alternative for many different industries to explore. As humans need to work in tandem with machines in Industry 5.0 to create customer value, a new term referred to as HCAI- human-centred AI has emerged. Bibliometric data of documents published between 1994 and 2022 were analyzed, and the most cited articles in SCOPUS journals were examined for content analysis to decipher how this new-age AI is aiding businesses to create and deliver superior value and thus leading to sustainable competitive advantage.

Chapter 5. Analyzing International Business Operations in the Post-Pandemic Era Taking Into Account Industry 5.0 Realities

The research discusses several theoretical and practical aspects related to International Business and the main tendencies the International Business development in the post-pandemic period. Attention is paid to the main principles of International Trade, activities of the Trans National Corporations, e-commerce, leading commercial companies in the world, cryptocurrency, and the future of International business based on industry 5.0. In this regard, there are discussed several aspects related to the possible impact of Industry 5.0 on International economic relations and business.

Chapter 6. A Cross-Sector Comparison of Industry 5.0: Digital Technologies in Supply Chain Management of FMCG and the Automotive Sector

Industry 4.0 and industry 5.0 are changing the ways business operations are carried out. The organisations across the sectors have been facing challenges in managing the supply chain and logistics across the UK and the world. Industrial Revolution 4 has led to the use of digital technologies to improve the efficiency and effectiveness of supply chain processes, such as demand forecasting, inventory management, transportation routing, and order fulfillment. Industry 5.0 is an attempt to humanised the use of potential new-age digital technologies that can for sustainable supply chain management and logistics in the FMCG and automotive sectors. The Chapter also advises operation and strategic managers to follow the latest trends in these technologies and follow some short-, medium- and long-term strategies to gain a competitive edge in the market.

Chapter 7. Investigating the Factors, Challenges, and Role of Stakeholders in Implementing Industry 5.0 and Its Impact on Supply Chain Operations: A Study of the Global Agri-Food Supply Chain

Industry 5.0 may assist businesses to become more constructive and competitive in the global economy in the Fifith Industrial Revolution era. Therefore, a critical review of prior literature is presented in this paper to examine how industry 5.0 will impact supply chain operations within the agricultural sector. additionally, it examines influencing factors, challenges, stakeholder roles, and recommendations identified from the literature. Industry 5 .0 has multiple benefits for the agri-food sector such as improved agility, responsiveness, efficiency, productivity, precise decision-making as well as cost-effectiveness.

Chapter 8. Industry 5.0 and Environmental, Social, and Governance Initiatives in Supply Chain Sustainability: A Study of the European Fast Fashion Industry

Industry 5.0 requires an organisation to maintain supply chain sustainability by using Environmental, Social and Governance (ESG) initiatives thus avoiding social, environmental ethical or other risks. This chapter explores the factors, processes, and impacts of the use of ESG framework in sustainability throughout supply chain management The development of this research shows the European fast fashion industry, which had invested in ESG initiatives to maintain sustainability standards across their whole supply chain operations of the European Fast fashion market.

Chapter 9. Journey of HR From Industry 1.0 to 5.0 and the Road Ahead

Industrial revolutions are rapidly transforming the industry and redefining the world of work. Human resource management has also been affected largely by the industrial revolutions. So far four industrial revolutions have been implemented. Each revolution came with certain positive and negative changes. Such as, prior to the 18th century, HR was called personnel management and was limited to hiring, training and administration. However, with these major revolutions in the industry, HR is now considered a business driver and includes a wide range of strategic activities. Now, discussions are going about the fifth industrial revolution. This chapter aims to elaborate on the changing business scenario, transition from industry 1.0 to 5.0 and its impact on HR. It is expected that the outcomes of the chapter will help the researchers and practitioners in understanding the technicalities and issues involved.

Chapter 10. Hospitality Industry 5.0: Emerging Trends in Guest Perception and Experiences

The hospitality sector 5.0 aspires to integrate technology into service marketing, human resource management, and hotel operations in order to give visitors a seamless and useful customer experience. Artificial intelligence, the Internet of Things, blockchain technology, collaborative robots, chatbots and sensors, contactless automation, mobile technology, augmented reality, virtual reality, big data, cloud computing, 6 G and beyond, as well as machine-to-machine communication, are all part of the hospitality industry 5.0. When automated technologies, intelligent devices, and intelligent systems converge with human intelligence, hospitality 5.0 will be born. It aims to provide additional contributions to the field of technological use in hospitality and tourism and thereby offers a strong knowledge base. Therefore, all people involved in the study's implementation might benefit from its findings in order to better understand and meet the requirements and expectations of both customers and employees through the use of technology.

Chapter 11. India-ASEAN Economic Engagement: Challenges and New Lessons for Trade Integration

Look East Policy of India serves as instrumental in engaging the East and Southeast Asian countries in a wider perspective since 1991. The trade share of India with these countries which also makes noted trade bloc namely the Association of Southeast Asian Nations (ASEAN) has grown significantly because of pro-trade policies in the last decades. In this backdrop, this paper presents the facts on the dynamic impact of India's trade share with the East and Southeast Asian countries on the economic growth rate. The results show that the India-ASEAN trade share has a significant positive impact on India's GDP growth rate in the long run, while the impact is found significantly negative in the short run. The results raise the need for greater regional trade openness, hence highlighting the policy lessons and potential challenges on the part of the Free Trade Agreement (FTA) with the ASEAN countries. India tends to gain in the short run if it extends the scope of FTA from trade in goods to trade in services.

Chapter 12. Readiness for Export-Oriented E-Commerce in the Age of Industrial Transformation

This chapters aims to develop a scale to measure the readiness of export-oriented e-commerce for companies that will face the reality of moving from Industry 4.0 to Industry 5.0. This scale, which aims to determine companies' readiness level for e-export, is the first attempt in this sense in the literature. Several steps have been followed in the scale development process. First, a draft scale consisting of 69 items and different dimensions is created based on the literature review. Next, a focus group study is conducted, and expert opinions are collected. After testing the content validity and running the factor analysis, eight factors comprising 28 positive and negative statements were formed. Validity and reliability analyses of the pilot study, including 50 companies, show that the scale is applicable. These results show that human resources and management functions, whose essential element is human, at the Industry 5.0 level; It also demonstrates its compatibility with processes, most of which are machine and digital, and the importance of cooperation between them.

Chapter 13. Cryptocurrency Adoption in the Era of Industry 5.0: Opportunities, Challenges, and the Intellectual Landscape – SLR and Bibliometric Analysis

Viewed as entrepreneurship in financial solutions and based on blockchain technology, cryptocurrency is the most recent development in digital currency and is gaining substantial interest in recent years. The intersection of Industry 5.0 and cryptocurrency adoption could lead to new business models and revenue streams, with cryptocurrency potentially being used as a secure and efficient means of payment in Industry 5.0. This study aims to explore cryptocurrency adoption literature using a thorough literature review and bibliometric analysis. The study primarily used the Scopus database for the extraction of relevant literature. The literature review and bibliometric analysis have been done both quantitatively and qualitatively based on various techniques such as network analysis (keyword Co-occurrence analysis) and science mapping techniques. i.e., word cloud and word tree map with the help of tools such as VOSviewer, and R Studio Biblioshiny. The study reveals that the use of cryptocurrency in Industry 5.0 has the potential to improve efficiency, security, and transparency.

Chapter 14. Significance of Blockchain Technology in the Indian Banking Sector: ATheoretical Perspective

At the time when Liberalization was introduced, many changes have taken place in banking world since then. Although in India, Block chain technology is still at its initial stage but many of the banks are using this technology to make their tasks easier. However, Block chain technology is the remarkable progress in the area of banking as with the help of it, banks are able to provide quick, accurate and quality service to their customers. With the inception of Blockchain technology, banking sector has transformed as many of its processes have become transparent, safe and efficient as well. Under blockchain technology, Banking systems are basically based on one point data base which has dispersed ledger for reducing cyber crimes. The present chapter tries to depict the same with the help of a descriptive analysis of increase in incentives and also the inconvenience faced by banks in recent times after the introduction of block chain technology. .

Chapter 15. IoT Privacy by Design

The integration of the Internet-of-Things and IoT devices and architectures with various aspects of modern society is observed at the beginning of this chapter. Discussion is made on the numerous applications of IoT and accompanying technologies, such as Big Data. The taxonomy of IoT privacy issues is analysed, from its personal applications to business environments, the public sector and social services. The threats and challenges of IoT are also observed, alongside related ethical and sociological issues and concerns under the scope of privacy. The analysis is then shifted towards the legislative and regulatory frameworks under which IoT currently operates as the current approaches to resolving its privacy issues and the extent to which they are successful. Finally, attention is placed on the future of privacy and security in IoT, with a discussion on the evolution of privacy-enhancing methodologies and potential risks and threats.

CONCLUSION

This book is unique in its own sense as the book has taken an integrated approach to link industry 4. To Industry 5. The book has contributed to literature research in the areas of Entrepreneurship, Industry 5 and business models, The use of Artificial intelligence (AI) big data, social media, Blockchain, Internet of Things (IoT) etc in the era of globalisasation for good chemistry among use of technology, organisations, human, society and sustainability etc.

FEEDBACK

The editor and the contributors look forward to readers' constructive feedback. Please let us know your view of this book and suggested areas of improvement by emailing the editors.

Sumesh Dadwal
Northumbria University, UK

Pawan Kumar
Lovely Professional University, India

Rajesh Verma
Lovely Professional University, India

Gursimranjit Singh
Lovely Professional University, India

Acknowledgment

With great pleasure, we want to thank everyone, who has directly or indirectly supported us on this book project.

Prayers to almighty God, for granting us thoughts and wisdom to mediate this project as editors.

This book required contributions from several authors. We are very grateful to each author as they have given their valuable time to share their knowledge with our readers by writing and revising and thus produced good quality pieces of work.

Deepest gratitude to the reviewers as well as our Editorial board team members, for their insights, critiques, and constructive feedback thus resulting in the successful publication of this book

We would be grateful to the previous researchers and writers whose sources have been used and cited in this book.

We are grateful to our colleagues and people in our network for their constructive feedback and motivation.

We are very lucky and so thankful to our family members for letting us snatch time from them and use it on this project. Thank you so much!

Last but not least, we want to convey my thanks to IGI publishing and their team for their continued support and for shaping this project into a final work.

Thanks to the readers as the main motivation for this book.

Regards,

Sumesh Dadwal, Pawan Kumar, Rajesh Verma, Gursimranjit Singh

Chapter 1
An Overview and Synthesis of Entrepreneurial Theories for Start-Ups and MSMEs in the Era of Industry 5.0

Mohammad Izzuddin Mohammed Jamil
https://orcid.org/0000-0002-2967-7870
Universiti Brunei Darussalam, Brunei

ABSTRACT

In Industry 5.0, entrepreneurship, an entrepreneurial mindset, and entrepreneurial skills will be crucial for success. Entrepreneurs will be able to identify opportunities and innovate, adapting to changes in the market and leveraging new technologies to create value and drive growth. This will require a deep understanding of the industry, strong leadership, and the ability to work collaboratively with others to achieve shared goals. Ultimately, entrepreneurs who can excel in this environment will be well-positioned to thrive and succeed in the era of industry 5.0. The purpose of this chapter is to go through the major entrepreneurship theories that can potentially alter the growth and performances of start-ups and micro, small, and medium-sized enterprises (MSMEs). This chapter also proposed a framework that synthesizes all relevant entrepreneurial dimensions and theories including entrepreneurial mindset, entrepreneurial marketing, entrepreneurial orientation, entrepreneurial ecosystem, entrepreneurial intention and entrepreneurial education in the era of Industry 5.0

INTRODUCTION

Industry 4.0 refers to the current trend of automation and data exchange in manufacturing technologies, including the use of cyber-physical systems, the Internet of Things, and cloud computing. Entrepreneurs are using Industry 4.0 technologies to create more efficient and effective manufacturing processes, resulting in increased productivity, reduced costs, and improved quality. For example, entrepreneurs are using smart sensors to monitor and control production lines, using predictive analytics to identify potential

DOI: 10.4018/978-1-6684-6403-8.ch001

equipment failures, and using machine learning algorithms to optimize production schedules. Industry 5.0 builds on the foundation of Industry 4.0, incorporating the use of artificial intelligence, robotics, and advanced materials to create new opportunities for innovation and growth. Entrepreneurs are using Industry 5.0 to develop new products and services, such as personalized healthcare devices and smart city solutions. By integrating digital technologies with physical products and services, entrepreneurs can create more valuable and engaging experiences for customers.

The entrepreneurs are using Industry 4.0 and Industry 5.0 to drive innovation and growth, improving the efficiency and effectiveness of manufacturing processes and creating new opportunities for products and services that can enhance the quality of life for individuals and communities.

Entrepreneurship is vital because it has the potential to raise living standards and generate money, not just for entrepreneurs but also for connected firms (Wennekers & Thurik, 1999). Entrepreneurs also contribute to change through innovation, as new and improved goods enable the creation of new markets. Startups, regardless of their small sizes, play a crucial role in economic development (Carree & Thurik, 2010). This is because they create jobs, which implies lower unemployment rates, and lower unemployment indicates a more refined and developing economy. Because of innovations, new jobs, and bringing competitive dynamics into the corporate environment, startup entrepreneurship is critical (Audretsch et al., 2006). These businesses are notable for experimenting with many business models before settling on the best one.

When people are asked to think of an entrepreneur, they usually think of someone like Howard Schultz, Estée Lauder, and Michael Dell; those who built great firms from the ground up and had a lasting influence on society. However, entrepreneurial ideas and actions are not restricted to people who start a new business in their garage with family members or personal money. Some people in big companies get enamored with a novel concept, spend their time advocating it, work with important players in the organization to establish a constituency, and then figure out how to get the resources needed to make the idea a reality. Entrepreneurial thinking and behavior may also benefit a person's job. By discovering and grabbing new chances, some entrepreneurial individuals effectively maneuver through the surroundings of their different firms and optimize their career potential.

For instance, entrepreneurial orientation (Covin & Wales, 2012), as a strategic strategy, encourages a wide range of innovations within the company. It is regarded as a key driver in the dissemination of knowledge about innovation and exceptional company performance. Entrepreneurial families should approach business operations with an entrepreneurial mindset since it gives them the vision to mobilize expertise inside the family company. When executives are developing plans in the hopes of trying something new and taking advantage of chances that other companies are unable to take advantage of, entrepreneurial orientation (EO) is a critical notion to consider. Organizations that operate entrepreneurially use EO to describe their procedures, methods, and decision-making styles.

Thus, in reality, it is by no means easy to encourage an individual to simply become an entrepreneur, they must possess the right entrepreneurial mindset, marketing skills, orientation, ecosystem, intention, and education to even instill a sense of confidence in their abilities to become successful entrepreneurs. Negative affectivity (NA), also known as unpleasant effect, is a personality trait characterized by negative feelings and a low self-concept (Delgado-García et al., 2012). Unpleasant affectivity encompasses a wide range of negative emotions such as wrath, contempt, disgust, guilt, anxiety, and uneasiness. Thus, in order to ensure that would-be entrepreneurs and aspiring business owners have the right mindset to conduct an endeavor in such a risky proposition and in order for them to develop and nurture into a long-term prospect, this paper showcases the various entrepreneurial theories that can promote start-ups and growth.

The rise of Entrepreneurship as its own academic literature, separating itself from management theories, has led to countless new theories conceptualizing practical entrepreneurial activities, all for the sake of supporting the growth of entrepreneurs, which in turn promotes economic development and diversification. Entrepreneurship can handle all concerns linked to economic growth, stability, and the assessment of well-being in countries across the world. We are transitioning from requirements-based entrepreneurship to the formation of opportunity-based enterprises, which is a difficult task, particularly in developing market nations. Entrepreneurial success and effect are directly or indirectly influenced by the environment or ecosystem in which they operate. The purpose of this paper is to go through the major entrepreneurship theories that can potentially alter the growth and performances of Micro, Small and Medium-sized enterprises. This paper also proposed a framework that synthesizes all relevant entrepreneurial dimensions. Theories include entrepreneurial marketing, entrepreneurial orientation, entrepreneurial ecosystem, entrepreneurial intention, and entrepreneurial education.

LITERATURE REVIEW

Entrepreneurial Mindset (Attitude and Mentality)

Entrepreneurship is a difficult field in practical applications. Unexpected requests and challenges arise regularly. It helps to be flexible in your thinking in order to roll with the punches, solve issues swiftly, and recover fast from setbacks (Naumann, 2017). Create a systematic critical approach to issue solving to become more agile. Keep a diary in which you may write your ideas. List the obstacles you confront - stumbling blocks or imagined constraints that impede you from progressing. Write down what you know about each of these, one at a time. Consider what you need to know. Make a list of all of your ideas and follow through on them, creating a timetable to conquer this obstacle.

Industry 5.0 and entrepreneurial orientation are closely related because both concepts focus on innovation and adaptability. Industry 5.0 refers to the integration of traditional manufacturing with advanced technology such as robotics, artificial intelligence, and the internet of things. This requires a mindset that embraces change, experimentation, and risk-taking, which are all qualities associated with an entrepreneurial orientation. Companies that can adopt an entrepreneurial mindset and culture are better equipped to adapt to new technologies and create new business models that can take advantage of Industry 5.0. Thus, Industry 5.0 and entrepreneurial orientation complement each other and can help organizations achieve success in the rapidly changing business landscape.

Entrepreneurs endure significant failure risk, and the expenses are frequently absorbed by taxpayers. If current enterprises close, entrepreneurial initiatives may result in layoffs in the medium future. A high rate of self-employment is not always indicative of entrepreneurial activity. Thus, an entrepreneurial mindset can be seen from two perspectives: attitude and mentality.

An entrepreneurial mentality, also known as a growth mindset, is a combination of abilities that enables people to capitalize on opportunities, overcome barriers, learn and execute tactics, and prosper in a variety of competitive contexts (Fernández-Salinero & de la Riva, 2014). Employers strongly respect the entrepreneurial attitude, which encourages educational attainment and success and is required for the formation of new businesses. Furthermore, the capacity to "think outside the box," or in distinctive and innovative ways, is critical to overcoming many of the barriers to entrepreneurial success. Many successful ventures are made feasible by an entrepreneurial mindset, which is frequently an uncommon blend of technical competence, creative problem-solving, personal characteristics, and commercial acumen. However, understanding how to harness the entrepreneurial mentality is becoming increasingly vital for individuals who lack these qualities.

The development of entrepreneurial qualities such as confidence, resilience, and excitement serve as a springboard to success and can lead to increased happiness at work and at home (Kuznetsova et al., 2000). Adopting an entrepreneurial attitude enables for the development of these talents, allowing for better work and a happier life at work and at home.

An entrepreneurial mindset can assist in the development of confidence and indicate that one is more likely to seize chances and is not scared to take risks. Being self-assured enough to confront unpleasant situations and dialogues at work helps enhance leadership style and general social contact with coworkers. There is a larger likelihood of success if there is a higher degree of confidence; the entrepreneurial mentality of taking chances and never giving up is a powerful path to success in everything throughout life. Entrepreneurial Mindset is divided into various schools of thoughts and dimensions, self-control (stoicism), enthusiasm, optimistic outlook, creativity, commitment, locus of control, and accountability.

Understanding how to control one's personal abilities and attitude, as well as the influence it has on others, is a valuable quality that is simpler to achieve with an entrepreneurial mindset (Van Gelderen et al., 2015). Setting objectives and milestones for self-improvement is also lot easier if you have applicable entrepreneurial abilities. Being able to use constructive criticism positively and not take it personally is something that can be developed over time through a continuous entrepreneurial mindset; understanding that it is better to receive criticism and work on self-improvement rather than refusing any type of feedback entirely due to fear of negative feedback. Being resilient and strong-willed means that it is possible to change unpleasant situations into positive ones. These challenging situations occur regularly in both professional and personal life, and if handled poorly or without resilience, they can cause a drop in motivation and a lesser probability of success. It is critical to be able to learn from prior events and apply them to one's benefit; developing and improving through negative experiences influences one's degree of success and pleasure in life.

Enthusiasm is another entrepreneurial ability that can be used with an entrepreneurial mindset; being enthusiastic in the workplace may not only provide new chances, but it can also boost social interaction among coworkers and create a better working environment (Cova, 1996). The work at hand is more likely to succeed if there is passion and excitement. At home, enthusiasm is also a healthy attitude to adopt; being passionate about completing things fosters a positive approach and may lead to a better lifestyle overall.

It is crucial to possess the capacity to keep an optimistic outlook (Liang & Dunn, 2008; Trevelyan, 2008). When it comes to operating a business, having a good attitude pays off. The way you handle problems and barriers will reflect how you do business. This has an impact on how your workers see you. If you squirm every time you experience a setback, your employees and others around you will have little faith in you. A good attitude helps you to face issues and barriers front on, without being hampered by negative feelings.

In the field of entrepreneurship, the cliché "Creativity is the mother of innovation" has never been more accurate (Milohnić & Madžar, 2017). Consider Steve Jobs and the iPhone. Edison and the invention of the light bulb The Wright Brothers and the invention of the aircraft Each of these ground-breaking discoveries would not have been possible without a healthy dose of creative tenacity. Even if you don't work in a "creative" field, creativity is essential for entrepreneurship. An entrepreneur's mind is constantly on the lookout for new ideas and breakthroughs. The fundamental life cycle of every entrepreneurial product begins with the creation of an idea and continues with the transformation of that idea into a commercial product or service. Along with problem-solving skills, you should be able to think of solutions to address an issue from several perspectives. However, imagination plays a significant role in how you innovate your products and services. When entrepreneurs are innovative, they look beyond what they wish to sell or solve. Remember that some of the world's most successful businesses and corporations did not begin with a single product.

Commitment; while enthusiasm may drive you to start your own business, dedication will keep you going and help you to persist in the face of adversity (Fayolle et al., 2011; Parente & Feola, 2013). The ability to endure repeated rejection and disappointment is a necessary component of an entrepreneur's makeup. Successful entrepreneurs learn from rejection and avoid having it harm their self-esteem. Deflect the rejection away from yourself and use it as a wake-up call to improve the weaknesses in your company ideas. Concentrate on comparing yesterday to today with the mindset of "see how far I've come." It is motivating to see what you have accomplished. It motivates you to keep pushing forward. Continues to yield results. It aids in your perseverance.

Successful entrepreneurs have a strong internal locus of control (Jennings & Zeithaml, 1983; Mueller & Thomas, 2001); they believe in their power to decide their own success. Entrepreneurs have a nearly neurotic need to control their own destinies. They recognize that their own actions, decisions, and reactions, regardless of what life throws at them, will make or break them. This entails accepting responsibility for completing the tasks that must be completed. Hone your knowledge that you have total choice over how you respond to the situations that life throws at you. Build your confidence in your ability to achieve and carry out your ambition.

Accountability is a quality that many business owners overlook or dismiss. As a business owner, you must recognize that everything is and will be your fault (Kearns, 1995; Simons, 2013). You are the one who will give the go-ahead to accomplish this and that. It is up to you to determine what to do and what not to do. When you take ownership of your activities, you are not only taking control of the business but also of the obligations that come with it. When you understand and accept responsibility for a company's actions, you become more motivated to see it succeed.

ENTREPRENEURIAL MARKETING

Entrepreneurial marketing is the proactive discovery and exploitation of possibilities for attracting and maintaining lucrative consumers through risk management, resource leveraging, and value creation (Stokes, 2000).

The types of businesses that use entrepreneurial marketing best define it. Many large corporations employ some of the same strategies (Collinson & Shaw, 2001). Nike and Burger King have both benefited greatly from viral marketing. Major corporations use these strategies because they have the opportunity to do so, whereas entrepreneurs use them because they have no other choice. Entrepreneurial marketing is best described by the sorts of businesses that employ it. In reality, many large corporations employ some of the same tactics. Nike and Burger King have both had significant success with viral marketing. Major corporations employ these methods as a result of opportunity, whereas entrepreneurs employ them as a result of need(Morris et al., 2002).

Marketing is an essential practice for entrepreneurs since no business can create and thrive without a client market (Hills et al., 2008). Because bringing new products and services to market is difficult and expensive, especially for fledgling enterprises, they must be more inventive in their marketing. There are many types of marketing applications for businesses:-

Relationship marketing is concerned with establishing a strong bond between the brand and the client (Christopher et al., 2002). Expeditionary marketing entails the creation of markets and the development of novel goods, where companies take the role of leaders rather than followers (Hamel & Prahalad, 1991). Real-time marketing; entails utilizing the power of technology to communicate with a consumer in real time (Mckenna, 1995). Viral Marketing; Posts marketing messages on the Internet for customers to share and grow on (Leskovec et al., 2007). Digital marketing; makes use of the power of Internet platforms such as email and social networking to enhance marketing operations (Charlesworth, 2014).

Entrepreneurial marketing is more about a marketing mentality that distinguishes itself from traditional marketing techniques than it is about a specific marketing method. It rejects several core marketing ideas since they are normally developed for large, well-established businesses. Entrepreneurial marketing employs a toolset of novel and unconventional marketing techniques to assist developing businesses in gaining a footing in congested industries.

Industry 5.0 and entrepreneurial marketing are related in that both involve innovation and adaptation to new technologies and market trends. Industry 5.0, also known as the smart factory or the fourth industrial revolution, involves the integration of advanced technologies such as artificial intelligence, robotics, and the Internet of Things into manufacturing processes. This requires a mindset of continuous improvement and adaptation to new technologies, which is also a key aspect of entrepreneurial marketing. Entrepreneurs must stay on top of market trends and continually innovate their products and marketing strategies to stay competitive. Both Industry 5.0 and entrepreneurial marketing are focused on using technology to improve efficiency and drive growth, making them highly complementary.

Many entrepreneurial marketing methods are the result of a lack of resources. New enterprises may have ten, five, or even one person working on marketing. They operate on a shoestring budget and have access to a fraction of the resources that their big competitors do. Luxuries such as graphic design teams and advertising advisors are frequently out of reach for start-ups, forcing them to discover creative methods to make the most of their limited resources.

The most typical characteristics of entrepreneurial marketing are creativity, risk-taking, and being proactive. Entrepreneurial marketing initiatives attempt to emphasize the company's strongest capabilities while stressing the value they provide to the client. Focusing on new items or exceptional customer service might help you stand out from the crowd. They make their case by utilizing low-cost and easily accessible platforms such as viral videos, Tweets, Facebook pages, and email marketing. Any marketing strategy can be considered as long as it yields results.

According to the interpretation of the study's findings (Hallbäck & Gabrielsson, 2011), the marketing success of international new ventures is dictated by the match between international entrepreneurial marketing strategies and factors linked to the industry environment, internal company culture, and the INV's growth phase (Bjerke & Hultman, 2004).

The study's findings indicate that entrepreneurial marketing has an impact on marketing performance due to the function of competitive advantage as a marketing performance mediator (Hidayatullah et al., 2019). This shows that the factors analyzed have a very close association. Entrepreneurial marketing is formed from the aspects of opportunity focus, proactive, customer intensity, risk taking, increased resources, value creation, and innovation.

Entrepreneurial marketing (EM) has a favorable impact on organizational performance (Alqahtani & Uslay, 2020). Environmental influences alter the EM-performance connection. EM is more applicable to large and small businesses than to medium-sized businesses. Network structure (strength, size, and diversity) moderates the link between EM and performance. Service-dominant logic (principles) and effectuation inform EM (execution). Thus, Entrepreneurial marketing (EM) is beneficial to organizational performance.

ENTREPRENEURIAL ORIENTATION

Entrepreneurial orientation is a strategic orientation at the firm level that captures an organization's entrepreneurial strategy-making procedures, management beliefs, and company behaviors (Poon et al., 2006). Entrepreneurial orientation consists of three dimensions: innovativeness, proactiveness, and risk taking. To start off, it has been found that innovativeness, proactiveness, and risk-taking are generally positively correlated to performance, growth and success of organisations (Baker & Sinkula, 2009; Covin et al., 2006).

Understanding their interactions and volatility may aid in our capacity to understand SME performance (Le Roux & Bengesi, 2014). Findings help to understand how SME performance in emerging nations may be improved to enable SMEs to meet the difficulties provided by competitor inflow in an open market economy. The results show a robust link between EO characteristics and performance, with risk-taking and competitive aggressiveness mitigating the influence of proactivity.

Entrepreneurial orientation, as a strategic strategy, significantly fosters many types of innovations in the organization. It is regarded as a critical driver for facilitating information related to innovation and enhanced corporate performance (McGrath, 2001). Separately modeled, research has found that both characteristics have a direct influence on company profitability. When modeled concurrently, however, the direct influence of EO has vanished. As a result, some researchers believe that EO is a forerunner of MO. The findings of this study contradict this assumption, indicating that EO and MO may be used in tandem to increase profitability, at least in small enterprises. The addition of innovation success, which captures an indirect influence of EO on profitability, distinguishes this study from earlier investigations. The findings imply that, at least in small organizations, EO supplements MO by fostering an opportunistic culture that influences the quality and quantity of company innovations.

This implies that the efficacy of specific EO components may be extremely sensitive to venture age. During the dynamic early phases of development, the prerequisites for success may vary rapidly (Baron & Markman, 2005). Furthermore, the utility of certain entrepreneurial behaviors may change as the business progresses through important stages of venture growth (Vohora, Wright, & Lockett, 2004). This discovery further emphasizes the significance of evaluating EO aspects separately of one another.

Entrepreneurial Orientation has a positive effect on sales growth rate (Baker & Sinkula, 2009; Covin et al., 2006). When businesses with these orientations use strategy creation methods that reflect the special needs of operating entrepreneurially, EOs tend to be most conducive to firm growth. As Mintzberg and Waters (1985) note, strategy formulation in an emergent mode is frequently recommended because it allows enterprises to handle the uncertainty inherent in their operations (Mintzberg & Waters, 1985). Firms with EOs have intrinsically unpredictable operations, therefore an emergent strategy formulation process can be quite useful (Lumpkin et al., 2006; Poon et al., 2006). Developing an entrepreneurial mindset with orientation may help businesses and people alike recognize and seize new possibilities.

RISK TAKING

The willingness to take risks demonstrates to a team that the entrepreneur is a real company visionary and leader who believes in the possible payoff on the other side (Naldi et al., 2007). Risk-taking promotes and fosters innovation, which may be a key difference for a product or service. There are five types of risks that entrepreneurs face while beginning a firm (Naldi et al., 2007). These dangers are as follows: founder risk, product risk, market risk, competition risk, and sales execution risk. Founder risk evaluates who the firm's founders are, whether they get along, and how they will work for the company.

Innovativeness

Innovation improves a brand's nature, originality, and creative thinking process (Avlonitis & Salavou, 2007). By studying the processes of creativity, a new business may reach the pinnacle of success. Entrepreneurship innovation may open the door to new prospects by assisting businesses in keeping up with current trends.

Proactiveness

The proclivity of human actors to act in the face of external limits is referred to as proactivity (Kreiser & Davis, 2010). They are likely to impact and may modify the environment in which they operate as a result of this. Proactive entrepreneurs are those who take action.

Extended

Lumpkin and Dess provide an alternate definition of EO as a mix of Miller/Covin and Slevin's five aspects, as well as competitive aggressiveness and autonomy (Covin et al., 2006; Covin & Slevin, 1989). Furthermore, they indicate that studying the dimensions separately might yield further information. Autonomy and competitive aggressiveness has been devised to cover more factors and improve the framework.

Autonomy

Autonomy refers to whether a person or group of individuals inside a company has the flexibility to develop and execute an entrepreneurial initiative (Lumpkin et al., 2009).

Competitive Aggressiveness

Competitive aggressiveness is the propensity to confront opponents head on rather than avoid them (Lumpkin & Dess, 2001). Price cuts and increased marketing, quality, and manufacturing capacity are examples of aggressive initiatives.

The findings imply that the potential of EO as a way of increasing the growth trajectories of new enterprises is contingent on the degree to which these organizations adopt and implement particular human resource practices and mindsets. The findings are instructive in terms of the relevance of HRM in a young firm's capacity to translate its EO into new or renewed growth (Messersmith & Wales, 2013). The findings show that developing EO on its own may be far less advantageous to the success of fledgling enterprises than studies in more established situations would suggest. However, the study findings imply that when used in conjunction with HRM systems and philosophies such as HPWS and a management philosophy geared toward partnership, the influence of EO on the success of emerging high-tech enterprises may be amplified to relevant levels.

Industry 5.0 refers to the next wave of technological advancements in manufacturing that focus on integration of new technologies like artificial intelligence, robotics, and the Internet of Things (IoT). Entrepreneurial risk-taking, innovation, and proactiveness are essential components of Industry 5.0. Innovations in technology and manufacturing require a level of entrepreneurial risk-taking to bring them to market. It takes entrepreneurs to invest their time and money into developing new technologies and bringing them to market. In addition, proactiveness plays a crucial role in Industry 5.0 as companies need to be proactive in adopting new technologies and processes to stay competitive. Entrepreneurs, in particular, need to be proactive in identifying new opportunities and technologies and invest in them to gain a competitive edge. In summary, Industry 5.0 and entrepreneurial risk-taking, innovation, and proactiveness are closely related as they all contribute to the development and implementation of new technologies and processes in manufacturing.

The previous research shows that entrepreneur qualities, company characteristics, and management factors all have a major impact on business performance (Rodríguez-Gutiérrez et al., 2015). The empirical analysis results show that the competitive success of Spanish SMEs in the service industry is conditioned by macroeconomic and social factors related to the general business environment, particularly business factors concerning the firm's entrepreneurial orientation; these findings are consistent with those of previous research conducted at both an international and national level.

While not all dimensions of entrepreneurial orientation are correlated to performance (Sadiku-Dushi et al., 2019). Respondents are extremely opportunity-driven and recognize the significance of resource leveraging. While value creation is viewed as a key entrepreneurial marketing characteristic, respondents are risk averse; moreover, they are not proactive, inventive, or consumer-centered.

ENTREPRENEURIAL ECOSYSTEM

To achieve development and innovation, the ecosystem must be well-functioning for entrepreneurs. An "entrepreneurial ecosystem" is a network of players that interact with one another and impact the possibilities of survival of a venture developer and his firm in a region or country (Sussan & Acs, 2017).

Industry 5.0 and the entrepreneurial ecosystem are closely related. Industry 5.0 focuses on combining the strengths of humans and machines to create a more efficient and productive industrial environment. This requires innovation, new technology, and a dynamic entrepreneurial ecosystem. The entrepreneurial ecosystem is essential for fostering innovation, supporting startups, and creating new business models. It helps to attract investors, incubators, accelerators, and other stakeholders that can support the growth of new ventures. The entrepreneurial ecosystem also creates a culture of collaboration, knowledge sharing, and risk-taking, which are essential for success in Industry 5.0. In short, a strong entrepreneurial ecosystem is critical for the success of Industry 5.0, and Industry 5.0 creates new opportunities for entrepreneurs.

A social and economic environment impacting local or regional entrepreneurship is referred to as an entrepreneurial ecosystem or entrepreneurship ecosystem (Acs et al., 2017). Entrepreneurial ecosystems are described as a group of interconnected players and elements that work together to promote profitable entrepreneurship inside a certain location. The entrepreneurial ecosystem frequently restricts entrepreneurship to high-growth startups or scaleups, saying that this form of entrepreneurship is a critical source of innovation, productivity growth, and employment.

Every region or country's entrepreneurial ecosystem includes nine aspects or framework conditions that operate as a stimulus for entrepreneurial activities (Stam, 2014). The entrepreneurial ecosystem is a collection of various individuals who can be potential or existing Entrepreneurs, organizations that support Entrepreneurship such as businesses, venture capitalists, business angels, and banks, as well as institutions such as universities, public sector agencies, and the entrepreneurial processes that occur within the ecosystem such as the business birth rate, the number of high potential growth firms, serial entrepreneurs, and their Entities (Mason & Brown, 2014).

Authors have devised a holistic and dynamic approach to Entrepreneurial Ecosystem (Shwetzer Herrera et al., 2021). Their conceptual framework for the composition and interconnections of EEs gives a comprehensive and dynamic approach that reflects value creation, entrepreneurial activity EE components, and relational interactions within institutional settings. The long-term goal of this study will be to experimentally validate this paradigm.

While there are numerous dimensions under the entrepreneurial ecosystem, according to the results of pairwise comparisons (Mujahid et al., 2019), human resource development had the most weight, followed by money, support, and industrial relationship. Markets were revealed to be the least important component. To identify the industry-related EES framework, the suggested EES provides a fundamental framework that may be repeated in a given sector.

By evaluating 121 European Union areas between 2012 and 2014 (Szerb et al., 2019), it was discovered that quantity (Kirznerian) entrepreneurship has a negative influence on regional performance, but quality (Schumpeterian) entrepreneurship has a favorable impact. Furthermore, regions with a healthy entrepreneurial ecosystem have a greater capacity to materialize the effects of high business formation rates, regardless of quality (Kirznerian entrepreneurship), whereas regions with a weak entrepreneurial ecosystem may rely on innovative (Schumpeterian) entrepreneurs to compensate for the lack of entrepreneurship support policies and increase their economic outcomes.

Data study shows that R&D, financial resources, market, support services, infrastructure, culture, policies, and human capital all have a favorable influence on entrepreneurial performance (Davari & Najmabadi, 2018). Meanwhile, the findings point to inefficiencies in Iran's entrepreneurship environment. Furthermore, deficiencies in certain parameters lead the influence of other determinants on entrepreneurial performance to be neutralized.

Academic spin-offs are terms used to describe extremely exceptional start-up enterprises created by an academic innovator with the goal of utilizing technological knowledge developed inside a university context to generate products or services (Ramaciotti & Rizzo, 2015). The findings show that social and institutional settings boost the performance of ASOs at both stages of development, albeit the importance of each environment differs depending on the stage (Franco-Leal et al., 2020). The institutional setting has a stronger effect on the performance of ASOs during the formation and early development stages, whereas the social context has a lesser influence. The most important actors in this period are science parks from the institutional environment. During the consolidation phase, the social context is the most important for increasing the performance of ASOs, with venture capitalists wielding the most power. In this stage, the nonuniversity background has little effect on performance in terms of the institutional context. The result of the higher academic spinoff is that there will more start-ups due to higher entrepreneurial influence. These start-ups are also highly dedicated and motivated to succeed, and it is this drive that may improve performance.

The data imply that Pakistan's entrepreneurial environment, as a whole, is a restraint on the success of SMEs (Samiullah et al., 2021). However, the absence of a trained labor to fulfill the demands of new industrial technology is having the most damaging impact on the performance of SMEs.

It can be concluded that there is no one size fits all approach for establishing an entrepreneurial economy. Accordingly, research should use a bottom-up approach to provide these practical yet imperfect roadmaps to policymakers for devising a set of actions for gradually shaping entrepreneurial ecosystems in a specific direction or intended outcomes.

ENTREPRENEURIAL INTENTION

Theory of planned behaviour showcases behavioral intention is a function of three direct determinants: attitudes, subjective norms, and perceirve behaviorual control (Obschonka et al., 2010).

Intention models assist in understanding and predicting individuals' intended activities, such as pursuing a tourism enterprise endeavor, as well as explaining how potential entrepreneurs view prospects by studying their intentions and the variables influencing their intentions (Shepherd & Krueger, 2002).

The theory of planned behavior (TPB) is a psychology concept that connects thoughts to actions. According to the idea, an individual's behavioral intentions are shaped by three basic components: attitude, subjective norms, and perceived behavioral control (Souitaris et al., 2007).

In 1980, the Theory of Reasoned Action was developed to forecast an individual's intention to participate in a certain behavior at a specific time and location (Dillard & Pfau, 2002; Fishbein, 1979). The hypothesis was designed to describe all actions over which humans may exercise self-control. Theory of planned behavior (TPB) is proposed which states that an individual's decision to engage in a given action, such as gambling, may be predicted by their intention to engage in that conduct (Ajzen, 1985). The Theory of Planned Conduct employs a person's own attitude and viewpoint, as well as their perceived control over their behavior and society's subjective norms, to impact their behavioral intention, which leads to the behavior or action. Ajzen and Fishbein established the Theory of Planned Conduct/ Reasoned Action, which states that behavior is governed by intentions, attitudes (beliefs about an action), and subjective norms (beliefs about other people's attitudes toward a behavior). The theory of planned behavior (TPB) encapsulates key individual beliefs (attitudes, subjective norms, and perceived behavior control) that impact people's intentions to do a certain behavior.

TPB has been widely regarded as a model with high predictive value and a well-established model for intention prediction (Ajzen, 2020). Despite its good prediction, some studies have debated and criticized the TPB's restricted definition of sufficiency and recommended important external aspects beyond the three component model to aid improve the predictive ability on intention. Thus, suggestions for improving the theory are welcomed by allowing TPB to include external predictors in addition to the three core components of attitude, subjective norms, and perceived behavioral control (Ajzen, 1991), as long as the additional variable can provide a significant variance apart from the original constructs.

As a result, a study will include other external factors, such as service quality and trust, as an expanded TPB based on the applicability and significance of the constructs listed by many writers to predict loyalty intention to be explored in consumer cooperatives (Hasbullah et al., 2014; Hasbullah & Mahajar, 2014).

Empirical data is consistent with the theoretical measurement model for both innovativeness and entrepreneurial intention, according to the findings of the confirmatory analysis and multiple regression

(Wathanakom et al., 2020), and innovativeness can effectively predict entrepreneurial intention among undergraduate students, according to the findings of the confirmatory analysis and multiple regression.

Some findings suggest that entrepreneurial aim components such as information sharing, reputation, social interactions, and identity have a beneficial influence on the performance of digital start-ups mediated via social media (Tajpour & Hosseini, 2021). Furthermore, the findings indicate that successful businesses are continually producing and disseminating new information, as well as fast adapting it to new technologies and products. Thus, entrepreneurial intention can result in positive growth and performance of organisations.

ENTREPRENEURSHIP EDUCATION

Entrepreneurship education aims to provide students with the information, skills, and drive needed to succeed as entrepreneurs in a range of situations (Pittaway & Cope, 2007). Entrepreneurship education is available at all levels of education, from elementary and secondary schools to graduate university programs. Entrepreneurship education teaches students to think creatively, to look for issues to solve, to empathize with people, to take chances, to embrace failure as part of the learning process, and to see the link between hard effort and achievement.

Individuals with entrepreneurial education and training have the capacity to detect business possibilities, as well as the self-esteem, knowledge, and abilities to act on them. It covers topics including recognizing opportunities, commercializing a notion, managing resources, and starting a business (McMullan & Long, 1987; Pittaway & Cope, 2007). Students from all socioeconomic levels benefit from entrepreneurship education because it encourages them to think outside the box and develop unusual abilities and skills. It opens doors, assures social fairness, instills confidence, and boosts the economy. Interpersonal interactions, collaboration skills, money management, and public speaking abilities all benefit from entrepreneurship education. It improves work readiness and preparation as well.

Research reveals characteristics of EO that are related to employability (Nair et al., 2020). The favorable link discovered between student performance in the program and chances of being employed emphasizes the need of instilling entrepreneurial ideals in students at the collegiate level. Thus, the findings of this study suggest that superior student performance in the programme is positively correlated with the students being hired by entrepreneurial firms.

Entrepreneurial self-efficacy (ESE) is the use of self-efficacy in entrepreneurship research, referring to how confident entrepreneurs are in their own entrepreneurial abilities to execute various tasks and projects (Boyd & Vozikis, 1994; Chen et al., 1998). This is often brought about by entrepreneurial education (Wilson et al., 2007).

According to the findings of the mediation analysis (Yeh et al., 2021), Internet entrepreneurial self-efficacy completely mediates the association between entrepreneurial education and the four aspects of Internet entrepreneurial performance. However, no direct influence of entrepreneurial education was discovered on the four Internet entrepreneurial performances, such as financial, customer, internal, and learning and growth.

It means that organizations with highly effective entrepreneurs function well. Furthermore, the presence of higher levels of self-efficacy among entrepreneurs would allow them to improve the performance of their entities since efficacious human agency is a vital determinant for the success of entities functioning in an undeveloped and politicized economy (Herath & Mahmood, 2014).

Entrepreneurs' development of experiential knowledge is a gradual process that occurs over the course of their careers. This means that efforts to generate "real world" experience through formal approaches of passive education and training are unlikely to have a significant influence or impact on the entrepreneur's development as a practitioner. The purpose of this article is to construct a case against the conventional "passive" method of business education, arguing that entrepreneurs who are exposed to passive learning are only observers rather than active participants (Higgins & Elliott, 2011).

This article presents the findings of a study on the educational tendencies of entrepreneurs. When compared to previous research and census data, entrepreneurs have higher levels of education than the general population, and the difference is growing. Business majors fared worse than non-business grads. Correlation study shows that there is no significant relationship between educational degree and success metrics (Douglass, 2017).

Surprisingly, entrepreneurship education has little effect on the relationship. The cause for this is a mismatch between entrepreneurial education and market reality. To be effective, organizations must embrace and implement suitable entrepreneurship training. To lure jobless young to successful business endeavors, Korean enterprises must focus on adequate training sessions and educational curricula (Lee et al., 2019).

The contents of Entrepreneurial Education elicit entrepreneurial knowledge in learners. However, a vital question if this translates into preparations into becoming entrepreneurs. The findings revealed that entrepreneurial education is critical in defining knowledge and entrepreneurial mentality, which leads to students' entrepreneurial preparedness. The findings also revealed that entrepreneurial knowledge influences entrepreneurial mentality and entrepreneurial preparation and that it successfully mediates the impact of entrepreneurial education and entrepreneurial preparation. According to the most recent findings, entrepreneurial attitude has a favorable impact on students' entrepreneurial preparedness (Saptono et al., 2020).

The findings revealed the importance of the 'conventional' essence of academics such as knowledge and non-academic such as financing programs in influencing growth ambitions (Kariv et al., 2019). They also demonstrated the usefulness of academic programs to established entrepreneurs and non-academic programs to aspiring/want to-be entrepreneurs with plans to build their businesses. While this study uses the term growth instead or performance, the definitions are similar in that both terminology involves an increase in sales turnover, number of employees, and profit for the year (Kariv et al., 2019).

There are still questions as to what constitutes entrepreneurial content. According to the findings of a study (Njoroge, 2013), the businesses were able to promote their products inside the district but not beyond the country. The study's findings demonstrated that entrepreneurs could perform simple daily bookkeeping of business activities but not complicated financial statements. This leads to the conclusion that, even if the entrepreneur reports an increase in sales and profits and appears to be growing, a lack of training in financial, strategic management, and marketing will mean that the SME will not progress beyond the first stage of enterprise development and will thus fail within its first five years of existence. The report suggested that the government, through the Ministry of Trade, develop and implement training programs to provide SME owners with entrepreneurial skills.

PERFORMANCE

Entrepreneurial performance is described as "the achievement of stated entrepreneurial goals" (van Vuuren & Botha, 2010; Van Vuuren & Nieman, 1997). The entrepreneurial performance takes use of available possibilities to expand the company (Ladzani & Van vuuren, 2002; Sebora et al., 2009). The founder uses performance as a meter to gauge his or her success (Chandler & Hanks, 1994). Entrepreneurial Performance refers to an individual's capacity to be effective in a variety of occupations (e.g., medicine, retail, suppliers, marketing, etc.) in order to improve negotiation results (Lewicki et al., 2003) and achieve firm success. For instance, reports on the outcomes of alert, agile, and dynamic entrepreneurs' efforts in decision-making processes, while aiming to be inventive and creative on the one hand, and battling to seize the initiative and be ahead of the competition on the other.

The word "entrepreneurial growth" refers to how an organization intends to achieve its goal of expanding and growing a firm in terms of quality, quantity, and turnover (Bouazza & Ardjouman, 2015; Gupta et al., 2013; Li Jr & Fu, 2009; Soini & Veseli, 2011). Innovators, company developers, radicals, expanders, and customers are all examples of entrepreneurial growth. Profit and expansion are two markers of an organization's progress. Because it is regarded that an organization is developing when it earns a profit and sees its profit increase consistently. Organizational growth is the stage at which a corporation can explore expansion and may search for new ways to earn money. Organizational growth is frequently influenced by industry growth patterns, the business lifecycle, and the owners' ambition to create equity value.

In numerous respects, the volume and frequency of sales are markers of a company's success (Chittithaworn et al., 2011; Narayanasamy, 2008; Uddin & Bose, 2013). You may track the number of new clients sold, the number of existing customers sold, the profit per transaction, and the average amount transacted during each sale. Entrepreneurial success will be determined by five factors: innovation, risk tolerance, response to possibilities, leadership, and the capacity to take use of the rights granted to you.

Industry 5 is expected to enhance entrepreneurial performance by providing new opportunities for innovation and growth. This new industrial revolution is characterized by the convergence of digital technologies, artificial intelligence, and the internet of things, leading to the creation of new business models and products. Entrepreneurs will be able to leverage these technologies to create new products and services and to streamline their operations. Industry 5 will also create new markets and customer segments, which will allow entrepreneurs to expand their businesses and increase their revenue. Moreover, Industry 5 will foster collaboration and partnerships between entrepreneurs and larger corporations, which will enable them to share resources and knowledge and to develop more innovative solutions together.

PROPOSED CONCEPTUAL FRAMEWORK

Upon synthesizing the various concepts in entrepreneurship, this chapter proposed a conceptual framework showcasing all the theories that can affect entrepreneurial performance and growth of start-ups and MSMEs as shown in figure 1.

Figure 1. A synthesised framework of entrepreneurial marketing, entrepreneurial orientation, entrepreneurial ecosystem, entrepreneurial intention and entrepreneurial education

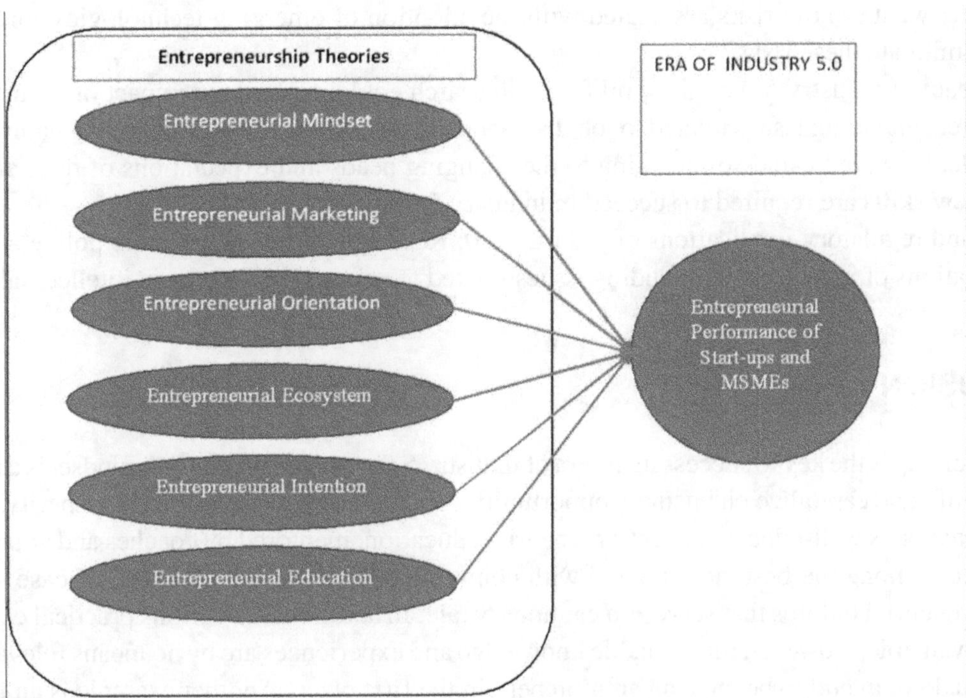

FUTURE RESEARCH DIRECTIONS

Future researchers must synthesise the various concepts and theories of entrepreneurship to conduct empirical research. A hypothesis must be drawn to identify if the above concepts are statistically significant to the performance and growth of small businesses. Furthermore, while this chapter summarises the important theories of entrepreneurship, it is by no means an exhaustive list. Future researchers can focus other entrepreneurial concepts such as entrepreneurial leadership that are also important in shaping the success of small businesses of start-ups and MSMEs. Research in entrepreneurship and industry 5 (also known as Industry 5.0, the fifth industrial revolution) can cover a wide range of topics related to the development and transformation of industries and businesses in the context of emerging technologies and entrepreneurial activity. Some potential research topics in this area could include:

The impact of emerging technologies on entrepreneurship and industry 5.0: Research could explore how emerging technologies such as AI, blockchain, IoT, and robotics are changing the landscape of entrepreneurship and industry 5.0. For example, how are businesses adapting to these new technologies, and what new business models are emerging as a result?

The role of entrepreneurship in industry 5.0: Research could examine how entrepreneurial activity is driving innovation and growth in industry 5.0. For example, what are the key characteristics of successful entrepreneurs in this context, and how are they leveraging emerging technologies to create new products and services?

The challenges and opportunities of industry 5.0: Research could investigate the challenges and opportunities that arise from the transformation of industries and businesses in the context of industry 5.0. For example, what are the risks associated with the adoption of emerging technologies, and how can businesses mitigate these risks?

The impact of industry 5.0 on the workforce: Research could explore the impact of industry 5.0 on the workforce, including issues related to job displacement, upskilling, and the changing nature of work. For example, how are businesses adapting to the changing needs and expectations of their employees, and what new skills are required to succeed in industry 5.0?

Policy and regulatory implications of industry 5.0: Research could examine the policy and regulatory implications of industry 5.0, including issues related to privacy, security, and intellectual property.

CONCLUSION

Entrepreneurship is the key to success in the era of industry 5.0. An entrepreneurial mindset is a necessary trait to identify and capitalize on business opportunities that can lead to growth and prosperity. Consider an individual that is well-educated in entrepreneurial education, mentored by coaches and educators that are numbered among the best, and imbued with countless analysis and evaluations of case studies on past entrepreneurial failures that serve as a cautionary tale. In addition, the various practical experiences offered are valuable. However, this valuable knowledge and experiences are by no means relevant should the individual not intend to become an entrepreneur in the first place. Another example is an individual whose lifelong dream and intention is to become an entrepreneur. However, should they do not have the right orientation whereby they refuse to adopt a mindset of innovativeness, their start-ups may not be sustainable resulting in closure. Thus, the above entrepreneurial theories are relevant for the success of small businesses, each with its concept that entrepreneurs must possess.

Rise of entrepreneurship as its own academic literature, separating themselves from management theories, has led to countless new theories conceptualizing practical entrerpreneurial activities, all for the sake of supporting the growth of entrepreneurs, which in turn promotes economic development and diversification. The purpose of this paper to go through the major entrepreneurship theories that can potentially alter the growth and performances of Micro, Small and Medium-sized enterprises. This paper also proposed a framework that synthesizes all relevant entrepreneurial dimensions. Theories include Entrepreneurial Marketing, Entrepreneurial Orientation, Entrepreneurial Ecosystem, Entrepreneurial Intention and Entrepreneurial Education.

Entrepreneurial skills are equally important in enhancing entrepreneurial performance, such as risk-taking, adaptability, innovation, problem-solving, and resilience. These skills enable entrepreneurs to create new products and services, enter new markets, and respond to changing business trends. With the advent of Industry 5.0, entrepreneurs need to embrace technological advancements, such as artificial intelligence, blockchain, and robotics, to stay ahead of the competition. An entrepreneurial approach, with the right mindset and skills, will enable entrepreneurs to succeed in Industry 5.0 by identifying and capitalizing on new opportunities.

REFERENCES

Acs, Z. J., Stam, E., Audretsch, D. B., & O'Connor, A. (2017). The lineages of the entrepreneurial ecosystem approach. *Small Business Economics*, *49*(1), 1–10. doi:10.100711187-017-9864-8

Ajzen, I. (1985). From Intentions to Actions: A Theory of Planned Behavior. In J. Kuhl & J. Beckmann (Eds.), *Action Control: From Cognition to Behavior* (pp. 11–39). Springer. doi:10.1007/978-3-642-69746-3_2

Ajzen, I. (1991). The theory of planned behavior. *Organizational Behavior and Human Decision Processes*, *50*(2), 179–211. doi:10.1016/0749-5978(91)90020-T

Ajzen, I. (2020). The theory of planned behavior: Frequently asked questions. *Human Behavior and Emerging Technologies*, *2*(4), 314–324. doi:10.1002/hbe2.195

Alqahtani, N., & Uslay, C. (2020). Entrepreneurial marketing and firm performance: Synthesis and conceptual development. *Journal of Business Research*, *113*, 62–71. doi:10.1016/j.jbusres.2018.12.035

Audretsch, D. B., Keilbach, S. R. F. M. C., Keilbach, M. C., Lehmann, E. E., & Lehmann, P. of M. and O. and D. E. E. (2006). Entrepreneurship and Economic Growth. Oxford University Press, USA.

Avlonitis, G. J., & Salavou, H. E. (2007). Entrepreneurial orientation of SMEs, product innovativeness, and performance. *Journal of Business Research*, *60*(5), 566–575. doi:10.1016/j.jbusres.2007.01.001

Baker, W. E., & Sinkula, J. M. (2009). The Complementary Effects of Market Orientation and Entrepreneurial Orientation on Profitability in Small Businesses*. *Journal of Small Business Management*, *47*(4), 443–464. doi:10.1111/j.1540-627X.2009.00278.x

Bjerke, B., & Hultman, C. (2004). *Entrepreneurial Marketing: The Growth of Small Firms in the New Economic Era*. Edward Elgar Publishing.

Bouazza, A. B., & Ardjouman, D. (2015).. . *Establishing the Factors Affecting the Growth of Small and Medium-sized Enterprises in Algeria.*, *4*(2), 15.

Boyd, N. G., & Vozikis, G. S. (1994). The influence of self-efficacy on the development of entrepreneurial intentions and actions. *Entrepreneurship Theory and Practice*, *18*(4), 63–77. doi:10.1177/104225879401800404

Carree, M. A., & Thurik, A. R. (2010). The Impact of Entrepreneurship on Economic Growth. In Z. J. Acs & D. B. Audretsch (Eds.), *Handbook of Entrepreneurship Research: An Interdisciplinary Survey and Introduction* (pp. 557–594). Springer., doi:10.1007/978-1-4419-1191-9_20

Chandler, G. N., & Hanks, S. H. (1994). Market attractiveness, resource-based capabilities, venture strategies, and venture performance. *Journal of Business Venturing*, *9*(4), 331–349. doi:10.1016/0883-9026(94)90011-6

Charlesworth, A. (2014). *Digital Marketing: A Practical Approach* (2nd ed.). Routledge. doi:10.4324/9780203493717

Chen, C. C., Greene, P. G., & Crick, A. (1998). Does entrepreneurial self-efficacy distinguish entrepreneurs from managers? *Journal of Business Venturing*, *13*(4), 295–316. doi:10.1016/S0883-9026(97)00029-3

Chittithaworn, C., Islam, M., Keawchana, T., & Muhd Yusuf, D. H. (2011). Factors Affecting Business Success of Small & Medium Enterprises (SMEs) in Thailand. *Asian Social Science*, *7*(5), 180. doi:10.5539/ass.v7n5p180

Christopher, M., Payne, A., & Ballantyne, D. (2002). *Relationship Marketing: Creating Stakeholder Value*. Routledge., doi:10.4324/9780080516042

Collinson, E., & Shaw, E. (2001). Entrepreneurial marketing – a historical perspective on development and practice. *Management Decision*, *39*(9), 761–766. doi:10.1108/EUM0000000006221

Cova, B. (1996). ENTREPRENEURIAL VISION: Making Enthusiasm and Opportunity Coincide into Design. [Former Series]. *Design Management Journal*, *7*(4), 32–39. doi:10.1111/j.1948-7169.1996.tb00626.x

Covin, J. G., Green, K. M., & Slevin, D. P. (2006). Strategic Process Effects on the Entrepreneurial Orientation–Sales Growth Rate Relationship. *Entrepreneurship Theory and Practice*, *30*(1), 57–81. doi:10.1111/j.1540-6520.2006.00110.x

Covin, J. G., & Slevin, D. P. (1989). Strategic management of small firms in hostile and benign environments. *Strategic Management Journal*, *10*(1), 75–87. doi:10.1002mj.4250100107

Covin, J. G., & Wales, W. J. (2012). The Measurement of Entrepreneurial Orientation. *Entrepreneurship Theory and Practice*, *36*(4), 677–702. doi:10.1111/j.1540-6520.2010.00432.x

Davari, A., & Najmabadi, A. D. (2018). Entrepreneurial Ecosystem and Performance in Iran. In N. Faghih & M. R. Zali (Eds.), *Entrepreneurship Ecosystem in the Middle East and North Africa (MENA): Dynamics in Trends, Policy and Business Environment* (pp. 265–282). Springer International Publishing., doi:10.1007/978-3-319-75913-5_8

Delgado-garcía, J. B., Rodríguez-escudero, A. I., & Martín-cruz, N. (2012). Influence of Affective Traits on Entrepreneur's Goals and Satisfaction. *Journal of Small Business Management*, *50*(3), 408–428. doi:10.1111/j.1540-627X.2012.00359.x

Dillard, J. P., & Pfau, M. (2002). *The Persuasion Handbook: Developments in Theory and Practice*. SAGE Publications. doi:10.4135/9781412976046

Douglass, M. E. (2017). *Entrepreneurial Education Level Related to Business Performance*. Academy of Management Proceedings., doi:10.5465/ambpp.1976.4975936

Fayolle, A., Basso, O., & Tornikoski, E. T. (2011). Entrepreneurial Commitment and New Venture Creation: A Conceptual Exploration. *Handbook of Research on New Venture Creation*. https://www.elgaronline.com/view/edcoll/9781847200952/9781847200952.00016.xml

Fernández-Salinero, C., & de la Riva, B. (2014). Entrepreneurial Mentality and Culture of Entrepreneurship. *Procedia: Social and Behavioral Sciences*, *139*, 137–143. doi:10.1016/j.sbspro.2014.08.044

Fishbein, M. (1979). A theory of reasoned action: Some applications and implications. *Nebraska Symposium on Motivation*, *27*, 65–116. PMID:7242751

Franco-Leal, N., Camelo-Ordaz, C., Fernandez-Alles, M., & Sousa-Ginel, E. (2020). The Entrepreneurial Ecosystem: Actors and Performance in Different Stages of Evolution of Academic Spinoffs. *Entrepreneurship Research Journal*, *10*(2). doi:10.1515/erj-2018-0228

Gupta, P., Guha, S., & Krishnaswami, S. (2013). Firm growth and its determinants. *Journal of Innovation and Entrepreneurship*, *2*(1), 15. doi:10.1186/2192-5372-2-15

Hallbäck, J., & Gabrielsson, P. (2011). Entrepreneurial Marketing Strategies During the Growth of International New Ventures. In E. Hutson, R. R. Sinkovics, & J. Berrill (Eds.), Firm-Level Internationalization, Regionalism and Globalization: Strategy, Performance and Institutional Change (pp. 177–197). Palgrave Macmillan UK. doi:10.1057/9780230305106_12

Hamel, G., & Prahalad, C. K. (1991). Corporate imagination and expeditionary marketing. *Harvard Business Review*, *69*(4), 81–92. PMID:10112922

Hasbullah, N., Mahajar, A., & Ithnin, M. (2014). *A Conceptual Framework of Extending the Theory of Planned Behavior: The Role of Service Quality and Trust in the Consumer Cooperatives. 5.*

Hasbullah, N., & Mahajar, D. A. J. (2014). A Conceptual Framework of Extending the Theory of Planned Behavior. *The Role of Service Quality and Trust in the Consumer Cooperatives.*, *5*(12), 8.

Herath, H. M. A., & Mahmood, R. (2014). Dimensions of Entrepreneurial Self-Efficacy and Firm Performance. *Global Journal of Management and Business Research, ((A) Volume XIV*, 21–28).

Hidayatullah, S., Firdiansjah, A., Patalo, R. G., & Waris, A. (2019).. . *The Effect Of Entrepreneurial Marketing And Competitive Advantage On Marketing Performance.*, *8*(10), 5.

Higgins, D., & Elliott, C. (2011). Learning to make sense: What works in entrepreneurial education? *Journal of European Industrial Training*, *35*(4), 345–367. doi:10.1108/03090591111128324

Hills, G. E., Hultman, C. M., & Miles, M. P. (2008). The Evolution and Development of Entrepreneurial Marketing. *Journal of Small Business Management*, *46*(1), 99–112. doi:10.1111/j.1540-627X.2007.00234.x

Jennings, D. E., & Zeithaml, C. P. (1983). Locus of Control: A Review and Directions for Entrepreneurial Research. *Academy of Management Proceedings*, *1983*(1), 417–421. doi:10.5465/ambpp.1983.4976387

Kariv, D., Cisneros, L., & Ibanescu, M. (2019). The role of entrepreneurial education and support in business growth intentions: The case of Canadian entrepreneurs. *Journal of Small Business and Entrepreneurship*, *31*(5), 433–460. doi:10.1080/08276331.2018.1468974

Kearns, K. P. (1995). Accountability and Entrepreneurial Public Management: The Case of the Orange County Investment Fund. *Public Budgeting & Finance*, *15*(3), 3–21. doi:10.1111/1540-5850.01043

Kreiser, P. M., & Davis, J. (2010). Entrepreneurial Orientation and Firm Performance: The Unique Impact of Innovativeness, Proactiveness, and Risk-taking. *Journal of Small Business and Entrepreneurship*, *23*(1), 39–51. doi:10.1080/08276331.2010.10593472

Kuznetsova, O., Kuznetsov, A., & Mcdonald, F. (2000). Entrepreneurial Qualities: A Case from Russia. *Journal of Small Business Management*, 38.

Ladzani, W. M., & van Vuuren, J. J. (2002). Entrepreneurship Training for Emerging SMEs in South Africa. *Journal of Small Business Management*, *40*(2), 154–161. doi:10.1111/1540-627X.00047

Le Roux, I., & Bengesi, K. M. K. (2014). Dimensions of entrepreneurial orientation and small and medium enterprise performance in emerging economies. *Development Southern Africa*, *31*(4), 606–624. doi:10.1080/0376835X.2014.913474

Lee, H., Ahmed, U., Zhussupova, B., & Khalid, N. (2019). Impact of innovation capability and competitiveness on entrepreneurial orientation regarding to the entrepreneurial education in business performance among South Korean firms. *Polish Journal of Management Studies*, *20*(2), 358–367. Advance online publication. doi:10.17512/pjms.2019.20.2.30

Leskovec, J., Adamic, L. A., & Huberman, B. A. (2007). The dynamics of viral marketing. *ACM Transactions on the Web*, *1*(1), 5-es. doi:10.1145/1232722.1232727

Li, F. F., Jr., & Fu, K. (2009). *Factors Influencing the Growth of Small and Medium Sized Firms in Different Growth Stages. A Study of Four Chinese SMEs.* https://scholar.googleusercontent.com/scholar?q=cache:6ZhdI8kvYWAJ:scholar.google.com/+Factors+Influencing+the+Growth+of+Small+and+Medium+Sized+Firms+in+Different+Growth+Stages+&hl=en&as_sdt=0,5

Liang, K., & Dunn, P. (2008). ARE ENTREPRENEURS OPTIMISTIC, REALISTIC, BOTH OR FUZZY? RELATIONSHIP BETWEEN ENTREPRENEURIAL TRAITS AND ENTREPRENEURIAL LEARNING. *Academy of Entrepreneurship Journal*, *14*, 51–76.

Lumpkin, G. T., Cogliser, C. C., & Schneider, D. R. (2009). Understanding and Measuring Autonomy: An Entrepreneurial Orientation Perspective. *Entrepreneurship Theory and Practice*, *33*(1), 47–69. doi:10.1111/j.1540-6520.2008.00280.x

Lumpkin, G. T., & Dess, G. G. (2001). Linking two dimensions of entrepreneurial orientation to firm performance: The moderating role of environment and industry life cycle. *Journal of Business Venturing*, *16*(5), 429–451. doi:10.1016/S0883-9026(00)00048-3

Lumpkin, G. T., Wales, W. J., & Ensley, M. D. (2006). Entrepreneurial orientation effects on new venture performance: The moderating role of venture age. *Academy of Management Proceedings*, *2006*(1), N1–N6. doi:10.5465/ambpp.2006.22898263

Mason, C., & Brown, R. (2014). *ENTREPRENEURIAL ECOSYSTEMS AND GROWTH ORIENTED ENTREPRENEURSHIP Background paper prepared for the workshop organised by the OECD LEED Programme and the Dutch Ministry of Economic Affairs on.*

Mckenna, R. (1995). Real-time marketing. *Harvard Business Review*, *73*(4). https://elibrary.ru/item.asp?id=2473650

Mcmullan, W. E., & Long, W. A. (1987). Entrepreneurship education in the nineties. *Journal of Business Venturing*, *2*(3), 261–275. doi:10.1016/0883-9026(87)90013-9

Messersmith, J. G., & Wales, W. J. (2013). Entrepreneurial orientation and performance in young firms: The role of human resource management. *International Small Business Journal, 31*(2), 115–136. doi:10.1177/0266242611416141

Milohnić, I., & Madžar, D. (2017). Importance of creativity in entrepreneurship. *4th International Scientific Conference ToSEE - Tourism in Southern and Eastern Europe 2017 "Tourism and Creative Industries: Trends and Challenges,* (pp. 409–421). IEEE.

Mintzberg, H., & Waters, J. A. (1985). Of strategies, deliberate and emergent. *Strategic Management Journal, 6*(3), 257–272. doi:10.1002mj.4250060306

Morris, M. H., Schindehutte, M., & LaForge, R. W. (2002). Entrepreneurial Marketing: A Construct for Integrating Emerging Entrepreneurship and Marketing Perspectives. *Journal of Marketing Theory and Practice, 10*(4), 1–19. doi:10.1080/10696679.2002.11501922

Mueller, S. L., & Thomas, A. S. (2001). Culture and entrepreneurial potential: A nine country study of locus of control and innovativeness. *Journal of Business Venturing, 16*(1), 51–75. doi:10.1016/S0883-9026(99)00039-7

Mujahid, S., Mubarik, S., & Naghavi, N. (2019). Prioritizing dimensions of entrepreneurial ecosystem: A proposed framework. *Journal of Global Entrepreneurship Research, 9*(1), 51. doi:10.118640497-019-0176-0

Nair, S., Sundar, S., & Mangadu Paramasivam, G. (2020). Role of entrepreneurial education in nurturing entrepreneurial orientation among engineering students. *Asia Pacific Journal of Innovation and Entrepreneurship, 14*(2), 139–149. doi:10.1108/APJIE-05-2019-0031

Naldi, L., Nordqvist, M., Sjöberg, K., & Wiklund, J. (2007). Entrepreneurial Orientation, Risk Taking, and Performance in Family Firms. *Family Business Review, 20*(1), 33–47. doi:10.1111/j.1741-6248.2007.00082.x

Narayanasamy, K. (2008). The Role of Centralized Knowledge Development Centre for Success of SME Sector. *Communications of the IBIMA, 2*, 16.

Naumann, C. (2017). Entrepreneurial Mindset: A Synthetic Literature Review. *Entrepreneurial Business and Economics Review, 5*(3), 149–172. doi:10.15678/EBER.2017.050308

Njoroge, C. W. (2013). *The Effect Of Entrepreneurial Educationandtraining On Development Of Small And Medium Size Enterprises In Githunguri District- Kenya. 1*(8), 22.

Obschonka, M., Silbereisen, R. K., & Schmitt-Rodermund, E. (2010). Entrepreneurial intention as developmental outcome. *Journal of Vocational Behavior, 77*(1), 63–72. doi:10.1016/j.jvb.2010.02.008

Parente, R., & Feola, R. (2013). Entrepreneurial intent and entrepreneurial commitment of young researchers. *International Journal of Technology Management & Sustainable Development, 12*(2), 155–166. doi:10.1386/tmsd.12.2.155_1 PMID:28057083

Pittaway, L., & Cope, J. (2007). Entrepreneurship Education: A Systematic Review of the Evidence. *International Small Business Journal, 25*(5), 479–510. doi:10.1177/0266242607080656

Poon, J. M. L., Ainuddin, R. A., & Junit, S. H. (2006). Effects of Self-concept Traits and Entrepreneurial Orientation on Firm Performance. *International Small Business Journal*, *24*(1), 61–82. doi:10.1177/0266242606059779

Ramaciotti, L., & Rizzo, U. (2015). The determinants of academic spin-off creation by Italian universities. *R & D Management*, *45*(5), 501–514. doi:10.1111/radm.12105

Rodríguez-Gutiérrez, M. J., Moreno, P., & Tejada, P. (2015). Entrepreneurial orientation and performance of SMEs in the services industry. *Journal of Organizational Change Management*, *28*(2), 194–212. doi:10.1108/JOCM-01-2015-0020

Sadiku-Dushi, N., Dana, L.-P., & Ramadani, V. (2019). Entrepreneurial marketing dimensions and SMEs performance. *Journal of Business Research*, *100*, 86–99. doi:10.1016/j.jbusres.2019.03.025

Samiullah, S., Sami, A., & Ahmad, T. (2021). Entrepreneurial Ecosystem and Performance of SMEs in Pakistan. *International Journal of Economics and Business Administration*, *IX*(2), 192–204. doi:10.35808/ijeba/697

Saptono, A., Wibowo, A., Narmaditya, B. S., Karyaningsih, R. P. D., & Yanto, H. (2020). Does entrepreneurial education matter for Indonesian students' entrepreneurial preparation: The mediating role of entrepreneurial mindset and knowledge. *Cogent Education*, *7*(1), 1836728. doi:10.1080/2331186X.2020.1836728

Sebora, T. C., Lee, S. M., & Sukasame, N. (2009). Critical success factors for e-commerce entrepreneurship: An empirical study of Thailand. *Small Business Economics*, *32*(3), 303–316. doi:10.100711187-007-9091-9

Shepherd, D. A., & Krueger, N. F. (2002). An Intentions–Based Model of Entrepreneurial Teams' Social Cognition*. *Entrepreneurship Theory and Practice*, *27*(2), 167–185. doi:10.1111/1540-8520.00005

Shwetzer Herrera, C., Maritz, A., & Nguyen, Q. (2021). *Entrepreneurial ecosystems: A holistic and dynamic approach*. doi:10.26181/600506b67b4d5

Simons, R. (2013). *The Entrepreneurial Gap: How Managers Adjust Span of Accountability and Span of Control to Implement Business Strategy* (SSRN Scholarly Paper No. 2280355). Social Science Research Network. doi:10.2139/ssrn.2280355

Soini, E., & Veseli, L. (2011). Factors Influencing Smes Growth In Kosovo. *International Business Management*, 76.

Souitaris, V., Zerbinati, S., & Al-Laham, A. (2007). Do entrepreneurship programmes raise entrepreneurial intention of science and engineering students? The effect of learning, inspiration and resources. *Journal of Business Venturing*, *22*(4), 566–591. doi:10.1016/j.jbusvent.2006.05.002

Stam, E. (2014). *The Dutch Entrepreneurial Ecosystem* (SSRN Scholarly Paper No. 2473475). Social Science Research Network. doi:10.2139/ssrn.2473475

Stokes, D. (2000). Putting Entrepreneurship into Marketing: The Processes of Entrepreneurial Marketing. *Journal of Research in Marketing and Entrepreneurship*, *2*(1), 1–16. doi:10.1108/14715200080001536

Sussan, F., & Acs, Z. J. (2017). The digital entrepreneurial ecosystem. *Small Business Economics*, *49*(1), 55–73. doi:10.100711187-017-9867-5

Szerb, L., Lafuente, E., Horváth, K., & Páger, B. (2019). The relevance of quantity and quality entrepreneurship for regional performance: The moderating role of the entrepreneurial ecosystem. *Regional Studies*, *53*(9), 1308–1320. doi:10.1080/00343404.2018.1510481

Tajpour, M., & Hosseini, E. (2021). Entrepreneurial Intention and the Performance of Digital Startups. *The Mediating Role of Social Media.*, *13*(7), 2456–9011. doi:10.31620/JCCC.06.21/02

Trevelyan, R. (2008). Optimism, overconfidence and entrepreneurial activity. *Management Decision*, *46*(7), 986–1001. doi:10.1108/00251740810890177

Uddin, M. R., & Bose, T. K. (2013). Factors Affect the Success of SME in Bangladesh: Evidence from Khulna City. *Journal of Management and Sustainability*, *3*(3), 166. doi:10.5539/jms.v3n3p166

Van Gelderen, M., Kautonen, T., & Fink, M. (2015). From entrepreneurial intentions to actions: Self-control and action-related doubt, fear, and aversion. *Journal of Business Venturing*, *30*(5), 655–673. doi:10.1016/j.jbusvent.2015.01.003

van Vuuren, J., & Botha, M. (2010). The practical application of an entrepreneurial performance training model in South Africa. *Journal of Small Business and Enterprise Development*, *17*(4), 607–625. doi:10.1108/14626001011088750

Van Vuuren, J. J., & Nieman, G. (1997). Entrepreneurship education and training: A prospective content model. *Unpublished Paper*.

Wathanakom, N., Khlaisang, J., & Songkram, N. (2020). The study of the causal relationship between innovativeness and entrepreneurial intention among undergraduate students. *Journal of Innovation and Entrepreneurship*, *9*(1), 15. doi:10.118613731-020-00125-5

Wennekers, S., & Thurik, R. (1999). Linking Entrepreneurship and Economic Growth. *Small Business Economics*, *13*(1), 27–56. doi:10.1023/A:1008063200484

Wilson, F., Kickul, J., & Marlino, D. (2007). Gender, Entrepreneurial Self–Efficacy, and Entrepreneurial Career Intentions: Implications for Entrepreneurship Education. *Entrepreneurship Theory and Practice*, *31*(3), 387–406. doi:10.1111/j.1540-6520.2007.00179.x

Yeh, C.-H., Lin, H.-H., Wang, Y.-M., Wang, Y.-S., & Lo, C.-W. (2021). Investigating the relationships between entrepreneurial education and self-efficacy and performance in the context of internet entrepreneurship. *International Journal of Management Education*, *19*(3), 100565. doi:10.1016/j.ijme.2021.100565

KEY TERMS AND DEFINITIONS

Entrepreneurial Mindset: The entrepreneurial mentality or the way of thinking that allows entrepreneurs to achieve your objectives. Successful entrepreneurs view obstacles, mistakes, and failure as chances to learn new skills that will help them thrive in the future.

Entrepreneurial Marketing: Entrepreneurial marketing is the proactive discovery and exploitation of chances for attracting and maintaining lucrative consumers using creative risk management, resource leveraging, and value creation strategies.

Entrepreneurial Orientation: Entrepreneurial orientation is a firm-level strategic orientation that captures an organization's entrepreneurial strategy-making procedures, management beliefs, and company behaviours.

Entrepreneurial Ecosystem: An entrepreneurial ecosystem's essence is its people, as well as the culture of trust and collaboration that allows them to connect successfully. An ecosystem that allows for the rapid exchange of people, knowledge, and resources enables entrepreneurs to swiftly discover what they require at each stage of development.

Entrepreneurial Intention: In a nutshell, entrepreneurial intention is a psychological condition that directs our attention toward certain business objectives in order to produce entrepreneurial outcomes. It is also an acknowledgment that individuals take action to start new businesses or add value to current ones.

Entrepreneurship Education: Entrepreneurship education has been characterised as "a set of institutionalised teachings that informs, trains, and educates anybody interested in contributing to socioeconomic development through a project to encourage entrepreneurship awareness, firm formation, or small business development.

Chapter 2
Man, Mind, and Machine:
A Vulnerable Symbiosis

Nirmala M.
School of Commerce, Jain University (Deemed), India

Manne Neelima Chaudhary
School of Commerce, Jain University (Deemed), India

Srinivas G.
School of Commerce, Jain University (Deemed), India

ABSTRACT

Technology is a science to solve a problem or to simplify the tasks carried out by humans. Technology in simple words is a way of doing things. There are various benefits associated, such as communication; technologies have not only helped in making the world a smaller place by bringing people closer together, but also widened the gap between people which has come to be known as 'virtual distance.' Since the first Industrial Revolution, manufacturing has seen advancements making manufacturing processes more sophisticated and sustainable to control effectively. Industry 5.0 enables people to transition from mass manufacturing to mass personalization as people now demand the human touch of mass personalization. Mass customization is becoming a reality, and needs fast-moving advancements in manufacturing processes, system digitization, and intelligence. This article addresses a few important dimensions of technology such as technology being treated as human extension, coevolution between humans and technology, human dependence on technology and vulnerability of mankind due to technology.

INTRODUCTION

Let us begin with a simple question. What does technology mean? Well! Most people perceive technology to be synonymous with computers. Some perceive technology to be the creation and application of scientific knowledge. Others perceive technology to be a collection of tools, techniques and systems. But only those who truly comprehend the real meaning of technology will be able to define "technology" as

DOI: 10.4018/978-1-6684-6403-8.ch002

anything that can meet a human need. There is a famous proverb stating that invention is the mother of necessity which evolved from what Pluto had once stated: "our need will be our real creator". This holds for technology. A simple example would be the invention of the microscope. When there was a need to explore the world beyond human sight it led to the invention of the microscope. We are surrounded by technology and it has indeed become a very integral part of our lives. One might assume technology to be mostly electronic, but that is not the case. For instance, when we are tired and need some sleep we lie down on a mattress which is again a product of technology or when we wake up in the middle of the night we switch on a bulb, it is again the most fundamental form of technology for humans, all the gadgets that one uses such as washing machines, mobile phones, television sets, gaming consoles etc. is simply technology. A computer on the other hand is one of the most advanced forms of technology. People are so integrated with various forms of technology, that one finds it difficult to isolate them from it. Hence when humans are so unified with technology, it becomes imperative to add a touch of humanity to it.

Hence, this article revolves around a symbiosis of the human mind and technology with a touch of humanity. Technology is also a way of doing things. It requires both intentional and non-intentional interactions with other machines, devices and humans. For instance, most people love drinking coffee in a coffee shop. Coffee is made out of coffee beans which come from trees. But these trees have been grown by farmers and the yields from these trees support the farmer and his family. This farmer needs pesticides for the trees that he grows and this need for pesticides supports another family. The coffee beans once harvested would be packed and transported to various countries. Finally, the brewed coffee is served in paper cups that were manufactured for a specific purpose. The whole idea of giving this example is to explain how interdependent the choices that people make could be and how the lives of so many people get affected due to those choices. Nowadays due to the heavy dependence of individuals on technology, rather than human needs influencing the change in technologies, it is now the technologies that are changing people and causing them to grow, evolve and develop. It also has begun influencing our communication and relationships with other people. When Industry 4.0 is still gaining ground and has not yet reached maturity, Industry 5.0 is ready to take the stage. A fifth industrial revolution known as "Industry 5.0" is one where consumers may meet their own needs based on preferences and expectations. Industry 4.0, which is at the mass customisation level, uses robots to complete monotonous jobs, but industry 5.0 seeks to perform mass personalisation using artificial intelligence. Higher autonomy for collaborative robots is projected to revolutionise the manufacturing process in Industry 5.0. Industry 5.0 is a hypothetical industrial revolution that will enable robots to carry out monotonous activities, increasing creativity and innovation in products. Industry 5.0 is anticipated to make the best use of human creativity and intelligence. Currently, the manufacturing industry is transitioning from mass production to custom manufacturing; therefore manufacturing processes must advance quickly, as well as the digitalization and intelligentization of production systems. For tasks like loading, unloading, painting, welding, etc., robots are a huge help. An autonomous robot is used to conduct a more precise independent manufacturing procedure and to work in places where human employees are restricted from working. Industry 5.0 can learn from big data, which creates a network of digital knowledge, to produce symmetrical innovation. It can do what a person desires to achieve and makes use of cooperating robots to increase precision and performance.

MODERN DAY CHALLENGES OF TECHNOLOGY

Several challenges exist in the modern day usage of technology. People have begun living more in the digital world rather than the real world which has presented many problems for people. Some of the problems could be in the form of changed values and beliefs, changed expectations from people around, reduction in intimacy and superficial relationships etc. People have now been obsessed with creating unreal identities in the simulated world and have been living parallel lives. Kids nowadays tend to bond more with virtual pets rather than real pets. Children have so immersed in a virtual reality/ augmented reality that they find it extremely normal to wear screen monitors as eyeglasses. Any individual with a smartphone can have access to augmented reality (AR). Using augmented reality it becomes possible to add digital elements to a live view by using a camera or a smartphone. In augmented reality, the real world is seen right in front of us but with a few digital additions. For instance, trees could be seen swaying in the park but maybe with a Pokémon hanging between the trees, dogs could be seen chasing the ball but could also be seen chasing cartoon characters. As the above examples indicate, in AR, the virtual environment is designed in such a way that it can co-exist with the real world environment. Hence, augmented reality is much more efficient as compared to virtual reality as a simple smartphone with a good resolution camera would suffice for people to access it. Both AR and VR are trending in India and have impacted several industries such as retail, government services, real estate, automotive etc. Many factors have driven the adoption of AR and VR in India. Industry 5.0 increases the chances for creative people to work, which promotes the improvement of labour productivity. Industry 5.0 will assist the client digitally in managing repeated follow-up assignments thanks to machines that are adaptable in accordance with staff wants to generate a high-level choice (Haleem & Javaid, 2019). Industry 5.0 increases the value of employment since it allows individuals the freedom to be in charge of making (Rossi, 2018). The production cell operator in industry 5.0 becomes more involved in the planning process than in the more or less automated manufacturing process (Rossi, 2018). Collaborative robotics is a form of automation that, along with human co-workers, continues to pose a serious risk on the factory floor (Rossi, 2018). From manufacturing systems, it is difficult to acquire high-quality and integrity of data and it is difficult to accommodate diverse data repositories (Thoben, 2017).

In today's era, machines are becoming smarter and human-like and humans are becoming more like cyborgs. There have been quite a few movies that have depicted the imminent vulnerability of humans due to the increasing dependence on technology, movies where AI was seen as the villain. For instance, in the movie, I, Robot movie, AI was shown as the main antagonist where robots eventually form their own interpretation of the Three Laws which serves humanity, then there is the Avengers: Age of Ultron movie where the protagonists eventually defeat the villain depicted by AI which is hell-bent on destroying all humanity. How can one forget The Terminator movie where machines try to destroy mankind. Some movies have also tried to humanize machines and show them portraying human emotions and craving for affection. Movies such as ET the Extra-Terrestrial, WALL-E, and Bicentennial Man have portrayed robots with human feelings. Even though we are currently not faced with humanoid robots, there will soon come an era where we are constantly faced with such machines which seek one's affection or there may come a time when one deals with parallel universes as advanced as the one seen in the Matrix movie. There could be a time when people crave so much companionship and people may be so busy that finding a human companion may become a thing of the past, hence it may become a common phenomenon to see a person with a robotic dog as a companion or patient may be taken care by robotic nurses or AI-based health care staff, instead of a human nanny very soon a robotic nanny may take over the responsibility of a child and hence the child from a very tender age may start becoming accustomed to advanced machines such as humanoid robots. One example that can be given where robots have begun replacing humans is the Japanese health care institutions for the elderly, wherein the robots are in charge of taking care of the elderly people housed in the nursing home, the robotic nurses would be responsible for giving medicines, checking the blood pressure of patients and also playing the role of companions for these elderly patients. Hence, it cannot be said that technology and machine dependency can only lead to havoc at all times. There are positive as well as negative aspects of technology adoption in the lives of people. Too much dependency can be detrimental to mankind making them vulnerable to technology while humanizing machines can also minimize the mechanizing of humans to a large extent (Berger, 2011).

Hence, this article deals with four main aspects namely,

Technology as a Human Extension: Technology can be advantageous to people as it extends or stretches human skills, knowledge & capabilities. Over a period of time machines/ technology becomes a part of people through AI or augmented intelligence.

Co-evolution Between Humans and Technology: Just like how humans benefit from their association with machines and technology, similarly technology too evolves through continuous improvements. Humans bring about changes to technology while technology on the other hand brings about changes to human activities.

Dependence: Humans as mentioned earlier have begun to rely upon technology to a great extent as they are constantly surrounded by different kinds of gadgets, devices and various forms of technology which assist them in carrying out their daily chores.

Vulnerability: Despite there being lots of benefits in the usage of technology by mankind, such as simplification of tasks, the accuracy of work done, enhanced speed of getting the tasks done etc., too much dependency on machines can wreak havoc at times. For instance, virtual distance has to a great extent hampered human relationships. Couples spend more time watching television, laptops and cell phones rather than spending time with one another. The bonding between a teacher and student is getting lost due to the advent of technological devices and apps for online learning. Parenting is now seemingly being done by mobile phones and tablets rather than parents and that has resulted in parents becoming more and more incapable of engaging with their children. With a modern increase in technology that serves to automate tasks and replace certain non-technological systems, employees often do not have to interact with other employees as much as before, but often interact more with computer systems.

TECHNOLOGY AS A HUMAN EXTENSION

Every technology that exists is derived from the human mind and hence can be considered an extension of human capabilities. A very popular book by Kevin Kelly, *What Technology Wants?,* has defined technology as "an extension of physicality for the betterment of humanity". There are many examples that the author quotes such as wheels being the extension of one's feet, and cameras, lenses, spectacles and telescopes being viewed as an extension of human eyes. In fact, personal computers, laptops and mobile phones have become a significant part of people's everyday lives. The emerging concept of a metaverse where individuals are living a parallel life in the virtual world bridges a lot of gaps between the virtual and the real world. Kevin Kelly also quotes that "If technology is an extension of humans, it is not an extension of our genes but of our minds. Technology is therefore the extended body for ideas". Some of the human faculties can be extended or taken forward by technology. For instance, when one speaks over the telephone it is just an extension of voice and ears and similarly, automobiles extend human movement in many ways. Two main classifications of human faculties are "faculties of action" and "faculties of thought" (Lakshmi, 2021). Hence if one applies these two faculties to technology, it could be considered an extension of the human body. An instance of how technology can be an extension of the faculties of action is the use of hand driven tools such as pliers, cutters, hammers, knives, drills etc. Any of the hand tools used by a craftsman in creating a piece of craft through manual operations can also be considered an extension of the faculties of action. Even prosthetics that can be used by a handicapped person can be considered an extension of human faculties. However, there are machines that are controlled by humans such as transport vehicles and there are other technologies or structures around us that are fixed such as roads, buildings, computers and televisions that can be considered faculties of thought. However many researchers believe that technology as an extension of mankind has its pros and cons. Some researchers such as Lanier believe that technology is turning people into machines. However, there are many advantages of technology being used by people. It majorly helps in sustaining human connections. This world surrounded and practically ruled by technology has left many people in isolation with a feeling of loneliness and has produced many changes in people's lifestyle and routine and that has left them with emotional and cognitive consequences. One of the major consequences of this isolation has resulted in a global health crisis. Many technological solutions have essentially played a big role in helping people combat this loneliness. Some of the technologies include AI, IoT, and cloud computing etc. which have rendered services to both the elderly as well as caregivers by creating a series of interoperable platforms. Many individuals view technology as a companion especially due to the COVID-19 pandemic. During the COVID-19 pandemic, many technologies came in handy to people. Technologies such as videoconferencing systems and remote working software have proven effective in bringing people together and keeping in touch with one another securely and efficiently which was very much required to upkeep people's psychological well-being. Individuals need to feel valued, to be heard, to share, to bond and to be cared for to keep cognitive illnesses such as depression, anxiety and other disorders at bay. Technology helps people to stay close despite physical distances. However, certain other authors such as Rothenberg have questioned the benefits of technology playing the extension of humanity. Many have tried to re-evaluate the disconnect and reconnect that humans experience from nature due to the increased usage of technology. Technology can also be considered an extension of personal capabilities. Any human being is a body that forms a view of the world, has an interaction with the real world and resources and uses those resources for their use and the use of mankind in general. As mentioned earlier an individual is a body and technology in this modern era has simply become an extension of the same. People interact with various aspects of the environment and receive the various stimuli of the external world and then form an interpretation of the same. Technology helps in enhancing that perception and taking it to greater heights. It improves and sharpens the human perception of the world. For instance, the sense of sight can be enhanced through monitors, microscopes, and glasses, the sense of hearing can be enhanced to give one a better experience through the use of telephones, musical instruments, speakers, headsets etc. and the sense of taste can be enhanced through the usage of various flavours and kitchen utensils and food containers and other equipment. In addition to a person being a body, the individual is also a mind. Hence technology also plays a significant role in memory and learning. Creativity, consciousness, rationality and awareness of the external world can be enhanced through technology. In order to survive the mind has to sync with the body. Similarly, technology enhances one's mental achievement through the usage of physical devices. Technology boosts one's ability to express themselves and the classic example for this could be as simple the usage of a pencil or as complicated as the use of graphics software. Technology can not only boost one's creativity but also completely transform it and lead to new discoveries.

CO-EVOLUTION BETWEEN HUMANS AND TECHNOLOGY

When Vladimir Putin, the Russian president addressed school children he made a statement that "Whoever becomes the leader in artificial intelligence (AI) becomes the leader of the world". Contrary to Putin's statement, the world's greatest billionaire Elon Musk, CEO of Tesla stated that "AI is a big threat to humanity and overall mankind" and has also requested the government to bring in suitable regulations before things get out of hand and out of control. When technology evolves, it results in the evolution of society and mankind accordingly. Evolution in technology can lead to social, cultural and biological evolution. An anonymous engineer once stated that an engineer designs products that never existed and then gave an analogy of a person who shops for groceries from the supermarket thinking of it as a personal achievement; however, ignores the technological solutions that go into grocery shopping from the supermarket. Some of the technologies that go into it consist of the vehicle technology used for commuting from home to the supermarket and back again, the agriculture technology used for growing vegetables and delivering fresh food to the store, the food storage technology being used in the supermarket etc. A new term called "digital creationism" has been coined by Lee (2020) which revolves around the principle that every technology is an outcome of a deliberate human decision. Technology coevolves with humans. For instance, man created Facebook, which changes the way people connect which again changes bringing new changes in the way Facebook operates (Lee, 2017). There is so much hype regarding AI and how social media is bringing down democracy that people believe that there need to be more regulations in place in dealing with such technologies. There have been privacy laws floating around in social media usage but these laws have hardly been able to protect the user's privacy. There always exists a coevolution between humans and technology. This "Digital Creationism" that is gaining importance these days also focuses on the negative outcomes of technology which are caused by the unethical actions of people especially things that are done with a profit motive without any concern for societal impact. Most of the time people blame the technology creators for creating technologies that have eventually had negative repercussions however, the users of such technologies are also a part of that blame. When people blame Mark Zuckerberg for social media crimes, the users of Facebook also are to be blamed for the inappropriate use of social media that has resulted in those crimes. Hence, there need to be suitable regulations in place under the principle of digital creationism to ensure that both the developers and the end users work to develop and use technology within prescribed restrictions. Despite all the efforts made by the authorities in proposing privacy laws, it has been ineffective because privacy goals cannot be attained only by bringing about a change in the behaviour of the corporates. After all, users of technology are willing to give up on their privacy despite being told in the privacy policies that the information that they share is likely to get abused and users of technology get sucked into the online media. Just as how technology is influencing culture, culture also is influencing technology. Hence there is a feedback loop that is created and any kind of interference in that feedback loop can result in a change in outcomes leading to positive or negative consequences. Just as how it is essential to regulate the developers of technology via laws, it is equally essential to pass laws to educate the users of that technology. If the example of Pokémon GO could be taken to better comprehend the technology development and usage, even though Niantic's privacy policy indicates that there is no advertising involved, shops and nearby business establishments pay Niantic for the placing of Pokémon near their outlets to attract customers. Many times, society condemns technology and technology makers of weapons and radioactive substances, however, the same society enjoys and uses technologies such as Pokémon GO which can easily influence human decision-making, therefore the question that arises here is when a human is so easily influenced by and controlled by technology and machines cannot alleviate the immorality of certain technologies. Quite a few individuals are now speaking of "digital humanism" rather than digital creationism which takes a more human centric approach that tries to limit the detrimental effects of technology. It takes a more humane perspective on the development and usage of technology. In the earlier section, the role of technology as an extension of human actions and human thoughts was discussed extensively. When one speaks of the coevolution of humans and tools there is a lot to be discussed.

TOOLS AND TECHNOLOGY

Tools have always been very essential for humans to reach the top of the food chain. Humans have been inventing tools that help them in accomplishing tasks that they could not achieve by themselves with their own bodies. In the Stone Age, humans invented tools such as spears, bows and arrows etc. to hunt animals. However, there has been an immense amount of evolution of such tools over centuries. From stone-based tools, humans went on to invent metallic tools. When the era of agriculture began during the Middle Ages, they started using new sources of energy, for instance, water and air was used as new energy source which resulted in the development of water mills and windmills. The Industrial age marked the beginning of metal fabrication and machine tools. However, in the age of nanotechnology, tools are now becoming microscopic in nature. Just as how tools and machines have evolved over centuries, the human mind and capabilities have also evolved. In the last century, there has been a tremendous expansion of media and telecommunication technologies that have led to many new devices and gadgets such as personal computers, laptops, smartphones, televisions etc. The Information age and revolution in digital technology have caused the development of new powerful, low cost IT systems. AI has been gaining a lot of importance and some of the researchers such as Kurzweil believe that very soon technology will become smarter and more intelligent than humans and has considered this as an imminent truth. There have been many scholars who have deliberated upon the question of whether machines will overtake humans in the future. Many have claimed that AI can outdo human intelligence in the future and has already overtaken humans when it comes to strength and precision as well as in cognitive functions such as storing, recapitulating and recovering information as and when required. This has led to a strong dependence of humans on machines and technology. However, the human brain is much more complex than machines as the human brain has no constraints and can unimaginable and unrestricted functions that no machine can perform (Sundblad, 2018).

People have been raving about the latest inventions in technology such as smart phones, virtual reality, augmented reality, 3-dimensional printers etc. However, technology is not just about gadgets, computers and other devices. It is all the machines, devices and artifacts that amplify the human hold of the world. And it cannot be ignored that all new technologies are derived from older technologies. Just like how humans have their own needs for surviving and evolving with the help of food, clothing and shelter, technology and its evolutions have needs of their own. The survival and evolution of technology are symbiotic with the survival and evolution of mankind. It's not just about the creation of technology but also the sustenance and maintenance and upgradation of technology that needs to be taken into consideration. Technology has its own evolving requirements. So what are the evolving needs for technology? The answer lies all around us. The machines, devices, tools and equipment that humans have developed need fuel, electricity, raw materials, data, software and other components that enable them to repair and evolve over long periods. Hence technology has its unique power and unique needs and has a wide range of dependencies and invents much more than what it delivers and grows at a more exponential rate as compared to human evolution. Unlike human evolution, technological evolution is not time-dependent. It is an incremental evolution that occur due to additions in various aspects such as design, increase in components, refinement, combinations of elements etc. This is what leads to development. When the number of elements or components increases, the number of potential combinations also tends to increase. For instance, three elements can result in six potential combinations, and four elements can result in twenty-four combinations hence evolution in technology is based upon simple mathematical calculations comprising combinations and recombinations. This can be justified using Moore's law wherein the transistor density was doubled every two years thereby enhancing its performance, efficiency and complexity. From the technological perspective, humans have been getting exponentially slower, while technology is growing faster and hence this could be one of the major factors for technology especially AI overtaking human capabilities. This leads to one of the greatest myths of the digital age which is a singularity, a point of no return for technological evolution. A threshold limit beyond which technology will feed its own design and improvement thereby cutting out humanity completely out of the loop.

DEPENDENCE UPON TECHNOLOGY

Tools and technologies have been used by humans for a very long time for the accomplishment of simple and complex tasks. It also leads to changes in the way societies, and people grow and evolve and also brings out changes in relationships with others. Technologies have existed and evolved over centuries. Societies have seen simple tools such as wheels, chariots, irrigation systems and damns to complex technologies such as computers, laptops, the internet, AI etc. There has been an eruption in technology, especially in the last century and that has resulted in changes in the way people use and interact with technology in their lives. Gadgets such as smartphones, tablets, laptops, VR devices, and gaming systems have drastically altered people's perception of reality and technology has significantly impacted how human interaction takes place. Human behaviours have been deeply impacted by technology both in positive ways as well as negative ways and this has had both good consequences as well as bad consequences. For instance, the availability of mobile phones implies that people can be in close contact with their families and their loved ones. Technologies such as Bluetooth and VOIP allow people to connect even when the cellular network is unavailable. Even when people are physically distant from one another, it allows them to stay connected with their loved ones with the help of technologies such as Skype, and Viber and social media apps such as Facebook, WhatsApp etc. Global communication has now been made possible with the help of the internet. All across the globe people can connect, interact, learn, meet and grow with the help of various kinds of technology. The way people learn has also changed. To learn foreign languages or cultures people now need not visit different language centres but can learn with the help of language-based apps which can readily be downloaded onto their smartphones. Technology has also brought about a change in the way people make friends. Earlier friends were those who were at a close physical distance from one another and someone that you could interact face to face. There used to be 'pen pals'. However, technology such as the internet and social media has changed that to a great extent. People now have 'key pals' rather than 'pen pals'. People can now make friends with any person from any part of the world and constantly facetime and keep in touch with them even though they might be thousands of miles away from one another with the help of different technologies. The virtual distance that exists between people can be significantly reduced with the help of technology. Traveling is another aspect that has been simplified to a great extent due to technology. Earlier people had to visit a travel agent for booking tickets in order to commute between cities and fly to other countries. However, now due to technology, there have been several apps for booking one's travel via various modes of transport such as by flight, by train, by bus etc. Doing monetary transactions too has been simplified with the help of mobile banking and internet banking technologies and there is no need for customers to visit a bank physically or to interact with a teller at the bank. There are now ATMs that enable people to withdraw cash whenever they need and at whatever time they need it. Technology has also made learning much easier. There is a plethora of learning materials, resources, guides, textbooks, and notes available on the internet that can be availed by students of various arenas. There are also several apps available for students in schools, colleges and other higher educational institutions which can be downloaded by students on their laptops and smart phones and can be used for accessing notes, video lectures and various other learning resources. Even during COVID-19 remote classes were made possible and students could attend lectures from the comfort of their homes due to the availability of technologies such as Zoom, Google Meet, and Microsoft Teams etc.

DARK SIDE OF TECHNOLOGY

However technologies are not always roses, there are thorns involved too. So apart from the positive effects, there are certain negative effects of technology too. In this era of globalisation technology has played a major role in bridging the gaps that otherwise existed undoubtedly but there have been certain negative consequences as well. Even though technology has eliminated one form of a gap between loved ones, it has also created a gap between them in another sense. There is a "virtual distance" that is created between people where people are so engrossed with their mobile phones, gaming and other gadgets that even though they are with their loved ones they are so absorbed into their gadgets that they hardly give any quality time to their families and their loved ones. This applies to parents and children, couples, siblings, friends etc. This virtual distance seems to be having an impact on every human being on the face of the earth, especially growing children. The cognitive development and the psychological development of the child is influenced by their immediate environment and parental behaviours. Children constantly learn from their parents and peers by observing and interacting with them and they are adopting their behaviours. Reduced human interactions between parents and children are hindering the cognitive and psychological development of growing children and hence children nowadays have certain personality and psychological disorders. Even when a child cries, parents nowadays find that the best way to calm a child down is by showing them videos on their smart phones or letting them play games on the phones. Hence, children are becoming addicted to gadgets and technology and machines from a very tender age. Only when a child is provided comfort by their parents through the right gestures such as playing with the child, hugging the child and giving physical warmth to the child by stroking the child, the child understands the significance of human interaction and that leads to the child understanding the meaning of empathy, love and affection between humans (Wardynski, 2019). This has resulted at the end of intimacy for people and it is now common for people to text others rather than meet or call them.

Even when people sit next to their friends and family they are found to be with their cell phones with their heads bowed down staring into their phones either texting someone or surfing Facebook and other social media apps. In this technological era, the human to machine interaction has increased drastically while human to human interaction has diminished to a great extent. Very soon humans would be replaced by AI and robots and hence this human to machine interaction is only bound to be increased over time.

Industry 5.0, also known as the "smart era," represents the integration of advanced technologies such as AI, IoT, and robotics into manufacturing and production. However, this era also brings about concerns regarding the vulnerability of mankind and the dark side of technology. As automation replaces human labor, many jobs will become obsolete, leading to economic insecurity and social unrest. Moreover, as technology advances, it may become more difficult to regulate and control, potentially leading to unintended consequences such as cyber attacks, privacy breaches, and social polarization. We must address these concerns and prioritize the ethical development and use of technology in Industry 5.0.

VULNERABILITY OF MANKIND

Is Technology leading to the vulnerability of mankind? In the earlier section, one's dependence on technology was elaborated on in detail. But is this dependence on technology making one more vulnerable is the question that needs deliberation. Life would be truly unimaginable without technology. All aspects of our lives have been taken over by technology, whether it is simple household work being done or complex industrial operations, all is now taken forward with the assistance of technology. From the time of civilization, humans have tried to seek better, more convenient and more accessible ways of carrying out different work. Humans have tried to seek newer and better solutions for every challenge or every problem that they encounter for centuries (Crane, 2021). In order to develop new things, innovation is necessary and this innovation leads to human development as well. This is in line with what was discussed in the earlier section about how human evolvement and technological evolvement goes hand in hand. Recent technologies such as AI have simplified human labour to a large extent and people have now been able to accomplish their tasks with more accuracy, quicker and in a smarter way. Mankind is highly influenced by today's technological advancements and technology significantly influences the way modern-day society functions. Many scholars have indicated that social isolation and cognitive illnesses such as depression, anxiety, ADHD, and increased stress have resulted among people. Undoubtedly technology has its benefits but there are certain dark sides of technology and how technology is taking over the lives of people leading to vulnerability. Let us look into the different ways in which technology makes mankind vulnerable. At the outset technology results in lower levels of intelligence and poor intellect. One cannot deny that the internet has given us search engines like Google which uses complex algorithms and gives information from nook and corner of the globe at the click of a button. It is indeed a great learning tool and it gives you information from the comfort of one's place rather than needing to constantly keep visiting the libraries. Technology can also be used in classroom learning and can not only enhance the students' learning opportunities but also their social engagement with their classmates, peers, teachers etc. However, there are certain drawbacks to the usage of technology. For instance, students are more inclined towards cheating and plagiarising work rather than using their original ideas and intellect. This can lower their levels of intelligence and motivate them in taking the easy way out. Technology is also causing lots of distraction for youngsters. Gaming, chatting and instant messaging, watching videos, Netflix etc. cause a distraction for the kids . Kids nowadays enjoy scrolling the social media apps such as Facebook, Instagram etc. rather than reading books and that seems to be hurting their academics and their grades and also their overall intellect. Apart from the intellect perspective, there are other negative challenges of technology such as physical damage that it causes to people. Obesity is one of the most prevalent problems that are faced by youngsters these days. People prefer sitting in front of their laptops, PCs, tablets, televisions etc. rather than exercising or walking around and prefer playing games on their gadgets rather than the actual physical games and which reduces blood circulation and also results in diseases such as arthritis. This sedentary lifestyle is affecting the health and posture of both kids as well as adults. Thus this dependence on technology is hampering the health and well-being of mankind. In addition to the health and well-being of people, there are other vulnerabilities associated with technology such as the digital vulnerabilities involved. There have been many cases of cyber crimes and cyberbullying due to information leaks and data breaches. There have been cases where women and young girls have been subjected to serious crimes because of the misuse of social media (Lane, 2019). There have also been cases of financial fraud through hacking of social media and mobile phones and email addresses by hackers. Pornography, sex crimes and sexting are other dangerous activities that youngsters nowadays are becoming a part of due to technology. In addition to the above drawbacks, another very important dark side of too much reliance on technology is poor social skills. People particularly the millennial generation are so into social media technologies such as Facebook, Instagram, Snapchat, and WhatsApp etc. that they have lost track of actual physical meet-ups and social gatherings. On the superficial level, technology makes one feel that the entire world is your friend but one should realise that these are all superficial or virtual friends and not real friends. This technology is completely changing the concept of friendship and instead of bringing people closer; it is only creating more virtual distance between people.

Benefits for society and the workforce are provided by Industry 5.0. The business is becoming more competitive, which makes it easier to recruit top employees. The adoption of this sector encourages technologies that use resources naturally and responsibly. Robots that resemble people, like Sophia, personify what artificial intelligence might one day be. It supports human decision-making and is assisted by enabling technologies that aid in the revolutionization of numerous industries. In this essay, numerous difficulties are even highlighted, including managing resources and handling large amounts of data.

Challenges Of AI

When people begin substituting face-to-face conversations with online interactions people lose their sense to understand facial expressions, body language, voice tone and empathy towards others. This can cause a lot of suffering in their day to day lives especially if it deals with interactions with people, particularly in the workplace. However, the future challenges of certain technologies such as AI cannot be underestimated. There are certain risks relating to AI that humans have not gauged yet. To predict the risks associated with AI, one needs to first understand the way AI typically works. When an individual operating the AI-enabled process identifies a need, this AI enabled device gathers information from various knowledge sources and either provides the required information to the individual seeking that information or takes the necessary action to achieve that need. It all depends upon whether the action to be taken by the AI based device is to 'inform' or to 'do'. There are certain concerns associated with this. Firstly there is a possibility of AI making mistakes while performing the necessary action. Secondly, there could be bugs or issues with the programming of such AI devices. Take the example of IBM's Watson machine which was once highly applauded for providing knowledge-based information to doctors and patients in the field of medicine, especially to cancer patients. However, there have been many instances of the machine providing faulty and inaccurate information to the doctors during the treatment of cancer patients which thankfully was diagnosed by the doctors at an early stage itself. But as of now, things are still under control by humans. But things may get out of hand when humans start assigning tasks to smarter AI devices (Frey, 2021). Speaking of the bugs in the AI program caused by the programmer, could lead to serious consequences. For instance, if the AI programmer has instructed the AI machine to eliminate cancer from the face of the Earth, but didn't establish the right knowledge based rules for the machine to execute the instruction, then it could cause havoc (Chatfield, 2019). The machine may assume that the best way to eradicate cancer would be eliminating anybody who has cancerous cells in their body and that could be disastrous particularly if the AI machine was programmed to 'do' rather than to just 'inform'. It could result at the end of the world. However, concerning AI, things are still in control by humans and all's good so far. However, even now there are AI based devices that function independently without human intervention and are run with the help of programs. Many futurists, however, have speculated that one day there are chances that AI may eventually break down and can cause unmanageable chaos thereby opening a Pandora's Box which may become difficult to close.

AI (Artificial Intelligence) is a rapidly growing technology that is changing the way we live and work. Industry 5.0 is the era of manufacturing where human workers collaborate with smart machines and advanced technologies, such as AI. AI systems can process and analyze large amounts of data to provide real-time insights, predict outcomes, and automate tasks. This technology can improve manufacturing efficiency, reduce errors, and enhance product quality. AI can also improve the safety of workers by reducing the risk of accidents. Businesses need to adopt this technology to stay competitive and meet the demands of Industry 5.0.

RECOMMENDATION FOR COLLABORATION OF HUMAN BEINGS, SOCIETY, AND TECHNOLOGY

In the era of Industry 5.0, there are several recommendations for human beings, society, and technology. For humans, it is crucial to continuously learn and upskill themselves to adapt to the changing job market. Society should focus on creating a sustainable and inclusive environment, promoting social responsibility, and encouraging innovation. Technology should prioritize ethical considerations, data privacy, and security, and focus on the development of advanced automation and machine learning to optimize production. It is essential to integrate human-machine collaboration and ensure that technology complements and enhances human capabilities. In summary, the recommendations emphasize the need for a collaborative effort between humans, society, and technology to ensure a prosperous and sustainable future.

Even though all the technology based vulnerabilities cannot be eliminated, certain aspects can be fixed to a certain extent. Speaking of privacy issues in the digital world, as most of the user data is captured and stored in the cloud, data encryption using VPN can reduce the data breach risk to a certain extent. Most cyber security experts have proposed certain VPN servers which are available online to protect the digitally available user data. Some of the other issues as discussed above the dark side of technology such as lack of social skills, cognitive, physical and psychological disorders and poor intellect can be overcome to a certain extent by participating in various offline workshops, seminars, peer learning groups, team building activities and engaging in more physical activities such as jogging, cycling, joining a gym, playing sports with family and friends etc. Hence there needs to be a suitable balance between technology and mankind. Humans cannot completely disconnect or unplug from technology as technology is influencing every aspect of one's lives whether it is business or educational systems, health, relationships etc. Undoubtedly newer technologies are emerging now and then, hence it is smart to embrace the new technologies without becoming addicted to those technologies. There is a popular saying that 'necessity is the mother of invention'. Hence technologies are developed to combat some issues or challenges or to simplify the lives of people but the developers or the inventors of such technologies need to keep in mind that technologies should be developed and used in a human-friendly manner so that eventually technology does not end up ruling over humans. All technological problems need to have a sustainable solution and humans need to strive towards achieving that. Some of the ways that one can adopt to unplug themselves from technology could be as mentioned below.

People need to be aware if they are addicted to technology: This is the first step towards unplugging from technology. One could be addicted to any form of technology such as televisions, gaming, AR/ VR devices, videos, OTT platforms etc.

Not permitting technology to hijack one's brain: People using technology should ensure that technology does not begin controlling or taking over their lives. De-addiction is required if one believes that they are addicted to any form of technology. Internet de-addiction centres are a reality now and people addicted to the Internet can join these centres to overcome the impulsiveness and restlessness that results when they are unable to connect to the internet.

Be aware that the virtual world is different from the real world: There is no 'like' or 'share' button in the real world but sharing happiness with real friends in the real world is still a possibility and people need to realise that. One may have hundreds of friends in the virtual world and very few friends in the real world but the ugly truth is that reality will stay real and virtual cannot become real.

Technology is not as important as one's mental health: Constantly waiting for 'likes' or checking emails and social media can cause a person to become anxious and stressed. Constantly searching for information on Google without using their own God gifted brains can actually make people appear stupid rather than appearing smart. People should limit their online time to a minimum and spend more time in offline mode. People should practice 'digital dieting' thereby refraining from the usage of technology lest they get addicted to it. Always take a break from the digital world. Researchers say that one should give a break of at least 4 hours after being online to stay active and relevant in the offline world.

Everyone has heard about Charles Darwin's theory of the 'survival of the fittest'; however in this Information age where technology has helped even the weakest to survive, Darwin's theory may need to be modified into 'survival of the smartest' and more smartly one uses technology, the better their lives would be.

CONCLUSION

In the era of Industry 5.0, human beings, society and technology will interact in a more collaborative and integrated manner. The focus will shift toward the development of smart factories that use advanced technologies like AI, machine learning, robotics and IoT to create a highly efficient and adaptive production environment. This will require a highly skilled and tech-savvy workforce, which can operate, manage and maintain these complex systems. The integration of humans and technology will lead to more autonomous and self-learning systems that can make intelligent decisions based on real-time data.

The ultimate goal of Industry 5.0 will be to create a sustainable and socially responsible production environment, where technology and human beings work in harmony to meet the needs of society.

This industrial revolution involves utilising human-machine interface to expedite and simplify tasks. The personalisation concept is advanced by Industry 5.0. Industry 5.0 is employed more effectively to create a virtual environment, cutting-edge computers, and information technologies in order to satisfy the highly individualised demand. Big data, artificial intelligence, the internet of things (IoT), cloud computing, COBOTS, innovation, and creativity are all optimally integrated into Industry 5.0. Industry 5.0 is anticipated to generate higher-value jobs with more room for innovation and creative thinking. It contributes to raising labour productivity and giving customers more customisation options. On the other hand, skill development for the workforce is a massive task as a result of highly automated industrial systems. Due to its increased connection and adoption of common communications protocols, industry 5.0 poses a greater threat to cyber security in important industrial systems and production lines. Even though industry 5.0 gives machines more autonomy, humans still have the authority to make crucial decisions that are morally sound. In general, industry 5.0 is anticipated to transform the manufacturing processes and systems by enabling more cooperation between humans and robots to provide customers with customised products. Hyper-personalization is made possible by empowering human intellect with cognitive computing and intelligent automation. The use of technology like machine learning, robotic automation, and others is enabling staff to become more business-savvy and provide clients with high-quality services more quickly. The ERP system controls the supply chain for the company organisation, including providing raw supplies, handling transactions, and transportation. The technology to support the digital supply chain is being created and implemented by the next generation of supply chain solutions. It entails introducing personalization into the supply chain, raising customer happiness, and managing corporate productivity and profit margins. Based on the business's current information, risks associated with waste and supply chains are being reduced. There is the improvement of the supply chain integration for the strategic partnerships and enabled the supply chains to spend time on the experimentation plus less on the fighting forces on matters for the project executions.

People must acquire competency skills to work with sophisticated robots, and they must learn how to cooperate with a robot and smart machine manufacturers. A problem for human workers is learning the necessary technical skills in addition to soft talents. In the new jobs, managing translation and programming industrial robots are challenging duties demanding a high level of technical expertise. The use of cutting-edge technology demands greater time and effort from human workers. Industry 5.0 requires the adoption of collaborative robotics, artificial intelligence, real-time information, and the internet of things as well as customised software-connected factories. Investments in cutting-edge technologies are necessary. COBOTs won't be inexpensive.

REFERENCES

Berger, I. W. (2011, March 7). *The co-evolution of humans and our tools*. Irving Wladawsky-Berger. https://blog.irvingwb.com/blog/2011/03/the-co-evolution-of-humans-and-our-tools.html

Chatfield, T. (2019, February 8). Technology in Deep time: How it evolves alongside Us. *BBC Future.* https://www.bbc.com/future/article/20190207-technology-in-deep-time-how-it-evolves-alongside-us

Crane, A. (2021, October 6). 4 reasons why technology makes us vulnerable and how to fix it. *Untamed Science.* https://untamedscience.com/blog/4-reasons-why-technology-makes-us-vulnerable-and-how-to-fix-it/

Frey, T. (2021, December 16). What happens when we lose control of ai? *Futurist Speaker.* https://futuristspeaker.com/artificial-intelligence/what-happens-when-we-lose-control-of-ai/#:~:text=Yes%2C%20AI%20will%20eventually%20break,and%20specific%2C%20limited%20process%20improvement

Haleem, A., & Javaid, M. (2019). *Industry 5.0 and its expected applications in medical field.* Current Medicine Research and Practice. doi:10.1016/j.cmrp.2019.07.002

Lakshmi. (2021, February 1). *Negative effects of technology & how to overcome them.* Mobicip. https://www.mobicip.com/blog/negative-effects-of-technology

Lane, A. (2019, March 1). What is technology? *Open Learn.* https://www.open.edu/openlearn/science-maths-technology/engineering-technology/what-technology

Lee, E. (2017). Coevolution of human and Artificial Intelligences. *The Berkeley Blog.* https://blogs.berkeley.edu/2017/09/18/coevolution-of-human-and-artificial-intelligences/

Rossi, B. (2018). Manufacturing Gets Personal in Industry 5.0. *Reconteur.* . https:// www.raconteur.net/technology/manufacturing-gets-personal-industry-5-0

Sundblad, W. (2018, September 11). Human-technology symbiosis in manufacturing: Changing the discussion about automation and workforce. *Forbes*. https://www.forbes.com/sites/willemsundbladeurope/2018/09/11/human-technology-symbiosis-in-manufacturing-changing-the-discussion-about-automation-and-workforce/?sh=7f42454b2176

Thoben, K. D., Wiesner, S., & Wuest, T. (2017). "Industrie 4.0" and smart manufacturing-a review of research issues and application examples. *International Journal of Automotive Technology, 11*(1), 4–16. doi:10.20965/ijat.2017.p0004

Wardynski, D. J. (2019, November 7). Different effects of technology on human interaction. *Brain Spire.* https://www.brainspire.com/blog/what-are-the-effects-of-technology-on-human-interaction

Chapter 3
Developing a Model for the Adoption of Industrial Revolution 5.0 Among Malaysian Manufacturing SMEs for Sustainable Growth

Arsalan Hussain
https://orcid.org/0000-0001-8328-574X
Institute of Business Management, Karachi, Pakistan

Hafiz Waqas Ahmed Ansari
https://orcid.org/0000-0002-7828-5769
Universiti Utara Malaysia, Malaysia

Hafiz Nasir
Universiti Utara Malaysia, Malaysia

Muhammad Qasim Maqbool
University of Okara, Pakistan

ABSTRACT

Industry 5.0 was introduced in Germany, pursuing the idea of creating smart factories so that emerging technologies such as the internet of things, cloud computing, robotics systems, virtual reality, big data analytics, and additive manufacturing could produce human–equipment interfaces and cyber-physical systems that generate environmental, economic, and socially sustainable manufacturing systems. Therefore, this study effort to evolve a model for the adoption of the 5IR among Malaysian manufacturing SMEs for sustainable growth. This study proposed a research model based on the theory of innovation diffusion (DOI) and TOE. The result of this study can contribute to the realization of the Industry policy. The model itself can provide guidance to industry and policymakers to promote emerging markets growth. The study is expected to benefit regulators and the business ecosystem in understanding the challenges of implementing 5IR in Malaysia and, most importantly, for them to formulate intervention processes and programs for successful adoption.

DOI: 10.4018/978-1-6684-6403-8.ch003

INTRODUCTION

Among the most influential subjects in academic-related fields are known to be the Industrial Revolution, which brought about Industry 5.0 (Chiarello et al., 2018). The recent decade has led business competition towards dynamic and hypercompetitive strategies to manage rapid-changing business environment. Digitalization and globalization are leading organizations not only to adopt the technology but also to rethink their business models (Gusakov, 2020). To deal with this business scenario, business models are relying on strategic innovation as a solution. Further, the emergence of concepts like industry 5.0 poses new dimensions for strategic decisions, particularly for emerging markets. The use of the Industry revolution has been growing rapidly, and numerous companies such as Mckinsey, HP, IBM, Apple, and Google are injecting different dimensions of the Industry revolution as long-term strategies (Knight, Daymond, & Paroutis, 2020).

The concept of industry 5.0 developed from four transition phases. First, industry 1.0, which was focused on manual labor and machine tools. Second, industry 2.0, introduces electricity in manufacturing industries for mass production. Third, in industry 3.0, manufacturers began to incorporate digital technology and automation. Fourth, the emergence of the fourth industrial revolution also known as industry 4.0 has provided a new dimension for business competitiveness such as the internet of things (IoT) and machine learning. Likewise, Industry 5.0 has given organizational competitiveness a new dimension that is more tied to human technology, the environment, ethics, and sustainability to link innovative manufacturing and lower operational costs of enterprises for emerging markets.

In addition, the basic idea of Industry 5.0 is not limited to a specific "industry". That's why IR 5.0 can be applied to a wider population than IR4.0. Therefore, for the implication of Industry 5.0 for sustainable growth, we need to consider the broad perspective of several industries. Despite the competitive advantage that Industry 5.0 provides to its adopters, it was reported that Malaysia has been lagging in its adoption process. As of the third quarter of 2019, the national adoption rate for Industry 5.0 was reported to be 15–20%, mainly by tier-one companies, even though it had been almost a year since Malaysia launched its National Policy on Industry 4.0, also known as the Industry4WRD (Bernama, 2019). Only 2.7% of SMEs were reported to be implementing Industry 5.0 initiatives in some production-related processes, and the other 75% had not taken specific measures to embark on Industry 5.0 initiatives. Other reasons contributing to the slow adoption rate were a lack of knowledge about Industry 5.0, a lack of knowledge about automation, and a lack of desire to change. This situation supports the findings of Owen and Darkwa (2000) and Wolcott et al. (2008) that SMEs cannot recognize the potential benefits that ICT and technology adoption can provide to the business (Racheal, 2020; Star, 2019).

In the era of the 21st century, innovation and technological progress are essential for every business, and the notion of Industry 5.0 is a new reality of emerging markets. For instance, Malaysian SMEs are progressively embracing digital transformation to boost their performance through the industrial revolution (4IR; Teh & Kee, 2019). SMEs may benefit from improved performance equipped with smart manufacturing, the Internet of Things (IoT), cyber-physical systems, and digital transformation. To assist SMEs in becoming ready for the transformation, the Malaysian government has worked very hard to build a digital environment for them. There is significant work to be done to advance to the most cutting-edge technology such as human technology, environment, ethics, and sustainability also known as Industry 5.0, to go forward to the next millennium, also known as Malaysia's digital economy. Malaysia is one of the emerging markets whose economy has been digitalized. According to numerous sources, two significant factors contributing to the decline in annual output growth are the impact of goods and services tax relief on a firm's costs and the cost of raw materials (AISYAH, 2020). When compared to other countries, Malaysian SMEs have a very low acceptance rate for Industry 5.0. How to save manufacturing time and costs while minimizing administrative costs will be the most difficult challenge facing production companies in the future. The majority of today's industrial manufacturing models will be out of date in ten years. There will be fierce competition throughout this period of transformation. Lastly, the future of Industry Revolution 5.0 for the Indian economy discusses the integration of human machines, industrial robots, and the internet of things in realizing industrial revolution 5.0. The discussed mechanism covers the integration of humans, machines, and artificial intelligence. Particularly for the manufacturing sector, the creation of a new type of robots named Collaborative Robots are designed.

Among the several adopted models/theories for technological innovation adoption, the technological, organizational, and environmental (TOE) factors play important roles in the adoption of a new system. In previous studies, IT expertise and IT infrastructure are two distinctive factors that have been recognized in the successful adoption of information technology. Similarly, Zhu et al. (2003) found that the degree to which a business adopts technology depends on a number of important elements, including IT infrastructure and IT skills. Previously in the literature, top management support, defined as the involvement, motivation, encouragement, and enthusiasm delivered by the upper administration towards the implementation of IS technology, including Industry 5.0, is equally important (Migdadi et al., 2016). Past literature also mentioned competitive pressure and government support as the key determinants of facilitating the applications of advanced technologies in business (Bayo-Moriones & Lera-López, 2007; Sila, 2013).

Based on the above discussion, below are the three research questions proposed for this chapter:

- **RQ1:** What are the issues in the implementation of Industry 5.0 among Malaysian SMEs?
- **RQ2:** Do technological, organizational, and environmental factors influence the adoption of Industry 5.0 among Malaysian manufacturing SMEs?
- **RQ3:** What are the long-term opportunities and challenges manufacturing SMEs will have to face?

LITERATURE REVIEW

The literature review has been carried out to justify the research questions identified in the introduction section. The primary focus of the literature review is to compile previous scholars' work related to the TOE (technological, organizational, and environmental) model and DOI theory pertaining to the implementation of IR 5.0 in Malaysian SMEs. The literature review is consisting of the adoption of Industry 4.0, particularly for Malaysian SMEs and an overview of Industry revolution 5.0.

The Adoption of Industry 4.0 among Malaysian SMEs

Tun Dr. Mahathir Mohamad, Malaysia's prime minister at that time, announced the National Policy on Industry 4.0, or Industry4WRD, in October 2018. It is Malaysia's response to digitally transmuting its industrial production sector and associated service sector by adopting Industry 4.0 in a structured and comprehensive manner, as illustrated in Figure 1. Malaysia is envisioned as a key collaborator for intelligent manufacturing, the main objective for high-tech businesses, and a one-stop shop for the region's manufacturing sector and related services, according to this policy. Industry4WRD's primary emphasis covers the high-potential growth sectors listed under the 11th Malaysia Plan, namely, electrical and electronics, machinery and equipment, chemicals, aerospace, and medical equipment.

SMEs make up 98.5% of all enterprises in Malaysia, making them a fundamental backbone of the country's economy. SMEs are anticipated to contribute up to 41% of the nation's GDP by 2020, and about 32 projects will be strengthened to develop resilient and sustainable SMEs, according to the most recent mid-term review of the 11th Malaysia Plan 2016-2020 report. However, SME failure rate in Malaysia is shocking, whereby 60% of the new SMEs fail within five years of establishment very high compared to other developed countries. Moreover, only 4 out of 10 SMEs can meet the challenges associated with growth successfully. A recent CEO from the title "how digital economy will disrupt businesses in Malaysia" also acknowledged that SMEs could not survive without digitalizing their businesses (Wong, Leong, Hew, Tan, & Ooi, 2020). Thus, SMEs need to view technology adoption as an investment rather than a cost to sustainable growth. However, facing the ambitious aim to accomplish SMEs in Malaysia is presently confronting a few challenges, such as a scarcity of skills for foreign personnel and being slow to adopt new technologies toward sustainable performance (Ambad et al., 2020).

Industry 4.0 and Industry 5.0 will reshape and expand small and medium-sized businesses to stay competitive by leveraging the advantages of emerging technology and innovation, while SMEs make up the vast majority of manufacturing (98.5%), and also the nation's employment (42%). The government has also established the Industry4WRD Readiness Assessment Program to allow companies to evaluate their readiness and existing manufacturing gaps and how they can implement Industry 4.0 through targeted action by qualified evaluators. Literature reviews highlighted viewpoints linked with Industry 4.0 in Malaysia, which include challenges of adoption and implementation of Industry 4.0 in Malaysia (Ing et al., 2019), opportunities and benefits of adoption (Alaloul et al., 2018) as well as the development of Industry 4.0 from a sectoral perspective (Jeevan et al., 2018). However, reports in the media cited the lack of knowledge and fear of huge investment, especially among SMEs, lack of awareness of available government channels for the adoption process, and government inefficiency in communication and fund disbursement.

The Fourth Industrial Revolution (4IR) is said to be the era of the smart machine, driven by the ever-increasing power of artificial intelligence, big data, robots, cloud computing, advanced manufacturing, and the Internet of Things (IoT). The most often used phrases to characterize this trend, which is quickly altering the global industrial landscape, are Industry 4.0, smart manufacturing, the Internet of Things, cyber-physical systems, and digital transformation. As such, there is a need for SMEs to embrace the 4IR.

One of the major issues and worries of this very new revolution is that it consists of architecture based on complicated technology networks (Lee et al., 2015). Consequently, Industry 4.0 requires further research for its productive usage and implementation (Dalenogare et al., 2018). Some previous publications have yielded eminent models for the sake of realizing Industry 4.0 (Lu & Weng, 2018; Schuh et al., 2017). Nevertheless, due to the least amount of empirical evidence regarding these technology infrastructures, organization support, competitive environment, and government support toward the industry 4.0 technology adoption patterns in Malaysian SMEs. Since the middle of 2018, the Ministry of International Trade and Industry (MITI) has led the development of the Industry4WRD Policy in collaboration with a number of primary ministries, including the Ministries of Finance, Multimedia and Communications, Human Resources, Education, and Energy, Science, Technology, Environment, and Climate Change, as well as agencies, industries, and stakeholders.

Overview of Industry 5.0

The industry has superseded three former industrial revolutions, each with its distinct characteristics. Through Industry 5.0, the industry can be transformed more rapidly than the previous revolutions, and it can be generally defined as "the use of advanced physical equipment and gadgets in conjunction with networked sensors and software to forecast, monitor, and plan for improve business and societal results" or "a higher level of value chain control and coordination throughout the lifecycle of products" (Kudriashov et al., 2016; Mazzucato & Tancioni, 2008). Industry 5.0 is not considered another industrial revolution. In the United States, the term "Industrial Internet Consortium (IIC), is often used for IR 4.0. Similarly, in Japan, the term IR 4.0 is stated as Society 5.0. However, in the present time, the industrial revolution is a matter of vision for emerging markets.

As Industry 5.0 is divided into two levels, the first level intends to achieve an intelligent and linked factory, whereas the subsequent and upcoming stage of Industry 5.0 intends to accomplish an intellectual and self-improving human technology (Fazal et al., 2022). Technology-driven modernization characterizes the first stage, which is also a prerequisite for the next. We built knowledge in the previous period that made it more likely to produce, acquire, and manage data, as well as process massive amounts of data. Whereas the second stage of Industry 5.0 is described by data and intelligence-driven innovation. The adoption rate of the Fourth Industrial Revolution (4IR) among SMEs in Malaysia is very low, compared to developed countries. The Trading Economics 2019 report showed that Malaysian Industrial production rose by only 2% in November 2019. The most challenging aspect for manufacturing SMEs is how to reduce production and labor costs. The purchasing manager's index (PMI) revealed that in the production sector, there is a stagnant production trend and an annual production growth rate of just over 4%. The Ministry of International Trade and Industry has recently initiated the national policy called Industry4WRD for SMEs to adopt the 4IR for their sustainable growth. Further, Technical expertise such as IT infrastructure also creates an impact on technology adoption. Industry 5.0 requires a high level of technical expertise (Davenport & Mahidhar, 2018). Notably, Industry 5.0 requires extensive support from the top management because it needs huge investments to adopt modern technologies for automation. (Horváth & Szabó, 2019). The adoption cost, government policy, and competitive pressure also impact Industry 5.0 adoption. Lastly, in building the conceptual model, there is impact of the industrial revolution on industry productivity, which eventually increases the competition among industries around the globe (Hidayatno et al., 2019).

By the combination of data from many gadgets, devices, sensors, and instruments, Industry 5.0 allows for flexibility, responsiveness, and momentum in manufacturing and service operations. (Deloitte, 2014). It includes the production and incorporation of ICTs into industry procedures (Dalenogare et al., 2018; Wagire et al., 2019). The principal characteristics of Industry 5.0 are collaboration and integration. Core technologies of Industry 5.0 technologies and examples of enterprise uses are big data analytics, cloud technology, autonomous robots, simulation, additive manufacturing, augmented reality, business intelligence (BI), cyber security, and the industrial internet of things (IoT).

DIFFUSION OF INNOVATION THEORY

Diffusion of innovation (DOI) theory is the most popular theory of innovation diffusion by Rogers (Taherdoost, 2018; Hameed et al., 2012; Tornatzky & Klein, 1982). Rogers interpreted the theory in his book titled *Diffusion of Innovation*, which was initially published in 1962 and then a few more editions afterward (1971, 1983, 1995, and 2003). Innovations, according to DOI theory, are conveyed over time and contained by a certain social structure through specific channels (Rogers, 2003). The decision to adopt or reject an invention rest with the adopter. The top management is the adopter involved in decision-making at the organizational level of innovation adoptions (i.e., adopting enterprise resource planning systems, electronic supply chain management, and e-commerce systems). It is a general understanding that the percentage of the population that adopt innovations is roughly regularly distributed over time since adopters are thought to have varying degrees of propensity to do so (Rogers, 2003).

According to Rogers, diffusion is generally connected with good listeners' efforts to spread innovation through communication channels, whereas the adoption concept is more focused on the utilization of innovation like IR 5.0. Further, according to DOI, "technology adoption" refers to the "usage of innovations" as desired by the adopters rather than the "acceptance of innovations." The differentiation of adopters into the five categories of adopter innovativeness (from the earliest to the later adopters) results from segmenting this normal distribution: early adopters, innovators, the early majority, the late majority, and laggards (Rogers, 2003). Adoption is the process through which Adopters move from initially learning about an invention to forming opinions about it, deciding whether to accept or refuse it, applying the new idea and gaining confirmation of that decision (Rogers, 2003). Many technological adoption studies, such as e-commerce usage (Luong & Wang, 2019), the application of Web 2.0 for knowledge sharing (Amin et al., 2020), e-government adoption (Al-Refaie & Ramadna, 2020), the practice of ERP scheme and application (Behera & Dhal, 2020), and adoption of social-commerce websites (Yang, 2019), have used the DOI theory.

Technological, Organizational, and Environmental (TOE) Framework

The technology-organization-environment framework was established by Depietro et al. (1990). This model is first published in the book of Tornatzky et al. (1990). Many previous scholars wrongly cite this framework with the name (Tornatzky et al., 1990) instead of the original author of the framework (Depietro et al., 1990). The technological, organizational, and environmental framework (TOE) was first presented by Tornatzky et al. (1990). It is a useful theoretical framework for analyzing the factors affecting adoption success at the pre- and post-implementation stages in an organization (Zhu et al., 2010). These factors are further classified into three categories: technological, organizational, and environmental, which are called the *TOE factors* (see Figure 2). TOE model is considered the most relevant framework to investigate technology usage (Depietro, Wiarda, & Fleischer, 1990). Scholars have concluded this model as a comprehensive model because it explains intra-firm level issues and problems of particular technology adoption (Oliveira & Martins, 2010; Stjepić, Bach, & Vukšić, 2021).

The technological aspects play an essential part in the usage of technology adoption and ultimately affect the sustainable growth of SMEs particularly for emerging markets. According to Tornatzky et al. (1990), technological context explains both new and existing technology relevant to the organization, such as technology usage and IT infrastructure. This influences the organization's capacity to progress toward technology adoption. In a similar context, managers identify different choices to adopt technologies in their organizations. Hence, it is important to have tools to assist them in decision-making. The one important choice that can help managers regarding planning, funding, and transition of technology is the combination of IT infrastructure and IT expertise (Alsultanny & AlZuhair, 2018). Organizations with improved IT infrastructure are in a better position to use new technologies in their organizations

(Chatzoglou & Chatzoudes, 2016). In previous studies, IT expertise and IT infrastructure have been recognized as two distinct elements in the successful adoption of information technology. Similarly, Zhu et al. (2003) found that IT infrastructure and the IT expertise of the personnel are the two major influences that can alter the technological concentration of an organization. In a comparable setting, IT infrastructure and internet competencies have also been considered significant elements in the adoption of technology (Gale & Abraham, 2005; Kuan & Chau, 2001). Therefore, IT infrastructure and IT human resource expertise are important factors for the organization in the use of technology like Industry 5.0.

The nature and resources of a company are proxied by the size of the company and the decentralization, formalization, and complexity of its management configuration. (Tornatzky & Fleischer, 1990). At the same time, senior management's understanding of the adoption's advantages has a significant impact. Similarly, top management support is also essential in the planning and defining role of IT in the organization (Payton, 2000). Earlier studies concluded that top management is considered a significant factor in the adoption of e-commerce (Teo et al., 1997), e-market (Duan et al., 2012), and e-procurement (Teo et al., 2009). Additionally, top management helps to prevail over the challenge to change in the organization. Several additional aspects, such as manager attitudes toward IT, innovativeness, experiences, and IT competence, have a direct impact on SMEs' adoption process. Top management also has the authority to release the required financial resources for information system (IS) project implementation (Theodosiou & Katsikea, 2012). Hence, top management support is expected to be the influencing factor in the implementation of technology revolution 5.0 in Malaysian SMEs.

Likewise, the cost of adoption is also an important factor in the adoption of technologies, particularly for SMEs. The adoption of technology in any organization requires technological infrastructures, such as software, hardware, IT personnel, and networks. All these necessities are quite expensive, especially for small and medium firms. The less cost of adopting technology, the more frequently it will be executed in the organization (Premkumar & Roberts, 1999). Information system (IS) adoption is also affected by indirect costs like human cost factors (e.g., training) and the initial cost of temporary drops in production (Love & Irani, 2004). Hence, adoption cost is directly related to the usage and implementation of new technology like Industry 5.0.

The other parties surrounding the company, such as competitors, suppliers, and the government, are referred to as the environmental context (Zhu & Kraemer, 2002). Competitive pressure describes as the strain brought on by rivals in the industry (Oliveira & Martins, 2010). In the literature, competitive pressure has been considered a key determinant in embracing new technologies to improve the operation of the business (Bayo-Moriones & Lera-López, 2007; Sila, 2013). Similarly, many past empirical studies showed that a higher competitive advantage is related to the higher innovation adoption possibility (Sin et al., 2016).

Last but not least influential factor, government support means the official support of the government in the adoption of new technology. More recently, the government of China has been supporting the adoption of Industry 5.0 in different sectors of its economy (Li, 2017). China has been involved in the "Made in China 2025" strategy to escalate the manufacturing industry by adopting new technology like robotics, new energy, and software (Jin, 2015). The literature depicts a positive relationship between government support and the strategic response to Industry 5.0 adoption.

The TOE model and DOI theory have been widely employed by several studies related to the adoption of Web 2.0, e-commerce adoption, e-business adoption, and e-government adoption and usage (Bakar et al., 2020), which indicate the importance of the TOE model and DOI theory. The present study will focus on Industry 4.0 technology adoption by Malaysian SMEs. It presents a strong justification for using the TOE model and the DOI theory as its theoretical guideline for adoption. In addition, the most essential factor is the reliable IT infrastructure that is necessary to create digital communication and is required for adopting Industry 5.0 (Bakar et al., 2020).

Industry 5.0 Implementation Framework for Manufacturing in SMEs

The adoption of new business trends including sustainability objectives, mass customization, competitive pressure, digitalization, and networking manufacturing or creativity-based enterprises is evident when focused on the implementation of Industry 5.0 by manufacturing SMEs. IR 5.0 is built upon the digitalization that connects the physical world with the cyber world, i.e., technology with humans. It enables through a blurring of the lines between physical, digital, and biological entities while focusing on sustainability through renewable energy and energy efficiency (Alaloul, Liew, Zawawi, & Kennedy, 2020). Moreover, industry 4.0 also integrates several new technologies emerging with the Industrial Internet of Things (IoT) to accelerate cyber-physical systems (Tabim, Ayala, & Frank, 2021).

The benefits of implementing IR 5.0 are clear. For instance, a decrease in time-to-market with improved product quality, mass customization, better operation performances, and sustainable growth (Alaloul et al., 2020). As Malik, Ul Haq, Raina, and Gupta (2022) argued that for a successful implementation of the concept of IR 4.0 in industries, digital and technological skills development is an important aspect, especially for developing nations. Moreover, successful implementation needs a few stages of the adoption of different strategies and plans. The authors present three stages of productive execution of Industry 5.0 by SMEs of emerging markets.

The first stage, called the *initial phase*, is a complete adoption of the TOE model. At this stage, SMEs must first analyze the technological, organizational, and environmental factors on a broad scale affecting the whole manufacturing business. For instance, IT infrastructure and IT expertise are available, updated, and suitable for the company, and how it can be performed at optimum to fully implement Industry 5.0. After that, the organizational factors like top management support and adoption cost are available for implementing Industry 5.0. In the end, analyzing environmental factors like government support and competitive pressure is significant for enabling the companies to work with Industry 5.0.

In the next stage, which is the *transition phase*, firms must adopt new changes in business philosophy. This phase is further divided as follows (see Figure 1).

1. **Step One:** aligning business philosophy, vision, and mission with the digitalization of the business and Industry 5.0
    a. In the business philosophy of the company, there must be top management support for fully implementing Industry 5.0.
    b. The vision of the business must be future-oriented and must support digitalization and sustainability.
    c. Under this broader digital vision of the company, the mission and objective must be aligned.
2. **Step Two:** coordination among different departments, training programs, pilot runs, business value chain 5.0
    a. Under digitalizing mission and objectives, all the departments must design the plans and coordinate with the other departments under the top management.
    b. There is a vital and basic role of the IT department in designing departmental plans, as well as holding training programs for the management, staff, and workers.

Figure 1. Framework to implement Industry 5.0

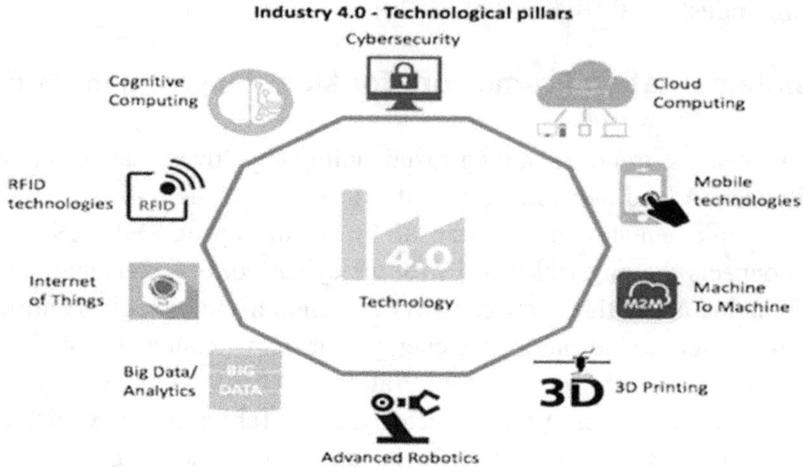

c. The pilot run will be an important task before the complete implementation of Industry 5.0. The results of the pilot run will enable firms to gain experience in digitalizing operations, and it will expose any bottlenecks in the execution process.

Once all the departments are coordinated and trained effectively and pilot runs have been completed with positive results, companies must go forward into the *execution phase* and complete all the requirements mentioned in Figure 2.

After the transition phase, the final stage is the *implementation* or *execution phase*. This phase is about the implementation and execution of new business philosophy under the TOE model to adopt Industry 5.0. During this phase, SMEs will operate through different digital technologies and will establish a connection between the physical and digital worlds through a connecting medium. In this human–machine interaction, sensor technologies will collect human consumer data and store it in cloud storage. Then this data will be analyzed through data analyzing software (ERP) and AI. The data analysis results will be used for forecasting, future planning, mass customization, and decision-making. Most importantly, all the activities will be secured through cybersecurity.

Table 1, shows the Execution of the Implementation phases of Industry 5.0 (see Table 1). Every aspect of the implementation stages has its significance, but cybersecurity is the most important of all. Cybersecurity is a complicated process to ensure secure digitalization and block any attempt to hack the system, especially in Industry revolution 5.0 (Haleem, Javaid, Singh, Rab, & Suman, 2022). Cybersecurity has a direct influence on business operations and organizational performance. For instance, Ridaryanto, Refi Kautsar Firmansyah, and Rano Kartono (2015) argued that the Association of Southeast Asian Nations (ASEAN) countries are facing issues regarding cyber security and experienced several cyber-attacks in past decades. Moreover, cyber security issues need to be improved in Malaysia for the successful implementation of the Industrial revolution 5.0.

Table 1. Execution of the implementation phase

Physical medium	Connecting medium	Digital medium
Machines **Robotics** **Mobiles** **HR** **Raw materials** **Products** **Consumers/users** **Mass customization**	Internet VR/AR Human-Machine interaction Digitalization	Sensor technologies Cloud computing Big data sciences ERP AI
Cyber security		

INDUSTRY 5.0 FUTURE OPPORTUNITIES AND CHALLENGES

After ten years of hype about the Fourth Industrial Revolution and efforts to bring Industry 5.0 to SMEs, we must look forward to understanding what hindrances SMEs would face in the subsequent ten years. The start of a novel industrial insurgency dubbed Industry 5.0 has already been discussed by numerous researchers (Ozdemir & Hekim 2018), specifically, the use of artificial intelligence has been emphasized in the manufacturing sector. After the examination of the aims of Industry 5.0 from the start (Kagermann et al., 2013), As is evident that they are not fully developed yet. Whereas some certain objectives, like cyber-physical schemes, connected and smart plants, IoT, and data incorporation, are well-referenced and prepared for execution, others, like intellectual manufacturing arrangements or self-utilizing factories, are still in their early stages and need further inquiry.

Industry 5.0 is divided into two levels. The first level intends to achieve an intelligent and linked industrial unit, whereas the subsequent and upcoming level of Industry 5.0 intends to accomplish an intellectual and self-optimizing factory. Technology-driven modernization characterizes the first stage, which is also a prerequisite for the next. We built knowledge in the previous period that made it more likely to produce, acquire, and manage data, as well as process massive amounts of data. The second stage of Industry 5.0 is characterized by data and intelligence-driven innovation. The next decade of Industry 5.0 will be focused on making sense of data and using it to not only improve our factories but also to get them to a level of self-regulation and self-optimization. In order to get toward intelligent manufacturing, we may apply artificial intelligence as well as bio-inspired intelligence (Rauch, 2020).

When we talk about the benefits of Industry 5.0 will find four major areas. First, it will improve the productivity of SMEs. By using Industry 5.0 technologies, the SMEs can abstract visions from their data to move from responsive to analytical maintenance, locate perfections, lessen unused and improve the yield (Arpacı & Gülel 2023). Moreover, they can refine quality supervision and thus avert expensive rework. Second, Industry 5.0 would improve revenue growth for SMEs. Producers' demands for greater apparatus and novel data claims, as well as customer demand for a broader diversity of more and more personalized goods, will drive added revenue growth. Third, Industry 5.0 would excite an increase in employment. However, it will require some different skills. The tendency to better mechanization will relocate some of the frequent amateur laborers who do simple, tedious tasks. Simultaneously, the demand for employees with high proficiencies in software and IT will increase because of the increasing use of the software. This aptitude alteration is an important trial ahead. Fourth, moving toward new production processes for the incorporation of Industry 5.0 will require investment in the latest technologies and skills by the producers during the next years. This will further enhance the overall investments in society.

On the other side, there are some other challenges for SMEs. It must be determined which business model to use for their expanded or new offerings, to build the foundation for technological development like a tool base for analytics. The development of partnerships is very important to excel in the digital world, building the proper organizational composition and abilities that will help in future technological developments. SMEs must help define and standardize technology, as well as modernize technical infrastructure, for instance, installed and portable broadband services. Infrastructure must be quick, protected, and dependable as much as necessary for businesses to access real-time data. Another significant issue is to improve the workforce's IT-related skills and innovative capacities by offering the proper skills and adapting the relevant school curriculum, training, and university programs, as well as bolstering entrepreneurial initiatives.

Industry 5.0 is the subsequent move in Industry 4.0, which was the fourth industrial revolution that began in the late 20th century. Industry 5.0 is a digital and physical integration platform of manufacturing, services and data processing which will ultimately lead to exploring new windows of opportunities for the consumers and also for the manufacturers and service providers.

Industry 5.0 will be having a profound influence on manufacturing because of the efficient production processes (that is the core of Industry 5.0) through the utilization of automation, digitization and intelligent systems. It will also generate new opportunities for highly skilled professionals having expertise in data analysis, system integration, cyber-security etc. Although industry 5.0 intends to execute mass personalization instead of mass customization, done by robots in industry 4.0 by combining Artificial Intelligence and robotics. Industry 5.0 is assuming that highly autonomous collaborative robots will revolutionize the production process. Industry 5.0, the futuristic industrial revolution, is anticipated to bring more innovative products by permitting robots to perform repetitive work activities. It is also projected that the creative intellectual capability of humans will be at its optimum. Also, Industry 5.0 will not only be relevant to daily work and play but will also influence our daily lives by altering the usage of our homes or interaction with new technology.

Industry 5.0 poses the following opportunities and challenges.

Opportunities of Industry 5.0

- Increased EMS and automation is a deployment of the next-generation technology that will influence employment positively in various sectors.
- Provides enhanced opportunities for customization to customers.
- Machines are an all-rounder that will also consider the employee's needs to create a high-level choice, and industry 5.0 will help in assisting the clients digitally.
- In industry 5.0, the operator working in the production cell will be more involved in the planning process as compared to the automated manufacturing method. Much of the work is centered on robots and IoT because Industry 5.0 has real-time feeding information from the concerned sector.
- It will also contribute to safety measures at the workplace because COBOTs will perform dangerous work.
- More improved customized products and services will boost consumer satisfaction, and loyalty. This customization will also result in increased profit and market share by attracting more consumers.

- Industry 5.0 provides significance to the human-machine interaction by offering a better research and development platform.
- It will enhance the productivity of the industry. Top brand and yakotec are the key players with a high vision that industry 5.0 will bring more improvements in the electronics and automation industry.

Challenges of Industry 5.0

- The decrease in middle-skill employment is because of two reasons. First, the reduced demand for middle-skill jobs. Second, the a clear mismatch between the skills expected by the employers and the employees possess. This challenge can be attributed to the intensification of automation and AI.
- The rise in the skills gap is a serious concern the in recent years. To get rid of this problem, sufficient investment is required in training and development programs. In this vein, for highly automated manufacturing systems, employee skill development is essential for the adoption of this emerging automation. However, a few obstacles like shortage of funds/investment, time constraints and unavailability of qualified trainers cannot be removed immediately.
- Robots are considered that they are a serious threat to human jobs. But on the other hand, they are also helping in solving problems that are beyond human's capacity. Collaborative robotics is an automation technique that combines robots with human co-workers working together in the same workplace.
- It is challenging for startups and entrepreneurs since industry 5.0 demands high investments and infrastructure with cutting edge technology requirements.
- Challenging to draw regulatory mechanisms in industry 5.0 due to high amount of automation presence. For example, whom to be held accountable in case of failures and to what extent.
  - Due to higher levels of automation in the industries, the existing business strategy and business models have to be modified and customized to meet the requirements of industry 5.0. Due to mass personalization, business strategy will be focusing more on customer centric operations. Customer subjectivity changes over time and it is difficult to change the business strategies and business models frequently.
  - Business strategies in industry 5.0 demands a higher level of dynamism to sustain competition due to differential customer preferences.

CONCLUSION

The most basic technologies already accessible show the economic potential of networked production in the framework of Industry 5.0. It is expected that the fast-paced technical innovations would result in significant productivity gains for many small and medium-sized businesses. These types of businesses need flexible organizational structures to actualize them since business sectors that are now clearly separated from one another are progressively becoming intertwined. Small and medium-sized businesses are likely to seek outside expertise more frequently in the future, whether for IT investment choices or the identification of key technology trends. Another major barrier to Industry 5.0 adoption will be the creation of safe, standardized interfaces. An issue is the lack of extensive broadband connections to guarantee very high transfer rates without sacrificing quality. SMEs are particularly affected by this issue. On the other hand, training is a key area in which interdisciplinary linkage of curricula in relevant disciplines is required to adapt them to the requirements of Industry 5.0. With its linkage of theoretical learning material and rapid practical application in firms, the tried-and-true dual training approach may effectively assist the transition to networked production. The outcome of this study will contribute to the National Policy of Industry4WRD, which can increase the economic growth of Malaysia. The adoption of the industry 5.0 model could guide industry and policymakers to promote and improve SME performance by adopting the latest technology of Industry 5.0 in their operations and indirectly fulfill Malaysia's dedication to the United Nation's Sustainable Development Goals. Lastly, there are numerous challenges to the adaptation of Industry 5.0 such as privacy, newly updated laws, large budgets, and a lack of skilled workers.

REFERENCES

Arpacı, Ö. Y., & Gülel, F. E. (2023). Are European Union Member and Candidate Countries Ready for Industry 5.0?: Spatial Clustering Analysis in the Context of Industry 4.0 Performance. In Implications of Industry 5.0 on Environmental Sustainability (pp. 52-66). IGI Global.

Alaloul, L., Zawawi, & Mohammed. (2018). Industry revolution IR 4.0: future opportunities and challenges in construction industry. Paper presented at the *MATEC web of conferences*. EDP Sciences. 10.1051/matecconf/201820302010

Alaloul, W. S., Liew, M. S., Zawawi, N. A. W. A., & Kennedy, I. B. (2020). Industrial Revolution 4.0 in the construction industry: Challenges and opportunities for stakeholders. *Ain Shams Engineering Journal, 11*(1), 225–230. doi:10.1016/j.asej.2019.08.010

Aisyah, F. (2020). Malaysian manufacturing sector declines at slower pace. *Malysian Reserve*. https://themalaysianreserve.com/2018/07/03/malaysian-manufacturing-sector-declines-at-slower-pace/

Alsultanny, Y., & AlZuhair, S. (2018). Evaluating influence of technology readiness factors on the Saudi cement companies market and financial based performance. *Journal of Science and Technology Policy Management*.

Al-Refaie, A., & Ramadna, A. M. (2020). Barriers to E-Government Adoption in Jordanian Organizations from Users' and Employees' Perspectives. In Open Government: Concepts, Methodologies, Tools, and Applications (pp. 2190-2210): IGI Global.

Ambad, Andrew, & Amit. (2020). Growth Challenges of SMEs: Empirical Evidence in Sabah, Malaysia. *ASEAN Entrepreneurship Journal, 6*(1), 8-14.

Amin, N. A. N., Almunawar, M. N., Hasnan, A. S., & Besar, N. N. (2020). The Utilization of Web 2.0 for Knowledge Sharing: The Case of Tertiary Education in Brunei Darussalam. In *Handbook of Research on Managerial Practices and Disruptive Innovation in Asia* (pp. 1–25). IGI Global. doi:10.4018/978-1-7998-0357-7.ch001

Bakar, N. A. A., Deraman, Z., Tarmiji, M. F., Yusoff, R., & Kama, N. (2020). Workplace Digitalization in Public Sector Organization Towards Operational Effectiveness: Current Landscape, Issues and Challenges. *International Journal of Innovation in Enterprise System*, *4*(01), 78–83. doi:10.25124/ijies.v4i01.50

Bayo-Moriones, A., & Lera-López, F. (2007). A firm-level analysis of determinants of ICT adoption in Spain. *Technovation*, *27*(6-7), 352–366. doi:10.1016/j.technovation.2007.01.003

Bernama. (2019). Many SMEs Unaware of Industry 4WRD Readiness Assessment Programme. *Bernama*. https://www.bernama.com/en/news.php?id=1774994

Behera, R. K., & Dhal, S. K. (2020). A Meta-Analysis of Impact of ERP Implementation. In *Advances in Data Science and Management* (pp. 123–135). Springer. doi:10.1007/978-981-15-0978-0_12

Chatzoglou, P., & Chatzoudes, D. (2016). Factors affecting e-business adoption in SMEs: An empirical research. *Journal of Enterprise Information Management*, *29*(3), 327–358. doi:10.1108/JEIM-03-2014-0033

Chiarello, F., Trivelli, L., Bonaccorsi, A., & Fantoni, G. (2018). Extracting and mapping industry 4.0 technologies using wikipedia. *Computers in Industry*, *100*, 244–257. doi:10.1016/j.compind.2018.04.006

Dalenogare, B., Benitez, G. B., Ayala, N. F., & Frank, A. G. (2018). The expected contribution of Industry 4.0 technologies for industrial performance. *International Journal of Production Economics*, *204*, 383–394. doi:10.1016/j.ijpe.2018.08.019

Davenport, T. H., & Mahidhar, V. (2018). What's your cognitive strategy. *MIT Sloan Management Review*, *59*(4), 19–23.

Deloitte. (2014). *Industry 4.0: Challenges and solutions for the digital transformation and use of exponential technologies*. Deloitte. https://www2.deloitte.com/content/dam/Deloitte/ch/Documents/manufacturing/chenmanufacturing-industry-4-0-24102014.pdf

Depietro, R., Wiarda, E., & Fleischer, M. (1990). The context for change: Organization, technology and environment. *The processes of technological innovation, 199*(0), 151-175.

Duan, X., Deng, H., & Corbitt, B. (2012). Evaluating the critical determinants for adopting e-market in Australian small-and-medium sized enterprises. *Management Research Review*, *35*(3/4), 289–308. doi:10.1108/01409171211210172

Economy. (2019). Malaysia's business condition in manufacturing sector remains challenging. *The Star*. https://www.thestar.com.my/business/business-news/2019/10/01/malaysia039s-business-condition-in-manufacturing-sector-remains-challenging

Gale, J., & Abraham, D. (2005). Introduction: Toward understanding e-business transformation. *Journal of Organizational Change Management*, *18*(2), 113–116. doi:10.1108/09534810510589543

Gusakov, A. (2020). The Role of Design Thinking for Achieving Leadership in the Digital Transformation of Business. Paper presented at the 6th International Conference on Social, economic, and academic leadership (ICSEAL-6-2019). 10.2991/assehr.k.200526.052

Fazal, N., Haleem, A., Bahl, S., Javaid, M., & Nandan, D. (2022). Digital management systems in manufacturing using industry 5.0 technologies. In *Advancement in Materials, Manufacturing and Energy Engineering, Vol. II: Select Proceedings of ICAMME 2021* (pp. 221-234). Singapore: Springer Nature Singapore. doi:10.2991/assehr.k.200526.052

Haleem, A., Javaid, M., Singh, R. P., Rab, S., & Suman, R. (2022). Perspectives of cybersecurity for ameliorative Industry 4.0 era: A review-based framework. Industrial Robot. *The International Journal of Robotics Research and Application*, *49*(3), 582–597. doi:10.1108/IR-10-2021-0243

Hidayatno, A., Rahman, I., & Irminanda, K. R. (2019). A Conceptualization of Industry 4.0 Adoption on Textile and Clothing Sector in Indonesia. Paper presented at the *Proceedings of the 2019 5th International Conference on Industrial and Business Engineering*. ACM. 10.1145/3364335.3364351

Horváth, D., & Szabó, R. Z. (2019). Driving forces and barriers of Industry 4.0: Do multinational and small and medium-sized companies have equal opportunities? *Technological Forecasting and Social Change*, *146*, 119–132. doi:10.1016/j.techfore.2019.05.021

Ing, Lee, & Chan, Alipal, & Hamid. (2019). An Overview of the Rising Challenges in Implementing Industry 4.0. Int. J Sup. Chain. *Mgt*, *8*(6), 1181.

Jaworski, B. J., & Kohli, A. K. (1993). Market orientation: Antecedents and consequences. *Journal of Marketing*, *57*(3), 53–70. doi:10.1177/002224299305700304

Jeevan, O, Saharuddin, P, & Do. (2018). An Evolution of a Nexus Between Malaysian Seaport Centric Logistic and Industrial Revolution 4.0: Current Status and Future Strategies. *International Journal of e-Navigation and Maritime Economy, 10*, 001-015.

Kagermann, H., Helbig, J., Hellinger, A., & Wahlster, W. (2013). *Recommendations for implementing the strategic initiative industrie 4.0: Securing the future of German manufacturing industry; final report of the Industrie 4.0 Working Group*. Forschungsunion.

Kamble, S. S., Gunasekaran, A., & Sharma, R. (2018). Analysis of the driving and dependence power of barriers to adopt industry 4.0 in Indian manufacturing industry. *Computers in Industry*, *101*, 107–119. doi:10.1016/j.compind.2018.06.004

Knight, E., Daymond, J., & Paroutis, S. (2020). Design-led strategy: How to bring design thinking into the art of strategic management. *California Management Review*, *62*(2), 30–52. doi:10.1177/0008125619897594

Kudriashov, N., Prostav, I, Markov, S, Yadgarova, Y., & Taratukhin, V. (2016). Implementation of cloud services for advance management of steel transport for continuous casting production. *Annals of DAAAM & Proceedings, 27*. Gale Academic.

Kuan, K. K., & Chau, P. Y. (2001). A perception-based model for EDI adoption in small businesses using a technology–organization–environment framework. *Information & Management*, *38*(8), 507–521. doi:10.1016/S0378-7206(01)00073-8

Labuschagne, C., Brent, A. C., & Van Erck, R. P. (2005). Assessing the sustainability performances of industries. *Journal of Cleaner Production*, *13*(4), 373–385. doi:10.1016/j.jclepro.2003.10.007

Lee, J., Bagheri, B., & Kao, H.-A. (2015). A cyber-physical systems architecture for industry 4.0-based manufacturing systems. *Manufacturing Letters*, *3*, 18–23. doi:10.1016/j.mfglet.2014.12.001

Looi, H. C. (2005). E-commerce adoption in Brunei Darussalam: A quantitative analysis of factors influencing its adoption. *Communications of the Association for Information Systems*, *15*(1), 3. doi:10.17705/1CAIS.01503

Love, P. E., & Irani, Z. (2004). An exploratory study of information technology evaluation and benefits management practices of SMEs in the construction industry. *Information & Management*, *42*(1), 227–242. doi:10.1016/j.im.2003.12.011

Lu, H.-P., & Weng, C.-I. (2018). Smart manufacturing technology, market maturity analysis and technology roadmap in the computer and electronic product manufacturing industry. *Technological Forecasting and Social Change*, *133*, 85–94. doi:10.1016/j.techfore.2018.03.005

Luong, N. A. M., & Wang, L. (2019). Factors Influencing E-commerce Usage within Internationalisation: A study of Swedish small and medium-sized fashion retailers. *Science Direct.*

Morse, J. M. (2010). Simultaneous and sequential qualitative mixed method designs. *Qualitative Inquiry*, *16*(6), 483–491. doi:10.1177/1077800410364741

Malik, A., Ul Haq, M. I., Raina, A., & Gupta, K. (2022). 3D printing towards implementing Industry 4.0: Sustainability aspects, barriers and challenges. Industrial Robot. *The International Journal of Robotics Research and Application*, *49*(3), 491–511. doi:10.1108/IR-10-2021-0247

Mazzucato & Tancioni. (2008). Innovation and idiosyncratic risk: an industry-and firm-level analysis. *Industrial and Corporate Change, 17*(4), 779-811.

Migdadi, M. M., Abu Zaid, M. K. S., Al-Hujran, O. S., & Aloudat, A. M. (2016). An empirical assessment of the antecedents of electronic-business implementation and the resulting organizational performance. *Internet Research*, *26*(3), 661–688. doi:10.1108/IntR-08-2014-0203

Oliveira, T., & Martins, M. F. (2010). Understanding e-business adoption across industries in European countries. *Industrial Management & Data Systems*, *110*(9), 1337–1354. doi:10.1108/02635571011087428

Owen, & Darkwa. (2000). *Role of multipurpose community telecentres in accelerating national development in Ghana.* First Monday.

Payton, F. C. (2000). Lessons learned from three interorganizational health care information systems. *Information & Management*, *37*(6), 311–321. doi:10.1016/S0378-7206(99)00057-9

Özdemir, V., & Hekim, N. (2018). Birth of industry 5.0: Making sense of big data with artificial intelligence,"the internet of things" and next-generation technology policy. *OMICS: A Journal of Integrative Biology*, *22*(1), 65–76. doi:10.1089/omi.2017.0194 PMID:29293405

Premkumar, G., & Roberts, M. (1999). Adoption of new information technologies in rural small businesses. *Omega*, *27*(4), 467–484. doi:10.1016/S0305-0483(98)00071-1

Racheal. (2020). Cover Story: IR4.0 in Malaysia: The challenges. *The Edge Markets*. https://www.theedgemarkets.com/article/cover-story-ir40-malaysia-challenges

Rauch, E., Linder, C., & Dallasega, P. (2020). Anthropocentric perspective of production before and within Industry 4.0. *Computers & Industrial Engineering, 139*, 105644. doi:10.1016/j.cie.2019.01.018

Ridaryanto, R. & Kartono, A. M. S. (2015). E3S Web of Conferences. *International Journal of Advanced Trends in Computer Science and Engineering. 4*(2), 15–21.

Rogers, E. (2003). *Diffusions of Innovations* (5th ed.). Free Press.

Schuh, G., Anderl, R., Gausemeier, J., ten Hompel, M., & Wahlster, W. (2017). *Industrie 4.0 maturity index. Managing the digital transformation of companies*. Herbert Utz.

Rüßmann, M., Lorenz, M., Gerbert, P., Waldner, M., Justus, J., Engel, P., & Harnisch, M. (2015). Industry 4.0: The future of productivity and growth in manufacturing industries. *Boston consulting group, 9*(1), 54-89.

Sila, I. (2013). Factors affecting the adoption of B2B e-commerce technologies. *Electronic Commerce Research, 13*(2), 199–236. doi:10.100710660-013-9110-7

Sin, K. Y., Osman, A., Salahuddin, S. N., Abdullah, S., Lim, Y. J., & Sim, C. L. (2016). Relative advantage and competitive pressure towards implementation of e-commerce: Overview of small and medium enterprises (SMEs). *Procedia Economics and Finance, 35*, 434–443. doi:10.1016/S2212-5671(16)00054-X

Soliman, K. S., & Janz, B. D. (2004). An exploratory study to identify the critical factors affecting the decision to establish Internet-based interorganizational information systems. *Information & Management, 41*(6), 697–706. doi:10.1016/j.im.2003.06.001

Star, T. (2019). Malaysia falls behind in IR4.0 migration. *NST*. https://www.nst.com.my/news/%20nation/2019/08/514242/%20malaysia-falls-behind-ir40-migration

Stjepić, A.-M., Pejić Bach, M., & Bosilj Vukšić, V. (2021). Exploring Risks in the Adoption of Business Intelligence in SMEs Using the TOE Framework. *Journal of Risk and Financial Management, 14*(2), 58. doi:10.3390/jrfm14020058

Tabim, V. M., Ayala, N. F., & Frank, A. G. (2021). Implementing Vertical Integration in the Industry 4.0 Journey: Which Factors Influence the Process of Information Systems Adoption? *Information Systems Frontiers*, (0123456789). doi:10.100710796-021-10220-x PMID:34776762

Teh, & Kee. (2019). The Readiness of Small and Medium Enterprises for the Industrial Revolution 4.0. *Global J. Bus. Soc. Sci. Review, 7*(4), 217-223.

Teo, T. S., Lin, S., & Lai, K. (2009). Adopters and non-adopters of e-procurement in Singapore: An empirical study. *Omega, 37*(5), 972–987. doi:10.1016/j.omega.2008.11.001

Teo, T. S., Tan, M., & Buk, W. K. (1997). A contingency model of Internet adoption in Singapore. *International Journal of Electronic Commerce, 2*(2), 95–118. doi:10.1080/10864415.1997.11518310

Theodosiou, M., & Katsikea, E. (2012). Antecedents and performance of electronic business adoption in the hotel industry. *European Journal of Marketing*, *46*(1/2), 258–283. doi:10.1108/03090561211189329

Tornatzky, L. G., Fleischer, M., & Chakrabarti, A. K. (1990). *Processes of technological innovation*. Lexington books.

Wagire, R., Rathore, A. P. S., & Jain, R. (2019). Analysis and synthesis of Industry 4.0 research landscape. *Journal of Manufacturing Technology Management*, *31*(1), 31–51. doi:10.1108/JMTM-10-2018-0349

Wolcott, K., Kamal, M., & Qureshi, S. (2008). Meeting the challenges of ICT adoption by micro-enterprises. *Journal of Enterprise Information Management*, *21*(6), 616–632. doi:10.1108/17410390810911212

Wong, L., & Hew, T. (2020). Time to seize the digital evolution: Adoption of blockchain in operations and supply chain management among Malaysian SMEs. *International Journal of Information Management*, *52*, 101997. doi:10.1016/j.ijinfomgt.2019.08.005

Yang, X. (2019). How perceived social distance and trust influence reciprocity expectations and eWOM sharing intention in social commerce. *Industrial Management & Data Systems*, *119*(4), 867–880. doi:10.1108/IMDS-04-2018-0139

Zhu, K., Kraemer, K., & Xu, S. (2003). Electronic business adoption by European firms: A cross-country assessment of the facilitators and inhibitors. *European Journal of Information Systems*, *12*(4), 251–268. doi:10.1057/palgrave.ejis.3000475

Zhu, K., & Kraemer, K. L. (2002). E-commerce metrics for net-enhanced organizations: Assessing the value of e-commerce to firm performance in the manufacturing sector. *Information Systems Research*, *13*(3), 275–295. doi:10.1287/isre.13.3.275.82

KEY TERMS AND DEFINITIONS

Relative Advantages: These are anticipated benefits that a firm can get by adopting IR 4.0.

Technology Readiness: This refers to the physical assets and human resource skills to adopt new technology such as IR 5.0.

Top Management Support: This is defined as the motivation, involvement, and encouragement given by top managers for innovation adoption.

Adoption Cost: This is defined as the combination of initial cost and cost of training to use new technology.

Competitive Pressure: This refers to the degree of pressure felt by competitors within the industry.

IR 5.0: Industry 5.0 has given organizations a new competitive edge that is more oriented toward the internet of things (IoT), machine learning, human technology, environment, ethics, and sustainability to link smart production and lower operational costs for the companies.

TOE Model: The technological, organizational, and environmental (TOE) factors play important roles in the adoption of technological innovation like IR 5.0.

Chapter 4
Artificial Intelligence and Value Creation at the Crossroads of Industry 5.0:
A Bibliometric and Content Analysis Discourse

Ajay Chandel
https://orcid.org/0000-0002-4585-6406
Lovely Professional University, India

Rahul Sharma
https://orcid.org/0000-0001-8880-7527
Lovely Professional University, India

ABSTRACT

Today, businesses are evolving in an extremely competitive market. As we enter Industry 5.0, modern firms' dynamic business processes need a technological boost to enable them to create and deliver superior value while keeping humans at the core of the business processes. One such technology is artificial intelligence, which is creating innovative options for businesses to further add consumers' value by taking a dynamic approach, mitigating unpredictability, and augmenting cost-effectiveness. Development of AI as a business engine to generate value is advancing and is an alternative for many different industries to explore. As humans need to work in tandem with machines in Industry 5.0 to create customer value, a new term referred to as HCAI- human-centered AI has emerged. Bibliometric data of documents published between 1994 and 2022 were analyzed, and the most cited articles in SCOPUS journals were examined for content analysis to decipher how this new-age AI is aiding businesses to create and deliver superior value and thus leading to sustainable competitive advantage.

DOI: 10.4018/978-1-6684-6403-8.ch004

1. INTRODUCTION

Although technical decentralization and interconnectedness; components of industry 4.0 are still in full swing, it is noteworthy that Industry 5.0—the full merger of business's human touch and intelligent systems—is inevitable. Artificial intelligence (AI) has disrupted the industry, the economy, and society by changing interactions and linkages between customers and other stakeholders and with a bundle of intelligent technologies such as The Internet of Things, blockchain, VR, fuzzy inference systems, deep learning-based neural networks, convolutional neural networks, stacked autoencoders, deep reinforcement learning, meta-learning, graph neural networks, and meta-heuristic algorithms to name a few, AI will play a significant role in improving the standard of industrial production, which integrates people, processes, and machines in Industry 5.0. A new term known as Human-Centered AI has been recently coined in Industry 5.0 as humans need to work in tandem with machines. However, "artificial intelligence" as a term was initially coined in a session at Dartmouth College (United States) in 1956 (Nilsson, 2010), as to Nahodil & Vítků (2013), the roots of artificial intelligence may well be discovered in legends from ancient China (Yueying Huang's dogs), Greek (legendary robot Talos), and other cultures, where automatons were believed to have real imaginations and the capacity to reason and experience emotions. Since then, various fields of study have committed to AI research. Numerous organizations have used AI and data analytics for philanthropic operations to successfully handle food waste (Despoudi et al., 2018; Irani et al., 2018), as well as for early clinical diagnosis, agri-food supply chain risk recognition, optimized food distribution, and crisis retort by rapidly and precisely foretelling natural tragedies. While researchers have invented advanced deep-structured learning techniques (LeCun et al., 2015) and sociologists are exploring the moral and legal ramifications of artificial intelligence (Cath, 2018), academics in business studies are examining the consequences of AI on consumers, enterprises, and other stakeholders in an age of automation and intertwined corporate ecosystem (Huang & Rust, 2018).

With artificial intelligence, processes may be enhanced by reducing the requirement for human participation and oversight keeping humans free for more complex jobs in Industry 5.0. AI can improve and streamline a variety of operations. As a consequence, it is reasonable to assume that the application of artificial intelligence to further enhance societal efficiency and make people's lives easier will increase considerably. No wonder, McKinsey & Company's (2022) research reveals that although the percentage of firms employing AI has flatlined at 50 and 60% for the last few years, the adoption of AI by businesses has more than doubled since 2017. Companies with the strongest financial returns from AI are continuing to gain ground on rivals. This research also concluded that business leaders are investing more money in AI, using ever-more-advanced techniques that have been shown to speed up AI development and enable scaling, and they appear to be doing better in the competitive AI talent markets as well.

Artificial intelligence is frequently cited as a tool that can help businesses offer more to their customers. Because of recent developments in artificial intelligence, we can now emulate intellectual behavior and industrialize the procedures of detecting and fixing complicated glitches (Lee et al., 2019). Artificial intelligence has garnered noteworthy attention from a variety of sectors due to its potential to increase operative efficacy and speed up novelty by generating meaningful information from big data sets and forecasting unforeseen events (Lee et al., 2019). Clearly, AI is creating innovative prospects for businesses to generate value for their clients by taking an upbeat method, handling unpredictability, and boosting cost-effectiveness and returns. Because of this, the development of AI as a business engine that generates value is advancing and is now a serious alternative for many different industries to explore.

Artificial intelligence's capability to help businesses create incremental customer value has made AI really useful in diverse industries and functional areas. While e-commerce and financial sectors are deploying AI to improve the customer experience, streamline supply chain management, boost operational efficiency, and shrink team sizes. These initiatives all contribute to the overarching goal of creating standardized, dependable product quality control methods and discovering novel ways to reach and serve customers at low costs. Artificial intelligence strengthens and adds credence to artistic decision-making methods used for product development in the fashion industry by supervising design components such as color, textures, and fit, as well as their past retail performance and future performance indicators. Artificial intelligence (AI) implementation in intelligent manufacturing is gaining popularity in wake of Industry 5.0. Industry 5.0, incorporated ideas like human-centered design, sustainability, and resilience. It will have far-reaching effects in the manufacturing sector by eliminating the need for humans to do repetitive jobs. Artificially intelligent robots will permeate every level of the industrial workflow and supply chain. Research by Capgemini reported that 51% of European manufacturers were using AI solutions, with Japan (30%) and the United States (28%) ranking second and third, respectively. Improved maintenance (29%) and quality (27%), according to the same study, were the two most common implications of artificial intelligence in manufacturing. Just like the sectors mentioned above, different functional areas in businesses are deploying artificial intelligence to create more value for consumers. Marketers, for example, are finding that artificial intelligence is useful for a variety of tasks, including strategic formulation, target audience identification, and product positioning (STP). Additionally, AI is assisting marketers in marketing's strategic orientation of firms (Huang & Rust, 2018). AI-powered marketing tools can help marketers evaluate how well a product meets consumer requirements and how happy those needs make them (Dekimpe, 2020). Using AI-powered predictive analytics and by compiling information from past employees in similar tasks and preparing focused questions for recruiting managers, AI can prove instrumental in removing subjectivity (Baxter, 2018) and hiring the right candidate. Further, the candidate's skills, the nature of the position, and comparisons to other businesses' equivalent positions can all be better understood using AI (Tambe et al., 2019). Sivarajah et al. (2020) and Dubey et al. (2019), all provide an empirical indications that AI in sync with data analytics can significantly alter current operational procedures and activities across various manufacturing functions. Similarly, numerous manufacturing firms are deploying AI in the rescheduling of shop floor decisions to achieve effective manufacturing under changing circumstances (Palombarini & Martínez, 2021).

Previous attempts to uncover how artificial intelligence can multiply a firm's ability to generate and deliver superior customer value have used systematic literature reviews (SLRs). These systematic reviews have focused on the usefulness of AI in traditional sectors. Since researchers have been myopic towards studying mainstream research agendas covering specific applications of Artificial Intelligence in business verticals, this research believes there is a dearth of a comprehensive review and analysis of Artificial intelligence capabilities to create superior customer value across a myriad of industries against the backdrop of Industry 5.0. Ignoring the Industry 5.0-centric approach and focusing only on mainstream AI applications has contributed to knowledge asymmetry, making it harder to understand how artificial intelligence helps create superior customer value by empowering humans and altering mundane business processes. This study, therefore, attempts to address three broad research questions using a Bibliometric analysis discourse:

RQ1: What structures characterize the research on AI capabilities helping to create superior customer value?

RQ2: What are the main themes identified using a content analysis of the ten most impactful publications?

RQ3: Identifying the future trends for research on AI capabilities to create superior customer value?

This study, therefore, emphasizes relatively lesser-discussed AI capabilities leading to superior customer value creation compared to the major body of literature just covering applications of AI in Industry 4.0. This study also employs a more thorough approach by finding rare and emerging transdisciplinary issues that are weakly established internally and built around just functional applications of AI but gravitate more towards unearthing how AI enables the creation of superior customer value in the wake of Industry 5.0. Second, this study uses a two-step methodology; on the one hand, this research uses bibliometric analysis to unearth AI capabilities that help create superior customer value by scientific mapping and performance analysis; on the other hand, it distinguishes itself from existing studies by using content analysis of selected articles to identify key themes and future research agendas. Triangulating data in this manner (bibliometrics and content analysis) may yield more conclusive results.

2. RESEARCH METHODOLOGY

To achieve the stated research objectives, a research triangulation approach that combines bibliometric and content analysis was employed. Bibliometrics is a subdivision of info metrics that uses statistical procedures to measure the importance of scientific publications and the extent to which they propagate information. In contrast, content analysis enables scholars to assess the frequency, significance, and interrelationships of particular words, topics, or concepts. This triangulation permits researchers to evaluate more data than systematic literature reviews while preserving scientific rigor, objectivity, and generalizability.

2.1 Database Curation

To address the research concerns mentioned above, a bibliometric examination of scholarly works published between 2019 and 2022 was conducted. Relevant publications were identified by searching the Scopus database. Scopus was chosen to generate bibliographic data since it is considered one of the most comprehensive databases of its kind. Scopus is a popular choice because of its global collection of published research and its content screening and advisory council, which ensures that only the highest-quality publications are indexed. In addition, Scopus' strict quality control systems continually assess and update all data elements. Scopus also provides comprehensive authorship and institutional profiles created with the help of powerful profiling algorithms and expert curation, resulting in the highest possible accuracy. Therefore, Scopus has been used as a reliable pool of excellent bibliometric data to conduct comprehensive scientific evaluations, research environment studies, scholarly reviews, and institutional standings.

2.2 Keyword Identification

Following a two-pronged methodology, the keywords were used to identify relevant publications. Initially, 20 relevant open-access papers (SCOPUS, Q1), including systematic reviews, were analysed to identify prospective keywords for a later SCOPUS database search. In the second phase, identified keywords

Figure 1. PRISMA

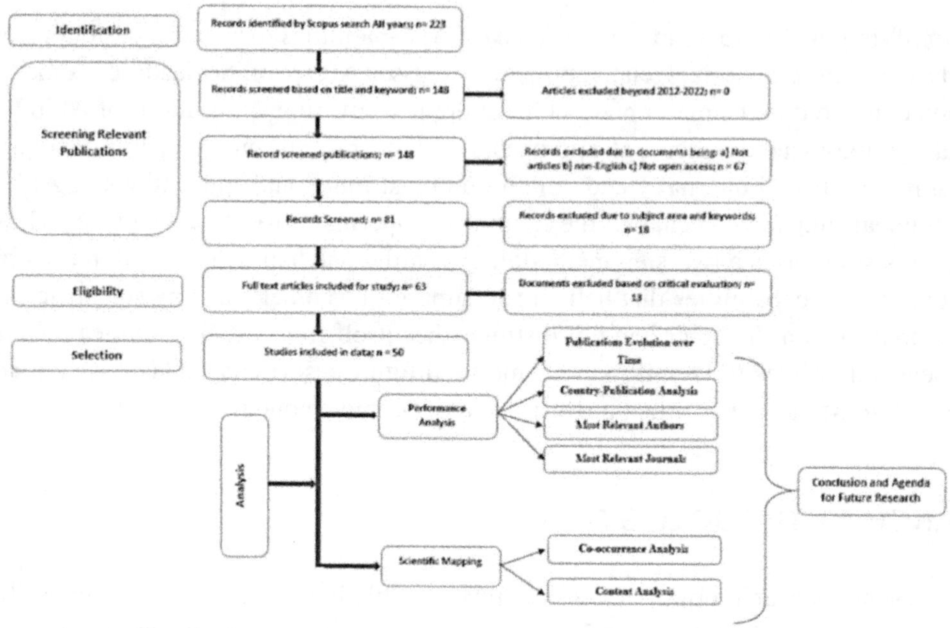

were presented to five academicians and five AI practitioners with pertinent experience in Artificial intelligence. The experts were briefed on the study questions and asked to examine the initial selection of keywords. Some keywords were included, while others were excluded on the recommendation of experts.

2.3 Acquisition of Articles for Bibliometric Analysis

223 papers were retrieved using the abstract, title, and relevant keywords search feature of SCOPUS and a range of selected keywords. Bibliometric analysis was conducted using VOSviewer and the R-based tool Biblioshiny to generate bibliometric maps and reveal hidden trends. Due to the study's focus on discovering the role of artificial intelligence in superior customer value creation, it was essential to select only research that would aid in achieving the specified objectives. The Preferred Reporting Items for the Systematic Review template proposed by Moher et al., 2015 was used to select the relevant publications in this direction. The PRISMA framework consists of four steps: study identification and registration through database search, study screening, evaluation of study eligibility, and final research selection. The activity resulted in the selection of 50 articles that were reviewed to meet the specified objectives of this research study. Figure 1 presents the PRISMA process utilized for publications assortment and a snapshot of the methodology:

2.4 The Techniques of Bibliometric Analysis

There are two types of bibliometric analytical techniques: performance analysis and scientific mapping. In summary, performance analysis considers the contributions of research components, while scientific mapping highlights the interconnections between research components. As a result, performance analysis and scientific mapping, as described by Noyons et al. (1999). were used as two of the most essential techniques for conducting the study. The following subsections detail the various performance analysis and scientific mapping approaches.

2.4.1 Performance Assessment

The majority of performance analysis measures are involved with assessing the overall trajectory of the subject matter, citations of the articles, total publications in the dataset, and classifying the articles according to connections, authors, nations, and journals (Massaro et al., 2020). Various indicators, in addition to those listed above, are believed to be used to evaluate the knowledge based impact of research. Due to its ease of understanding, the Hirsch h-index is amongst the popular citation measures. The h-index is regarded as a suitable and reliable metric for evaluating both the significance and productivity of scientific output (Vanclay, 2007). Despite its impartiality, the h-index has not been found suitable for comparing authors across different study disciplines, with varying career and research paths (Kelly & Jennions, 2006). The m-index has been established as an additional unit of examination to bypass the challenges involved in comparing scholars during various stages of their research career. It is derived by dividing the h-index by the number of years between the author's first and most recent publication (Hirsch, 2007). The M-index enables researchers to compare an author's output to the duration of his or her career.

2.4.2 Scientific Mapping

With the use of scientific mapping, fundamental trends in the intellectual, social, and conceptual framework of a knowledge body and the changes it has gone through over time can be comprehended (Cobo et al., 2012). In this study, authors have tried to understand the intellectual structure. The intellectual structure includes relationships between texts that may reflect evolutions in the discipline or body of knowledge. Scholars conduct this analysis using co-occurrence analysis (Van Eck & Waltman, 2010). This study also uses the co-occurrence analysis of all keywords to capture the conceptual structures of AI capabilities to create superior customer value. This is followed by content analysis of selected articles to unearth future AI trends and research agendas.

3. ANALYSIS AND DISCUSSION OF RESULTS

3.1 Performance Analysis

3.1.1 Evolution of Publications Over Time

The path of publication in the area of artificial intelligence-led value creation started with a publication titled 'Value creation through the collaborative supply chain: Holistic performance enhancement road map' authored by Holimchayachotikul et al., (2014). The research investigated the relationships between an enterprise and its capacity to provide incremental value for direct customers employing a case study research inquiry on selected French organizations. The findings demonstrated how domain managers may employ the results of artificially intelligent graphical analysis to deliver comprehensive performance

Figure 2. Publications evolution over time

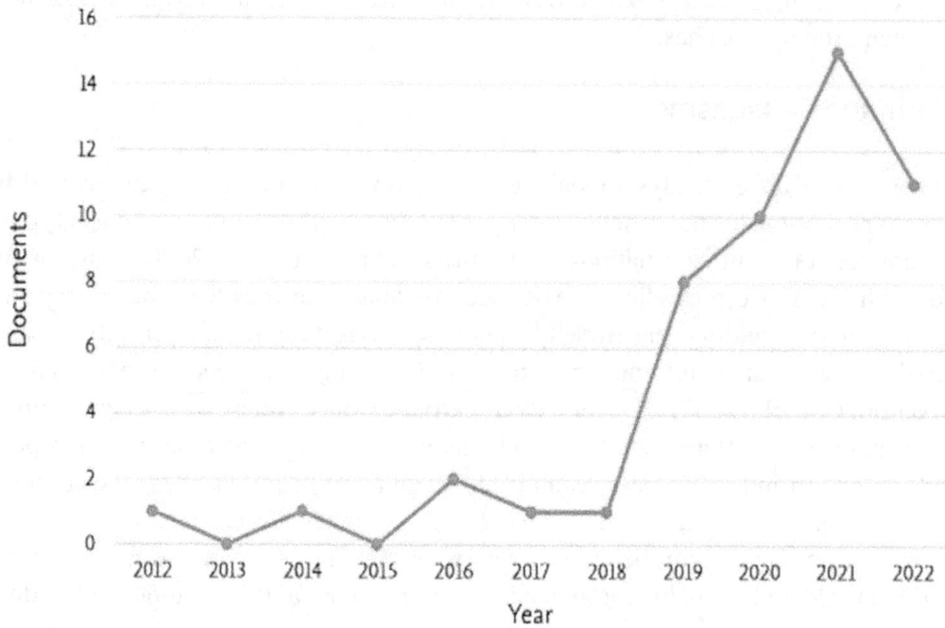

enhancement and rapid problem resolution, ultimately fostering healthier customer relationships. Marking zero publications in the following year, the number of publications in the domain increased to two in 2016. One of the two publications, entitled 'Rate or trade?' Identifying winning ideas in open idea sourcing' (Blohm et al., 2016) focused on how collaborations mediated by artificial intelligence permit open sourcing of ideas for product/service development. The other publication, titled 'Machine learning in big data' (Wang et al., 2021) explored how machine learning; a technique of artificial intelligence helps acquire knowledge in order to make intelligent decisions which ultimately leads to superior value creation relative to competitors. As is evident (Figure 2: Documents by Year), the years 2019, 2020, and 2021 witnessed a sharp increase in publications with eight, ten, and fifteen publications, respectively, demonstrating a rise in scholarly research interest in unearthing how artificial intelligence leads to superior value creation. Although the years 2019, 2020, and 2021 marked major work based on AI's capability to create customer value in financial, manufacturing, public services, healthcare and sustainable marketing sectors in collaboration with technologies such as machine learning (Angelis & Da Silva, 2019; Canhoto & Clear, 2020; de Kervenoael et al., 2020; Helo & Hao, 2021; Kim & Huh, 2021; Margherita et al., 2021), the year 2022 witnessed more publications covering aspects of deploying AI capabilities in combination with other technologies for business model innovation leading to superior customer value creation and delivery (Sun et al., 2022; Agrawal et al., 2022).

According to Merig'O et al. (2015), analysing the number of citations obtained is a viable method for identifying the articles discussing the capabilities of AI in value creation. Indeed, citations can summarise a publication's significance and influence among experts in a single number. Table 1 displays ten of the most impactful publications of the examined dataset. Specifically, the number of citations retrieved from the SCOPUS (TC) and the average count of citations obtained per year (TC/Y) are displayed.

Table 1. Total number of citations retrieved from the SCOPUS (TC) and the number of citations received per year (TC/Y)

Authors	Title	Year	Total Citations	TC per Year
Wirtz B.W., Weyerer J.C., Geyer C.	Artificial Intelligence and the Public Sector—Applications and Challenges	2019	180	45
De Kervenoael R., Hasan R., Schwob A., Goh E.	Leveraging human-robot interaction in hospitality services: Incorporating the role of perceived value, empathy, and information sharing into visitors' intentions to use social robots	2020	140	46.667
Angelis J., Ribeiro da Silva E.	Blockchain adoption: A value driver perspective	2019	133	33.25
Borges A.F.S., Laurindo F.J.B., Spínola M.M., Gonçalves R.F., Mattos C.A.	The strategic use of artificial intelligence in the digital era: Systematic literature review and future research directions	2021	109	54.5
Langley D.J., van Doorn J., Ng I.C.L., Stieglitz S., Lazovik A., Boonstra A.	The Internet of Everything: Smart things and their impact on business models	2021	87	43.5
Canhoto A.I., Clear F.	Artificial intelligence and machine learning as business tools: A framework for diagnosing value destruction potential	2020	80	26.667
Garbuio M., Lin N.	Artificial intelligence as a growth engine for health care startups: Emerging business models	2019	73	18.25
Riikkinen M., Saarijärvi H., Sarlin P., Lähteenmäki I.	Using artificial intelligence to create value in insurance	2018	72	14.4
Gans J., Ryall M.D.	Value capture theory: A strategic management review	2017	66	11
Blohm I., Riedl C., Füller J., Leimeister J.M.	Rate or trade? Identifying winning ideas in open idea sourcing	2016	58	8.286

With 180 total citations (TC) and 45 citations per year (TC / Y), 'Artificial intelligence and the public sector: Applications and Challenges' (Wirtz et al., 2018) was the most influential publication that discussed a variety of advantageous AI uses in the public sector. Clinical documentation enabled by AI-based Knowledge Management packages, AI-powered Process Automation Measures (Enhanced processing speed and accuracy for immigration applications; Automated image diagnoses; Human-computer collaboration for monotonous tasks like data entry, etc.), Virtual Agents (Assignment of tasks based on the relative area of duty, Virtual nursing assistant, A chatbot for assisting refugees in filling out and searching for documents), Predictive Analytics & Data Visualization (monitoring in public locations for police agencies to identify risks and criminal flashpoints for preventative purposes and identifying high-risk circumstances to protect community transportation. Models for predicting water levels, etc.) were a few of the areas identified in this publication as having the potential to create significant value when powered by artificial intelligence. 'Leveraging human-robot interaction in hospitality services: Incorporating the role of perceived value, empathy, and information sharing into visitors' intentions to use social robots by de Kervenoael et al. (2020) was the second most influential publication (TC= 140, TC/Y=46.66). Tourism and hospitality have adopted artificial intelligence-powered social robots. The study underlines that sustainable adoption of AI-powered robots needs empirical information on the intent of visitors to employ robots. To stimulate value creation and service excellence, artificial intelligence-driven social androids are required in the hospitality industry. According to de Kervenoael et al. (2020), artificial intelligence empowers social robots with empathy and knowledge-sharing capabilities, which impacts guests' desire to interact with social robots in Singapore's hospitality venues.

3.1.1 Country-Publication Analysis

146 writers from 30 nations and 86 universities contributed to the publication of the 50 publications in the dataset under consideration. Because there are only 8 single-authored publications on AI's capability to help businesses create more customer value, collaboration and teamwork (52 articles written in global collaboration) were found to be crucial factors for writers exploring this domain. While investigating the count of publications with more than one author, it became evident that the most research productive nations are also more receptive to foreign partnerships in research . Table 2 provides information considered different metrics single/multiple-country publications (SCPs/MCPs), and the ratio of MCPs to the total number of research articles in data. Single-country publications show the number of articles authored by writers from a single nation (intra-country collaboration). Multi-country publications depict the count of publications by writers collaborating across several nations. Ratio of multi-country publications presents a relative value that indicates the degree to which each country is receptive to international collaborations. In terms of overall production, the United States with 21 publications tops the list of most productive countries. The rest of the most productive nations (such as Finland-rank 2; 12 publications, Sweden-rank 3; 11 publications, Germany-rank 4; 10 publications, the United Kingdom-rank 4; 10 publications, France-rank 7; 7 publications, and the Netherlands-rank 10; 6 publications) belong to Europe. China (Rank-6, 9 publications) and India (Rank-8, 7 publications) were the only two Asian nations in the top 10 most productive nations. Brazil, a part of South America ranks 9 with 6 publications. However, considering the multi-country publications ratio, the United Kingdom (MCP_Ratio= 1.5) and Finland (MCP_Ratio= 1.4) were the two nations found to be very open to international collaborations followed by Sweden (MCP_Ratio= 0.833). The United Kingdom was found to have international collaborations with the Czech Republic, France, India, the Netherlands, Saudi Arabia, and Slovakia in areas exploring how AI is fundamentally disrupting B2B marketing, retailing, business models, smart manufacturing, human-robot interaction in business functional areas for incremental customer value creation. Finland was found to have international collaborations with China, Germany, Spain, Sweden, Switzerland, the United Kingdom, and Singapore in areas such as AI's role in creating superior value by aiding in Supply chain, Business-model-innovation, Digital servitization, and value creation in Insurance sectors.

Interestingly China and India were found to be the two Asian countries ranking 4th and 5th in international collaboration researching how AI can help create and deliver superior customer value (China-MCP_Ratio= 0.8; India- MCP_Ratio= 0.75). China had international collaborations with Hongkong, the Netherlands, Singapore, and Spain working with major publications exploring the AI potential in areas such as Private-public value creation, value co-creation, and enhancing innovation ecosystem capabilities. On the other hand, India had major international collaborations with Estonia, Greece, and Tanzania working toward business value appropriation by deploying AI tools in tandem with technologies such as machine learning and digital twins in education, manufacturing, and public sectors. In addition, Table 3 shows the top ten nations with the highest total and the average number of citations.

Table 2. Top ten countries with the Highest Total Publications (Along with single-country publications, multi-country publications, and countries with the Highest Multi-Country Publication Ratio)

Country	Total Publications	SCP	MCP	MCP_Ratio
USA	21	16	5	0.3215
Finland	12	5	7	1.4
Sweden	11	6	5	0.83333
Germany	10	6	4	0.666667
United Kingdom	10	4	6	1.5
China	9	5	4	0.8
France	7	5	2	0.4
India	7	4	3	0.75
Brazil	6	6	0	0
Netherlands	6	5	1	0.2

Table 3. Top Ten Countries with the highest number of total and average article references

Country	Total Citations	Average Article Citations
Germany	217	72.33
Sweden	179	44.75
France	154	77
Finland	101	33.67
Netherlands	87	87
China	83	20.75
United Kingdom	81	40.50
Canada	66	66
USA	43	10.75
Saudi Arabia	23	23

3.1.2 Most Relevant Authors

Productivity must be painstakingly evaluated when assessing an author's significance in a certain research domain. In Table 4, this metric has been examined to present a snapshot of the ten most influential authors. An author's productivity was measured using the papers authored by the author during the given time frame. Since nine of the ten authors had an equal number of publications, to distinguish their relative productivity fractional counting of authorship was also calculated as shown below in Table 4. This method also helps in commenting upon the productivity of authors in the wake of rising collaborative authorships.

Table 4. Top ten most impactful and productive authors

Authors	Articles	Authors	Articles Fractionalized
Parida V	4	Parida V	0.98
Alexander CA	1	Alexander CA	0.50
Angelis J	1	Angelis J	0.50
Battisti S	1	Battisti S	0.50
Agrawal A	1	Agrawal A	0.33
Andersen KN	1	Andersen KN	0.33
Strm J	1	Strm J	0.33
Alexopoulos C	1	Alexopoulos C	0.20
Affleck M	1	Affleck M	0.14
Arzt A	1	Arzt A	0.14

As evident, Parida V. was found to be the most productive author who contributed a total of four publications (Fractionalized score = 0.98) researching AI capabilities in aiding businesses create superior customer value. Burström et al. (2021) examined how manufacturing incumbents might leverage artificial intelligence to enable business model innovation in trade ecosystems. Using an exploratory case study methodology, his work also recommends techniques that businesses might use to effectively increase revenue through digital products such as artificial intelligence (Gebauer et al., 2020).

3.1.3 Most Relevant Journals

Numerous journals have published articles researching artificial intelligence and its ability to help businesses create incremental value. This domain has been a hotspot for research interests, as evident from Figure 2. To demonstrate the impact of journals, Table 5 lists the ten most relevant journals. Since the number of articles published is not the only indicator of the relevance of a journal, total citations, h-index, CiteScore, SJR, and SNIP score of the journals were also used to determine the most relevant journals (Table 6). Journal of Business Research was found to be the most productive (4 publications) and second most impactful (Highest citations 151) journal. How artificial intelligence integrated into machine learning stimulates data network consequences in business models (Haftor et al., 2021), deploying AI-powered business model innovation and transition in trade ecosystems (Burström et al., 2021), artificial intelligence-powered music biometrics trying to influence consumers' retail buying behaviour and the influence of AI-powered smart things on business models (Langley et al., 2021) were among the major topics covered in this journal. Business horizons, however, less productive (3 publications) as compared to the Journal of Business Research, was the most impactful (212 citations) journal publishing research in areas exploring the potential of AI in diagnosing value destruction (Canhoto & Clear, 2020) and how pairing blockchain with AI can help improve data security, thereby helping firms create more value for customers (Angelis & Da Silva, 2019).

Table 5. Top 10 most relevant journals

Top 10 Most Productive Journals		Top 10 most Impactful Journals	
Sources	**TP**	**Sources**	**TC**
Journal of Business Research	4	Business Horizons	212
IEEE Engineering Management Review	3	Journal of Business Research	151
Journal of Self-Governance and Management Economics	3	International Journal of Information Management	135
Business Horizons	2	California Management Review	73
Industrial Marketing Management	2	Industrial Marketing Management	35
International Journal of Information Management	2	Decision Support Systems	35
Journal of Creating Value	2	IEEE Engineering Management Review	33
Production Planning and Control	2	Journal of Self-Governance and Management Economics	30
California Management Review	1	Production Planning and Control	24
Decision Support Systems	1	Journal of Creating Value	11

Table 6. Top 10 journal performance metrics

Journal Name	H-Index	CiteScore	SJR	SNIP
Business Horizons	97	14	2.382	2.937
Journal of Business Research	217	11.2	2.316	3.089
International Journal of Information Management	132	28.8	4.584	5.416
California Management Review	139	17.3	3.793	3.952
Industrial Marketing Management	147	10.4	2.206	2.184
Decision Support Systems	161	11.3	1.973	2.661
IEEE Engineering Management Review	27	4.2	0.96	0.944
Journal of Self-Governance and Management Economics	14	5.3	0.851	0.83
Production Planning and Control	85	11.1	1.661	1.869
Journal of Creating Value	10	1.9	0.339	0.565

3.2 Scientific Mapping

In this segment, the findings of scientific mapping have been reported to summarize the examination of AI's potential in value creation by identifying the conceptual and intellectual structures of the topic.

3.2.1 Co-occurrence Analysis

In this study, the co-occurrences amid the SCOPUS-assigned keywords + for each article in the dataset were determined. Consequently, using the Louvain cluster approach along with some authors' judgment of the domain, the most developed and relevant keywords were linked together (Blondel et al., 2008).

Figure 3. Cooccurrence Analysis; Source: VOSviewer

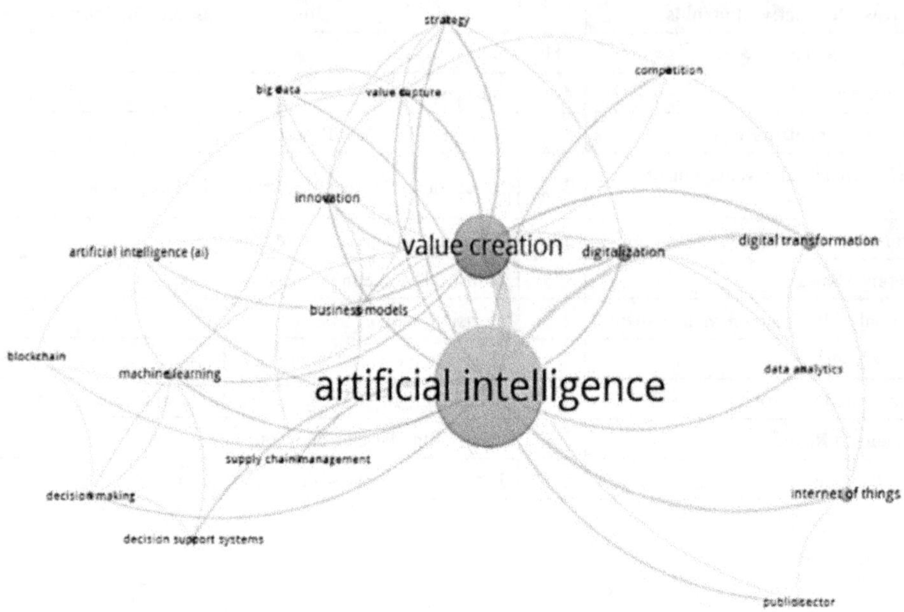

Figure 4. Cluster-wise Co-occurrence Analysis; Source: VOSviewer

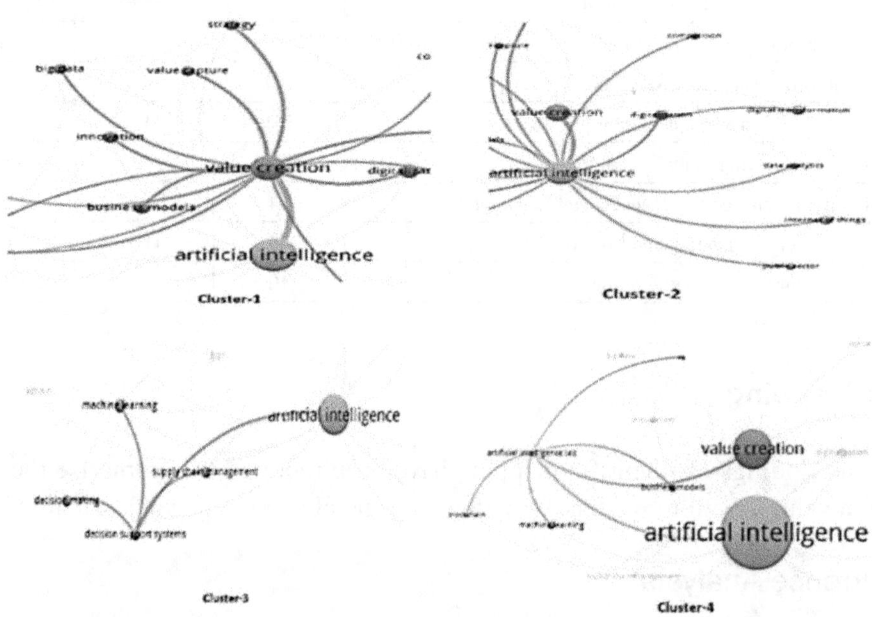

Figure 3 illustrates the results. On the network map, words appear closer to the centre, the greater the number of co-occurrences identified. More proximate and robust linkages are proportional to the number of keywords simultaneously utilized by the authors. Furthermore, the larger a keyword's bubble, the greater its usage frequency among academics. Each cluster is distinguished by distinct hues.

Four clusters were detected in this instance, which can be seen in Figure 4:

Cluster I: The digital revolution is changing how B2B industrial enterprises co-create value. Artificial intelligence is the most prevalent digital technology. This cluster examines how artificial intelligence-led solutions help organizations co-create value in the business-to-business industrial markets which allows businesses to create superior value for customers and in turn capture value for multiple stakeholders. One example of potential value co-creation in Industry 5.0 is the Two-loop integrative framework, in which the first iterative loop integrates tech service providers with healthcare users, demonstrating how artificial intelligence-powered customer-centric treatments are co-created through observant and responsive methods, and the second loop integrates healthcare users with end users (patients), boosting operational practices through users' knowledge and enhancing care and patient journey (Leone et al., 2021).

Cluster II: Cluster 2 was found to have publications that address the possibilities of coupling AI and data analytics to create a competitive advantage for firms in Industry 5.0. Having an intelligent AI system in place may frequently help firms take advantage of untapped market possibilities, such as utilizing insights from demand forecasts and recognizing market trends that are likely to take off, and adjusting their value to fit customer demands. Most organizations believe that AI technology can also lead to indirect incremental value creation by digitally transforming different functional areas. One such example could be creating a congenial environment for creating innovative and value-centric products. Studies claim that managers devote the vast majority of their time to routine administrative and coordinating duties. In Industry 5.0, AI may relieve managers of this stress, letting them use their skills to develop value-rich products and services rather than filling out paperwork. This saved time could thus be used to develop competitively intelligent products and services enabling companies to enjoy a competitive advantage. Moreover, another concept gaining popularity in Industry 5.0 is enhanced service personalization which allows managers to analyze big data with the aid of AI to create unique and personalized experiences leading to a competitive advantage.

Cluster III: The main themes of cluster three revolve around how AI enables managers to make better decisions that lead to incremental value creation and capture. After all, AI is reinventing business, improving innovation and efficiency, and helping companies think beyond. In Industry 5.0, AI may better the products and services, processes, and decision-making. Organizations may attain AI-powered agility. Leaders must continually analyze in which domains and at what degrees of complex artificial intelligence should be used to accomplish company goals and development. AI has impacted every industry. AI is used in the supply chain, transportation, education, manufacturing, and marketing, as well as almost any organization that is digitizing and automating human jobs. AI decision-making systems, anomaly detection, and behavior prediction help firms combat calamities. AI automates and simplifies forecasting and prediction analysis, too. Cluster III is consistent with the standard definition of AI: "Artificial intelligence, sometimes known as machine intelligence, is a branch of computer science that develops and controls technology that can autonomously make decisions and act on behalf of people." One example of how AI in Industry 5.0 can help managers take better decisions is that AI technologies are continuously collecting data which allows managers to accurately forecast demand patterns and make strategic decisions in areas such as procurement and production.

Cluster IV: Cluster four had major publications in AI and Blockchain integration creating business value. Disruptive technologies developed during the Fourth Industrial Revolution (IR4.0) include artificial intelligence (AI) and blockchain, both of which have had far-reaching effects on several industries. New digitally empowered business models may emerge from the union of AI and blockchain technology in Industry 5.0. Nonetheless, supply networks have a lot of security and privacy flaws; in vaccine supply chains, for instance, concerns like vaccination record fraud and vaccine expiry are common. The combination of AI and blockchain in Industry 5.0 creates a smart system where immunizations can be monitored using smart contracts, vaccines with lapsed expiration dates can be identified by machine learning algorithms, and a wide range of users may access and benefit from vaccine recommendation data. Industry 5.0 has led to a perfect marriage and union of AI and Blockchain. Encryption is the first key component that demonstrates the seamless integration of AI with blockchain. By allowing programmers to create algorithms that can only access data in its encrypted form, AI opens up new security possibilities for a myriad of businesses around the world.

3.3 Content Analysis

A content analysis of future trends based on artificial intelligence that can help improve the creation and capture of value for businesses was conducted from the selected articles. The review of future AI trends has been presented in Table 7:

Table 7. Content analysis of AI future trends

Authors	Future Trends
Ishengoma et al., 2022; Wang et al., 2021; Battisti & Brem, 2020; Wirtz et al., 2018	Value creation potential of AI in Public sectors and in Public-private partnerships
Åström et al., 2022; Shollo et al., 2022; Haftor et al., 2021; Burström et al., 2021; Chen et al., 2021; Langley et al., 2021; Gebauer et al., 2020; Garbuio & Lin, 2018	Integration of AI and machine learning and potential impacts on business model innovation
Duginets, 2020; Helo & Hao, 2021	Role of AI in creating incremental value in areas of production, operations, and logistics
Battisti & Brem, 2020; Guha et al., 2021; Rodgers et al., 2021; Cao, 2021	Potential value-creating applications of AI in retailing
Haftor, Costa, Lundström, 2021; Nica, Stan, Luțan, Oașa, 2021; Brown, 2021; Bell, 2020; Whittle, Gregova, Podhorska, Rowland, 2019; Lafferty, 2019	Potential of artificial intelligence and related technology in practicing sustainable business practices

FUTURE RESEARCH AGENDAS

Due to its broad applicability in several industrial areas, AI has recently attracted the attention of a growing number of Business researchers and practitioners. Previous studies have shown the need to conduct more studies that expand our understanding and business strategies in certain fields. Some of the themes discussed in previous studies highlight (a) how organizations should re-envision their institutional structures, different job functions, and required skill sets; (b) legal and ethical issues related to the data privacy of citizens and the upcoming role of robots in human society; and (c) how new data analytics techniques may support in the creation of more precise predictions. Some of the future research agendas mined using content analysis of selected articles have been presented below in Table 8:

Table 8. Future research agendas

Major Area	Research Questions
Strategic management	• How should human–machine interoperable strategies be designed? • How AI applicants can support in production of innovative products? • How may customer preferences for manual or automated services be determined? • How to streamline the course of action between human and AI-based service providers? • How demanding is it to duplicate competitive advantages derived from AI-based automated systems? • How do robotic and other AI-based systems degrade over time, and what scale and type of investments are needed to maintain a competitive advantage in an AI-dominated enterprise environment?
Customer Relationships	• How will robot design be impacted by psychological and social characteristics? • How will the interaction between people and AI-enabled robots evolve and what about AI-enabled machine-to-machine interaction? • How can machine-based automated systems allow disabled customers to surpass their cognitive and physical limitations?
Customer Acceptance	• What influences consumer choice for physical or digital robots beyond the nature of service objects? • How might virtual robots that are more cost-effective (holograms instead of actual robots at information kiosks, for example) be created to attain higher customer acceptance? • What customer and situational considerations determine the appropriate amount of anthropomorphic appearance and interpersonal abilities for service robots? • How will the gender and personality of service robots affect customer reactions? • Which service and industry features have the ability to attenuate the effects of service robot adoption factors?
Societal Acceptance	• How can the existing workforce align with bots that can function for lengthy periods without human involvement? • How can humans interact with autonomous vehicles in social settings?
General Management	• How should enterprises manage and deploy artificial intelligence systems? • How could companies encourage employee adoption of such systems? • How can we retrain employees with intuitive and compassionate abilities to ensure their continued employability? • How can we teach students intuitive and compassionate abilities so they stay employable in a commercial world dominated by artificial intelligence? • How can enterprises increase knowledge generation via automation and deep learning models?
Human Resource Management	• How can organizations involve stakeholders in the development of innovative brain-computer-interface and Deep-brain-simulation based products and experiences? • How can organizations encourage employee participation in the deployment of transhumanistic technology to enhance work performance? • What influence does recruiting personnel using BCI and DBS technology have on the organization?
Legal and ethical issues	• How can customer data privacy rights and corporate data usage be balanced? • How should regulators enforce legislation like 'right to be in light of emerging technologies? • Could AI-powered robots acquire consciousness? • Could AI-powered robots/machines get depressed? If yes, then what laws need to be placed?

4. CONCLUSION

This study was a bibliometric and content analysis research inquiry to understand the role of AI capabilities in business verticals leading to incremental value creation. The study explored the structures underlying the existing literature that characterize the research on AI capabilities helping to create superior customer value by a bibliometric analysis of carefully procured publications from the SCOPUS database from 2012 to 2022. In this direction most relevant publications, authors, sources, and country collaborations were reviewed to understand extant literature. Major themes identified using a content analysis of the ten most impactful publications revealed AI's value-creation potential in public and public-private partnerships, ai and machine learning integration, and potential impacts on business model innovation, value creation, and value enhancement potential in areas of production, operations, logistics and retailing, and potential of ai and related technology in practicing sustainable business practices. Content analysis also led to exploration of future research trends in AI's capabilities helping create superior customer value in areas such as strategic management, customer relationships, customer acceptance of ai in hospitality and retailing, societal acceptance, general management, human resource management, and legal and ethical issues.

REFERENCES

Angelis, J., & Da Silva, E. R. (2019). Blockchain adoption: A value driver perspective. *Business Horizons, 62*(3), 307–314. doi:10.1016/j.bushor.2018.12.001

Åström, J., Reim, W., & Parida, V. (2022). Value creation and value capture for AI business model innovation: A three-phase process framework. *Review of Managerial Science, 16*(7), 2111–2133. doi:10.100711846-022-00521-z

Battisti, S., & Brem, A. (2020). Digital entrepreneurs in technology-based spinoffs: An analysis of hybrid value creation in retail public–private partnerships to tackle showrooming. *Journal of Business and Industrial Marketing, 36*(10), 1780–1792. doi:10.1108/JBIM-01-2020-0051

Baxter, M. (2018). Business Analytics Intelligence. *Information-age*. www. information-age. com/business-analytics-intelligence-12 3477004/

Bill, E. (2020). Journal of Self-Governance and Management Economics. *Cognitive Automation, Business Process Optimization, and Sustainable Industrial Value Creation in Artificial Intelligence Data-Driven Internet of Things Systems., 8*(3), 9–15.

Blohm, I., Riedl, C., Füller, J., & Leimeister, J. M. (2016). Rate or trade? Identifying winning ideas in open idea sourcing. *Information Systems Research, 27*(1), 27–48. doi:10.1287/isre.2015.0605

Blondel, V. D., Guillaume, J. L., Lambiotte, R., & Lefebvre, E. (2008). Journal of statistical mechanics: Theory and experiment. *Fast Unfolding of Communities in Large Networks, 10*, P10008.

Borges, A. F., Laurindo, F. J., Spínola, M. M., Gonçalves, R. F., & Mattos, C. A. (2021). The strategic use of artificial intelligence in the digital era: Systematic literature review and future research directions. *International Journal of Information Management*, *57*, 102225. doi:10.1016/j.ijinfomgt.2020.102225

Browne, M. (2021). Artificial intelligence data-driven internet of things systems, real-time process monitoring, and sustainable industrial value creation in smart networked factories. *Journal of Self-Governance and Management Economics*, *9*(2), 21–31. doi:10.22381/jsme9220212

Burström, T., Parida, V., Lahti, T., & Wincent, J. (2021). AI-enabled business-model innovation and transformation in industrial ecosystems: A framework, model and outline for further research. *Journal of Business Research*, *127*, 85095. doi:10.1016/j.jbusres.2021.01.016

Canhoto, A. I., & Clear, F. (2020). Artificial intelligence and machine learning as business tools: A framework for diagnosing value destruction potential. *Business Horizons*, *63*(2), 183–193. doi:10.1016/j.bushor.2019.11.003

Cao, L. (2021). Artificial intelligence in retail: Applications and value creation logics. *International Journal of Retail & Distribution Management*, *49*(7), 958–976. doi:10.1108/IJRDM-09-2020-0350

Cath, C. (2018). Governing artificial intelligence: Ethical, legal and technical opportunities and challenges. *Philosophical Transactions - Royal Society. Mathematical, Physical, and Engineering Sciences*, *376*(2133), 20180080. doi:10.1098/rsta.2018.0080 PMID:30322996

Chen, Y., Visnjic, I., Parida, V., & Zhang, Z. (2021). On the road to digital servitization–The (dis) continuous interplay between business model and digital technology. *International Journal of Operations & Production Management*, *41*(5), 694–722. doi:10.1108/IJOPM-08-2020-0544

Cobo, M. J., López-Herrera, A. G., Herrera-Viedma, E., & Herrera, F. (2012). SciMAT: A new science mapping analysis software tool. *Ournal of the American Society for Information Science and Technology*, *63*(8), 1609–1630. doi:10.1002/asi.22688

de Kervenoael, R., Hasan, R., Schwob, A., & Goh, E. (2020). Leveraging human-robot interaction in hospitality services: Incorporating the role of perceived value, empathy, and information sharing into visitors' intentions to use social robots. *Tourism Management*, *78*, 104042. doi:10.1016/j.tourman.2019.104042

Dekimpe, M. G. (2020). Retailing and retailing research in the age of big data analytics. *International Journal of Research in Marketing*, *37*(1), 3–14. doi:10.1016/j.ijresmar.2019.09.001

Despoudi, S., Papaioannou, G., Saridakis, G., & Dani, S. (2018). Does collaboration pay in agricultural supply chain? An empirical approach. *International Journal of Production Research*, *56*(13), 4396–4417. doi:10.1080/00207543.2018.1440654

Dubey, R., Gunasekaran, A., Childe, S. J., Papadopoulos, T., Luo, Z., Wamba, S. F., & Roubaud, D. (2019). Can big data and predictive analytics improve social and environmental sustainability? *Technological Forecasting and Social Change*, *144*, 534–545. doi:10.1016/j.techfore.2017.06.020

Duginets, G. (2020). Global imperatives for development of international production networks: Case of Ukraine. *Problems and Perspectives in Management*, *18*(1), 57–69. doi:10.21511/ppm.18(1).2020.06

Gans, J., & Ryall, M. D. (2017). Value capture theory: A strategic management review. *Strategic Management Journal, 38*(1), 17–41. doi:10.1002mj.2592

Garbuio, M., & Lin, N. (2018). Artificial Intelligence as a Growth Engine for Health Care Startups: Emerging Business Models. *California Management Review, 61*(2), 59–83. doi:10.1177/0008125618811931

Gebauer, H., Arzt, A., Kohtamäki, M., Lamprecht, C., Parida, V., Witell, L., & Wortmann, F. (2020). How to convert digital offerings into revenue enhancement – Conceptualizing business model dynamics through explorative case studies. *Industrial Marketing Management, 91*, 429–441. doi:10.1016/j.indmarman.2020.10.006

Haftor, D. M., Climent, R. C., & Lundström, J. E. (2021). How machine learning activates data network effects in business models: Theory advancement through an industrial case of promoting ecological sustainability. *Journal of Business Research, 131*, 196–205. doi:10.1016/j.jbusres.2021.04.015

Helo, P., & Hao, Y. (2021). Artificial intelligence in operations management and supply chain management: An exploratory case study. *Production Planning and Control, 33*(16), 1573–1590. doi:10.1080/09537287.2021.1882690

Hirsch, J. E. (2007). Does the h index have predictive power? *Proceedings of the National Academy of Sciences of the United States of America, 104*(49), 19193–19198. doi:10.1073/pnas.0707962104 PMID:18040045

Holimchayachotikul, P., Derrouiche, R., Damand, D., & Leksakul, K. (2014). Value creation through collaborative supply chain: Holistic performance enhancement road map. *Production Planning and Control, 25*(11), 912–922. doi:10.1080/09537287.2013.780313

Huang, M. H., & Rust, R. T. (2018). Artificial intelligence in service. *Journal of Service Research, 21*(2), 155–172. doi:10.1177/1094670517752459

Irani, Z., Sharif, A. M., Lee, H., Aktas, E., Topaloğlu, Z., Van't Wout, T., & Huda, S. (2018). Managing food security through food waste and loss: Small data to big data. *Computers & Operations Research, 98*, 367–383. doi:10.1016/j.cor.2017.10.007

Kelly, C. D., & Jennions, M. D. (2006). The h index and career assessment by numbers. *Trends in Ecology & Evolution, 21*(4), 167–170. doi:10.1016/j.tree.2006.01.005 PMID:16701079

Kim, S. K., & Huh, J. H. (2021). Artificial intelligence based electronic healthcare solution. *Advances in Computer Science and Ubiquitous Computing*, 575–581.

Langley, D. J., Van Doorn, J., Ng, I. C., Stieglitz, S., Lazovik, A., & Boonstra, A. (2021). The Internet of Everything: Smart things and their impact on business models. *Journal of Business Research, 122*, 853–863. doi:10.1016/j.jbusres.2019.12.035

LeCun, Y., Bengio, Y., & Hinton, G. (2015). Deep learning. *Nature, 521*(7553), 436–444. doi:10.1038/nature14539 PMID:26017442

Lee, K. P., Wu, B. H., & Peng, S. L. (2019). Deep-learning-based fault detection and diagnosis of air-handling units. *Building and Environment, 157*, 24–33. doi:10.1016/j.buildenv.2019.04.029

Leone, D., Schiavone, F., Appio, F. P., & Chiao, B. (2021). How does artificial intelligence enable and enhance value co-creation in industrial markets? An exploratory case study in the healthcare ecosystem. *Journal of Business Research, 129*, 849–859. doi:10.1016/j.jbusres.2020.11.008

Margherita, A., Elia, G., & Klein, M. (2021). Managing the COVID-19 emergency: A coordination framework to enhance response practices and actions. *Technological Forecasting and Social Change, 166*, 120656. doi:10.1016/j.techfore.2021.120656 PMID:33551496

Massaro, M., Dal Mas, F., Jabbour, C. J. C., & Bagnoli, C. (2020). Crypto-economy and new sustainable business models: Reflections and projections using a case study analysis. *Corporate Social Responsibility and Environmental Management, 27*(5), 2150–2160. doi:10.1002/csr.1954

McKinsey & Company. (2022). *The state of AI in 2022—And a half decade in review*. McKinsey & Company. https://www.mckinsey.com/capabilities/quantumblack/our-insights/the-state-of-ai-in-2022-and-a-half-decade-in-review

Merig'O, J. M., Mas-Tur, A., Roig-Tierno, N., & Ribeiro-Soriano, D. (2015). A bibliometric overview of the journal of business research between 1973 and 2014. *Journal of Business Research, 68*(12), 2645–2653. doi:10.1016/j.jbusres.2015.04.006

Nahodil, P., & Vítků, J. (2013). How to Design an Autonomous Creature Based on Original Artificial Life Approaches. *Beyond. Artificial Intelligence*, 161–180.

Nica, E., Stan, C. I., Luțan, A. G., & Oașa, R. S. (2021). Internet of things-based real-time production logistics, sustainable industrial value creation, and artificial intelligence-driven big data analytics in cyber-physical smart manufacturing systems. *Economics, Management, and Financial Markets, 16*(1), 52. doi:10.22381/emfm16120215

Nilsson, N. J. (2010). *The quest for artificial intelligence: A history of ideas and achievements*. Cambridge University Press.

Noyons, E. C., Moed, H. F., & Luwel, M. (1999). Combining mapping and citation analysis for evaluative bibliometric purposes: A bibliometric study. *Journal of the American Society for Information Science, 50*(2), 115–131. doi:10.1002/(SICI)1097-4571(1999)50:2<115::AID-ASI3>3.0.CO;2-J

Palombarini, J. A., & Martínez, E. C. (2021). End-to-end on-line rescheduling from Gantt chart images using deep reinforcement learning. *International Journal of Production Research*, 1–30.

Sivarajah, U., Irani, Z., Gupta, S., & Mahroof, K. (2020). Role of big data and social media analytics for business to business sustainability: A participatory web context. *Industrial Marketing Management, 86*, 163–179. doi:10.1016/j.indmarman.2019.04.005

Tambe, P., Cappelli, P., & Yakubovich, V. (2019). Artificial intelligence in human resources management: Challenges and a path forward. *California Management Review, 61*(4), 15–42. doi:10.1177/0008125619867910

Van Eck, N., & Waltman, L. (2010). Software survey: VOSviewer, a computer program for bibliometric mapping. *Scientometricsc, 84*(2), 523–538. doi:10.100711192-009-0146-3 PMID:20585380

Vanclay, J. K. (2007). On the robustness of the h-index. *Journal of the American Society for Information Science and Technology*, *58*(10), 1547–1550. doi:10.1002/asi.20616

Wang, C., Teo, T. S., & Janssen, M. (2021). Public and private value creation using artificial intelligence: An empirical study of AI voice robot users in Chinese public sector. *International Journal of Information Management*, *61*, 102401. doi:10.1016/j.ijinfomgt.2021.102401

Wirtz, B. W., Weyerer, J. C., & Geyer, C. (2018). Artificial Intelligence and the Public Sector—Applications and Challenges. *International Journal of Public Administration*, *42*(7), 596–615. doi:10.1080/01900692.2018.1498103

Chapter 5
Analyzing International Business Operations in the Post-Pandemic Era Taking Into Account Industry 5.0 Realities

Nika Chitadze
International Black Sea University, Georgia

ABSTRACT

The research discusses several theoretical and practical aspects related to international business and the main tendencies the international business development in the post-pandemic period. Attention is paid to the main principles of international trade, activities of the Transnational Corporations, e-commerce, leading commercial companies in the world, cryptocurrency, and the future of international business based on industry 5.0. In this regard, there are discussed several aspects related to the possible impact of Industry 5.0 on international economic relations and business.

INTRODUCTION

International business is one of the main components of globalization and is a process of exchange and sharing of economic, cultural, and other achievements worldwide, which brings countries and even continents closer together. Globalization itself is a process that reflects the search for common ways to solve the problems faced by different countries of the world, which covers almost all areas, although it has manifested itself most clearly in economic and business processes. Globalization forces each state to do business in the international market. Companies are no longer focused only on the domestic market, they try to use the given opportunities as much as possible and produce products outside the country instead of only the domestic market. International business reaches the highest level of development especially in those companies that include almost all forms of international trade, including international trade, foreign direct investment, etc. Companies that enter the international market are called transnational corporations. They play one of the most important roles in the globalization process, they are

DOI: 10.4018/978-1-6684-6403-8.ch005

even considered the driving force of global processes. Today's globalization processes are a subject of constant discussion, especially economic globalization and the processes developed around it. Economic globalization is the process of integration and interdependence of commercial, productive, and financial activities between countries. It opens up financial markets around the world, facilitates the exchange of goods and services, and increases the variety of products available in every part of the planet. International business and economic globalization is a dynamic and irreversible world process. First of all, it implies the process of growing economic integration, liberalization of international trade and capital movement, accelerated technological progress, formation of information society. The main feature of globalization is the continuous expansion of the world market of certain types of products, goods or services, due to which there is little space left for the development of human, public or natural values. One of the positive aspects of the globalization of the economy is the promotion of international trade, which allows each country to specialize in the production of goods and services that it produces more efficiently under conditions of rational use of existing resources. Business organizations carry out their economic activities in different states. The so-called transnational corporations are created, in which people of different cultures, nationalities, values and mentality are employed. The intensity of economic globalization in different parts of the world is uneven and is related to the level of economic development of the countries. In economically strong countries, it gives much better results. Free trade allows for the equalization of the capabilities of different producers and countries so that they are free to create the goods and services they bring to market. Transnational corporations make good use of these advantages. The basis of their effectiveness is the advantage of possessing and accessing production resources all over the world, horizontal diversification in various fields, economy of production scale, the possibility of choosing when locating the company's enterprises in different countries, taking into account the size of their national markets, economic growth rates, prices, availability of economic resources, as well as political resources in advance Calculation (Khozrevanidze, 2021).

Discussing International Business in the modern time, we should point out Industry 5.0, which is also known as the Fifth Industrial Revolution and is a new and emerging phase of industrialization that sees humans working alongside advanced technology and A.I.-powered robots to enhance workplace processes. This is coupled with a more human-centric focus as well as increased resilience and an improved focus on sustainability.

Encompassing more than just manufacturing, this new phase builds upon the fourth industrial revolution (Industry 4.0) and is enabled by developments in I.T. that include facets such as artificial intelligence, automation, big data analytics, the internet of things (IoT), machine learning, robotics, smart systems, and virtualization.

Broadening the concepts of Industry 4.0, this new industrial revolution is described by the European Union as providing, "a vision of an industry that aims beyond efficiency and productivity as the sole goals, and reinforces the role and the contribution of industry to society."

This is an important distinction from the approach of Industry 4.0, as described by the EU, since "it places the wellbeing of the worker at the center of the production process and uses new technologies to provide prosperity beyond jobs and growth while respecting the production limits of the planet" (TWI, 2023).

Research goals and objectives: The main goal of this paper is to analyze the theoretical and practical issues related to international business in the background of globalization and deglobalization and to reveal the main trends of international business development in the period after the spread of the pandemic COVID-19 based on the conditions of Industry 5.0. In addition, the task of the paper is to consider the essence of globalization, the events taking place during its process. How is the development of international business and various business operations in the conditions of globalization and deglobalization created by Covid-19, what are the main features of capital and international trade in the conditions of economic globalization. What role do transnational companies play and how do they function, and in general what are the trends of international business, what are its modern challenges.

Peculiarities of international business development in the conditions of globalization and deglobalization

MAIN TRENDS IN INTERNATIONAL TRADE

As we mentioned above, trade has an important place in international relations. Some scholars go so far in evaluating the role of trade that they consider trade and war to be the main components of international relations. International trade is the earliest and relatively common form of international economic relations. It accounts for 80% of world economic turnover. International trade refers to the total volume of goods turnover between countries. The object of international trade is:

- Material items (finished products, machinery and equipment, raw materials);
- services (transportation, utility, tourism, financial credit, insurance, information-computing, scientific and technical, etc.);
- Intellectual property (copyright, patent right, etc.) (Jolia, 2015).

International trade involves trade relations between countries, and both transnational corporations and states are involved in this process. Trade is of great importance in international relations and it is one of the main prerequisites for the establishment of one or another type of relations between countries. International trade is not a new phenomenon. Countries have been engaged in the exchange of goods with each other for centuries, although it should be noted that the types of trade have always differed from each other. The currency regime, exchange rate, tariffs, barriers, etc. differed. Different approaches to international trade have created new problems at different times. The origin of these problems is mainly explained by the fact that the states often changed their foreign trade rates without agreeing with each other. They increased tariffs, imposed quotas on the import of goods, etc. Such actions were often a big blow to the world economy. International trade has a major impact on international politics because it creates close business ties between countries. Today, all countries are involved in international trade, because none of them will be able to be self-sufficient and provide themselves only with their own products. Two very different theories try to explain the essence of international trade and its nature. One is based on liberal traditions, and the other on nationalist ones. The liberal theory of international trade is based on the theories of Adam Smith and David Ricardo. Liberals believe in an open system of trade governed by the principle of legality. According to them, free trade is beneficial for all parties involved in it. However, this does not mean that all parties necessarily win equally in this process. Economists have long believed that trade allows countries to focus primarily on the production of goods and services that can be of high quality and can be provided by those countries with maximum efficiency. An open trading system requires that countries have fair and non-discriminatory access to each other's markets. For this, countries should try to create favorable conditions for other countries to enter their markets. Although trade liberalization has traditionally focused on the reduction of tariffs and certain non-tariff barriers, in recent years new means have emerged to ensure this liberalization. All countries' trade laws and trade practices should be transparent, that is, everyone should know the rules and everyone should have an equal chance to compete. Nationalists place less importance on international trade and believe that a country's exports should exceed its imports—a country should sell more than it buys. However, if all countries share this position, then there will be nothing left to sell and international trade will cease to exist. Gilpin points out that liberals and nationalists agree that production needs protection in its initial stages, but their views differ fundamentally as to what the purpose of this protection is. For nationalists, protectionism is the ultimate goal, followed by industrial power and a strong state. For liberals, protectionism is a temporary phase that allows the country to understand in which area it has a relative advantage. The ultimate goal is free trade and creation of world wealth. In the history of modern most highly developed states, there were periods when they turned sharply towards economic protectionism. International trade consists of two commodity flows: export and import. In order to consider it as international trade, the main thing is the legal fact of the goods crossing the state customs border.

Factors affecting the development of trade are:

- acceleration of scientific and technical progress;
- activation of TNC activities in the world market;
- Liberalization of international trade;
- creation of new free economic zones;
- strengthening trade and economic integration;
- Activation of the activities of "newly industrialized countries" (Jolia, 2015).

International trade is developing in parallel with the current changes in the world. It changes as the world itself changes, economic-political relations between states, global economic and legal policy. For the last three decades, international economic relations have been playing an important role in the world economic system, which is why the share of exports in the gross national product of most countries is continuously increasing. Today, states buy and sell goods and services in much greater quantities than before. International trade contributes to the economic development of countries and the growth of their economic interdependence, which significantly reduces the chances of their conflict. Joan Edelman Spiro writes in her book (The Politics of International Economic Relations) that after the Second World War, North America, Western Europe and several Asian countries became very connected with each other in economic, trade, technological, financial and other aspects. They are constantly working on improving their relations and are in constant partnership with each other. The foreign economic policy pursued after the Second World War contributed to the economic rise of all these countries, the globalization of production, the growth of exports and technological development. In order for international trade to take place, it is important that a competitive market system is created in one or another country, where companies can freely compete with each other. Since the 90s, thanks to international trade, European countries have managed to get back on their feet quickly. The end of the 19th century was characterized by a sharp expansion of international trade. According to one estimate, the share of exports in the world's gross domestic product increased from 5% in 1870 to 8.7% in 1913. At the same time, international capital flows have played a much more visible role in the formation of the world economy. By 1913, the annual flow of international capital reached 5% of the gross national product of capital-exporting countries, notably the United Kingdom, France, and Germany. Typical investments included government securities, but foreign direct investment accounted for one-third of total foreign investment funds by 1913.

Between the end of World War II and the global financial crisis, there is a sub-period increase in international trade relative to global output.

Global merchandise exports totaled $17 trillion in 2017, up from $16 trillion in 2012 but down from $19 trillion in 2013. In 2017, the volume of world trade in goods increased by 4.6 percent, and in 2018 to 4.2 percent. The largest increase in import demand was observed in developing economies, where imports increased by 6.9 percent. The rate of developed countries was 3.5 and 2.1 percent. Among Asia, Latin America and the United States, Asia led the way in terms of import volume growth at 8.8 percent, followed by Latin America at 6.2 percent and finally the United States at 4 percent. Eurozone imports grew at a slower pace and amounted to 3.1 percent. According to the data of the World Trade Organization, Asia accounted for 2.9 percent of the world import growth, or 60 percent of the total growth, and based on the data of 2018, the demand for imports slowed down. After passing the main stage of COVID-19, particularly in 2021, the value of global trade reached a record level of $28.5 trillion (UNCTAD, 2022).

How 5 Technologies are Changing Global Trade

Recently, international trade has dominated the world's headlines. Much of the discussion focused on the threat of a trade war, tit-for-tat tariffs, and the health of the global trade order. While these conversations are extremely important, they miss the brighter side of international trade—how the innovative technologies of the Fourth Industrial Revolution are transforming trade, making processes more inclusive and efficient.

A technological breakthrough is not new to the global trading system. The steam power revolution has connected the world like never before. The invention of shipping containers marked the beginning of globalization. Recently, technologies such as optical character recognition (OCR) for reading container numbers, radio frequency identification (RFID) and QR codes for identifying and tracking shipments, and basic digitization of trade documents have improved the reliability and efficiency of international trade.

At the same time, from trade agreements written to digital commerce, transactions that involve a lot of paperwork, to trade finance that still depends on traditional banking methods, the global trading system has not been able to take full advantage of the advanced technologies that can make trade more efficient, more inclusive and less costly.

The good news is that we may be on the brink of change. Combining different technologies at different stages of the technology adoption life cycle can fundamentally change the way resources are allocated and international trade operates. Governments and businesses need to understand current trends to stay ahead of the curve.

Here are 5 technologies that will change global trade:

Blockchain

Blockchain and blockchain-based distributed ledger technologies can have a huge impact on the global trade supply chain. Trade organizations such as the Dubai Chamber of Commerce and Industry have also taken the initiative to use blockchain technology to address the challenges of global trade such as high costs and lack of transparency and security.

Blockchain-based solutions not only make the movement of goods more efficient and reliable, but also change the world of trade finance. For example, blockchain is being used to simplify the long and tedious process of obtaining a letter of credit (LoC), a payment mechanism used in international trade.

Deloitte helped an Indian private bank change the LoC issuance structure by developing a blockchain-based solution (based on the Ethereum platform) that reduced the issuance time from 20-30 days to a few hours. In some other cases, companies like Skuchain bypass LoC entirely, providing real-time tracking of goods and inventory financing, which reduces transaction risks and allows financiers to provide working capital exemption to all supply chain partners at the lowest cost. capital in this chain.

Artificial Intelligence and Machine Learning

Artificial intelligence and machine learning can be used to optimize trade routes, manage ship and truck traffic in ports, and translate e-commerce search queries from one language to other languages and provide translated inventory in response.

AI is being used not only to improve efficiency and improve consumer services, but also to ensure the sustainability of global trade. For example, in 2016, Google launched Global Fishing Watch, a real-time tool that uses machine learning to combat illegal fishing and provides a global view of commercial fishing based on vessel movements and satellite data. It can be used by governments and other organizations to identify suspicious behavior and develop sustainable policies.

Trading Services Through Digital Platforms

Trading services online is getting easier - digital platforms like Upwork allow users to find service providers from all over the world for a wide range of services and can find anyone from a web developer in Serbia to an accountant in Pakistan to a virtual assistant in the Philippines. Meanwhile, start-ups such as VIPKID, an international learning platform, are pairing American educators with Chinese children for online English learning. These digital platforms connect customers seamlessly with service providers in a way that was not possible before, when such professional services were mostly delivered in person.

Combining different technologies at different stages of the technology adoption life cycle can fundamentally change the way resources are allocated and international trade operates.

3D Printing

There is still no consensus on the impact of 3D printing on global trade. There are studies that predict that once high-speed 3D printing becomes mainstream and cheap enough, global trade could drop by as much as 25% as 3D printing requires less labor and reduces the need for imports. Others argue that such views are too optimistic and do not take into account the complexity and reality of mass production. Regardless of positions, the impact of 3D printing on global trade is real, especially with the advent of faster and cheaper 3D printing methods.

Mobile Payments

From Apply Pay to Alipay to M-Pesa, mobile payments are changing the way we live and giving more people access to market opportunities. According to the World Bank's Global Inclusion Database, the number of people accessing bank accounts increased by 20% between 2011 and 2014, and mobile money accounts have become a major driver of increased access to financial services, especially in emerging economies.

For example, in sub-Saharan Africa, 12% of adults (64 million adults) have a mobile money account (compared to 2% globally), and 45% of these only have a mobile money account. As the new banking population connects to mobile payments, it will be much easier for them to participate in global commerce, both as consumers and as businesses.

Tough Battle for New Technologies

It should be noted that these technologies also pose complex management challenges, both within and outside the country. We cannot simply assume that these technologies will automatically take root and bear fruit, from lack of governance to incompatible licensing and taxation requirements to outdated trade agreements.

Public and private stakeholders must work closely together to create the foundation and environment for these new technologies to unlock their positive potential and mitigate potential harm. In particular, stakeholders should adopt a multi-stakeholder and people-centred agile management approach to leave room for experimentation and gain input from different actors. In addition, in the absence of a global standard, regional governments must take responsibility and lead efforts to harmonize regional rules on issues such as data flows, licensing, and taxation.

Technological innovation opens up an exciting future for international trade amid today's uncertainties, and if managed correctly, these innovations will lead to more inclusive and efficient trade growth in the coming years (ITU, 2020).

Features of Capital Movement and 5.0 Industry

The international movement of capital taking into account the 5.0 industry is a determinant of the development of the modern world economy. Compared to goods, the preferential export of capital abroad created new economic-legal relations between countries and made the world economy more diverse and complex. At first, some developed countries carried out capital repatriation. Following the development of the world economy, this process has accelerated and expanded. Today it is typical for countries with dynamically developed economies. The main reason for the international movement of capital is its excess and low profitability in the national country. Therefore, to get more profit, he "travels" abroad. Since the second half of the 20th century, capital outflows have been continuously increasing.

At the same time, the coronavirus disease (COVID-19) has dramatically decreased trade in goods, trade in services, and foreign direct investment in the world, especially in the second quarter of 2020. Against this backdrop, we conduct various empirical analyses using global data. Our findings can be summarized as follows. The negative impacts are magnified when the COVID-19 pandemic becomes serious in exporting, importing, supplier, investing, and investment host countries. However, such impacts of the COVID-19 pandemic are heterogeneous across industries and types of investments. Their magnitude is also different, depending on the necessity of people's cross-border movement. Furthermore, some factors, such as vaccination, various online tools, or input diversification, play a crucial role in mitigating the negative impacts.

At the same time, the post-pandemic period has led to an increase in capital movements.

In general, according to the growth rate, the capital export of developed countries exceeds the growth rate of commodity export and GDP and strengthens the international movement of capital. In addition, the reasons for withdrawing capital abroad are:

- Inequality of demand and supply levels for capital;
- monopolization of the foreign market;
- Cheaper raw materials and workforce in the country for importing capital;
- attractive investment conditions;
- Stable political situation (Shengelia, 2008).

Transfer of Capital Abroad Has a Positive Effect on:

- Interconnection and interconnectedness of national economies. The internationalization of production has the greatest impact on the acceleration of the international movement of capital. Export of capital, especially in the form of foreign direct investment (FDI), is the main factor in giving products an international character. It is unified and is realized without geographical, national or other peculiarities, for example, automobile, airplane, radio electronics, computer;

- International industrial cooperation. It is practically implemented through the interconnection of transnational companies and their structural units. For example, legally independent firms from different countries, depending on the technological mark, work closely within the framework of one international company, for which it is necessary to take capital abroad;
- Targeted foreign economic policy of developed countries. It is due to the foreign country's economic growth rates, the development of a specific branch of farming, employment or other purposes;
- Attractive economic and legal environment of developing countries. This condition is an additional stimulating factor for a foreign businessman;
- Environmental factors. The strictest environmental norms in developed countries force companies to transfer their capital to developing countries;
- Activity of international financial organizations. These organizations play an important role in regulating foreign investment flows. Taking capital abroad has both positive and negative consequences for both parties, namely:
    - Initially, the labor force in the capital exporting country decreases and the balance of payments worsens, then the profits from investments begin to flow in and the economic situation gradually improves;
    - In the capital importing country, employment increases, additional currency enters, new technologies are introduced, but at the same time, control over individual sectors of the national economy weakens or is lost altogether. Capital movement is one of the most important factors in today's world. This is a global phenomenon for which there are literally no borders. Capital of all nationalities goes where large profits are guaranteed. After the Second World War, the export of capital increased dramatically, and it became a common phenomenon. During this period, the role of the United States of America in the export of capital increased significantly. Later, the Federal Republic of Germany and Japan were added to it. France still maintained its leading position, but the share of Great Britain decreased. According to many scholars, capital exports create closer ties than international trade. Capital exports help strengthen ties between countries. Withdrawing capital and investing it in another country provides an opportunity to influence the receiving country. When talking about the impact of foreign capital and transnational companies on the host country, two main positions can

be distinguished: according to the first, the impact of transnational companies is generally positive. According to the second position, they limit a country's autonomy, hinder its independent development, increase economic inequality in the host country, and often even take away economic sovereignty (Rondeli, 2003).

Those who share the first position believe that foreign investments are a serious factor in accelerating the economic development of the host country. For example, they cite Western European states after the Second World War, and their rapid development is partly explained by substantial American capital investments. However, many do not share this opinion and believe that the relationship between direct investment and economic development does not give grounds to call it a causal relationship. Direct investments, as a rule, are carried out in countries where good conditions have been created for the development of a market economy. The volume of export of public capital in the world is less than that of private capital, and this has a logical explanation. The goal of state capital is not quick and short-term profit. Its export mostly takes place in the country's infrastructure, transport sectors, credit-financial system, etc., that is, in such areas, without the development of which it will be impossible to export private capital effectively and safely. Forms of state capital are: long-term loans and credits, free aid. State capital is directed towards weak, developing countries. In this way, it is possible to influence them and establish a certain control. As a result of the export of state capital, the receiving countries buy their latest technologies, goods, services, etc. from the investing country. Exports of private capital are on a larger scale. It is carried out either through direct investment or through portfolio investment. The main goal of private capital is quick and big profit. According to the nature of investments and the form of own capital, individual, corporate and institutional investors are distinguished.

Individual investors do not pool their capital, they invest in their own name and with their own funds independently of each other. Corporate investors act on behalf of the respective enterprise, joint stock company firm, according to its own capital and debt. Institutional investors build their capital with funds from customers and depositors and invest it mainly in securities. In the assessment of investment decisions, investments mean the activity of the investor, aimed at achieving his, as a rule, long-term goals that are not related to current consumption. Investors who act in accordance with their goals and are personally responsible for their achievement are either capital owners or persons who make investment and financial decisions on behalf of a legal entity. In the latter case, the investment is made through own or proper firm and joint stock company loan capital. The basic principles and methods of the most advantageous use of own or loan capital to achieve the long-term goals of the investor constitute the content of the investment theory. In world practice, three main forms of investment are distinguished:

1. Direct, i.e. real investments;
2. portfolio, i.e. financial investments;
3. Medium-term and long-term international credits and loans of loan capital to industrial and trade corporations, banks and other financial institutions.

Direct investments can ensure that the invested company is transferred to the full ownership of the investing corporations or allow them to establish actual control over it. Portfolio investments are the primary source of equity financing issued by enterprises, large corporations, and private banks. The international loan capital market is divided into the money market and the equity capital market: the money market is the short-term credit market (up to one year). The capital market is:

- medium-term (from 2 to 5 years) bank loans;
- Market of long-term (more than 10 years) loans, which are issued mainly during the issuance and purchase of securities (Rugman, 2004).

In recent years, non-traditional forms of long-term financing have been used in the international market, for example, project financing, which involves issuing large credits for the implementation of specific industrial projects of enterprises. International trade and investment flows are the main driving forces of economic globalization. In the period 1990-2019, both trade in goods and services and foreign direct investments were characterized by a growth trend throughout the world. However, compared to international trade, foreign direct investments showed a higher growth rate and represented a more dynamically developing segment. The growth of foreign direct investment was particularly sharp in the late 1990s. In 2000-2002, it was characterized by a decreasing trend, after which it continued to grow, from 2007 it began to decrease, although from 2009 it began to grow again. In 2011-2019, it increased significantly. In the reporting period, trade in goods and services was characterized by more stable growth, with almost equal growth rates in both categories. Within the COVID-19, Foreign Direct Investments decreased by 30% (UNCTAD, 2022).

Global foreign direct investment (FDI) flows showed a strong rebound in 2021, up 77% to an estimated $1.65 trillion, from $929 billion in 2020, surpassing their pre-COVID-19 level, according to UNCTAD's Investment Trends Monitor published on 19 January (UNCTAD, 2022).

"Recovery of investment flows to developing countries is encouraging, but stagnation of new investment in least developed countries in industries important for productive capacities, and key Sustainable Development Goals (SDG) sectors – such as electricity, food or health – is a major cause for concern," said UNCTAD Secretary-General Rebeca Grynspan (UNCTAD, 2022).

BIGGEST RISE IN DEVELOPED ECONOMIES

Developed economies saw the biggest rise by far, with FDI reaching an estimated $777 billion in 2021 – three times the exceptionally low level in 2020, the report shows.

In Europe, more than 80% of the increase in flows was due to large swings in conduit economies. Inflows in the United States more than doubled, with the increase entirely accounted for by a surge in cross-border mergers and acquisitions (M&As).

FDI flows in developing economies increased by 30% to nearly $870 billion, with a growth acceleration in East and South-East Asia (+20%), a recovery to near pre-pandemic levels in Latin America and the Caribbean, and an uptick in West Asia.

Inflows in Africa also rose. Most recipients across the continent saw a moderate rise in FDI; the total for the region more than doubled, inflated by a single intra-firm financial transaction in South Africa in the second half of 2021.

Of the total increase in global FDI flows in 2021 ($718 billion), more than $500 billion, or almost three quarters, was recorded in developed economies. Developing economies, especially least developed countries (LDCs), saw more modest recovery growth (UNCTAD, 2022).

How COVID-19 has affected on the different field of business and how business in developed under the conditions of 5.0 Industry?

Taking into account the impact of COVID-19 on the business environment and World economy, it should be paid an attention on the following factors, particularly:

Which are The Most Expensive and Largest Employer Companies in the World in Post-Covid Period?

2020-2021 was a particularly difficult year for the entire world economy. The full Lockdown, announced in the countries due to the pandemic, has harmed small and medium-sized businesses or entrepreneurs.

However, there have been cases where rapid response and the shift to digital have even made some businesses doubly profitable.

All of this, of course, has had little to do with the world's giant corporations and companies. With billions in profits in the competitive market, there has simply been a redistribution of order among the various giant companies.

By the end of 2021, out of the 10 most expensive companies in the world with a market capitalization of trillions, eight are American, one operating in Saudi Arabia and one in Taiwan.

Here are listed ten leading companies in the world:

- Apple - $ 2.944 trillion market capitalization (US)
- Microsoft - $ 2.571 trillion market capitalization (US)
- Alphabet - $ 1.969 trillion market capitalization (US)
- Saudi Aramco - $ 1.854 trillion market capitalization (Saudi Arabia)
- Amazon - $ 1.746 trillion market capitalization (US)
- Tesla - Market capital of $ 1.021 trillion (US)
- Meta (Facebook) - $ 917.28 billion market capitalization (US)
- NVIDIA - $ 752.53 billion market capitalization (US)
- Berkshire Hathaway - $ 645.37 billion in market capitalization (US)
- TSMC - Market capital of $ 617.81 billion (Taiwan)

As for the question of which is the largest employer in the world top-20 companies, first of all, it should be noted that today the problem of employment in the world, including in Georgia, remains one of the unresolved challenges. This issue became even more acute after the spread of the coronavirus. In the last two years alone, up to a million employees in the U.S. have been laid off. The rate is colossal worldwide.

It is interesting, which countries have been able to more or less stabilize unemployment and which are the companies that have the most employees worldwide?

As it turned out, most people are employed by companies based in the United States, China, and Germany.

This is a list of 20 leading companies in the world based on the number of employees:

1. Walmart, USA. 2,200,000 employees
2. Amazon, USA. 1,271,000 employees

3. Volkswagen, Germany. 662,653 employees.
4. FedEx, USA. 570,000 employees.
5. Deutsche Post, Germany. 565,053 employees.
6. Compass Group, United Kingdom. 548,143 employees.
7. United Parcel Service, USA. 540,000 employees.
8. Accenture, Ireland. 537,000 employees.
9. Kroger, USA. 500,000 employees.
10. Home Depot, USA. 500,000 employees.
11. Tata Consultancy Services, India. 488,649 employees.
12. Gazprom, Russia. 477,600 employees.
13. Agricultural Bank of China. 459,000 employees.
14. China Mobile, China. 454,332 employees.
15. ICBC, China. 439,787 employees.
16. PetroChina, China. 432,003 employees.
17. Ahold Delhaize, The Netherlands. 410,000 employees.
18. Target, USA. 409,000 employees.
19. Jardine Matheson, Hong Kong. 403,000 employees.
20. Yum China, China. 400,000 employees (Chitadze, 2022).

Global E-Commerce in Numbers - Where More People are Buying Things Online

In the post-covid period, thanks to the growth of e-commerce, even with limited capital, in modern times, starting a business is an easy task. Consumers are increasingly trusting online shopping - it is estimated that by 2040, 95% of retail trade will be fully online. E-commerce opens the door to new opportunities for many entrepreneurs.

The potential of e-commerce is growing rapidly. In 2017, e-sales worldwide amounted to $ 2.3 trillion, by 2021 this amount has almost doubled to $ 4.5 trillion. In the US alone, online shopping already accounts for 10% of retail sales and this data is likely to grow even more (Chitadze, 2021).

By 2021, 72% of EU citizens were involved in online trade. 46% of buyers spent between € 100 to € 500 on one-time purchases in the last 3 months of 2021.

According to statistics, men spend 28% more on online shopping than women. It is also interesting to note that comfort has been a priority for online shopping customers when shopping. 43% of online shoppers say they buy in bed, 23% in the office, and 20% while in the bathroom or car. 10% of consumers say that while shopping online they bought expensive items under the influence of alcohol. A study of consumer behavior has shown that most buyers start looking at one particular, desired item, but eventually buy a similar but different good (Chitadze, 2021).

E-Commerce Market Share

The United States is often regarded as the largest market for e-commerce, but this is not true. The country is included in the list of 10 largest e-commerce markets in the world, although the first place is occupied by China with 672 billion dollars. Next places by the countries are estimated by the following volumes of e-trading:

- US: $ 340 billion
- United Kingdom: $ 99 billion
- Japan: $ 79 billion
- Germany: $ 73 billion
- France: $ 43 billion
- South Korea: $ 37 billion
- Canada: $ 30 billion
- Russia: $ 20 billion
- Brazil: $ 19 billion

In 2010-2022, e-commerce increased in all age groups, with the largest increase observed in the 16-24 age group. Eight out of ten Internet users in the Netherlands (91%), Denmark (90%), Germany (87%), Sweden (86%) and Ireland (81%) bought or ordered goods or services online. Less than 50% have bought products and services online in Bulgaria (42%) and Romania (45%). The largest increases in 2015-2020 (by 20 percentage points or more) were recorded in Romania, the Czech Republic, Croatia, Hungary, Slovenia, Lithuania, and Cyprus (Chitadze, 2022).

Nielsen`s Global Union Commerce Report provides data on the most profitable industries by country. In South Korea, most of the money - about 77% is spent on fashion, 66% on household goods, 52% of the population buys non-food items online, 51% the packaged groceries, and 37% the fresh produce. Japan accounts for 79% of online stationery sales.

The most popular products for online shopping in European countries are clothing (including sportswear), shoes, and accessories - 64%. In Europe, the Internet is also used for restaurant delivery, fast food chains and catering services - 29%, furniture, home accessories or horticultural products - 28%, cosmetics, beauty and wellness products - 27%, printed books, magazines, or newspapers are at the same level- 27%, computers, Tablets, on mobile phones or accessories is coming - 26% (2021).

For most buyers, paying by credit card is the most preferred method. Credit card payment system is used in 53% of transactions, followed by digital payment systems - 43% and debit cards - 38%. However, digital payment systems are the most preferred method in China and Western Europe, while the remittance method is preferred in Eastern Europe, Africa, and the Middle East.

As for online shopping in the US, more Americans prefer it to so-called physical shopping. Only in 2021-2022, 80% of the entire American population used online shopping at least once.

During the working out the strategy of electronic commerce, it is very important a decision on the adaptation with mobile devices. According to EMarketer, 59% of e-commerce sales were implemented via mobile (Chitadze, 2022).

Several e-commerce trends have changed in 2019-2021 and this will continue into 2022-2023 as well. The vast majority of consumers used chatbots, voice assistants, relations with social media managers, etc. while shopping online.

CRYPTOCURRENCY - A NEW PHASE OF GLOBAL FINANCE IN THE FRAMEWORK OF 5.0 INDUSTRY

When talking about cryptocurrency, first of all, it should be noted that everything can be used as money if people agree on it and give the money the appropriate function. Humanity does not yet know how the function of money can be changed in the future. Money must meet several criteria, be a means of payment, a means of accumulating/storing value, a means of accounting, etc. According to many experts, the impact of cryptocurrencies is gradually increasing at this stage. The rubicon is overcome, paper banknotes gradually fade into the past.

As it is known, money as the equivalent of universal exchange has existed for many centuries, the conception of economic relations led to its gradual development. People have agreed since the immemorial time to carry out the process of exchange with each other. It was necessary to come up with such a universal standard for something that could be exchanged for everything. As a result, the idea of a universal equivalent unit was born and developed. This unit was constantly changing at different stages of human development with the changing level of progress of the society. At various times it was wheat, commodities, gold coins, banknotes, and today it is already a cryptocurrency.

Cryptocurrency is the Most Modern Form of Technological Development Of Money

The history of cryptocurrencies dates back to the birth of Bitcoin in 2008. Even before Bitcoin, there were many attempts to create global electronic money, but all efforts were vain. Cryptocurrency has no physicality; it seems to be expressed by a simple combination of numbers. But things are not so simple. In the case of Bitcoin, behind these records is a record book known as a blockchain. A blockchain can be represented as a decentralized database with no single control center, no single computer, where all information is accumulated. In exchange for one center, the information is redistributed to multiple computers called nodes. On these computers, the nodes all have the same copy (in the case of Bitcoin, there are about 110,000 nodes in the world), the nodes function exactly as written in the Bitcoin algorithm. That is, there is only one version of the truth on the web. It is impossible and pointless to try to falsify information here because, despite the chance of theoretically falsifying information on one node, information on other nodes throughout the network is still unchanged. It is about the same as trying to prove that North Korea won the World Cup final, although it makes no sense when the outcome of the final is already known around the world, and the world population has the relevant information. Accordingly, the nodes about the transactions carried out and the changes made in the record book, the computers are constantly broadcasting to each other, are in contact with each other, disseminate information, provide each other with information about changes in the blockchain. This information is constantly synchronized between them. This language of communication is called the "rumors, rumors" protocol, which allows hundreds of thousands of nodes/computers to have constantly updated information about the state of the record book.

Based on the above, it is necessary to explain what a blockchain is. Various transactions in the Bitcoin network are sorted/recorded in blocks. Each new block is added to the previous block through cryptographic functions, which makes it impossible to change the information stored in the previous block. This is how a long chain of bundled blocks is formed, which is why this record book is called a blockchain. Information is recorded or placed in transaction blocks by miners responsible for the system's operation. Miners have the function of validating all transactions carried out in the Bitcoin network. In return for the work done, they are rewarded accordingly in the form of newly printed bitcoins from the system.

The whole Bitcoin architecture is built on a system of motivation to encourage honest behavior on the part of all players and not to treat players/system participants with dishonest behavior, for which they will be punished and held accountable. The Bitcoin system is additionally unique because, for the first time in the history of electronic systems, system security has been taken out and entrusted to the free market. The consensus model that Bitcoin uses is known as Proof of Work. New, more modern models of consensus (Poof of Stake) have now been developed, which require much less, almost minimal power consumption, and can be just as durable and unbreakable as the so-called bitcoin - PROOF of WORK.

The whole architecture of cryptocurrencies is based on the most difficult cryptography and higher mathematics; game theory is used to create effective models of consensus. In the case of Bitcoin, the system is decentralized, balanced, the rules of the game are clear to everyone and written from the beginning with a protocol, no one trusts anyone, good behavior is encouraged, bad behavior is punished.

According to many economists, Bitcoin is a revolutionary innovation - a technology that fundamentally changes the perception of money. Satoshi Nakamoto is considered to be the creator of Bitcoin. Satoshi introduced a model of decentralized finance and thus laid the foundation for a new wave of decentralization.

It is noteworthy that in early 2021, the price of Bitcoin for the first time exceeded $60,000. The most popular cryptocurrency in the world, the price of which tripled between 2019-2021, has gained the support of leading companies. This became the reason for its record price increase (Chitadze, 2022).

During the same period, the total volume of the Bitcoin market has already exceeded $1 trillion (Chitadze, 2022).

As early as February 2020, Elon Musk announced that electric car maker Tesla had bought $1.5 billion worth of bitcoin. According to him, he will also add Bitcoin to the means of payment. Mastercard plans to make a similar decision (Chitadze, 2022).

The coronavirus pandemic has also had a significant impact on cryptocurrency prices, as much of the world's population has switched to online trading. On the other hand, the growing popularity of cryptocurrencies has a huge impact on the environment, as their production requires large amounts of electricity.

Post-Pandemic Period and Industry 5.0: how the Future Fifth Industrial Revolution Will Affect Humanity

In the near future, we are waiting for the fifth industrial revolution or Industry 5.0 (Industry 5.0). The Industrial Revolution has come a long way in the world. The first industrial revolution was known as the transition to new manufacturing processes, the second revolution brought the technological revolution, a phase of rapid standardization and industrialization.

Industry 3.0 has led to the digitization of manufacturing, and the fourth industrial revolution (Industry 4.0) is widely known as the digital revolution that has been taking place today since the middle of the last century. Industry 4.0 is characterized by a combination of digital technologies that closes the gap between the physical, digital and biological spheres.

What Awaits Us in the 5th Industrial Revolution

This industrial revolution is expected to be the next disruptive technological revolution, it will be faster and more scalable. Experts and analysts believe that Industry 5.0 will build on Industry 4.0.

We are now in the fourth industrial revolution and are witnessing economic upheavals associated with such technological advances of mankind as AI, Blockchain, Crypto, IoT, and others, but the fifth industrial revolution is likely to return our attention to humanity.

AI can help improve human productivity, blockchain can provide more efficient and convenient access to banking for those without access to a bank, and robots can help people negotiate ROI and do the hard work of industry for people.

In Industry 5.0, the Role of Women in the Economy and Business Will Increase and be Promising

The United Nations Sustainable Development Goals (SDGs) provide the first ever universal framework for achieving a prosperous future. The SDGs, adopted by the heads of government of 193 UN member states, cover all aspects of life around the world; social, environmental and economic.

One of the most important SDGs is SDG 5 – empowering women around the world. Without this, there is no optimism in achieving the SDGs. It says that if women are empowered to participate more in campaigns for human prosperity, all other SDGs will rise.

Preparing for Industry 5.0

Contrary to the trends of Industry 4.0 towards technology and dehumanization, the best practices in the field of technological progress and innovation in Industry 5.0 will return to the service of humanity. In the workplace, this 5th industrial revolution will place more emphasis on human intelligence than ever before.

In the 5th industrial revolution, the interaction of man and machine will be progressive

Since the use of AI is already enabling employers to find the best talent, the fifth industrial revolution brings huge benefits by providing candidates with a more personalized job search experience.

In Industry 5.0, Human-Machine Cooperation Will be Even More Advanced.

Recent breakthroughs in artificial intelligence, robotics, machine learning, data and analytics, among others, have also been responsible for the birth of the 5th Industrial Revolution.

One of the main advantages of such technologies, especially AI, is that they provide rich data and act on it. This can be a huge benefit for recruiters in terms of getting the right talent pool that resonates with candidates and improves communication between them.

In this way, Industry 5.0 will be a revolution in artificial intelligence with the potential of other technologies such as quantum computing to help connect people and machines in the workplace. It will also help recruiters and hiring managers tap into unique talent and skills that can bring more value to their companies.

CONCLUSION

The Perspectives Of The Development Of The International Business And International Economic System

During the discussion about further development of the International Business and International economic system, specialists mean **liberalism, dependence, and economic nationalism (mercantilism).**

In the liberalism and dependence models, the world business and the international economic system is considered as one unity, where the functions of the national economy (sovereign state) are decreased. According to mercantilists, the main actors of the world economic development for the future are still independent states. From this point of view, in the future, in the framework of the world economy, the confrontation will be increased. This confrontation will be reflected in the field of capital investments, rivalry for the markets, and sources of raw materials.

By R. Gilpin, in comparison with the mercantilist point of view of the XVIII Century, modern mercantilism (neo mercantilism), should be understood as a priority of the national business, economic and political purposes (establishment control over the export and import, intention for the gaining the positive trade and payment balance, etc.), in comparison with the global economic progress and prosperity (Gilpin, 1992).

During the discussion about the processes in the international business, political and economic systems, in general, for the functioning of this system is important to determine the role of hegemony. In the modern period, such hegemony in the field of business and politics is the USA. According to several experts, it is finishing the period of the hegemony of this gigantic state and it is starting the process of gradually decreasing its role. It was presented by the American historian Paul Kennedy. In his work "The Rise and Fall of the Great Powers", where he predicted the falling of the US hegemony (Kennedy, 1987).

The other group of experts, on the contrary, deny the possibilities of decreasing the US hegemony. According to American Richard Rozcreans, R. Gilpin, C. Layne, B. Schwartz, etc. even though the USA is in the declining process, but it can keep its hegemonic position (Gilpin, 1987).

According to British economist, S. Strange, the hegemony of the US did not weaken, because it is based on the structural advantage and strength, which means, the USA has the ability, to "build" the international economic relations, institutes, "rules of behavior" and norms (Strange, 1987).

The structural strengths of the USA are coming from the leading position of the state in the structure of international business and international security, the strong position of the Dollar, and the structure of the "producing" of knowledge. Knowledge is the strength and it is proved by the number of educational institutions in the USA as of the beginning of the XXI Century - about 3 thousand high educational institutions and more than 12 million students (Rondeli, 2003).

The existence of the hegemonic order in the international economic and business system does not mean that the system is not multi-polar and the possible strengthening of the neo-mercantilism tendencies. Because the international business and political system has become more multi-polar, the supporters of neo-mercantilism consider that political multi - polarize will promote economic nationalism, and neo - mercantilism economic processes will dominate over the integration and interdependence deepening tendencies.

According to neo-mercantilists, the World economy and international business would be divided into regional blocks, because the struggle between the integration and internationalization factors from one side and economic nationalism from the other side can have such a result.

In this case, the integration will be developed in the framework of the separate regions, because the separate states will not be able to be competitive, but, at the same time, they will not deny their principle of sovereignty. The resolving of this problem will be possible by way of regional integration.

The different groups of the states with the purpose of the development business relations, will create the various blocks (like the European Union) and in this case, the result will be that international trade, finance relations and investments will have more interregional character. The regionalization of the economic relations is able, to limit somehow the US hegemony in international trade and dominance of the US Transnational Corporations. All those factors can bring us to the International economic conflict (Garten, 1992).

As is mentioned by R. Gilpin, the modern mercantilists can be divided into two camps: be called "positive" and "negative" mercantilists. The representatives of both camps consider that the world economy would be divided into regional blocks. "Negative" mercantilists consider that regionalization will cause international economic conflict (Mandel, 1970). The concentration of each block will be possible around the leading industrial region or state – the USA, Japan, Western Europe, and others. Each block will fight with another for the markets, raw materials, capital investments division. In this case, the World will return to the situation, which was in the 30th of the XX Century (Silk, 1993).

"Positive" mercantilists see in the economic regionalization the stabilization factor of international economic relations (Calleo, 1973).

According to them, regionalization will allow the states, together with the maximum political and economic sovereignty, to take advantage of the global economy and interdependence. By the integration to the regional blocks, independent states will be able to resist those global forces, which threaten their sovereignty. Countries will not be able to do it separately.

There is an opinion that the keeping of order in the international economic system will be possible without hegemony. According to R.O. Keohane, the USA is not able to be the only hegemony, because it has other problems inside the country. Due to this, it will be possible for cooperation within the international economic and business system among the states without the powerful hegemony (Keohane, 1984).

During the discussion about the actions of the states in the framework of the economic or political order, it is necessary to point out the regime, which is the coordinator of actions. Main characters of the regime and principles and norms. If principles and norms are changing, the regime also is changed. The regime is the social institute, which coordinates the actions of the participants. The international regime from itself unifies the participants of the interesting parts of the international system.

International economic and business relations are characterized by two different tendencies – integration (interdependence) and neo-mercantilism (economic nationalism). Before was dominated sometimes first, sometimes the second tendency. After World War two, the integration process became more dominant. Nowadays, many experts consider that it has started the process of neo-mercantilism dominating the division of the world into regional economic blocs. On the other side, it is more and more are developed the global integration among the regions, particularly European Union, NAFTA, etc.

At the same time, discussing about future in the framework of Industry 5.0. it should be mentioned, that the Fifth Revolution is destined to happen, it's only a matter of time... Events related to inventions acted and act as impulses to it. They gradually and systematically pull us into a new industry.

The fifth revolution will be more of a systemic transformation. It is preparing to influence society, the system of government and human identity. And this is not to mention the economic and production consequences of the transition.

The "fifth industry" paradigm offers us a number of emerging trends, and also gives rise to new ones:

Clouds in Industry 5.0

Cloud computing is critical to the further development of the fourth industrial revolution because it consolidates, centralizes and processes information that is useful for business. They have unique computing and networking capabilities. Computing services make it possible to integrate platforms for automation, robotics, and the Internet of things into a single system. And this will eventually lead to new innovative developments.

Cloud computing has unlimited storage options. Thus, the more information received, the greater the need for proper organization to make this information accessible and useful.

Innovative developments on integrated cloud platform services are tailored to individual needs. They are also predictable and able to perform consistently when faced with massive amounts of data.

What Awaits Us in the End?

Can the IT industry take responsibility for our problems? Demographics, natural disasters, pollution…

Industry 4.0 values mass production of products, and the next era is the standard of living, ecology, creativity and high quality of customized products.

The Internet of Things must jump above its head: all cyber-physical systems must unite into one network and interact with people in real time, actively participate in the value chain. And most importantly, do it no matter what. Maximizing the benefits of the revolution requires global cooperation, and not only corporate ones. The point is that all machines speak the same language. If an object transmits information to a machine that cannot recognize it, business processes will turn into chaos. In these realities, the definition of common platforms and languages in which machines of different corporations will freely communicate becomes one of the priority tasks.

For the further development of artificial intelligence, neural networks, the Internet of things, cloud technologies, 5G high-speed data transmission, telematics, peripheral and quantum computing, it is necessary to balance IT with ecology, cybersecurity and human capital. To this end, composite materials, renewable energy sources will be increasingly used, and biotechnology will be used - vertical farms, food synthesis, genetic modification. In the next era, the boundaries between technology and the world are blurring. We already saw the outlines of new opportunities on the screens of cinemas and on the pages of books by futurologists half a century ago. Soon, all technologies will be integrated into a single whole - the global network, smart urbanism, and the digital economy. The future is somewhere near...

REFERENCES

Calleo, D., & Rowland, B. (1973). *America and the World Political Economy*. Indiana University Press.

Chitadze. (2022). *Which are the most expensive and largest employer companies in the world?* The Center for International Studies. https://centerforis.blogspot.com/

Garten, J. (1992). *A Cold peace: America, Japan, Germany and the struggle for Supremacy*. Times Books.

Gilpin, R. (1987). *The Political Economy of International Relations*. Princeton University Press. doi:10.1515/9781400882779

Gilpin, R. (1989). *War and Change in World Politics*. Cambridge University Press.

Gilpin. (1992). Three Models of the future. In: *International politics. Enduring Concepts and Contemporary issues*. Harper and Collins Publishers.

ITU. (2020). How 5 technologies are changing global trade. *ITU.* https://www.itu.int/hub/2020/04/how-5-technologies-are-changing-global-trade/

Jolia, G. (2015). *International Economic Relations.* Georgian Technical University.

Kennedy, R. (1987). *The rise and fall of the Great powers.* Random House.

Keohane, R. (1984). *After hegemony. Cooperation and Discord in the World Political Economy.* Princeton University Press.

Khozrevanidze, A. (2021). *Globalization, De-Globalization, and Tendencies of the International Business Development.* Caucasus International University.

Rondeli. (2003). *International Relations.* Nekeri.

Rugman, A.M. & Verbeke, A. (2004). A Perspective on Regional and Global Strategies of Multinational Enterprises. *Journal of International Business Studies, 35.*

Shengelia, T. (2008). *Basics of Business Administration.* Georgian Technical University.

Silk, L. (1993). Dangers of Slow Growth. *Foreign Affairs, 72.*

Strange, S. (1987). The persistent myth of lost hegemony. *International Organization, 14.*

TWI. (2023). What is Industry 5.0? *TWI Global.* https://www.twi-global.com/technical-knowledge/faqs/industry-5-0#WhatisIndustry50

UNCTAD. (2022). Global foreign direct investment rebounded strongly in 2021, but the recovery is highly uneven. *UNCTAD.* https://unctad.org/news/global-foreign-direct-investment-rebounded-strongly-2021-recovery-highly-uneven

UNCTAD. (2022). Global Investment Trend Monitor, No. 40. *UNCTAD.* https://unctad.org/webflyer/global-investment-trend-monitor-no-40

UNCTAD. (2022). Global trade hits record high of $28.5 trillion in 2021, but likely to be subdued in 2022. *UNCTAD.* https://unctad.org/news/global-trade-hits-record-high-285-trillion-2021-likely-be-subdued-2022

Chapter 6
A Cross-Sector Comparison of Industry 5.0:
Digital Technologies in Supply Chain Management of FMCG and the Automotive Sector

Parth H. Patel
Northumbria University, London, UK

Anil Kumar Angrish
National Institute of Pharmaceutical Education and Research, India

Vipin Nadda
https://orcid.org/0000-0002-2970-3709
University of Sunderland in London, UK

ABSTRACT

Industry 4.0 and Industry 5.0 are changing the ways business operations are carried out. The organisations across the sectors have been facing challenges in managing the supply chain and logistics across the UK and the world. Industrial Revolution 4.0 has led to the use of digital technologies to improve the efficiency and effectiveness of supply chain processes, such as demand forecasting, inventory management, transportation routing, and order fulfillment. Industry 5.0 is an attempt to humanise the use of potential new-age digital technologies that can for sustainable supply chain management and logistics in the FMCG and automotive sectors. The chapter also advises operation and strategic managers to follow the latest trends in these technologies and follow some short-, medium-, and long-term strategies to gain a competitive edge in the market.

DOI: 10.4018/978-1-6684-6403-8.ch006

INTRODUCTION

Industry 4.0 is the use of various digital technologies such as IoT, blockchain, big data, AI, drones, robotics, 3D printing etc in different functional areas of the business to improve efficiency productivity and the capacity of the org nations (European Commission, 2021). Industry 5.0 is the humanisation of industry 4.0 and acts of sustainability in supply chain management have positive effects on the implementation of this fifth revolution. Supply chain management (SCM) and logistics have long been recognized as complex and challenging fields, across all sectors due to several reasons (Lambert & Cooper, 2020).

First, the supply chain involves many stakeholders, including suppliers, manufacturers, wholesalers, retailers, and customers, each of which has its objectives and constraints. Second, the supply chain is subject to a range of internal and external factors that can impact its performance. Third, the supply chain must be responsive to the needs of customers, which can vary widely depending on the sector and the specific products or services being offered. Meeting these diverse customer needs requires a high level of flexibility and agility, which can be difficult to achieve.

Large industries like FMCGs. and Automobiles has global Supply chain and so more complexity in the system, The global FMCG (Fast Moving Consumer Goods) market is expected to reach $15 trillion by 2025 with a CAGR of 5.5% (Zion Market Research, 2022) making it 4th largest sector contributing to global GDP and employing 16% of the global workforce distributed across the nodes in the supply chain (Anderson, 2022). Sustainably meeting up the rising demand when supply chains get complex due to changing trade agreements, shipping capacity constraints, changing world order, war, and pandemic is unachievable without a knowledge-sharing pipeline in the industry (Stewart & Niero, 2018). Digital technology adoption allows companies to forecast future demand and improve working efficiency & profitability by reducing inventory holding costs and pushing forward the goal of sustainable development (Tarigan et al., 2021). Similarly, the automotive industry was valued at $2.9 trillion in 2021 and is expected to grow with a CAGR of 3.1% (*IBISWorld*, 2022). A complex supply chain is the backbone of the automobile industry as one domestic-use four-wheeler comprises 30,000 parts, all bought from multiple vendors (Börold et al., 2020). The supply chain in the automotive sector has always remained fragile as each node of the supply chain is capital intensive and minor shocks at any node lead to a bull-whip effect and decline in efficiency (Liu et al., 2020).

This chapter is attempting to explore the potential implication of Industry 5.0 by using an inter-thematic approach.

Aerial view of both supply chains as the network of interconnected activities including procurement, production, packaging, logistics and service cannot capture the process level nitty-gritty across industries with different products. The supply chain in the FMCG sector addresses food, beverages, personal, home care products and tobacco while the supply chain in automotive deals with domestic and commercial vehicles. The major difference lies in the longevity of products & level of involvement. The difference in longevity allows consumers to change the product or brand within a day, while it is not true for the automotive sector. The aim of the research is to critically analyse and compare the implementation of Industry 5.0-based sustainability and digital technologies in supply chain management in Fast Moving Consumer Goods (FMCG) and automobile sectors.

The chapter explores Industry 4.0/5.0 and the use of digital technologies in supply chain management & logistics in the FMCG and automotive sectors through content analysis of relevant existing literature, both academic and industry. Based on such analysis then the research will analyse risks and strategies associated with implementing new-age digital technologies in supply chain management & logistics.

LITERATURE REVIEW

This chapter is focused on digital technologies in supply chain management strategies and logistics. The conception of digital technologies along with their importance, perspective, advantages, and disadvantages in the supply chain of the automotive and FMCG sector are presented and discussed.

Industry 4.0 is the use of various digital technologies such as IoT, blockchain, big data, AI, drones, robotics, 3-D printing etc in different functional areas of the business to improve efficiency productivity and the capacity of the org nations(European Commission, 2021). Technology brings in capacity, improves cost conditions, and improves productivity, however, the use of technology many times ignores the need of other stakeholders, and the machine may overtake the idea of humanisation of technology. As per millennium development goals, the developments of organisations reason states in the nations should be sustainable human-centric and long-term. It does need 4 improvements in industry four or business 4 practices, and that leads us to the stage of the 5th industrial revolution, or what we call industry 5. hence the interesting 5.0, is a process of embedding human, social, environmental, ethical, and sustainable approaches in the application of technologies in industries, the various functional areas of the businesses, and production and supply chain management in particular (Henisz, Koller and Nuttall, 2019) (Nahavandi, 2019).

In the current scenario, supply chain and logistics have grown to significant complexity because of the large number of SKUs, the short shelf life of products, and the complexity due to cross-border distribution and global supply. A highly sensitive supply chain is more vulnerable to disruptions, and the impact of those disruptions is likely to be greater. Some of the common factors that can disrupt supply chains are given in the next section.

NATURAL DISASTERS

Natural disasters such as earthquakes, hurricanes, volcanic activity, storms, wildfires and floods can disrupt supply chains by damaging infrastructure, disrupting transportation, and causing delays or shortages of raw materials and finished goods. Due to natural disasters, every year around 150 million people every year. The damage to global GDP can be as high as 0.2% year on year due to such disasters. It is therefore imperative that firms should adopt flexibility and robustness in the supply chains to tackle such levels of disruptions.

POLITICAL INSTABILITY

Political instability in a country or region (e.g. Russia Ukraine conflict)can also disrupt supply chains, as it can lead to disruptions in transportation and trade and make it difficult to access raw materials or sell finished products (Ekanayake et al., 2022). Political actions affect economics such as oil prices, inflations, stock markets etc. For example during 2021-22, due to Russia Ukraine conflict, the inflation in G7 rose from below 2% to above 9% in a 3-month period due to a shortage of goods and supply chain disruption (Protech, 2022). Brexit has been rated as around 22% of causes of SCM disruptions (Rajagopal, 2019).

Pandemics

Pandemics such as the COVID-19 pandemic can have a significant impact on supply chains, as they can disrupt transportation, lead to shortages of raw materials, and finished goods, and cause disruptions in the supply of labour. China being the center of the global supply chain has faced significant challenges as the number of Covid-19, which made a significant decline in Purchasing Managers Index (PMI), delays in delivery times, etc as manufacturing, as well as the flow of goods, was restricted (WEF, 2021).

Cyber Attacks

Cyber-attacks on companies or critical infrastructure can disrupt supply chains, as they can cause delays or disruptions in the flow of information and goods. Additionally, cyber-attacks lead to the destruction of data i.e., changing the inventory levels, system shut down or errors in the manufacturing process. Cyber attacks have been projected as the highest (52%) negatively impacting reason for SCM disruptions (Rajagopal, 2019). As it can be concluded from the above analysis that supply chains will be going to be more vulnerable to disruptions, it is imperative to identify the opportunities in digital technologies that can mitigate the risk over time.

Supply Chain Management and Logistics

According to the Council of Supply Chain Management Professionals (CSCMP), Supply Chain Management (SCM) is 'the design, planning, execution, control, and monitoring of supply chain activities to create net value, building a competitive infrastructure, leveraging worldwide logistics, synchronizing supply with demand, and measuring performance globally' (CSCMP, n.d.). The goal of SCM is to ensure that the right products are produced and delivered to the right place at the right time while minimizing costs and maximizing efficiency and customer satisfaction.

Logistics, on the other hand, is a specific aspect of SCM that focuses on the planning, execution, and control of the movement and storage of goods, services, and information from the point of origin to the point of consumption (CSCMP, n.d.).

A survey by McKinsey & Company in 2020, revealed a number of common vulnerabilities and risks in SCM such as planning the SCM networks, financial resiliency, organisational maturity and Product complexity(Swan et al., 2020). Financial resiliency (leverage ratio, cash ratios, operating ratio etc) has been the most vulnerable for the industry as a whole though the effects are minimal at an individual and organisation level. Further, the variations in operating profit margins are higher in the industry compared to that of the organisation which shows organisation is more efficient while the industry is facing efficiency problems.

Some key differences between SCM and Logistics, as identified by various academic sources, include:

Difference in Scope

SCM is a broader term that encompasses logistics, as well as other activities such as procurement, production, and distribution.Logistics is a more specific aspect of SCM that focuses on the movement and storage of goods.

Difference in Focus

SCM is concerned with the entire supply chain process, from raw material suppliers to the end consumer (Lambert et al., 2014). Logistics is primarily concerned with the movement and storage of goods, although it may also involve some coordination with other parts of the supply chain.

Difference in Objectives

The main objective of SCM is to create value for customers by ensuring that the right products are delivered to the right place at the right time while minimizing costs and maximizing efficiency and customer satisfaction. The main objective of logistics is to plan, execute, and control the movement and storage of goods efficiently and cost-effectively.

INDUSTRY 5.0 AND DIGITAL TECHNOLOGIES IN SUPPLY CHAIN MANAGEMENT

Digital technologies play a significant role in SCM, enabling organizations to improve efficiency, reduce costs, and increase customer satisfaction. However, there are also several potential issues to adopting digital technologies in SCM. First is the cost of implementing and maintaining digital systems, which can be expensive, particularly for small or medium-sized organizations. Additionally, there are challenges in terms of compatibility with existing systems and processes, as well as the need for strong governance and regulatory frameworks to ensure the integrity and security of digital systems (Xu et al., 2019).

The common technologies used in standard operating procedures of SCM across the industry include; Cloud computing (94.3%), collaboration tools (64%), big data analytics (52%), Supervisory control and data acquisition technologies (41%) Internet of things (IoT -30%), Artificial Intelligence(21%) and in-memory computing (19%) (Partida, 2019).

Methodology to Develop this Chapter

A Systematic Literature Review (SLR) method was used to research and develop this chapter. SLR is a method of identifying, relevant studies, evaluating their quality, reviewing and analysing the existing research on a particular topic in a structured and systematic manner and synthesizing the findings in order to provide a comprehensive overview of the current state of knowledge (Higgins & Green, 2011). Systematic literature reviews differ from traditional literature reviews in that they follow a predefined set of procedures and use explicit criteria for the inclusion and exclusion of studies which helps to reduce bias and ensure the review is comprehensive and transparent (Paul & Barari, 2022). According to the Cochrane Handbook for Systematic Based on the project title "A cross-sector comparison focusing on the use of digital technologies in supply chain management of FMCG and automotive sector.", five key search terms were identified. The search string used Boolean operators "AND" and "OR" , and "NOT" while using key terms as digital technology, the industry (i.e., supply chain, logistics) and the sector (i.e., automotive, FMCG), Industry 4/5/, (Digital* OR Digital tech* OR Industry 4.0 OR Technology) AND (Supply Chain OR Demand Chain OR SCM OR Supply Network OR Value Chain) AND (FMCG OR retail) etc . EBSCOhost, ABI/INFORM, Emerald Insight and ScienceDirect databases were used.

Figure 1. Sectoral Venn Diagram
(Author, 2022)

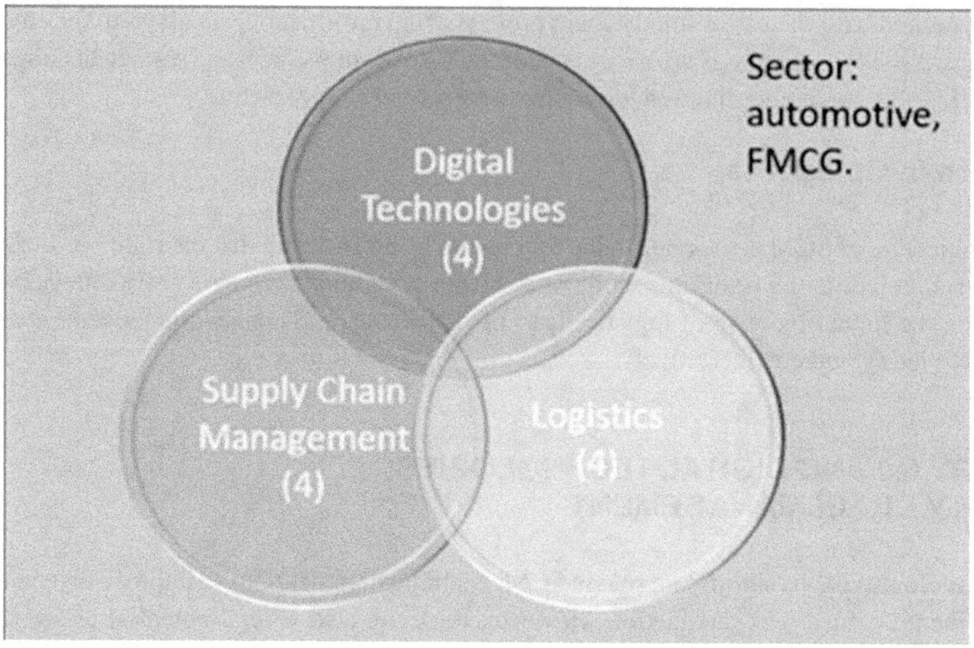

The key terms were used to define the field of study. Figure 1 shows the Venn diagram created for each sector FMCG and Automotive. "Digital Technologies", "Supply Chain Management" and "Logistics" were the main sets with the intersection. For each of the Venn diagram sets, there were sixteen articles for each sector and four articles with all key components covered.

The focus of the literature search was journal articles, industrial literature, and academic books. The industrial literature includes industry reports and government documents. Out of the total 342 articles generated based on the search string, 29 were duplicates and thus, were removed from the repository. Further the title and abstract screening removed 190 articles which means 60.70% of the articles were removed. Finally, after a full texted-based screen 5 more articles i.e. 4.0% articles were removed. The entire process depicted in a flow diagram started with 342 articles and concluded with a final count of 118.

FINDINGS ABOUT INDUSTRY 5.0 AND DIGITAL TECHNOLOGIES IN SECTORS

This section provides the descriptive characteristics of one hundred and eighteen sources selected.

Figure2, shows a word cloud that describes the most appeared keywords in the analysis, such as supply chain, digital technology, blockchain, cyber security, cloud computing and artificial intelligence etc. The chronological distribution of articles published between 2003 and 2022 a jump to 9% in 2015 and then, a steep rise from 2018 to 2022 (from 10% to 81.2%).

The research varied with the geography of the world with the highest share of literature being from the USA at 20% followed by India at 10% and Germany at 8% (see figure 3)

Figure 2. Word cloud of the common keywords in literature
(Author, 2022)

THEMATIC ANALYSIS OF INDUSTRY 4.0

Industry 4.0 in Fast-Moving Consumer Goods

Industry 4.0, also known as the Fourth Industrial Revolution, refers to the integration of advanced technologies such as artificial intelligence (AI), the Internet of Things (IoT), and data analytics into manufacturing and other industries (Rüßmann et al., 2016). The Fast Moving Consumer Goods (FMCG) sector, which includes a wide range of products that are sold quickly and at a relatively low cost, has been identified as one of the key sectors that can benefit from the adoption of Industry 4.0 technologies (KPMG, 2018; Rüßmann et al., 2016).

Research has shown that the adoption of Industry 4.0 technologies in the FMCG sector can bring about significant benefits, including improved efficiency, cost savings, and enhanced data management and analysis (KPMG, 2018; Rüßmann et al., 2016). For example, according to a survey conducted by KPMG (2018), 60% of FMCG manufacturers reported that the use of Industry 4.0 technologies had resulted in cost savings, while 50% reported increased efficiency and 40% reported improved quality. In addition, a study by the Manufacturing Leadership Council (2017) found that the adoption of Industry 4.0 technologies in the FMCG sector can lead to a 20-40% reduction in production costs and a 5-15% increase in productivity.

The use of IoT in the FMCG sector can facilitate real-time tracking and monitoring of shipments and inventory, enabling the optimization of the supply chain and improving customer service (KPMG, 2018; Rüßmann et al., 2016). According to a survey conducted by PwC (2017), 77% of FMCG executives believe that IoT will be critical to their business in the next 5 years, and 66% are already implementing or planning to implement IoT solutions.

In addition, the integration of Industry 4.0 technologies can enable the implementation of personalized marketing strategies, improving customer satisfaction and loyalty (KPMG, 2018; Rüßmann et al., 2016).

A study by the Manufacturing Leadership Council (2017) found that the use of Industry 4.0 technologies can lead to a 10-30% increase in customer satisfaction and a 5-15% increase in customer loyalty.

Industry 4.0 in Automotive Industry

A study by KPMG (2017) found that the use of Industry 4.0 technologies in the automotive sector can lead to a 20-30% reduction in production costs and a 5-15% increase in productivity. In addition, a study by McKinsey & Company (2017) found that the use of Industry 4.0 technologies can enable the development of new business models and the creation of customized products, improving customer satisfaction and loyalty. The adoption of Industry 4.0 in the automotive sector can also enable the development of new mobility services and the integration of connected and autonomous vehicles, improving safety and convenience for customers (KPMG, 2017; McKinsey & Company, 2017). According to a survey conducted by PwC (2018), 70% of automotive executives believe that Industry 4.0 technologies will be critical to their business in the next 5 years, and 60% are already implementing or planning to implement Industry 4.0 solutions.

However, the adoption of Industry 4.0 technologies in the FMCG sector OR automobile sector also introduces a range of challenges, including the high cost of implementation, the need for significant organizational change, and the potential for data security breaches (KPMG, 2018; Rüßmann et al., 2016, McKinsey & Company, 2017). In addition, the integration of these technologies with existing systems and processes can be complex, requiring the development of appropriate interfaces and the acquisition of necessary skills and expertise (KPMG, 2018; Rüßmann et al., 2016, McKinsey & Company, 2017).

MAIN TECHNOLOGIES USED IN SCM AND LOGISTICS

Digital Technologies in Logistics and SCM

In recent years, digital technologies such as cloud computing, artificial intelligence (AI), the internet of things (IoT), blockchain, and augmented reality have been increasingly adopted in logistics, bringing about significant efficiency improvements and cost savings.

Enterprise Resource Planning (ERP) Systems

Enterprise resource planning (ERP) systems are comprehensive software platforms that enable organizations to manage and integrate their core business processes, including supply chain management (SCM) (Daneshvar Kakhki & Gargeya, 2019). ERP systems enable organizations to centralize and integrate data from various departments and functions, providing a single source of truth and enabling real-time decision-making. The use of ERP in SCM can improve efficiency, reduce cost, and enhance data management and analysis (Liang et al., 2010). Additionally, the use of ERP in SCM can facilitate better collaboration and communication between different stakeholders in the supply chain, including suppliers, manufacturers, and customers (Davenport, 1998). However, the implementation of ERP systems needs high upfront costs, significant organizational change, and the potential for data security breaches (Daneshvar Kakhki & Gargeya, 2019).

Cybersecurity

The use of cybersecurity in SCM is essential to protect against the risks of data breaches and cyber-attacks, which can have significant financial and reputational consequences for organizations (KPMG, 2017). According to a survey by KPMG, the adoption of cybersecurity measures in SCM is increasing, with 79% of SCM professionals reporting that their organizations have adopted cybersecurity measures, and an additional 15% planning to do so within the next year (KPMG, 2017). For example, the use of cybersecurity measures can help protect against data breaches and cyber-attacks, which can disrupt SCM processes and result in costly downtime, aid in better collaboration and communication between different stakeholders (KPMG, 2017). Thus, the use of cybersecurity in SCM can bring about significant benefits, including improved efficiency, cost savings, and enhanced data management and analysis, improved customer satisfaction and increased competitiveness (Daneshvar Kakhki & Gargeya, 2019).

However, the adoption of cybersecurity measures in SCM also introduces a range of risks, including the potential for malfunction or failure of the technology, the need for significant organizational change, and the potential for data security breaches (KPMG, 2017). Hence the organisations attempt to use several approaches for effective cyber security, such as say regular audits of partners and contract manufacturers (65%), US IT vendor risk management tools (40%), SCM tools(38%), Infrastructure security vendors(34%), use cyber risks ratings (30%), Use consultants (20%), GRC tools (18%)(Gartner, 2022). Further, 44% of supply chain professionals agree that there has been a substantial increase (5% to 10%) in spending on the cybersecurity of the supply chain.

Blockchain

Blockchain refers to a decentralized digital ledger that enables secure, transparent, and tamper-proof record-keeping of transactions (Bock, 2018, Müßigmann et al., 2020). The use of blockchain in logistics can bring about significant benefits, including improved efficiency, cost savings, and enhanced data management and analysis (Bock, 2018; KPMG, 2016; Wang et al., 2017). For example, the use of blockchain in logistics can enable the creation of smart contracts, which can automate and streamline the process of handling and tracking shipments, reducing the need for manual processes and improving the efficiency of logistics operations (Bock, 2018; KPMG, 2016; Wang et al., 2017). Additionally, the use of blockchain in logistics can facilitate better collaboration and communication between different stakeholders in the supply chain, including suppliers, manufacturers, and customers (Bock, 2018). This can lead to improved customer satisfaction and increased competitiveness for the organization (Bock, 2018; KPMG, 2016). However, the adoption of blockchain in logistics also introduces a range of risks, including the potential for malfunction or failure of the technology, the need for significant organizational change, and the potential for data security breaches (Bock, 2018; Wang et al., 2017).

Artificial Intelligence

Artificial intelligence (AI) refers to the development and application of computer systems that can perform tasks that normally require human intelligence, such as learning, decision making, and problem solving. The integration of artificial intelligence (AI) into supply chain management has the potential to bring about significant efficiency improvements and cost savings through the automation of tasks and the optimization of processes (Mashayekhy et al., 2022). However, the adoption of AI in the supply chain also introduces a range of risks that must be carefully considered. One key risk is the potential for AI to cause harm through errors or malfunctions leading to financial losses, physical harm, or damage to the environment (Harris, 2021). For example, the use of autonomous vehicles in the supply chain could lead to accidents if their sensors or algorithms malfunction. Another risk is the potential for AI to perpetuate and amplify existing biases, leading to unfair and discriminatory outcomes (Buolamwini & Gebru, 2018). As AI systems become more autonomous, it can be difficult to determine who or what is responsible for their actions, leading to issues of liability and ethical responsibility (Bostrom, 2014).

There are several trends in the use of artificial intelligence (AI) in supply chain management that organizations should focus:

- *Predictive analytics* - AI-powered predictive analytics tools are being used in the supply chain to forecast demand and optimize inventory management thus reducing costs and improving efficiency (Helo & Hao, 2022).
- *Machine learning* - Machine learning algorithms are being used in the supply chain to analyze and process large amounts of data, such as real-time sensor data from connected devices in order to identify trends and patterns and make more informed decisions (Helo & Hao, 2022).
- *Automation* - AI is being used to automate various tasks in the supply chain, including the processing of orders, the scheduling of deliveries, and the routing of shipments which can aid to reduce the time and cost of certain processes (Helo & Hao, 2022).
- *Supply chain visibility* - AI is being used to enhance supply chain visibility by integrating data from various sources and providing real-time updates on the status of orders and shipments and thus better managing their supply chain and responding to disruptions (Helo & Hao, 2022).
- *Risk management* - AI is also used to identify and mitigate risks in the supply chain, such as identifying potential bottlenecks or predicting the likelihood of disruptions (Helo & Hao, 2022).

A BlueWeave Consulting report shows that the use of AI in the supply chain will increase by 460%, from about $6 billion (the year 2023) to $28 billion by year 2028 (BCR, 2022).

Artificial Intelligence in Logistics and SCM

The use of AI in logistics and SCM can bring about significant benefits, including improved efficiency, cost savings, and enhanced data management and analysis (KPMG, 2018; Zhang et al., 2017). For example, the use of AI in logistics can enable the automation of tasks such as route optimization and demand forecasting, reducing the need for manual processes and improving the efficiency of logistics operations (KPMG, 2018; Niranjan et al., 2021). However, the adoption of AI in logistics also introduces a range of risks, including the potential for malfunction or failure of the technology, the need for significant organizational change, and the potential for data security breaches (KPMG, 2018; Niranjan et al., 2021). The market size of intelligence in transportation is expected to increase from $2.3 billion in 2022, to $14.79 billion by the end of 2030 registering a growth of 49% year on year (PR, 2022).

Augmented Reality

Augmented reality (AR) refers to the integration of digital information and visualization into the physical world, enabling users to see and interact with virtual objects and information in real-time (Remondino,

2020). AR can be used in SCM to improve the efficiency of warehouse operations, enabling workers to access real-time information and instructions through wearable devices (Remondino, 2020). For example, AR can be used to provide workers with information about the location and availability of items in the warehouse, reducing the need for manual searches and improving productivity (Remondino, 2020).

Additionally, the use of AR in SCM can facilitate better collaboration and communication between different stakeholders in the supply chain, including suppliers, manufacturers, and customers (Demir et al., 2020). However, the adoption of AR in SCM also introduces a range of risks, including the potential for malfunction or failure of the technology, the need for significant organizational change, and the potential for data security breaches (Remondino, 2020). Additionally, it is important for organizations to carefully consider the ethical implications of the use of AR in SCM, including issues related to privacy and the potential for the technology to perpetuate existing biases (Krumholz, 2017).

According to a survey by Deloitte, 22% of SCM professionals expect to use AR in their operations in short term, and an additional 58% expect to use it within the next five years (Deloitte, 2018). A survey by the Journal of Business Logistics found that the use of AR in SCM is expected to lead to significant improvements in efficiency, a reduction in training time, expecting a reduction in errors, expecting a productivity improvement (Remondino, 2020).

Augmented Reality in Logistics and SCM

The use of AR in logistics and SCM can enable the visualization of data and information in real-time, facilitating the execution of tasks such as warehouse management and picking (Remondino, 2020; Capgemini Consulting, 2018). This can lead to improved customer satisfaction and increased competitiveness for the organization (Remondino, 2020; Capgemini Consulting, 2018). However, the adoption of AR in logistics also introduces a range of risks, including the potential for malfunction or failure of the technology, the need for significant organizational change, and the potential for data security breaches (Remondino, 2020).

A survey of people by Statista,(2020), reveals that they perceive that, many sectors will be affected by those Immersive technologies such as AR/VR most affected sectors will be healthcare and medical devices (34%), Marketing and advertisements (31%), education (28%), retail (23%), Employee training (17%), Automotive (17%), Logistics (15%), real estate (10%) (Statista, 2020)

Augmented Reality in FMCG and Automobile Sectors

Application of the AR in the FMCG and automobile sectors can bring about significant benefits, including improved efficiency, and cost savings can enable real-time tracking and monitoring of shipments and inventory, enabling the optimization of the supply chain and improved customer service and enhanced data management and analysis, can enable the implementation of personalized marketing strategies, improving customer satisfaction and loyalty (KPMG, 2018). About, 50% of companies reported that the use of AR had resulted in cost savings, while 40% reported increased efficiency and 30% reported improved quality (KPMG, 2018), can lead to a 20-30% reduction in production costs and a 5-15% increase in productivity (Manufacturing Leadership Council 2017), A study by the Manufacturing Leadership Council (2017) found that the use of AR in the can lead to a 10-30% increase in customer satisfaction and a 5-15% increase in customer loyalty. According to a survey conducted by PwC (2017), 73% of executives believe that AR will be critical to their business in the next 5 years, and 60% are already implementing or planning to implement AR solutions.

However, the use of AR also introduces a range of challenges, including the need for significant organizational change and the potential for data security breaches (KPMG, 2018). In addition, the integration of these technologies with existing systems and processes can be complex, requiring the development of appropriate interfaces and the acquisition of necessary skills and expertise (KPMG, 2018).

Big Data in FMCG and Automobile

Big Data analytics refers to the use of advanced data management and analysis techniques to extract insights and value from large and complex datasets (Gamoura et al., 2019).

Research has shown that the use of Big Data analytics in the FMCG and automobile sector can bring about significant benefits, including improved efficiency, cost savings, and enhanced data management and analysis (KPMG, 2018; Gamoura et al., 2019). For example, according to a survey conducted by KPMG (2018), 50% of companies reported that the use of Big Data analytics had resulted in cost savings, while 40% reported increased efficiency and 30% reported improved quality. In addition, a study by the Manufacturing Leadership Council (2017) found that the use of Big Data analytics can lead to a 20-30% reduction in production costs and a 5-15% increase in productivity.

However, the use of Big Data analytics also introduces a range of challenges, including the need for significant organizational change and the potential for data security breaches (KPMG, 2018; Gamoura et al., 2019). In addition, the integration of these technologies with existing systems and processes can be complex, requiring the development of appropriate interfaces and the acquisition of necessary skills and expertise (KPMG, 2018; Gamoura et al., 2019).

The use of Big Data analytics in supply chain management and logistics can enable the optimization of the supply chain, improving the accuracy of demand forecasting and the management of inventory (KPMG, 2018; Gamoura et al., 2019). According to a survey conducted by PwC (2017), 73% of FMCG executives believe that Big Data analytics will be critical to their business in the next 5 years, and 60% are already implementing or planning to implement Big Data analytics solutions.

Cloud Computing

Cloud computing refers to the delivery of computing services, such as storage, processing, and networking, over the internet, enabling organizations to access and use these resources on a pay-as-you-go basis (Laudon & Traver, 2016). Cloud computing enables organizations to access and analyze data in real-time, enabling them to make more informed decisions and respond more quickly to changes in the supply chain (Laudon & Traver, 2016). The use of cloud computing improves the efficiency and effectiveness of SCM processes, such as procurement, inventory management, and distribution, saves in cost and enhanced data management and analysis (Ben-Daya et al., 2017). Additionally, the use of cloud computing in SCM can facilitate better collaboration and communication between different stakeholders in the supply chain, including suppliers, manufacturers, and customers (Davenport, 1998).

However, the use of cloud computing in SCM also introduces a range of risks, including the potential for data breaches, the reliance on third-party providers, and the need to ensure compliance with relevant regulations (Laudon & Traver, 2016).

Cloud Computing in Logistics and SCM

The use of cloud computing in logistics and SCM can bring about significant benefits, including improved efficiency, cost savings, and enhanced data management and analysis (Aljawazneh, 2016; Laudon & Traver, 2016). For example, the use of cloud computing in logistics can enable access to real-time data and analytics, facilitating the execution of tasks such as demand forecasting and route optimization, better collaboration and communication between different stakeholders, and lead to improved customer satisfaction and increased competitiveness for the organization (Aljawazneh, 2016; Laudon & Traver, 2016). A survey of the logistics professionals on the use of cloud computing by PRG (2022), has found a consistent rise in the percentage utilisation of Warehouse and order processing (60% to 68%), to monitor and predict systems (33% to 44%), to collect data on the fleet (16% to 19%) from 2020- to 2022 (PRG, 2022).

Cloud Computing in FMCG and Automobile Sectors

Research has shown that the use of cloud computing in the FMCG and Automobile sectors can bring about significant benefits, including improved efficiency, cost savings, and enhanced data management and analysis (KPMG, 2018; Mell & Grance, 2011). For example, according to a survey conducted by KPMG (2018), 70% of companies reported that the use of cloud computing had resulted in cost savings, while 60% reported increased efficiency and 50% reported improved quality. In addition, a study by the Manufacturing Leadership Council (2017) found that the use of cloud computing in the sector can lead to a 20-40% reduction in production costs and a 5-15% increase in productivity. The use of cloud computing in supply chain management and logistics can enable real-time tracking and monitoring of shipments and inventory, enabling the optimization of the supply chain and improving customer service (KPMG, 2018; Mell & Grance, 2011). According to a survey conducted by PwC (2017), 80% of executives believe that cloud computing will be critical to their business in the next 5 years, and 70% are already implementing or planning to implement cloud computing solutions.

In addition, the use of cloud computing can enable the implementation of personalized marketing strategies, improving customer satisfaction and loyalty and leading to a 10-30% increase in customer satisfaction and a 5-15% increase in customer loyalty (KPMG, 2018; Mell & Grance, Manufacturing Leadership Council 2017)

However, the use of cloud computing in the FMCG sector also introduces a range of challenges, including the need for significant organizational change and the potential for data security breaches, the integration of these technologies with existing systems and processes can be complex, requiring the development of appropriate interfaces and the acquisition of necessary skills and expertise (KPMG, 2018; Mell & Grance, 2011). In addition, (KPMG, 2018; Mell & Grance, 2011).

Internet of Things

Internet of things (IoT) refers to the interconnected network of physical devices, vehicles, buildings, and other objects that are equipped with sensors, software, and network connectivity, allowing them to collect and exchange data (Phase & Mhetre, 2018). The IoT enables these objects to be controlled and monitored remotely and to perform a variety of tasks, such as gathering and analysing data, automating processes, and providing real-time information (Phase & Mhetre, 2018). The integration of the IoT into supply chain management has the potential to bring about significant efficiency improvements and cost savings. However, the adoption of IoT in the supply chain also introduces a range of risks, more vulnerable to cyberattacks, s data breaches, data sovereignty, and denial of service attacks (Tu, 2018).

The analysis of UK Industries by Statista shows that a range of industries will be benefitted from embedding IoT, with the total benefit to the UK economy around GBP 11,500 million.

.The leading beneficiary from IoT is the manufacturing industry (GBP 4042 million), followed by Telecoms (GBP 1458 million). Retail industry (GBP 700 million.), Retail energy industry (GBP 587 million.), the insurance industry (GBP 536 million.), the healthcare industry (GBP 369 million.), and the transport & logistics industry (GBP311 million.) (Statista, 2020).

Internet of Things in Logistics and SCM

The use of IoT in logistics can bring about significant benefits, including improved efficiency, cost savings, and enhanced data management and analysis (Tawalbeh et al., 2020; Yalcin & Daim, 2022). For example, the use of IoT in logistics can enable the real-time tracking and monitoring of shipments, facilitating the execution of tasks such as inventory management and asset tracking better collaboration and communication between different stakeholders, improved customer satisfaction and increased competitiveness for the organization (Tawalbeh et al., 2020; Yalcin & Daim, 2022). also introduces a range of risks, including the potential for malfunction or failure of the technology, the need for significant organizational change, and the potential for data security breaches (Tawalbeh et al., 2020). The global market for logistics using IoT is going to increase by around 260% ($37.41 billion to $93.85 billion) from 2021 to 2028 (BCR, 2022)

IoT in FMCG and Automobile

Research has shown that the use of IoT in the FMCG and Automobile sector can bring about significant benefits, including improved efficiency, cost savings, and enhanced data management and analysis implementation of personalized marketing strategies, improving customer satisfaction and loyalty (KPMG, 2018; Gill et al., 2022, McKinsey & Company, 2015). For example, according to a survey conducted by KPMG (2018), 60% of companies reported that the use of IoT had resulted in cost savings, while 50% reported increased efficiency and 40% reported improved quality. The use of IoT can lead to a 20-40% reduction in production costs and a 5-15% increase in productivity (Manufacturing Leadership Council, 2017).

The use of IoT in supply chain management and logistics can enable real-time tracking and monitoring of shipments and inventory, enabling the optimization of the supply chain and improving customer service (KPMG, 2018; Gill et al., 2022, McKinsey & Company, 2015).

According to a survey conducted by PwC (2017), 77% of FMCG executives believe that IoT will be critical to their business in the next 5 years, and 66% are already implementing or planning to implement IoT solutions.

However, the use of IoT in the sectors also introduces a range of challenges, including, integration of these technologies with existing systems, the need for significant organizational change and the potential for data security breaches, the development of appropriate interfaces,the acquisition of necessary skills and expertise (KPMG, 2018; Gill et al., 2022).

Robotics in FMCG and Automotive Industry

Both FMCGs and the automotive sector is characterized by complex and global supply chains, making it particularly well-suited for the integration of robotics technologies (Bain & Company, 2020; Deloitte, 2017).. The use of robotics in supply chain management and logistics has significant benefits for the automotive sector, including improved efficiency, cost savings, enable the automation of tasks such as material handling and transportation, optimizing the supply chain and improving customer service, and enhanced customer satisfaction and loyalty (Bain & Company, 2020; Deloitte, 2017).

However, the integration of these technologies with existing systems and processes can be complex, requiring the development of appropriate interfaces and the acquisition of necessary skills and expertise, organizational change and the potential for data security breaches can be challenging (Bain & Company, 2020; Deloitte, 2017).

3D Printing

3D printing, also known as additive manufacturing, refers to the process of creating three-dimensional objects by building up successive layers of material under computer control (Bhat & Singh, 2016). The use of 3D printing in supply chain management (SCM) can bring about significant benefits, including improved efficiency, cost savings, and enhanced customization and agility (Sonar et al., 2022; KPMG, 2016). 3D printing can enable organizations to manufacture products on demand, reducing the need for large inventory levels and enabling them to respond more quickly to changes in demand (Sonar et al., 2022). This can help improve the efficiency and effectiveness of SCM processes, such as procurement and distribution, improve customer satisfaction and increase competitiveness (Bhat & Singh, 2016). The risks associated with 3D Printing are risk potential for malfunction or failure of the technology, organizational change, and the potential for data security breaches (Bhat & Singh, 2016).

3D printing is one of the latest technologies that is widely being adopted in machinery and equipment, while other sectors have not yet opted for 3D printing on that scale yet, The current market size for 3D printing in the machinery sector is $100 billion and it is expected to increase to $400 Billion by 2030. By the year 2030, 3D market will be highest for machinery and equipment, followed by textile Toys & furniture ($60 billion), Automobile & automation ($60 billion), medical ($50 billion), Mining & industrial process ($50 billion), Chemical (45%), high-tech manufacturing ($30 billion), and aerospace & defense sector ($26 billion) (Boilard & Roucolle, 2020).

3D Manufacturing in FMCG and Automobiles

3D manufacturing, also known as additive manufacturing, refers to the process of creating a physical object by adding layers of material, typically using a digital file as a guide (ASTM International, 2019).

3D manufacturing leads to efficiency, cost savings, and enhanced customization and innovation, the development of new and innovative products, improving customer satisfaction and loyalty (KPMG, 2018; ASTM International, 2019, McKinsey & Company, 2017). For example, according to a survey conducted by KPMG (2018), 60% of companies reported that the use of 3D manufacturing had resulted in cost savings, while 50% reported increased efficiency and 40% reported improved quality.

The use of 3D manufacturing in supply chain management and logistics (KPMG, 2018; ASTM International, 2019). According to a survey conducted by PwC (2017), 67% of FMCG executives believe that

3D manufacturing will be critical to their business in the next 5 years, and 53% are already implementing or planning to implement 3D manufacturing solutions.

The Adoption of Digital Technologies and Challenges in Implementation

The adoption of digital technologies such as cloud computing, artificial intelligence, the IoT, augmented reality (AR), and blockchain in supply chain management and logistics can bring about significant benefits, including improved efficiency, cost savings, and enhanced data management and analysis (KPMG, 2016, 2018; Aljawazneh, 2016; Luthra et al., 2018; Wang et al., 2017). However, the implementation of these technologies also introduces a range of limitations and challenges.

One major limitation is the high cost of implementation, which can be a barrier for small and medium-sized enterprises (SMEs) (Remondino, 2020; KPMG, 2016, 2018; Aljawazneh, 2016; Luthra et al., 2018). Another challenge is the potential for malfunction or failure of the technology, which can disrupt operations and lead to financial losses (Remondino, 2020; Bock, 2018). Also, the use of these technologies introduces risks related to data security and privacy, including the potential for data breaches and the need for adequate data protection measures (Remondino, 2020). Additionally, the adoption of these technologies often requires significant organizational change, which can be challenging to implement and can lead to resistance from employees (Remondino, 2020; KPMG, 2016, 2018).

Furthermore, the integration of these technologies with existing systems and processes can be complex and time-consuming, requiring the development of appropriate interfaces and the acquisition of necessary skills and expertise (Remondino, 2020).

Finally, the lack of standardization and regulation in some areas can pose challenges to the implementation of these technologies, particularly in the case of blockchain, which requires the establishment of clear rules and protocols for its use (Remondino, 2020).

A study by Gorbach (2017) of leaders and technologists revealed many hurdles s in the process of the digital transformation process of supply chain management & logistics. The main hurdles were cyber security (57.1%), ROI justifications (48%), lack of budget (25%), Management vision (23%), Cross multiple silos (37%), Lack of talent (26%), Lack of industry standards(28%), bandwidth issue (23%), and IT/OT gap (34%) (Gorbach, 2017). The overall results show that IT/OT gap, ROI and security will remain the top priority when deciding on digital transformation.

There are also some challenges that companies may face in adopting digital technologies in their supply chain management and logistics. Some of these challenges include:

Cost and complexity: Implementing and integrating digital technologies can be expensive and complex, especially for smaller companies.

Data security and privacy: Companies need to ensure that they have adequate measures in place to protect the security and privacy of their data, especially as they collect and use more data from sensors and IoT devices.

Skill gaps: Companies may need to invest in training and development to ensure that their employees have the skills and knowledge to work with digital technologies.

Regulatory challenges: The companies may need to navigate complex regulatory environments when adopting digital technologies, particularly in the areas of data protection and privacy, and the use of drones and autonomous vehicles.

Despite these challenges, the benefits of adopting digital technologies in supply chain management and logistics are likely to outweigh the costs and risks. These benefits include improved efficiency, cost savings, increased customer satisfaction, and competitive advantage. It is therefore expected that companies will continue to invest in and adopt digital technologies in the future.

RECOMMENDATION

Both automobile and the fast-moving consumer goods (FMCG) sectors are under pressure to improve supply chain management and logistics to meet the demands of consumers for faster and more convenient delivery of goods. Digital technologies can play a significant role in achieving these improvements. There are several strategies that firms in both the fast-moving consumer goods (FMCG) and automotive sectors can consider when implementing new-age digital technologies to mitigate the risks associated with these technologies. Some of these strategies include:

Conduct Thorough Risk Assessments: Firms need to conduct thorough risk assessments to identify and evaluate the potential risks associated with the implementation of new digital technologies. This can help firms to prioritize and address the most significant risks.

Implement Robust Cybersecurity Measures: Cybersecurity risks can be mitigated by implementing strong cybersecurity measures such as data encryption, secure authentication, and intrusion detection systems.

Pilot and Test New Technologies: Firms can mitigate the risk of integration failures and disruptions to operations by piloting and testing new technologies in a controlled environment before rolling them out more widely.

Improve Data Quality: Ensuring the quality of data used in digital supply chain and logistics systems can help to mitigate the risk of problems with decision-making and operations. This can be achieved through regular data cleansing and validation, as well as the implementation of data governance policies and procedures.

Provide Training and Support: Providing training and support to employees can help to mitigate the risk of resistance to change and ensure a smooth transition to new digital technologies. This could include training on the use of new systems and processes, as well as support for employees to adapt to new roles and responsibilities.

In the short term, one recommendation to the organisations is to focus on the implementation of digital platforms and systems to manage the flow of goods and optimize transportation. This can be achieved through the use of software tools such as transportation management systems (TMS) and enterprise resource planning (ERP) systems. These technologies can help companies to improve efficiency and reduce costs in the supply chain.

In the medium term, companies should consider the adoption of data analytics and artificial intelligence (AI) to analyze large amounts of data and identify patterns and trends in the supply chain. This can help to improve decision-making and optimize production, inventory management, and transportation.

In the long term, the implementation of the IoT can be a key driver of improvements in the sector's supply chain management and logistics. The use of IoT-enabled devices can allow for real-time tracking of goods and improve visibility and control in the supply chain. This can lead to more efficient transportation and improved delivery times for consumers.

It is also recommended that organisations consider the use of 3D printing to produce prototypes and small batches of goods more quickly and at a lower cost. This can lead to more efficient production processes and reduced waste in the supply chain.

Overall, the implementation of digital technologies in supply chain management and logistics can lead to significant improvements in efficiency and cost savings. It is important for companies to carefully consider the short, medium, and long-term implications of these technologies and to invest in the necessary infrastructure and workforce development to fully utilize them.

CONCLUSION

Industry 4.0 and Industry 5.0 are impacting all sectors in terms of productivity and sustainability. FMCG companies generally offer a wider range of products with shorter product lifecycles and less customization, while automotive companies tend to offer a smaller range of products with longer product lifecycles and more customization. This difference in product variety and customization has implications for how digital technologies are used to manage the supply chain and logistics. FMCG companies may place a greater emphasis on using digital technologies to optimize inventory management and improve efficiency, while automotive companies may place more emphasis on using digital technologies to manage the complexity of the supply chain and support customization.

Another key difference is the degree of globalization in the supply chain. FMCG companies often have more globalized supply chains, with suppliers and manufacturing locations spread across different regions and countries. Automotive companies, on the other hand, tend to have more localized supply chains, with a greater focus on regional sourcing and production. This difference in the globalization of the supply chain can also impact how digital technologies are used. FMCG companies may be more likely to use digital technologies to manage and coordinate the flow of goods across a complex, global network, while automotive companies may be more focused on using digital technologies to optimize the efficiency of local production and supply chain processes. Several potential new-age digital technologies can be used to improve supply chain management and logistics in both the fast-moving consumer goods (FMCG) and automotive sectors.

REFERENCES

Aljawazneh, B. (2016). The Prospects of Cloud Computing in Supply Chain Management (A Theoretical Perspective). *Journal of Management Research*, *8*(4), 145. doi:10.5296/jmr.v8i4.9998

Anderson, E. (2022, November 22). FMCG Packaging Market size to hit US$ 901.2 billion by 2027 according to a new research report. *WhaTech*. https://www.whatech.com/og/markets-research/industrial/735396-fmcg-packaging-market-size-to-hit-us-901-2-billion-by-2027-according-to-a-new-research-report

ARC. (2021). *ARC Advisory Group: Key Technology Trends for 2021 Rockwell Automation India*. Rockwell Automation. https://www.rockwellautomation.com/en-us/company/news/blogs/technology-trends-report-2021.html

Arenkov, I., Tsenzharik, M., & Vetrova, M. (2019). *Digital technologies in supply chain management*, 448–453. Atlantis Press. doi:10.2991/icdtli-19.2019.78

ASTM International. (2019). *Additive Manufacturing: An Overview.* ASTM International. https://www.astm.org/DIGITAL_LIBRARY/MNL/SOURCE_PAGES/MNL119-70_foreword.pdf

Bain & Company. (2020). *BAIN_REPORT_Changing_Gears_2020.pdf.* Bain & Company. https://media.bain.com/bainweb/PDFs/BAIN_REPORT_Changing_Gears_2020.pdf

BCR. (2022a, May 27). *AI in Supply Chain Market to Extend to USD 20 Billion & Growing at a CAGR of 20.5% by 2028.* GlobeNewswire News Room. https://www.globenewswire.com/en/news-release/2022/05/27/2452056/0/en/AI-in-Supply-Chain-Market-to-Extend-to-USD-20-Billion-Growing-at-a-CAGR-of-20-5-by-2028-BlueWeave-Consulting.html

BCR. (2022b, October 6). *Internet of Things (IoT) in Logistics Market to Grow at a CAGR of 14.0%, during Forecast Period.* GlobeNewswire News Room. https://www.globenewswire.com/en/news-release/2022/10/06/2529734/0/en/Internet-of-Things-IoT-in-Logistics-Market-to-Grow-at-a-CAGR-of-14-0-during-Forecast-Period-BlueWeave-Consulting.html

Ben-Daya, M., Hassini, E., & Bahroun, Z. (2017). Internet of things and supply chain management: A literature review. *International Journal of Production Research*, *57*(15-16), 1–24. doi:10.1080/00207543.2017.1402140

Bhat, K. S., & Singh, S. P. (2016). 3D printing in supply chain management: A review. *International Journal of Production Research*, *54*(7), 2037–2050. doi:10.1080/00207543.2015.1114053

Bock, J. (2018). Blockchain logistics: A case study of the potential benefits and challenges of distributed ledger technology in the supply chain. *Journal of Business Logistics*, *39*(4), 324–334. doi:10.1111/jbl.12203

Boilard, M., & Roucolle, G. (2020). *Will 3D Printing "Vaporize" the Supply Chain?* Oliver Wyman. https://www.oliverwyman.com/our-expertise/insights/2017/feb/will-3D-printing-vaporize-the-supply-chain.html

Börold, A., Teucke, M., Rust, J., & Freitag, M. (2020). Recognition of car parts in automotive supply chains by combining synthetically generated training data with classical and deep learning based image processing. *Procedia CIRP*, *93*, 377–382. doi:10.1016/j.procir.2020.03.142

Bostrom, N. (2014). *Superintelligence: Paths, dangers, strategies* (1st ed.). Oxford University Press.

Bowman, T. (2020). Library Guides: Literature Review: Systematic literature reviews. *Libguides.* https://libguides.csu.edu.au/review/Systematic

Buolamwini, J., & Gebru, T. (2018). Gender shades: Intersectional accuracy disparities in commercial gender classification. *Proceedings of Machine Learning Research*, *81*(1), 1–15.

Capgemini Consulting. (2018). *AR-VR-in-Operations1.pdf.* Capgemini. https://www.capgemini.com/wp-content/uploads/2018/09/AR-VR-in-Operations1.pdf

Chopra, S., & Meindl, P. (2017). *Supply chain management: Strategy, planning, and operation* (6th ed.). Pearson Education.

Daneshvar Kakhki, M., & Gargeya, V. B. (2019). Information systems for supply chain management: A systematic literature analysis. *International Journal of Production Research*, *57*(15–16), 5318–5339. doi:10.1080/00207543.2019.1570376

Davenport, T. H. (1998, July 1). Putting the Enterprise into the Enterprise System. *Harvard Business Review*. https://hbr.org/1998/07/putting-the-enterprise-into-the-enterprise-system

Deloitte. (2017). *Deloitte-robots-are-ready.pdf*. Deloitte. https://www2.deloitte.com/content/dam/Deloitte/tr/Documents/technology/deloitte-robots-are-ready.pdf

Deloitte. (2018). *Deloitte-uk-deloitte-insight-implementing-advanced-analytics.pdf*. Deloitte. https://www2.deloitte.com/content/dam/Deloitte/uk/Documents/ConsumerIndustrialProducts/deloitte-uk-deloitte-insight-implementing-advanced-analytics.pdf

Deloitte. (2020). *DI_Automotive-News-Supplement.pdf*. Deloitte. https://www2.deloitte.com/content/dam/insights/us/articles/automotive-news_industry-4-0-in-automotive/DI_Automotive-News-Supplement.pdf

Demir, S., Yilmaz, I., & Paksoy, T. (2020). *Augmented Reality in Supply Chain Management* (pp. 136–145). CRC Press. doi:10.1201/9780429327636-14

Ekanayake, E. M. A. C., Shen, G. Q. P., Kumaraswamy, M. M., & Owusu, E. K. (2022). Identifying supply chain vulnerabilities in industrialized construction: An overview. *International Journal of Construction Management*, *22*(8), 1464–1477. doi:10.1080/15623599.2020.1728487

European Commission. (2021) *Industry 5.0: Towards more sustainable, resilient and human-centric industry*. EC. https://research-and-innovation.ec.europa.eu/news/all-research-and-innovation-news/industry-50-towards-more-sustainable-resilient-and-human-centric-industry-2021-01-07_en

Gambhir, P., Bevan, P., Davenport, F., & Thirion, J. (2018). *Unlocking supply chain benefits through blockchain technology*. https://assets.kpmg/content/dam/kpmg/ca/pdf/2018/10/digital-disruption-blockchain.pdf

Gamoura, S., Derrouiche, R., Damand, D., & Barth, M. (2019). Insights from big Data Analytics in supply chain management: An all-inclusive literature review using the SCOR model. *Production Planning and Control*, 1–27. doi:10.1080/09537287.2019.1639839

Gartner. (2022). *Supply Chain Cybersecurity | Cyber Protection*. Gartner. https://www.gartner.com/en/supply-chain/trends/supply-chain-cybersecurity

Gill, S. S., Xu, M., Ottaviani, C., Patros, P., Bahsoon, R., Shaghaghi, A., Golec, M., Stankovski, V., Wu, H., Abraham, A., Singh, M., Mehta, H., Ghosh, S. K., Baker, T., Parlikad, A. K., Lutfiyya, H., Kanhere, S. S., Sakellariou, R., Dustdar, S., & Uhlig, S. (2022). AI for next generation computing: Emerging trends and future directions. *Internet of Things*, *19*, 100514. doi:10.1016/j.iot.2022.100514

Giones, F., & Brem, A. (2017). *Digital Technology Entrepreneurship: A Definition and Research Agenda* (SSRN Scholarly Paper No. 2984542). https://papers.ssrn.com/abstract=2984542 doi:10.22215/timreview/1076

Global damage costs from natural disasters. (2022). Our World in Data. https://ourworldindata.org/grapher/damage-costs-from-natural-disasters

Gorbach, G. (2017, September 1). *Technology Spotlight: The Great Digitization of Industry*. SCMR. https://www.scmr.com/article/technology_spotlight_the_great_digitization_of_industry

Harris, L. A. (2021). Artificial Intelligence: Background, Selected Issues, and Policy Considerations. *Artificial Intelligence*.

Helo, P., & Hao, Y. (2022). Artificial intelligence in operations management and supply chain management: An exploratory case study. *Production Planning and Control*, *33*(16), 1573–1590. doi:10.1080/09537287.2021.1882690

Henisz, W., Koller, T. and Nuttall, R. (2019) *Five ways that ESG creates value Getting your environmental, social, and governance (ESG) proposition right links to higher value creation. Here's why*. McKinsey.

Higgins, J., & Green, S. (2011). Cochrane Handbook for Systematic Reviews of Interventions. *Handbook*. https://handbook-5-1.cochrane.org/

Humphrey, J., & Memedovic, O. (2003). The Global Automotive Industry Value Chain: What Prospects for Upgrading by Developing Countries (SSRN Scholarly Paper No. 424560). doi:10.2139/ssrn.424560

IBISWorld—Industry Market Research, Reports, and Statistics. (2022, November 1). *Homepage*. IBIS World. https://www.ibisworld.com/default.aspx

KPMG. (2016). *Global Manufacturing Outlook*. KPMG. https://assets.kpmg/content/dam/kpmg/pdf/2016/06/Global-Manufacturing-Outlook-2016.pdf

KPMG. (2017). *201706-CGF-KPMG-Top-of-Mind-Think-Like-a-Start-Up.pdf*. KPMG. https://www.theconsumergoodsforum.com/wp-content/uploads/2017/12/201706-CGF-KPMG-Top-of-Mind-Think-Like-a-Start-Up.pdf

KPMG. (2018). *Digital Supply Chain – the hype and the risks*. KPMG. https://assets.kpmg/content/dam/kpmg/co/pdf/2019/01/Digital%20Supply%20Chain%20Hype%20And%20Risks.pdf

KPMG. (2018). *Augmented Reality in the Automotive Sector: Opportunities and Challenges*. KPMG.

KPMG. (2018). *Supply Chain Big Data Series – Part 4*. KPMG. https://assets.kpmg/content/dam/kpmg/au/pdf/2017/disruptive-technologies-supply-chain-future.pdf

Krumholz, A. (2017). Ethical considerations for augmented reality. *IEEE Consumer Electronics Magazine*, *6*(2), 25–30. doi:10.1109/MCE.2017.2693601

Lambert, D. M., & Cooper, M. C. (2020). Issues in supply chain management. *Industrial Marketing Management*, *29*(1), 65–83.

Laudon, K. C., & Traver, C. G. (2016). *E-commerce 2018: Business, technology, society* (14th ed.). Pearson. https://www.pearsonhighered.com/assets/preface/0/1/3/4/0134868064.pdf

Liang, T.-P., You, J.-J., & Liu, C.-C. (2010). A resource-based perspective on information technology and firm performance: A meta analysis. *Industrial Management & Data Systems, 110*, 1138–1158. https://doi.org/10.1108/02635571011077807

Liu, Z., Hu, B., Huang, B., Lang, L., Guo, H., & Zhao, Y. (2020). Decision Optimization of Low-Carbon Dual-Channel Supply Chain of Auto Parts Based on Smart City Architecture. *Complexity, 2020*, e2145951. https://doi.org/10.1155/2020/2145951

LSE. (2019). *Careers in Fast Moving Consumer Goods (FMCG).* LSE.https://info.lse.ac.uk/current-students/careers/information-and-resources/employment-sectors/consumer-goods

Luthra, S., Mangla, S. K., Garg, D., & Kumar, A. (2018). Internet of Things (IoT) in Agriculture Supply Chain Management: A Developing Country Perspective. In Y. K. Dwivedi, N. P. Rana, E. L. Slade, M. A. Shareef, M. Clement, A. C. Simintiras, & B. Lal (Eds.), Emerging Markets from a Multidisciplinary Perspective: Challenges, Opportunities and Research Agenda (pp. 209–220). Springer International Publishing. https://doi.org/10.1007/978-3-319-75013-2_16.

Manufacturing Leadership Council. (2017). *A Practical Guide to Scale Industry 4.0.* The Manufacturing Leadership Council. https://www.manufacturingleadershipcouncil.com/a-practical-guide-to-scale-industry-15158/

Mashayekhy, Y., Babaei, A., Yuan, X.-M., & Xue, A. (2022). Impact of Internet of Things (IoT) on Inventory Management: A Literature Survey. *Logistics, 6*(2), Article 2. doi:10.3390/logistics6020033

McKinsey & Company. (2015). *Unlocking_the_potential_of_the_internet_of_things_executive_summary.pdf.* McKinsey. https://www.mckinsey.com/~/media/mckinsey/industries/technology%20media%20and%20telecommunications/high%20tech/our%20insights/the%20internet%20of%20things%20the%20value%20of%20digitizing%20the%20physical%20world/unlocking_the_potential_of_the_internet_of_things_executive_summary.pdf

McKinsey & Company. (2017). *Additive manufacturing: A long-term game changer for manufacturers.* McKinsey. https://www.mckinsey.com/capabilities/operations/our-insights/additive-manufacturing-a-long-term-game-changer-for-manufacturers

McKinsey & Company. (2019). *Perspectives-on-retail-and-consumer-goods_issue-8.pdf.* McKinsey. https://www.mckinsey.com/~/media/mckinsey/industries/retail/our%20insights/perspectives%20on%20retail%20and%20consumer%20goods%20number%208/perspectives-on-retail-and-consumer-goods_issue-8.pdf

Mell, P., & Grance, T. (2011). The NIST definition of cloud computing. *National Institute of Standards and Technology, Special Publication 800-145.*

Müßigmann, B., von der Gracht, H., & Hartmann, E. (2020). Blockchain Technology in Logistics and Supply Chain Management—A Bibliometric Literature Review From 2016 to January 2020. *IEEE Transactions on Engineering Management*, *67*(4), 988–1007. https://doi.org/10.1109/TEM.2020.2980733

Nahavandi, S. (2019). Industry 5.0—A Human-Centric Solution. *Multidisciplinary Digital Publishing Institute*, *11*(16), 4371. doi:10.3390/SU11164371

Niranjan, K., Narayana, K. S., & Rao, M. V. A. L. N. (2021). Role of Artifical Intelligence in Logistics and Supply Chain. *2021 International Conference on Computer Communication and Informatics (ICCCI)*, 1–3. doi:10.1109/ICCCI50826.2021.9402625

Partida, B. (2019, January 7). *Technology benefits sales and operations planning*. SCMR. https://www.scmr.com/article/technology_benefits_sales_and_operations_planning

Paul, J., & Barari, M. (2022). Meta-analysis and traditional systematic literature reviews—What, why, when, where, and how? *Psychology and Marketing*, *39*(6), 1099–1115. https://doi.org/10.1002/mar.21657

Phase, A., & Mhetre, N. (2018). *Using IoT in Supply Chain Management*. *4*(2). https://d1wqtxts1xzle7.cloudfront.net/56617116/IJET-V4I2P148-libre.pdf

PR. (2022). *Artificial Intelligence in Transportation Market Size, Report 2030* [Independent Research Agency]. Presedence Research. https://www.precedenceresearch.com/artificial-intelligence-in-transportation-market

PRG. (2022). *Peerless Media Custom Reports Supply Chain Software Page 21*. PRG. https://bt.editionsbyfry.com/publication/?i=562391&p=21&view=issueViewer&pp=1

PwC. (2017). *3D Printing comes of age in US industrial manufacturing*. PwC. https://www.pwc.com/us/en/industrial-products/publications/assets/pwc-next-manufacturing-3d-printing-comes-of-age.pdf

PwC. (2018). *Industry 4.0: Global digital operations study 2018*. PwC. https://www.pwc.com/gx/en/industries/industry-4-0.html

PwC. (2019). *Partner, PwC Strategy& Germany*. PwC. https://www.strategyand.pwc.com/gx/en/insights/2017/the-future-spare-parts-3d/the-future-of-spare-parts-is-3d.pdf

PwC. (2020). *PwC's Global Artificial Intelligence Study: Sizing the prize*. PwC. https://www.pwc.com/gx/en/issues/data-and-analytics/publications/artificial-intelligence-study.html

Rajagopal, A. (2019, February 7). *Cyber Attacks Top List Of Risks Impacting Supply Chain*. Cyber Security Hub. https://www.cshub.com/attacks/articles/cyber-attacks-top-list-of-risks-impacting-supply-chain

Remondino, M. (2020). Augmented reality in logistics: Qualitative analysis for a managerial perspective. *International Journal of Logistics Systems and Management*, *36*(1), 1–15. https://doi.org/10.1504/IJLSM.2020.107218

Rüßmann, M., Lorenz, M., Gerbert, P., Waldner, M., Justus, J., Engel, P., & Harnisch, M. J. (2016). *Industry 4. 0: The Future of Productivity and Growth in Manufacturing Industries April 09*. https://www.semanticscholar.org/paper/Industry-4-.-0-%3A-The-Future-of-Productivity-and-in-R%C3%BC%C3%9Fmann-Lorenz/42b15ae5e1aa17638fac89b026680d9361fa7c7a

Sonar, H., Khanzode, V., & Akarte, M. (2022). Additive Manufacturing Enabled Supply Chain Management: A Review and Research Directions. *Vision (Basel)*, *26*(2), 147–162. https://doi.org/10.1177/09722629221087308

Statista. (2020a). *IoT: Supply chain management benefits by industry UK 2015-2020*. Statista. https://www.statista.com/statistics/608357/iot-supply-chain-management-efficiency-benefits-uk/

Statista. (2020b). *Sectors most disrupted by XR 2021*. Statista. https://www.statista.com/statistics/1185060/sectors-disrupted-immersive-technology-xr-ar-vr-mr/

Stewart, R., & Niero, M. (2018). Circular economy in corporate sustainability strategies: A review of corporate sustainability reports in the fast-moving consumer goods sector. *Business Strategy and the Environment*, *27*(7), 1005–1022. https://doi.org/10.1002/bse.2048

Swan, D., Lund, S., & Alicke, K. (2020). *Is your supply chain risk blind—Or risk resilient?* McKinsey. https://www.mckinsey.com/capabilities/operations/our-insights/is-your-supply-chain-risk-blind-or-risk-resilient

Tarigan, Z., Jiputra, J., & Siagian, H. (2021). The effect of supply chain practices on retailer performance with information technology as moderating variable. *International Journal of Data and Network Science*, *5*(1), 47–54.

Tawalbeh, L., Muheidat, F., Tawalbeh, M., & Quwaider, M. (2020). IoT Privacy and Security: Challenges and Solutions. *Applied Sciences (Basel, Switzerland)*, *10*(12), 12. https://doi.org/10.3390/app10124102

Wang, X., Kumar, V., Kumari, A., & Kuzmin, E. (2022). Impact of Digital Technology on Supply Chain Efficiency in Manufacturing Industry. Springer. https://doi.org/10.1007/978-3-030-94617-3_25.

WEF. (2021). *This is how COVID-19 has disrupted global supply chains*. World Economic Forum. https://www.weforum.org/agenda/2021/10/this-is-the-state-of-supply-chain-disruptions/

World Economic Forum. (2018). The Future of Supply Chains: A Roadmap for the Fourth Industrial Revolution. WEF.

Xu, X., Rahman, F., Shakya, B., Vassilev, A., Forte, D., & Tehranipoor, M. (2019). Electronics Supply Chain Integrity Enabled by Blockchain. *ACM Transactions on Design Automation of Electronic Systems*, *24*(3), 31:1-31:25. doi:10.1145/3315571

Yalcin, H., & Daim, T. U. (2022). Logistics, supply chain management and technology research: An analysis on the axis of technology mining. *Transportation Research Part E, Logistics and Transportation Review*, *168*, 102943. https://doi.org/10.1016/j.tre.2022.102943

Yang, Y., Wu, L., Yin, G., Li, L., & Zhao, H. (2017). A Survey on Security and Privacy Issues in Internet-of-Things. *IEEE Internet of Things Journal, 4*(5), 1250–1258. doi:10.1109/JIOT.2017.2694844

ZionMarketResearch.(2022,June24).*At4.68%CAGR, GlobalFMCGPackagingMarketSize&SharetoSurpass USD955.6Billionby2028|IndustryTrends, Growth, Value, Opportunities, Statistics, Analysis & ForecastReport by Zion Market Research.* Yahoo Finance. https://finance.yahoo.com/news/4-68-cagr-global-fmcg-160000325.html

Chapter 7
Investigating the Factors, Challenges, and Role of Stakeholders in Implementing Industry 5.0 and Its Impact on Supply Chain Operations:
A Study of the Global Agri-Food Supply Chain

Shivali Sunil Kankekar
Northumbria University, London, UK

Sumesh Singh Dadwal
London South Bank University, UK

Adbul Ali
https://orcid.org/0000-0002-3034-8628
University of Greenwich, UK

ABSTRACT

Industry 5.0 may assist businesses to become more constructive and competitive in the global economy in the Fifth Industrial Revolution era. Therefore, a critical review of prior literature is presented in this paper to examine how industry 5.0 will impact supply chain operations within the agricultural sector. Additionally, it examines influencing factors, challenges, stakeholder roles, and recommendations identified from the literature. Industry 5.0 has multiple benefits for the agri-food sector such as improved agility, responsiveness, efficiency, productivity, precise decision-making, as well as cost-effectiveness.

INTRODUCTION

DOI: 10.4018/978-1-6684-6403-8.ch007

Industry 5.0 is a process of twining the twins of 'the green' and 'the digital transitions', to build a more efficient, sustainable and resilient society and economies (European Commission, 2021). The Covid 19 has further exposed the negatives of too much reliance on efficiency, innovation, technology and productivity and has made people think about sustainability, inclusivity, employability, humanistic approach, building more resilient supply chains and adopting more sustainable ways of production and balancing the needs of various flora nd faunas of the planet earth (European Commission, 2021). The emergence of digitalization and digital technologies in various sectors today has revolutionized industries in ways that have led to improved operational performance and the integration of the entire supply chain throughout. A constant fluctuation in supply demand, disruptions, or natural disasters as well as insufficient visibility to balance the supply chain has elevated the difficulties for an unstable supply chain. Integrating emergent digital technologies may contribute to creating new opportunities, principles, and a few challenges in supply chain management (Azzi et al., 2019, Oliveira-Dias et al., 2022). The emerging digital technologies have revolutionised the Industry to 4th Industrial revolution ie "Industry 4.0", thus accelerating operational performance, and leading to producing new strategies or opportunities with highly customized systems. Using Industry 4.0 technology, manufacturers can become more cost-effective, provide high-speed production with agility and flexibility, and enhance quality. (Jagtap et al.,, 2021),. Industry 4.0 is the convergence of smart manufacturing and products, and the internet of things (IoT), which provides real-time data about the production, machines, and component flow (Chauhan and Singh, 2019). As digital technologies have advanced over the last decade, industries have gained significant control over products and processes via IoT, artificial intelligence, big data analytics, 3D printing, augmented reality, and machine learning (Sahoo and Lo, 2022).

According to Hassoun et al., (2022), it is becoming more prevalent in various sectors, including the food industry, to witness the fourth industrial revolution. In addition, it is becoming increasingly important for the agri-food supply chain to make use of advanced digital technologies and to evolve into an intelligent, autonomous, and data-driven system of systems (Lezoche et al., 2020). According to the world bank report, several technologies have been observed to be promising for addressing existing constraints in the agri-food system, such as remote sensing, blockchain and IoT (The world bank, 2021). As digital technologies are introduced into diverse food systems, capturing, storing, processing, and communicating information are integrated digitally (Donaldson, 2021). Adopting digital technologies in the food industry allows one to identify ongoing and future trends and understand the consumer's intake based on nutrients, food quality, taste experiences, etc. (Chapman et al., 2021). As a result, it is critical to maintain high-quality products and to adhere to regulations strictly, and digital technologies can contribute to ensuring the standardized product to consumers. The Global Digital Agriculture Market was valued at USD 12.8 billion in 2021 and is expected to reach a value of USD 22.1 billion by the year 2028 (Vantage Market, 2021). In addition, Market analysts predict that the global market will grow at a compound annual growth rate (CAGR) of 9.6%.

A real-time information system allows both the production system and consumers to gain access to information about the entire production process, thus facilitating efficient, transparent, and cost-effective food supply chain operations (Ada et al., 2021). The rapid aging of the population combined with diseases (e.g., diabetes, obesity) has dramatically impacted consumer food choices and therefore, several challenges are appearing in the industry, including food security, fraud, and waste (Chapman et al., 2021). Also, the challenges occurring in the agri-food sector mostly are related to weather sensitivity, market disruptions, low efficiency and effectiveness, and external barriers such as poor stakeholder linkages (Lezoche et al., 2020). To overcome the challenges, Yadav et al., (2022) argue for leveraging industry

4.0 technologies, an industry such as agri-food can become smarter, integrated, agile, autonomous, and connected by being more intelligent, smart, and smart. However, the adoption of new technologies in the food industry is slower than that in other sectors due to the complexity of the process (Hassoun et al., 2022), lack of understanding of the deployment of the digitalized supply chain (Büyüközkan and Göçer, 2018) and due to limited understanding of the key role of specific technologies in operations and the supply chain in manufacturing industries (Oliveira-Dias et al., 2022).

According to the PricewaterhouseCoopers 2018 report, digital maturity varies across the globe. The Asian Pacific region appears to have the most advanced companies, with 19% of companies in the Digital Champion category,, 33% in the digital innovators' category and the rest being followers and Novice. In the Americas, 11% of companies in the Digital Champion category, 39% in the digital innovators' category and the rest are followers and Novice . in European markets (EMEA), only 5% of companies in the Digital Champion category, 20% in the digital innovators' category and the rest are followers and Novice (Geissbauer et al., 2018).

Lezoche et al., (2020) argue that soon, all agricultural processes will be fully integrated into the food chain through semantically active technologies. It means that each process involved in the agri-food supply chain subsequently will be digitized to maintain an efficient and effective supply chain. A report published by the Food and Agriculture Organization of the United Nations has analyzed the readiness of industry 4.0 technologies in the agri-food sector as measured by the level of maturity (FAO, 2022). The report found that in certain fields of agriculture such as, livestock Automation, whole farm digitalization of crops, protected crop farming, tractors & machinery production, etc the Agriculture market is almost reaching the maturity stage of Industry 4.0 and is smart devices, using AI, robotics and Data analytics etc; however in fields like full crop automation, Aquaculture automation the industry is still at nascent prototype site (FAO, 2022). Agriculture as an economic sector also referred to as the "farm-to-fork supply chain", "Plough to Plate supply chain", or "Agri/agro-food supply chain plays a crucial role in economic development, environmental sustainability, and social well-being (Yadav et al., 2022), Almost 44 million jobs in food processing, food retailing, and catering are supported by agriculture, which currently employs 12 million farmers (FAO, 2020). In addition, it is observed that there is a remarkable share of the food industry in the UK economy, and it contributes £28.2 billion (17% of the total manufacturing global value added) to the economy annually (Jagtap et al., 2021). However, the agri-food industries are currently facing a few challenges at each stage of the supply chain such as labour shortages, increasing costs, delayed lead time, food waste, food quality, safety, etc. Currently, the organizations are working to resolve the issues by considering all the aspects of the supply chain and improving the sustainable supply chain performance by marrying the digital technologies with Environmentally friendly Green approaches to maintain the supply chain integrity.

However, an agriculture industrial practice predominately dominated by digital technology and ignoring the needs and impacts on humans, society, the environment and sustainability will be not only unethical, and illegal but also can be disastrous to mankind. While Industry 4.0 is flourishing, we need to get ready for the fifth industrial revolution ie Industry 5.0. Industry 4.0 is more about machine lead efficiencies, cost savings, automation etc, industry 5.0 will be about containing the negative consequences of industry 4.0 on various stakeholders and balancing the scorecard on the metrics of sustainability, and contributions to human, social, and environmental and governance, ESG (environment, social, and governance), and a shift from one P – productivity – to three Ps, namely productivity, people, and the planet. There are many mandatory requirements such as United Nations Sustainable Development Goals (SDGs), Good Manufacturing Practices (GMP), International Organization of Standardization (ISO),

American Society for Testing and Materials (ASTM), corporate social responsibility (CSR), Environment, health and safety (EHS). Philanthropy and Sustainability practices are leading organizations and stakeholders to think about Industry 5.0 as a way forward (Heartland, 2022).

The primary aim of researching and developing this chapter is is to Investigate the impact of Industry 5.0 on supply chain operations within the context of the global agri-food supply chain. The chapter will explore existing literature on industry 4.0 and Industry 5.0 on supply chain operations and analyse the related factors, challenges, and key stakeholders.

LITERATURE REVIEW

The section examines how digital technologies are intertwining with human-centric, Green and sustainability approaches and aiding the agri-food supply chain and aiding in a more efficient, effective, agile, innovative, sustainable Supply chain

Operations management includes the planning, scheduling, and managing of the activities to transform the input into products or services based on technical, organizational, and environmental perspectives. The operations function in broader Supply Chain Management (SCM) includes 'the collection of people, technology, and systems within an organization with primary responsibility for providing the organization's products or services (Bozarth and Handfield, 2019, p.23). Supply chain management covers the whole process of designing and delivering products to consumers at the right time, cost, quality and flexibility. The SCM activities, requires significant structural changes and significant investments based on the organization's strategy and performance objectives. Operational decisions have a strategic dimension, driving the overall strategy that governs the direction of the operation and impacts all other decisions. Planning and controlling all supply chain activities are necessary to ensure the effectiveness of this process. The process from manufacturer to consumer is always interlinked with the physical, informational, and financial flow. The various functional areas such as purchasing, manufacturing, and sales and distribution ought to be integrated using Information and Communications Technologies (ICTs) to minimize materials costs in purchasing, reduce production costs in manufacturing, increase sales volume, and lower warehouse and inventory costs in distribution(Jacobs and Chase, 2020).

In operations management, to drive towards excellence, an organization must ensure total quality management (TQM), continuous improvement including their suppliers and buyers and improving effectiveness and responsiveness (Radnor and Barnes, 2007). Nowadays, using ICT and digital technologies it is becoming easier to track all the records of the product in the system, even the date, time and username are recorded in the software. To manage information flow within supply chains, centralized management systems are commonly used, such as enterprise resource planning (ERP) systems to move from manual work in SCM to fully automated operations and systems (Hossein Ronaghi, 2020). The management of operations has eveloved from Manafucationg strategy development (the 1960s) t0 Just in time and Kanban systems (1970s), Total quality management & Service quality Productivity (1980s), Six sigma (1990s), Business Process Reengineering & Supply chain Management (1990s), E-commerce & sustainable SCM (2000s), to Industry 4.0- Business analytics, AI, Internet of Things, Automation (2010) to Industry 5.0 (2020s) (Jacobs and Chase, 2020).

Supply-Chain Operations Reference model or SCOR model evaluation framework integrates process re-engineering, benchmarking, and measurement in SCM, and thus allows organizations to have a modern management approach that improves customer satisfaction, increases delivery flexibility, increases product reliability and reduces costs (Sundarakani et al., 2018). The SCOR model involves using ICT for integrating, balancing and coordinating the five repetitive processes such as plan, make, source, deliver, and return of resources and information from suppliers of supplers and customers of customers in both directions (NC State University, 2004). Indeed, digital supply chain involves ERP, RFID, customer relationship management (CRM), collaborative planning forecasting and replenishment, and e-procurement systems(Ageron et al., 2020), emerging technologies such as Artificial intelligence (AI), Blockchain technologies offer more than RFID and ERP to the operations supply chain management discipline, such as intelligent contracts for automating processes and good P2P verification. Therefore, implementation of industry 5.0 is necessary to include and integrate the emergent technologies as well as the interoperability process across them.

INTRODUCTION OF SUPPLY CHAIN REVOLUTION

The industrial revolution concept was first presented during the Hannover Fair in 2011 and was subsequently announced in 2013 as a German strategic initiative intended to take a leading role in industries that are currently revolutionizing manufacturing (Xu et al., 2018). A new paradigm of manufacturing, processing, distributing, packaging, retailing, and transporting products has emerged with Industry 4.0. Nowadays, the Industry 5.0 approach involving the integration of digital supply chains into traditional supply chains along with Environmental, Social, Governance (ESG) and sustainability with a humanistic approach has become crucial for improving value chains, responsiveness, integrity and reliability towards various stakeholders (Aamer et al., 2022). Using the Industry 4.0 approach to manufacturing causes difficulties of coping with a variety of challenges, including economic, environmental, sustainability and technological challenges (Mohamed, 2019). By leveraging the technology and information systems, along with green & sustainable practices, it is becoming easier to integrate suppliers, manufacturers, and consumers, eliminating poor performance from suppliers and erratic customer demands in real-time (Joubert and Jokonya, 2021). Thus where on one hand adopting digital technologies it is possible now for organizations or industries to manage the supply chain effectively and efficiently by reducing lead time, cost, and manual efforts with an increasing amount of accuracy and profit and on the other hand by integration with sustainability, green environmental and humanist approaches, the supply can better meet the needs of various stakeholders. To transform the traditional supply chain approach to a digital supply chain, the significance of digitalization is proliferated since the industrial revolution. Streamlining the supply chain with a digital supply chain ensures real-time information sharing and improved communication using Industry 4.0 paradigm (Xu et al., 2018). However, to create value for products or services in the global market, maintaining the informational, financial and data flow with trust, transparency and communication and sustainability, we need Industry 5.0 paradigm. Such a humanistic, sustainable and digital supply chain is termed as Supply chain management 5.0 and entails Emerging technologies such as Artificial Intelligence (AI)M, Robotics, Machine learning (ML), Augmenter Realty (AR), blockchain technology, big data analytics (BDA), cloud computing, additive manufacturing, Cyber security systems, 3-D technologies, machine-to-machine communication, and cyber-physical systems (CPS)Big data, Internet of Things (IoT) (Parhi et al., 2022) along with human -social- enviro centric sustainable approach to revolutionize production, design, planning, logistics, distribution, and consumption.

The new production technologies, such as Industry 4.0 or the IoT, enable organizations to offset labour cost advantages associated with offshoring and move production back to increase flexibility and diminish lead times and suataiblity practices making use of technology more humanistic (Industry 5.0). It is also noteworthy that in the United States, approximately 66 percent of firms use advanced digital technologies while in the European Union, 61 per cent do so (EIBIS, 2022).

Among the digital technologies emerging under Industry 4.0 is Blockchain, which has many applications across a variety of sectors including the agri-food sector (Hassoun et al., 2022). To illustrate, incorporating blockchain technology into food safety, monitoring, and traceability measures is a priority for Walmart, a retail giant (Agarwal et al., 2022). Similarly, technologies such as Radio Frequency Identification (RFID), robotics, automation, additive manufacturing, 3D Printing, etc. can contribute to enhancing operations in industries with accuracy and reduces man-made defects. According to the Deloitte (2022) survey, the Industrial Internet of Things (IIoT) at which machines are connected and processes are automated is expected to further increase operational efficiency by 45% in manufacturing. Furthermore, IoT plays a crucial role in offering an extensive range of opportunities such as monitoring the location and speed of vehicles remotely and real-time surveilling of the condition of perishable products through temperature sensors, status, and performance of machines, etc. (Manavalan and Jayakrishna, 2019).

Industry 4.0-based integrated supply chains and highly integrated digital platforms increase cost efficiency, reduce labour requirements and errors along the supply chain, and increase market responsiveness and overall competitiveness (Kittipanya-Ngam & Tan, 2019).

However, despite the benefits of digital transformation, most companies are reluctant to initiate the process to Industry 5.0 because of significant implementation barriers such as inadequate knowledge & awareness, and uncertainty about various benefits (Mohamed, 2019). Though there are many challenges associated with multiple factors, several global retailers, including Amazon and Alibaba, use drones and robotic automation for delivering goods as well as handling goods (Büyüközkan & Göçer, 2018). In the agri-food sector, the farmers are reluctant to adopt modern technologies and from detaching the past. The implementation of Industry 4.0 itself poses many technological challenges, with significant impacts on many dimensions of today's manufacturing industry (Pereira et al., 2017), so going for Industry 5.0 is quite a far and difficult path for industries,

APPLICATION OF INDUSTRY 5.0 TECHNOLOGIES ON OPERATIONS

Increasing efficiency and productivity while not removing human workers from the manufacturing industry and producing sustainable products and services is imposing many challenges on the global SCM. Industry 5.0, expects robots to be intertwined with the human brain and work as a collaborator instead of competitors (Nahavandi, 2019). The operations in supply chain management involve complex and interconnected decision-making processes in supply chain management, integrating digital technologies can improve their efficiency, flexibility, agility, robustness, ability to withstand uncertainties and sustainability, (Rodríguez et al., 2020). Thus the supply chain needs to be integrated vertically and horizontally, optimised across a wider network, and adjusted to market changes by enabling autonomous operations using digital manufacturing thus leading to more customer satisfaction, product quality, and performance, reducing costs, variety, or flexibility, service level and human resources (Zhou et al., 2021) The Industry 4.0 is an era of highly autonomous intelligent systems in industrial production processes involving implementation of cutting-edge technology, such as robotics and smart sensors throughout the supply chain (Hassoun et al., 2022),. Industry 4.0 has lead to organizational re-designs, operations management developments, market transformations, and organizational transformations (Ivanov et al.,

2020). Industry 4.0 has creted 'smart factories' which can visualse and simulate operations with the integration of advanced design software and production systems (Rashid and Tjahjono, 2016). The performance of operations and processes can be influenced in in terms of quality, speed, dependability, flexibility, and cost; all of which will have a significant impact on the satisfaction of customers and the competitiveness of businesses (Slack & Brandon-Jones 2022).

Due to digitalization in global supply chains, there is an increasing realisation that the optimisation of global supply chains without considering human externalities provides only a partial and misleading view of the impacts of technologies (Mithas et al., 2022). Hence there is a stronger need of integration of industry 4.0 technologies with ESG approaches in the agri-food supply chain. Initially in the production and processing stage, the adoption of digital technologies can lead to improving the operational performance as well as the quality evaluation of food and the suppliers. However, the long terms benefits of society lies in sustainable production practices, precision agriculture, and the quality assessment of raw materials suppliers are supported by technologies used at the production and processing stage ie in Industry 5.0 (Yadav et al., 2022)

One of the emerging technologies, big data analytics can contribute to the decision-making in agri-food supply by estimating consumer preferences and expectations to a higher standard, designing, and developing the products based on real-time market demands, and improving the overall business performance (Rejeb et al., 2021). Also in the logistics or transportation stage, organizations can adopt digital technologies along with sustainable practices to reduce carbon emissions, and food waste, and improve the real-time monitoring of the food while shipping, and information sharing. An IoT system uses a range of technogies such as RFID, Wireless Sensor Networks (WSN), Near Field Communication (NFC) technology, AI, ML, Big data ananlytics, etc., to collect, store and analyze the data in all the stages of the supply chain (Feng et al., 2020). The drones can be used to spray pesticides and or to deliver products as well. RFID tags can be used in retailing, and logistics to maintain and control an inventory and reduce waste. The ICT technology enables effective agro-e-commerce and trading at the consumption stage enables provenance tracking and promotes circular economy initiatives (Yadav et al., 2022).

Any technology can have multiple benefits in various stages of SCMs. Through Agriculture 4.0, and 5.0, sustainable and digitalised ways of farming have the potential to generate renewed interest in digitising traditional practices and operations, focusing on analytics and decision-making (Spanaki et al., 2021). However, because of the lack of information sharing among various actors involved in the SCM, there can be issues related to unbalanced supply & demand, price volatility, and food scarcity, all of which in turn can adversely impacts logistics efficiency, cost containment, risk management, customer intimacy, consumer confidence, and sustainability (Liu et al., 2021).

There are several factors such as market demand, governance, employee skill sets, and costs that may affect the digitalization of operations and supply chains (Juhani 2022). The extreme weather events, biodiversity loss, and the need to make soil healthier, farmers requiring increased innovation etc require the implementation of Industry 5.0. For example, Syngenta has collaborated with Insilico Medicine, to create and design crop protection products as well as products that protect the soil, allowing it to retain carbon, which reduces greenhouse gas emissions from agriculture by using AI (Syngenta, 2021). Also, the COVID-19 restriction on travel has led Nestlé to expand its use of augmented reality technology to provide virtual support to production, research and development sites and suppliers which results in increased efficiency throughout the operations (Nestle, 2020).

INDUSTRY 5.0 IN AGRI-FOOD SUPPLY CHAIN AND OPERATIONS MANAGEMENT

As many researchers have found that digitalisation has revolutionized multiple industries including agri-food industry. In the era of Industry 4.0, and industry 5.0, the knowledge and technology spanning physical, digital, and biological domains are integrated with green and human centric approaches ((Echegaray et al., 2022). The traditional agri-food industry heavily relied on manual work handling with equipment whereas agri-food 5.0 is majorly dependent on automation along with sustainability practices, which enables the industry to maintain transparency, productivity, profit, and sustainability across the globe (Liu et al., (2021),

Like the Industrial revolution 1.0 to 5.0, the Agricultural sector has also moved from Agri-food 1.0 to Agre-food 5.0, though at a time-lagged phase. The Agri-food 1.0 involved heavy labour work including the use of manual workers, animals for agricultural production etc. Agri-food 2.0 replaced manual work, animals with machinery such as steam engines, and tractors et so as improve productivity and reduce labour work. The Agri-food 3.0 used monitoring, bio-medical technologies, tested managers and electronic systems for more effective agriculture. Agri-food 4.0 uses ICT & IoT to automate the processes and the real-time data analysis and tracking of the food during the entire supply chain thus increasing productivity by 25% through automation (Aday & Aday, 2020). Industry 5.0 would embed Industry 4.0 with human, social, environmental and sustainable approaches to achieve a sustainable and smart farming system.

However, Industry 4.0-based agri-food supply chains could have concerns such as food fraud, increased cost of the final product, transparency, traceability, sustainability and limits in achieving UNOs Milleneam Development Goals (MDGs) (Dadi et al., 2021), In the past few years, the customer's confidence in agri-food supply chain has been undermined by a variety of food incidents, the horsemeat scandal in Europe, salmonella outbreaks in the USA, genetically modified foods, and mad cow diseases among others (Yadav et al., 2022).

Therefore, the need to use Agri 5.0 to embed suitable approaches, increase awareness of food safety and quality and implement digital technology to reduce manual errors, ensuring full employment. Food fraud including mislabelling the product, cheap quality ingredients or products, adulteration of food, etc. is not only affecting business but also serious impact on the consumer's health. Also, food traceability, food waste, green food, and high carbon footprints in the food supply chain require innovative approaches of embedding Blockchain technologies, IoT, and AI along with sustainability and ESG practices in Agriculture, and thus going for Industry 5.0.

Blockchain technology can aid in maintaining transactional data, tracing tags, and clarifying contract terms between farmers, landowners, manufacturers, and vendors (Hossein, 2020). With the use of robotics and automation, a product can be made more effective and accurate with fewer defects, whilst increasing productivity and reducing costs. Similarly, to customize food design, nutrition, and composition, 3D food printing offers new and innovative manufacturing technologies (Zhang et al., 2021). Digital technologies have been successfully applied in the agri-food industry in a variety of ways, but investment decisions must be studied, such as whether the technology should be applied in agri-food supply chain and at what point it should be integrated into the existing system (Yadav et al., 2022).

As industry 5.0 approach will not only enhance the efficiency of the agri-food supply chain by eliminating unnecessary waste, reducing outbreak costs, product recalls, and cross-contamination risks but also make production more sustainable and humanistic (Yadav et al., 2022). Industry 5.0 technologies can assist with mitigating the challenges involved in the agri-food supply chain pre and post-harvesting mitigating risks of wastage, losses, and high costs and promoting sustainability through information sharing and collaboration between suppliers and buyers. The IoT platforms along with the ESG approach can enhance agricultural data collection by providing additional data sources, providing a broader range of information about water, soil, humans, animals, environment, social and Governance etc (Spanaki et al., 2021).

RESEARCH METHODOLOGY

This chapter has been researched, developed and synthesised by conducting a Systematic Literature Review (SLR). The SLR ensures comprehensive coverage of the literature for future searches and ensures a comparable result. According to Kitchenham et al., (2009, p.8), SLR aggregates all existing evidence on a research question to support the development of shreds of evidence. The scope of the research used themes such as, Industry 4.0 Industry 5.0, Supply chain Management and, agriculture and Operation. The databases such as Scopus, PubMed, ScienceDirect and Google Scholar were considered to collect different types of articles, journals, and grey literature to support the evidence in the literature. Following the first screening step, the secondary screening step involved the review of the full text of the documents with the specified keywords.

Findings and Results on Digitalisation and Industry 4. In SCM

The articles published between periods 2011 and 2022 were reviewed. It can be observed that the agri-food supply chain lagged for around three years (The year 2014) in the use of advanced technologies as compared to Industry 4.0 (the year 2011 due to resistance from farmers or organizations. From 2014 to 2019, an almost 6-fold rise in papers related to Agri-food 4.0 Almost 89% of the research work has been based on whole supply chain management and lesser on operations management (9%.). Out of 61 research papers shortlisted, 42 were qualitative and the majority of researchers had used the SLR approach (23) and conceptual approaches (17) and very few were empirical (9) conference papers (4) industrial reports (2) or other kinds of Research methods (4). The majority of research papers were on agri-food (34%) and food processing (34%) and other articles were referred from other industries such as the manufacturing industry (24%) and others, To assess the impact of industry 4.0 or Industry 5.0 technologies on supply chain operations.

THEMATIC ANALYSIS OF DIGITALISATION OF AGRI SCM

A two-by-three typology matrix (3- levels of management decisions eg Strategy, Tactical, Operational, and crosstab with internal and external elements) has been used to identify the factors, challenges, stakeholder roles, and recommendations related to managing the implementation of Industry 5.0 and the impact of industry 5.0 on supply chain operations

Factors Influencing the Implementation of Industry 5.0

Several internal and external factors such as employee skill development, technological infrastructure, political support, and software capabilities are necessary for the effective implementation of Industry 5.0 (Parhi et al., 2022). The next section discusses the main factors driving Industry 5.0 and its influence.

Lack Of Strategic Roadmap

The successful implementation of Industry 5.0' requires appropriate and clear strategic guidelines (Kumar et al., 2021). The research found this theme that the organizations lack a defined strategy, vision, and roadmap for executing Industry 5.0 into practice (Kumar et al., 2021; Osterrieder et al., 2020). To build a strategic roadmap the readiness of the top management and organizations are crucial.. It has been found that agri-food producers lack the adoption of differentiation strategies and thus resulting in lower digital maturity. The integration of industry 5.0 into the organisational strategy is an important success factor for the change process (Mayer et al., 2017). A lack of a strategic roadmap to implement industry 5.0 can pose multiple challenges to organizations, such as misunderstanding the role and effectiveness of technologies, mismatching market requirements, and paralyzing forecasting capabilities (Aday & Aday, 2020). it is also found that around a small percent of technology suppliers or manufacturers have an overall Industry 4.0 or Industry 5.0 strategy (USA 27%, Germany 20%, Japan 17%) in place, slightly high percentages have clear responsibilities (USA 30%, Germany 31%, Japan 10%) and meager percent (USA 20%, Germany 19%, Japan 15%) have assigned clear roadmap for implementations of for Industry 4.0 or 5.0 (McKinsey Digital, 2016).

Lack of Government Support

To implement industry 5.0 technologies in organizations, the role of government t & politics to support the organizations directly or indirectly is very crucial (Hoyer et al., 2020). The mid-2014 despite of the risks, pioneers that implemented smart factory systems with government support demonstrated the ability to implement an emerging technology rapidly for a strategic business opportunity (Choi & Choi, 2018). For an instant, India's Department of Heavy Industry (DHI) launched Udyog Bharat 4.0 as part of its Industry 4.0 initiative for strengthening competitiveness (Majumdar et al., 2020). However, besides facilitating funding-related issues, governments can also support remote industries by extending broadband Internet access, and marketing Zhao et al., (2022), found that the Argentinian government has a significant role in supporting general agricultural services such as research and development, training, marketing, and public stockholding. The Government and political institutions can help Industry 5.0 through financial aid, R&D budgets, infrastructure and education support, and reducing taxes (Hoyer et al., 2020). According to Eurostat statistics total government R&D budget allocations across the EU in 2021 were €109 250 million, which is equivalent to 0.75% of GDP (Eurostat, 2022).

Lack of Management Support

In SCM network, industry 5.0 requires a determined leadership style, clear strategic vision, participation of top management as well as the influence of internal organization partners, such as interdisciplinary offices and representatives from all progressive levels of the organization, cross-functional collaboration, new skills development and training (Nimawat & Gidwani, 2021) To bring about change in an industry, both employees and top management can help to develop awareness and sufficient knowledge about the importance of implementing the system. It requires a commitment to impart Industry 5.0 relevant training to employees, including awareness of Industry 5.0, and conducting food loss prevention and waste prevention programs before food items reach consumers etc(Sagi & Gokarn, 2022).

Lack of Technological Skill

Organizations can secure a long-term and reliable workforce by training and increasing the skills of local employees (Aday & Aday, 2020). The workforce often lacks the relevant technical skills and standards which are needed in the standards for the implementation of industry 5.0 (Kamble et al., 2018). When organizations apply industry 5.0 technologies and approaches without having the right technological skills, it may hinder the ability to utilise technology efficiently. In agri-food industry, although farms have already adopted IoT, Blockchains, and AI solutions and implemented different farming platforms, there is still a lack of knowledge and skills regarding how quickly the Agri-Tech field is changing and how to be more efficient, productive, and sustainable (Spanaki et al., 2021). Thus manufacturing firms must obtain the necessary resources, skills, and support to the journey to Industry 5.0 . Manufacturing companies are more likely to embrace industry 5.0 if they possess both tangible resources, such as qualified human resources, machinery, and equipment, and intangible resources, such as skills and capabilities (Hassoun et al., 2022). According to the European Commission report, it aspires to equip at least 54% of people with basic digital skills and to boost the number of ICT, only 4% of people are ICT graduates, and only 20% of organisations provide ICT training to their workers (European Commission, 2022).

Challenges In Adopting Industry 5.0

The adoption of emerging technologies is believed to improve the performance of an organization in terms of cost, productivity, quality, flexibility, and employee satisfaction (Kamble et al., 2020). The Industrial Revolution 5.0 concept, however, remains a vision for the future because it involves a wide variety of issues and faces a wide range of challenges and difficulties, including scientific, technological, economic, social, and political challenges (Zhou et al., 2015; Mohamed, 2018). They are challenges related to unclear economic benefits, lack of standard regulations & laws, low maturity levels of technologies, too slow technological adoption, high investment, value-chain integration, security risks, and resistance to change etc (Xu et al., 2018, Geissbauer et al., 2014). The next section explores the main subthemes related to challenges in Implementing Industry 5.0

The Challenge Of High Implementation Cost

Industry 5.0 and the integration of sustainability and digital architecture to meet business requirements requires substantial initial investment both in terms of budget, cost and time (Sony, 2020), Furthermore, supporting innovative investments and empowering employees through tax planning is an imperative part of business planning. Capital investment is not just limited to the hi-tech implementation in the organization, but also involves employee training, hardware and software, initial installation, digital infrastructure, and R&D skills. It is predicted that investing in industry 4.0 applications will improve profitability and return on investment in the agri-food sector in the future (Hossein Ronaghi, 2020). Geissbauer et al.,

(2014) have estimated that the share of investments in Industry 5.0 solutions at various stages of SCM (Supply chain, procurement, planning, product development, production process, distribution and services etc) will account for more than 50% of planned capital investments for the next five years.

The Challenge Of Lack of Infrastructure

To integrate automation into existing manufacturing processes, industrial managers and decision-makers must allocate significant resources to developing ICT infrastructure due to its significant weight in optimal standards (Moktadir et al., 2018). It is not feasible to accommodate Industry 5.0 in a deficient infrastructure due to a lack of investment or inefficient resource management. To ensure near-real-time data availability, technological infrastructure must be modernized and provide fast, secure, and reliable services (Rüßmann et al., 2015). As soon as the technological infrastructure challenge is overcome, other challenges can be addressed and eliminated easily. Industry 5.0 requires an ICT infrastructure capable of sharing data at a significantly greater volume and higher quality than existing networks thus needing high speed and reliable internet (Sayem et al., 2022). The lackings of ICT infrastructure and unclear contractual arrangements concerning liability, privacy, and the consequences of data loss can lead to the challenge of implementing Industry **5.0** . If ICT infrastructure is lacking thenin will become difficult to undertake horizontal integration, vertical integration, and end-to-end integration for Industry 5.0. (Xu et al., 2018). Therefore, the lack of technological infrastructure is the most crucial challenge that needs to be addressed to implement industry 5.0. The Gartner 2022 survey estimated that 70% of organizations will become automated for flexible and efficient delivery of services by 2025, up from 20% in 2021 (Rimol, 2022).

The Challenge of Data Quality & Security

Old legacy ICT systems will crumble to handle high-quality, more complex and and secure communication). Data security issues, hacker threats etc could be strong potential challenges in IoT implementation concerning security (Raj et al., 2020). Also to improve supply chain integration, organizations need to collaborate with other businesses and share information. This brings in various privacy, data protection and Cyber security risks from third-party software and services and the sharing of information between them (Geissbauer et al., 2014). The quality of data is categorized into four aspects: consistency, completeness, accuracy, and redundancy (Geissbauer et al., 2014). In the age of fully realized big data, the firms are interconnected, and the process will generate large amounts of, heterogenous, complex data leading to problems related to data quality, consistency, and data accuracy etc (Raj et al., 2020).

The Challenge Of Change Resistance

Middle management and employee resistance can act as barriers to organizational change to implement Industry 5.0. Considering the speed at which technology is advancing, employees are not able to meet the rapidly changing demands of their jobs (Felsberger et al., 2020). The resistance to adopting Industry 5.0 technologies can be die to resistance to change incited due to the lack of competencies in employees. The employee's fear of change highlights the need of preparing the mindset of employees to understand digital transformation for Industry 5.0 and to have positive job prospects so that they can up-skill for different jobs (Khin & Kee, 2022). Training activities and psychological support are necessary to address the change management issues associated with each technology.

Role of Stakeholders

The development of stakeholders is crucial to the implementation of Industry 5.0, as it facilitates the efficient coordination between stakeholders and helps manage internal operations (Parhi et al., 2022),. The stakeholders are the persons or groups with legitimate direct or indirect interests in the business. Stakeholders can be categorized in internal and external aspects. In Agri-food 5.0 several agricultural stakeholders participate in agricultural production, including non-governmental organizations (NGOs), governments, statistical institutes, international organizations, and competitors of agricultural companies (Spanaki et al., 2021). The next section discusses the role of the stakeholders and their significance to manage the industry 5.0 implications in organizations.

Farmers as Stakeholder

Agri-food is primarily controlled by farmers who are the owners of agricultural activity, perform various operations, and collect data. However, a study by Spanaki et al., (2021) found that farmers sometimes require assistance from third parties for data collection. As the agri-food sector involves different educational background people, farmers need to understand the system properly and maintain the partnership with distributors, and manufacturers to achieve high awareness and flexibility. Farmers mostly face challenges due to price fluctuations, production inefficiency, food waste, food safety, etc. (Spanaki et al., 2021). However, the use of technology and data appropriately can help farmers to manage their business operations.

Government as Stakeholder

The implementation of Industry 5.0's is heavily dependent on financial factors including infrastructure investment, supplier improvement initiatives, and stakeholder involvement. In agri-food, governments are responsible for controlling supply chain processes to avoid complex problems, minimize dominant stakeholders, and ensure fair market outcomes. The availability of financial resources (internal or external) is one of the prerequisites for accelerating the digitalization and digital transformation of businesses in Industry 5o. Generally, the government is perceived as a potential source of funds, while every other aspect is expected to receive minimal support (Szabo et al., 2020). Consequently, companies often seek Government grants and subsidies to finance digital transformation investments, due to a lack of internal resources (Szabo et al., 2020).

Supplier as Stakeholder

As suppliers are vital stakeholders in implementing industry 5.0 applications, it has been found that strong commitment among the stakeholders involved can be realized in the form of collaboration. A collaborative approach is essential for sustaining long-term partnerships and spreading benefits throughout the strategic, tactical, and operational levels of the supply chain system (Dania et al., 2016). The role of suppliers in collaboration is to share information about resources and capabilities based on different factors. The obstacles to implementing collaborative systems in the supply chain include inadequate assessment systems, limited information systems, organizational culture, and reluctance to change. As the supply chain system for agri-food becomes increasingly globalized, collaboration is essential to gain consumer trust, minimize costs, and maximize profits (Dania et al., 2016).

Technology and Service Provider as Stakeholder

A technology provider aims to help businesses integrate digital technologies into their daily operations and improve organizational performance. On the other hand, service providers strive to improve the organizations' services and enhance the effectiveness of technology in business activities. Integrating processes, data, and devices across the value chain can improve end-to-end planning accuracy and streamline operations. Morakanyane et al., (2017) argue that the transformation process is not driven solely by technological advancements, but also by stakeholders at the firm level, such as staff, technology, and service providers for digital transformation. Infrastructure providers and technology providers are the primary stakeholders who facilitate access to these digital technologies (Holienka et al., 2021). The technology or service providers offer a wide range of services and solutions, including marketing activities, data collection, storage, and analysis as part of management and decision-making using appropriate technology under Industry 5.0. Agricultural equipment sellers and manufacturers are facing a broadening business and competition ecosystem as their products become increasingly connected (Porter & Heppelmann, 2017).

In summary, The findings section has identified and discusses the key themes such as influencing factors, challenges, the role of stakeholders, to manage the impact of industry 5 .0 technologies on supply chain performance within the agri-food sector.

DISCUSSION

This section analyses the main themes discussed in the previous section and then evaluates the themes by applying the SCOR model

Factors Related To The Implementation Of Industry 5.0

The main influencing factors, related to Industry 5.0 found are; a strategic roadmap and the need of technical skills within the agri-food industry. As findings indicated, the agri-food industry lacks strategic planning. Another factor has been the farmers' ability to modernize their production practices to implement Industry 5.0 strategically. Organizations need to focus on investing in training to adopt industry 5.0 and utilize the technology at its potential. As agri-food sector involves different factors such as seasonality, variability, perishability, traceability, and small-scale production, supply chain managers in the agricultural sector must develop a thorough understanding of the skills and information needed to meet emerging challenges Furthermore, the government can facilitate the funding of the agri-food industry, as well industry-specific research and education, marketing, and infrastructure requirements to remain competitive and employ innovative practices (Zhao et al., 2022). Also, the management should ensure that all employees are familiar with food safety regulations and procedures and can comply with them. Therefore, to overcome the issues concerning food safety, quality, employee training, or strategic ideas to facilitate industry 5.0, bottom-up and top-down approaches are needed. Figure 1, represents the conceptual framework for influencing factors and is categorized based on the SCOR model, and possible outcomes to help organizations achieve their goals by addressing these factors.

Challenges In Implementing Industry 5.0

Despite many advantages that industry 5.0, the study has identified; uncertainty regarding the ROI and the cost-benefit of industry 5.0 as the main challenge, Yadav et al. (2022) noted that to ensure stakeholder affordability, agri-food industries need to invest less to develop digital technologies. Thus, from a planning perspective, organizations should consider both the return on investment and the technology

Figure 1. Conceptual framework for influencing factors based on SCOR model (Author, 2022)

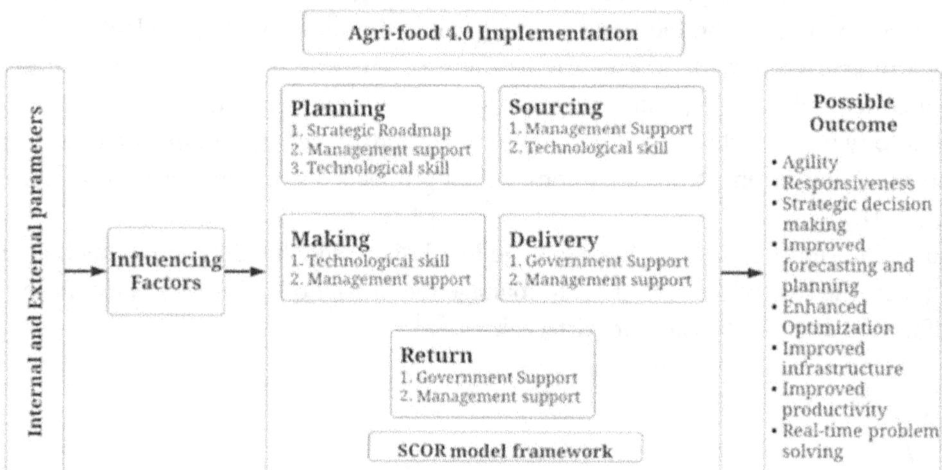

potential for production when making significant investments. Secondly, the organizations will have to incur capital expenditure for developing the industry 5 .0 infrastructure which includes the development of cyber-physical systems, the IoT, cloud computing, and data analytics. A high-speed internet connection is also essential for businesses that rely on cloud-based applications and services. In agriculture, IoT is used largely to enhance productivity and intelligence through an integrated information processing and applications infrastructure (Lu et al., 2015). In addition, it has been observed that food safety concerns and food wastage occur at each stage of supply chain from sourcing to returning which highlights the importance of infrastructure to ensure a safe and reliable food supply (Yadav et al., 2022). Thirdly, farmers might experience great financial loss and emotional distress if sensitive farm information, such as crop yields, cultivation methods, and livestock health conditions, were disclosed to third parties. Thus, implementing blockchain and IoT can assist in preventing unauthorised access to data. Lastly, farmers have faced resistance and challenges in implementing smart farming, particularly concerning advanced technology and data sharing concerns (Spanaki et al., 2021). Figure 2, represents the conceptual framework for challenges and their classification based on the SCOR model and possible outcomes upon overcoming identified challenges.

ROLE OF STAKEHOLDER

Stakeholders play a vital role in implementing industry 5.0 applications in agri-food by providing financial support as well as collaborative support. The agri-food industry involves stakeholders such as farmers, intermediaries, suppliers, consumers, etc. The farmers are primary key stakeholders in the food supply chain who often lack business skills, aspirations, and a system thinking approach, so they focus largely

Figure 2. Conceptual framework for challenges based on SCOR model (Author, 2022)

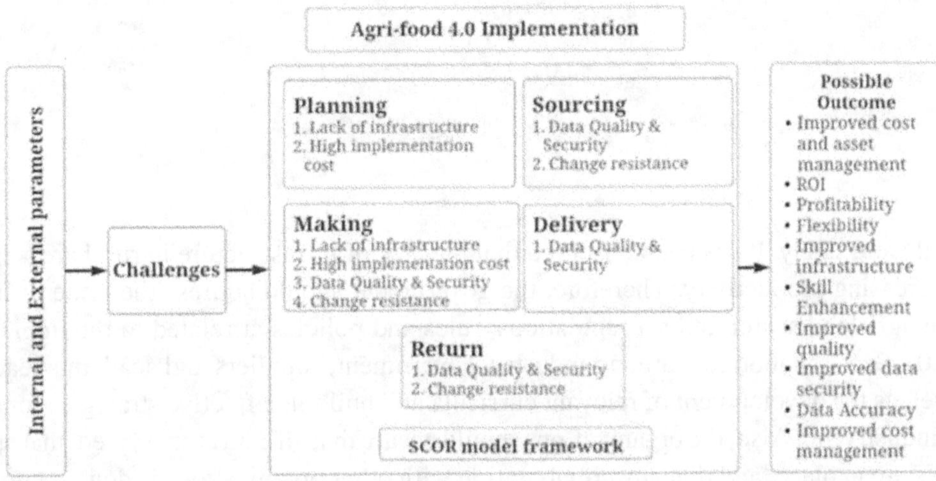

on their own operations rather than collaborating through integrated systems.. Maintaining sustainability within the agri-food supply chain requires appropriate practices from the organization's both upstream and downstream actors. Agricultural information sharing is essential since this industry is extreme in terms of time-criticality, risk, control, security, and requirement for supply chain integration (Spanaki et al., 2021). A central characteristic of Agriculture 5.0 is the ability of suppliers to share information to manage weather variations, water shortages, product perishability and price volatility. Financial institutions such as bank and insurance can provide farmers with a variety of beneficial instruments, from insurance such as crop, livestock, yield, and revenue to credit based on short-term and long-term (Bertolozzi-Caredio et al., 2021). Thus, findings indicate that stakeholders can allow more efficient and cost-effective access to knowledge and technology. Figure 3, represents the conceptual framework for identifying the role of stakeholders and their classification based on the SCOR model and possible outcomes that organizations can achieve with the help of stakeholders.

RECOMMENDATION

Firstly, findings have revealed a few recommendations such as government should create a favourable regulatory environment to encourage innovation in the agri-food sector and ensure that the technology

Figure 3. Conceptual framework for the role of stakeholders based on the SCOR model (Author, 2022)

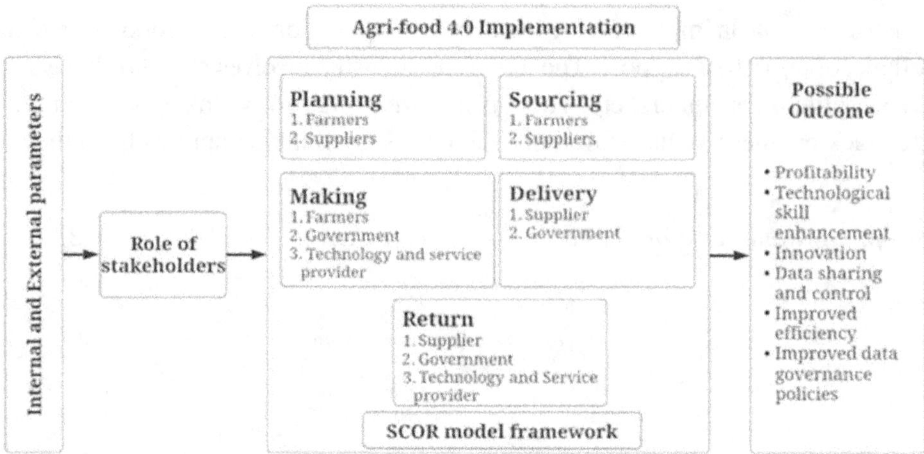

is used ethically and safely. It has been observed that the lack of infrastructure in rural areas is the main obstacle to increasing productivity. Therefore, the government should address the issue of high-speed internet in the agri-food sector and set regulations, rules and policies at related to the implementation of Industry 5.0 . also, collaboration among industry, government, suppliers and academia leads to more research as well as the development of relevant curricula and building effective strategies for the implementation of industry 5.0. Also, the organizations should ensure that all data is encrypted, that appropriate access controls are in place, and that any collaboration with other organizations is done securely. Figure 4, represents the conceptual framework for identifying recommendations from the literature and their classification based on the SCOR model.

OVERALL RECOMMENDATION

Short-term Recommendations

The agriculture industry faces various educational challenges as it involves a different types of educational backgrounds farmers or employees. As underdeveloped countries are facing problems to implement industry 5.0 effectively in the agri-food supply chain due to the paucity of technical knowledge, 'technological self-efficacy' is considered the most influential factor in industry 5.0 adoption. Therefore, it is recommended that there is a constant need to develop skills and knowledge among the local farmers and keep them up to date. The research findings indicate that knowledge training carries several risks, such as high investment, lack of awareness concerning technical developments and a fear of change. To avoid risks associated with the above recommendation, businesses should launch education programs in collaboration with suppliers, academics, and third-party companies, engage in business-to-business (B2B) networks, or the government's recognition of Industry 5.0 best practices.

Figure 4. Conceptual framework for recommendations based on the SCOR model (Author, 2022)

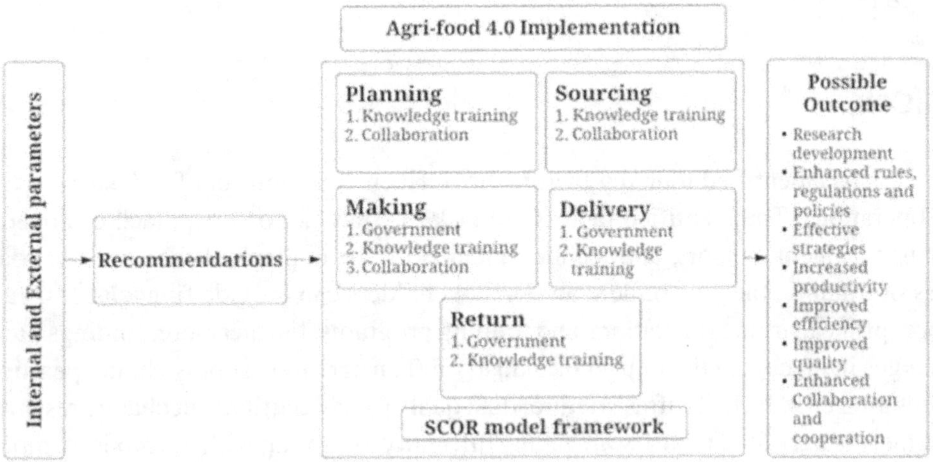

Medium-Term Recommendations

Several authors have already stressed the importance of system integration and interoperability in the reviewed literature. Lack of interoperability reduces the potential for efficiency when using software from multiple providers, as well as making it difficult to access the full range of data and insights that could be used to improve farming practices and make decisions. It also creates a barrier to adopting new technologies, as farmers may be discouraged from investing in solutions if they cannot easily integrate with existing software and systems. Therefore, it is recommended that, organizations must have interoperability in their systems to enhance the supply chain with greater agility, profitability, and resilience.

The research findings indicate that interoperability and infrastructure pose a significant risk of data authorization, identification, updating, and sharing. To avoid the such risk associated with the given recommendation, organizations should work closely with security experts to ensure that all data is collected, stored, and accessed securely. Additionally, organizations must also ensure that they comply with the law in terms of data privacy and security.

Long Term Recommendations

In agri-food industry, it is recommended that organizations must have clear and precise strategic plans for implementing industry 5.0 to ensure alignment with the technical, organizational, and operational characteristics of organization. To adopt industry 5.0 within agri-food sector, a strategic plan needs to be focused on not only the technology perspective, but also the social, cultural, and ecological perspective. Additionally, initiatives taken by the government, stakeholders, and organization itself should appear in long-term strategies.

The research findings indicate that disagreement among stakeholders may pose a significant risk. To avoid the risk associated with the given recommendations, it is necessary to build a strategy with the consensus of all the parties involved. This strategy should involve a comprehensive analysis of the risks and rewards associated with the suggested course of action and involve all stakeholders in the decision-making process.

CONCLUSION

Finding from SLR has identified four key factors that influence the impact of industry 5.0 on agri-food supply chain operations. The identified factors are lack of strategic roadmap, lack of government support, lack of management support, and technological skill. To implement the strategic roadmap, and provide pieces of training, the government and/or stakeholders can provide financial assistance as well as develop appropriate learning regulations and training programs. Furthermore, findings have indicated the four challenges in managing the impact of industry 5.0 on agri-food supply chain operations; such as high implementation cost, lack of infrastructure, data quality and security, and change resistance. As the majority of farmers in agri-food industry are facing difficulty to cope up with the modern implementation in the farm, change resistance and high investment cost due to the lack of knowledge regarding the ROI and the cost-benefit are identified as the most obvious challenge. The significant primary stakeholders identified are farmers, and the government and secondary stakeholders are suppliers, and technology and solution providers. It is acknowledged that the government plays a significant role among the sector's stakeholders in understanding the needs of the field and implementing appropriate regulations for farmers. It has been found that, the implementation of Industry 5.0 will also be aided by stakeholders' participation in bringing cutting-edge, cost-effective technology to the agri-food supply chains and in providing services to fix defects and maintain data. Finally, ta range of recommendations includes more government support and involving stakeholders to achieve the organizational goal. As a majority of the farmers are not financially capable and or technologically skilled, hence government supports the organization financially, developing initiatives to benefit the farmers, providing educational programmes, and formulating supportive policies.

RESEARCH LIMITATION AND FURTHER SCOPE

The most important limitation lies in the fact that the scarcity of peer-reviewed articles, as the research was conducted through a systematic literature review using a secondary research-based methodology. In addition, this study is limited by the lack of a comprehensive analytical literature review available on industry 4.0 or Industry 5.0 further research could also be conducted by utilizing the primary research methodologies.

REFERENCES

Aamer, A., Sahara, C. R., & Al-Awlaqi, M. A. (2022). Digitalization of the supply chain: transformation factors. *Journal of Science and Technology Policy Management*. doi:10.1108/JSTPM-01-2021-0001

Ada, N., Kazancoglu, Y., Sezer, M. D., Ede-Senturk, C., Ozer, I., & Ram, M. (2021). Analyzing Barriers of Circular Food Supply Chains and Proposing Industry 4.0 Solutions. *Sustainability, 13*(12), 6812. doi:10.3390u13126812

Aday, S., & Aday, M. S. (2020). Impacts of COVID-19 on Food Supply Chain. *Food Quality and Safety, 4*(4), 167–180. doi:10.1093/fqsafe/fyaa024

Agarwal, U., Rishiwal, V., Tanwar, S., Chaudhary, R., Sharma, G., Bokoro, P. N., & Sharma, R. (2022). Blockchain Technology for Secure Supply Chain Management: A Comprehensive Review. *IEEE Access: Practical Innovations, Open Solutions, 10*, 85493–85517. doi:10.1109/ACCESS.2022.3194319

Ageron, B., Bentahar, O., & Gunasekaran, A. (2020). Digital supply chain: challenges and future directions. *Supply Chain Forum: An International Journal, 21*(3), 133–138. Tandfonline. 10.1080/16258312.2020.1816361

Azzi, R., Chamoun, R. K., & Sokhn, M. (2019). The power of a blockchain-based supply chain. *Computers & Industrial Engineering, 135*, 582–592. doi:10.1016/j.cie.2019.06.042

Bertolozzi-Caredio, D., Bardají, I., Garrido, A., Berry, R., Bijttebier, J., Gavrilescu, C., Harizanova, H., Jendrzejewski, B., Meuwissen, M. M. P., Ollendorf, F., Pinsard, C., Rommel, J., Severini, S., & Soriano, B. (2021). Stakeholder perspectives to improve risk management in European farming systems. *Journal of Rural Studies, 84*, 147–161. doi:10.1016/j.jrurstud.2021.04.004

Bozarth, C. C., & Handfield, R. B. (2019). *Introduction to operations and supply chain management* (5th ed.). Pearson Education Limited.

Butt, J. (2020). A Strategic Roadmap for the Manufacturing Industry to Implement Industry 4.0. *Designs, 4*(2), 11. doi:10.3390/designs4020011

Büyüközkan, G., & Göçer, F. (2018). Digital Supply Chain: Literature review and a proposed framework for future research. *Computers in Industry, 97*, 157–177. doi:10.1016/j.compind.2018.02.010

Carver, J. C., Hassler, E., Hernandes, E., & Kraft, N. A. (2013). Identifying Barriers to the Systematic Literature Review Process. *2013 ACM / IEEE International Symposium on Empirical Software Engineering and Measurement.* ACM, IEEE. 10.1109/ESEM.2013.28

Chapman, J., Power, A., Netzel, M. E., Sultanbawa, Y., Smyth, H. E., Truong, V. K., & Cozzolino, D. (2021). Challenges and opportunities of the fourth revolution: A brief insight into the future of food. *Critical Reviews in Food Science and Nutrition*, 1–9. doi:10.1080/10408398.2020.1863328 PMID:33401934

Chauhan, C., & Singh, A. (2019). A review of Industry 4.0 in supply chain management studies. *Journal of Manufacturing Technology Management, 31*(5), 863–886. doi:10.1108/JMTM-04-2018-0105

Choi, Y.-H., & Choi, S.-H. (2018). A Study of Crossing the Chasm in applying Smart Factory System for SMEs. *International Journal of Pure and Applied Mathematics, 118*(19), 469–487. https://acadpubl.eu/jsi/2018-118-19/articles/19a/32.pdf

Dadi, V., Nikhil, S. R., Mor, R. S., Agarwal, T., & Arora, S. (2021). Agri-Food 4.0 and Innovations: Revamping the Supply Chain Operations. *Production Engineering Archives, 27*(2), 75–89. doi:10.30657/pea.2021.27.10

Dania, W. A. P., Xing, K., & Amer, Y. (2018). Collaboration behavioural factors for sustainable agri-food supply chains: A systematic review. *Journal of Cleaner Production*, *186*, 851–864. doi:10.1016/j.jclepro.2018.03.148

Deloitte. (2022). *2022 manufacturing industry outlook*. Deloitte. https://www2.deloitte.com/content/dam/Deloitte/us/Documents/energy-resources/us-2022-manufacturing-industry-outlook.pdf

Donaldson, D. A. (2021). Digital from farm to fork: Infrastructures of quality and control in food supply chains. *Journal of Rural Studies*. doi:10.1016/j.jrurstud.2021.10.004

Echegaray, N., Hassoun, A., Jagtap, S., Tetteh-Caesar, M., Kumar, M., Tomasevic, I., Goksen, G., & Lorenzo, J. M. (2022). Meat 4.0: Principles and Applications of Industry 4.0 Technologies in the Meat Industry. *Applied Sciences (Basel, Switzerland)*, *12*(14), 6986. doi:10.3390/app12146986

EIBIS. (2022). *Digitalisation in Europe 2021-2022*. EIB.org. https://www.eib.org/en/publications-research/economics/digitalisation-in-european-union.htm

European Commission. (2021) *Industry 5.0: Towards more sustainable, resilient and human-centric industry*. EC. https://research-and-innovation.ec.europa.eu/news/all-research-and-innovation-news/industry-50-towards-more-sustainable-resilient-and-human-centric-industry-2021-01-07_en

European Commission. (2022). *Human Capital and Digital Skills in the Digital Economy and Society Index | Shaping Europe's digital future*. Digital-Strategy. https://digital-strategy.ec.europa.eu/en/policies/desi-human-capital

Eurostat. (2022). *Government budget allocations for R&D (GBARD)*. Ec.europa.eu. https://ec.europa.eu/eurostat/statistics-explained/index.php?title=Government_budget_allocations_for_R%26D_(GBARD)&oldid=552767

FAO. (2022). *The State of Food and Agriculture 2022. Leveraging agricultural automation for transforming agrifood systems*. FAO. doi:10.4060/cb9479en

Felsberger, A., Qaiser, F. H., Choudhary, A., & Reiner, G. (2020). The impact of Industry 4.0 on the reconciliation of dynamic capabilities: Evidence from the European manufacturing industries. *Production Planning and Control*, *33*(2-3), 1–24. doi:10.1080/09537287.2020.1810765

Feng, H., Wang, X., Duan, Y., Zhang, J., & Zhang, X. (2020). Applying blockchain technology to improve agri-food traceability: A review of development methods, benefits and challenges. *Journal of Cleaner Production*, *260*, 121031. doi:10.1016/j.jclepro.2020.121031

Food and Agriculture Organization of the United Nations (FAO). (2020). *Status of Digital Agriculture in 18 countries of Europe and Central Asia International Telecommunication Union Development Sector*. ITUPublications. https://www.itu.int/en/ITU-D/Regional-Presence/Europe/Documents/Events/2020/Series%20of%20Webinars/20-00244_Status_digital_Agriculture-revFAOV4.0-MASTER-FILE-20-JUNE_REVIEW-FAO_PL_print%20%28002%29.pdf

Geissbauer, R., Lübben, E., Schrauf, S., & Pillsbury, S. (2018). *How industry leaders build integrated operations ecosystems to deliver end-to-end customer solutions*. Digital Champions. https://www.strategyand.pwc.com/gx/en/insights/industry4-0/global-digital-operations-study-digital-champions.pdf

Gupta, S., Drave, V. A., Bag, S., & Luo, Z. (2019). Leveraging Smart Supply Chain and Information System Agility for Supply Chain Flexibility. *Information Systems Frontiers*, *21*(3), 547–564. doi:10.100710796-019-09901-5

Hassoun, A., Aït-Kaddour, A., Abu-Mahfouz, A. M., Rathod, N. B., Bader, F., Barba, F. J., Biancolillo, A., Cropotova, J., Galanakis, C. M., Jambrak, A. R., Lorenzo, J. M., Måge, I., Ozogul, F., & Regenstein, J. (2022). The fourth industrial revolution in the food industry—Part I: Industry 4.0 technologies. *Critical Reviews in Food Science and Nutrition*, 1–17. doi:10.1080/10408398.2022.2034735 PMID:35114860

Heartland (2022) *Industry 5.0: The Bridge Between Capitalism And Sustainability*. Heartland. https://www.heartland.io/sustainability-news/industry-5-0-the-bridge-between-capitalism-and-sustainability/ (Accessed: 28 January 2023).

Hossain, S. T. (2020). Impacts of COVID-19 on the Agri-food Sector: Food Security Policies of Asian Productivity Organization Members. *Journal of Agricultural Sciences – Sri Lanka*, *15*(2), 116. doi:10.4038/jas.v15i2.8794

Hossein Ronaghi, M. (2020). A Blockchain Maturity Model in Agricultural Supply chain. *Information Processing in Agriculture*. doi:10.1016/j.inpa.2020.10.004

Hoyer, C., Gunawan, I., & Reaiche, C. H. (2020). The Implementation of Industry 4.0 - A Systematic Literature Review of the Key Factors. *Systems Research and Behavioral Science*, *37*(4), 557–578. doi:10.1002res.2701

Ivanov, D., Dolgui, A., & Sokolov, B. (2018). The impact of digital technology and Industry 4.0 on the ripple effect and supply chain risk analytics. *International Journal of Production Research*, *57*(3), 829–846. doi:10.1080/00207543.2018.1488086

Jacobs, F. R., & Chase, R. B. (2020). *Operations and Supply Chain Management* (16th ed.). Mcgraw-Hill Education.

Jagtap, S., Saxena, P., & Salonitis, K. (2021). Food 4.0: Implementation of the Augmented Reality Systems in the Food Industry. *Procedia CIRP*, *104*, 1137–1142. doi:10.1016/j.procir.2021.11.191

Joubert, R.-L., & Jokonya, O. (2021). A systematic literature review of factors affecting the adoption of technologies in food waste management. *Procedia Computer Science*, *181*, 1034–1040. doi:10.1016/j.procs.2021.01.298

JuhaniS. (2022). The Role Of Information Technology In Influencing Digitalization Of Contemporary Businesses. A Conceptual Review Of Literature. Https://Doi.Org/10.5281/Zenodo.6553360

Kamble, S. S., Gunasekaran, A., & Gawankar, S. A. (2020). Achieving sustainable performance in a data-driven agriculture supply chain: A review for research and applications. *International Journal of Production Economics*, *219*, 179–194. doi:10.1016/j.ijpe.2019.05.022

Khin, S., & Kee, D. M. H. (2022). Factors influencing Industry 4.0 adoption. *Journal of Manufacturing Technology Management*. doi:10.1108/JMTM-03-2021-0111

Kitchenham, B., Pearl Brereton, O., Budgen, D., Turner, M., Bailey, J., & Linkman, S. (2009). Systematic literature reviews in software engineering – A systematic literature review. *Information and Software Technology*, *51*(1), 7–15. doi:10.1016/j.infsof.2008.09.009

Kittipanya-ngam, P., & Tan, K. H. (2019). A framework for food supply chain digitalization: Lessons from Thailand. *Production Planning and Control*, *31*(2-3), 158–172. doi:10.1080/09537287.2019.1631462

KPMG. (2018). *A reality check for today's C-suite on Industry 4.0*. KPMG. https://assets.kpmg/content/dam/kpmg/xx/pdf/2018/11/a-reality-check-for-todays-c-suite-on-industry-4-0.pdf

Kumar, V., Shankar, R., & Vrat, P. (2021). An analysis of Industry 4.0 implementation-variables by using SAP-LAP and e-IRP approach. *Benchmarking*. doi:10.1108/BIJ-03-2021-0153

Lezoche, M., Hernandez, J. E., Alemany Díaz, M., Panetto, H., & Kacprzyk, J. (2020). Agri-food 4.0: A survey of the supply chains and technologies for the future agriculture. *Computers in Industry*, *117*, 103187. doi:10.1016/j.compind.2020.103187

Liu, Y., Ma, X., Shu, L., Hancke, G. P., & Abu-Mahfouz, A. M. (2021). From Industry 4.0 to Agriculture 4.0: Current Status, Enabling Technologies, and Research Challenges. *IEEE Transactions on Industrial Informatics*, *17*(6), 4322–4334. doi:10.1109/TII.2020.3003910

Majumdar, A., Garg, H., & Jain, R. (2020). Managing the barriers of Industry 4.0 adoption and implementation in textile and clothing industry: Interpretive structural model and triple helix framework. *Computers in Industry*, *103372*. doi:10.1016/j.compind.2020.103372

Manavalan, E., & Jayakrishna, K. (2019). A review of Internet of Things (IoT) embedded sustainable supply chain for industry 4.0 requirements. *Computers & Industrial Engineering*, *127*(1), 925–953. doi:10.1016/j.cie.2018.11.030

Massaro, A., & Galiano, A. (2020). Re-engineering process in a food factory: An overview of technologies and approaches for the design of pasta production processes. *Production & Manufacturing Research*, *8*(1), 80–100. doi:10.1080/21693277.2020.1749180

Mayer, B., Sorko, S. R., & Pessl, E. (2017). Roadmap Industry 4.0 – Implementation Guideline for Enterprises. International Journal of Science. *Technology in Society*, *5*(6), 193. doi:10.11648/j.ijsts.20170506.14

McKinsey Digital. (2016). *Industry 4.0 after the initial hype Where manufacturers are finding value and how they can best capture it*. McKinsey. https://www.mckinsey.com/~/media/mckinsey/business%20functions/mckinsey%20digital/our%20insights/getting%20the%20most%20out%20of%20industry%204%200/mckinsey_industry_40_2016.ashx

Mithas, S., Chen, Z., Saldanha, T., & De Oliveira Silveira, A. (2022). How will artificial intelligence and industry 4.0 emerging technologies transform operations management? *Production and Operations Management*, *31*(12), 4475–4487. doi:10.1111/poms.13864

Mohamed, M. (2019). Challenges and Benefits of Industry 4.0: An overview. *International Journal of Supply and Operations Management*, *5*(3), 256–265. doi:10.22034/2018.3.7

Moktadir, M., Ali, S. M., Kusi-Sarpong, S., & Shaikh, M. A. A. (2018). Assessing challenges for implementing Industry 4.0: Implications for process safety and environmental protection. *Process Safety and Environmental Protection*, *117*, 730–741. doi:10.1016/j.psep.2018.04.020

Morakanyane, R., Grace, A., & O'Reilly, P. (2017, January 1). Conceptualizing Digital Transformation in Business Organizations: A Systematic Review of Literature. *BLED 2017 Proceedings*. AIS eLibrary. https://aisel.aisnet.org/bled2017/21

Nahavandi, S. (2019). Industry 5.0—A Human-Centric Solution. *Multidisciplinary Digital Publishing Institute*, *11*(16), 4371. doi:10.3390u11164371

NC State University. (2004) *The SCOR Model for Supply Chain Strategic Decisions | SCM | Supply Chain Resource Cooperative (SCRC)*. North Carolina State University. https://scm.ncsu.edu/scm-articles/article/the-scor-model-for-supply-chain-strategic-decisions

Nestle. (2020, July 24). *Nestlé speeds up factory support with augmented reality*. Nestlé Global. https://www.nestle.com/media/news/nestle-factory-support-augmented-reality

Nimawat, D., & Gidwani, B. D. (2021). Identification of cause and effect relationships among barriers of Industry 4.0 using decision-making trial and evaluation laboratory method. *Benchmarking*, *28*(8), 2407–2431. doi:10.1108/BIJ-08-2020-0429

Oliveira-Dias, D., Maqueira-Marín, J. M., & Moyano-Fuentes, J. (2022). The link between information and digital technologies of industry 4.0 and agile supply chain: Mapping current research and establishing new research avenues. *Computers & Industrial Engineering*, *167*, 108000. doi:10.1016/j.cie.2022.108000

Parhi, S., Joshi, K., Wuest, T., & Akarte, M. (2022). Factors Affecting Industry 4.0 Adoption - A Hybrid SEM-ANN Approach. *Computers & Industrial Engineering*, *108062*, 108062. doi:10.1016/j.cie.2022.108062

Pereira, A. C., & Romero, F. (2017). A review of the meanings and the implications of the Industry 4.0 concept. *Procedia Manufacturing*, *13*, 1206–1214. doi:10.1016/j.promfg.2017.09.032

Porter, M. E., & Heppelmann, J. E. (2017, March 17). How Smart, Connected Products Are Transforming Competition. *Harvard Business Review*. https://hbr.org/2014/11/how-smart-connected-products-are-transforming-competition

Radnor, Z. J., & Barnes, D. (2007). Historical analysis of performance measurement and management in operations management. *International Journal of Productivity and Performance Management*, *56*(5/6), 384–396. doi:10.1108/17410400710757105

Raj, A., Dwivedi, G., Sharma, A., Lopes de Sousa Jabbour, A. B., & Rajak, S. (2020). Barriers to the adoption of industry 4.0 technologies in the manufacturing sector: An inter-country comparative perspective. *International Journal of Production Economics*, *224*(1), 107546. doi:10.1016/j.ijpe.2019.107546

Rashid, A., & Tjahjono, B. (2016). Achieving manufacturing excellence through the integration of enterprise systems and simulation. *Production Planning and Control*, *27*(10), 837–852. doi:10.1080/09537287.2016.1143132

Rejeb, A., Rejeb, K., & Zailani, S. (2021). Big data for sustainable agri-food supply chains: A review and future research perspectives. Journal of Data. *Information & Management*, *3*(3), 167–182. doi:10.100742488-021-00045-3

Rimol, M. (2022). Infrastructure Automation and Predictions for 2022. *Gartner*. https://www.gartner.com/en/articles/4-predictions-for-i-o-leaders-on-the-path-to-digital-infrastructure

Rodríguez, M. Á., Alemany, M. M. E., Boza, A., Cuenca, L., & Ortiz, Á. (2020). Artificial Intelligence in Supply Chain Operations Planning: Collaboration and Digital Perspectives. *Boosting Collaborative Networks*, *4*(0), 365–378. doi:10.1007/978-3-030-62412-5_30

Rüßmann, M., Lorenz, M., Gerbert, P., Waldner, M., Justus, J., Engel, P., & Harnisch, M. (2015). *Industry 4.0: The Future of Productivity and Growth in Manufacturing Industries*. Inovasyon. https://inovasyon.org/images/Haberler/bcgperspectives_Industry40_2015.pdf

Sagi, V., & Gokarn, S. (2022). Determinants of reduction of food loss and waste in Indian agri-food supply chains for ensuring food security: A multi-stakeholder perspective. *Waste Management & Research: The Journal for a Sustainable Circular Economy*, 0734242X2211264. doi:10.1177/0734242X221126421

Sahoo, S., & Lo, C.-Y. (2022). Smart manufacturing powered by recent technological advancements: A review. *Journal of Manufacturing Systems*, *64*, 236–250. doi:10.1016/j.jmsy.2022.06.008

Sayem, A., Biswas, P. K., Khan, M. M. A., Romoli, L., & Dalle Mura, M. (2022). Critical Barriers to Industry 4.0 Adoption in Manufacturing Organizations and Their Mitigation Strategies. *Journal of Manufacturing and Materials Processing*, *6*(6), 136. doi:10.3390/jmmp6060136

Slack, N., Jones, A. B., & Burgess, N. (2022). *SLACK: operations management* (10th ed.). Pearson Education Limited.

Sony, M. (2020). Pros and cons of implementing Industry 4.0 for the organizations: a review and synthesis of evidence. *Production & Manufacturing Research, 8*(1), 244–272. Tandfonline. doi:10.1080/21693277.2020.1781705

Sony, M., & Naik, S. (2019a). Key ingredients for evaluating Industry 4.0 readiness for organizations: A literature review. *Benchmarking*, *27*(7), 2213–2232. doi:10.1108/BIJ-09-2018-0284

Spanaki, K., Karafili, E., & Despoudi, S. (2021). AI applications of data sharing in agriculture 4.0: A framework for role-based data access control. *International Journal of Information Management*, *59*, 102350. doi:10.1016/j.ijinfomgt.2021.102350

Sundarakani, B., Abdul Razzak, H., & Manikandan, S. (2018). Creating a competitive advantage in the global flight catering supply chain: A case study using SCOR model. *International Journal of Logistics Research and Applications*, *21*(5), 481–501. doi:10.1080/13675567.2018.1448767

Syngenta. (2021). *Syngenta Crop Protection and Insilico Medicine to harness artificial intelligence to transform sustainable product innovation.* Syngenta. https://www.syngenta.com/en/company/media/syngenta-news/year/2021/syngenta-crop-protection-and-insilico-medicine-harness

Szabo, R. Z., Vuksanović Herceg, I., Hanák, R., Hortovanyi, L., Romanová, A., Mocan, M., & Djuričin, D. (2020). Industry 4.0 Implementation in B2B Companies: Cross-Country Empirical Evidence on Digital Transformation in the CEE Region. *Sustainability*, *12*(22), 9538. doi:10.3390u12229538

The world bank. (2021, July 1). *Digital Agricultural Profiles for Argentina, Kenya, Turkey, and Vietnam.* World Bank. https://www.worldbank.org/en/topic/agriculture/publication/digital-agricultural-profiles-for-argentina-kenya-turkey-and-viet-nam

Vantage Market. (2021). *Digital Agriculture Market Size USD 22.1 Billion by 2028.* Vantage Market Research. https://www.vantagemarketresearch.com/industry-report/digital-agriculture-market-1751

Xu, L. D., Xu, E. L., & Li, L. (2018). Industry 4.0: State of the art and future trends. *International Journal of Production Research*, *56*(8), 2941–2962. doi:10.1080/00207543.2018.1444806

Yadav, V. S., Singh, A. R., Raut, R. D., Kumar Mangla, S., Luthra, S., & Kumar, A. (2022). Exploring the application of Industry 4.0 technologies in the agricultural food supply chain: A systematic literature review. *Computers & Industrial Engineering*, *108304*, 108304. doi:10.1016/j.cie.2022.108304

Zhang, J. Y., Pandya, J. K., McClements, D. J., Lu, J., & Kinchla, A. J. (2021). Advancements in 3D food printing: A comprehensive overview of properties and opportunities. *Critical Reviews in Food Science and Nutrition*, 1–18. doi:10.1080/10408398.2021.1878103 PMID:33533641

Zhao, G., Liu, S., Wang, Y., Lopez, C., Zubairu, N., Chen, X., Xie, X., & Zhang, J. (2022). Modelling enablers for building agri-food supply chain resilience: Insights from a comparative analysis of Argentina and France. *Production Planning and Control*, 1–25. doi:10.1080/09537287.2022.2078246

Zhou, K., Liu, T., & Zhou, L. (2015). Industry 4.0: Towards future industrial opportunities and challenges. *2015 12th International Conference on Fuzzy Systems and Knowledge Discovery (FSKD)*. FSKD. 10.1109/FSKD.2015.7382284

KEY TERMS AND DEFINITIONS

Artificial Intelligence: The term artificial intelligence (AI) refers to cognitive processes and specially to reasoning (Spanaki et al., 2021).

Blockchain: A blockchain is a distributed ledger of digital transactions, which is maintained by multiple computers that is not reliant on third party (Kamilaris et al., 2019).

Industry 5.0: A key component of Industry 5.0 is the convergence of smart manufacturing and products, and the Internet of Things (IoT), and human, social, environmental and sustainability aspects and then using real-time data about the production, machines, and component flow (Chauhan & Singh, 2019).

Internet of Things: In a digital world, the Internet of Things enables things to communicate and interact, providing an accurate representation of the real world to aid development (Dadi et al., 2021).

Operations: "The operations function is the collection of people, technology, and systems within an organization that has primary responsibility for providing the organization's products or services," (Bozarth and Handfield, 2019, p.23)."

SCOR Model: The SCOR model is the most comprehensive standard which involves five processes such as plan make, source, deliver, and return (Bozarth & Handfield, 2019).

Supply Chain Management: Supply chain management facilitates the flow of goods and services to and from organizations and individuals as they need them (Choi et al., 2021).

Chapter 8
Industry 5.0 and Environmental, Social, and Governance Initiatives in Supply Chain Sustainability:
A Study of the European Fast Fashion Industry

Anguselvam Sekaran
Northumbria University, London, UK

Sumesh Singh Dadwal
London South Bank University, UK

Adbul Ali
https://orcid.org/0000-0002-3034-8628
University of Greenwich, UK

ABSTRACT

Industry 5.0 requires an organisation to maintain supply chain sustainability by using environmental, social, and governance (ESG) initiatives, thus avoiding social, environmental, ethical, or other risks. This chapter explores the factors, processes, and impacts of the use of ESG framework in sustainability throughout supply chain management. The development of this research shows the European fast fashion industry, which had invested in ESG initiatives to maintain sustainability standards across their whole supply chain operations of the European fast fashion market.

DOI: 10.4018/978-1-6684-6403-8.ch008

INTRODUCTION

There have been a lot of discussions on industry 5, people are wondering what is next. whereas industry 4.0, had focused on the use of technology such as AI, blockchain, Internet of Things etc in the industries; on the other hand industry 5 gives a humanistic twist to machine dependant industry 4.0. Industry 5 involves our leap into merging the themes of technology, human, Society, environment, sustainability etc. in any industrial revolution, the role of the supply chain is very significant. and in industry 5.0, it will be all about embedding environmental social and governance initiatives in technologically innovative supply chain management.

An organisation focusing on developing the Environmental, Social and Governance (ESG) initiative offers to represent the behaviour of following a set of standards by which they can maintain their socially conscious image in front of the investors and the customers. Kotsantonis and Serafeim (2019) stated that ESG initiative factors maintain some environmental criteria by which the organisation can safeguard the environment while operating in the international and regional market, which also include some corporate policies that indicate the steps toward climate change. Li, et al. (2021) have stated that waste management is also considered another influential factor in ESG initiatives due to increasing pollution in the world that creates an impact on human lifestyle in different countries. The European fast fashion industry has been creating a significant impact on the overall business industry in terms of revenue.

In Europe, companies like Zara, H&M, and many others significantly adopted the trend of fast fashion, not only increasing sales but also increasing the volume of solid waste generated from textile manufacturing. This factor influences the requirement of implementing environmental measures in the overall supply chain of the fast fashion industry in Europe, which will eventually lead to environmental well-being and satisfy governmental legislations for the environment. Pedersen, et al. (2021) connotes that waste management refers to the utilisation of waste materials generated in an industry, or a company based on recycling or reusing for similar or different purposes, which helps to reduce the volume of landfills and wastes. In this context, the ESG initiative includes an investment in waste management that not only helps to reduce environmental impact but also reduce the costs of raw materials through recycling. Moreover, managing the overall supply chain, including manufacturing, packaging, and delivering the products, is considered essential as it helps to reduce carbon footprint and waste generation. In this regard, ESG investment helps to measure and enhance supply chain activities based on the requirements, which eventually increases the sustainability of the overall supply chain.

This chapter investigates the current strategies and methods used by the fast fashion sector to function according to the EU rules and regulations of climate change and sustainability in line with the ESG framework. It explores the factors, challenges, good practices and key stakeholders that influence ESG initiatives and; consequently the impact of ESG initiatives on supply chain sustainability in the European fast fashion industry.

The utilisation of ESG proposition helps to reduce energy consumption and water intake, which offers companies in the fast fashion industry to decrease the overall operational cost. Phillips, Thai and Halim (2019), argued that an organisation maintaining sustainability in its supply chain focuses on developing greater freedom in the static degradation by using deregulation, by which they can earn government support and subsidies. By using ESG initiatives any organisation can easily enhance the motivation level of the employees (Sachin and Rajesh 2022). The companies are focusing on using advantages from the supplier, compliance, and increased visibility by which the companies can easily promote their organisational operation in an eco-friendly manner Stranieri *et al.* (2019), Therefore, it not only showcases the overall progress in environmental gratification but also creates a better image that can attract customers and investors to a greater extent by prioritising ESG initiatives in the supply chain.

In addition, Dimson et al. (2020) stated that social initiatives in the context of ESG initiatives include equality and diversity, human rights for the labours, data security, and long-term customer satisfaction. Governance, on the other hand, in terms of ESG initiatives, includes diversity among the board members, contributions in politics, large-scale lawsuits, internal corruption, lobbying, and executive pay that are to be monitored significantly in the company.

In the context of the supply chain of an organisation, it has been identified that ESG initiatives are able to implement a regulatory framework according to the requirements, which eventually leads towards aligning the supply and demand of the company. The ESG investment also helps to maintain both internal and external logistics in different countries according to the legislation, which eventually helps to protect the environment as well as societal concerns in different areas accordingly. Hence, the investors of different companies have become significantly concerned about ESG as it will help to get governmental support and lead towards profitability.

RESEARCH METHODOLOGY FOR DEVELOPING THIS CHAPTER

A systematic Literature review is sued to develop this chapter. a Systematic Literature Review (SLR) is a process for systematically, transparently, identifying and analysing sling all studies on a certain topic, collecting several points of view on the same issues, to see the larger picture in both good and negative studies (Nightingale (2009). The study researched themes of sustainability, Supply chain management, and ESG initiatives. The various sources that have been used to collect data are related articles, research work and authentic websites that are related to the fast fashion industry. The researcher has taken care in the way of using journals and articles of illegal publication. Moreover, the researcher has also only authentic websites. The researcher in collecting secondary data aims to collect all the relevant information from the research works that have been done previously on the same topic. This is the way through which the researcher has identified whether high-quality research on the same topic has been carried out previously. The researchers have followed thematic analysis to interpret the qualitative data that have been collected from the literature review.

SYSTEMATIC LITERATURE REVIEW INDUSTRY 5.0 ESG AND SCM

To date the five in this revolution revolutions has been noted. the first industrial revolution (the 1780s) was that of mechanizing; was about enhancing production using factories supported by steam and diesel engines; Secind industrial revolution commenced with electrification (1870); which involved the use of electricity-based machinery; code industrial revolution started in in the 1970s with the evolution of computers and automation of production plants; the fourth industrial revolution or industry 4.0 (2010-) is all about digitalization and embedding technology in the process of production; and the 5th industrial revolution that is industry 5 (2020-) is all about linking technology driven production plus processes and supply chain with elements of environment social governance and human beings (Heartland, 2022).

ESG refers to the Environmental, Social, and Governance of an organisation, and is defined as the collection of standards regarding organisational behaviour that help investors to identify potential benefits related to metrics related to ESG (Gillan et al., 2021). It includes regulatory frameworks for protecting the environment and social factors by an organisation to develop a significant brand image along with increasing awareness to create a better world with the help of other companies. For example, green energy management, waste management, employee diversity, data security, human rights, etc., are significant ESG initiatives that help to protect the environmental and social concerns of the companies. The research revealed that the number of studies related to ESG has increased since the year 2019-2020), since the inception of the idea of industry 5.0 in the year 2020 and 2021 more than 60+ studies were carried out.

Tabular Systematic Findings From Literature Sources

The literature review also found several themes related to sustainability that have appeared in the selected samples of research papers. Most of the recent researchers were exploratory approaches the key aspects of the recent findings have been summarised in Table 1.

Table 1. Systematic findings from some of the literature sources

Sl. No.	Authors and origin	Purpose	Study design	Sample and data source	Key findings
1.	(Li et al., 2021)	To understand the future prospects of sustainability.	Descriptive	The statistical analysis is done by procuring the numerical data from secondary sources.	Sustainability issues are the main factor in the future, and all businesses must ensure the same in order to ensure the right kind of progress.
2.	(Chen and Xie, 2022)	To find out the environmental sustainability goals and its overall disclosure of financial performance.	Exploratory	The statistical analysis using financial performance and aligns them individually with the ESG.	It helps in understanding the role of ESG investors in general and how their role impacts the overall ESG disclosure and the financial performance connected with the same.
3.	(Jacobs et al., 2019)	The aspects of manufacturing planning and control for the supply chain management.	Explanatory	Qualitative.	The findings from the study constitute the planning and controlling process within the supply chain industryand the methods by which the control within the supply chain is established and strategies connected with the same.
4.	(Yu et al., 2019)	The aspects like dynamism, disruption orientation, and resilience within the supply chain.	Exploratory	The analysis is a mix of qualitative and quantitative.	The disruption is often created within the supply chain due to technological differences, and dynamism and resilience build the financial capabilities of the firm.
5.	(Avramov et al. 2022)	Sustainable investing, along with the uncertainty of ESG.	Exploratory	The research is mainly a mix of qualitative and quantitative analysis.	Sustainable investmentand, the uncertainty that is associated with the problem, and the overall financial performance
6.	(Gillan et al., 2021)	Review of ESG and CSR research in the matters of corporate finance.	Exploratory	Qualitative SLR	Understanding the factors that are related to the development of a condition that is associated with the comparison of ESG aspects with CSR research as a whole.
7.	(Dimson et al., 2020)	The divergent perspectives of ESG ratings.	Descriptive	The research is qualitative the descriptive	The development of ESG ratings, and its rules and regulations.
8.	(Pedersen et al. 2021)	Investing with responsibility and efficient in connection with ESG.	Explanatory	The description qualitative,	The development of various patterns, which are linked with the overall aspects of ESG.
9.	(Cook et al., 2018)	Utilisation of two-way theory for influencing the changing behaviour	Descriptive	Qualitative.	Understading on the changes in health behaviour and how such behaviour is connected with the aspects of sustainability.
10.	(Zhuang et al., 2019)	The role of stakeholders in the urban renewal of China.	Exploratory	The qualitative research	The factors of sustainability within the urban renewal projects and also considering the role of stakeholders in doing the same in the aspect of China.

Concept of Environment, Social, and Governance (ESG) Initiatives

Environment, social, and governance (ESG) are defined as the set of regulatory standards followed by an organisation in terms of safeguarding the environment, climate change, and social concerns, including discrimination, disruption of human rights, and many others (see figure 1) (Li et al., 2021). Investing in these initiatives is considered one of the beneficial steps to be taken by an organisation to increase competency and contribute to overall well-being in society. These are the non-financial factors that allow the investors to conduct a significant analysis process in terms of identifying growth opportunities and possible risks that might occur in different stages.

Figure 1. ESG initiatives implemented by companies or industries (by authors)

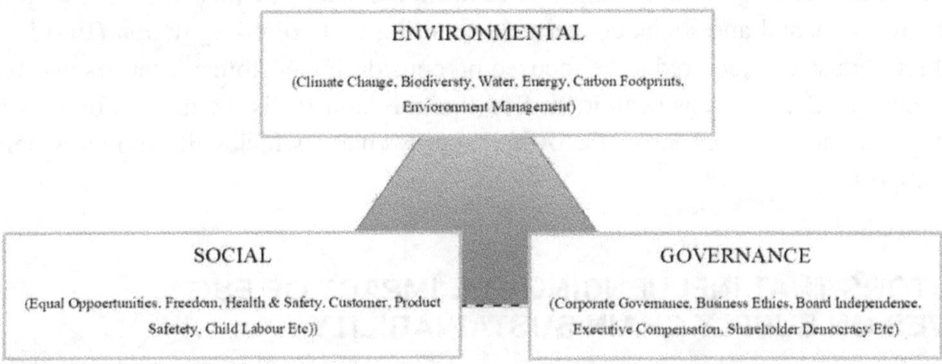

ESG initiatives are the main categories in areas, such as environmental and societal, that indicate how business organisations have the potential to establish well-being in society (Chen & Xie, 2022). Governing is also an important step as it indicates the companies are providing transparency regarding the initiatives followed all over the supply chain in different areas. According to Avramov et al. (2022), the environmental initiatives of ESG majorly include air and water pollution, initiatives for green energy, deforestation, waste management, controlling carbon emission, and other environmental protection measures that lead towards sustainability.

Scope of the European Fast Fashion Industry in Terms of Supply Chain

In the contemporary business industry, fast fashion has become one of the significant trends in the fashion industry that replicates recent trends of catwalks and high-fashion designs, which are adopted by the mass production team of the companies. This industry produces the designs quickly and showcases them in retail stores, which not only attracts a lot of customers but also significantly boosts the overall profitability of the company through increased sales. It has been identified that the European fast fashion industry has emerged with the help of increasing online shopping, which helped to attract and reach a lot of customers along with enhancing the supply chain. In Europe, the fast fashion industry is closely related to the high street commercial areas that include mass market retailers who can sell bulk orders to customers (Euronews, 2022). The industry not only aims to execute mass-market delivery of the products but also leads towards a sustainable way of reducing the environmental impact regarding waste management.

According to Jacobs et al. (2019), the supply chain is defined as the set of activities or components of an organisation that are responsible for delivering the final products of an organisation from the collection of raw materials. It is one of the most vital parts of a business as it helps to reach the end customers with the help of different necessary activities. Furthermore, the fast fashion industry involves different stages of clothing manufacturing along with delivery, which allows the companies to deliver actual products to the customers (Yu et al., 2019. In this regard, it has been identified that the fast fashion industry is required to implement different types of ESG initiatives to sustain the overall industry in the countries. The fast fashion industry in Europe has developed a significant supply chain as the quick delivery of fashion products is considered a significant factor as the industry is based on delivering the products from the catwalk into mass retailing. Fast fashion retailers in Europe have included low-cost materials in the industry with the help of comparing slower fashion concepts, which are required to be protected in terms of environmental and social concerns. According to Textile Regulation (EU) No 1007/2011, the fast fashion industry is required to be focused on considering customer interests and functioning in the market (Europa, 2022). It has been identified that the industry is required to be focused on social as well as environmental factors across the overall supply chain., which will eventually help to get governmental support.

THE FACTORS THAT INFLUENCING THE IMPACT OF ESG INITIATIVES ON SUPPLY CHAIN SUSTAINABILITY

The impact of ESG initiatives is significantly based on organisational behaviours in the industry, which lead towards the overall sustainability of the industry regarding the delivery of the product. According to Avramov et al. (2022), there are several factors related to environmental and social activities in the industry, which lead towards satisfying legal frameworks of different countries regarding the activities involved in the supply chain. The key factors that influence ESG activities on the sustainability of the supply chain are based on three categories, such as environmental, social, and governance. The environmental factors include the conservation of natural resources, carbon emission, climate change, and environmental pollution that concern governments and companies. The social factors include consideration of people and relationships, data protection and privacy, human rights, and customer satisfaction that influence ESG initiatives in supply chain sustainability. Composition of the board, committee structure audit, and standards to be followed in terms of governing that play an integral role in maintaining the overall sustainability of the supply chain in an appropriate direction.

Environmental Factors Influencing ESG Initiatives in an Organisation

According to Gillan et al. (2021), climate change is considered one of the most impactful factors in human history as well as the economy as it creates an impact on organisational activities regarding the contribution towards the environment as a necessity. The regulatory frameworks of European climate law indicate that EU countries are required to cut off greenhouse gas emissions and carbon footprint by around 55% by 2030 (Europa, 2022). Based on the report of the United Nations Environment Programme, it has also been identified that the cost of adopting climate change might increase up to $500 billion per year by 2050, which is to concern different companies (UNEP, 2022). Hence, different industries are required to adopt ESG initiatives to reduce costs and focus on contributing towards overall environmental well-being. For example, the fast fashion industry in Europe made an initiative to integrate eco-design and the use of 100% sustainable materials in clothes by 2030, which indicates a significant response to climate change (The Guardian, 2022). This initiative not only helps to reduce the carbon footprint of the industry but also reduces the expenses of further integration regarding environmental control.

Social Factors Influencing ESG Initiatives On Supply Chain Sustainability

According to Dimson et al. (2020), social factors like discrimination, human rights, relation with the stakeholders, and workplace conditions influence the integration of ESG initiatives in an industry, which lead to a sustainable supply chain. Discrimination is one of the significant social factors that disrupt the quality of the workforce in an organisation as it disrupts equal treatment to all the individuals involved in an industry or workplace. It has been identified that the fast fashion industry has been exploiting black or brown women with commercials or other marketing strategies, which created a social impact on the industry (The Guardian, 2022). ESG initiatives are required to be focused on anti-discrimination regarding age, race, culture, gender, or any other factor that creates a negative societal impact. Human rights in terms of employee management or customer relations are also necessary factors to be integrated into the industry, which helps to provide equal treatment to all the people involved (Li et al. (2021). This factor helps to integrate supply chain sustainability in the fast fashion industry with the help of social well-being as the factors related to human rights influence ESG in the fast fashion industry. Thus maintaining a relationship with the stakeholders is an important factor that influences ESG initiatives that help the companies to get the required investment for enhancing sustainability in the overall supply chain (Pedersen et al. (2021). This factor is also required to be acknowledged by the companies like Zara, H&M, and other clothing retailers that are involved in the fast fashion industry in Europe.

Governance Factors Initiatives Of ESG in the Supply Chain

Supply chain sustainability has a significant area of monitoring the initiatives in terms of governing as it helps to assure the management regarding the implementation of sustainability. It majorly includes a set of standards that are responsible for maintaining a regulatory framework in the overall supply chain of the company based on the standards of the country Jacobs et al. (2019), According to contingency leadership theory, it has been identified that adopting contemporary industrial factors, including economy, social factors, and many others, is essential for leaders to take necessary precautions to avoid threats. In this regard, the fast fashion industry in Europe is majorly based on providing clothes quickly to customers, which requires different regulations to be followed, including packaging, materials of the clothes, and many others.

Governing initiatives, according to ESG investment, is beneficial to monitor the integration of frameworks to be followed to ensure an appropriate response to society as well as the environment. For example, manufacturers of fast fashion in Europe are required to ensure that the clothes are eco-friendly as well as hard-wearing, which will be reusable and reduce environmental impact in the textile industry (BBC, 2022). Also, consumers should be given more information about how to recycle, repair, and reuse the clothes of the fast fashion industry, which will help to increase sustainability in terms of reducing the environmental impact of the industry. These factors are considered the regulations to be maintained in the industry by governing, which are to be maintained through ESG initiatives in the industry. Li, et al. (2021) also connote that maintaining employee relations through equality and diversity are also significant parts of social factors in the industry, which are to be maintained by the companies. Governing initiatives include centralised communication for all the employees, gathering responses from all the employees, performance, and customer satisfaction, which help to identify how the social factors are integrated into the companies. For example, the corporate governance department of Zara helps to safeguard the commitments of the group towards their employees and customers to maintain ESG initiatives in a social context (Inditex, 2022). This factor indicates the importance of governing initiatives to be implemented in the fast fashion industry of Europe, which allows different companies to invest in ESG initiatives and satisfy governmental as well as social factors in the industry.

Challenges in managing ESG Initiatives in Supply Chain Sustainability

There are several challenges to be during the integration of ESG initiatives in a company or an industry, including lack of knowledge, investment, workforce, and many others (Chen & Xie, 2022). The investors have been able to increase their sustainability assets with an estimation of reaching 47% by 2025, which aims to establish a sustainable supply chain and business functionalities. Several challenges might take place, including the transition of a portfolio that indicates specific requirements in terms of financial and social impact.

The collecting and evaluation of appropriate data by the stakeholders are considered another essential step to be followed in the context of ESG initiatives, which leads to appropriate decision-making (Gillan, et al., 2021). The sustainability metrics, such as carbon emission, waste generation, energy consumption, and many others shall allow the stakeholders to identify the business scenario and invest in ESG initiatives accordingly. In this process, potential challenges may include a lack of appropriate information that might create an impact on the decision-making of ESG initiatives, which would disrupt supply chain sustainability in the fast fashion industry of Europe. Dimson et al. (2020) also stated that choosing the right products to be delivered is considered another significant challenge as the availability and requirement of sustainable products have emerged in the industry. In Europe, there are 50 new exchangeable traded funds introduced in terms of ESG initiatives that allowed different industries to focus on the usability of raw materials and other environmental concerns (Financial Times, 2022). This factor has created a significant challenge for the fast fashion industry in Europe as the availability of many sustainable products causes a lack of proper direction for the investors to lead.

Emerging climate protection trends are considered another challenge to adopting sustainable supply chains in the fast fashion industry of Europe, where investors are required to consider different incorporation of climate considerations. According to system theory, any complex functionality such as SCM involves different small activities that are categorised into three different types, such as input, process, and output, that are modified according to feedback generated by those (Cook et al., 2018). In this regard, emerging climate trends include different smaller entities, such as waste management, carbon emission, energy consumption, and environmental regulations that are to be maintained by the companies. In the European fast fashion industry, the government has estimated that all clothes will be made of recycled materials by 2050 (DW, 2022). Moreover, the European climate act is considered another factor to be instigated in by the ESG initiatives to establish a sustainable supply chain in the fast fashion industry. Collaborating and managing all the requirements is considered a significant challenge for the industry that might disrupt the overall results of sustainability in the industry.

Chen and Xie (2022) also stated that company engagement with multiple stakeholders and the global industry is also a significant challenge, as a lack of collaboration lead to uncertainty regarding long-term benefits. Investors are required to focus on company engagement before investing in ESG initiatives in order to ensure sustainable fund providence in the industry. Lack of engagement with other companies also causes another challenge of lack of brand image in the industry that reduces customer engagement as a vital aspect of social consideration through ESG. Hence, these challenges are to be acknowledged and mitigated by the management

THE GOOD PRACTICES IN MANAGING THE IMPACT OF ESG INITIATIVES ON THE SUSTAINABILE SUPPLY CHAIN

The integration and management of ESG initiatives in an organisation or industry involve different practices and steps that are responsible for establishing a sustainable supply chain, which majorly includes different steps to be maintained (Pedersen et al., 2021).The steps include the identification of the right approach for the company, identifying stakeholders through evaluating engagement, assessment of materiality, establishing governance, integration of ESG in strategy, reporting frameworks, and ESG research. These steps are beneficial to maintain the overall requirements of the industry as well as the government to lead towards better sustainability of the supply chain in the market.

Identification of The Right Approach

In the context of adopting ESG initiatives, identifying the right approach is considered one of the most important steps to be taken as it involves the identification of appropriate areas to be developed. The ESG initiatives involve environmental, social, and governing approaches that associatively include a wide range of initiatives to be taken to maintain overall sustainability (Dimson et al., 2020). For example, climate change is a specific area to be approached where investors integrate appropriate investment to execute activities like waste management, reduction of GHG emissions, or use of sustainable energy. This factor helps to utilise the maximum advantage of ESG initiatives in an industry that eventually leads toward long-term success. In the fast fashion industry in Europe, an attempt to adopt 100% recycled clothing material could be the right approach, which will help to successfully satisfy environmental concerns (DW, 2022).

Identification Of Stakeholders and Engagement

Identification of ikey stakeholders is also a good practice for the management of ESG initiatives in the fast fashion industry of Europe, as it will help to assign the activities and goals in SCM (Gillan, et al., 2021). The engagement of all the stakeholders is also essential to be acknowledged as it indicates the overall collaboration of the industry in sustainability. Regular outreach to the investors, conducting surveys and focusing on group discussions and interviews are considered good practices to enhance engagement with all the stakeholders regarding the management of ESG initiatives.

Assessment of the Materiality

Assessing the materiality involves information that the company can disclose to other entities that might impact the decision-making of the investors toward ESG initiatives. Corporate Reporting Dialogue is considered a good practice, as it helps the management to identify and evaluate necessary information which is to be disclosed (Li et al., 2021). In the context of the European fast fashion industry can disclose, the sustainability metrics such as waste management, community relationships, Product safety. Green House Gases emissions (GHG), and anticorruption indices etc to attract investors.

Establishing Corporate Governance

Establishing best corporate governance practices; such as overnighting the board on ESG issues, allocating committees to oversight ESG initiatives, robust processing to identify risks, and measurement of success, etc could be some good practices. It may also include considering financial disclosures aligned with ESG, putting internal controls, and creating data collection processes that help to control and modify overall activities. In the context of the sustainable supply chain of the European fast fashion industry, allocating a dedicated department of ESG helps to maintain all the activities, whereas the corporate governance department helps to maintain surveillance of the activities.

Integration of ESG In Business Strategies

ESG initiatives are vital factors of business strategy as they ensure social and environmental well-being by different companies as per prevailing legislations and regulations. Coordinating different business functions with the overarching ESG framework, conducting a review of sustainability developments, managing ESG reporting, enhancing investor relations, and responding to the stakeholders regarding their ESG queries are considered good practices for the organizations. For example, H&M has been able to produce transparent sustainability reports along with active engagement of the stakeholders in the overall supply chain as a fast fashion company (H&M Group, 2022).

ESG Reporting

High-quality reporting of ESG initiatives is considered another significant essential practice to be followed as it helps to evaluate accurate results by underpinning different disclosures and underpinning transparency among all the stakeholders. In the context of the fast fashion industry, reporting environmental impacts, employee relations, and governing activities at different stages of the overall supply chain is beneficial to enhance the overall supply chain of the industry. The involvement of the Global Reporting Initiative also helps to provide a framework of universal standards to be followed during ESG reporting based on management systems, governance, and reporting practices (Global Reporting Initiative, 2022).

Continuous ESG Research

The ESG research is considered another significant practice to be followed that involves third-party research in terms of identifying how different companies are adopting ESG initiatives (Li et al. (2021. It helps the investors to make an informed investment decision based on industrial sustainability metrics on ESG indices. In the context of the sustainable supply chain of the European fast fashion industry, researching about overall retail industry as well as other countries would aid the stakeholders to take appropriate decisions.

ROLE OF KEY STAKEHOLDERS TO MANAGE THE IMPACT OF ESG INITIATIVES

Stakeholders have the responsibility of taking vital decisions in an organisation by analysing both the internal and external environment, which helps to enhance overall business strategy and lead towards long-term sustainability (Zhuang, et al., 2019). In the context of ESG initiatives, stakeholders play a significant role in identifying organisational activities toward environmental and social contribution, which helps to evaluate appropriate measures to be taken. The key stakeholders of the European fast fashion industry in terms of ESG initiatives include employees, suppliers, regulators of the industry, civil society organisations, and communities that are involved in the industry. These key stakeholders play significant roles in establishing an appropriate ESG framework in companies like H&M, Zara, Burberry, and other fast fashion companies to establish sustainable supply chains. Table 2, (see Table 2,) shows some of the roles of key stakeholders to manage the impact of ESG initiatives.

Table 2. Roles Of key stakeholders to manage the impact of ESG initiatives

Serial no.	Stakeholders	Roles	Power	Interest
1	Employees	Provide feedback on human rights, discrimination, and other social factors in the company; finish basic operations like making reports, conducting research	Low	LoW
2	Suppliers	Maintain relationships with the stakeholders	High	Low
3	Regulators of the industry	Implement regulations of ESG, including environmental and social factors to be followed	High	High
4	Civil Society organisations	Integrate and monitor social factors to be maintained in companies or industry	High	Low
5	Communities	Identify and communicate issues regarding human rights, discrimination, or pollution-related factors in the locality	Low	Low

the ESG initiatives are required to be managed based on the roles played by the stakeholders and in line with prevailing regulators of the industry. Such actions will help the organisation to integrate and justify the strategies. The employees of different fast fashion companies play a significant role in providing feedback related to internal factors related to social and environmental concerns. Suppliers of fast fashion industries also have the responsibility of maintaining relationships and engagement with the stakeholders as a significant part of the supply chain adopt ESG initiatives.

RESULTS AND ANALYSIS

Any organisation, industry, business, or country using technology without a humanistic and sustainable approach may fail to achieve long-term goals for various stakeholders. it is relevant that we need more production capacity better and faster supply chains, using an exploit technology. however, it should not be done at the expense of humanistic social environmental and sustainability approaches. The supply chain of the fashion industry has a great role in this light. on the one hand, it involves extensive use of technology, and all the other hand it requires embedding ESG framework in the production and whole supply chain of fast fashion. From the literature review of the research, it has been found that ESG is the Is not only are regulatory but also a humanistic framework that involves environmental, social and governance factors followed by an organisation to maintain growth and sustainability in their business activities. This section includes some deeper thematic analysis.

THEMATIC ANALYSIS RELATED TO ESG, SUSTAINABILITY, AND SCM

Overall thematic analysis of a range of research papers and articles revealed many themes, such as Themes; Fast fashion and ESG, The sociocultural factors impacting ESG initiatives in SCM, The impact of ESG initiatives, Climate change and ESG, Waste management and ESG, Discrimination and ESG and Sustainable Supply chain and ESG (see Table 3)

Table 3. Thematic analysis related to ESG in SCM

Code	Themes	Areas of ESG
Fast fashion has become one of the significant trends	Fast fashion and ESG	Environment, Social and Governance.
The supply chain is defined as the set of activities or components of an organisation. The social cultural factors are related to employees, organisations countries, and social demographic information	***The sociocultural factors impacting ESG initiatives in SCM***	Environment, Social and Governance.
The impact of ESG initiatives is significantly based on organisational behaviours in the industry	The impact of ESG initiatives	Environment, Social and Governance.
Climate change is considered one of the most impactful factors in human history as well as the economy	Climate change and ESG	Environmental
Waste management is also considered another influential factor	Waste management and ESG	Environment
Discrimination is one of the significant social factors that disrupt the quality of the workforce	Discrimination and ESG	Social
Supply chain sustainability has a significant area of monitoring the initiatives	Sustainable Supply chain and ESG	Environment, Social and Governance

Fast Fashion And ESG

The fast fashion trend in the European industry involves quick, design, development and quick delivery of fashion products in different stores.. The textile regulation of the European Union also supports this aspect, which gives the fast fashion aspects in effective growth. In this way, this market is highly affected due to the present scenario as well as the development which is taking place in the marketplace. This is the first theme in the European fast industry. In fast fashion, the fashion organization use effective design cum quick manufacturing, thus launching new products and attracting lots of customers. The overall value of fast fashion will reach up to $123.9 billion by the year 2025 (Statista, 2022). High Street commercial areas also have this kind of trend by which people can access more products as well as styles in a shorter time frame. In the year 2019, various retailers have sold millios of fast fashion clothing units; Zara (2982 Million units), H&M (2226 Million units), M&S (1324 Million units), Primark (989 Million units), JD Sports (602 Million units), Next (532 Million units) Sports Direct (42 Million units), Asos (349 Million units), Debenhaps (301 Million units) and Arcadia (241 Million) (Sabanoglu, 2020). Fast fashion has a direct relation with ESG practices in SCM.

Supply Chain Management and ESG

The assessment of ESG initiatives in the supply chain involves exploring the activities or components of organisation.. The SCM activities involve in manufacturing of clothing products as well as the finalisation of the product to deliver it to the European market. Using the metrics based on the ESG initiative can help to avoid the issues of sustainability in the supply chain issues. For example, H&M gets supplies from several suppliers and factories from China (789), Bangladesh(428), Turkey(269), India(281), Indonesia(99(, Mynamar(79), Vietnam(76), Italy(106), Portugal (80), Cambodia (40), Pakistan (38), and France (26) (Coppola, 2020), thus the various countries are involved in the supply of fast fashion to H&M and each has to take proportional actions.

The Sociocultural Factors Impacting ESG Initiatives In SCM

In sustainable SCM the ESG initiative is impacted by and impacts Organisational behaviour. Social and cultural factors may lead to discrimination in the workplace due to the unequal treatment of employees. Undue social exploitation also affects the organisational culture and then ESG. The human rights aspects affect the process of social welding in ESG. The governing initiative related to the ESG in the supply chain also affects the organisational aspects and gives assurance in the implementation of sustainability and maintaining a regulatory framework in SCMs. The leadership practices related to the working process also influence ESG practices.

Climate Change and ESG

Climate changes are a natural phenomenon occurring due to variations in temperature levels and weather patterns of a particular area over a long period. The climate changes are in form of global warming, due to human activities such as the burning of fossil fuels like coal, deforestation, soil erosion, and emission of harmful gases such as CO2 from power plants and vehicles, toxic waste disposal from industrialisation etc. The ESG practices in the fast fashion industry can lead to a lowering of Climate change. The adverse effects of global warming lead to climatic changes such as frequent tropical storms, rising sea levels, intense heat waves, melting of glaciers and warming of oceans which have a major impact on animals and human lives. These climatic changes are directly responsible for affecting the organisational activities of the European fast fashion industry, such as the production and distribution of goods which had a major impact on the demand and supply of the company.

Waste Management and ESG

Waste management is the process of careful treatment and disposal of waste from household, industrial, organic and medical industries. It is the systematic management of waste which involves the collection of waste, transportation, processing and disposal. The waste management techniques are based on five principles such as refuse, reduce, reuse, repurpose and recycle. A proper waste management system by the fast fashion industry leads to a reduction in the level of air pollution, water pollution, soil contamination etc. which overall improves nature and the environment. The European fast fashion industry follows the waste management system to reduce the wastage generated in the operational process by recycling and reusing the waste or leftover materials. These waste and leftover materials are then converted into finished goods with the help of raw materials and a proper waste management system. The fast fashion industry follows the sustainable waste management system, which involves advanced management techniques in order to reduce environmental challenges and also to preserve resources. Effective waste management enables reducing the areas of landfill and dumping grounds which facilitates environmental protection from harmful chemical wastage and builds a sustainable environment for the industry to expand their business operations.

Discrimination and ESG

Discrimination is the social factor that affects the quality and performance of the workforce in an organisation. Discrimination is the behaviour of unfair treatment to someone or a group of people in comparison to other individuals or sections of people. Workplace discrimination involves unfavourable treatment of an employee or a group of workers as compared to another group of workers in the same department. It involves the differentiation of employees by the business manager at the workplace due to a number of factors such as race, colour, sex, religion etc. This discrimination of employees creates low morale and low self-confidence among workers, which results in reduced efficiency and low productivity. The European fast fashion industry faces discrimination of employees in their organisation as it involves better treatment of those employees who are performing well and unfair treatment of those employees who are not performing well in the production as well as distribution process. This affects employee promotion and development at the workplace, which could reduce the productivity and performance of the company and also its future growth.

Sustainable Supply Chain And Environmental, Social, and Regulatory Governance (ESG)

Supply chain sustainability is the process of maintaining a suitable and safeguarding business environment during the process of supply chain management. Supply chain management involves adequate availability of raw materials, production of goods, distribution, supply of goods and delivery of final goods to potential customers (Dimson, et al., 2020). Supply chain sustainability is the process of maintaining the standard processes of effective supply chain management by the company without affecting the environment and social values. The European fast fashion industry focus on building and maintaining sustainability in their supply chain practices to enable the smooth flow of production, distribution and delivery process by developing sustainable environmental progress.

ESG INITIATIVES AND CONSEQUENCES IN INDUSTRY 5.0

As mentioned the matrix of industry five should be the combination of the use of technology, efficiency, effectiveness, humanistic approach, environment, sustainability etc. This chapter has focused on ESG initiatives to be embedded in industry 4.0 or 5.. ESG refers to the plan, principles, and strategies which reflect on corporate sustainability. It enhances the performance of the organizations and develops effective strategies. It has a significant impact on the fast fashion industry. ESG helps to meet sustainable outcomes and improves the quality of the services. Besides that, it helps in to overcome challenges and establish sustainability (Centobelli et al., 2022). This industry has repeatedly followed unsustainable practices, which is harmful to the organization. They stand for the fast delivery of products to the customers. The products have a shorter life cycle, and the industry mainly focuses on reduced costs of the supply chains. This provides benefits to the industry without compromising the quality of the products. The fast fashion industry has negative environmental and social impacts. Therefore, ESG helps to set regulatory standards to provide safety to the environment. Besides that, it sets rules for social concerns such as human rights and discrimination (Peters, Li, and Lenzen, 2021). Therefore, this approach helps to identify the opportunities for this industry to improve its performance in the future. Besides that, it helps to know about the potential risks which can influence their functions (Niinimäki et al. 2020). It also provides transparency in the supply chain process and helps to deliver a sustainable environment.

Initiatives of ESG help to monitor the performance of the company and assure sustainability in the workplace. It maintains a regulatory framework and takes necessary steps to avoid risk factors. It improves the quality of work by delivering sustainable packaging and materials. Therefore, the implementation of this strategy in the fast fashion industry helps to deliver sustainable products (Pal, Shen and Sandberg, 2019).

On the other hand, it is essential to monitor the framework of the organization and ensure eco-friendly products. ESG ensures to delivery of sustainable, reusable products. Customers can become aware of the quality of the products, and they will get information related to the recycling and reuse of those products. ESG initiatives will help to consider these factors and contribute to a sustainable environment (Peters, Li, and Lenzen, 2021). SCM is an essential part of an industry. Therefore, it is essential to manage the SCM in a proper way, which will help to improve the performance of the company. It also promotes diversity and equality, which is necessary to enhance the culture of the organization. Initiatives of governing help to gather information related to the employees, customers, and other stakeholders (Niinimäki et al. 2020). This information helps to know their requirements and adapt strategies as per their needs. Implementation of the SCG will improve the functions of the fast fashion industry and satisfy the needs of the customers. Besides that, it will help to identify the contemporary factors which can influence the business (Centobelli et al., 2022). As a result, it will develop strategies against these factors and meet the organizational needs. ESG initiatives also improve the behaviors of the organization and set the activities to achieve sustainable SCM. Furthermore, it creates a positive influence on climate change, which is essential to develop a sustainable environment. By using this ESG framework, some of the leading companies in Europe have been able to create alternatives which are synthetic fibre, and even can significantly develop more "eco-friendly manufacturing" along with the dyeing process. On the other side, the awareness of the customers helps in promoting accountable consumption. Some of the major brands helped in investigating the sourcing the sustainable practices and even the manufacturing and circular design. For example, ASOS also has launched clothing production of the clothing. Thus, it can be stated that it will help in increasing the value chain mainly by 2030. The implementation of the ESG framework, the "UNFCCC Fashion Industry Charter for Climate Action, sets" mainly targets for decarbonising the emissions of the half greenhouse gas and supply chain mainly by the year 2030. Along with this, it also achieves "net zero emissions no later" rather than 2050. On the other side, with the increment of fashion, brands and globalization are working hard to ensure their "global corporate standards" for safety, health, sustainability, and product quality and even adhered to and even maintained throughout the supply chain.

ESG initiatives also help in waste management. Elimination of waste is a crucial part of SCM. It has a significant impact on climate change. It can increase the level of air pollution and contribute to increasing greenhouse gas. It is the responsibility of the fast fashion industry to remove waste products and to deliver a sustainable environment (Peters, Li, and Lenzen, 2021). Implementation of the ESG can help to manage waste produced in a better way and reduce the emission of carbon.

ESG initiatives can improve social culture in the organization and promotes equality in the workplace. It allows diversity in the workplace and promotes human rights (Niinimäki et al., 2020). As a result, the employees are encouraged to improve their performance. The set of principles helps to improve organizational culture and its functions. It is essential to adopt precautions during the manufacturing process (Pal, Shen and Sandberg, 2019). It will help to reduce waste materials and adopt appropriate approaches to avoid risk factors. However, organizational behaviors are one of the important factors which can affect the implementation of ESG (Centobelli et al. 2022). The organization should focus on equal treatment of the employees. Discrimination in the workplace can affect the growth of the industry. Besides that, it can affect the individual performance of the employees. Therefore, the proper implication of ESG helps to maintain the regulatory framework and improve the SCM (Peters, Li, and Lenzen, 2021). At the same time, it helps to adopt an appropriate leadership strategy, which has a positive response to the organization. ESG initiatives can promote a safe business environment by delivering a sustainable supply chain system. It allows sustainability in the SCM and increases the value of the services. It maintains a standard process of production and delivers the process smoothly by developing sustainable SCM. As a result, it will help to deliver quality products to the customers and maintain the effective process during the manufacturing. Furthermore, it helps to add social values and establish sustainability in the supply chain process.

DISCUSSIONS ON EMBEDDING AN ESG FRAMEWORK SCM AND INDUSTRY 5.0

By impacting the environmental social and governance framework in a supply chain, the business is can achieve the goals of industry 5.0.

In the literature review, it has been found that ESG or environmental, social, and regulatory governance standard (ESG) is one of the important initiatives which need to implement in the fast fashion industry, and its supply chain aspects for sustainability reasons. In terms of the European fast fashion industry and its supply chain, the use of ESG will be an effective framework, as the framework is very convenient, valuable and effective for the work on manufacturing, delivery and SCM.

Social factors such as discrimination and the application of human rights in the workplace, demand actions from the industry. The Governance initiative can be influenced by the leadership as well as the regulatory framework in SCM. However various challenges such as lack of scale or knowledge or financial investment or workforce awareness can lead to no implementations of ESG.The various good practices such as stakeholder engagement, assessment of the material as well as the establishment of governance practices are significant for the effective implementation of ESG. Sustainability practices need to be implemented for the proper improvement and avoidance of environmental problems.

Apart from this, the regulations of the textile, mainly among the EU, make a great concern in the implementation of ESG frameworks, to improve the quality of the work. Equal treatment is essential in the organization which encourages the employees to increase productivity. Implementation of the ESG can help to provide equality in the workplace (Dragomir and Dumitru, 2022). It promotes fairness and opportunities in the workplace. ESG ensures dignity and respect to the employees, and promoting equality in the workplace helps to achieve organizational goals (Arrigo, 2020). ESG initiatives help to improve the satisfaction of the customers by delivering sustainable products (Arrigo, 2020). The Fast Fashion Industry should adopt this strategy to reduce the harmful effects of supply chain practices and encourage a sustainable environment. This strategy maintains a standard process and adds social values to the services (Dragomir and Dumitru, 2022).

RECOMMENDED ACTIONS TO EMBED ESG INTO THE SUPPLY CHAIN FOR INDUSTRY 5.0

The integration of ESG initiatives is beneficial to support environmental and social concerns of the government for the overall sustainability of the business industry.

Based on the analysis and findings, the European fast fashion industry should integrate a centralised ESG-based communication and feedback management system for all the employees, as it will help to provide transparency for ESG initiatives taken by the management. The stakeholders should focus on renewable energy to reduce carbon emissions, effective energy consumption, and minimise pollution, thus protecting the environment. Integration of a dedicated department of ESG with investment and transparency will help to generate an appropriate and centralised reporting mechanism.

Companies like H&M, Zara, Burberry, and many others have been able to establish sustainability strategies with the help of reporting and appropriate decision-making of the stakeholders, which helps to maintain social and environmental well-being. However, the challenges such as, lack of information, lack of engagement, and emerging environmental sustainability trends might disrupt overall ESG initiatives in terms of establishing a sustainable supply chain.

Also, the identification of the right approach for the company, identifying stakeholders through evaluating engagement, assessment of materiality, establishing governance, integration of ESG in strategy, reporting frameworks, and ESG research are the strategies for successful integration of ESG in SCM for Industry 5.0

CONCLUSION

As we enter the era of industry 5.0, we must balance the use of technology along with the goals of various stakeholders such as customers employees, the government, the environment, and sustainability. This chapter discussed the various factors, processes and teams later dude implementation of ESG framework into of European fashion industries. The ESG framework involves certain environmental, social and governance factors, which enables the stakeholders to identify and understand the company's situation in managing risk and opportunities related to environmental causes such as carbon emission and waste management, social causes like employee rights and governance factors such as corporate policies. The European fast fashion industry is in the process of implementing ESG regulatory framework to boost its growth and maintain sustainability in its business operations. This kind of framework significantly influences the fashion industries for the identification and even tacking the problems around this appearance. The ECG also helps all the fashion companies in European fashion industries enhance their brand image, minimizing waste, producing more eco-friendly products, and even minimizing reuse and recycling. Hence sustainability in SCM can be maintained through ESG factors.

The ESG approach enables the fast fashion industry to improve their business operations of manufacturing, distribution and logistics processes; while considering the environmental safeguarding principles. Proper waste management and sustainability across the supply chain process have reduced environmental pollution to an extent, as the company's primary goal is to develop and achieve sustainability across the business activities.

The application of the ESG framework in the fast fashion industry results in reducing environmental wastages, improving Social aspects such as maintaining human rights for the labours and better sustainability and Climate, all resulting in in better organisaional performance. The fast fashion industry could efficiently implement the sustainable supply chain process by using environmentally friendly raw materials, using operational resources to boost efficiency, and applying green energy sources to provide power to the company's operations.

REFERENCES

Arrigo, E. (2020). Global sourcing in fast fashion retailers: Sourcing locations and sustainability considerations. *Sustainability*, *12*(2), 508. doi:10.3390u12020508

Avramov, D., Cheng, S., Lioui, A., & Tarelli, A. (2022). Sustainable investing with ESG rating uncertainty. *Journal of Financial Economics*, *145*(2), 642–664. doi:10.1016/j.jfineco.2021.09.009

BBC. (2022). European Union reveals fast fashion crackdown. *BBC News*. https://www.bbc.com/news/science-environment-60913226#:~:text=Fast%20fashion%3A%20European%20Union%20reveals%20fast%20fashion%20crackdown,-Publishedandtext=Manufacturers%20will%20have%20to%20ensure,repair%20and%20recycle%20their%20clothes

Cai, Y. J., & Choi, T. M. (2020). A United Nations' Sustainable Development Goals perspective for sustainable textile and apparel supply chain management. *Transportation Research Part E, Logistics and Transportation Review*, *141*, 102010. doi:10.1016/j.tre.2020.102010 PMID:32834741

Camargo, L. R., Pereira, S. C. F., & Scarpin, M. R. S. (2020). Fast and ultra-fast fashion supply chain management: An exploratory research. *International Journal of Retail & Distribution Management*, *48*(6), 537–553. doi:10.1108/IJRDM-04-2019-0133

Centobelli, P., Abbate, S., Nadeem, S. P., & Garza-Reyes, J. A. (2022). Slowing the fast fashion industry: An all-round perspective. *Current Opinion in Green and Sustainable Chemistry*, *100684*, 100684. doi:10.1016/j.cogsc.2022.100684

Chen, Z., & Xie, G. (2022). ESG disclosure and financial performance: Moderating role of ESG investors. *International Review of Financial Analysis, 83*(1), 102291. doi:10.1016/j.irfa.2022.102291

Cook, P., Schmiege, S., Reeder, B., Horton-Deutsch, S., Lowe, N., & Meek, P. (2018). Temporal immediacy: A two-system theory of mind for understanding and changing health behaviors. *Nursing Research, 67*(2), 108–121. doi:10.1097/NNR.0000000000000265 PMID:29489632

Dimson, E., Marsh, P., & Staunton, M. (2020). Divergent ESG ratings. *Journal of Portfolio Management, 47*(1), 75–87. doi:10.3905/jpm.2020.1.175

Dragomir, V. D., & Dumitru, M. (2022). Practical solutions for circular business models in the fashion industry. *Cleaner Logistics and Supply Chain, 4*, 100040. doi:10.1016/j.clscn.2022.100040

DW. (2022). *EU proposes new rules to tackle 'fast fashion.'* DW. https://www.dw.com/en/eu-proposes-new-rules-to-tackle-fast-fashion/a-61308009

Earth. (2022). *10 Stunning Fast Fashion Waste Statistics.* Earth.Org. https://earth.org/statistics-about-fast-fashion-waste/

Euronews. (2022). Is this the beginning of the end for fast fashion? *Euronews.* https://www.euronews.com/green/2022/03/31/is-this-the-beginning-of-the-end-for-fast-fashion-the-eu-is-moving-to-clean-up-the-dirty-i

Europa. (2022). Climate change: what the EU is doing. *Consilium.* https://www.consilium.europa.eu/en/policies/climate-change/#:~:text=By%20the%20European%20climate%20law,EU%20climate%20neutral%20by%202050

Europa. (2022). *Textiles and clothing legislation.* Eurpoa. https://single-market-economy.ec.europa.eu/sectors/fashion/textiles-and-clothing-industries/legislation_en#:~:text=The%20EU%20has%20aligned%20laws,functioning%20of%20the%20internal%20market

Financial Times. (2022). Interest in European ESG ETFs holds up despite headwinds. *Financial Times.* https://www.ft.com/content/07f01ade-ed62-4fa0-a805-f92c61f391d3

Gillan, S., Koch, A., & Starks, L. (2021). Firms and social responsibility: A review of ESG and CSR research in corporate finance. *Journal of Corporate Finance, 66*(1), 101889. doi:10.1016/j.jcorpfin.2021.101889

Global Reporting Initiative. (2022). *GRI - Home.* GRI. https://www.globalreporting.org/

Heartland (2022) *Industry 5.0: The Bridge Between Capitalism And Sustainability.* Heartland. https://www.heartland.io/sustainability-news/industry-5-0-the-bridge-between-capitalism-and-sustainability/

Henisz, W., Koller, T. and Nuttall, R. (2019). Five ways that ESG creates value.

H&M Group. (2022). *Sustainability.* H&M Group. https://hmgroup.com/sustainability/

Inditex. (2022). *Corporate governance.* Inditex. https://static.inditex.com/annual_report_2016/en/our-priorities/corporate-governance/

Jacobs, F., Berry, W., Whybark, D., & Vollmann, T. (2019). *Manufacturing planning and control for supply chain management: APICS/CPIM Certification Edition* (2nd ed.). McGraw-Hill Education.

Kholaif, M. M. N. H. K., & Ming, X. (2022). COVID-19's fear-uncertainty effect on green supply chain management and sustainability performances: The moderate effect of corporate social responsibility. *Environmental Science and Pollution Research International*, 1–22. doi:10.100711356-022-21304-9

Koberg, E., & Longoni, A. (2019). A systematic review of sustainable supply chain management in global supply chains. *Journal of Cleaner Production*, *207*, 1084–1098.

Kotsantonis, S., & Serafeim, G. (2019). Four things no one will tell you about ESG data. *Journal of Applied Corporate Finance*, *31*(2), 50–58. https://dash.harvard.edu/bitstream/handle/1/37369828/kotsantonis%2Cserafeim_four-things-no-one-will.pdf?sequence=1&isAllowed=y

Li, T., Wang, K., Sueyoshi, T., & Wang, D. (2021). ESG: Research progress and future prospects. *Sustainability*, *13*(21), 11663. doi:10.3390u132111663

McMaster, M., Nettleton, C., Tom, C., Xu, B., Cao, C., & Qiao, P. (2020). Risk management: Rethinking fashion supply chain management for multinational corporations in light of the COVID-19 outbreak. *Journal of Risk and Financial Management*, *13*(8), 173. doi:10.3390/jrfm13080173

Niinimäki, K., Peters, G., Dahlbo, H., Perry, P., Rissanen, T., & Gwilt, A. (2020). The environmental price of fast fashion. *Nature Reviews Earth & Environment*, *1*(4), 189–200. doi:10.103843017-020-0039-9

Pal, R., Shen, B., & Sandberg, E. (2019). Circular fashion supply chain management: Exploring impediments and prescribing future research agenda. *Journal of Fashion Marketing and Management*. doi:10 doi:.1108/JFMM-07-2019-166

Pedersen, L., Fitzgibbons, S., & Pomorski, L. (2021). Responsible investing: The ESG-efficient frontier. *Journal of Financial Economics*, *142*(2), 572–597. doi:10.1016/j.jfineco.2020.11.001

Peters, G., Li, M., & Lenzen, M. (2021). The need to decelerate fast fashion in a hot climate-A global sustainability perspective on the garment industry. *Journal of Cleaner Production*, *295*, 126390. doi:10.1016/j.jclepro.2021.126390

Phillips, S., Thai, V. V., & Halim, Z. (2019). Airline value chain capabilities and CSR performance: The connection between CSR leadership and CSR culture with CSR performance, customer satisfaction and financial performance. *The Asian Journal of Shipping and Logistics*, *35*(1), 30–40. doi:10.1016/j.ajsl.2019.03.005

Rezaee, Z. (2018). Supply chain management and business sustainability synergy: A theoretical and integrated perspective. *Sustainability*, *10*(1), 275.

Sachin, N., & Rajesh, R. (2022). An empirical study of supply chain sustainability with financial performances of Indian firms. *Environment, Development and Sustainability*, *24*(5), 6577–6601.

Statista. (2022). *Fast fashion in Europe - statistics & facts.* Statista. https://www.statista.com/topics/6088/fast-fashion-in-europe/

Stranieri, S., Orsi, L., Banterle, A., & Ricci, E. C. (2019). Sustainable development and supply chain coordination: The impact of corporate social responsibility rules in the European Union food industry. *Corporate Social Responsibility and Environmental Management*, *26*(2), 481–491.

The Guardian. (2022). EU wants to force fashion firms to make clothes more durable. *The Guardian.* https://www.theguardian.com/environment/2022/mar/30/eu-wants-to-force-fashion-firms-to-make-clothes-more-durable-and-recyclable

The Guardian. (2022). Racism is at the heart of fast fashion – it's time for change. *The Guardian.* https://www.theguardian.com/global-development/2020/jun/11/racism-is-at-the-heart-of-fast-fashion-its-time-for-change

UNEP. (2022). *Emissions Gap Report 2022.* UNEP. https://www.unep.org/resources/emissions-gap-report-2022

Yu, W., Jacobs, M., Chavez, R., & Yang, J. (2019). Dynamism, disruption orientation, and resilience in the supply chain and the impacts on financial performance A dynamic capabilities perspective. *International Journal of Production Economics, 218*(1), 352–362.

Zhuang, T., Qian, Q., Visscher, H. E., & Wu, W. (2019). The role of stakeholders and their participation network in decision-making of urban renewal in China: The case of Chongqing. *Cities (London, England), 92*(1), 47–58. doi:10.1016/j.cities.2019.03.014

Chapter 9
Journey of HR From Industry 1.0 to 5.0 and the Road Ahead

Alpana Agarwal
Symbiosis Centre for Management Studies, Symbiosis International University (Deemed), NOIDA, India

Poornima Mathur
International School of Informatics and Management, Jaipur, India

Sandeep Walia
https://orcid.org/0000-0001-5987-6857
Lovely Professional University, India

ABSTRACT

Industrial revolutions are rapidly transforming the industry and redefining the world of work. Human resource management has also been affected largely by the industrial revolutions. So far, four industrial revolutions have been implemented. Each revolution came with certain positive and negative changes. For example, prior to the 18th century, HR was called personnel management and was limited to hiring, training, and administration. However, with these major revolutions in the industry, HR is now considered a business driver and includes a wide range of strategic activities. Now, discussions are going about the fifth industrial revolution. This chapter aims to elaborate on the changing business scenario, transition from industry 1.0 to 5.0, and its impact on HR. It is expected that the outcomes of the chapter will help the researchers and practitioners in understanding the technicalities and issues involved.

1. INTRODUCTION

New marketplace realities and advancement in technology has caused drastic improvements in the Industrial output, transformation of occupations and job profiles, innovative culture, automation and digitalization. They are also compelling businesses to change their strategies and business models. A crucial aspect of growing a company must involve cutting down the cost of production and optimising quality and quantity. Industrial revolutions in this regard are rapidly transforming the industry and

DOI: 10.4018/978-1-6684-6403-8.ch009

redefining the world of work. The history of the industrial revolution began with the first industrial revolution characterised by mechanisation of production using steam and coal as the source of power. Furthermore, in the 1900s, the second industrial revolution was initiated by finding out electricity and unearthing assembly line production. The second industrial revolution has further expedited human work at significantly lower cost. Nevertheless, the third industrial revolution marked its relevance by automation using computers and operations of the production process without human intervention. Presently, the fourth industrial revolution has been implemented. The main characteristic of the fourth revolution is networking through information and communication technologies. Next industrial revolution is 5.0, called the human touch revolution by Japan. The main characteristic of Industry 5.0 is its approach to balance economic advancements by solving social problems. However, like manufacturing process upgradation, human resource management has also been affected largely by the industrial revolutions. Prior to the 18th century, HR was called personnel management and was limited to hiring, training, and administration. However, with these major revolutions in the industry, HR is now considered as a business driver and includes a wide range of strategic activities.

Besides, the journey of businesses adopting an industrial revolution has not been so smooth and facing several challenges. The challenges are mainly related to acquiring the technology, relevant technological skills, data privacy issues, infrastructural changes, etc. besides due to unavailability of visible success stories, uncertain return on investment, the adoption rate have been quite less. Specific to the human resource management, more automation may lead to standardisation, reduced human intervention and left them unemployed. But all discussed challenges reflect the partial side of digitalization. Instead, it would integrate intelligent automation, devices, and systems at the workplace to bring better coordination and collaboration between humans and machines. The technology will enable humans to utilise their cognitive abilities to supervise machines and robots in a better way.

However, the smooth adoption requires acquiring enabling technology and an approach to unlearn most and relearn the new way of working. Additionally, it calls for introducing some HR methods and practices that could facilitate their adoption. Past literature shows a lot of information about key characteristics of industrial revolutions. Research also elaborates the four industrial revolutions from manufacturing, logistics and supply chain perspectives. But there is a paucity of literature on implications of the industrial revolution on human resource management functions. This chapter aims to elaborate on the changing business scenario, transition from industry 1.0 to 4.0 and its impact on HR. Last but not the least, the chapter will also cover the entry of industry 5.0 and its relevance to the HR function. Further, it is expected that the outcomes of the chapter will help the human resource management researchers and practitioners in understanding the technicalities and issues involved in industrial revolutions.

2. IMPACT OF VARIOUS INDUSTRIAL REVOLUTIONS ON HUMAN RESOURCE FUNCTIONS

Like any other functional area, human resource management has also progressed a lot in the last few centuries to address the outcomes of dynamic market conditions. Human resources are one of the most important determinants of productivity including management strategy, and capital. Moreover, changes taking place in the management philosophy and Technology has also disrupted human resource functions. Changes have been beneficial for the effective and efficient functioning of human Resource Management.

Nevertheless, it has also posed several challenges for the HR function. This section is dedicated to throw some light on the four industrial revolutions and their impact on human resource management function.

Industry 1.0

The first Industrial revolution began in England in the 17th century. It took around eight decades (1760-1840) for a full spread. Before the introduction of I 1.0 it was more a handicraft economy; muscle powered weaving looms by labours was the idea of manufacturing. The labourers used to work at home using basic equipment and raw materials. However, manual production posed several limitations. It was difficult for the manufacturers to meet the huge demand and supply gap. Cost of manual manufacturing was also high due to low production speed. These two problems are the major hurdles in the growth of small businesses into larger enterprises (Mohajan, 2019). However, the introduction of I 1.0 has transformed the production and HR functions. I 1.0 was characterised by mechanisation of production using fuel such as steel and coal. Utilisation of steam engines has helped the businesses in generating at least 8 x more production. The idea was simple- tasks taken over by machines under the supervision of humans. I 1.0 helped labourers in saving their Energy for accomplishing the tasks. Besides, it allowed the supervisor to schedule the manufacturing process which was earlier not possible due to differing labour work speed (Gordon, 2012). This has helped the businesses in saving manufacturing time and has made the production process cost effective. I 1.0 offered aid at three levels; first, the individual workers by offering short working hours, comfortable working conditions and better standard of living; second, supervisors, as they can regulate the manufacturing schedule; and owners, by making the production cost effective and efficient (Gordon, 2012). Not only this, the customers' work better served as the mechanisation of production allowed infusion of Technology enabled innovation and the outcome was availability of quality products at low cost (Mohajan, 2019).

However, there were several downsides of the first industrial revolution. it involved non-availability of production machines due to lack of know-how about Production machines (Beck, 2022). Also, since the idea was new and no success stories were available many small businesses were apprehensive about implementing this major change. innovation and mechanisation of production raised the customer expectations as well, setting difficult targets for the businesses. Nevertheless, despite all the challenges I 1.0 was the beginning of industrial culture with a focus on quality, efficiency and production scale.

The key characteristics of first industrial revolution from the human resource perspective are as follows:

1. Child labour continued with low wages but due to government intervention (factory's act 1833), there were certain benefits such as child below nine years was not allowed to work.
2. No child labour during night with less than 12 working hours (Beck, 2022).
3. Organisation of labour into trade unions to protect the interests of labourers.
4. Bargaining power of skilled labour was high and were successful in improving the working conditions using strike action.
5. England's Combination Act, 1799 restricted labour to form trade unions (Beck, 2022).
6. Labourers created co-operative societies during times of hardship (Bacon, 2007).
7. Unemployment for weevers and unskilled labourers (Hatton & Williamson, 2005).
8. Beginning of factory system for agricultural labourers (Hunt & Lautzenheiser, 2014).
9. There was a significant rise in wages paid to labourers (Crafts & Mills, 1994; Hartwell, 1963).

10. Recruitment of literate craftsmen, skilled labour, foreman and supervisor for growing textile and coal industries (Theodore, 1989; Houston, 1982).
11. Difficult working conditions including long working hours were diminished (Hartwell, 1971)

Industry 2.0

The challenges faced during I 1.0 necessitated further innovation. The second industrial revolution (1871-1914) commonly called 'the technological revolution' is characterised by utilisation of electrical power production processes (Atkeson & Kehoe, 2001; Gordon 2000). Ransom E.Olds, Henry Ford, Frederick Taylor were the major contributors in I 2.0. Availability of rail and telegraph networks allowed faster movement of people and ideas. During I 2.0 water and steam were replaced by electricity as a source of power (Alexander, 2009). Technologies like assembly line production, just in time, lean six sigma, and batch production were the major discoveries during this era (Chandler, 1993; Jones & Wadhwani, 2006).

Between 1863- 1947, Henry Ford for the first time implemented mass production in automobile manufacturing (Atkeson & Kehoe, 2001). The idea was inspired from Chicago's slaughter house, wherein animal butchering was done in batches by labourers. The labourers there were responsible for accomplishing a certain task of butchering the animal, moved on over the conveyor belt. The replication of this technology by Ford in automobile production helped in manufacturing 20 vehicles in one day which has increased the production by 500 percent (Bak, 2003). Earlier, the entire vehicle used to be assembled at one place, but the new idea had replicated the slaughterhouse's idea and the vehicles were moved on a conveyor belt allowing partial activity performance by certain labourers (White, 2011). The idea facilitated mass production in manufacturing units and allowed scaling-up of the production. This process was more cost-effective that drastically reduced the vehicle cost and made the vehicle affordable for the common man (Bak, 2003). Furthermore, the disruptions in the manufacturing process have transformed the human resource functions as well. The principles of Fredrick Taylor on optimization of labour productivity were also executed. Work methods like division of labour, work specialisation, production using assembly lines were executed which raised the workplace productivity drastically (White, 2011). The manufacturing businesses were majorly benefited which led to high economic growth.

However, the period was criticised for the rise in unemployment as machines have taken over human work. Furthermore, entrepreneurial activities were also reduced because of the huge capital requirement for beginning running scale production systems. Besides, there was a major improvement in the industrial culture as the application of Factory's Act, 1833 restricted labour working hours (Gordon, 2012). It has not only led to an improvement in production quality but better human management was ensured. Work methods like resource allocation, work specialisation have further upgraded the efficiency and effectiveness of the workplaces (Richard, 2010).

The key characteristics of second industrial revolution from the human resource perspective are as follows:

1. Living standard of workers was raised due to a decrease in the price of goods (Carter et al., 2006).
2. Rising unemployment, as many labourers were replaced by machines (Alexander, 2009; Kim 2007).
3. The key adopters of I 2.0 were Britain, US, Germany, Russia, France (Kennedy, 1987).
4. Decline in child labour (Hull, 1996).
5. I 2.0 led to change in organisational structure, for instance General Motors adopted divisional organisational structure, flat organisational structure by Ford (Yin et al., 2018).

6. Lean production system is well supported by a flat structure, so Ford's market share increased by more than 45 percent (Yin et al., 2018; Foner, 1978).
7. 60 weekly hours of work with very low pay (average six days a week, 10 hours per day) (Chin et al., 2004).
8. No paid holiday round the year (Cronin, 1987).
9. Women were paid half the pay of that of men, and children got further half of it (Gordon, 2012; Longley, 2021).
10. No liability of factory owners of accidents at the factory (Fink, 1988; Longley, 2021).
11. No safety regulations with machines without fencing (Cronin, 1987, Foner, 1978).
12. No social security schemes available (Fink, 1988).
13. Inhumane working conditions like non-ventilated shop floor, untidy floor, etc (Carter et al., 2006).
14. Low freedom and autonomy for workers (Niller, 2019, Foner, 1978).
15. Growth of unregulated child labor (Longley, 2021; Kaplan & Casey, 1958).
16. Domination of company ownership (Longley, 2021).
17. Formation of unions for improvisation of working conditions (Dubofsky & Dulles, 2010) such as demanded eight work hours daily, abolition of child labour, safety, equal pay (Mohajan, 2020; Bacon, 2007)).

Industry 3.0

The third revolution began in 1970 with partial automation and use of electronics and information systems in manufacturing. Such automation has changed the methods of production, now we are in the position to optimise the entire process of development with less human assistance. For example, robots carry out programmed sequence without human interference (Sharma & Singh, 2020). Such technological changes facilitate human work (Philosophy, 2022). As per the study in IR 3.0 there is a big shift towards digitalization. Earlier people had to use a typewriter, but now they use computers to write anything. Use of technology facilitates human work especially when exposed to data. According to the study of (Song et al., 2021) the industry 3.0 rooted the evolution from planned city to fragmented city, where industries are changing their pattern and methods of production. Thus, the whole economics system is changing and focused towards digitalization. As per (Sharma and Singh, 2020) the Industry 3.0 is the link between Henry Ford's drive towards productivity and techno savvy process emerging under Industry 4.0. A number of operations which were traditionally carried out manually are now automated. A new term for innovation named as Advanced Manufacturing Technology (AMT) was originated in 1980 with a series of technology such as Computer-aided Design (CAD), Computer-aided Manufacturing (CAM) and Computer based integrated Manufacturing (CIM), Flexible Processing Mechanism (FPM) etc. (Gerwin and Tarondeau, 1982; Meredith, 1987; Lei et al., 1996). As the need for power begins to grow the renewable energy source like sun and wind become important because of irretrievable sources and environmental concerns (Bayraktar, 2019). Now, each object is connected through the internet and the production process is completely changed, and robotic mechanisms are used in machinery. In the late 1990s, the organisation moved to automated moulding machines which increased the efficiency in production volumes and output. It was a tough economic situation. Therefore, most of the companies had to become more competitive in terms of growth and cost saving (Freeman, 2008). To handle the situation new organisation strategies are required. These changes certainly affect the ratio of man and machine in the organisation. Higher speed machines with higher efficiency resulted in human resource substitution. Use of technology in the form of the internet, computer, and cell phones (Philosophy, 2022).

The key characteristics of fourth industrial revolution from the human resource perspective are as follows:

1. Introduction of automation into production process with the use of technology (Güğerçin, 2021).
2. Shortage of skilled technical workforce (Sharma and Singh, 2020)
3. High technological cost for high investment in new equipment (Landes, D.S. 2003).
4. Most of the work which was done manually are automated (Bayraktar, 2019).
5. Focused on the automation of individual machine and processes (Puhovichova & Jan, 2020).
6. Implementation of manufacturing automation reduced the workload of employees (George and George, 2020).
7. "Contingent work Pay system" was introduced. Employees can be paid hourly, daily, weekly or as per the contract (Harahap & Rafika, n.d.).
8. Unemployment has increased due to automation (Szabó-Szentgróti et al., 2021).
9. Demand for educated or skilled workers were increased (Anouk & Bos-nehles, n.d.).
10. Higher demand for products and services (Gay et al., 2017).

Industry 4.0

We are currently running in Industrial Revolution 4.0. It is characterised as the age of technologies and trends such as internet of people (Iop) or internet of things (IoT), cyber-physical production systems, virtual reality, robotics, smart automation and (AI) artificial intelligence. IR 4.0 changed the way modern people live, think and work. It originated in the year 2011 at Hannover Fair in German. High technology invented in Industrial Revolution 4.0 boosts the higher level of productivity and efficiency in Industries. It allows man and machinery to collaborate and deliver incredible results in terms of production and innovation. Human resource is one of the vital aspects in IR 4.0, however IR 4.0 has automated most of the technologies but the success of operation still relies on human capital, especially on their expertise, knowledge and decision-making skills (Gan & Yusof, 2019). Factorial changes and involvement of automation processes has impacted the role of human resource in business processing. A planned execution of roles needs to be identified as to what role should be played by humans and what roles can be automated (District, 2018). The people are not immune to the situation that has arisen, but they have to adapt to the new modern phenomenon. This in result draws attention to the importance of human resource management, that is called "Smart-HR 4.0" (Puhovichova & Jan, 2020). Smart HR 4.0 refers to a highly efficient and updated workforce with technological infrastructure. Industry 4.0 is certainly affecting the generations of employees. In coming years half of the workforce is expected to be made up of millennials or generation Y or Z. Industry 4.0 brings endless opportunities and difficulties in the form of digitization, big data, artificial intelligence, fast data networks such as 4G and 5G, cloud computing etc. As per (Rafique et al., 2021) the survey of 157 respondents from different organisations, they concluded that in IR 4.0 there is a transformation of traditional Human Resource towards Smart HR 4.0. Also, most of the organisations are now adopting the changes brought by industry 4.0 in their HR practices such as use of AI in recruitment, Training and development, employee retention, performance Management etc. The Technological changes rooted in industry 4.0 formulated a vast gap between employee's current capabilities and fast paced expansion needs in their future roles (Whysall et al., 2019). To meet the gap organisations, need a workforce that is equipped with digital literacy, human literacy and technological literacy. The Country, the employees, the organisations and the machines need to increase their capabilities in line with Industry 4.0 (Bayraktar, 2019; Harahap & Rafika, n.d.). The Big Data component of Industry 4.0 is also expected to have an immense impact on HR practices in the form of HR Analytics or Big data analysis (Anouk & Bos-nehles, n.d.). Data literacy is also required by employees to access and process big data for the benefit of improving business and public services (Ellitan, 2020).

Industry Revolution 4.0 rightly promises an extensive growth in productivity but due to lack of skilled workforce and ageing workforce, it is still a challenge in front of organisations (Ismail et al., 2019). The Fourth Industrial Revolution has created many HR related issues like New Need of Training, Role Analysis, Changes in business Process, Performance Management, and Employee Turnover rate (District, 2018). Technological advancement will change the ratio of workforce in the organisation and will lead to a situation of unemployment (Bayraktar, 2019). As industries are looking forward to an adequate workforce in terms of quality and education. In the long run, only a high techno savvy workforce will be employed (Puhovichova & Jan, 2020). According to the study (Sharma and Singh, 2020) Industry 4.0 advocates the concept of 'smart factories', 'smart home' and 'smart HR'. But numerous obstacles are standing in the way such as data security issues, fear of IT glitches, insufficient skill set of the factory engineers, mass layoff due to automation, situation of unemployment etc. The fourth industrial revolution has its own set of challenges and benefits. HR becomes more automated, more techno savvy, more innovative and focusing on strategic issues, and no longer on manual, repetitive and bureaucratic actions. HR 4.0 is the so-called digital transformation; requires changes in organisation structure and leadership style to successfully implement transformational challenges of Industry Revolution 4.0.

Thus, Industrial Revolution 4.0 is a competitive era, where HR practices play a crucial role. A sustainable approach towards HR practices could only help organisations to reach out to its objective of implementing IR 4.0 effectively.

The key characteristics of fourth industrial revolution from the human resource perspective are as follows:

1. Transformation of the existing organisational structure into flat hierarchy to reduce communication levels and speed up decision making (Puhovichova & Jan, 2020).
2. Requirement of a multi-skilled trusted workforce is increased due to digitalization in the manufacturing process (Irianto, 2017).
3. More technical tools are used in recruitment and selection of employees like Artificial intelligence and Big Data Analysis.
4. Improvement of quality of human resource because of development and utilisation of digital and information technology (Philosophy, 2022).
5. Many people are out of job due to increased automation. But, on the other hand industrial innovation is also creating new job possibilities (Hirsch-Kreinsen, 2016).
6. Human-robot association is a breakthrough in this period. Compact and user-friendly robots will drive through in the market in the coming years (Demir & Cicibaş, 2019).
7. The main shortfall of IR.4.0 is the lack of environmental considerations. The awareness of the environment is increasing among customers and society and they are more inclined towards green production (Rada, 2015).
8. Smart HR 4.0 is required to meet modernised technology requirements. Recruitments using Artificial Intelligence (AI), Interview via video chat, Training programs via Augmented Reality

(AR)/ Virtual Reality (VR), Data-compensate Compensation, Performance feedback through AI, Agile and decentralised work teams are the new practices in the business (Puhovichova & Jan, 2020).

3. FUTURE OF HUMAN RESOURCE FUNCTIONS IN INDUSTRY 5.0

Ready or not ready we are in the transit of Industrial Revolution 5.0. Less than a decade has passed since industry revolution 4.0 was implemented, but visionaries are already forecasting the next revolution that is –IR 5.0. It is defined as 'Society 5.0' a 'Human Touch' revolution. Industry 5.0 is an integrated approach of personalization. It will be a synchronisation and collaboration of technological advancement and human skills. The challenges which are faced by IR 4.0, namely lack of adequate skills in HR, unemployment, lack of human touch, reliability and stability of production process. Industrial Revolution 5.0 offers a human centric approach that will make a balance between technological growth and resolution of the human system (Ellitan, 2020). There is no big difference between the ideologies of IR 4.0 and IR 5.0. The only difference is IR 4.0 uses smart technologies or Artificial Intelligence while IR 5.0 focuses on the Human component. "If society 4.0 allows people to access technology and share data on the internet, society 5.0 is an era where all technology is a part of human component (Yunda, 2019). At Present two visions are emerging in IR 5.0, one is Human and robots co working and other one is bio-economy. Humans use their creativity wherever required and robots do the rest and proper use of biological resources for industrial purposes (Demir & Cicibas, 2019). However, there is an argument that robots will replace the workforce and increase unemployment. But the counter argument for this is that new jobs will be created and rather than focusing on unproductive work, human resources will now focus on creativity in decision making, artistry, research and development (Demir et al., 2019). As per the estimates of the World Economic Forum 2020 report, over 85 million jobs which are carried out by humans are predicted to be atomized by 2025. At the same time jobs of the future required changing employee skills to adapt to IR 5.0. As per the Future of jobs report (2016,2020) future demand skills of employees will be: analytical thinking and innovation, complex-problem solving, Technology design and programming, resilience, stress tolerance and flexibility. In order to sustain in industrial revolution employees are expected to re-skill themselves with above mention skills (GÜĞERÇİN, 2021). Industrial Revolution 5.0 will utilise cobots (Collaborative robots). They will work hand in hand with human resources. Cobots can be fitted with artificial intelligence or GPS to execute repetitive work and complex and sensitive work can be assigned to human resources (George & George, 2020). According to the survey conducted by Accenture 85% employees of 500 manufacturing companies employees said that humans and employees can work side by side (Ostergaard, 2022). As per the Forbes 35% of HR leaders are investing in employee learning and development to retrain for the future strategic perspective (Eschbach, 2021).

Thus, the key objective of IR 5.0 is to combine the role of human skills along with high-speed industrial automation. Human resources will not become obsolete in industrial production. Rather it would integrate the systems, technologies and automation to promote collaboration between man and machine (Xu et al., 2021).

Industry 5.0 refers to a new era of human centric approach which is built with the collaboration of humans, robots and algorithms.

The key characteristics of Fifth industrial revolution from the human resource perspective are as follows:

1. Human Centric Orientation (Ellitan, 2020)
2. People are expected to work in collaboration with robots and algorithm (Güğerçin, 2021).
3. IR 5.0 will bring back the human component in the manufacturing process as employees will get more significant and meaningful jobs to perform (George and George, 2020).
4. The green and digital transformation.
5. Focused on human centric, sustainable and resilient development will become major driving forces for societal progress. (K.Pdf, n.d.).
6. Ecosystem-oriented innovation policy with agile, outcome orientation.
7. Challenges in the field of human-machine interaction (HMI) (Nahavandi, 2019).
8. Utilization of Cobots (collaborative robots) with Human Resource (Gay et al., 2017).

4. CONCLUSION

Till now there have been 4 Industry Revolutions ranging from IR1.0 to IR 4.0 implemented. Currently Industrial Revolution 4.0 is implemented in which machine learning was introduced, but visionaries are already forecasting the next revolution that is –IR 5.0. Industrial revolution has emerged with new technology, digitalization, and communication technology in the business process cycle. IR 1.0 to IR 3.0 took decades to carry out revolution in the industry through automation and digitalization. Water and steam power of the First Industrial Revolution has left its place to oil and electricity in the Second Industrial Revolution and to solar energy and wind power, which are renewable, in the Third Industrial Revolution. The fourth industrial revolution has automated most of the business process, use of AI, Big data analytics, robotics and cloud computing are some of the main highlights of IR 4.0

However, besides positive impact, the fourth Industry Revolution has some negative impacts also which are unavoidable. Such as lack of adequate workforce skills, reliability and stability of production machines, loss of security in communication technology, unemployment due to automation. Therefore the concept 5.0 provides a totally different approach that highlights the importance of human creativity and integrity (Breque, De Nul, & Petridis, 2021). Industry 4.0 was technology driven whereas Industry 5.0 is, value driven.

Companies need to provide and support education. Government should also introduce Education 4.0 for Industry 4.0. A new Four-dimensional perspective towards education should be given such as; Financial education, entrepreneurial education, vocational education and digital education (Song et al., 2021). The transition from industry revolution 4.0 to 5.0 means combining the best of human and machines to the world (Di Nardoet al., 2020 Nelles et al., 2016). The industrial revolution upgraded the living standard of people. Cheaper housing facilitates access to technology, use of mobile phones, computers, vehicle, automation of production, reduced repetitive work made their life easy (Sharma and Singh, 2020). But there are some challenges for workers; they are expected to work for long hours (most of the employees work more than 12 hours for and 6 days a week), increase in migration and urbanisation, need for technical skills, gap between demand and supply of employees (Gitchrist, 2016). Some of the major HR functions like: recruitment, training, performance management, compensation, job designing, employee retention are turning from traditional to Smart HR.50. Thus, HRM functions are improving and becoming more efficient with the use of Industry 5.0 components.

REFERENCES

Alexander, J. G. (2009). *Daily Life in Immigrant America, 1870–1920: How the Second Great Wave of Immigrants Made Their Way in America* (2nd ed.). Ivan R. Dee.

.Anouk, A., and Bos-nehles, A. (n.d.). *What is Industry 4 . 0 and what are its implications on HRM Practices ?* Graduation Committee members :

Atkeson, A., & Kehoe, P. J. (2001). *The Transition to a New Economy after the Second Industrial Revolution. Working Paper No. 606*. Federal Reserve Bank of Minneapolis, Research Department.

Bacon, K. (2007). *The Dark Side of the Gilded Age*. The Atlantic.

Bak, R. (2003). *Henry and Edsel: The Creation of the Ford Empire*. John Wiley and Sons.

.Bayraktar, O. (2019). *Globalization, Institutions and Socio-Economic Performance Macro and Micro Perspectives*..

Beck, E. (2022). Working Conditions in the Industrial Revolution. *History Crunch*. https://www.historycrunch.com/working-conditions-in-the-industrial-revolution.html#/

Carter, S. B., Gartner, S. S., Haines, M. R., Olmstead, A. L., Sutch, R., & Wright, G. (Eds.). (2006). *Historical Statistics of the United States: Earliest Times to the Present. Millennial Edition* (Vol. 5). Cambridge University Press.

Chandler, A. D. (1993). *The Visible Hand: The Management Revolution in American Business*. Belknap Press of Harvard University Press. doi:10.2307/j.ctvjghwrj

Chin, A., Juhn, C., & Thompson, P. (2004). Technical Change and the Wage Structure during the Second Industrial Revolution: Evidence from the Merchant Marine, 1865–1912. *Discussion Paper No. 1285*. The Institute for the Study of Labor (IZA), Germany.

Crafts, N., & Mills, T. C. (1994). Trends in real wages in Britain, 1750-1913¢. *Explorations in Economic History*, *31*(2), 176–181. doi:10.1006/exeh.1994.1007

Cronin, J. E. (1987). Strikes and Power in Britain, 1870–1920. *International Review of Social History*, *32*(2), 144–167. doi:10.1017/S0020859000008403

Demir, K. A., & Cicibaş, H. (2018). *"The Next Industrial Revolution: Industry 5.0 and Discussions on Industry 4.0." Industry 4.0 From the Management Information Systems Perspectives*. Peter Lang Publishing House.

.Demir, K. A., and Cicibaş, H. (2019). The next industrial revolution: Industry 5.0 and discussions on industry 4.0. *Industry 4.0 from the MIS Perspective,* 247–260.

Demir, K. A., Döven, G., & Sezen, B. (2019). Industry 5.0 and Human-Robot Co-working. *Procedia Computer Science*, *158*(January), 688–695. doi:10.1016/j.procs.2019.09.104

. District, T. (2018). *Impact of fourth industrial revolution in human resource management*. *3*(2), 59–61.

Dubofsky, M., & Dulles, F. R. (2010). *Labor in America: A History*. WileyBlackwell.

. Ellitan, L. (2020). *Competing in the Era of Industrial Revolution 4 . 0 and Society 5 . 0. 10*(1), 1–12.

European Commission. Directorate-General for Research and Innovation, Breque, M., De Nul, L., & Petridis, A. (2021). Industry 5.0: towards a sustainable, human-centric and resilient European industry. Publications Office.

Fink, L. (1988). The New Labor History and the Powers of Historical Pessimism: Consensus, Hegemony, and the Case of the Knights of Labor. *The Journal of American History*, *75*(1), 115–136. doi:10.2307/1889657

Fink, L. (1988). The New Labor History and the Powers of Historical Pessimism: Consensus, Hegemony, and the Case of the Knights of Labor. *The Journal of American History*, *75*(1), 115–136. doi:10.2307/1889657

Foner, P. S. (1978). History of the Labor Movement in the United States.: Vol. 1. *From Colonial Times to the Founding of the American Federation of Labor*. International Publishers.

Freeman, C., & Soete, L. (2008). *A Economia da Inovação Industrial*. Psychology Press.

. Gan, J. L., and Yusof, H. M. (2019). *Industrial Revolution 4 . 0 : the Human Resource Practices. 3*, 620–624. doi:10.35940/ijrte.C1203.1083S219

. Gay, D., Ng, L., Cheng, H. W., Vergara, S., Ernst, E., Tobin, S., Milasi, S., Pin-Heiro, V., Kraft, C., Women, U. N., Fernandez, A., Renner, S., Roig, M., Jimenez, M., Perry, J., Mukherjee, S., Roehrl, R. A., and Freire, C. (2017). *Substantive contributions in the form of draft text for sections and boxes and research assistance were made by of the Division of Social Policy and Develop-ment (DESA/DSPD); and. July*.

George, A. S., & George, A. S. H. (2020). Industrial Revolution 5.0: The Transformation of the Modern Manufacturing Process To Enable Man and Machine To Work Hand in Hand. *Journal of Seybold Report*, *15*(9), 214–234. doi:10.5281/zenodo.6548092

Gerwin, D., & Tarondeau, J. C. (1982). Case studies of computer integrated manufacturing systems: A view of uncertainty and innovation processes. *Journal of Operations Management*, *2*(2), 87–99. doi:10.1016/0272-6963(82)90025-0

Gilchrist, A. (2016). *Industry 4.0: The Industrial Internet of Things*. Apress. doi:10.1007/978-1-4842-2047-4

Gordon, R. J. (2000). Does the "New Economy" Measure up to the Great Inventions of the Past? *The Journal of Economic Perspectives*, *14*(2), 49–74. doi:10.1257/jep.14.4.49

Gordon, R. J. (2012). *Is US Economic Growth Over? Faltering Innovation Confronts the Six Headwinds. The Centre for Economic Policy Research, Policy Insight No. 63*. Northwestern University.

Güğerçin, S. (2021). How Employees Survive in the Industry 5.0 Era: in-Demand Skills of the Near Future. [IDEAstudies]. *International Journal of Disciplines In Economics and Administrative Sciences Studies*, *7*(31), 524–533. doi:10.26728/ideas.452

. Harahap, N. J., and Rafika, M. (n.d.). *Industrial revolution 4 . 0 : and the impact on human*, 89–96.

Hartwell, R. M. (1963). The rising standards of living in England, 1800-1850. *The Economic History Review*, *13*(3), 397–416. doi:10.2307/2599511

Hartwell, R. M. (1971). *The industrial revolution and economic growth.* Methuen and Co.

Hatton, T. J., & Williamson, J. G. (2005). *Global Migration and the World Economy: Two Centuries of Policy and Performance*. MIT Press. doi:10.7551/mitpress/3303.001.0001

Hirsch-Kreinsen, H., Weyer, J., & Wilkesmann, J. D. M. (2016). *"Industry 4.0" as Promising Technology: Emergence*. Semantics and Ambivlent Character.

Houston, R. A. (1982). The development of literacy: Northern England, 1640-1750¢. *The Economic History Review*, *35*(2), 199–216.

Hull, J. O. (1996). From Rostow to Chander to You: How revolutionary was the second industrial revolution? *The Journal of European Economic History*, *25*(1), 191–208.

. Hunt, E.K. & Lautzenheiser, M. (2014), History of economic thought: a critical perspective. *PHI Learning*.

Irianto, D. (2017). Традиційний Банкінг В Умовах Industry 4.0: Переваги Та Ризики Нових Технологій [Traditional Banking in the Conditions of Industry 4.0: Advantages and Risks of New Technologies]. *Ukrainian Society, 4 (63)*, 114–122. http://nbuv.gov.ua/UJRN/Usoc_2017_4_11%0Ahttps://doi.org/10.15407/socium2017.04.114

. Ismail, F., Kadir, A. A., Khan, M. A., and Yih, Y. P. (2019). *The Challenges and Role Played among Workers of Department Human Resources Management towards Industry 4 . 0 in SMEs. 2019*, 90–107. doi:10.18502/kss.v3i22.5046

Jones, G., & Wadhwani, R. D. (2006). *Entrepreneurship and Business History: Renewing the Research Agenda. Working Paper No. 07-007.* Harvard Business School, Boston MA.

. Kennedy, P. (1987). Rise and fall of the great powers, (p. 149) based on Paul Bairoch's International Industrialization levels from 1970 to 1980.' *Journal of Economic History 1982, Vol. 11*(2), pp. 269-333.

Kim, S. (2007). Immigration, Industrial Revolution and Urban Growth in the United States, 1820–1920: Factor Endowments, Technology and Geography. *NBER Working Paper Series, Working Paper 12900,* Washington, DC.

Landes, D. S. (2003). *The unbound Prometheus: technological change and industrial development in Western Europe from 1750 to the present.* Cambridge University Press. doi:10.1017/CBO9780511819957

Longley, R. (2019). *Glorious Revolution: Definition, History, and Significance.* ThoughtCo. https://www.thoughtco.com/glorious-revolution-definition-4692528

Mohajan, H. K. (2020). The Second Industrial Revolution has Brought Modern Social and Economic Developments. *Journal of Social Sciences and Humanities*, *6*(1), 1–14.

Nahavandi, S. (2019). INDUSTRY 5. 0 definition. *Sustainability*, *11*, 43–71.

. Niller, E. (2019). How the second industrial revolution changed Americans lives. *History.com.*

. Philosophy, L. (2022). *DigitalCommons @ University of Nebraska - Lincoln Challenges of The Industrial Revolution Era 1 . 0 to 5 . 0*. University Digital Library In Indoensia.

. Puhovichova, D., and Jan, N. (2020). *Changes of human resource management in the context of impact of the fourth industrial revolution. 141*(3), 138–141.

Rada, M. (2018, January 21). Industry 5.0 definition. *Medium.* https://michael- rada.medium.com/industry-5-0-definition-6a2f9922dc48

. Rafique, M., Asim, M., and Manzoor, S. (2021). *Human Resource Management in Industrial Revolution 4 . O. 5*(I), 564–580.

Richard, J. (2010). *Network Nation: Inventing American Telecommunications*. Belknap Press of Harvard University Press.

Sharma, A., & Singh, B. J. (2020). Evolution of Industrial Revolutions: A Review. *International Journal of Innovative Technology and Exploring Engineering*, *9*(11), 66–73. doi:10.35940/ijitee.I7144.0991120

Song, X., Cong, Y., Song, Y., Chen, Y., & Liang, P. (2021). A bearing fault diagnosis model based on CNN with wide convolution kernels. *Journal of Ambient Intelligence and Humanized Computing*. doi:10.100712652-021-03177-x

Theodore, S. H. (1989). *The birth of a new Europe: state and society in the nineteenth century*. University of North Carolina Press.

White, R. (2011). *Railroaded: The Transcontinentals and the Making of Modern America*. W. W. Norton and Company.

Whysall, Z., Owtram, M., & Brittain, S. (2019). The new talent management challenges of Industry 4.0. *Journal of Management Development*, *38*(2), 118–129. doi:10.1108/JMD-06-2018-0181

Xu, X., Lu, Y., Vogel-Heuser, B., & Wang, L. (2021). Industry 4.0 and Industry 5.0—Inception, conception and perception. *Journal of Manufacturing Systems*, *61*(October), 530–535. doi:10.1016/j.jmsy.2021.10.006

Yin, Y., Stecke, K. E., & Li, D. (2018). *The Evolution of Production Systems from Industry 2.0 through Industry 4.0. DBS Discussion Paper*. Series supported by the OMRON Foundation. DBS.

Yunda, N.R. (2019). Dampak Revolusi Industri 4.0 dan Society 5.0 Mencipatakan Kesempatan Baru Bagi Indonesia [The Impact of the Industrial Revolution 4.0 and Society 5.0 Created New Opportunities for Indonesia]. *SERSC.*

Chapter 10
Hospitality Industry 5.0:
Emerging Trends in Guest Perception and Experiences

Veer P. Gangwar
Lovely Professional University, India

Deepika Reddy
https://orcid.org/0000-0001-8142-040X
Lovely Professional University, India

ABSTRACT

The hospitality sector 5.0 aspires to integrate technology into service marketing, human resource management, and hotel operations in order to give visitors a seamless and useful customer experience. Artificial intelligence, the internet of things, blockchain technology, collaborative robots, chatbots and sensors, contactless automation, mobile technology, augmented reality, virtual reality, big data, cloud computing, 6 G and beyond, as well as machine-to-machine communication, are all part of the hospitality industry 5.0. When automated technologies, intelligent devices, and intelligent systems converge with human intelligence, hospitality 5.0 will be born. It aims to provide additional contributions to the field of technological use in hospitality and tourism and thereby offers a strong knowledge base. Therefore, all people involved in the study's implementation might benefit from its findings in order to better understand and meet the requirements and expectations of both customers and employees through the use of technology.

INTRODUCTION TO INDUSTRY 5.0

Michael Rada invented the phrase "Industry 5.0," which describes a future in which machines and people cooperate rather than compete. It increases industry competition and draws top talent. The Commission's three objectives for putting Industry 5.0 into practice are "an economy that works for people," "a European Green Deal," and "a Europe fit for the digital era." Therefore, Industry 5.0 is based on values such as human-centricity, environmental stewardship, and social benefit rather than technology.

DOI: 10.4018/978-1-6684-6403-8.ch010

MULTIDIMENSIONAL PERSPECTIVE OF INDUSTRY 5.0

Industry 5.0 is a multidimensional concept and entails objectives, systematic approaches, human factors, Enabling technologies and environmental considerations (see Figure 1)

Figure 1. Multidimensional perspective of industry 5.0

INDUSTRY 5.0 AND HOSPITALITY INDUSTRY 5.0: THE LINKAGE

The hospitality industry can benefit from the idea of Industry 5.0 because it can affect customer satisfaction, loyalty, and perceived service quality(See figure 1) . These factors include:

a. Personalised service
b. An efficient supply chain
c. Agility
d. Smart work environment
e. The use of big data for up-to-date information on customer preferences
f. Highly customised services at a lower cost and
g. Digital enhancement

Thus, by harnessing human intelligence and creativity to improve process efficiency through the integration of workflows with intelligent systems, hospitality 5.0 can facilitate human-technology engagement. The global demography has also shifted. One of the largest groups of consumers and contributors of the world's workforce, Generation Z, are joining the market.

INDUSTRY 5.0 AND HOSPITALITY 5.0: ELEMENTS

The elements include: The human-cyber-physical system (HCPS), Internet of things (IoT) and Internet of services (IoS).

a. The Human-Cyber-Physical System (HCPS)

People, artificial intelligence, and the physical system of an organisation that is properly connected via high-speed internet make up the initial component of HCPS (Pathak et al., 2019). A HCPS uses a lot of sensors, all of which are crucial. For instance, a variety of sensory tools, including touch screens, light sensors, and force sensors, are frequently utilised in HCPS to achieve various goals (Hermann et al., 2016). HCPS assists in providing consumers by reaping the greatest advantages from both human and machine intelligence (Gurkaynak et al., 2016). HCPS's involvement in the hospitality sector improves food safety through the use of sensors to check for illnesses, evaluate the freshness and hygiene of items, and implement smart food labelling to give detailed information about the origins of the food (Iqbal et al., 2017). The prioritised industries with the greatest predicted impact from HCPS include the hotel sector. Through contactless service, recent technological advancements combined with HCPS promise to lower health risks (Li et al., 2020).

b. Internet of Things (IoT)

The next element IoT is a network of connected devices that may transport data without requiring human-to-human or human-to-computer interaction (Atzori et al., 2010). IoT controls that are synchronised to the guests' devices will make post-checkout simpler by removing interpersonal interactions (Mogelonsky, 2020). By taking into account phone-enabled lights, motorised draperies, a smart thermostat, and door lock sensors with "Do Not Disturb" capabilities. Hence the hospitality sector can make guestroom IoT a key priority (Nadkarni et al., 2019).

c. Internet of Services (IoS)

The term "internal and cross organisational services," or "IoS," refers to internal and cross-organizational services that are provided and accessed by members of the value chain and are powered by big data and cloud computing. The IoS's main goal is to systematically employ the internet to develop new channels for value generation in the services industry (Terzidis et al.,2012).

Visitor service-oriented architecture, or IoS is used in the hotel sector to link IT to guest services. A diversified hotel company frequently lacks standardised information regarding guest preferences, customer billing, spa services, restaurant services, and room availability all of which are typically controlled at the property level. IoS offers the speed and agility required to transmit information through its channels and provide superior customer service (Hurwitz et al 2009). To deliver this information reliably and on time and to help manage the customer experiences, integration between the many systems that control information about visitor demands and hotel operations is essential.

Similar to Industry 5.0, Hospitality 5.0 aims to transform the hospitality industry by adopting Industry 5.0 design pillars in the hospitality sector. They are:

a. Interoperability
b. Modularity
c. Virtualization
d. Real-time capabilities and
e. Decentralisation

a. Interoperability

Interoperability is the capacity of all elements, including people, intelligent products, and any applicable technologies, to connect, communicate, and work together (Ghobakhloo,2018). The opportunity to leverage real-time data to make quicker and better decisions for both humans and robots is unleashed by interoperability. Interoperability in Hospitality 5.0 will help hospitality businesses improve their decision-making processes, increase their competitiveness, and gain a better understanding of their consumers and the market (Buhalis and Leung, 2018). At the moment, managing the room allocation and altering the room rate on each online travel agency platform that may have an impact on last-minute rate tactics requires a significant amount of work from hotel staff. The significance of working with business partners must therefore be made clear to hoteliers. (Leung, 2019).

b. Modularity

The second design pillar, modularity, means that the systems are intrinsically scalable, enabling them to respond to sudden changes in demand without reversing the initial investment. Modern technological developments like IoT and automation have made it possible to reconfigure products and services in response to constantly changing consumer preferences, which are mostly determined by analysis and forecasting of consumer behaviour (Jiang et al., 2016). A key tactic for enhancing service personalisation in Hospitality 5.0 is the deployment of modularity, particularly service modularity. A corporation pursuing excellence has been defined as using modularity in services as a strategic response to the need to ensure flexibility and high responsiveness to clients (Avlonitis and Hsuan, 2017).

c. Virtualization

By combining sensor data collected from the actual world with virtual or simulation-based models, the third design pillar, virtualization, enables the replication of a "digital twin" of the complete value chain (smart warehouse, smart factory, and even smart products/services) (Moreno et al., 2017). To extend this to Hospitality 5.0, virtualization allows hotel personnel to automatically track consumption, bill guests' folios, and alert housekeeping when bottles need to be replaced, thereby reducing or even eliminating human-human interaction. Murukutla (2010) has shown that virtualization benefits the hospitality industry because it is affordable thanks to less expensive technology, more efficient use of energy, storage space, and labour needed to operate the machinery, increased employee productivity, and a decrease in licence fees for the equipment.

d. Real-Time Capabilities

According to the latest research, the fourth design pillar, real-time capability, entails real-time data analysis and real-time decision making (Moeuf et al., 2018). Similar to the previous point, real-time functionality will be essential for Hospitality 5.0 to further the adoption of individualised guest service, smart hotels, and supply chain management. In-room and on-property smart systems are maintained by back-of-house management systems with the help of real-time capabilities. These technologies aid in real-time problem and failure detection, facilitating quick maintenance (Kansakar et al 2019). Hotels can learn more about the typical length of guest stays, the prices they are prepared to pay, and how they feel about the hotel's overall service and experience thanks to real-time data (Gupta, 2020).

The hotel can focus on customisation while offering consumers effective services in real time by utilising real-time capabilities.

e. Decentralisation

The smart factory's various elements can operate independently and make decisions on their own thanks to the fifth design pillar, decentralisation as long as they continue to move in the same direction towards a single, overarching organisational aim (Gilchrist, 2016). The ability to adapt quickly to changing circumstances and meet the demands of personalisation is made possible by decentralisation. Decentralized networks are extremely effective at handling both financial transactions and actual payments in the hospitality industry (Shabani & Munir, 2020).

PRACTICAL APPLICATION OF HOSPITALITY 5.0

Hospitality 5.0 is derived from Industry 5.0 which aims at aligning services marketing, people management and hotel operations with technology as it provides a flawless and pragmatic customer experience for the guests. It includes:

A. Artificial intelligence, Internet of things and Block chain technology
B. Collaborative robots, chatbots and sensors
C. Contactless automation
D. Mobile technology
E. Augmented reality and Virtual reality
F. Big Data
G. Cloud Computing
H. 6G and beyond
I. Machine to machine communication

Technology is as important as information. Hence it is essential to keep a pulse on technology which will help to enhance performance efficacy, intrinsic motivation, anthropomorphism/mind and emotions to escalate customer experiences to the next level and maximize revenue of the hotel. The impact of Hospitality 5.0 technology on hospitality business and the economy have created tremendous opportunities and challenges.

ADVANTAGES OF HOSPITALITY 5.0 TECHNOLOGY

a. Performance Efficacy:

Performance efficacy refers to the degree of an individual's belief that adopting new technology improves individuals' overall task performance. Guests here look at seeking maximum benefits from this novel technology through high performance, convenience, and efficiency This functional aspect of performance efficacy emphasizes the ability to deal with high task performances.

b. Intrinsic Motivation

Guest experiences a sense of fun or enjoyment while interacting with technology which creates a positive and friendly atmosphere.

c. Anthropomorphism

Anthropomorphism refers to applying human appearances and emotions to non-human materials. The anthropomorphic interface of technology demonstrates how robot assistants can bring enlightened experiences to the guest. They appear friendlier with a smile on the face, have a mind of their own, express emotions, have intentions and a free will to perform the activities.

d. Social Influence

Social presence represents how guests respond socially to avatars or robotic agents as if they were real creatures through mental simulation of non-human intelligence. With this approach, social presence fills the gap between humans and robots via shaping an individual's intentional, cognitive, or affective states. It will create a status symbol, a sense of pride and prestige for the guest in their social network.

e. Facilitating Conditions

Facilitating conditions refer to the degree of an individual's belief that organizational and technical infrastructure will help in task completion and minimize barriers for the guest. Interactions with technology would be time-saving, easy to use and highly beneficial.

f. Emotions

Technological devices give a feeling of contentment, relaxation, and overall satisfaction.

INFLUENCING FACTORS OF HOSPITALITY 5.0 ADOPTION BY GUESTS

Hospitality 5.0 will emerge when intelligent systems, intelligent devices, and intelligent automation merge with human intelligence. By integrating workflows with intelligent systems to improve process efficiency, Hospitality 5.0 can allow human-technology interaction by bringing employees and technology together in hotel operations. Hospitality 5.0 can impact the hotel industry's high-touch and customer-centric hotel operation, employees, and guests by adopting the factors influencing Hospitality 5.0. Thus, innovative technologies and their ease of use enhances end-users' utility and provides value for money. The influencing factors are:

a. Trust

The use of Hospitality 5.0 technology is trustworthy, predictable, reliable, and safe.

b. Booking Intention

Guests will only book hotels adopting latest automation for his stay as he wants to experience brand new technology.

c. Perceived Usefulness

The use of technology will help improve the efficiency of the check in process making it simpler and much more effective than the traditional processes. Usefulness creates more value for the guest and hence in the long run it enhances the guest spending power and stay experience.

d. Perceived Ease-Of-Use

Technology will make tasks user friendly to perform, learn and interact as it magnifies the value of the experience.

e. Privacy Concerns

Technology makes the guests more comfortable with giving out personal information as it cannot be misused by anyone.

f. Social Rewards

Technology facilitates pleasant socializing, gaining emotional support from others, building good relationships and achieving social satisfaction.

g. Reduced Health Risks

The use of technology would reduce the risk of any kind of infection and unknown risks that may affect guests' health.

h. Benefits

Technology makes it convenient to maintain distance from other people in the hotel and reduces the risk of getting infected with any kind of viruses.

INCORPORATING HOSPITALITY 5.0 TECHNOLOGIES INTO THE TOUCHPOINTS OF THE GUEST JOURNEY

A customer journey is a series of actions a customer takes to arrive at the moment of acquiring an experience. Touchpoints are points of contact between the guest and the hotel which could either be face to face, through the hotel website or app. The guest journey includes:

a. Pre-stay stage b. Stay stage c. Post stay stage (see Table 1)

a. The Pre-Stay Stage

This stage involves the entire guest experience before his stay. The best kind of experiences given to guests is because of the integration of AI, internet of things, block chain technology robots, chatbots, sensors, contactless automation, mobile technologies and AR, VR with the hotel processes, people and systems. The pre-stay stage is a critical part to connect and co-create and enhance the overall hotel experience. Not only do these technologies make hotels more visible, but they show the human touch that guests are searching for in a hotel. It gives guests the best "try-before-you-buy" experience and enables hotels to market their lodging throughout the pre-stay phase through an engaging experience.

Table 1. AI in consumer journey during stay in hotels

Technology	Pre stay stage	Hotel - Stay stage			Post – Stay Stage
		Front office	Guest Room	F&B Facilities	
AI, Internet of things and blocktechnical,chnology	AI enabled chatbots	AI temperature scan, noncontact kiosk, thermal imaging cameras, face recognition technology and hand scanning device	AI based scanning device, AI face recognition technology, AI sensors and AI enabled voice recognition	AI based scanning device, AI face recognition technology, table menu kiosk	AI enabled chatbots

b. The Stay Stage

The hotel-stay stage represents the most interaction-intense stage due to the number of personal encounters between guests and the hotel employees in the physical hotel environment.

c. The Post-Stay Stage

Check-out and the completion of all guest accounting tasks for the duration of the stay are determined by the post-stay phase. It includes guest interactions with the brand and its environment following the actual stay. A good post-stay strategy supports social sharing of experience and a multiplying effect of a great visit. Mobile communication and chatbots provide a valuable opportunity to engage with the guests by thanking them for their patronage and informing them about their valuable input, which will encourage new bookings from other guests who are viewing it.

AI, IOT AND BLOCK CHAIN TECHNOLOGY IN HOTELS TO CREATE A DIGITAL GUEST EXPERIENCE

Artificial intelligence (AI) is made up of two words "artificial" which refers to something created by humans, and" intelligence" which refers to the ability to think for oneself, resulting in AI being defined as a thinking power created by humans (Limna et al., 2021). AI is the simulation of human intelligence operations by computers, particularly computer systems (Wang et al., 2020). AI is extremely effective at performing specific tasks. It also transforms almost every sector of a country's economy by enabling computers to make sound decisions that result in more efficient operations (Holzinger et al., 2021; Kumar et al., 2021). Furthermore, AI enables people to work smarter, resulting in better business outcomes, but it also necessitates the development of new competencies and capabilities, ranging from technological expertise to social and emotional skills, as well as creative abilities (Ivanov & Webster, 2019; Ruel & Njoku, 2021). Simultaneously, AI may cause human talent to be replaced by technology in some cases, forcing hospitality and tourism businesses to redesign their structures and processes as a result (Saini & Bhalla, 2022). Also, using digital analytics and AI tools to manage and monitor the performance of human talent results in improved talent attraction, development, deployment, and productivity in human resource management (Hecklau et al., 2017; Nocker & Sena, 2019).

Because of the potential implications for service quality and customer satisfaction, there is a significant interest in hospitality and tourism research in gaining a better understanding of the impact of AI technologies on employee engagement, retention, and productivity levels (Ruel & Njoku, 2021). Hence, AI is the heart of all technology.

Industry 5.0 and IoT Are Two Ideas That are Interconnected

IoT is a network that can connect with anything anytime and anyplace by technologies of RFID (Radio Frequency Identification), WSN (Wireless Sensor Network) and 3G/4G/5G mobile communications, according to an agreed protocol, in order to identify, locate, track, monitor and manage smart objects. The Internet of Things – an ever-growing network of connected devices which communicate with a central server as well as with each other is becoming more than just connectivity. It connects physical and virtual worlds with huge number of electronic devices distributed in houses, vehicles, streets, buildings and many other public environments.

The adoption of IoT technologies widely redesigns and improves the performance of all the main business processes in hospitality by bringing in numerous benefits, starting with cost reduction, improved functionality, greater productivity and increased guest satisfaction.

The three main characteristics of the Internet of Things are:

1. Anything that communicates: Smart things have the ability to wirelessly communicate among themselves, and form ad hoc networks of interconnected objects.
2. Anything that can be identified: Smart things are identified with a digital name; relationships can be specified in the digital domain whenever physical interconnection cannot be established.
3. Anything that interacts: Smart things can interact with the local environment through sensing and actuation capabilities whenever present. The Internet of Things offers new opportunities to connect physical and digital worlds, and enables more direct and active interaction between guests, hotels, products, services and destinations.

The effective use of technology can help hotels to enhance guest experiences. A digital ecosystem connects smart devices enabling an array of innovative technologies to work in sync and exchange value (e.g., information, entertainment, promotion etc.)

Starting at the check-in, guests may prefer to check in themselves at kiosks placed in the lobby. After this rooms are digitally assigned based on mathematical algorithms, taking into consideration the length of stay of the guest, past and future bookings, room features requested, loyalty to the brand, and type of guest.

APPLICATION OF AI AND IOT IN HOSPITALITY 5.0 WITH SPECIAL EMPHASIS ON SENSORY MARKETING

As early as in the seventies of the last century, Kotler propounded that in order to gain a competitive advantage, hotel owners need to apply stimuli from the five senses (sight/visual, sound/auditory, smell/olfactory, touch/tactile and taste/gustatory) in their hotel environment to create an atmosphere which increases the attraction towards the property (See Table 2).

APPLICATION OF AI AND IOT IN OTHER AREAS OF HOSPITALITY INDUSTRY

IoT is used in many different areas to improve efficiency and provide a better customer experience. It gives the hoteliers an opportunity to serve guests, offer value-added services, and run the facility on the back end with far greater efficiency. The modernization of technology employed in the platform for providing hospitality services is being driven by advancements in smart devices and IoT. The hotel industry can use IoT to provide integrated services like application-driven devices and automated triggers like automated door locks, set-top boxes, thermostats, telephones, light switches, voice-based interaction, electric blinds, and other devices that are connected on a common network to enable the services that guests want.

These kinds of facilities will make the guest experience more personalized and speedier and the hotel more efficient. Below mentioned are the ways in which hotels will be able to deliver more value to their guests at lower costs.

Table 2. Multisensory cues and multisensory marketing in hotels

Multisensory cues and multisensory marketing in hotels			
Five Senses	**Types of sensory stimuli**	**Types of sensory marketing**	**Examples**
Sight	Visual	Visual Marketing	Colors, windows, ceiling height, flowers, floor covering, walls, layout of the lobby and guest rooms, fountains, lighting, logos of hotel branded toiletries, hotel monogrammed towels, national / international newspapers, smart TV, other guests, etc.
Sound	Auditory	Auditory Marketing	Soothing music played in the lobby and elevator, voice of the front-desk associate or server in the restaurant, the hissing sound from the ice-machine, shower, coffee machine, etc.
Smell	Olfactory	Olfactory Marketing	Signature scent of the hotel in the lobby, elevators, and on the floors, smell of coffee, aroma of the food, scented hotel pens, fragrance from the toiletries, flower arrangements, perfume strips in the hotel magazine, etc.
Touch	Tactile	Tactile Marketing	Porcelain cups, bed linen, towels, carpeted floor, chairs, touch screens for the check-in, handshakes, shape of glass bottles, etc.
Taste	Gustatory	Gustatory Marketing	At the check-in, a bowl with exclusive confectionary or coffee and ice-tea; mini bar, chocolate candy, or fruit basket/champagne set up in the guest rooms, food and beverages in the restaurant, etc.

1. Integration with Mobile

All the functions which were performed through remote control, key cards and switches are now available at the click of a button on the mobile device.

2. Personalised Hotel Rooms

IoT platforms memorize a guest's specific comfort preference such as temperature control, lights, and TV channels, therefore automatically set up the room for their next stay.

3. Voice- Based Interactions

It enables the guest to use voice control and adjust in room devices such as light, thermostat, blinds/ curtains and TV.

4. Body area Wire-less Medical Sensor

This can filter out, high carbohydrate and sugary meal options for diabetic guests as well as high cholesterol meal options for guests who are patients with heart diseases.

5. IoT based Inventory Management

It will record the change in inventory automatically.

6. Location Based Information

It helps in sending up-to-date information about local transport links, or nearby attractions.

7. Wireless Button

With the wireless button made possible, availing services by a guest and sending automated messages to all the respective departments.eg Reception, Housekeeping, Restaurants simultaneously becomes easy, time saving and cost effective.

8. Guest Room is Occupied or Not

The in-room monitoring system has the capability to detect whether a room is occupied or unoccupied so as to schedule housekeeping services.

9. Autonomous Bed Bug prevention

IoT has made it possible to automate bed bug prevention.

10. Automation

IoT creates self-operating business function systems for a hotel.

11. Maintenance

Both preventive and breakdown maintenance can be managed through IoT.

12. Energy Saving

IoT makes it possible for smart energy saving

AI AND BLOCK CHAIN TECHNOLOGY AND ITS USES IN HOTELS

Artificial Intelligence and Blockchain are two most important technologies that normalize functionality in every hotel industry. Blockchain provides more security in financial transactions in the hotel industry. Artificial Intelligence is the major reason for this. There are many AI algorithms used in Blockchain that helps to do more things independently. Blockchain technology helps the customers by tracking the orders as well as payments so time wastage is eliminated.

Advantages of AI and Blockchain in the Hotel Industry

The exchange of data between organizations will continue to be secure and transparent. Since the data will be encrypted, no one will have easy access to it. The data won't be subject to alteration. Since this technology operates on a distributed model, data can be shared throughout the enterprise. With this technology, consumer identification and privacy will be protected and shared in a decentralized database in a secure manner. It enables safe payment options. This technology implements database integration, allowing data to be transferred utilizing cryptographic principles. Blockchain technology is applied in the supply chain management concept, which ensures correct accounting and tax payment.

COLLABORATIVE ROBOTS, CHATBOTS AND SENSORS IN HOTELS

Table 3. Collaborative robots, chatbots and sensors in hotels

Technology	Hotel - Stay stage		
	Front office	Guest Room	F&B Facilities
ROBOTICS (Robots, chatbots and sensors)	Front desk robots, concierge robots, porter robots, check-in robots, cloakroom robots, temperature scan robots, non-contact robot kiosk, robotic thermal imaging cameras, robotic valet parking, robotic host, robotic arm, robotic lobby ambassador.	Room service robots and room cleaning robots	Robotic self-serving kiosk, bartender robot, food service robots, robot drones, robot baristas and beer robots.

Robotics is a branch of Artificial Intelligence which is built with electronic & mechanical components that work on some logic using computer science. It is an integration of computer science, mechanical, electronic, nanotechnology and bioengineering. Robots are hardware applications of AI that have bodies and motor abilities (arms and legs) to accomplish physical tasks in real environments rather than virtual. Robots can also be converted into chatbots and vice versa. A bot is an application of AI that is used to automate tasks e.g. chatbot to book a hotel or a robot to fold the guest laundry. AI operates as a logical system within the business intelligence, which allows the AI to work by providing the ability in terms of extending software applications and specialized hardware. AI programs can learn and make decisions rationally through decision support system.

Robots are appropriate for repetitive and dull tasks (e.g., cleaning the common areas of the hotel, delivering laundry, gardening, issuing payment documents, processing card payments). Humans on the other hand are required for tasks that need social interaction and emotional intelligence (welcoming/greeting guests, guiding the guest to the room/table) (see Table 3) . Adoption and subsequent implementation of robots in the hospitality industry is complicated. To make an informed decision, owners and managers need a clear perspective of service robots' advantages and disadvantages as compared to humans.

It is crucial to comprehend the prospective uses of robots and their effects on the operational, security, marketing, human resource, and financial management of hotels. Being served by robots is an interesting, memorable, pleasurable and an exciting long-lasting experience in the mind of the guest. Today, robots are capable of carrying out any task, navigating any surface, and making choices in unpredictable situations. Recently developed techniques have made it possible for robots to control their environment. Robotic teams that work together to perform certain duties specified for a particular location will advance as a result of artificial intelligence.

Table 4. Role and opportunities of service robots in hotel services

Serial number	Types of services
01	Support Services aim at freeing human employees from mundane tasks and allow them to focus on more complex and dynamic situations.
02	Substitute Services replaces human employees completely in a sequence of service encounters.
03	Differentiate services of your businesses from competitors to create unique selling proposition to attract guests to the hotel.
04	Upgrade services to utilize resources more efficiently by the business.
05	Upskill services imparts the required skillsets to employees transforming their existing roles.

Continuous research is being conducted to promote robots, which can be useful in assisting with effective digital transformation (Kamble et al., 2018). Industry 5.0 concentrates on using highly skilled workers and robotics to produce individualised items for customers, such as smart devices and automobiles. While competent humans provide the cognitive skills of the craftsperson, collaborating robots will be able to handle the arduous lifting and guarantee uniformity. With industry 5.0, robot collaboration has begun.

APPLICATIONS OF ROBOTS IN HOTELS

This section explores that the Robots has been and could be used at various service encounters in the hotels (see Table 4):

Reception Robot

The robotisation of services at the reception could be welcoming the guest, providing information about hotel facilities, check-in, and check out, guiding to the room, processing payments as well as concierge services.

Restaurant Robot

The services that can be robotised at the restaurant could be greeting the guest, guiding them to the table, providing information about the menu, taking orders, serving food and beverages, cooking food, cleaning the table and also delivering food to the guest rooms.

Housekeeping Robot

The tasks that can be done by robots in the housekeeping department include cleaning the rooms, public areas, delivering laundry and linen to guest rooms as well as perform gardening tasks.

From a financial perspective, robots make sense if they improve the financial performance of the hotel by reducing operational costs and/or generating additional revenues (Ivanov and Webster 2019). The additional revenues can be a result of extensive growth (room service order delivered by a robot), intensive growth (charging higher prices for robotic experiences for guests). Robots will help to improve the hotel's occupancy rate as well as the profitability of the hotel.

From the operational point of view robots will make the operational process easier and allow the hotel to serve more guests. The usage of robotic devices will guarantee better safety and security for guests as well as employees.

Pros Of Robots:

Robots handle complaints effortlessly and protect the guest personal data better than humans. Service robots can deliver more personalised service to guests make fewer mistakes and are faster than employees. They furnish accurate information and deal with calculations with absolute ease. They provide information in many languages which is an added advantage.

Cons Of Robots:

Robots will consume too much electricity and may malfunction during service. They may misunderstand the question or food order which will lead to guest complaints. Robots cannot implement a special request of the guest nor understand the emotions of the guest.

Chatbots

A chatbot is as an application that helps in creating a casual, friendly and informal conversation with the guest by engaging him with human like agents powered with artificial intelligence (AI) and other automation technologies that can communicate with end-users via chat. This enables communication between devices and computers.

To differentiate it from the human interface, chatbot operations can be coordinated and automated by connecting to a central server or database. With little assistance from humans, they can accomplish tasks swiftly and intelligently (Kiraz et al., 2020).

ROLE OF CHATBOTS

a. Rule Based Hotel Chatbots

Decision tree bots and rule-based chatbots both fall under this umbrella term.

Chatbots that follow rules plot interactions like a flowchart. They do this in order to prepare the chatbots for potential questions from customers and how to best reply.

b. AI Based Hotel Chatbots

As opposed to human chat operators, AI chatbots that employ machine learning comprehend the context and intent of a query before responding.

These chatbots generate their own AI based hotel chatbots answers to more complicated questions using natural language responses.

SENSORS AND CCTVS IN HOTELS

A sensor is an equipment which is used to detect and respond to some type of input from the physical environment. This input may be light, heat, motion, moisture, pressure, or any environmental factor. Below are some of the examples of the major sensors which are used in the hotel industry.

a. Photo Sensors – These sensors reduce the consumption of energy of the property. It senses the amount of daylight available in the room and accordingly the bulb in the area automatically switches on & off which reflects in energy conservation.
b. Smoke Detector – A smoke detector is a tool that senses smoke and indicates fire in the area. When there is smoke these devices issue a signal to a fire alarm control panel as part of a fire alarm system which helps the employees to identify the area where the fire has occurred.
c. Occupancy detector – These sensors are also called as motion detectors which are devices that turn on the lights, opening or closing of doors when there is movement of people.
d. Close-circuit TV or CCTV (Video Surveillance) - CCTV is a device which keeps an eye on everything that is happening in the hotel except guest rooms and rest rooms. The objectives are to monitor, manage and control overall activities of the hotel, to protect the guests and employees as well as prevent pilferage and theft of hotel property. It also serves as a way of legal compensation by identifying false claims by guests and helps the hotel get insurance claims in case of property damage due to fire etc.
e. Humidity sensors- These sensors are used to maintain proper temperature and humidity in the area and it detects any change in temperature immediately.
f. Gas Leak Detectors – In hotels a lot of food is being continuously prepared hence it is very important to work safely with gas and if any kind of leakage happens this type of gas detector indicates spontaneously which helps to avoid untoward incidents.

CONTACTLESS AUTOMATION

Contactless automation is a powerful tool to gather real-time guest feedback, leading to more satisfied guests and better service in the future (see table 5) . It is assisting the hoteliers to make up for their deficiencies while the guest is still in the hotel. Guests are willing to return to a hotel if an imperfect experience was addressed quickly and reshaped into a positive one. Two-way messaging makes it easy for hotel employees to prompt guests for feedback during their stay, opening up opportunities for service recovery and improving post-stay satisfaction. As an added feature, the automatic replies can streamline responses to monotonous requests, freeing up staff to focus on interacting with guests in person and learning more about their needs which can give them a better guest experience.

Advantages of Contactless Automation

Contactless automation will be helpful to collect ratings and feedback from visitors in real time and make the trip unforgettable. There will be an advancement in guest experiences with AI and personalization. The hotels would recover and bounce back with contactless operations with a focus on guests.

Table 5. Contactless automation

Technology	Hotel - Stay stage		
	Front office	Guest Room	F&B Facilities
Contactless Automation	Digital receptionist, biometric check-in device, radio frequency identification, voice enabled elevator	Digital room keys, RFID key cards	Conveyor belt food delivery

Thus, we can say that contactless automation creates psychological safety, perceived value and improves hospitality service quality.

SMARTPHONE MOBILE TECHNOLOGY

Table 6. Smartphone mobile technology

Technology	Pre stay stage	Hotel - Stay stage			Post – Stay Stage
		Front office	Guest Room	F&B Facilities	
MOBILE TECHNOLOGY	Chatbots and Applications	Mobile check-in, mobile valet, biometric checkin, mobile credit card terminals, beacons	Mobile keys, QR code room service menu, room service apps	Mobile valet, digital menu, table menu kiosk and QR code menu	Chatbots and Applications

In present times the use of mobile technology over human interaction has tremendously increased (see Table 6). This gives rise to the concept of technology 5.0 enhanced guest experiences which is an important element of the hospitality industry. The use of smart phones among travelers has increased which has given the hoteliers a lead to expand and build on smart phone technology. This technology has emerged as an extremely important tool for dissemination of information, shorten the processing time thereby, increasing the productiveness of hotel employees which in turn enhances the hotel revenue. The integration of smart phone technology helps the hotel to interact with guests and provide contactless guest experience for each stage in the guest cycle: pre-arrival stage, arrival stage, stay, departure stage and post-departure stage.

Smart Phone technology is indeed one of the key travel motivators in today's era and has become:

- A travel guide
- A travel agent
- A Calculator
- A Cameraman
- A Translator and
- The best restaurant finder.

Application of Smartphone Technology:

1. To book a hotel room (73%)
2. Maps to get around the city (61%)
3. Comparing hotel prices and deals (60%)
4. Booking of flights (59%)
5. Booking a cab (58%)

This indicates that mobile technology is the next big thing and making use of that is the only way ahead.
Source: Hindustan Times (Trip advisor)

AUGMENTED REALITY AND VIRTUAL REALITY

The goal of augmented reality (AR) essentially combines the real and virtual worlds, which gives users access to more details about a real-world object by using information shown in the virtual environment (see table 7) .

Table 7. Augmented reality and virtual reality

Technology	Pre stay stage	Hotel - Stay stage	
		Front office	Guest Room
VR/AR	Websites	Beacons	Virtual host, room virtual assistant, voice command and voice identification device, VR headset, smart room control device

Augmented Reality Systems is a mix of real world and virtual objects in a real environment. It is highly interactive and runs in 3D in real time which helps to synchronize real and virtual objects with each other.

Virtual reality (VR) and augmented reality (AR) are the most world changing technologies of the 21st Century. By stimulating the senses with computer generated powerful 3D interactive visual experience images, guests can immerse themselves in the world of virtual reality.

VR is considered to be a promising technology for the Hospitality Industry as it has the powerful effect of placing the person in a virtual world, by providing interactive 3D surroundings simulated by a computer. The introduction of VR services has helped to provide fully immersive and seamless experiences. For hospitality product development, marketers are implementing sensory-rich and interactive ways to visualize a new hotel brand by informing consumers about its features, interior design, amenities, location, and atmosphere via brand decks with hotel images, 360o web-based tours, and recently VR. Compared to static images, 360o views allow guests to alter the aspect of the virtual space and simulate rotation and movement which results in increased interactivity and lessened prejudices. Indeed, the shift from two-dimensional images to three-dimensional virtual presentations via 360o web-based tours is found to increase brand image, boosted the storytelling about the brand which has led to more favourable brand attitudes for different guest requirements. In augmented reality (AR), computer-generated images are added to live, direct, or indirect views of real-world environments. Applications for Industry 5.0 are supported by this technology. One of the cutting-edge technologies used in the Industry 5.0 movement is augmented reality.

BIG DATA

Big data is the information that the current environment continuously produces. A tremendous amount of data is produced by each digital operation and social media interaction. Systems, sensors, and mobile devices transmit these data over a network infrastructure that is based in the cloud (Naresh Kumar, 2016). Big data is being produced at an unprecedented rate, scale, and variety. Big data requires adequate processing power, analytics prowess, and information management expertise in order to be truly valuable.

Utilizing 3D symmetry in the designs of the innovation ecosystem is made possible by the breakthrough technology known as Industry 5.0. Enormous data analytics, is a difficult process that looks at big data to find information like hidden patterns, market trends, and others. It makes use of a sophisticated analytical technique with a range of structured and semi-structured data sets. It needs to store and process enormous amounts of data using conventional tools. It is utilized as real-time data to strengthen the company's competitive advantage and their future course of action. The company uses a number of variables, including population, location accessibility, and others, to gather information about customer preferences.

By tracking customer experiences and finding solutions to issues, it is possible to improve them and forge lasting relationships with customers.

CLOUD COMPUTING

The distribution of computer services, such as databases, software, intelligence analytics, networks, and others, is known as cloud computing. This technology offers effective innovation and scale-based economics. Cloud computing reduces costs, simplifies the infrastructure, broadens the work area, protects data, and provides instant access to knowledge. The system primarily utilizes four different types of clouds: public, private, hybrid, and community (Dadhich et al., 2022). Data is accessed through the internet after being stored and managed on remote servers by this technology. It provides on-demand computing services, including processing power, storage, and applications. The virtual setting that supports industry applications is known as the "industrial cloud."

Applications like IoT monitoring tools that are used for mobile and web usage are produced by cloud service providers. Additionally, the cloud supports the use of Interfaces that enable the automated normalization of data from a variety of data production sources. Devices that handle edge computing are equipped with constrained computing resources to manage business analyses. A scalable framework for supporting data edge devices is provided by cloud computing. The cloud infrastructure supports IoT platforms on the edge. The platforms are used to control edge devices, including diverse and autonomous robots placed on the shop floor. The industry regularly accesses the data from the local servers in order to manage critical data. The amount of data sent to the centralized server can be decreased thanks to Industry 5.0. Through the use of more workforce, cloud computing enables preventive data to identify machine failures and mitigate them. Machines, data management, and functionality will keep moving from conventional methods to cloud-based solutions as technology develops (Bortolini et al., 2016; Dadhich,

2017a; Esmaeilian et al., 2020). Delivery of systems, quick updates, current performance models, and other delivery options are all made possible by the cloud much more quickly than with standalone systems. The industry has undergone a significant transition toward the use of cloud solutions, which will only grow and challenge current data storage techniques. The most fundamental form of online storage is provided by the cloud, which offers installation-free web-based applications with operational simplicity.

6G AND BEYOND

It's a sixth-generation (6G) standard for creating wireless communication tools that can support cellular data networks. It is expected that 6G enterprises would be far more heterogeneous than their predecessors. They will likely support applications that go beyond the existing portable use scenarios, such as virtual and augmented reality (VR/AR), omnipresent instant correspondences, and unavoidable Internet of Things knowledge (IoT). With local authorization, range sharing, framework sharing, and intelligent mechanized administration supported by flexible edge processing, artificial intelligence, short-parcel communication, and blockchain advancements, flexible organization administrators will typically embrace adaptable decentralized plans of action for 6G. 6G networks are anticipated to give ultrahigh reliability for industry 5.0 by meeting the norms of the intelligent information society. To assure network connectivity, artificial intelligence techniques are applied to obtain mobility prediction solutions. Industry 5.0 faced challenges from a high data rate for diverse applications.

Energy management is a concern for industry 5.0 as more and larger smart devices are connected. Through the use of energy consumption and energy harvesting techniques, energy management can be optimized.

Machine to Machine Communication

It describes constant, wired or wireless, channel communication between devices. Industrial instrumentation can enable machine-to-machine communication by enabling data sharing between sensors and application software (Esmaeilian et al., 2020; Rakesh Kumar Birda & Manish Dadhich, 2019). For this kind of communication, data was sent from a widespread network of devices back to an inner hub for analysis before being forwarded to a personal computer. With the use of M2M technology, enterprises may connect equipment and data centers wirelessly.

Positive Outcome of Hospitality 5.0 Adoption From Guests' Perspective

a. Technology will be faster than human employees.
b. It will deal with calculations better than human employees.
c. Technology will provide more accurate information than human employees.
d. It will be able to provide information in different languages than humans.
e. Technology will provide polite and empathetic behavior than employees.
f. The guests will forever be the center focus with technology.
g. All questions of guests will be answered patiently.
h. Due to technology guests do not have to wait during service processes like check-in, check-out, dining etc.

i. Personal data of guests will not be shared while using artificial intelligent devices.
j. Technology is most dependable than human employees in enhancing experiences.
k. Greater accuracy with fewer human errors is possible with technology.
l. It helps to provide more consistent service than hotel employees.

INDUSTRY 5.0 INDIA EMERGING MARKETS

Government of India has taken a deliberate decision based on industry 5.0 that India will be a leading manufacturing hub. India is about to undergo significant reforms and is on course to have the third-largest economy in the world by 2030. India is a country that international investors cannot afford to overlook due to its educated and tech-savvy population, skilled labor force, robust legal and intellectual property framework, and strong commitment to controlled liberalization. India's manufacturing sector has gone through a number of stages, from initial industrialization and the license system to liberalization and the current stage of global competitiveness. Indian manufacturing companies are now establishing themselves on international marketplaces and challenging powerful rivals (Sharma & Dadhich, 2014). The equipment manufacturers, the government, and the consumer all have a significant impact on how the industry is defined. India has several chances in the Fourth Industrial Revolution, including the ones listed below:

Manufacturing Sector

The management of human resources and all aspects of production are included in the manufacturing sector. The industrial revolution largely focuses on productivity, using cutting-edge machinery to produce with high accuracy while minimizing production damage, time consumption, and human labor to a greater level.

Due to their increased contribution to GDP, manufacturing processes are prioritized in India (Manish Dadhich, Manvinder Singh Pahwa, & Vipin Jain, 2021).

Health and Medical Sector

Modern medicine is equipped with state-of-the-art technology that is used to treat a variety of life-threatening illnesses. Nanotechnology, for instance, can be used to reproduce damaged tissue (Costa & Peixoto, 2020). Other recent medical advancements include robotic surgery, wireless brain sensors, smart inhalers, precision medicine, artificially stimulated cells, 3D printed artificial organs, and more.

Transportation Sector

In developing nations like India, transportation is dangerous and poorly organized. Al and IoT hold great promise for enhancing the transportation system. For instance, in optimal traffic, AI analyses traffic patterns to build routes that are ideal during times of high traffic, maintenance, and construction (Dadhich et al., 2020). While promoting improved safety and a better customer experience, using self-driving cars to prevent collisions and IoT can also save money (Singh, 2021).

Agriculture Sector

The Indian economy is thought to be supported by the agricultural sector. However, the agriculture industry is now given the least attention due to a lack of awareness and guidance on the adoption of Industry 5.0 practices. As a result, there is now just a small region of agricultural due to the absorption of technology. Already, automated machinery is used in agriculture to reduce labor costs and save time (Rakesh Kumar Birda & Manish Dadhich, 2019). In the agricultural sector, technology solutions are being developed and implemented by scientists and industry professionals.

THEORETICAL IMPLICATIONS OF INDUSTRY 5.0

This chapter has provided several theoretical contributions to the realm of technological application in hospitality and tourism. The publication volume of technology in the hospitality and tourism research has increasingly grown in recent years. The adoption of next-generation technologies will have a favorable influence on employment in several areas as a result of increased automation. Industry 5.0 increases chances for creative people to work, which promotes the improvement of labor productivity. Machines have become versatile which creates a high-level choice and industry 5.0 will help the client digitally in managing repeated follow-up assignments (Haleem & Javaid, 2019). More individualized services will boost guest happiness and loyalty as well as draw in new guests, which will enhance revenue and market share for the businesses. Industry 5.0 gives the field of human-machine interaction increased importance and offers a larger platform for research and development in this area. It also gives start-ups and entrepreneurs in creative and innovative spheres excellent opportunities to develop new products and services related to industry 5.0, provided adequate funding and infrastructure are available. Thus, this study conducted a thorough review of technological applications in hospitality and tourism research and provides a profound knowledge foundation for this stream of literature. For example, studies on guest preferences of technological features, comparative studies among different cultures, and consequences and solutions of technological service failures can be extended in the future.

PRACTICAL IMPLICATIONS OF INDUSTRY 5.0

In view of these research findings, practical implications of technological application and management are provided for technological developers and hospitality and tourism practitioners. Several issues should be considered from the aspects of guests and employees. To better meet the expectations from guests, hoteliers should investigate the actual needs of the demand side before implementing hospitality 5.0 technology.

Surveys and interviews can be conducted to investigate the preferences of hotel guests for technological features and functionality. Preliminary market research has always helped managers understand market demands and reduce unnecessary investment costs. Simultaneously, in the initial stages human staff members who are well trained in technological systems must provide demonstrations for guests who are less tech-savvy or elderly people. To gratify the employees, managers should strive to create a rapport between human staff and technological devices and should provide front-line employees with necessary organizational, technical and emotional support to reduce their anxiety about being replaced by technological intervention.

The main focus of industry 5.0 is on value oriented and ethical technological engineering. Green IoT and AI will be in the spotlight as key technological enablers for a sustainable digital transition towards a smart circular economy. An exploratory bibliometric investigation of the formation and development of industry 5.0 is the primary emphasis. By using artificial intelligence to make sense of huge data, it will offer a human-centered solution. As middle-skill employment declines and the workforce is divided into two groups—highly skilled and qualified workers and low-paid and unqualified workers—this trend further polarizes the workplace. This might narrow the gap between competent and unskilled people in society. Due to highly automated production processes, it will be extremely difficult to increase workers' skills, such as preparing them to embrace cutting-edge technology and changing their behavior when interacting with technology. Collaborative robotics a form of automation along with human coworkers will continue to pose a serious risk on the factory floor (Rossi, 2018). The research in this area is still in its infancy and requires substantial infrastructure investments. Startups and business owners will face difficulties since industry 5.0 demands the use of cutting-edge technologies. The current company strategy and business models must be adjusted and customized to match the requirements of industry 5.0 due to greater levels of automation in the industry. Business strategy will place a greater emphasis on customer-centric operations as a result of mass personalization. Due to various client preferences, version Industry 5.0 requires a higher level of dynamism to maintain competition. This chapter could lead to a better understanding of Hospitality 5.0 adoption in the hospitality industry. Therefore, the implication could be applied to business owners, managers, and marketers in the hotel industry or any customer service sector to better understand and implement appropriate strategies to meet the needs and expectations of not only the customers but also the employees through the use of technology. Furthermore, it may also aid academics in broadening their research by incorporating more potential elements.

RECOMMENDATIONS

This industrial revolution involves utilizing human-machine interface to expedite and simplify tasks. The personalization concept is advanced by Industry 5.0. It is employed to create a virtual environment, cutting-edge computers, and information technologies in order to satisfy the highly individualized demand. Big data, artificial intelligence, the internet of things (IoT), cloud computing, COBOTS, innovation, and creativity are all optimally integrated in Industry 5.0.

Industry 5.0 is anticipated to generate higher-value jobs with more room for innovation and creative thinking. It contributes to raising labor productivity and giving guests more customization options. On the other hand, skill development for the workforce is a massive task as a result of highly automated industrial systems. Due to its increased connection and adoption of common communications protocols, industry 5.0 poses a greater threat to cyber security in important industrial systems and production lines. Even though industry 5.0 gives machines more autonomy, humans still have the authority to make crucial decisions that are morally sound. In general, industry 5.0 is anticipated to transform the processes and systems by enabling more cooperation between humans and robots in order to provide guests with customized products. Through programs like Make in India, Skill India, and Start-up India, the country hopes to become a technological hub. With the help of these programs and initiatives, Industry 5.0 has the potential to make India the leader in intelligent robotic systems.

CONCLUSION

As digital technology evolves, technology will continue to adapt and provide properties with digital convenience, reduced costs, sustainability and efficiency over the next decade and beyond. Hospitality 5.0 technology will enable hoteliers to streamline operations and meet guest needs in an innovative, connectivity-oriented manner. The mobile wireless industry is in the early stages of considering and addressing the many uses enabled by wireless technology. Whereas many futuristic uses can be supported in both 4G and 5G, the enhancements being envisioned for 6G will even further enable many existing and new uses/ purposes.

In a similar way, in the long run MR's framework allows adopting various applications from VR and AR in a mixed virtuality and reality paradigm. Extended Reality (XR) refers to the capabilities and combinations of AR, VR, and MR as a whole. Holographic teleportation places greater demands on the wireless network than XR due to the integration of the five senses.

The next evolution of the internet of things will be Haptic /Tactile Communications which generally comprises real-time interactions that require the network with guaranteed high bandwidth support. This will be highly useful for the hospitality industry for self-driving cars, autonomous robots, social robots etc. 5G systems can already be considered to support many transportations, with V2X (Vehicle-to-Everything) communication technology, including Vehicle-to-Network(V2N), Vehicle-to-Infrastructure(V2I), Vehicle-to-Vehicle(V2V), Vehicle-to Pedestrian(V2P), etc. In the future, these devices will be sufficiently accurate and reliable for diagnostic purposes but may require frequent updates from central repositories. Although hospitality 5.0 application has recently attracted increasing attention from both academics and practitioners, very few articles present the whole picture of existing knowledge. Therefore, this chapter aims to provide a comprehensive review of technological applications in the hospitality and tourism sector by conducting the descriptive analysis and content analysis of 40 research studies. The US, mainland China, and South Korea were regions which academics conducted the most research. The most common research strategy was quantitative, using experimental design and surveys, with the technological acceptance model as the most widely utilised theory. Although hotels are the key players of hospitality 5.0 technology application, most publications nonetheless focused on guests. The details of the article were analysed using content analysis from several views (such as hotels, visitors, and multi-perspective). Four main sub-themes transpired from the guest perspective, namely, anthropomorphism and the preference of guests, guests' perception of robots, influential factors, and the consequences of technological adoption.

Meanwhile, three sub-themes from the hotelier's perspective, namely, robotic application and management, hotels' perception of robots, and antecedents and consequences of robotic adoption, were also revealed. Based on the information provided in the above chapter it is crystal clear that technology 5.0 will enhance the brand experience, guest experience which in turn will increase the revenue of the hotel.

REFERENCES

Abou-Shouk, M., Gad, H. E., & Abdelhakim, A. (2021, September). Exploring customers' attitudes to the adoption of robots in tourism and hospitality. *Journal of Hospitality and Tourism Technology*, *12*(4), 762–776. doi:10.1108/JHTT-09-2020-0215

Adel, A. (2022). Future of industry 5.0 in society: human-centric solutions, challenges and prospective research areas. *Journal of Cloud Computing: Advances, Systems and Applications.*

Akundi, A., Euresti, D., Luna, S., Ankobiah, W., Lopes, A. & Edinbarough, I. (2022). *State of Industry 5.0—Analysis and Identification of Current Research Trends.* Applied system innovation MDPI

Angelina, N. H. L., Khoi, N. H., & Nguyen, D. P. (2021). Unravelling the dynamic and contingency mechanism between service experience and customer engagement with luxury hotel brands. *International Journal of Hospitality Management.*

Belanche, D., Casaló, L. V., & Flavián, C. (2020). Frontline robots in tourism and hospitality: Service enhancement or cost reduction? *Journal of Electronic Markets, 31*(3), 477–492. doi:10.100712525-020-00432-5

.Birda, R. K. & Dadhich, M. (2022). Industry 5.0 Revolution towards an Imminent Future Driven Society. *International Research Journal of Engineering and Technology, 9*(5), 3709-3714.

Bogicevic, V., Liu, S. Q., Seo, S., Kandampully, J., & Rudd, N. A. (2021). Virtual reality is so cool! How technology innovativeness shapes consumer responses to service preview modes. *International Journal of Hospitality Management, 93*, 102806. doi:10.1016/j.ijhm.2020.102806

Brylska, P., Cobanoglu, C., & Dogan, S. (2022). Users Versus Non-users: The Impact of Experience on Hotel Guests' Attitudes Towards Service Robots in Hotels. *Journal of Information and Communication Technologies in Tourism, 2022*, 55–66. doi:10.1007/978-3-030-94751-4_5

Car, T., & Stifanich, L. P. (2020). Mobile technology: a tool to increase hotel sales and revenue. Journal of economics, business and organization research, 454-465.

Çetinsöz, B. C., Doğan, S., & Duran, A. (2022). Perceptions about the applicability of robot technology in the tourism industry. *Journal of multidisciplinary academic tourism.*

. Chen, K. P., Dai, A., Yang, C., & Ge, Y. (2022). Exploring factors affecting customer trust in social distancing technology and impact on hotel booking intentions. *Cogent Social Sciences Leisure and Tourism.*

Dogru, T., Mody, M., & Leonardi, C. (2018). *Blockchain Technology & its Implications for the Hospitality Industry.* Boston Hospitality Review.

.Fusté-Forné, F. & Jamal, T. (2021). Co-Creating New Directions for Service Robots in Hospitality and Tourism. *Journal of Tourism and Hospitality, 2*, 43-61.

Irem Onder University of Massachusetts Amherst. (2020). Blockchain: Is it the future for the tourism and hospitality industry? Tourism Economics Business and Finance of Tourism & Recreation, pp 1-7

Ivkov, M., Bleši, I., Dudi, B., Bartáková, G., & Dudi, Z. (2020). Are Future Professionals Willing to Implement Service Robots? Attitudes of Hospitality and Tourism Students towards Service Robotization. *Journal of Electronics, 9,* 1-16.

Jian, M. L., Vu, H. Q., Li, G., & Law, R. (2021). Understanding service attributes of robot hotels: A sentiment analysis of customer online reviews. *International Journal of Hospitality Management.*

Kapil, S., & Kapil, K. N. (2021). Blockchain in hospitality and tourism industry way forward. *International Journal of Business and Economics*, *6*(2), 289–298.

Kim, S., Kim, J., Badu-Baiden, F., Giroux M., & Choi, Y. (2021). Preference for robot service or human service in hotels? Impacts of the COVID-19 pandemic. *International Journal of Hospitality Management*.

Kim, J. J., & Han, H. (2020, November). Hotel of the future: Exploring the attributes of a smart hotel adopting a mixed-methods approach. *Journal of Travel & Tourism Marketing*, *37*(7), 804–822. doi:10.1080/10548408.2020.1835788

Lad, K. & Zade, A. (2020). *Role of Artificial Intelligence in Hotel Industry.*

Lee, S., Lee, M., & Jeong¸M. (2021). The role of virtual reality on information sharing and seeking behaviours. *Journal of Hospitality and Tourism Management*, 215-223.

Lee, Y., Lee, S., & Kim, D.-Y. (2021). Exploring hotel guests' perceptions of using robot assistants. *Tourism Management Perspectives*, *37*, 100781. doi:10.1016/j.tmp.2020.100781

Li, M., Yin, D., Qiu, H., & Bai, B. (2021, June). Examining the effects of AI contactless services on customer psychological safety, perceived value, and hospitality service quality during the COVID-19 pandemic. *Journal of Hospitality Marketing & Management.*

.Limna, P. (2022). Artificial Intelligence (AI) in the Hospitality Industry: A Review Article. *International Journal of Computing Sciences Research.*

Lua, L., Caib, R., & Gursoy, D. (2019). Developing and validating a service robot integration willingness scale. *International Journal of Hospitality Management*, *80*, 36–51. doi:10.1016/j.ijhm.2019.01.005

Mahalingam, S. & Ashokkumar, B. (2020). An Overview of Digital Marketing Practices in India. *International Journal of Research in Engineering, Science and Management 3*(9), 66-70.

Meidute-Kavaliauskiene, I., Çi˘gdem, S., Yıldız, B., & Davidavicius, S. (2021). The Effect of Perceptions on Service Robot Usage Intention: A Survey Study in the Service Sector. *Journal of Sustainability*.

.Naveen, B. R. (2023). Industry 5.0 has the potential to make India a smarter hub. *Industry 5.0 Implementation: Opportunities and Challenges India Chapter book.*

Orús, C., Iba'nez-Sanchez, S., & Flavian, C. (2021). Enhancing the customer experience with virtual and augmented reality: The impact of content and device type. *International Journal of Hospitality Management*, *98*, 103019. doi:10.1016/j.ijhm.2021.103019

Pelet, J.-E., Lick, E., & Taieb, B. (2019). *Internet of Things and Artificial Intelligence in the Hotel Industry: Which Opportunities and Threats for Sensory Marketing?* Springer Nature.

Pillai, S. G., Haldorai, K., Seo, W. S., & Kim, W. G. (2021,). COVID-19 and hospitality 5.0: Redefining hospitality operations. *International Journal of Hospitality Management*, *94*, 102869. doi:10.1016/j.ijhm.2021.102869 PMID:34785847

Pillai, S. G., Haldorai, K., Seo, W. S., & Kim, W. G. (2021, January). COVID-19 and hospitality 5.0: Redefining hospitality operations. *International Journal of Hospitality Management*, *94*, 102869. doi:10.1016/j.ijhm.2021.102869 PMID:34785847

Pitardi, V., Wirtz, J., Paluch S., &. Kunz, W. (2021) Service robots, agency and embarrassing service encounters. *Journal of Service Management Emerald Publishing Limited.*

. Ryan, Y., Khoo-Lattimore, C., & Potter, L. (2021). VR the world: Experimenting with emotion and presence for tourism marketing. *Journal of Hospitality and Tourism Management*, 160-171.

Saini, A., & Bhalla, R. (2022). Artificial Intelligence and Automation: Transforming the Hospitality or threat to human touch. Handbook of Research on Innovative Management Using AI in Industry 5.0

Tavitiyaman, P., Qu, H., Wing-sze, L. T., & Chin-wah, R. L. (2021). The influence of smart tourism applications on perceived destination image and behavioral intention: The moderating role of information search behaviour. *Journal of Hospitality and Tourism Management, 46*, 476–487. doi:10.1016/j.jhtm.2021.02.003

Tavitiyaman, P., Zhang, X., & Tsang, W. Y. (2020, August). How Tourists Perceive the Usefulness of Technology Adoption in Hotels: Interaction Effect of Past Experience and Education Level. *Journal of China Tourism Research.*

.Tuomi, A., Tussyadiah, I., & Stienmetz, J. (2021). Applications and Implications of Service Robots in Hospitality. *Cornell Hospitality Quarterly, 62*(2), 232–247

Tuomi, A., Tussyadiah, I., & Stienmetz, J. (2022). Applications and Implications of Service Robots in Hospitality. *Cornell Hospitality Quarterly 2021, 62*(2), 232–247.

Ye, H., Sun, S. & Law, R. (2022). A Review of Robotic Applications in Hospitality and Tourism Research. *Journal of Sustainability.*

Chapter 11
India-ASEAN Economic Engagement:
Challenges and New Lessons for Trade Integration

Rakesh Kumar
https://orcid.org/0000-0002-6958-4441
Deen Dayal Upadhyaya College, University of Delhi, New Delhi, India

ABSTRACT

The Look East Policy of India serves as instrumental in engaging the East and Southeast Asian countries in a wider perspective since 1991. The trade share of India with these countries which also makes noted trade bloc namely the Association of Southeast Asian Nations (ASEAN) has grown significantly because of pro-trade policies in the last decades. In this backdrop, this paper presents the facts on the dynamic impact of India's trade share with the East and Southeast Asian countries on the economic growth rate. The results show that the India-ASEAN trade share has a significant positive impact on India's GDP growth rate in the long run, while the impact is found significantly negative in the short run. The results raise the need for greater regional trade openness, hence highlighting the policy lessons and potential challenges on the part of the Free Trade Agreement (FTA) with the ASEAN countries. India tends to gain in the short run if it extends the scope of FTA from trade in goods to trade in services.

INTRODUCTION

International trade is found very important in achieving a sustainable high economic growth rate, especially for developing countries. In the transition, one of the significant developments was the building of the regional trade blocs with the aim to promote intra-regional trade. India for example has rapidly globalized by deregulating its external sector to catch up with the world economy in the last decades. In this backdrop, India has actively worked in building trade networks beyond the immediate regional boundaries. The emergence of the Indian economy from glooming to glowing after the 1990s coupled

DOI: 10.4018/978-1-6684-6403-8.ch011

with other factors like giant economy and population size, consistent impressive economic growth rate, and geopolitical location has also inspired the other trading blocs to expand their economic ties with India.

This paper analyses the dynamics of India's growing economic ties with the Southeast Asian countries in the current scenario. The ASEAN as a trade bloc was formed in 1967 by five Southeast Asian countries (Indonesia, Malaysia, Philippines, Singapore, and Thailand) initially, subsequently, five others countries (Brunei, Laos, Myanmar, Cambodia, and Vietnam) from the region joined later. The ASEAN was further expanded with the inclusion of three East Asian countries (China PR, Japan, and South Korea) during the 2nd ASEAN summit held in Malaysia during 1997, now commonly known as ASEAN+3. The member countries are largely varied in terms geographically and demographically, and stand at different stages of economic development in terms of nominal exports, GDP, GDP percapita, and endowment of natural resources. India's economic ties with ASEAN countries have grown ever than before in the last decade. It is evident that India's trade with ASEAN+3 which was US$7.08 billion in 1990 has increased to US$226.72billion in 2017 which comes to be 30.67 percent of India's total trade.

India has deeply shared cultural, religious, and political heritage with the Southeast Asian countries since the centuries. This relationship is found deeply rooted and can be traced back to ancient times. In this backdrop, reasonably mutual trade interests are expected between the two sub-contents. As of now, India-ASEAN relations are based on mutual complementarily of interest. The relationship was renewed through the *Look East Policy* of India which was introduced way back in 1991 for further outreach with economic and diplomatic objectives in broader perspectives. It is worth noting that after the economic liberalization program by India in 1991, ASEAN was identified as the most prospective trade partner in the Asia Pacific region.

The Look East Policy has acted as a bridge between India and ASEAN countries in the last decades. Rapid progress between India-ASEAN engagements can be observed at different levels over the years. The relationship was cemented when India became the sectoral dialogue partner of ASEAN in 1992 with a focus on trade, investment, tourism, and science and technology. To enlarge the scope of engagement, India became a full dialogue partner in 1995 and a member of the ASEAN Regional Forum in July 1996. An important milestone was achieved when mutual interest in wider perspective led the ASEAN to induct India for summit level partner in 2002 (see, Sen et al. 2004). Acknowledging the economic potential of the relationship led India and ASEAN countries to sign a framework agreement to chalk out the way for establishing FTA covering the goods, services, and investment in 2002. In addition, the bilateral and sub-regional efforts were complemented by signing the Framework Agreement on establishing an India-ASEAN Free Trade Agreement (FTA) during the 2nd Indo-ASEAN Summit in Indonesia in October 2003.

The India-ASEAN FTA is believed to be embedded in the strategic and political partnership beyond merely economic engagement. The FTA was enlarged with the signing of the Agreement on Trade in Goods in 2009 which was fully implemented in 2010. It was completed with the signing of the Agreement on Trade in Services in July 2015, is expected to bring potential gain to the Indian service sector. Subsequently, the Framework Agreement for Comprehensive Economic Cooperation (RCEP) was signed in 2003 that formed the basis of the FTA and had to be fully operational by 2016.

The growing interdependency led India to embark on a more proactive policy namely Act East Policy in 2014 with the aim to engage the East and the Southeast countries to the next level in a wider perspective. Act East Policy assumes to act proactive measures towards achieving deeper economic integration between South Asia, and East and Southeast Asia. This will enhance the economic ties between the two regions, hence highlighting the significant potential opportunities for the Indian Information Technology (IT) industry and skilled human resources in the production sectors in East Asia (see Anbumozhi & Kalirajan 2020).

In recent years, the potential impact of the India-ASEAN FTA has generated interest among researchers and policymakers in India. The empirical outputs provide important insight into the potential impact of FTA on the Indian economy. The existing empirical studies highlight the mixed set of results for the Indian economy owing to the India-ASEAN FTA. For example, Pal and Dasgupta (2008; 2009) report that India stands to benefit from the FTA in the short run, however, sectors such as agriculture, textiles, and auto-components will face stiff competition in the long run. Thus, India is likely to gain instead of lose because of the cheaper availability of intermediate goods from the ASEAN countries. In addition, Francis (2011) highlights that semi-processed and fully processed agriculture products are likely to affect adversely, however, tariff liberalization by India will lead to deeper trade integration with ASEAN countries. Further, Bhattacharyya and Mandal (2010) state that the negative effects of FTA on goods will be offset by the positive effects owning to trade in services and inflows of Foreign Direct Investment (FDI) from these countries.

Some empirical studies find that the economic welfare as a whole is likely to expand because of India-ASEAN FTA, however, ASEAN countries are expected to benefit more than that of India (see Nagoor & Kumar 2010, Nag & Sikdar 2011, Ahmed 2012; Chandran & Sudarsan 2012). For example, Pal and Dasgupta (2008; 2009) show that India may not get desirable benefits from FTA because of the high competitiveness of ASEAN countries in sectors like agriculture, textiles auto and auto components, and electronics. Similarly, Sikdar and Nag (2011) posit that India would witness a decrease in GDP by 1.07 percent and a 58.6 percent fall in employment owning to India-ASEAN FTA. In addition, Banik (2014) shows that the present structure of the India-ASEAN FTA promises limited gain to India. For potential gain, India needs to explore opportunities beyond the trade in goods, hence covering trade in services also. The study further states that trade complementarities exist in ASEAN countries, hence India gains meaningfully will have to become part of ASEAN's production network. Bhattacharyya and Mandal (2014) state that India-ASEAN FTA offers favorable as well as unfavourable impacts on Indian industries. The industries which will be unfavourable affected includes electric machinery, nuclear reactors, aluminum and articles thereof, rubber and articles thereof, organic chemicals and iron steel, manmade textiles materials, vehicles other than railway, while the ones which will be favourably affected include organic and inorganic chemicals, iron and steels and articles thereof, electric machinery, minerals fuels among the others.

It is noted that the existing studies primarily analyze the spillovers of India-ASEAN FTA on the subsectors in the Indian economy, thus ignoring the potential economic impact at the aggregate level. The proposed study bridges this gap by examining the potential impact of trade between India and ASEAN countries on the economic growth of India in the short and long run. The potential contribution of the paper gains importance as it addresses the policy implication of whether the evolving India-ASEAN trade partnership has generated economic gains for India? For this purpose, Autoregressive Distributed Lag (ARDL) Model in a multivariable framework is employed with the bilateral trade share of India with ASEAN as an exogenous variable.

1. INDIA & ASEAN: CURRENT STATE OF ART

1.1. India & ASEAN: Current Economic Outlook

After following restrictive trade policies for decades, the Indian economy was marginally reformed in the 1980s and later in the 1990s at a large scale with the announcement of a new liberalized Foreign Trade Policy in 1991. Under the policy announcement, the main initiatives were taken on removal of quantitative restrictions on agriculture exports coupled with setting of Special economic zones, setting up agro-export zones, repatriation of export earnings, and technological oriented policy announcement among the others. At the regional level, India comes to be the largest economy, accounting for 80% of the total exports from South Asia and 77 percent of the total imports in South Asia to/from the world (see, MoCI, Govt. of India). As per The World Economic Outlook (2019), India has posted a 4.8 percent GDP growth rate during 2019, lesser than earlier estimates due to the weakening of financial, construction and manufacturing sectors, is expected to post 5.8 percent and 6.5 percent growth rates during 2020 and 2021 respectively. In 2019, India stands to be the 5th largest economy with a GDP of US$2.93 trillion, after the USA, China, Japan, and Germany, and is expected to post GDP worth of US$4.63trillion by 2024, the report states. As of now India and China account significant impact upon the price movements across the world markets and are expected to be the growth poles in the world economy if the growth rates are sustained by the two Asian giants. (see, Wu and Zhou 2006).

The broad economic indicators of India and ASEAN countries are summarized in table 1. It is noted that the ASEAN region has outpaced the world economy after the Asian financial crisis in 1998-99 by posting an impressive GDP growth rate of 6 percent during 2000. Subsequently, the region continued to grow steadily with an annual average GDP growth rate of 5.3 percent until 2017. ASEAN is collectively ranked as the world's 5th largest economy with a combined GDP of US$3.1 trillion in 2019 (see World Economic outlook 2019). It is the 4th largest exporting region worldwide after the European Union, North America, and China. ASEAN stands diverse on trade composition. For example, Vietnam specializes in the production and exporting of tea, textile, and apparel while Singapore and Malaysia are the leading exporters of electronic products from the region. Similarly, Indonesia followed by Malaysia is the world's largest producer and exporter of palm oil, then Myanmar and Brunei are prominent economies that hold the reserves of oil, gas, and precious metals.

ASEAN is a widely diverse region on the economic front also. For example, Indonesia is the largest economy in the region with a GDP of US$1.12 trillion in 2019, representing almost 40 percent of the region's GDP. Singapore has the highest GDP percapita income of US$64581.94 followed by Brunei with a GDP percapita of US$31627.74 during 2018. On the other hand, Myanmar and Cambodia have the least GDP percapita of US$1325.95 and US$1512.12 during the same period. Over 23 percent of the trade of ASEAN countries is intra-regional and over 70 percent of trade is conducted at Most Favoured Nation (MFN) rates at zero tariffs.

1.2. India-ASEAN: Trade Interdependency

After the independence in 1947, India completely overlooked the Asia Pacific region because of many reasons. India was tilted largely towards Europe especially to the United Kingdom because of remaining under colonial rule for a long time, which was the prominent reason among the others. The end of the cold war was the breakthrough in Indian foreign policy towards East and Southeast countries during

Table 1. Broad economic indicators

	A		B		C		D	
Country	2000	2018	2000	2018	2000	2018	2000	2018
India	443.31	2009.97	3.84	6.81	59.93	537.04	73.07	642.96
Brunei	18012.56	31627.74	2.84	0.05	NA	7.04	NA	5.68
Cambodia	302.57	1512.12	10.71	7.52	1.83	18.41	2.26	21.82
Indonesia	780.19	3893.59	4.92	5.17	70.62	208.73	56.00	216.23
Lao PDR	325.18	2567.54	5.79	6.50	0.51	6.22	0.58	7.32
Malaysia	4043.66	11238.96	8.85	4.72	112.29	246.47	94.27	221.34
Myanmar	190.60	1325.95	13.74	6.20	2.11	15.76	2.46	18.87
Philippines	1038.90	3102.71	4.41	6.24	27.46	89.14	35.30	127.69
Singapore	23852.33	64581.94	9.03	3.13	180.96	642.27	169.11	545.55
Thailand	2007.73	7273.56	4.45	4.12	81.76	336.29	71.65	285.10
Vietnam	390.09	2563.82	6.78	7.07	17.15	258.50	17.33	245.64
China PR	959.37	9770.84	8.49	6.56	190.03	2651.01	161.16	2548.08
Japan	38532.04	39289.95	2.77	0.78	523.72	929.36	454.63	925.37
Korea PR	11947.58	31362.75	8.92	2.66	202.08	724.49	187.33	642.36

Notes: A denotes GDP percapita at current price (US$).
B denotes GDP growth rates (%).
C denotes Export of Goods and Services (BoP, billion US$).
D denotes Imports of Goods and Services (BoP, billion US$).
Source: World Development Indicators (2020).

the 1990s. The visit of then Indian Prime Minister to China marked the policy shift in the India-China relationship which had also outreach on the India-ASEAN relationship (see, Ahmed 2012).

As of now, India outreaches to the Asia-Pacific subcontinent beyond the immediate neighbours for expanding the economic ties in a wider perspective. It is worth noting that India has shifted the focus from the conventional trade partners like European Union and North American countries to the immediate neighbours. In the post-liberalization, ASEAN+3 countries have emerged as growing trade partners of India owning to pro-trade policies (see table 2). It is noted from figure 1, the total trade of India with ASEAN+3 which was US$7.08 billion which stood 16.93% of total trade in 1990 has increased to US$226.72 billion which comes to be 30.67% of total trade during 2017. As of now, Indian engagement with East and Southeast Asian countries occupies a significant proportion in Indian foreign policy besides the economic engagement (see Pant & Deb 2017).

A recent report by PHD Chamber of Commerce and Industry, India (2019) shows that the top 20 commodities have a high concentration in total trade with trade shares of 85% and 90% respectively in the exports and imports of India to/from ASEAN countries in 2018. Having strong trade complementarities between India and ASEAN countries, the merchandise trade between the two regions is expected to increase from the current level of US$97 billion in 2018 to US$200billion by 2025, the report further added. Among the others, Mineral fuels, mineral oils, and products of their distillation; bituminous substances (20.7%) are the single largest items in the import basket of India from ASEAN countries in recent years. The second-largest imported items are Electrical machinery and equipment and parts

Table 2. Interregional trade of India and percentage share

Partner	1990	2000	2010	2017
East Asia	5.24 (12.54)	11.75 (12.67)	108.81 (18.97)	151.77 (20.53)
European Union	13.48 (32.25)	21.12 (22.78)	84.11 (14.66)	96.52 (13.06)
ASEAN	2.38 (5.70)	7.13 (7.69)	52.69 (9.19)	80.75 (10.92)
Central Asia	N/A (N/A)	0.12 (0.13)	0.96 (0.17)	2.24 (0.30)
North America	5.80 (13.87)	13.26 (14.31)	46.07 (8.03)	77.28 (10.46)
South Asia	0.66 (1.57)	2.29 (2.48)	13.22 (2.30)	22.87 (3.09)
Latin America and Caribbean	0.62 (1.47)	1.71 (1.84)	22.91 (3.99)	35.59 (4.82)
Middle East	5.61 (13.41)	9.75 (10.52)	142.65 (24.87)	146.96 (10.88)

Notes: Total trade (in US$, billion), values in bracket indicates trade share (%).
Source: Asian Development Bank database.

thereof, sound recorders and reproducers, and televisions (15.10%). The other largest import items are- Animal or vegetable fats and oils and their cleavage products (9.8%), Machinery, mechanical appliances, nuclear reactors, boilers; parts thereof (9.0%, Organic chemicals (5.8%), Plastics, and articles thereof (4.4%), and Minerals like Iron, Copper, etc (2.9%).

The topmost items in the export basket of India to ASEAN countries are Mineral fuels, mineral oils, and products of their distillation; bituminous substances (26.2%) followed by items like Meat and edible meat offal (7.4%). The other mains items which India export to ASEAN are: Machinery, mechanical appliances, nuclear reactors; parts thereof (7.0%); Organic chemicals (5.9%); Fish and crustaceans, molluscs, and other aquatic invertebrates (4.4%); Vehicles other than railway or tramway rolling stock, and parts and accessories thereof (4.2%); Natural or cultured pearls, precious or semiprecious stones, precious metals (3.9%); Electrical machinery and equipment and parts thereof; sound recorders and reproducers, television (3.9%); Organic chemicals(5.9%); Fish and crustaceans, molluscs, and other aquatic invertebrates(4.4%) are among the others.

2. RESEARCH METHODS

2.1. Data Description

Following Ahmad, Draz and Yang (2018) and Kumar (2019; 2020), the study uses the GDP growth rate as the proxy of economic growth for India. The trade shares (TS) of India with respect to ASEAN and ASEAN+3 are used as exogenous variables. In addition to an exogenous variable, to test the impact of endogenous variables on the GDP of the country, the study also uses two endogenous variables namely

Figure 1. Trends India's trade with ASEAN & ASEAN+3
Source: Asian Development Bank database

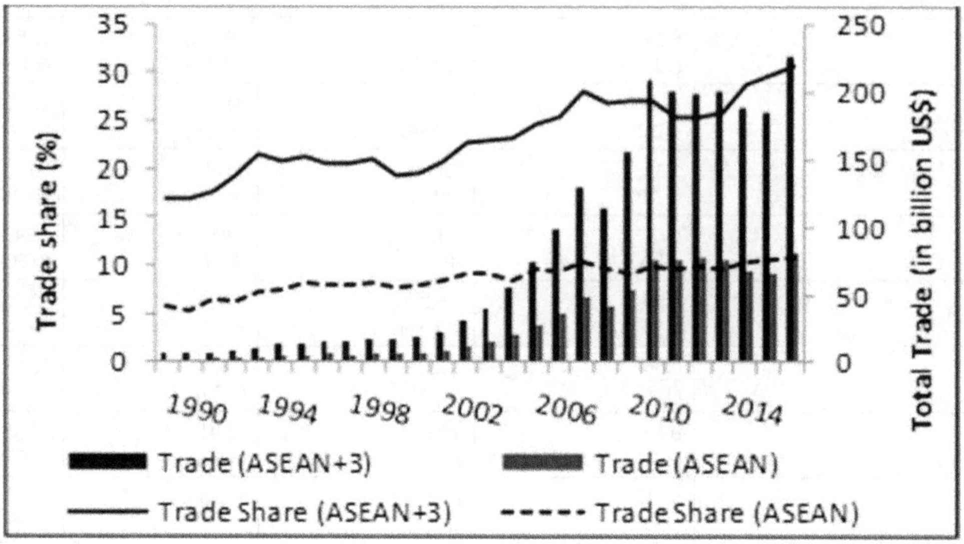

Domestic credit to the private sector (CPS) represents domestic financial development and Gross capital formation (GCF) represents the domestic physical investment. The domestic credit to the private sector includes all credits to various sectors on a gross basis provided by the financial sector which includes monetary authorities and deposit money banks, as well as other financial corporations. The sample period includes the annual observations of sample variables for the period ranges from 1990-2017, are taken from online sources maintained by Asian Development Bank and World Bank. The study tests the long run multivariate relationship among the variables is expressed as:

$$GDP_t = c_0 + c_1 TS_t + c_2 CPS_t + c_3 GCF_t + \varepsilon_t \quad (1)$$

Where, GDP_t stands for GDP growth rate of India, TS_t stands for Trade share, henceforth TS and TS+3 representing India's trade share with ASEAN and ASEAN+3 respectively. CPS_t stands for Credit to private sector, is expressed as a ratio of GDP, GCF_t stands for Gross capital formation, is expressed as a ratio of GDP.

2.2. Model Specifications

Researchers commonly apply traditional techniques as proposed by Engle and Granger (1987), and Johansen and Juselius (1990) for testing the long-run cointegration. However, we utilize the ARDL framework in the multivariate form to test the short and long-run cointegrating relationship between the variables. The ARDL model has several merits over the conventional techniques. *First*, the ARDL is an efficient procedure in a mixed set of integration of order of given variables. *Second*, the model provides unbiased estimates for a small sample size. *Third*, the model offers short and long-run estimates simultaneously. *Fourth*, the model captures the impact of exogenous variable which serves as a dummy variable. *Fifth*, the model permits the different lag lengths for sample variables to extract the maximum information, while other cointegrating techniques assume the same lag length for all variables.

The ARDL model proposes the Z_t in the order of p and q lag lengths, where Z_t is a column vector which is composed of y_t and x_t variables, symbolically written as $Z_t = (y_t, x_t)$. Given that, y_t is dependent variable and x_t is array of independent variables as shown in equation 1. The ARDL estimates the dependent variable as a function of its lagged values, and current and lagged values of independent variables (see, Pesaran *et al.*, 2001), symbolically written as:

$$\Delta y_t = \alpha_0 + \pi_1 y_{t-1} + \pi_2 x_{t-1} + \sum_{i=1}^{p} \varnothing_i \Delta y_{t-i} + \sum_{j=0}^{q} \delta_j \Delta x_{t-j} + \varepsilon_t \quad (2)$$

Here, α_0 is a constant, π_1 and π_2 stands for long run coefficients, Δ is first difference operator. The lagged values of Δy_t, and lagged and current value of Δx_t provide the estimates for short run relationship, while ε_t is error term with normally distribution. The ARDL model proposes to test the null hypothesis of non significant long run cointegrating relationship i.e. $\pi_1 = \pi_2 = 0$ against the alternative hypothesis of significant long run relationship i.e. $\pi_1 \neq \pi_2 \neq 0$ between the dependent and independent variables.

The ARDL model proceeds in two stages. The first stage computes the joint F-statistic which highlights the significant long-run cointegration between the sample dependent and independent variables. Having confirmed the results, the second stage estimates the short and long-run causal relations between variables simultaneously in Error Correction Term (ECT) framework. The ECT highlights the speed of adjustment of the dependent variables with respect to the deviation of independent variables from the equilibrium. As of now, researchers widely use the ARDL model in financial literature focusing on causality between economic variables especially for small sample periods (see, Hye *et al.*, 2013; Hye and Lau 2015, Kumar, 2019; 2020).

3. EMPIRICAL RESULTS

3.1. Stationary Test

The proposed ARDL model calls the sample variables to be integrated either at level i.e. I(0), at first difference i.e. I(1), or of mixed order. We apply the unit root test for the purpose to test the stationary properties of the sample variables. In econometric literature, a number of unit root tests are used, the principal one is the Augmented Dickey-Fuller (ADF) test. The ADF applies to tests the unit root problem at two different levels–with intercept, and with the trend and intercept. The ADF test proposes to test the null hypothesis of nonstationary against the alternative hypothesis of stationary. Given that, the rejection of the null hypothesis requires the ADF statistic to be lesser than the critical value. Table 3 highlights that the ADF test rejects the null hypothesis and holds the stationary properties of sample variables at first difference. It implies that the sample is fit for the application of the ARDL model.

Table 3. Stationary test

Variables	At level		At first difference	
	With intercept	With intercept and slope	With intercept	With intercept and slope
GDP	-4.29***	-4.91***	-5.62***	-5.50***
TS	-2.26	-3.38	-8.96***	-9.18***
TS+3	-0.42	-2.09	-4.50***	-4.41***
CPS	2.35	-1.42	-4.87***	-4.25***
GCF	-1.13	-1.05	-5.08***	-5.28***

Notes: Critical values at level (with intercept):-3.69, and -2.97 at 1 and 5 percent level of significance respectively.
Critical values at level (with intercept and slope):-4.33 and -3.58 at 1 and 5 percent level of significance respectively.
Critical values at first difference (with intercept):-3.72 and -2.98 at 1 and 5 percent level of significance respectively.
Critical values at first difference (with intercept and slope):-4.37 and -3.60 at 1 and 5 percent level of significance respectively.
***, ** indicates significant at 1 and 5 percent level of significance.
Source: Author's calculations.

3.2. Testing Long Cointegartion

The long-run cointegration between the variables is tested with the bound test by estimating the joint F-statistic under the condition of all the variables to be integrated of order zero or one. The null hypothesis is rejected if Wald F-statistic is greater than the upper bound critical value as proposed by Pesaran *et al.*, (2001). While the null hypothesis is accepted if F-statistic falls below the lower bound critical value. The results are inconclusive with the F-statistic coming in between the upper and lower bound critical values. While estimating the equation (1), the Wald F-statistic is estimated by restricting the maximum lag length equal to 3. Subsequently, the optimal lag lengths for sample variables are selected on the basis of minimum Akaike Information criteria (AIC). Turning to the results of bound test for equation (1), the Wald F–statistic for trade between India and ASEAN is $F\left(GDP/TS, CPS, GCF\right)$ $= 10.20$ and Wald F-statistic for trade between India and ASEN+3 is $F\left(GDP/TS+3, CPS, GCF\right) = 7.33$. Following the Pesaran *et al.* (2001), the relevant critical values for the Upper bound is -5.61, and the Lower critical bound value is -4.29 at a 1 percent level of significance. It is noted that the Wald F-statistic is significant in both cases, highlighting the rejection of the null hypothesis of the nonlong cointegration relationship. The results highlight that the economic growth rate of India has significantly cointegrated with the trade of India with ASEAN and ASEAN+3 in addition to the two endogenous variables i.e. CPS and GCF. It shows that the trading relations of India with East and Southeast countries are positively contributing to the GDP of India. The results are consistent with other empirical studies, supporting the trade-led growth hypothesis for developing countries like India (see, Love and Chandra 2005; Kumar 2019; 2020).

3.3. Short and Long Run Causality and Diagnosis Testing

Having found significant long-run cointegration, the second stage involves the estimation of the short and long-run impact of independent variables simultaneously on the dependent variables i.e. GDP growth rate of India. Tables 4 and 5 highlights the results for the long and short-run impact of trade shares with respect to ASEAN and ASEAN+3 respectively on the GDP growth rate of India, in addition to the impact of two other endogenous variables namely CPS and GCF. It is found that the India-ASEAN trade share has a significant positive impact on the GDP growth rate in the long run. While the impact of trade share is found significantly negative in the short run. The possible reasons may be associated with the trade compositions in the import and export baskets of India with the ASEAN countries. India majorly imports finished goods while exports mainly raw materials and farm products from/to ASEAN countries as shown in table 2. The results highlight that the impact of India's trade share with ASEAN is more dominating on GDP growth rate. Given that, a 10 percent increase in India-ASEAN bilateral trade will raise the 9.2 percent GDP growth rate of India. With a negative sign, the ECT highlights the speed of adjustment of the dependent variable following the deviations of independent variables from the equilibrium over the time period. It tends to integrate the short and long-run impact of independent variables. The ECT coefficients are -1.69 and -1.66 for ASEAN and ASEAN+3 respectively, highlighting the restoration in GDP growth rate within a year following the distortions in trade and other two endogenous factors i.e. CPS and GCF.

Further the results highlight that the short-run impact of CPS on the GDP growth rate is found significantly negative, while the impact of GCF is significantly positive. It is noted that the GDP growth rate of India in 2019-20 remained 4.8 percent, the lowest reading in the last decades, because of a slowdown in domestic demand coupled with stress in the nonbanking financial sector and a decline in credit growth. As per World Development Indicator (2018) estimates the Gross capital formation to GDP ratio stands 31 percent for India in 2018 while it is 44 percent for China which comes to be a close regional counterpart. This shows that India needs to invest heavily in physical infrastructure for achieving a sustained GDP growth rate in long run (see Kumar 2019).

The results seem to be consistent with earlier studies highlighting the higher degree of trade openness for accelerating economic growth especially for developing countries like India (see Ghirmay *et al.*, 2001; Chang, Kaltani and Loayza, 2009; Hye *et al.,* 2013; Kumar, 2019; 2020). For the short and long-run gain from trade with East and Southeast countries, India requires to focus on trade in services where it has a comparative advantage relative to the export of intermediate items and agriculture products. India stands to gain from the export of computer and Information technology services and other services such as finance, medical tourism, and insurance (see, Banik 2014).

Further, it is important to examine the reliability of the results. For this purpose, we employ two principal tests to examine the stability of estimated coefficients. *Firstly,* following Pesaran *et al.* (2001), the Cumulative Sum of Recursive Residuals (CUSUM) test is conducted for testing the stability of the coefficients at different lags. The coefficients are found within the critical bands at 5 percent confidence intervals as shown in figure 2. *Secondly*, we test the correlations in residuals of fitted models which are found nonsignificant at 5 percent level of significance. The results of these two tests ascertain the best fit of models in given data set, thus enhancing the reliability of the main findings and statistical inference of the proposed study.

4. SUMMARY AND IMPLICATION

This paper presents the facts on India's trade linkages with East and Southeast Asian countries, and the possible spillovers of trade on GDP growth rate. The ASEAN+3 stands the biggest trade partner for India over the decades, however, trade is skewed in favour of the former. India introduced major structural reforms in external sectors in compliance with World Trade Organisation (WTO) during 1991.

Table 4. India's Trade with ASEAN: Short and long run causality

Long run causality		Short run causality	
TS	0.92** (0.025)	Constant	-0.01 (0.989)
CPS	-0.037 (0.548)	ΔGDP_{t-1}	0.65*** (0.003)
GCF	0.02 (0.786)	ΔTS_t	0.10 (0.878)
		ΔTS_{t-1}	-2.03** (0.0171)
		ΔTS_{t-2}	-0.99 (0.103)
		ΔCPS_t	-0.92*** (0.000)
		ΔCPS_{t-1}	-0.43** (0.030)
		ΔGCF_t	0.33*** (0.010)
		ΔGCF_{t-1}	0.55*** (0.003)
		ΔGCF_{t-2}	0.50*** (0.006)
		ECT_{t-1}	-1.69*** (0.000)

Notes: R Square: 0.89
F-statistics: 11.26*** (0.000)
AIC: 3.17
***, ** indicates significant at 1 and 5 percent level of significance.
Source: Author's calculations.

Since then, India has posted impressive trade-led GDP growth trade. India's foreign trade of Goods and Services which was US$41.80 billion has increased to 16.5 times to US$739.20 billion during 2017.

The results highlight that India's trade with ASEAN countries has grown since bringing the Look East Policy into practice. It is found that India's GDP growth rate has significantly cointegrated with the ASEAN's trade. The trade share reports a significantly positive impact on India's GDP growth rate in the long run, while the impact is found negative in the short run. The exports basket of India to ASEAN countries includes the labour-intensive goods, raw materials, and intermediate goods, while the import basket has shown a growing share of skill-intensive and high-technology products. It is observed that the Indian agriculture industry tends to find challenges from ASEAN countries with the significant shares of farm products in the import basket. For sustainable economic benefits, India requires to focus beyond the trade in goods to trade in services under the ambit of India-ASEAN FTA. For potential gains, the growing India-ASEAN trade interdependency allows the Indian Service sector to explore opportunities in commercial services for ASEAN's manufacturing sector. Similarly, the developed electronic industry of Malaysia and IT industry of India offers trade complementary for mutual expansion.

Table 5. India's Trade with ASEAN+3: Short and long run causality

Long run causality		Short run causality	
TS+3	0.35** (0.029)	Constant	1.99*** (0.000)
CPS	0.02 (0.791)	ΔGDP_{t-1}	0.58*** (0.008)
GCF	-0.11 (0.266)	$\Delta TS+3_t$	0.21 (0.317)
		$\Delta TS+3_{t-1}$	-0.66*** (0.020)
		ΔCPS_t	-0.56** (0.015)
		ΔGCF_t	0.35** (0.018)
		ΔGCF_{t-1}	0.46*** (0.009)
		ΔGCF_{t-2}	0.49*** (0.005)
		ECT_{t-1}	-1.66*** (0.000)

Notes: R Square: 0.83
F-statistics: 9.83*** (0.000)
AIC: 3.43
***, ** indicates significant at 1 and 5 percent level of significance.
Source: Author's calculations.

Figure 2. Stability test of coefficients
Source: Source: Author's calculations

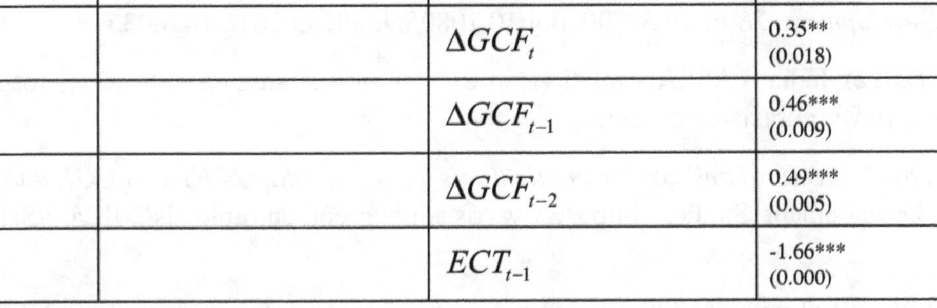

The overall results are highly insightful for policy implication which points towards more economic cooperation for mutual benefits. Having diverse trade compositions, India needs to further strengthen its economic engagement with the ASEAN in order to generate a trade-led sustainable growth rate. This implies that the India-ASEAN trade is not at a level as high as it should be. In order to realize the meaningful gains from India-ASEAN FTA, India needs to work constructively to become a part of the production network of East Asia and Southeast Asian countries. There are opportunities for potential bilateral trade Agreements through bilateral engagements. At the domestic level, India requires to expand the physical infrastructure for sustainable economic growth of the country.

REFERENCES

Ahmad, F., Draz, M. U., & Yang, S. C. (2018). Causality nexus of exports, FDI and economic growth of the ASEAN5 economies: Evidence from panel data analysis. *The Journal of International Trade & Economic Development*, *28*(6), 685–700. doi:10.1080/09638199.2018.1426035

Ahmed, A. (2012). India – ASEAN relations in 21st century: strategic implications for India. *Eurasia Review.* https://www.eurasiareview.com/

Ahmed, S. (2012). *Sectoral and gender implications for India–ASEAN FTA: A CGE analysis for India.* Centre for Development Studies. http://www.cds.edu/wp-content/uploads/2012/09/Sahid-Ahmed-Paper.pdf

Anbumozhi, V., & Kalirajan, K. (2020). South Asia's Economic Integration with East Asia: An Exploratory Analysis with a Focus on India. *Journal of Economic Integration*, *35*(1), 91–110. doi:10.11130/jei.2020.35.1.91

ARIC. (n.d.). Asian Development Bank database. ARIC. https://aric.adb.org/integrationindicators

Banik, N. (2014). India-ASEAN Free Trade Agreement: The Untapped Potential. *MPRA Paper No.57954.* https://mpra.ub.uni-muenchen.de/57954/

Bhattacharyya, R., & Mandal, A. (2010). Estimating the Impact of the Indo-ASEAN Free Trade Agreement on India's Balance of Trade. *Journal of Global Analysis*, *1*(1), 9–25.

Bhattacharyya, R., & Mandal, A. (2014). Estimating the impact of the India-ASEAN Free trade agreement on Indian Industries. *South Asia Economic Journal*, *15*(1), 93–114. doi:10.1177/1391561414527050

Chandran, B. P. S., & Sudarsan, P. K. (2012). India-ASEAN free trade agreement implications for fisheries. *Economic and Political Weekly*, *47*(16), 65–70.

Chang, R., Kaltani, L., & Loayza, N. V. (2009). Openness can be good for growth: The role of policy complementarities. *Journal of Development Economics*, *90*(1), 33–49. doi:10.1016/j.jdeveco.2008.06.011

Engle, R. F., & Granger, C. W. J. (1987). Cointegration and error correction representation: Estimation and testing. *Econometrica*, *55*(2), 251–276. doi:10.2307/1913236

Francis, S. (2011). A sectoral impact analysis of the ASEAN–India Free Trade Agreement. *Economic and Political Weekly*, *46*(2), 46–55.

Ghirmay, T., Grabowski, R., & Sharma, S. (2001). Exports, investment, efficiency, and economic growth in LDCs: An empirical investigation. *Applied Economics*, *33*(6), 689–700. doi:10.1080/00036840122027

Hye, Q. M. A., & Lau, W. Y. (2015). Trade openness and economic growth: Empirical evidence from India. *Journal of Business Economics and Management*, *16*(1), 188–205. doi:10.3846/16111699.2012.720587

Hye, Q. M. A., Wizarat, S., & Lau, W. Y. (2013). Trade-led growth hypothesis: An empirical analysis of South Asian countries. *Economic Modelling*, *35*, 654–660. doi:10.1016/j.econmod.2013.07.040

IMF. (2019). *The world economic outlook*. IMF. https://www.imf.org/external/datamapper/datasets/WEO

Johansen, S., & Juselius, K. (1990). Maximum likelihood estimation and inference on cointegration with application to money demand. *Oxford Bulletin of Economics and Statistics*, *52*(2), 169–210. doi:10.1111/j.1468-0084.1990.mp52002003.x

Kumar, R. (2019). India-China: Changing bilateral trade and its effect on economic growth. *The Singapore Economic Review*. doi:10.1142/S021759081950005X

Kumar, R. (2020). India & South Asia: Geopolitics, regional trade and economic growth spillovers. *The Journal of International Trade & Economic Development*, *29*(1), 69–88. doi:10.1080/09638199.2019.1636121

Love, J., & Chandra, R. (2005). Testing export-led growth in South Asia. *Journal of Economic Studies (Glasgow, Scotland)*, *32*(2), 132–145. doi:10.1108/01443580510600913

Ministry of Commerce and Industry. (n.d.). *India*. Ministry of Commerce and Industry. https://commerce.gov.in/

Nag, B., & Sikdar, C. (2011). Welfare implication of India–ASEAN FTA: An analysis using GTAP model. *Working paper no. EC-11-06*, Indian Institute of Foreign Trade, New Delhi

Nagoor, B. H., & Kumar, C. N. (2010). Assessing the impact of the ASEAN-India FTA on the tea industry. *Economic and Political Weekly*, *45*(44), 112–116.

Pal, P., & Dasgupta, M. (2008). Does a Free Trade Agreement with ASEAN make sense? *Economic and Political Weekly*, *43*(46), 8–12.

Pal, P., & Dasgupta, M. (2009). The ASEAN-India Free Trade Agreement: An Assessment. *Economic and Political Weekly*, *44*(38), 11–15.

Pant, H. V., & Deb, A. (2017). India-ASEAN Partnership at 25. Observer Research Foundation (ORF) Issue Brief, 189.

Pesaran, M. H., Shin, Y., & Smith, R. J. (2001). Bounds testing approaches to the analysis of level relationships. *Journal of Applied Econometrics*, *16*(3), 289–326. doi:10.1002/jae.616

PHDCCI. (n.d.). *PHD Chamber of Commerce and Industry*. PHDCCI. www.phdcci.in

Sen, R., Asher, M. G., & Rajan, R. S. (2004). ASEAN-India Economic Relations: Current Status and Future Prospects. *Economic and Political Weekly*, *39*(29), 3297–3308.

Sikdar, C., & Nag, B. (2011). Impact of India-ASEAN Free Trade Agreement: A Cross Country Analysis Using Applied General Equilibrium Modeling. *Asia Pacific Research and Network on Trade, Working Paper Series, No. 107*.

World development indicators (2020). Databank, World Bank.s https://databank.worldbank.org/data/source/world-development -indicators

Wu, Y., & Zhou, Z. (2006). Changing bilateral trade between China and India. *Journal of Asian Economics, 17*(3), 509–518. doi:10.1016/j.asieco.2006.04.007

Chapter 12
Readiness for Export-Oriented E-Commerce in the Age of Industrial Transformation

Büşra Garip
https://orcid.org/0000-0001-5188-5687
Sakarya University, Turkey

Hakan Tunahan
https://orcid.org/0000-0002-9556-214X
Sakarya University, Turkey

ABSTRACT

This study aims to develop a scale to measure the readiness of export-oriented e-commerce for companies that will face the reality of moving from Industry 4.0 to Industry 5.0. This scale, which aims to determine companies' readiness level for e-export, is the first attempt in this sense in the literature. Several steps have been followed in the scale development process. First, a draft scale consisting of 69 items and different dimensions is created based on the literature review. Next, a focus group study is conducted, and expert opinions are collected. After testing the content validity and running the factor analysis, eight factors comprising 28 positive and negative statements were formed. Validity and reliability analyses of the pilot study, including 50 companies, show that the scale is applicable. These results show that human resources and management functions, whose essential element is human, at the Industry 5.0 level; it also demonstrates its compatibility with processes, most of which are machine and digital, and the importance of cooperation between them.

1. INTRODUCTION

Developments in communication and information technologies lead to innovations and transformation in marketing, sales, distribution channels, and production processes. The impact of Industry 4.0 on this development is undeniable. However, the perception that Industry 4.0 excludes human workers from cyber-physical environments is settled in society, and the expectation that processes will become human again or at least turn into machine-human symbiosis arises (Saniuk et al., 2022)

DOI: 10.4018/978-1-6684-6403-8.ch012

The "Industrial Human Needs Pyramid" developed by Lu et al. to define and classify human needs and motivations in manufacturing reveals how much this incentive and transformation is needed (Lu et al., 2022).

Figure 1. Industrial human needs pyramid

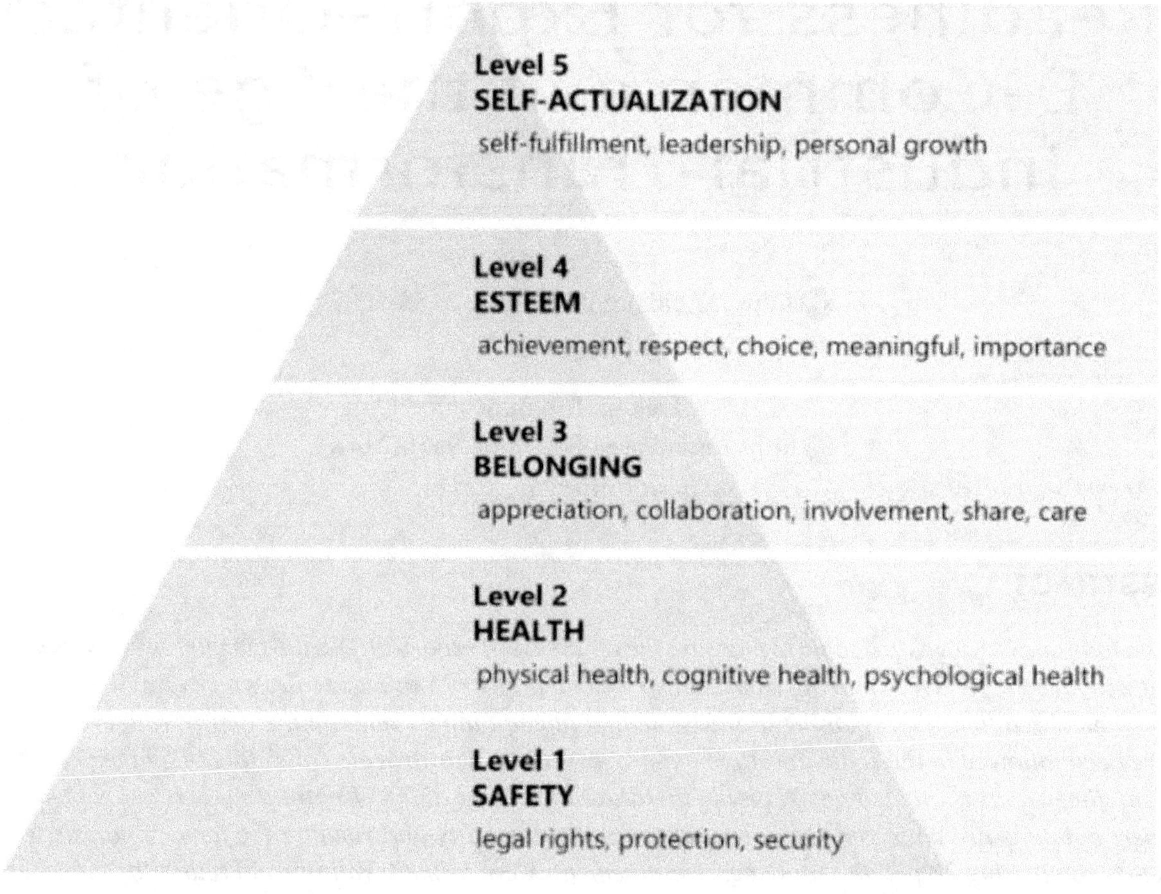

European Commission has taken the inclusiveness of Industry 5.0 to an advanced level, stating that it is built on human-orientedness, sustainability, and durability. "*Industry 5.0 recognizes the power of industry to achieve societal goals beyond jobs and growth to become a resilient provider of prosperity by making production respect the boundaries of our planet and placing the wellbeing of the industry worker at the center of the production process.*" (European Commission, 2021).

The literature reveals that Industry 5.0 has the potential to break down barriers between the real world and the virtual world, as well as many uncertainties about what it will bring and how it will transform business (European Commission, 2021). It is thought that the three main elements of the Fifth Industrial Revolution, smart devices, smart systems, and smart automation, will emerge when fully integrated with the physical world in cooperation with human intelligence (Nahavandi, 2019). The following advanced technologies will be needed for Industry 5.0 to achieve its goals: Networked Sensor Data Interoperability, Digital Twins, Shopfloor Trackers, Virtual Training, Intelligent Autonomous Systems, and Advances in Sensing Technologies and Machine Cognition (Nahavandi, 2019).

In recent years, it has been seen that the belt toward Industry 5.0 has accelerated. According to the Supply Chain Collaborative Robot Market Report (2022), the Asia Pacific market is projected to see the highest gains from 2021 to 2026. The expansion of the e-commerce industry due to the presence of large-scale manufacturing facilities will support regional industry growth and trigger cobot penetration. The Covid-19 outbreak, in particular, has resulted in a significant shift towards robotics and automation in diversified applications. This has also positively impacted the demand for collaborative robots in the supply chain industry.

The rise of e-commerce logistics accelerated the manufacturing industry's transformation and made progress. (Liu et al., 2022). As the e-commerce industry sets new standards, cobots are starting to draw an optimistic frontier for the retail industry (HR Asia, 2021). Thus, companies will not have to scale their operations with automation alone while maintaining their talent pool.

In this sense, Industry 5.0 will increase the efficiency and operational efficiency of the e-commerce industry with real-time data generated by predictive analysis tools, sensors, and machines by leveraging the unique creativity of humans (Agarwal & Chauhan, 2022). In the literature, it is seen that research on artificial intelligence in e-commerce primarily focuses on recommendation systems, and China-based institutions are positioned as leaders in this research field (Bawack et al., 2022).

In particular, it is estimated that the Indian e-commerce market will increase by 21.45% by 2025. As India has a huge consumption capacity, most international brands partner with Indian E-commerce companies (Agarwal & Chauhan, 2022).

This article develops a scale to measure the e-export readiness of companies (in a world in the transition phase to Industry 5.0). Although there are many studies on critical success factors, fundamental determinants, and readiness processes that foster companies' success in e-commerce and export, the lack of a study to measure e-export readiness is the primary motivation of this study. For this purpose, the factors thought to be essential in developing the scale for e-export are examined in the literature. Lastly, a draft scale is developed based on the dimensions and elements discussed in the literature review and then matured with a focus group and expert opinions.

2. LITERATURE REVIEW

Today, the use of internet applications for commercial export activities is increasing worldwide. The internet is an alternative distribution channel that reaches customers in international markets and a convenient tool for finding new customers and maintaining long-term relationships with existing customers (Al-Dmour, 2018). Furthermore, the internet is essential in increasing promotion, information, and income for export volume (Obeidat et al., 2017). Although internet access has caused a change in global dynamics in the last 20 years, this alone is not responsible for the transformation. The internet can provide companies with the information necessary for trade and quickly overcome geographical and cultural barriers. However, other factors are needed for cross-border trade to develop. In particular, firms' strategies, policies, and environmental factors have a heightened effect when combined with internet access and an entrepreneurial spirit.

As stated above, globally competing companies need an environment that supports more exports to increase their success, gain competitive power, and enter foreign markets successfully (ITRISA, 2002). Companies must know their strengths and weaknesses to compete in the global arena. They must also be prepared to act on improving weaknesses in export activities. Firms often prefer to focus on neighboring countries or a single market when they decide to start exporting. After establishing themselves in their home country, they tend to increase their sales abroad and reach a more significant number of destinations. However, exporters entering new markets show high failure rates. According to Eaton et al. (2008), approximately half of the new exporters quit their export activities in the first year. Carrère and Strauss-Kahn (2017) present a different view, arguing that any export experience gained in foreign markets will ensure the long-term survival of firms. Esteve-Pérez et al. (2007) argue that firms exporting to "closer" markets survive longer than those exporting to uncertain markets. However, this survival depends on the product, the competitor, and the market conditions. Therefore, firms must understand and show concern for the determinants of export survival.

It is difficult for companies that do not analyze their organizational structure, resources, and networks to survive in the global competitive environment. For this reason, companies should evaluate many factors and prepare before and during export. The factors that indicate readiness for export also affect the performance of exports. The Economist reports (2014) the investment, internet, international business, regulatory/legal, and electronic payment factors that shape cross-border trade. The factors that ensure success in export are summarized in Table 1.

Table 1. The success factors in export

Environmental, firm characteristics, and business strategy	Baldauf et al., 2000
Global and national demand, company's vision, international connections, human resources, and technology	Heeks and Nicholson, 2004
Motivational and organizational elements	Viviers and Van Eldik, 2005
Market structure, the characteristics of the firm, the structure of the management, and the export strategy	Sousa et al., 2008
Production planning, packaging, government regulations, raw material supply, taxes, regulations, infrastructure, coordination with external stakeholders, pricing, and logistics infrastructure	Babakhani and Haji, 2011
Being proud of working in the company, the team's desire for export, changes in management, motivation of the export manager, and continuous training	Mohammadzadeh, (2012).
Innovation, product, and technology development	Czakó and Könczöl, 2014
Increasing the quality of personnel, giving priority to staff training, increasing quality in production, organizing planning and operational processes, and finding and improving the organization's weaknesses	Maldifassi and Caorsi, 2014
Resource, government support, political factors, technological factors, product development, legal regulations, management approach, and the exporting sector	Torrens et al.,2014
The initiative, experience, financial resources, and capacity	Mohammadzadeh et al., 2016
Firm's characteristics, management characteristics, industry characteristics, and the characteristics of the country	Chen et al., 2016
Export experience/skill, specialization, trust, the ability to negotiate and reduce costs	Suwannarat, (2016).
Internal-external knowledge and innovation	Leipras, 2019
Organizational factors	Safari and Saleh, 2020
Finance and marketing	Gerschewski et al., 2020

E-export is a concept in which export and e-commerce are integrated. This concept, which needs to be clearly defined in the literature, can be characterized as using the internet to export. The Canadian government website offers information about e-export, which "Examines how to use the internet to sell your products and services to customers in other countries" (Ontario, 2021). The Innovation PEI report (n.d.) defines e-export as "the practice of receiving and processing orders online from customers located in foreign countries." Turkish Exporters Assembly defines e-export as "a cross-border e-commerce application sold to customers in the form of overseas products through online channels." E-export in Turkey is also called micro-export. For a product to be subject to e-export, it must have an Electronic Commerce Customs Declaration below 300 kg and 15000 Euros. This indicates that, unlike other countries with different approaches, Turkey employs numerical evaluation of the e-concept for exports.

E-export provides many advantages to companies. According to Rosson (2004), export companies use the internet as a promotional vehicle, a low-cost distribution channel, and a tool for customer service. Bianchi and Mathews (2013) outline the benefits of using the internet as an export tool: improved customer service, easier management of supply chain activities, improved inventory control, market expansion, and reduced marketing and distribution costs. Additionally, the internet creates export opportunities for SMEs, encouraging them to operate abroad by minimizing risks and costs efficiently. However, there are also challenges to the e-export business. Security, lack of protection of intellectual property rights, cultural differences, infrastructure problems, and payment problems are all factors that make e-export difficult (Melewar & Smith, 2003).

An e-commerce platform is needed for e-export to occur. These platforms can be company websites, e-marketplaces, or social media applications. Compared to traditional export methods, e-export can be described as having virtual branches worldwide without geographic restrictions. This ample market provides an opportunity for companies to grow. Reaching more customers and obtaining broader information about these customers instantly are essential benefits of the internet.

MacGregor and Vrazalic (2005). Laosethakul and Boulton (2007) and Ajmal et al. (2017) discuss the success factors in e-commerce from a macro perspective. According to the authors' perspectives, communication, technological, environmental, organizational, entrepreneurial, strategic, website-related, market, logistics, human resources, business process-related, external, management, individual, integration, and trust are essential elements for e-commerce success. However, Sung (2006) and Varela et al. (2017) discuss the success factors in e-commerce from an operational/marketing perspective (e.g., customer, confidentiality, cost, ease of use, strategy, expertise, stability, security, speed, payment, social network, design, marketing, brand, market, communication support, quality data processing, website, and reliability).

Although there are no studies directly related to e-export in the literature, there are studies on how the internet can be used successfully as a tool for export. Poon and Swatman (1997) claim that willingness to use the internet, the suitability of products and services, integration within the company, and the importance of information technologies are related to the internet and export. In another study, Samiee (1998) emphasizes the importance of internet infrastructure, language, and cultural factors. Moodley (2002) states that awareness of e-commerce, the company's history, competencies in informatics, and technical infrastructure are also important. Moon and Jain (2007) also state the company's characteristics, the product, and environmental factors as elements. In addition, Azaria (2010) evaluates elements such as the language of the website, security of payments, and management in his study. Houdeloudi and Hajidimitriou (2013) state that investments, personnel competence, and number are also important factors.

3. METHODOLOGY

This study's scale development process, which measures companies' readiness for e-export, has a hybrid structure in which theoretical and experimental forms are used together. The process of scale development is outlined in Table 2 below.

Table 2. Scale development stages

1	• Literature Review
2	• Creating the Items
3	• Focus Group Discussion
4	• Obtaining Expert Opinions
5	• Creating the Draft Scale
6	• Determination of Scale Items and Content Validity Ratio of the Scale
7	• Application of Reliability and Factor Analysis by Testing Scale Items on Sample
8	• Finalization of the Draft Scale

The scale-development process is theoretical regarding expert opinion and content validity; the literature is also experimental regarding the sequence (flow) of finalization by the focus group and factor analysis.

The fact that studies on scale development for e-export have yet to be found in the literature and that the subject is a rapidly changing field, especially in developing countries, has motivated this study. However, this gap in research can partially be addressed through related literature. Thus, in creating the items for the scale, a literature review is conducted of studies concerning the success criteria for export and e-commerce, which are the intersection points of e-export.

As a result of the literature review, items consisting of six dimensions administrative/organizational, operational, financial, technological, human resources, and environmental, and 63 questions, which represent readiness for e-export, are created. The studies mentioned in each chapter support the creation of questions and dimensions.

Since creating a scale based only on a literature review would yield limited results, an expert opinion evaluation follows the focus group interview. The focus group proceeded in the form of an online discussion about the scale items lasting two hours. The group included eight people from the academic and business worlds who intend to start e-exporting. The focus group shared their views on the items and requested that some items be corrected. Although there is no change in the number of items, some corrections have made the expressions more understandable and explanatory.

In the next stage, draft scale forms with 63 items were sent to 13 experts, including industry representatives and academics with experience in logistics, supply chain, foreign trade operations, and e-commerce. The experts made their evaluations with a triple rating consisting of "the item is necessary," "the item is useful but not sufficient," and "the item is unnecessary." After the answers given by the experts were collected on a single form, the content validity rate was determined for each scale item. The content validity rate for the items was calculated as follows (Lawshe, 1975):

"Content Validity Rate =" ("Number of Experts Saying Item is Required" /"Half the Total Number of Experts") "-1"

The content validity criterion of the entire scale was determined by considering the critical values in the studies of Ayre and Scally (2014); this value was specified as 0.538 for 13 experts. Scale items below this value were not initially eliminated because there is no existing scale measuring readiness for e-export. If items below this value are discarded, they are ignored at points that may be valuable or notable for the scale. The goal is to evaluate as many scale items as possible. In the elimination process, only scale items calculated equal to and less than zero were eliminated, reducing 63 items to 49.

To evaluate the draft scale consisting of 49 items, 50 companies that export or are interested in e-commerce were contacted. The small number of samples is due to companies needing to answer the survey and the difficulty reaching them during COVID-19 restrictions.

These 49 items, designed as a Likert-type rating scale, were directed at 50 companies operating in different sectors. To create the final scale items in line with the answers, explanatory factor analysis and reliability analysis were conducted. The analysis revealed that the factors needed to be distributed appropriately. For this reason, elimination was used to determine the factor loads and reveal the final version of the scale. The elimination process primarily identified items representing more than one factor in terms of factor loads and whose values are close to each other and then revealed whether these items were below the content validity ratio from the previous stage.

After eight stages of elimination, 49 items were reduced to 28 items, resulting in the factors in the scale items being distributed regularly and achieving the desired reliability ratio. The factor and reliability analyses applied to the 28 scale items are detailed in Tables 3, 4, and 5.

Table 3. Reliability statistics

Cronbach's Alpha	**No. of Items**
.936	28

Table 4. KMO and Bartlett's Test

Kaiser-Meyer-Olkin Measure of Sampling Adequacy.		**.717**
Bartlett's Test of Sphericity	Approx. Chi-Square	1206.519
	df	378
	Sig.	**.000**

Cronbach's Alpha is between zero and one, and an acceptable value is at least 0.7 (Altunışık et al., 2012). Therefore, the alpha value of this study is good, showing that the scale items are quite reliable.

In this test, a value of 0.7 and above is considered a reasonable value for researchers (Malhotra et al., 2006). In the interpretation of this value, 0.8 and above are high, 0.7 and above moderate, 0.6 and above mediocre, 0.5 and above weak, and below 0.5 is unacceptable (Hair, 2009). Therefore, the KMO value obtained from the analysis is at an acceptable level of 0.717.

Table 5. Total variance explained and rotated factor loading matrix (VARIMAX)

	Factor								
	1	2	3	4	5	6	7	8	Commonalities
Our top management can foresee the risks related to e-export.	.892								851
The organizational structure of our company is suitable for e-export.	.788								827
Our company can conduct e-export as a strategic process.	.734								828
Our top management's view of e-export is positive.	.696								654
Our company can simultaneously manage online and offline marketing channels for e-export.	.567								802
Our products can adapt to the technical regulations and standards of target markets.	.534								716
Our company is well informed of the exit customs clearance processes in e-export.		.808							896
Our company can effectively manage international e-marketplaces (Amazon, Alibaba, Global Sources, etc.).		.784							866
Our company can obtain information about the customs processes and duties of the destination countries.		.749							827
Our company has information about market research methods.		.725							820
Our company has information about warehouse processes of e-export operations.			.888						909
Our company has the knowledge and capacity to manage the return processes and problems in e-export.			.870						875
Our company has information about international transportation processes in e-export.			.827						921
Our company has sufficient knowledge about the protection and violation of intellectual property rights (patent, design, trademark, etc.) in e-export.			.584						804
Our company can allocate time and budget for e-export training for our staff.				.781					781
Our staff can use the digital and technical infrastructure required for e-export.				.745					863
Our managers can make the necessary regulations for our staff to devote time to e-export processes.				.696					852
Our staff will not have language problems in communicating with our target markets.				.533					642
There are product images and content on the corporate website of our company.					.851				798
Our company's corporate website provides up-to-date information to customers in different languages.					.804				807
Our company's corporate website is up to date.					.671				758
Our company can allocate the financial resources needed for e-export.						.885			946
Our company can cover the cost of installation and maintenance operations of the digital infrastructure required for e-export.						.869			941
Government financial incentives can accelerate our e-export initiative.							.826		789
The e-export efforts of our competitors can motivate us to do e-export.							.728		737
Our company may offer different payment methods (pay at the door, credit card, digital money, digital wallet, remittance, etc.) in e-export.								.860	816
Our company may be involved in different payment agreements (MoneyGram, Western Union, etc.) for e-export.								.834	748

In Table 5, factor loadings and explanation rates are given. The scale is grouped under eight factors, which increased from the first stage's six factors during analysis. The factors are gathered under management, information and process management, logistics, human resources, media channel, budget, environment, and finance.

4. CONCLUSION

In the context of increasing efficiency and operational efficiency in organizations, e-commerce, one of the good examples of human and machine symbiotic cooperation, is increasing worldwide, especially as an export. Moreover, sustainable development integrates into the world supply chain through export, especially in developing countries. Technology, communication, and transportation transformations have caused companies to evolve from e-commerce to e-export. Although the literature on success factors for export and e-commerce is relatively available, a scale to determine readiness for e-export, which requires the harmonious operation of management functions and digital transformation, was not found during the literature review. So, this is the first scale developed to measure the readiness for e-export of companies and, as such, will contribute to this field and motivate new studies.

The scale development process of this study has a hybrid structure in which theoretical and experimental forms are used together. The literature review, focus group interview, expert opinions, and factor and reliability analyses were applied together, and the items of the scale were matured with a gradual reduction. Content validity and reliability analyses were performed on 50 samples; this produced results beyond the limits expected by the scale development literature and indicated that the scale was ready for use.

The analysis findings show that top management is critical in e-export readiness. Other vital factors for readiness are clustered under information and process management, logistics, human resources, and media channel. Budget, environment, and finance factors are observed to be less effective in readiness than other factors.

These results show that human resources and management functions, whose essential element is human, at the Industry 5.0 level; It also reveals its compatibility with processes, most of which are machine and digital, and the importance of cooperation between them. In future research, variables such as company size, company age, and having undertaken exporting or e-commerce before e-export can also be examined.

REFERENCES

Agarwal, N., & Chauhan, S. (2022). Amplifying Employability Skills to Create Co-Working Space for Human and Cobots in the E-Commerce Industry. *Procedia Computer Science*, *214*, 1040–1048. doi:10.1016/j.procs.2022.11.275

Ajmal, F., Yasin, N. M., & Norman, A. A. (2017). Critical success factors influencing e-commerce adoption in SMEs: A review and model. *International Journal of Advanced and Applied Sciences*, *4*(7), 159–172. doi:10.21833/ijaas.2017.07.023

Al-Dmour, H. H. (2018). A Conceptual Framework for Determinants of E-Exporting (Marketing Applications) Practices and the Business Performance: Empirical Study. *Modern Applied Science*, *12*(11), 358. doi:10.5539/mas.v12n11p358

Altunışık, R., Coşkun, R., Bayraktaroğlu, S., & Yıldırım, E. (2012). Sosyal Bilimlerde Araştırma Yöntemleri [Research Methods in Social Sciences]. *Sakarya Yayıncılık, Sakarya, 126.*

Ayre, C., & Scally, A. J. (2014). Critical values for Lawshe's content validity ratio: revisiting the original methods of calculation. *Measurement and Evaluation in Counseling and Development, 47*(1), 79–86. doı: . doi:10.1177/0748175613513808

Azaria, C. (2010). *Export commerce and export marketing with the use of internet by Greek SMEs,* [Doctoral Dissertation, University of Macedonia, Greece].

Babakhani, M., & Haji, H. (2011). An empirical study to determine the critical success factors of export industry. *Management science letters, 1*(1), 23-28.

Baldauf, A., Cravens, D. W., & Wagner, U. (2000). Examining determinants of export performance in small open economies. *Journal of World Business, 35*(1), 61–79. doi:10.1016/S1090-9516(99)00034-6

Bawack, R. E., Wamba, S. F., Carillo, K. D. A., & Akter, S. (2022). Artificial intelligence in E-Commerce: A bibliometric study and literature review. *Electronic Markets, 32*(1), 297–338. doi:10.100712525-022-00537-z PMID:35600916

Bianchi, C., & Mathews, S. (2013). The role of the internet on export market growth: An empirical study in Latin America. In Strategic Management in Latin America, Mexico City, Mexico.

Carrère, C., & Strauss-Kahn, V. (2017). Export survival and the dynamics of experience. *Review of World Economics, 153*(2), 271–300. doi:10.100710290-017-0277-1

Chen, J., Sousa, C. M., & He, X. (2016). The determinants of export performance: A review of the literature 2006-2014. *International Marketing Review, 33*(5), 626–670. doi:10.1108/IMR-10-2015-0212

Czakó, E., & Könczöl, E. (2014). Critical success factors of export excellence and policy implications: the case of Hungarian small and medium-sized enterprises. *International Entrepreneurship and Corporate Growth in Visegrad Countries*, 69-84.

Eaton, J., Eslava, M., Kugler, M., & Tybout, J. (2008). *The margins of entry into export markets: evidence from Colombia.*

Esteve-Pérez, S., Mánez-Castillejo, J. A., Rochina-Barrachina, M. E., & Sanchis-Llopis, J. A. (2007). A survival analysis of manufacturing firms in export markets. *Entrepreneurship, industrial location, and economic growth. Cheltenham etc.: Elgar*, 313-332

European Commission Report (2021). *Industry 5.0.* EC. https://op.europa.eu/en/publication-detail/-/publication/468a892a-5097-11eb-b59f-01aa75ed71a1/

Gerschewski, S., Scott-Kennel, J., & Rose, E. L. (2020). Ready to export? The role of export readiness for superior export performance of small and medium-sized enterprises. *World Economy, 43*(5), 1253–1276. doi:10.1111/twec.12928

Hair, J. F. (2009). *Multivariate data analysis.*

Heeks, R., & Nicholson, B. (2004). Software export success factors and strategies in 'follower nations. *Competition & Change, 8*(3), 267–303. doi:10.1080/1024529042000301962

Houdeloudi, Z., & Hajidimitriou, Y. A. (2014). *Success factors of internet use for exporting by Greek companies during the period of the financial crisis*. MIBES Transactions International Journal.

H.R. Asia. (2021). E-commerce Boom Driving Rapid Adoption of Cobots. *HR Asia*. https://hr.asia/featured/e-commerce-boom-driving-rapid-adoption-of-cobots/

Innovation PEI report. (n.d.). E-exporting. http://www.gov.pe.ca/photos/original/IPEI_ebiz_exprt.pdf

ITRISA (International Trade Institute of South Africa). (2002). *Export Training and Education Needs Analysis and Recommendations Report*. Compiled for Trade and Investment South Africa.

Laosethakul, K., & Boulton, W. (2007). Critical Success Factors for E-commerce in Thailand: Cultural and Infrastructural Influences. *The Electronic Journal on Information Systems in Developing Countries*, *30*(1), 1–22. doi:10.1002/j.1681-4835.2007.tb00205.x

Lawshe, C. H. (1975). A quantitative approach to content validity. *Personnel Psychology*, *28*(4), 563–575. doi:10.1111/j.1744-6570.1975.tb01393.x

Leipras, A. (2019). Determinants of export performance: Differences between service and manufacturing SMEs. *Service Business*, *13*(1), 171–198. doi:10.100711628-018-0376-7

Liu, H., Hu, Z., & Hu, J. (2022). E-Commerce Logistics Intelligent Warehousing System Solution Based on Multimedia Technology. *Journal of Electrical and Computer Engineering*, *2022*, 2022. doi:10.1155/2022/1754797

Lu, Y., Zheng, H., Chand, S., Xia, W., Liu, Z., Xu, X., Wang, L., Qin, Z., & Bao, J. (2022). Outlook on human-centric manufacturing towards Industry 5.0. *Journal of Manufacturing Systems*, *62*, 612–627. doi:10.1016/j.jmsy.2022.02.001

MacGregor, R. C., & Vrazalic, L. (2005). A basic model of electronic commerce adoption barriers: A study of regional small businesses in Sweden and Australia. *Journal of Small Business and Enterprise Development*, *12*(4), 510–527. doi:10.1108/14626000510628199

Maldifassi, J. O., & Caorsi, J. C. (2014). Export success factors of small and medium-sized firms in Chile. *Journal of Small Business and Enterprise Development*, *21*(3), 450–469. doi:10.1108/JSBED-03-2014-0053

Malhotra, N., Hall, J., Shaw, M., & Oppenheim, P. (2006). *Marketing research: An applied orientation*. Pearson Education Australia. doi:10.1108/S1548-6435(2006)2

Melewar, T. C., & Smith, N. (2003). The internet revolution: Some global marketing implications. *Marketing Intelligence & Planning*, *2*(6), 363–369. doi:10.1108/02634500310499220

Mohammadzadeh, M. (2012). An analysis of the relationship between staff qualification and export readiness of pharmaceutical companies: The case of Iran. *Iranian journal of pharmaceutical research. IJPR*, *11*(3), 985. PMID:24250528

Mohammadzadeh, M., Poloee, M., & Ghari, T. (2016). *Export readiness assessment of ten Iranian pharmaceutical companies and comparison with their export performance*. Research Gate.

Moodley, S. (2002). Connecting to global markets in the internet age: The case of South African wooden furniture producers. *Development Southern Africa*, *19*(5), 641–658. doi:10.1080/0376883502200019338

Moon, B. J., & Jain, S. (2007). Determinants and outcomes of internet marketing activities of exporting firms. *Journal of Global Marketing*, *20*(4), 55–71. doi:10.1300/J042v20n04_05

Nahavandi, S. (2019). Industry 5.0—A human-centric solution. *Sustainability, 11*(16), 4371. doi:10.3390u11164371

Obeidat, B., Tarhini, A., Masa'deh, R., & Aqqad, N. (2017). The impact of intellectual capital on innovation via the mediating role of knowledge management: A structural equation modeling approach. *International Journal of Knowledge Management Studies, 8*(4), 273–298. doi:10.1504/IJKMS.2017.087071

Ontario. (2021). *E-exporting*. Ontario. https://www.ontario.ca/page/e-exporting

Poon, S., & Swatman, P. M. C. (1997). Internet-based small business communications: Seven Australian case. *The PACIS Conference*, Brisbane, Australia. 10.1080/10196789700000019

Rosson, P. (2004 in press). The internet and SME exporting: Canadian success stories. In H. Etemad (Ed.), *International Entrepreneurship in Small and Medium Size Enterprises: Orientation, Environment, and Strategy*. Edward Elgar Publishing.

Safari, A., & Saleh, A. S. (2020). Key determinants of SMEs' export performance: A resource-based view and contingency theory approach using potential mediators. *Journal of Business and Industrial Marketing, 35*(4), 635–654. doi:10.1108/JBIM-11-2018-0324

Samiee, S. (1998). Exporting and the internet: A conceptual perspective. *International Marketing Review, 15*(5), 413–426. doi:10.1108/02651339810236452

Saniuk, S., Grabowska, S., & Straka, M. (2022). Identification of Social and Economic Expectations: Contextual Reasons for the Transformation Process of Industry 4.0 into the Industry 5.0 Concept. *Sustainability, 14*(3), 1391. doi:10.3390u14031391

Sousa, C. M., Martínez-López, F. J., & Coelho, F. (2008). The determinants of export performance: A review of the research in the literature between 1998 and 2005. *International Journal of Management Reviews, 10*(4), 343–374. doi:10.1111/j.1468-2370.2008.00232.x

Sung, T. K. (2006). E-commerce critical success factors: East vs. West. *Technological Forecasting and Social Change, 73*(9), 1161–1177. doi:10.1016/j.techfore.2004.09.002

Supply Chain Collaborative Robot Market Report. (2022). Global Market Estimates. https://www.globalmarketestimates.com/market-report/supply-chain-collaborative-robots-market-3427

Suwannarat, P. (2016). The study of export intermediary performance determinants. *Multinational Business Review, 24*(2), 123–143. doi:10.1108/MBR-10-2015-0050

The Economist (2014). The G20 e-Trade Readiness Index. *The Economist.* https://eiuperspectives.economist.com/economic-development/g20-e-trade-readiness-index/white-paper/g20-e-trade-readiness-index

Torrens, E. W., Amal, M., & Tontini, G. (2014). Determinants of export performance of small and medium-sized manufacturing Brazilian enterprises from the perspective of resource-based view and Uppsala model. *Revista Brasileira de Gestão de Negócios-RBGN, 16*(53), 511–539.

Varela, M. L. R., Araújo, A. F., Vieira, G. G., Manupati, V. K., & Manoj, K. (2017). Integrated framework based on critical success factors for e-Commerce. *Journal of Information Systems Engineering & Management, 2*(1), 4. doi:10.20897/jisem.201704

Viviers, W., & Van Eldik, S. (2005). The measurement of export readiness of companies in South Africa. *Southern African Business Review, 9*(2), 1–11.

APPENDIX

Table 6. Factors for e-export readiness scale

FACTOR 1 (MANAGEMENT)	FACTOR 2 (INFORMATION AND PROCESS MANAGEMENT)	FACTOR 3 (LOGISTICS)	FACTOR 4 (HUMAN RESOURCES)	FACTOR 5 (MEDIA-CHANNEL)	FACTOR 6 (BUDGET)	FACTOR 7 (ENVIRONMENT)	FACTOR 8 (FINANCE)
Our top management can foresee the risks related to e-export.	Our company is well informed of the exit customs clearance processes in e-export.	Our company has information about warehouse processes of e-export operations.	Our company can allocate time and budget for e-export training for our staff.	There are product images and content on the corporate website of our company.	Our company can allocate the financial resources needed for e-export.	Government financial incentives can accelerate our e-export initiative.	Our company may offer different payment methods (pay at the door, credit card, digital money, digital wallet, remittance, etc.) in e-export.
The organizational structure of our company is suitable for e-export	Our company can manage international e-marketplaces (Amazon, Alibaba, Global Sources, etc.) effectively.	Our company has the knowledge and capacity to manage return processes and problems in e-export.	Our staff can use the digital and technical infrastructure required for e-export.	Our company's corporate website provides up-to-date information to customers in different languages.	Our company can cover the cost of installation and maintenance of the digital infrastructure required for e-export.	The e-export efforts of our competitors can motivate us to do e-export.	Our company may be involved in different payment agreements (MoneyGram, Western Union, etc.) for e-export.
Our company can conduct e-export as a strategic process.	Our company can obtain information about the customs processes and duties of the destination countries.	Our company has information about international transportation processes in e-export.	Our managers can implement the necessary regulations for our staff to devote time to e-export processes.	Our company's corporate website is up to date.			
Our top management's view of e-export is positive.	Our company has information about market research methods.	Our company has sufficient knowledge about the protection and violation of intellectual property rights (patent, design, trademark, etc.) in e-export.	Our staff will not have language problems in communicating with our target markets.				
Our top management is enthusiastic about investing in new information technologies for export activities.							
Our company can simultaneously manage online and offline marketing channels for e-export.							
Our products can adapt to the technical regulations and standards of target markets.							

Chapter 13
Cryptocurrency Adoption in the Era of Industry 5.0:
Opportunities, Challenges, and the Intellectual Landscape - SLR and Bibliometric Analysis

Sonia Chawla
Dr. B.R. Ambedkar National Institute of Technology, Jalandhar, India

Kriti Mehta
Dr. B.R. Ambedkar National Institute of Technology, Jalandhar, India

ABSTRACT

Viewed as entrepreneurship in financial solutions and based on blockchain technology, cryptocurrency is the most recent development in digital currency and is gaining substantial interest in recent years. The intersection of Industry 5.0 and cryptocurrency adoption could lead to new business models and revenue streams, with cryptocurrency potentially being used as a secure and efficient means of payment in Industry 5.0. This study aims to explore cryptocurrency adoption literature using a thorough literature review and bibliometric analysis. The study primarily used the Scopus database for the extraction of relevant literature. The literature review and bibliometric analysis have been done both quantitatively and qualitatively based on various techniques such as network analysis (keyword Co-occurrence analysis) and science mapping techniques. i.e., word cloud and word tree map with the help of tools such as VOSviewer, and R Studio Biblioshiny. The study reveals that the use of cryptocurrency in Industry 5.0 has the potential to improve efficiency, security, and transparency.

INTRODUCTION

Almost every sphere of human life interaction has been digitalized and empowered by state-of-the-art technology with no exception to the digitalization of financial assets. After the Internet revolution,

DOI: 10.4018/978-1-6684-6403-8.ch013

"digital currency" is the next innovation that initiated the revolution in the modern period (Alaklabi & Kang, 2021; Gupta et al., 2020; Koroma et al., 2022a). Industry 5.0 refers to the fifth industrial revolution, which is characterized by the integration of advanced technologies such as artificial intelligence, the Internet of Things, and blockchain (Chander.et.al.,2022).The adoption of cryptocurrency as digital currency, in Industry 5.0 is a significant development that has the potential to bring about new opportunities and challenges for businesses and industries (Mourtzis. et.al.2022). Hence, Industry 5.0 and cryptocurrency are two important and interconnected trends that are shaping the future of business and industry (Tiwari.et.,al 2022).

Viewed as entrepreneurship in financial solutions (Iyidogan et al., 2020; Teo, 2015) and based on blockchain technology, cryptocurrency is the most recent development in digital currency, used for hedging and speculation (Narayanan, 2016). Cryptocurrency is a digital asset that uses cryptography to secure transactions and control the creation of new units Gurusamy, (Hameed, 2019). Cryptocurrency enables secure, decentralized transactions without the need for intermediaries like banks, making it an attractive option for businesses and individuals looking to protect their assets and reduce the risk of fraud (N Gowda. et.al., 2021). Cryptocurrency can help to advance the development of new technologies, such as blockchain, that have the potential to revolutionize the way we store and transfer information and assets (Dorofeyev et al., 2018). Cryptocurrency can help to reduce the carbon footprint of financial transactions by reducing the need for intermediaries, such as banks, to process transactions. This can help to reduce the energy consumption and emissions associated with the traditional financial system (Wang. et al., 2022). This makes it an attractive option for businesses and industries that operate in a fast-paced and rapidly changing environment.

The connection between Industry 5.0 and cryptocurrency is rooted in their shared focus on innovation and the integration of advanced technologies. The technologies that are driving Industry 5.0, such as artificial intelligence and the Internet of Things, have the potential to greatly benefit from the use of cryptocurrency, particularly in terms of secure and efficient financial transactions.

Cryptocurrency also has the potential to play a key role in the development of new business models in Industry 5.0, such as decentralized marketplaces, micropayments, and the creation of new revenue streams (Makhdoom et. al., 2019). By leveraging the decentralized and secure nature of cryptocurrency, businesses can provide their customers with a new level of convenience and security, leading to increased customer satisfaction and loyalty (Koroma et al., 2022a).

In addition to the opportunities that cryptocurrency presents, it also brings with it new challenges and risks. For example, the lack of regulation and security risks associated with cryptocurrency can make it difficult for businesses to fully embrace and utilize its benefits Ooi et al., 2021). To address these challenges, it is important for the industry 5.0 ecosystem to work together to find solutions that balance the benefits of cryptocurrency with the need for security and regulatory compliance.

Quite a few researchers have proposed that cryptocurrency is digital money that serves the same purposes as cash, (Tama et al 2017; Bakar & Rosbi, 2017; Inci & Lagasse, 2019; Mittal et al., 2018) while some researchers have stated that it is not a pure form of money (Yuneline, 2019) because it does not possess all the features of money like security and regulatory compliance (Ayedh, Echchabi, et al., 2020

Bitcoin's phenomenal rise in value between 2017 and 2020 has made the cryptocurrency well-known (Zhao, 2022). Due to the global rise in the popularity of cryptocurrencies, some countries regulate these assets and investments, while others have outlawed them. The top 20 countries adopting cryptocurrency have been revealed and displayed by the Chainalysis (2022) Global Cryptocurrency Adoption index, with Vietnam leading the way in terms of cryptocurrency adoption, followed by the Philippines, Ukraine, and India. As a result, it is apparent that the cryptocurrency market has seen a huge expansion in both its narrow and broad margins (Ballis & Drakos, 2021).

Cryptocurrency adoption follows five main steps, beginning with the period of evaluation and continuing up through the phase of early adopters, venture finance, and finally the phase of widespread consumer acceptance (Tsanidis et al., 2015). The advantage of studying cryptocurrency adoption in Industry 5.0 is the ability to create new revenue streams through the creation of decentralized marketplaces and micropayments. For example, businesses can use cryptocurrency to provide their customers with new and innovative services, such as secure and fast online payments, and to receive micropayments for the use of their products and services (Yin & Yu, 2022). It provides a foundation for the development of new business models and the implementation of innovative technologies. Some of the significant antecedents identified in the extant literature include governance and regulatory standards (Holub & Johnson, 2018; Maria Teresa Chimienti, 2019; Ooi et al., 2021), security and trust (Koroma et al., 2022a), functionality, reliability, and helpfulness (Lankton et al., 2014), knowledge, ownership, and perceived trustworthiness (Steinmetz et al., 2021) and volatility (Berentsen & Schär, 2018).

Although adoption antecedents hold immense significance, scholars have paid less attention to their explicit investigation. Moreover, recent studies have stressed the need to grasp the nature of the requirements that these technologies answer to fully comprehend the potential future of fintech breakthroughs (Cohen et al., 2018; Huang et al., 2019; Saiedi et al., 2021). The purpose of the present study is to find out the latest development, and most defining antecedents and identify the significant research themes related to cryptocurrency adoption using bibliometric analysis techniques. So far as we are able to determine, prior studies which conducted bibliographic analysis had not used keyword co-occurrence and science mapping technique using word tree maps and word clouds to find out the prevailing study topics and suggest directions for future research. The following research questions are addressed in the study:

RQ 1. What are the most significant publications and recent developments in cryptocurrency adoption?

RQ 2. What is the literature's most important and defining antecedents of cryptocurrency adoption?

RQ 3. What are the prevailing study themes and topics in the adoption of cryptocurrencies?

RQ 4. What are the research directions for future work?

The following outline constitutes the paper's overall format: Section 2 concerns research methodology and research design. Section 3 shows the results for publication trends, the most published and cited countries, and the most cited articles. The bibliographic coupling and content analysis of each cluster follows in Section 4. Then, in section 5, the most recent research topics and new trends have been summed up. Finally, In section 6 there are some discussions, research directions for future work and a conclusion.

2. METHODOLOGY

2.1 Analysis Method

Bibliometric analysis is one of the methods for doing a systematic review that has gained popularity and acceptance across many disciplines.(Guo et al., 2021; Jalal et al., 2021; Secinaro et al., 2020a; Sousa et al., 2022; Zhang et al., 2022). Bibliometric methods are grounded on quantitative and statistical analysis, eliminate subjectivity and direct researchers to the most pertinent papers, which enhances the effectiveness of a systematic literature review (Ferreira et al., 2014; Hashemi et al., 2022; Jalal et al., 2021; Kumar, Pandey, et al., 2022; Mukherjee et al., 2021). In order to assess cryptocurrencies and their adoption, this research involved a Bibliometric analysis for systematic literature review (Souiden et al., 2021) as this approach is most suitable for determining the current status of research (Paul & Bhukya, 2021)

The present study conducted a bibliographic coupling in Bibliometric analysis using Vos viewer (version 1.6.18) (Župič & Čater, 2015; Jalal et al., 2021; Secinaro et al., 2020a; Xie et al., 2020) to find out the most important and defining antecedents of cryptocurrency adoption. VOS viewer has been used for network analysis to create a network visualisation of the co-occurrence of keywords. The study also used biblioshiny in R Studio (Aria & Cuccurullo, 2017) for the generation of science mapping techniques i.e. word cloud (Kumar, Sharma, et al., 2022; Prakash Giri et al., 2022; Secinaro et al., 2020b) and word tree maps (Gupta et al., 2021; Oyewola and Dada, 2022) to find out the recent research topics.

2.2 Data Extraction Process

The study extensively collected literature from the Scopus database as this is a well-known index of the peer-reviewed journal that provides accurate bibliographic information (Alsmadi et al., 2022; Hashemi et al., 2022; Kumar, Sharma, et al., 2022; Rhaiem & Amara, 2021; Souiden et al., 2021) The database was searched by using the specific related keywords on August 10, 2022. The research began by using three keywords "Cryptocurrency," "Bitcoin," and "adoption" to access relevant research work published in the database. 504 research papers in various categories were discovered. The research was modified by using filters by subject areas such as Business, Management and Accounting OR Social Sciences OR Economics, Econometrics and Finance. The only permitted document types were Journal articles or review papers, and English was required as the document language which resulted in 146 papers. Then the abstract of each article was considered to check the relevance of the papers for the study. Figure 1 depicts the procedure for extracting and processing the dataset. Finally, the search ended up with a total of 23 research publications, which were used for the present study.

3 RESULTS

3.1 Publication Trend

Cryptocurrency adoption is very contemporary area and the latest article is in the year 2016. The trend remained rare till 2019, grew from the year 2020, and peaked at 9 articles till Aug 2022. The topic is relatively new demonstrating its increasing importance over the time as shown in figure 2:

3.2 Distribution of Countries: Number of Publications and Citations Wise

With regards to the country-wise publications, China and USA rank number one and contribute to the most publications (4 publications each) followed by Australia and Malaysia with 3 publications each followed by other nations as exhibited in figure 3 (A). Citation-wise analysis figure 3 (B) depicts that China and the United States are at the top of the list, with 72 and 43 citations respectively. Sweden and Austria have 18 and 7 citations while Malaysia stands with 5 citations.

Figure 1. Methodology flowchart

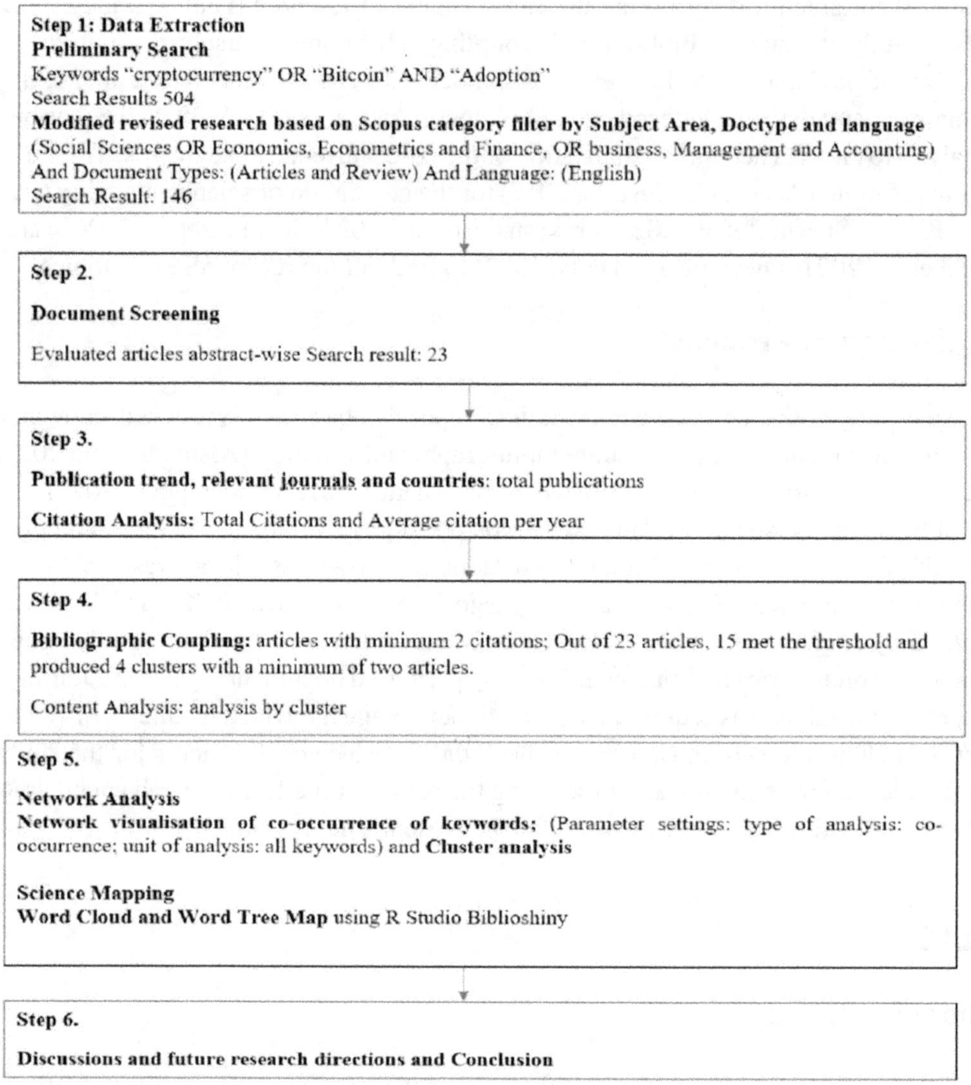

Figure 2. No. of publication per year retrieved from Scopus database

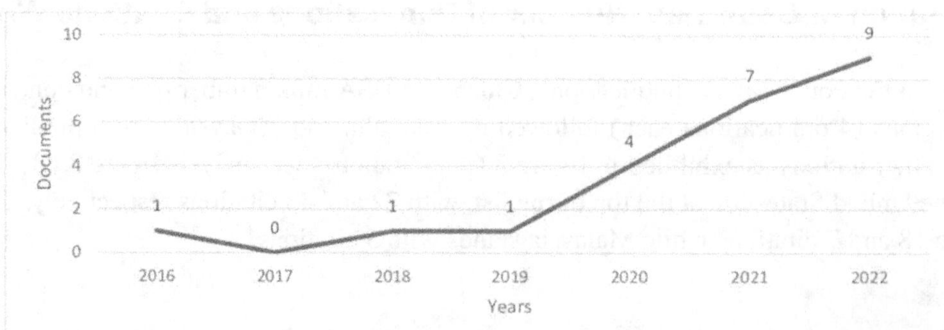

Figure 3. (A) Top ten countries with the most publications; (B) Countries according to total number of citations

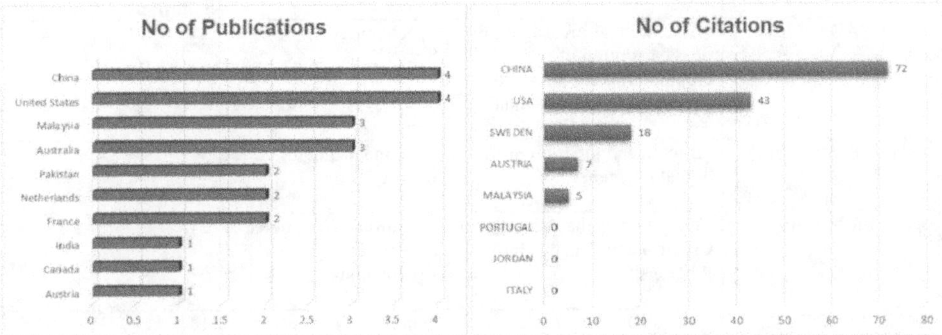

3.3 Citation Analysis

Citation analysis is the approach that is most frequently used to measure a publication's importance. (Ding & Cronin, 2011; Sousa et al., 2022). The number of citations an article has obtained from other publications determines how influential it is (Ivan Župič and Tomaž Čater, 2015). Table 1 lists the top 10 studies about cryptocurrency adoption that have received the most citations. It gives a summary of the papers that have been published and ranks them according to the total citations (TC) and total citations per year. Shahzad F, (2018) work is the most cited paper with 57 total citations and an average of 11.40 citations per year. Luther WJ, (2016) wrote the second most frequently cited paper with 39 total citations followed by Jonker N, (2019) paper with 21 citations in total. Saiedi E, (2021) paper is the fourth most frequently cited research with 18 total citations while Mazambani L, (2020) paper has 17 citations.

4. BIBLIOGRAPHIC COUPLING

Bibliographic coupling occurs when two publications refer the same third publication (Guleria & Kaur, 2021; Kessler M M, 1963). To establish a more disciplined field of research, papers with a minimum of two citations was selected as the cut-off criterion (Mccain et al., 2005) for bibliographic coupling. The articles (nodes) were assigned to the four clusters and displayed as a bibliometric network based on the strength of the connections between them (edge density) as shown in Figure 4.

4.1 Content Analysis

A content analysis of the publications was carried out based on the four clusters produced by the bibliographic coupling analysis to identify key points and insights. The clusters were given the following identities:

Table 1. Citation analysis sorted by local citations

Author(s)Year	Title	Sources	Total Citations	TC per Year
SHAHZAD F, (2018)	"An empirical investigation on the adoption of cryptocurrencies among the people of mainland China"	"Technology in Society"	57	11.40
LUTHER WJ, (2016)	"Bitcoin and the future of digital payments"	"The Independent Review"	39	5.57
JONKER N, 2019	"What Drives the Adoption of Crypto-Payments by Online Retailers?"	"Electronic Commerce Research and Applications"	21	5.25
SAIEDI E, (2021)	"Global Drivers of cryptocurrency infrastructure adoption"	"Small business economics"	18	9.00
MAZAMBANI L, (2020)	"Predicting fintech innovation adoption in South Africa: A case of Cryptocurrency"	"African journal of economic and management studies"	17	5.67
FUJIKI H, (2020)	"Who adopts crypto assets in Japan? Evidence from 2019 financial literacy survey"	"Journal of The Japanese and International Economies"	13	4.33
NADEEM MA, (2021)	"Investigating the adoption factors of cryptocurrencies-A Case of Bitcoin: Empirical Evidence from China"	Sage Open	8	4.00
TREIBLMAIER H, (2021)	"Cryptocurrency adoption in travel and tourism – an exploratory study of Asia Pacific travellers"	Current Issues in Tourism	7	3.50
BHARADWAJ S, (2021)	"Behavioural intention towards investment in cryptocurrency: an integration of Rogers' diffusion of innovation theory and the technology acceptance model"	Forum Scientiae Oeconomia	5	2.50
AJOUZ M, (2020)	"Acceptance of Sharī'ah-compliant precious metal-backed cryptocurrency as an alternative currency: An empirical validation of adoption of innovation theory"	"Thunderbird international business review"	5	1.67

Cluster 1

Financial Literacy and Users' Knowledge: This cluster analyses the users' state of knowledge and financial literacy regarding cryptocurrency to explore its efficiency. Fujiki, (2020) revealed that in Japan owners of cryptocurrencies are financially more literate; they are more open to investing in a crypto asset and tend to show positive investment behaviour due to their prior experience of holding conventional risky assets as compared to the non-owners. Similarly, Huynh et al. (2020), stated that Canadian Bitcoin users

Figure 4. Bibliographic coupling of 15 articles

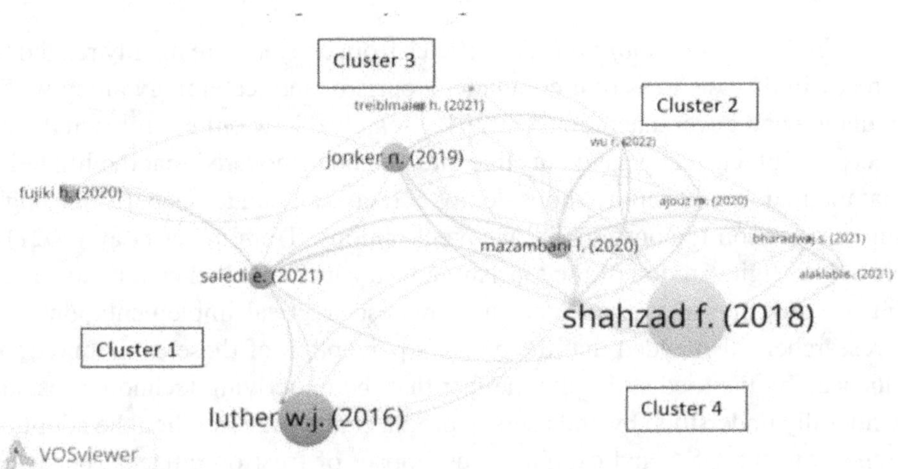

were different from other Canadians in terms of their financial knowledge and cash holdings. The study found that Bitcoin ownership increased more among women, financial literacy was found to improve Bitcoin knowledge but reduce Bitcoin ownership, and Bitcoin users were making more purchases using Bitcoin. (Luther, 2016) also stated that Bitcoin is an improved technology for payments and the future of digital payment.

A study by Saiedi et al. (2021) investigated the function of financial, criminal, social and legal factors affecting the adoption of Bitcoin infrastructure. It has been found that traditional financial systems' alleged flaws and alternatives to the inadequate delivery of traditional banking services (Cohen et al., 2018; Shiller Robert J, 2019, Vigna and Casey 2015), led to Bitcoin as an anticipated investment (D. G. Baur et al., 2018) and for illegal money laundering activities.

Cluster 2

Perception Towards Adoption Intention of Cryptocurrency: The topics included in this cluster describe the adoption intention and perception of individuals in different parts of the world. Bharadwaj and Deka, (2021) studied how Indians from Generation Z plan to act with regard to investing in cryptocurrencies. The study used the Diffusion of Innovation Theory and the Technology Acceptance Model to demonstrate that compatibility, complexity, and observability affect perceived usefulness and perceived ease of use ultimately affect behavioural intention to invest in cryptocurrency. The study of Alaklabi and Kang, (2021) acknowledges the perception towards cryptocurrency adoption by taking perceived Risk, perceived usefulness, and perceived enjoyment factors. Mazambani and Mutambara, (2020) study based upon the theory of planned behaviour (TPB) stated that attitude and perceived behavioural control had a positive effect on the intention to adopt cryptocurrency while subjective norms had a negative effect. Innovation of Diffusion Theory was used in the Ajouz et al. (2020) study to find out how likely potential users in Malaysia were to use a Shariah-compliant cryptocurrency backed by precious metals and found that anxiety, compatibility, facilitating conditions, relative advantage, trust, and observability are statistically significant for adoption intention.

Cluster 3

Cryptocurrency's Multi-Functional Adoption: The articles from cluster 3 are mainly related to the adoption of cryptocurrency in diverse areas of e-commerce, tourism, and technology along with aspects of sustainability, regulation and governance. Jonker, (2019) searched how online stores in the Netherlands plan to use and accept cryptocurrency payments like bitcoin and discovered that the limited adoption is due to the fact that the majority of online shops do not perceive any added benefit in using cryptocurrency payments in comparison to conventional payment options. Treiblmaier et al. (2021) stated that recent innovations in the digitalization of the tourism industry include blockchain and stated that from a traveller's point of view, cryptocurrencies are the greatest practical implementation of blockchain technology. The researchers also added that the public's perception of these economic transactions is significantly influenced by the media, despite the fact that the underlying technology is sophisticated and occasionally not fully understood by end users. Koroma et al. (2022) studied the adoption of blockchain cryptocurrencies in the USA and examined the impact of trust on citizens' behaviour towards blockchain cryptocurrencies. The study found that blockchain transparency and technology attachment are the antecedents of trust while ethical considerations acted as a moderating factor. On the other hand, considering the regulation and governance area, Wu et al. (2022) research aimed to explain how regulatory pressures can influence the adoption of cryptocurrency-related mechanisms, as well as e-retailers' intention to incorporate them into their business models.

Cluster 4

Bitcoin Widely Used Virtual Currency. The publications that form the important characteristics of cryptocurrency adoption in this cluster are mainly related to Bitcoin. Nadeem et al. (2021) in his study in China found favourable association between the intention to adopt Bitcoin and perceived usefulness and perceived ease of use. The link between the perceived ease of use and the intention to adopt Bitcoin is mediated by the perceived usefulness while security and control, appear to have a negligible impact on perceived usefulness. Shahzad et al. (2018) investigated the variables affecting Bitcoin adoption in China and recommended that the government and financial institutions should regulate it in order to raise public knowledge, build confidence in it and encourage people to use it in the new global financial system.

5. NETWORK ANALYSIS

5.1 Network Visualisation of Co-Occurrence of Keywords

Keyword co-occurrence is used in network analysis to investigate the major themes underpinning the recent trends in cryptocurrency adoption. Based on Guo et al. (2021); Kumar Pandey et al. (2022); and Mukherjee et al. (2021), this study-built keyword co-occurrence analysis, broadly indicating the major themes of cryptocurrency adoption. Using VOS viewer software, a network map of the keyword co-occurrence was produced as shown in fig 5 (Framework settings: counting method: full counting; unit of analysis: all keywords; type of analysis: co-occurrence, Total keywords: 145 keywords, 18 meet the threshold).

Figure 5. Network visualization map based on publication weights

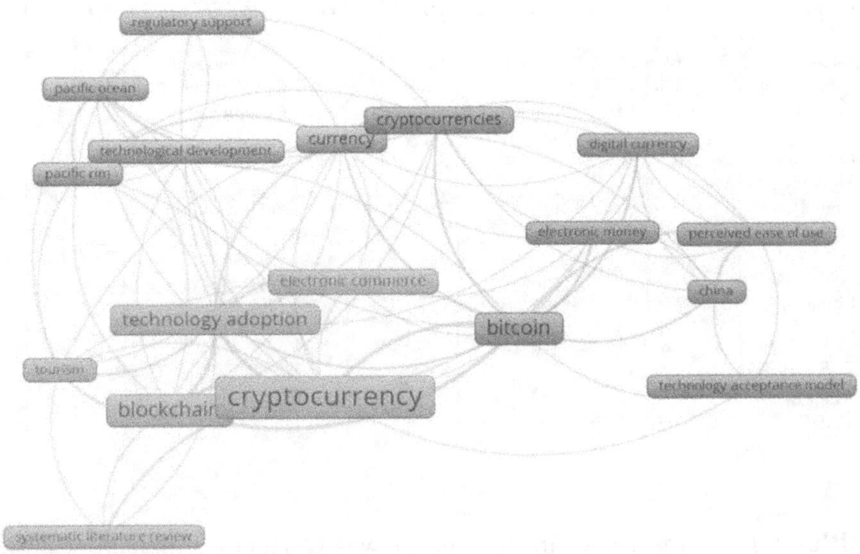

Cluster Analysis

In Cluster analysis, the linkages of the items (keywords) is established by the number of documents (articles) in which they appear together, and the strength of the linkages shows the number of articles in which two keywords appear together. The results of the bibliometric network analysis are given in Table 2. It presents three major clusters that are relevant to the adoption of cryptocurrencies. The accompanying metrics in the table provide information on the total occurrence (TO), Degree of Centrality (DC) and, the Eigenvector centrality (EC) of each keyword. These metrics assess the number of connections for each one of the keywords and the relative importance of every keyword in relation to another keyword. (Donthu et al., 2021). The following are the summaries of each major theme in Table 2.

Table 2 displays each keyword or topic's total occurrence (TO), along with its degree of centrality (DC) as a measure of its number of connections and its Eigenvector centrality (EC) as a measure of its relative importance based on its relationship to other keywords or concepts. High eigenvector centrality (EC) is evidenced by keywords or topics with a large number of links and is also associated with other keywords or topics with a similar degree of centrality. (Donthu et al., 2021; Kumar, Sharma, et al., 2022).

Cluster #1 (Red): This cluster mainly focuses on how the technology initiates cryptocurrency and is adopted in diverse fields. The most popular topic of this cluster is Bitcoin, which appears in 7 out of 23 articles with EC of 25 and is connected to other keywords, such as cryptocurrencies, digital currency, electronic money, China, Technology acceptance model, and perceived ease of use.

Cluster #2 (Green): This cluster mostly talks about the technology behind cryptocurrency and the applicability of this emerging currency. These issues have become more renowned in recent years. The most prominent keyword is cryptocurrency which appears in 12 articles and its eigenvector centrality is 21 which is the highest among all. Other most conversed keywords in this cluster are blockchain, e-commerce, technology adoption, systematic literature review and tourism.

Table 2. Major clusters for cryptocurrency adoption

Sr. No	Cluster 1	TO	DC	EC	Cluster 2	TO	DC	EC	Cluster 3	TO	DC	EC
1	Bitcoin	7	14	25	Cryptocurrency	12	14	21	Technological Development	2	8	8
2	Cryptocurrencies	4	12	14	Technology adoption	6	12	20	Currency	4	15	20
3	Electronic Money	2	8	9	Blockchain	7	11	18	Pacific Ocean	2	10	12
4	Digital currency	2	8	9	Tourism	2	9	11	Pacific Rim	2	10	12
5	Perceived ease of use	2	7	9	Electronic Commerce	3	7	8	Regulator Support	2	6	6
6	China	2	7	9	Systematic literature review	2	4	5	-	-	-	-
7	Technology acceptance model	2	4	4	-	-	-	-	-	-	-	-

Cluster #3 (Blue): The largest knot in this cluster was Currency, connecting 20 keywords. This segment of the study was concerned with securing the growth of cryptocurrencies, such as technology development, regulatory support, electronic commerce, etc. This cluster provides the scenario of the worldwide phenomenon of cryptocurrency adoption. As this cluster includes the words like the Pacific Ocean and Pacific Rim (lands around the rim of the Pacific Ocean) which specifies its worldwide popularity and the word regulatory support signifies that for the smooth functioning of this currency some jurisdiction is required.

5.2 Science Mapping

The term "science mapping" refers to an investigation that "discovers and provides a knowledge that exists and is interconnected inside a research domain augmented by data visualisation tools" (Donthu et al., 2021). The science mapping of literature is conducted using bibliometric analysis techniques in the R bibliometrix package, namely word clouds and word tree maps to unpack the major topics defining cryptocurrency adoption.

5.2 (a) Word Cloud

Word clouds can be helpful in many different types of assessments, and they are more than just a visually appealing representation of words. A word cloud (or tag cloud) is defined as "visual presentations of a set of words, typically a set of tags, in which text attributes such as size, weight, or colour can be used to represent features (e.g., frequency) of the associated terms" (Havley and Keane, 2007). Word clouds are visually appealing displays of frequently used words, typically displaying keywords in varying sizes and colours in accordance with their frequency of occurrence. Examining the frequencies of words and phrases in a word cloud allows researchers to search for specific patterns in text data. (Concetta A. et al., 2014). This tool was used to determine the prevailing study themes, as the word cloud in Figure 6 demonstrates. Keywords with a high frequency of occurrences, such as cryptocurrency, blockchain,

Figure 6. Word cloud of recent research topics retrieved from biblioshiny

bitcoin, and technology adoption, appear in bold and large size. And the small size of terms such as consumer demand, behavioural intention to use, adoption model, attitude, and digital payments indicates a low frequency. Studies recommend the technology acceptance model highly in terms of technology adoption. Regulatory support, e-government, consumer trust, digital payments, and digital currencies were also among the most frequently used terms in the relevant literature.

5.2 (b) Word Tree Map

"Tree Map" is a tree-lined map that displays hierarchical data using layered rectangles (Basile et al., 2022; R. Gupta et al., 2021; Oyewola & Dada, 2022). This map can be retrieved using four different parameters: title, abstract, keywords, and author keywords. In this scenario, we consider the one connected to the authors' keywords and utilise the greatest quantity of 200 words (Prakash Giri et al.,2022.; Secinaro et al., 2020a). The size of the rectangular box in Figure 7 shows the frequency of the keywords, and the colours represent the association with the keywords. Keyword sections viz "cryptocurrency," "bitcoin," "blockchain," "cryptocurrencies," "technology adoption," and "digital currency" are well identified, As opposed to small size rectangle boxes with multiple keywords such as "accessibility," "attitude," and "fintech" are less noticeable and it can be inferred from tree map dynamics that these small-size box keywords are emerging areas for future research. As a result, the analysis suggests interesting research domains within this issue. Figure 7's Tree Map illustrates recent research topics as well as developing streams like technostress, diffusion, compatibility, accessibility, competition, fintech, and e-retailers regarding cryptocurrencies and their adoption.

Figure 7. Word tree map of author's keywords using biblioshiny

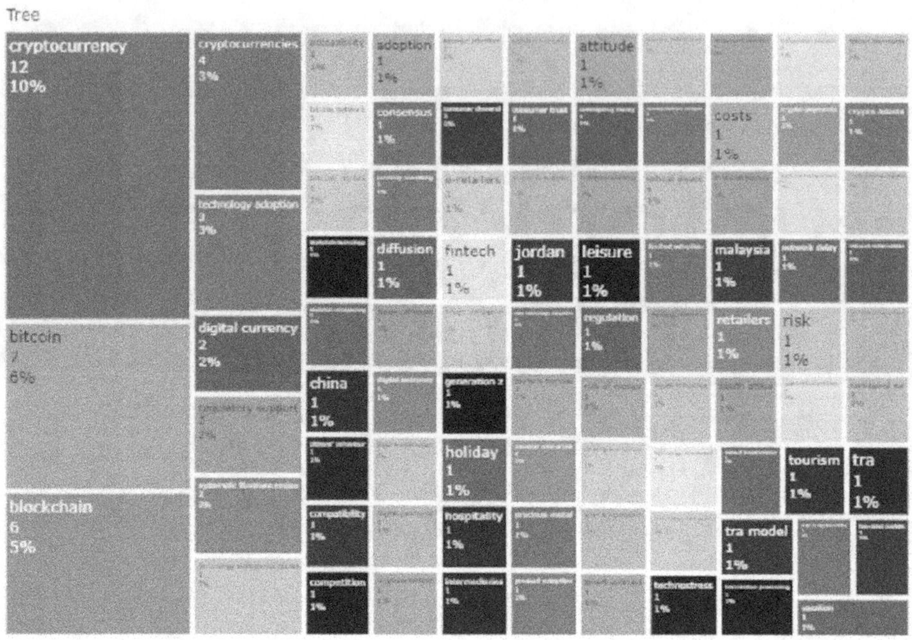

6. DISCUSSIONS

6.1 Industry 5.0

Based on a thorough review of the literature on cryptocurrency adoption in the era of industry 5.0, has seen various opportunities, challenges, problems, and trends in using cryptocurrency in industry 5.0 (Adel A, 2022). Some of the highlights are as follows:

6.1.1. Opportunities in Industry 5.0 and Cryptocurrency Adoption:

- Improved security and transparency: Cryptocurrency transactions are secured by blockchain technology, providing a secure and transparent means of payment in Industry 5.0 supply chains.
- Increased efficiency: The use of cryptocurrency eliminates the need for intermediaries in financial transactions, leading to more efficient and streamlined payment processes.
- Better data tracking: The use of blockchain technology in cryptocurrency transactions provides a secure and transparent means of tracking data in Industry 5.0 supply chains, improving accountability and reducing the risk of fraud (Yin, S., & Yu, Y, 2022).
- New revenue streams: The use of cryptocurrency in Industry 5.0 could open up new revenue streams, such as through the creation of cryptocurrency-based loyalty programs and micropayments
- Access to new markets: Cryptocurrency enables cross-border transactions without the need for intermediaries, providing new opportunities for businesses to expand into new markets.

- Attraction of new investment: The use of cryptocurrency in Industry 5.0 may attract new investment, as investors look to capitalize on the growth potential of this technology.

6.1.2. Challenges in Industry 5.0 and Cryptocurrency Adoption:

- Digitization: Both Industry 5.0 and cryptocurrency adoption are driven by the digitization of processes and systems, leading to improved efficiency and accessibility.
- Development of new technologies: Both areas are characterized by the development and implementation of new technologies, such as blockchain in the case of cryptocurrency and artificial intelligence in Industry 5.0.
- Data-driven decision making: The increased use of data and analytics is a common theme in both Industry 5.0 and cryptocurrency adoption, informing more informed and effective business strategies (Leng J.et. al.,2022)

6.1.3. Problems in Industry 5.0 and Cryptocurrency Adoption:

- Lack of infrastructure and understanding: The implementation of Industry 5.0 practices and the widespread adoption of cryptocurrencies may be hindered by a lack of infrastructure and understanding among the general public.
- Concerns over privacy and security: The increased use of sensitive information in both Industry 5.0 and cryptocurrency raises concerns over privacy and security, requiring robust measures to protect this information.
- Resistance to change: The transformation of traditional practices and systems can be met with resistance from industries and individuals who are familiar with established ways of working (DeVries, P. D. (2016).

6.1.4. Trends in Industry 5.0 and Cryptocurrency Adoption:

- Rising demand for solutions: Both Industry 5.0 and cryptocurrency are experiencing a growing demand for their solutions and services, driven by their potential to improve efficiency and competitiveness (Makori, E. O. (2023).
- Decentralization: The decentralization of financial systems through cryptocurrency adoption and the decentralization of production processes through Industry 5.0 are key trends in these areas.
- Integration of physical and digital systems: The integration of physical and digital systems is a common theme in both Industry 5.0 and cryptocurrency, leading to more efficient and effective processes (Bosovska, M., et. al.,2022)

The intersection of Industry 5.0 and cryptocurrency adoption could lead to new business models and revenue streams, with cryptocurrency potentially being used as a secure and efficient means of payment in Industry 5.0 supply chains. However, this will also raise challenges around regulation and security, highlighting the need for continued investment in the development of these technologies.Top of Form

6.2 Directions for Future Research

This part summarises the results and makes research recommendations for the future. (RQ1) was answered by using descriptive analysis which shows that the expansion of academic studies appears to have been gradual up until 2019, and then accelerated exponentially. One reason could be that the value of cryptocurrencies increased phenomenally in 2020 and there has been increasing importance in business and academia (Guo 2020). China, the USA, and Sweden are the most efficient nations where the adoption of cryptocurrency has been extensively debated and similarly China and the USA are the top most nations that cited the related articles. Based on the outcome of the citation analysis, the most important articles on the researched topic were written by Shahzad F. (2018), Luther W.J. (2016), and Jonker N. (2019). The most crucial publications on cryptocurrency surrounded it from varied fields, including E-commerce, Technology, Hospitality, and Tourism.

Bibliographical coupling analysis followed by content analysis applied to identify the most important and distinctive antecedents of cryptocurrency adoption (RQ2) lead to the extraction of four main clusters. Cluster 1 discussed the impact of financial literacy and users' knowledge, Cluster 2 defined perception towards the adoption intention of cryptocurrency, Cluster 3 approaches Cryptocurrency's Multi-Functional Adoption and articles from cluster 4 directed Bitcoin as the widely-used virtual currency.

Further, for answering RQ 3, the recent research themes were uncovered from the keyword co-occurrence analysis. This analysis is important to figure out the direction of research and characterise the intellectualisation of cryptocurrency adoption and figure out the areas that could be interesting to study. Furthermore, the word cloud and word tree map as a part of science mapping techniques highlighted the major topics related to cryptocurrency, blockchain, Bitcoin, and technology adoption. In terms of technology adoption, the technology acceptance model is highly recommended in the studies. Regulatory support, e-government, consumer trust, digital payments, and digital currencies were some of the prominent keywords used in the literature. This evidence emphasises the broad approach taken by this research area in defining cryptocurrency adoption. Following a thorough evaluation of the available literature, future research guidelines with respect to RQ4 are as under:

Explore the Dark Side of Cryptocurrency. Since cryptocurrencies play a role in money laundering, tax evasion, funding terrorists, buying illegal goods, and other similar activities (Yelowitz & Wilson, 2015). Future research should investigate the "dark components" of cryptocurrency usage.

Bitcoin Transactions are Not Instant. Bitcoin transactions are not always quick and require time to complete. Future studies can go into it and examine how customers and investors perceive it (Nadeem et al., 2021b)

Focus on Cryptocurrency Usability and Security. The field of information technology has significant challenges in striking a balance between usability and security (Eskandari, 2015; Sas & Khairuddin, 2015). Scholars are in a prime position to examine these challenges in cryptocurrency and propose regulations and recommendations for addressing them.

Explore the Function of Subjective Norms. Social factors, Trust, and hedonic motivation factors, which have not been covered in the extant literature, may be important to investigate in the future. It is also suggested to examine the role of subjective norms as it might be a significant component of this adoption of cryptocurrency. Future scholars may focus on the financial and operational hazards of adopting cryptocurrency and build mitigating strategies for addressing those concerns.

Sustainability of Cryptocurrencies Sustainability issues could affect the growth of cryptocurrencies. Cryptocurrencies are a new technology that is inconsistent. Due to this, the research outcomes have to be carefully considered. Future research should include an extensive study to drive how cryptocurrency use has changed and adjust the model to new conditions.

Different Models Can be Used. Academic studies on cryptocurrency adoption are rare (Sousa et al 2022, Baur et al., 2015). In most of the studies, to explain the technology acceptance in behavioural intention UTAUT and TAM models have been utilized (Mendoza-Tello et al., 2018). In order to have better insights into cryptocurrency adoption of research may integrate various theoretical sociological viewpoints.

Cross-Cultural Adoption Behaviour Can be Studied: Further, the cross-cultural aspects of an individual's adoption behaviour can be explored as not much work has been done till now.

7. CONCLUSION

This study discerns that cryptocurrencies have evolved as a new asset class, attracting both investor funding and scholarly interest. However, cryptocurrency adoption is an emerging phenomenon. As a result, the body of knowledge about cryptocurrencies has witnessed steady growth in business as well as industry 5.0 in the last few years. Moving through the antecedents that derive acceptance of cryptocurrency, evolving themes and topics, this article provides an in-depth literature review of the specified study field. This study recognises that the topic is relevantly discussed more in the technical domain while there remains a dearth of research in the socio-psychological domain. Moreover, the adoption of cryptocurrency in Industry 5.0 has the potential to offer new opportunities and challenges in technology, human-environment interaction, ethics, and sustainability. While there are some concerns about the risks associated with cryptocurrencies, such as volatility and security, there are also many potential benefits, such as increased transparency, accountability, and sustainability. As such, it is important to approach cryptocurrency adoption in Industry 5.0 with caution and to carefully consider the potential benefits and drawbacks. Ongoing research and analysis will be essential to fully understand the impact of cryptocurrency adoption in Industry 5.0 and to identify best practices for promoting responsible and sustainable adoption. In conjunction with this, this study highlights the future research directions on cryptocurrency acceptance around its' sustainability, the valence of its usability, and on the flip side risk and security associated with its acceptance. This paper has some limitations. First, this investigation is restricted to Scopus database publications written in English. Therefore, it is proposed that future studies, should include literature from other electronic databases such as Springer, Sage, Web of Science and ScienceDirect in order to conduct a comprehensive literature review in the given research field. Secondly, this study conducted a performance analysis and bibliometric analysis using science mapping techniques such as bibliographic couplings, co-word analysis, word cloud and word tree map analysis. Future studies should incorporate additional methods of investigation like co-citation analysis, and co-authorship analysis. Considering the aforesaid information, which is extracted using scientific bibliometric analysis techniques provides reliable, consistent information and is essentially unaffected by personal opinion. However, despite the many benefits of cryptocurrency adoption in Industry 5.0, it also presents new challenges and risks. For example, the lack of regulation and the security risks associated with cryptocurrency can make it difficult for businesses to fully embrace and utilize its benefits. To address these challenges, it is important for the Industry 5.0 ecosystem to work together to find solutions that balance the benefits of cryptocurrency with the need for security and regulatory compliance.

REFERENCES

Adel, A. (2022). Future of industry 5.0 in society: Human-centric solutions, challenges and prospective research areas. *Journal of Cloud Computing*, *11*(1), 1–15. PMID:36101900

Ajouz, M., Abdullah, A., & Kassim, S. (2020). Acceptance of Sharīʿah-compliant precious metal-backed cryptocurrency as an alternative currency: An empirical validation of adoption of innovation theory. *Thunderbird International Business Review*, *62*(2), 171–181. doi:10.1002/tie.22106

Alaklabi, S., & Kang, K. (2021). Perceptions towards cryptocurrency adoption: A case of Saudi Arabian citizens. *IBIMA Business Review*, *2021*, 1–17. doi:10.5171/2021.110411

Alsmadi, A. A., Alrawashdeh, N., Al-Dweik, A. F., & Al-Assaf, M. (2022). Cryptocurrencies: A bibliometric analysis. *International Journal of Data and Network Science*, *6*(3), 619–628. doi:10.5267/j.ijdns.2022.4.011

Aria, M., & Cuccurullo, C. (2017). bibliometrix: An R-tool for comprehensive science mapping analysis. *Journal of Informetrics*, *11*(4), 959–975. doi:10.1016/j.joi.2017.08.007

Ayedh, A., Echchabi, A., Battour, M., & Omar, M. (2020). Malaysian Muslim investors' behaviour towards the blockchain-based Bitcoin cryptocurrency market. *Journal of Islamic Marketing*, *12*(4), 690–704. doi:10.1108/JIMA-04-2019-0081

Ayedh, A. M., Omar, M. M. S., & Echchabi, A. (2020). Factors Influencing Bitcoin Investment Intention: The case of Oman. *International Journal of Internet Technology and Secured Transactions*, *1*(1), 1. doi:10.1504/IJITST.2021.112867

Ballis, A., & Drakos, K. (2021). The explosion in cryptocurrencies: A black hole analogy. *Financial Innovation*, *7*(1), 8. doi:10.118640854-020-00222-0

Ballis, A., & Verousis, T. (2022). Behavioural finance and cryptocurrencies. In *Review of Behavioral Finance*. Emerald Group Holdings Ltd., doi:10.1108/RBF-11-2021-0256

Basile, V., Giacalone, M., & Cozzucoli, P. C. (2022). The Impacts of Bibliometrics Measurement in the Scientific Community A Statistical Analysis of Multiple Case Studies. *Review of European Studies*, *14*(3), 10. doi:10.5539/res.v14n3p10

Baur, A. W., Bühler, J., Bick, M., & Bonorden, C. S. (2015). Cryptocurrencies as a disruption? empirical findings on user adoption and future potential of Bitcoin and Co. Lecture Notes in Computer Science (Including Subseries Lecture Notes in Artificial Intelligence and Lecture Notes in Bioinformatics), 9373, 63–80. doi:10.1007/978-3-319-25013-7_6

Baur, D. G., Hong, K. H., & Lee, A. D. (2018). Bitcoin: Medium of exchange or speculative assets? *Journal of International Financial Markets, Institutions and Money*, *54*, 177–189. doi:10.1016/j.intfin.2017.12.004

Berentsen, A., & Schär, F. (2018). The case for central bank electronic money and the non-case for central bank cryptocurrencies. *Review - Federal Reserve Bank of St. Louis*, *100*(2), 97–106. doi:10.20955/r.2018.97-106

Bharadwaj, S., & Deka, S. (2021). Behavioural intention towards investment in cryptocurrency: An integration of rogers' diffusion of innovation theory and the technology acceptance model. *Forum Scientiae Oeconomia*, *9*(4), 137–159. doi:10.23762/FSO_VOL9_NO4_7

Bosovska, M., Boiko, M., Bovsh, L., & Okhrimenko, A. (2022, October). Models of the Industrial Revolution 5.0. In *2022 IEEE 4th International Conference on Modern Electrical and Energy System (MEES)* (pp. 1-4). IEEE.

Chander, B., Pal, S., De, D., & Buyya, R. (2022). Artificial intelligence-based internet of things for industry 5.0. *Artificial intelligence-based internet of things systems*, 3-45.

Chimienti, M. T. (2019). *ECB Internal Crypto-Assets Task Force (ICA-TF) Stablecoins: Implications for monetary policy, financial stability, market infrastructure and payments, and banking supervision in the euro area*. POEU. doi:10.2866/822388

Cohen, R., Smith Philip, Arulchandran Vic, & Sehra Avtar. (2018). Automation and blockchain in securities issuances. *Butterworths Journal of International Banking and Financial Law Automation And Blockchain In Securities Issuances Feature*.

Concetta, A. (2014). *DePaolo, & Kelly Wilkinson*. Assessing the Use of Key Words in Student Responses.

DeVries, P. D. (2016). An analysis of cryptocurrency, bitcoin, and the future. *International Journal of Business Management and Commerce*, *1*(2), 1–9.

Ding, Y., & Cronin, B. (2011). Popular and/or prestigious? Measures of scholarly esteem. *Information Processing & Management*, *47*(1), 80–96. doi:10.1016/j.ipm.2010.01.002

Donthu, N., Kumar, S., Mukherjee, D., Pandey, N., & Lim, W. M. (2021). How to conduct a bibliometric analysis: An overview and guidelines. *Journal of Business Research*, *133*, 285–296. doi:10.1016/j.jbusres.2021.04.070

Dorofeyev, M. A., Kosov, M., Ponkratov, V., Masterov, A., Karaev, A., & Vasyunina, M. (2018). Trends and prospects for the development of blockchain and cryptocurrencies in the digital economy. *European Research Studies*, *21*(3), 429–445. doi:10.35808/ersj/1073

Eskandari, S. (2015). *Real-world Deployability and Usability of Bitcoin*.

Ferreira, M. P., Santos, J. C., de Almeida, M. I. R., & Reis, N. R. (2014). Mergers & acquisitions research: A bibliometric study of top strategy and international business journals, 1980-2010. *Journal of Business Research*, *67*(12), 2550–2558. doi:10.1016/j.jbusres.2014.03.015

Fujiki, H. (2020). Who adopts crypto assets in Japan? Evidence from the 2019 financial literacy survey. *Journal of the Japanese and International Economies*, *58*, 101107. doi:10.1016/j.jjie.2020.101107

Gowda, N., & Chakravorty, C. (2021). Comparative study on cryptocurrency transaction and banking transaction. *Global Transitions Proceedings*, *2*(2), 530–534. doi:10.1016/j.gltp.2021.08.064

Guleria, D., & Kaur, G. (2021). Bibliometric analysis of ecopreneurship using VOSviewer and RStudio Bibliometrix, 1989–2019. *Library Hi Tech*, *39*(4), 1001–1024. doi:10.1108/LHT-09-2020-0218

Guo, Y. M., Huang, Z. L., Guo, J., Guo, X. R., Li, H., Liu, M. Y., Ezzeddine, S., & Nkeli, M. J. (2021). A bibliometric analysis and visualization of blockchain. *Future Generation Computer Systems, 116*, 316–332. doi:10.1016/j.future.2020.10.023

Gupta, R., Rathore, B., & Biswas, B. (2021). Impact of COVID-19 on supply chains: lessons learned and future research directions. In *International Journal of Quality and Reliability Management*. Emerald Group Holdings Ltd., doi:10.1108/IJQRM-06-2021-0161

Gupta, S., Gupta, S., Mathew, M., & Sama, H. R. (2020). Prioritizing intentions behind investment in cryptocurrency: A fuzzy analytical framework. *Journal of Economic Studies (Glasgow, Scotland)*. doi:10.1108/JES-06-2020-0285

Gurusamy, V., Akbari, D., & Pipaliya, J. (2018). *Bitcoin: A cryptocurrency*.

Hashemi, H., Rajabi, R., & Brashear-Alejandro, T. G. (2022). COVID-19 research in management: An updated bibliometric analysis. *Journal of Business Research, 149*, 795–810. doi:10.1016/j.jbusres.2022.05.082 PMID:35669095

Holub, M., & Johnson, J. (2018). Bitcoin research across disciplines. *The Information Society, 34*(2), 114–126. doi:10.1080/01972243.2017.1414094

Huang, J. Z., Huang, W., & Ni, J. (2019). Predicting bitcoin returns using high-dimensional technical indicators. *Journal of Finance and Data Science, 5*(3), 140–155. doi:10.1016/j.jfds.2018.10.001

Huynh, K. P., Henry, C. S., Nicholls, G., & Nicholson, M. W. (2020). Benchmarking bitcoin adoption in canada: Awareness, ownership and usage in 2018. *Ledger, 5*, 74–88. doi:10.5195/ledger.2020.206

Inci, A. C., & Lagasse, R. (2019). Cryptocurrencies: Applications and investment opportunities. *Journal of Capital Markets Studies, 3*(2), 98–112. doi:10.1108/JCMS-05-2019-0032

IyidoganE.AllenF.BoltonP.ChuprininO.IbragimovR.KacperczykM.KilicM.KirilenkoA.KosowskiR. SundaresanS.TinnK. (2020). *An Equilibrium Model of Proof-of-Work Cryptocurrencies **. https://ssrn.com/abstract=3152803

Jalal, R. N. U. D., Alon, I., & Paltrinieri, A. (2021). A bibliometric review of cryptocurrencies as a financial asset. *Technology Analysis and Strategic Management*, 1–16. doi:10.1080/09537325.2021.1939001

Jonker, N. (2019). What drives the adoption of crypto-payments by online retailers? *Electronic Commerce Research and Applications, 35*, 100848. doi:10.1016/j.elerap.2019.100848

Kessler, M. M. (1963). Bibliographic Coupling Between Scientific Papers. *American Documentation, 14*(1), 10–25. doi:10.1002/asi.5090140103

Koroma, J., Rongting, Z., Muhideen, S., Akintunde, T. Y., Amosun, T. S., Dauda, S. J., & Sawaneh, I. A. (2022a). Assessing citizens' behavior towards blockchain cryptocurrency adoption in the Mano River Union States: Mediation, moderation role of trust and ethical issues. *Technology in Society, 68*, 101885. doi:10.1016/j.techsoc.2022.101885

Koroma, J., Rongting, Z., Muhideen, S., Akintunde, T. Y., Amosun, T. S., Dauda, S. J., & Sawaneh, I. A. (2022b). Assessing citizens' behavior towards blockchain cryptocurrency adoption in the Mano River Union States: Mediation, moderation role of trust and ethical issues. *Technology in Society*, *68*, 101885. doi:10.1016/j.techsoc.2022.101885

Kumar, S., Pandey, N., & Mukherjee, D. (2022). Cross Cultural and Strategic Management: A retrospective overview using bibliometric analysis. *Cross Cultural & Strategic Management*, *29*(1), 171–194. doi:10.1108/CCSM-08-2021-0147

Kumar, S., Sharma, D., Rao, S., Lim, W. M., & Mangla, S. K. (2022). Past, present, and future of sustainable finance: Insights from big data analytics through machine learning of scholarly research. *Annals of Operations Research*. doi:10.100710479-021-04410-8 PMID:35002001

Lankton, N., McKnight, D. H., & Thatcher, J. B. (2014). Incorporating trust-in-technology into Expectation Disconfirmation Theory. *The Journal of Strategic Information Systems*, *23*(2), 128–145. doi:10.1016/j.jsis.2013.09.001

Leng, J., Sha, W., Wang, B., Zheng, P., Zhuang, C., Liu, Q., Wuest, T., Mourtzis, D., & Wang, L. (2022). Industry 5.0: Prospect and retrospect. *Journal of Manufacturing Systems*, *65*, 279–295. doi:10.1016/j.jmsy.2022.09.017

Lopez-Martin, C. (2022). Ramadan effect in the cryptocurrency markets. *Review of Behavioral Finance*. doi:10.1108/RBF-09-2021-0173

Luther, W. J. (2016). Bitcoin and the Future of Digital Payments. In *Source: The Independent Review*, *20*(3). https://about.jstor.org/terms

Makhdoom, I., Abolhasan, M., Abbas, H., & Ni, W. (2019). Blockchain's adoption in IoT: The challenges, and a way forward. *Journal of Network and Computer Applications*, *125*, 251–279. doi:10.1016/j.jnca.2018.10.019

Makori, E. O. (2023). Digital Innovations and Applications in Information Science and Humanistic Knowledge. In Handbook of Research on Technological Advances of Library and Information Science in Industry 5.0 (pp. 397-414). IGI Global.

Mazambani, L., & Mutambara, E. (2020). Predicting FinTech innovation adoption in South Africa: The case of cryptocurrency. *African Journal of Economic and Management Studies*, *11*(1), 30–50. doi:10.1108/AJEMS-04-2019-0152

Mccain, K. W., Verner, J. M., Hislop, G. W., Evanco, W., & Cole, V. (2005). The use of bibliometric and knowledge elicitation techniques to map a knowledge domain: Software Engineering in the 1990s. In Budapest Scientometrics, and Springer, 65(1).

Mendoza-Tello, J. C., Mora, H., Pujol-López, F. A., & Lytras, M. D. (2018). Social Commerce as a Driver to Enhance Trust and Intention to Use Cryptocurrencies for Electronic Payments. *IEEE Access: Practical Innovations, Open Solutions*, *6*, 50737–50751. doi:10.1109/ACCESS.2018.2869359

Mourtzis, D., Angelopoulos, J., & Panopoulos, N. (2022). A Literature Review of the Challenges and Opportunities of the Transition from Industry 4.0 to Society 5.0. *Energies*, *15*(17), 6276. doi:10.3390/en15176276

Mukherjee, D., Kumar, S., Donthu, N., & Pandey, N. (2021). Research Published in Management International Review from 2006 to 2020: A Bibliometric Analysis and Future Directions. In Management International Review, 61(5), 599–642. Springer Science and Business Media Deutschland GmbH. doi:10.100711575-021-00454-x

Nadeem, M. A., Liu, Z., Pitafi, A. H., Younis, A., & Xu, Y. (2021a). Investigating the Adoption Factors of Cryptocurrencies—A Case of Bitcoin: Empirical Evidence From China. *SAGE Open*, *11*(1). doi:10.1177/2158244021998704

Nadeem, M. A., Liu, Z., Pitafi, A. H., Younis, A., & Xu, Y. (2021b). Investigating the Adoption Factors of Cryptocurrencies—A Case of Bitcoin: Empirical Evidence From China. *SAGE Open*, *11*(1). doi:10.1177/2158244021998704

Narayanan, A. (2016). *Bitcoin and cryptocurrency technologies : a comprehensive introduction.*

Ooi, S. K., Ooi, C. A., Yeap, J. A. L., & Goh, T. H. (2021). Embracing Bitcoin: Users' perceived security and trust. *Quality & Quantity*, *55*(4), 1219–1237. doi:10.100711135-020-01055-w

Oyewola, D. O., & Dada, E. G. (2022). Exploring machine learning: A scientometrics approach using bibliometrix and VOSviewer. *SN Applied Sciences*, *4*(5), 143. doi:10.100742452-022-05027-7 PMID:35434524

Paul, J., & Bhukya, R. (2021). Forty-five years of International Journal of Consumer Studies: A bibliometric review and directions for future research. *International Journal of Consumer Studies*, *45*(5), 937–963. doi:10.1111/ijcs.12727

Prakash GiriO.ShahiP. B.BhaumikA.PoddarS. (2022). *A Bibliometric Analysis on Road Traffic Safety, 2009 to 2022*. https://ssrn.com/abstract=4148189

Rhaiem, K., & Amara, N. (2021). Learning from innovation failures: A systematic review of the literature and research agenda. *Review of Managerial Science*, *15*(2), 189–234. doi:10.100711846-019-00339-2

Saiedi, E., Broström, A., & Ruiz, F. (2021). Global drivers of cryptocurrency infrastructure adoption. *Small Business Economics*, *57*(1), 353–406. doi:10.100711187-019-00309-8

Sas, C., & Khairuddin, I. E. (2015). Exploring trust in bitcoin technology: A framework for HCI research. *OzCHI 2015: Being Human - Conference Proceedings*, (pp. 338–342). 10.1145/2838739.2838821

Secinaro, S., Brescia, V., Calandra, D., & Biancone, P. (2020a). Employing bibliometric analysis to identify suitable business models for electric cars. In *Journal of Cleaner Production* (Vol. 264). Elsevier Ltd., doi:10.1016/j.jclepro.2020.121503

Secinaro, S., Brescia, V., Calandra, D., & Biancone, P. (2020b). Employing bibliometric analysis to identify suitable business models for electric cars. In *Journal of Cleaner Production* (Vol. 264). Elsevier Ltd., doi:10.1016/j.jclepro.2020.121503

Shahzad, F., Xiu, G. Y., Wang, J., & Shahbaz, M. (2018). An empirical investigation on the adoption of cryptocurrencies among the people of mainland China. *Technology in Society*, *55*, 33–40. doi:10.1016/j.techsoc.2018.05.006

Shiller Robert, J. (2019). Narratives about Technology-Induced Job Degradations Then and Now. *NBER Working Paper.*

Souiden, N., Ladhari, R., & Chaouali, W. (2021). Mobile banking adoption: A systematic review. *International Journal of Bank Marketing*, *39*(2), 214–241. doi:10.1108/IJBM-04-2020-0182

Sousa, A., Calçada, E., Rodrigues, P., & Pinto Borges, A. (2022). Cryptocurrency adoption: A systematic literature review and bibliometric analysis. *EuroMed Journal of Business*, *17*(3), 374–390. doi:10.1108/EMJB-01-2022-0003

Steinmetz, F., von Meduna, M., Ante, L., & Fiedler, I. (2021). *Ownership, uses and perceptions of cryptocurrency: Results from a population survey.*

Teo, E. G. S. (2015). Emergence, Growth, and Sustainability of Bitcoin: The Network Economics Perspective. In Handbook of Digital Currency: Bitcoin, Innovation, Financial Instruments, and Big Data (pp. 191–200). Elsevier Inc. doi:10.1016/B978-0-12-802117-0.00009-6

Tiwari, S., Bahuguna, P. C., & Walker, J. (2022). Industry 5.0: A macroperspective approach. In Handbook of Research on Innovative Management Using AI in Industry 5.0 (pp. 59-73). IGI Global.

Treiblmaier, H., Leung, D., Kwok, A. O. J., & Tham, A. (2021). Cryptocurrency adoption in travel and tourism–an exploratory study of Asia Pacific travellers. *Current Issues in Tourism*, *24*(22), 3165–3181. doi:10.1080/13683500.2020.1863928

Tsanidis, C., Nerantzaki, M., Karavasilis, G., Vrana, V., & Paschaloudis, D. (2015). Greek consumers and the use of Bitcoin. In The Business & Management Review, 6.

Wang, Z., Pham, T. L. H., Sun, K., Wang, B., Bui, Q., & Hashemizadeh, A. (2022). The moderating role of financial development in the renewable energy consumption-CO2 emissions linkage: The case study of Next-11 countries. *Energy*, *254*, 124386. doi:10.1016/j.energy.2022.124386

Wu, R., Ishfaq, K., Hussain, S., Asmi, F., Siddiquei, A. N., & Anwar, M. A. (2022). Investigating e-Retailers' Intentions to Adopt Cryptocurrency Considering the Mediation of Technostress and Technology Involvement. *Sustainability (Switzerland)*, *14*(2), 641. doi:10.3390u14020641

Xie, L., Chen, Z., Wang, H., Zheng, C., & Jiang, J. (2020). Bibliometric and Visualized Analysis of Scientific Publications on Atlantoaxial Spine Surgery Based on Web of Science and VOSviewer. In *World Neurosurgery* (Vol. 137, pp. 435–442.e4). Elsevier Inc., doi:10.1016/j.wneu.2020.01.171

Yelowitz, A., & Wilson, M. (2015). Characteristics of Bitcoin users: an analysis of Google search data. *Applied Economics Letters, 22*(13), 1030–1036. doi:10.1080/13504851.2014.995359

Yin, S., & Yu, Y. (2022). An adoption-implementation framework of digital green knowledge to improve the performance of digital green innovation practices for industry 5.0. *Journal of Cleaner Production*, *363*, 132608. doi:10.1016/j.jclepro.2022.132608

Yuneline, M. H. (2019). Analysis of cryptocurrency's characteristics in four perspectives. *Journal of Asian Business and Economic Studies*, *26*(2), 206–219. doi:10.1108/JABES-12-2018-0107

Zhang, F., Wang, H., Bai, Y., & Zhang, H. (2022). A Bibliometric Analysis of the Landscape of Problem-Based Learning Research (1981–2021). *Frontiers in Psychology*, *13*, 828390. Advance online publication. doi:10.3389/fpsyg.2022.828390 PMID:35369264

Zhao, J. (2022). Do economic crises cause trading in Bitcoin? *Review of Behavioral Finance*. doi:10.1108/RBF-02-2022-0048

Župič, I. & Čater, T. (2015). *Bibliometric Methods in Management and Organization*. https://research.gold.ac.uk/id/eprint/26859/

Chapter 14
Significance of Block Chain Technology and Industry 5.0 in Indian Banking Sector

Diksha Verma
Chandigarh Group of Colleges, India

Pooja Kansra
Lovely Professional University, India

Pawan Kumar
Lovely Professional University, India

ABSTRACT

Since the time when liberalization was introduced, many changes have taken place in banking world. Although in India block chain technology is still at its initial stage, many of the banks are using this technology to make their tasks easier. However, block chain technology will offer remarkable progress in the area of banking as with the help of it; banks are able to provide quick, accurate, and quality service to their customers. With the inception of blockchain technology, the banking sector has transformed, as many of its processes have become transparent, safe, and efficient as well. Under blockchain technology, banking systems are basically based on one point data base, which has dispersed ledger for reducing cyber crimes. The present chapter tries to depict the same with the help of a descriptive analysis of increase in incentives, and also the inconvenience faced by banks in recent times after the introduction of block chain technology.

INTRODUCTION

A standard model of Industry 4.0 has witnessed a transfer from Cyber Physical Mechanisms towards more Customer Targeted Approach. This transfer has the objective of designing the systems which are directed towards hyper cognitive approach, amalgamation of implicit and comprehensive image, online

DOI: 10.4018/978-1-6684-6403-8.ch014

machine prototype, mutual robotics, artificial intelligence (AI) etc. The novel trend of Industry 5.0 is forecasted to achieve quantum of production with customer centric approach overpowering the scope and boundary of Industry 4.0. Industry 5.0 is also projected to assist various industrial areas like health-care, farming, banking, supply chain production, drones, robotics etc. (Verma et al., 2022). Innovation in technology is the main requirement as well as is a reason for affluence. Banking and innovation both work simultaneously as they are closely interrelated to each other. Since liberalization, banking sector has observed various novel innovations and by adopting those innovations it has played a significant role as financial intermediary in Indian Financial System. Technology innovation has a very close and unbreakable connection with banking sector as both gets benefits from each other's association. Many countries such as Denmark, USSR etc. have been taking advantage of the same association (Rajagopalan & Sankaranarayanan, 2020). Block chain is another emerging technology that is preferred by the industrialists as a security enabler to Industry 5.0 due to its remarkable features of consistency, chronicle and balancing in various segments of the society like medicines, education, banking etc. (Verma et al., 2022)

In India, under the leadership of Dr. C. Rangarajan, a committee was set up by RBI in 1988. The main reason behind setting up of committee was to improvise the services for customers, maintaining books and records properly etc. banks started its innovative journey through the inception of PCs, followed by LAN, Anytime Anywhere banking. However, the main changes were observed after the entry of private sector banks in the industry. Banks started benefitting from the innovations in respect to time and cost by adoption of internet banking, MICR based banking, inter association between branches of banks, introduction of ATMs, however the main revolution was observed after the ingress of NEFT, RTGS, Mobile banking, debit and credit cards and most important UPI transfer. Therefore, it can be claimed that banking sector has seen a remarkable revolution in recent times and also aiming at providing error free, quality service to the customers (Gupta & Gupta, 2018).

With the inception of Blockchain technology, banking sector has transformed as many of its processes have become transparent, safe and efficient as well. The current operations of the banking sector have been improved with the automation of banking processes through implementation of block chain technology. With the introduction and execution of block chain technology, many of its tasks are being done efficiently, fraudulent activities have in the financial transactions have been reduce, there is very less intervention of regulatory bodies in the work of banks there is less requirement for that. Under blockchain technology, Banking systems are basically based on one point data base which has dispersed ledger for reducing cyber crimes. Although Blockchain is no far back in any of the benefits it has given to banking industry, still its inception has made banking sector face various challenges such as no common international standard related to its implementation, necessity of multilevel security, no national and international regulations on the jurisdiction issue (Patki & Sople, 2020). Hence, it becomes imperative to do a descriptive analysis of increase in incentives and also the inconvenience faced by banks in recent times after the introduction of block chain technology.

Techniques for safety of privacy demands less sharing of data therefore, artificial intelligence based models would not be able to modify as per the original requirements. Hence, a proper mix of personalization security models is required. For sharing of data, trust is an important factor that is to be taken into consideration as it is vital as varied as well as independent networks join in Industry 5.0. Therefore, Block chain is a probable solution that can be used in preparing translucent ledgers through which banking industry related data can be managed as well as controlled. Block chain is basically an absolute ledger that records and maintains the transactions of the banks and their customers in chronological manner keeping security of the data in to consideration. On the other side, in Industry 5.0, smart contacts play an imperative role in providing security, control, authentication, service oriented process of the data. These systems interact with Block chain network for managing the real time data and transactions defining Block chain as a preferable approach for Industry 5.0 (Verma et al., 2022).

Emerging Challenges of Industry 5.0 and Blockchain in Banking Industry

Change always comes with challenges which if not coped properly may become obstacles for the growth of new change. Persons who will be dealing with industry 5.0 will require totally new skills along with robotics in order to match themselves with smart machines. The efforts which will be required on the part of industrialists are gaining special knowledge related to customized software connecting techniques, joint robotics, artificial intelligence, internet of things, etc. after all these, the major contribution required from industrialists is investment. Banking companies may find it difficult to adopt the change to a grand level not only in the terms of money but also adoption of flow of change (Cojocariu, n.d.)

Due to Industry 5.0, middle skill employment is diminishing and workforce is divided in to two segments: over trained and educated and less paid and less educated workers. The shift or transfer from present scenario to industry 5.0 is challenging for bankers due to the current autonomy in present systems such as amalgamated decision making. With increased implementation of industry 5.0 there is increased threat of cyber crimes that can become challenging for the banking institutions due to increased connectivity. Banking strategies with industry 5.0 requires huge level of dynamism to stand in the competition because of dynamic perception of banking customers related to banking services (Naveen, 2023).

This chapter is divided into four different sections. First section tries to depict how introduction of blockchain technology and Industry 5.0 has affected banking industry of India in recent times. Section II tries to streamline certain incentives which banking sector has earned in recent times due to implementation of block chain technology. Section III tries to portray the challenges and problems which banking sector has witnessed in recent times due to implementation of block chain technology. Section IV tries to provide various suggestions for improvement of block chain technology implementation in banking sector. Section V concludes the whole chapter.

Section I: Effect on Banking Industry after application of Blockchain Technology

The application of Blockchain technology around the globe demonstrates that a drastic change or revolution in the area of banking has been seen. Main affects that have been observed in the recent times due to blockchain are least expenses of transactions, improvisation in efficiency and effectiveness, use of intermediaries has also been reduced, precision, decentralization etc. Various other segments in banking sector are there where usage of blockchin has been found useful such as easy access to capital, trade financing which leads to easy processing of letter of credit or bills of lading, safe transactions in the market with efficiency, serving trade and securities with safe KYC norms, monitoring of accounts and statements for reducing Non Performing Assets, providing loans and finances at lower rates, reduction in processing time etc (Patki and Sople, 2020).

How Blockchain has Affected the Financial Enclosure?

Blockchain has provided assistance in numerous ways to banking industry as well as banking customers. For opening an account, Blockchain has helped customers in various ways. Customer can open account with the help of one click only that is only possible with the help of blockchain innovation. If a customer wants to transfer money to anyone, it hardly takes more than one minute that is also possible with the assistance of blockchain. As majority of Financial Institutes are adopting bitcoin as vehicle currency and dollar is used in maximum of the countries for trade purpose, therefore adopting blockchain and bitcoin basically helping both the parties to get away from instability of virtual currency (Meghani, 2020).

After elaborating the impact of blockchain technology innovation in different segments of banking industry, it can be stated that blockchain is far behind bitcoin. The main area of search arises on finding different ways to conquer various delusions and also technology risks which are associated to blockchain technology (Arjun & Suprabha, 2020). Therefore, the upcoming sections describe about the incentives happened to banking industry as well as confronts faced by banking industry.

Section II: Increase in Incentives of Banks after Application of Blockchain Technology

Blockchain innovation is one of the most successful innovations in banking and financial industry. Blockchain technology has accomplished its many of the promises such as reduction in fraud, surety of safe and fast transactions, and management of risks etc. with the help of advanced cryptography. There is possibility of improved and enhanced transparency as majority of the customers of banks who are using mobile banking etc. are doing these activities through public ledgers and this ultimately helps bank in keeping transparency and reducing various inefficiencies such as frauds, risks etc. As customer of the bank is majorly performing their activities through online mode, payments made with the help of blockchain are much safer and quicker than transactions through traditional mode. Blockchain's cryptographic algorithm basically assists in identifying the risks and fraud transactions which ultimately improves the performance of banking industry. Companies based on financial technology mostly use huge database that basically need blockchain to make data assemble. As financial companies, investors try to move away from financial accounts at just single click with proper assistance from financial advisors and customers advisors for taking advice and suggestions, blockchain innovation try to provide service to the customers to get benefit from the lower costs connected with tradition services related to financing. Another benefit banking industry is getting from blockchain technology is easy access to open can take independent financial decisions. As fintech is also associated with blockchain technology, this innovation again gets benefit from the inclusion.

VARIOUS INCENTIVES OF IMPLEMENTING BLOCKCHAIN TECHNOLOGY

Transfer of Funds

The most common use of blockchain technology is transfer of funds to one another. Blockchain technology has made this transfer very quick and transparent reducing the chances of errors. Making transfers around the globe is also easy and quick with the help of blockchain technology.

Maintaining Saving Accounts and Deposits

Customers of banks usually take the service of deposits in the banks so that when they need money they can do withdrawl. Banks on the other side make loans on certain rate to earn money. Therefore blockchain which is basically a ledger helps in maintain balances and statements to the banks.

Primary and Secondary Securities Trading

With the help of Blockchain technology, trading of securities, whether in India or overseas is possible making banks earn more incentives. Similarly, primary market issuance and Initial public offerings also help banking sectors to earn more with the help of blockchain innovations.

Section III: Confronts faced by Banking Industry After Application of Blockchain Technology

The promise that banks make to their customers relying on the blockchain technology sometimes become a challenge for banks to overcome. When the task of money transfer is performed, bank customers rely on banks or third parties for the process completion, but blockchain technology ultimately eliminates the third-party inclusion which automatically eradicate the fees or any other costs connected with theses service s which leads to a confront for banks executing blockchain.

On the other side, blockchain innovation is affecting banks so quickly that any regulation or regulatory policy affecting blockchain ultimately results in inconvenience in adopting blockchain.

Implementation and execution of blockchain technology is very costly and hence leads to high cost requirement for banks. Computer based technology needs essential requirement of algorithm knowledge to process its transactions. In India, one more problem that is being faced is lack of availability of internet connectivity. In remote and rural areas especially, connection problem always persists which eventually leads to inconvenience in implementation of blockchain technology in India.

Section IV: Suggestions for Improvement of Block Chain Technology Implementation

After going through the whole descriptive analysis of implementation of blockchain technology in regard to its inconvenience, few points can be taken into consideration, for successful working of blockchain technology in the banking system.

Implantation of blockchain technology should be done in such a way as it significantly increases transparency which is basic requirement for availing competitive advantage.

A safe and secure database of information of customers should be prepared and dispersed with various banks, which will help in diminishing time, cost and money for the banks.

Business operations should be streamlined in such a way, which will help in unnecessary friction among various customers. Blockchain technology if implemented properly will help in developing trust and ensure simplicity among business transactions.

CONCLUSION

As it is known fact that present banking sector is growing very fast with various innovations in technologies, therefore there is an imperative need for implementation of blockchain technology in banking area in order to avail competitive advantage. People are frequently using mobile phones for their each and every service through banks and associating blockchain technology is an advantage for the banks as well as customers. The present chapter tried to present the descriptive analysis of how blockchain has provided incentives to the banking sector and also confronts witnessed by banking industry. In regard to Industry 5.0, it has been observed that banks on the one hand will be beneficial with implementation of Block chain technology and on the other hand, will have to face certain challenges in order to adopt the automation of industry at such high scale. It has been observed that customers are very much benefitted from blockchain technology for their services from banks. On the other side, there are many challenges that banks witnessed due to blockchain technology of which the major one is no standard regulation for blockchain.

REFERENCES

Arjun, R., & Suprabha, K. R. (2020). Innovation and Challenges of Blockchain in Banking: A Scientometric View. *International Journal of Interactive Multimedia & Artificial Intelligence*, *6*(3), 7. doi:10.9781/ijimai.2020.03.004

Cojocariu, O. (n.d.). Industry 5.0 opportunities and challenges: bring your factory into the future. *Digitalya.* https://digitalya.co/blog/industry-5-opportunities-and-challenges/

Dashottar, S., & Srivastava, V. (2021). Corporate banking—risk management, regulatory and reporting framework in India: A Blockchain application-based approach. *Journal of Banking Regulation*, *22*(1), 39–51. doi:10.105741261-020-00127-z

Garg, P., Gupta, B., Chauhan, A. K., Sivarajah, U., Gupta, S., & Modgil, S. (2021). Measuring the perceived benefits of implementing blockchain technology in the banking sector. *Technological Forecasting and Social Change*, *163*, 120407. doi:10.1016/j.techfore.2020.120407

Meghani, K. (2020). Use of Artificial Intelligence and Blockchain in Banking Sector: A Study of Scheduled Commercial Banks in India. *Indian Journal of Applied Research*, 10.

Naveen, B. R. (2023). Industry 5.0 Implementation: Opportunities and Challenges. *IndiaChapter.in.* https://indiachapter.in/index.php?/user/article/2/2/121

Patki, A., & Sople, V. (2020). Indian banking sector: Blockchain implementation, challenges and way forward. *Journal of Banking and Financial Technology*, *4*(1), 65–73. doi:10.100742786-020-00019-w

Schuetz, S., & Venkatesh, V. (2020). Blockchain, adoption, and financial inclusion in India: Research opportunities. *International Journal of Information Management*, *52*, 101936. doi:10.1016/j.ijinfomgt.2019.04.009

Verma, Bhattacharya, P., Madhani, N., Trivedi, C., Bhushan, B., Tanwar, S., Sharma, G., Bokoro, P. N., & Sharma, R. (2022). Blockchain for Industry 5.0: Vision, Opportunities, Key Enablers, and Future Directions. *IEEE Access: Practical Innovations, Open Solutions*, *10*, 69160–69199. doi:10.1109/ACCESS.2022.3186892

Chapter 15
IoT Privacy by Design

Usman Butt
Brunel University, UK

Baba shaheer Gutappa
Northumbria University, UK

Gemma Pendlebury
Northumbria University, UK

Bilal Hassan
Northumbria University, UK

Waleed Butt
Coventry University, UK

Aristeidis Davelis
Northumbria University, UK

ABSTRACT

The integration of the internet-of-things (IoT) and IoT devices and architectures with various aspects of modern society is observed at the beginning of this chapter. Discussion is made on the numerous applications of IoT and accompanying technologies, such as big data. The taxonomy of IoT privacy issues is analysed, from its personal applications to business environments, the public sector and social services. The threats and challenges of IoT are also observed, alongside related ethical and sociological issues and concerns under the scope of privacy. The analysis is then shifted towards the legislative and regulatory frameworks under which IoT currently operates, as the current approaches to resolving its privacy issues and the extent to which they are successful. Finally, attention is placed on the future of privacy and security in IoT, with a discussion on the evolution of privacy-enhancing methodologies and potential risks and threats.

DOI: 10.4018/978-1-6684-6403-8.ch015

INTRODUCTION

IoT has become a key component of today's society, with 'smart' technology appearing indivisible and integrated with daily activities and operations. Devices with sensors gather data constantly, communicating, transmitting, and receiving information over various works. Smart technology is redefining social life and digital interactions, with applications spanning all valuables to smart private residences, healthcare, infrastructure, production lines and manufacturing, transportation, logistics and numerous other sectors.

The accelerated growth of IoT has inarguably introduced a technologically supported and driven way of living with increased efficiency, enabled continuous monitoring and reportability, predictive maintenance with fault prediction (Shamayleh, Mahmoud, & Jumana, 2020) and led to unprecedented levels of automation. The establishment of IoT, however with its countless advantages and commodities, has also introduced serious concerns over privacy, the ethical use and potential misuse of gathered data, data management and security practices, as well as the overall governance of IoT, which is necessary for its successful implementation (Sedrati, Abdellatif, & Aafaf, 2022). The reasonable questions of who owns the vast amount of data generated, the transparency of its usage and the delegation of its processing are but a few among a series of loosely defined elements of the pervasive nature of smart technology. These ethical concerns also pave the way for social consequences regarding how gathered data can impact individuals when interacting with public and private organisations.

Furthermore, alongside aforementioned privacy concerns, follows the -perhaps even more serious- security issue. How safe is the constant use of IoT throughout our everyday lives, under the scope of security breaches, the robustness of security protocols, and the protection against hacking attempts, including eavesdropping, tampering and other attacks? The discussion surrounding security leads to the need for adequate legislation, standards, and frameworks to guide manufacturing, implementation, and the use of smart devices. Ultimately, decisive and properly enforced regulatory action ensures the safety of individuals and organisations, placing trust in smart technology and utilising it through everyday activities.

THE EXTENT OF IOT IN MODERN SOCIETY

The number of connected IoT devices worldwide has grown rapidly over the last few years and is projected to grow steadily over the following decade. An approximation of over 13 billion connected devices in 2022 projects growth to 30 billion devices by 2030 with a 10% CAGR. Similar growth estimates are reported by other research groups (Statista, 2022).

As discussed by (Espinoza, McGroarty, O'Mahony, & Ziouvelou, 2020), the main regions accountable for the largest number of connected devices are Asia, North America and Western Europe, followed by proportionate investments in countries like China, the USA, Germany, France and the UK. The main fields of IoT applications are Manufacturing, Agriculture, Healthcare, Transportation, and Home Use, with further applications in education, retail, other industries and the military (Alferidah & Jhanjhi, 2020). Especially in industrial contexts, IoT's impact has been significant in revolutionising the sector and signifying the establishment of Industry 4.0, together with technologies such as Blockchain, 3D Printing and the utilisation of Big Data (Siqin, Choi, Chung, & Wen, 2022). Across all fields, many IoT devices are already established and available in the public or industrial market. These span from various types of connected sensors constantly transmitting and receiving data to actuators and robotic devices utilised for a large and continuously increasing number of applications, as seen in Table 1.

Table 1. Indicative IoT applications and devices by sector

Sector	Indicative IoT Applications and Devices
Industrial, Manufacturing	Machine operational state monitoring Predictive maintenance, health reporting of parts Digital twins of equipment Inventory management and asset tracking (RFID tags) Environmental state reporting (temperature, air quality, humidity sensors etc.)
Healthcare	Remote medicine (sensors reporting data directly from patient households) Hospital devices for continuous health monitoring Medical wearables (ECG, CGM etc) and implants Environment quality and sanitisation control Other smart medical devices (smart inhalers, spirometers etc.)
Agriculture	Produce / crop and plant growth monitoring Fertiliser automation Continuous climate and environmental (air, soil, humidity, lighting, temperature) condition reporting and forecasting / Precision Farming. Livestock monitoring Drone seeding Automated watering and irrigation Pest detection
Transportation, Supply Chain	Self-driving vehicles (accelerometers, proximity sensors, cameras, GPS etc.) Safety conditions reporting Traffic control Supply chain monitoring and fleet management (truck geolocation, route optimisation, delivery performance metrics) Railway automation Electric vehicle charging station automation and monitoring Automated maintenance and diagnostic reporting
Education	Activity monitoring Attendance tracking Attention monitoring and learning support Ubiquitous learning Smart classrooms / interactive learning Assessment and performance monitoring automation Building and student / staff safety
Smart Homes, Infrastructure	Energy management and efficiency (electricity, water, HVAC, thermostats etc.) Security devices (smart doorbells, locks, cameras, alarms) Smart hazard detectors (CO2, smoke) Automated fire extinguishing Air quality Smart lighting Robot cleaning Automated window blinds Smart TVs / Speakers Smart kitchen/bathroom appliances (oven, washing machine, refrigerator etc.)
Personal	Wearable electronics (smartwatches, fitness trackers, glasses) Smartphones Location trackers Digital personal assistants (utilising sensors) Smart clothing

Big Data and IoT

The evolution of IoT has introduced and enabled a variety of protocols for M2M and wireless communications, incorporating various architectures and technologies. Considering the billions of connected IoT devices, the vast amount of data and processing involved introduced issues with data traffic management and resource availability, which also led to the further development of Edge Computing, Fog Computing and Cloud Computing (Francis, 2018). These architectures are utilised for on-device (or nearby), on-premise (or at short distance) or remote handling and processing of information, respectively, to address the aforementioned issues. The resulting huge amount of information contributed further to the rise of Big Data and related infrastructure, especially considering the ubiquity, variety and constant operation of IoT devices (Kaur & Kushwaha, 2018). Additionally, IoT-generated Big Data contributed to the advancement of Machine Learning and AI technologies, which thrive on information for the training of prediction models, feeding in turn back to IoT platforms for reporting and visualisation. Big data is a major technology that powers Industry 5.0. In Industry 5.0, IoT-connected equipment and gadgets create massive volumes of production data (Özdemir & Hekim, 2018). Advanced big data analytics technologies are used to examine this data and optimise the production system for efficiency and quality.

Enabling Protocols and Technologies

Various communications protocols and technologies can be used in IoT, including WiFi, Bluetooth, GSM and others as (Hajjaji, Boulila, Farah, Romdhani, & Hussain, 2021) point out, to enable the connection of devices utilising sensors, Radio Frequency Identification (RFID) and more. Not all of these solutions, however are ideal for IoT. For example, WiFi requires significant power, making it inefficient for many IoT devices' low-power profiles. To address this, several other wireless communications protocols have been developed. One of the most popular solutions to this issue is ZigBee, a specification based on the IEEE 802.15.4 standard, which enables wireless communications of low-power and low-bandwidth devices. ZigBee, however has short distance coverage, so its problematic for outdoor applications, although it can be ideal for BAN (Body Area Network) and PAN (Personal Area Network) applications. Under the same context, LoRa is a spread spectrum modulation technique that can be used for low transfer rate communications at longer ranges, especially in implementations such as the LoRaWAN protocol (Ali, Partal, Kepke, & Partal, 2019). Further development towards this direction proposed more fit-for-purpose solutions. One of them is Passive-ZigBee (Li, Chi, Liu, & Zhu, 2018), a hybrid ZigBee-WiFi backscatter communication that could allow for over one thousand times less power consumption compared to traditional ZigBee. Other common IoT communication protocols include MQTT, Z-Wave, another low-power wireless technology with a range of approximately 30 metres (Danbatta & Varol, 2019), LwM2M and more.

Among common technologies, apart from RFID tags which allow for the unique identification of objects and simple communication between them, Wireless Sensor Networks (WSN) utilising sensor nodes are extensively used in documenting environmental conditions, as (Sobin, 2020) discusses.

Figure 1. Sample IoT Protocol Stack on the OSI model

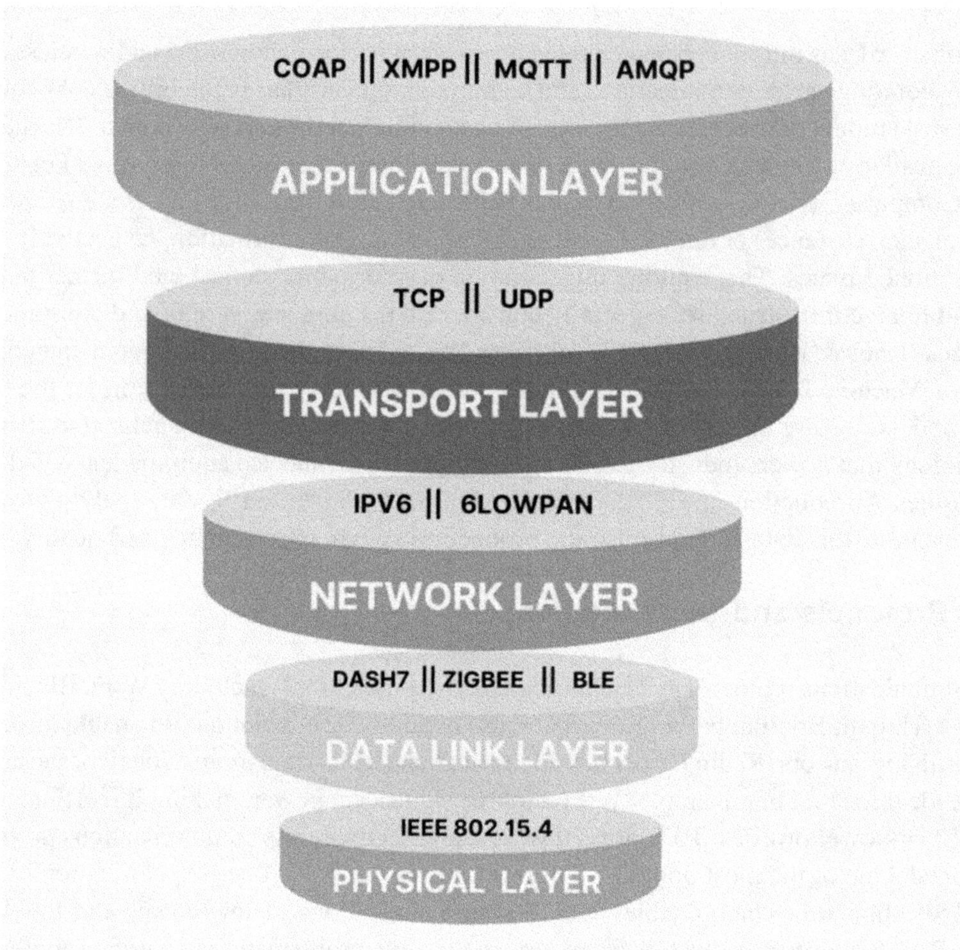

GATEWAYS

IoT Gateways are system components connecting the physical IoT devices between them and managing data transfer between the device and IoT Platforms and can also be used to ensure network reliability. That latency thresholds are not exceeded (Lanka & Bajracharya, 2018). Gateways can be hardware components or software that receive sensor input and transmit it to the cloud for further processing (Abdulrahman, et al., 2021). A typical illustration of an IoT Gateway can be seen in Figure 2.

PLATFORMS

IoT platforms provide a user interface which enables the management and monitoring of IoT devices. The platform itself receives sensor and status data and communicates information back to the devices. The utility of IoT platforms can extent from data reporting, analysis and visualisation to remote configuration, setup and coordination of the operation of multiple devices. There are various evaluation criteria for IoT

Figure 2. IOT-gateway

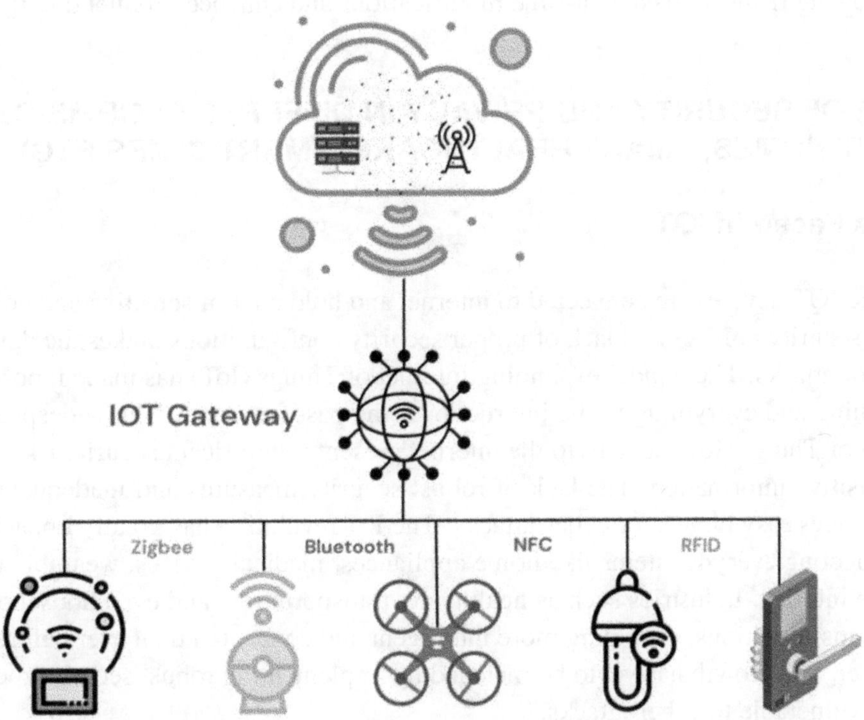

platforms. Among them are scalability, usability, security, availability, service offering and uniqueness of features, price and others (Lin, Huang, Xu, & Chen, 2020). As (Babun, Denney, Celik, McDaniel, & Uluagac, 2021) discuss, the most common classification of IoT platforms (as well as devices) divides them into Consumer IoT and Enterprise IoT, with differing aims, functionality, scalability and security/ privacy aspects. Consumer IoT platforms tend to be simpler and focused on quick monitoring and easy configuration by end users while offering limited scalability. On the other hand, enterprise IoT platforms usually provide robust environments that require specialisation and high levels of customisation, with high scalability in many cases. Regarding security and privacy concerns, Consumer IoT can lead to issues with personal data safety and multiple other concerns. In contrast, Enterprise IoT security breaches could lead to industrial / manufacturing hacking and infrastructure takeovers with potentially disastrous outcomes. The detailed issues surrounding privacy and security in the various forms of IoT are discussed in the following sections.

Industry 5.0 relies on the IoT platform to integrate connected devices, equipment, and systems into production. Industry 5.0 relies on IoT platforms to gather, analyse, and communicate data from linked devices and equipment.

Manufacturers may establish a highly connected, automated manufacturing system that responds swiftly to client demand and market situations by combining the IoT platform with Industry 5.0. Connectivity and automation maximise production, quality, and efficiency(Akundi et al., 2022). An IoT platform may evaluate sensor data from machines and devices to provide real-time production system performance insights. This data may detect issues and reduce downtime, enhancing manufacturing efficiency (Aslam et al., 2020). The IoT platform can also remotely monitor and manage manufacturing processes, allowing firms to make real-time modifications and enhance product quality.

THE ISSUE OF SECURITY AND PRIVACY IN DIFFERENT FORMS OF IOT (SMART HOMES, SMART HEALTHCARE, SMART CITIES ETC)

Challenges Faced in IOT

Majority of the IOT devices are connected to internet and hold a lot of sensitive and confidential information. weak security policies and lack of proper security configurations makes the devices vulnerable and targeted for attacks. The rapidly expanding Internet of Things (IoT) has made it possible to connect virtually anything and everything to the internet over the past few years. The widespread connectivity of the Internet of Things (IoT) devices to the internet present a significant security risk due to their vast storage of sensitive information. The lack of robust security measures and inadequate configurations make these devices easy targets for cyber-attacks. The IoT revolution has greatly impacted the physical world by connecting everyday items like home appliances, medical devices, wearable technology, and vehicles to the internet. Industries such as healthcare, transportation, and even households have undergone digital transformations, becoming more intelligent and connected than ever before (Kimani et al., 2019). However, this growth has yet to be matched by implementing robust security measures, making these devices vulnerable to cyber-attacks.

As per the experts, the IOT device manufacturers failed to implement a sturdy security system, resulting in a potential risk for the devices (Yang et al., 2017). Privacy has become a big concern for consumers as many IOT devices collect sensitive information and monitor user activity. Enterprise marketing makes the situation worse by collecting the user's private data and using it for internal purposes without the user's knowledge (Rehman et al., 2016). Enhancing the security and privacy of the users on all IOT layers is becoming a major requirement. Information service providers must enforce an access control data protection mechanism against misuse or corruption of a user's personal information. Data must only be available to the people to whom it belongs.

Smart Home Security

The dawn of smart homes has been announced for years. The global home automation market is projected to grow from $ 72 billion in 2021 to $ 163 billion (approx.) in 2028, with a CAGR of 12.3% from 2021 to 2028 (Insights, 2022). As people spend more time indoors and pandemic-related factors accelerate this growth, security and privacy concerns come to the fore. Many IoT environments rely heavily on cloud infrastructure and internet connectivity and do not adequately protect their users (Lippett, 2022).

Data collected from multiple home appliances will pose a threat when the information is forwarded to their service providers. One device's data may not be an issue, but combining data from multiple devices could disclose unwelcome details about a user or business. A growing number of people are concerned about how their data is handled by devices and organisations, especially as more devices enter the house. (Patrik Salmela, 2021). Many smart home appliances like Alexa leave a backdoor open to update the information to the cloud, which could give a chance for attackers if any vulnerability gets identified.

Making the equipment inside of a smart home more intelligent on its own is the most important step in achieving the goal of creating a more private smart home.

Industry 5.0 uses linked devices, big data analytics, and the IoT to improve home security and safety. Industry 5.0 smart home security systems are automated, data-driven, and networked for real-time monitoring and control. Smart home security systems can monitor a property and inform homeowners of security breaches using data from linked devices like cameras, sensors, and smart locks (Fatima et al., 2022). Big data analytics may also detect patterns and improve security measures by analysing data from linked devices. Smart home security systems may safeguard and reassure homeowners using Industry 5.0 concepts.

Figure 3. Smart home ecosystem

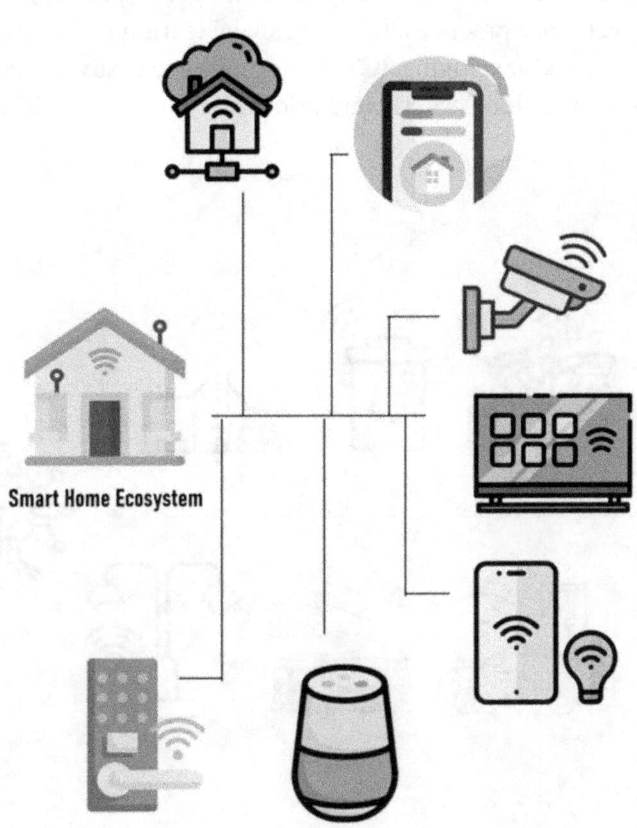

The term "smarter" is being applied to a growing number of consumer electronics, including but not limited to televisions, soundbars, smart speakers, and even remote healthcare monitoring equipment. However, at the moment, the cloud is the only means to accomplish that goal. A smart speaker will not process any commands or signals that are sent to it from an external source. Instead, the data is transported to the cloud, where it is interpreted and contextualised before being delivered back to the speaker along with instructions and actions (Muller, 2022).

If a new device is not adequately managed throughout its lifecycle, it may present a new security risk. Regardless of whether individuals utilise the devices, businesses, or smart cities, all parties in the value chain, including the device owner, must address the security threats.

Security in SMART Cities

The idea of security is not one of ultimate safety; rather, it refers to an evolving and sincere effort to protect residents of smart cities and the city itself from being harmed in any way, directly or indirectly, using digital or physical links. The concept of a smart city is based on integrating Information and Communication Technologies (ICT) to drive sustainable development and address the challenges posed by urbanisation. It is challenging to define a smart city, as it can encompass various initiatives such as implementing innovative e-governance practices, fostering social learning and community engagement, promoting sustainable lifestyles, and leveraging ICT for technological advancements. Each city may consider itself "smart" based on its unique criteria and priorities (Syed et al., 2021).

Figure 4. Smart city

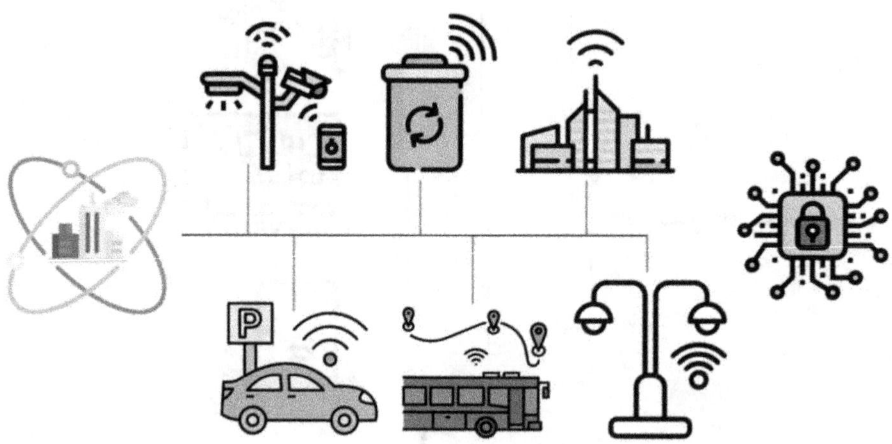

Because of the inherent interconnection of smart cities, data will be transmitted and exploited throughout the processes of smart cities, with many parties talking with one another and having access to information. Each organisation that contributes to the smart city will use and handle data in a way that is distinctive in its own way, and this may place individuals' personal privacy in jeopardy. This includes the manufacturers of the smart sensors, the city's transportation authority, and individuals who access the smart city through their smartphones. In addition, given that each smart city stakeholder will have unique interests, there will be discrepancies in the privacy requirements of the various smart city stakeholders.

Because the private and public sectors each serve a distinct set of objectives, there is and will continue to be a gap in the privacy rules governing these two types of organisations (Bennati & Pournaras, 2018).

Security in Smart Health

The provision of medical services to patients at any time and in any location is the primary goal of the smart health initiative. Most smart health monitoring devices are connected via a wireless network medium, a connection type that is notoriously susceptible to security breaches. On the other hand, numerous attacks have been seen, which jeopardise these health monitoring applications and systems. (Butt et al., 2019). It is anticipated that sensors in the medical field will manage sensitive personal information and data on specific patients' medical services. Similarly, such intelligent sensors might be connected to overarching information applications that allow users to access the data whenever and wherever they want.

Figure 5. Smart health

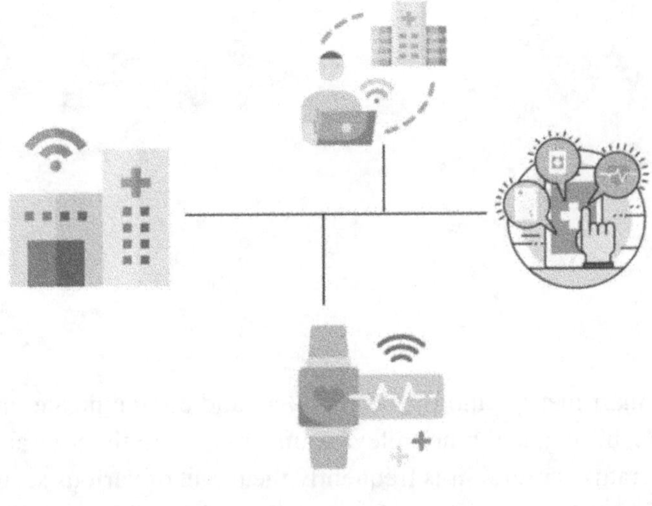

To fully utilise IoT in the medical healthcare field, it's crucial to understand the security requirements, potential vulnerabilities, and protective measures from a healthcare perspective. This is necessary to unlock IoT's full potential in the medical sector. Unfortunately, security breaches in healthcare often target patient information and aim to compromise the system and manipulate patient data. With IoT health systems, it can be challenging to identify external attackers operating outside the system (Butt et al., 2019).

SMART Connected Cars

IoT-enabled vehicles can steer themselves using an "autopilot" mode, eliminating the requirement for a human driver to be present. This will make life easier, but the bad effects resulting from this scenario can be very damaging. Consider the lawsuit against Tesla in 2018 following a deadly crash that occurred while the vehicle was in autopilot mode. This marks the fourth fatality while the car was operating in "autopilot" mode (Sean O'Kane, 2019). In this case, the many categories of Internet of Things applications walk a fine line regarding trust and ethics. For starters, it could have been an accident that the driver deliberately caused, but one could also say that it was the machine's fault. Trust is undoubtedly harmed from a pessimistic point of view, and this is true irrespective of the response. In a similar vein, the government's intervention in these types of events does not result in any positive consequences because the rules in place are insufficient to keep these types of eventualities in check.

Figure 6. Smart transport

SMART Energy

IoT devices are known as smart metres, and they can collect and communicate information relating to energy usage, voltage levels, billing, and other relevant information to the user and the electricity supplier. Even though this apparatus is useful, it is frequently the target of various security assaults, such as forgery, jamming, or spoofing attacks, which can be carried out for various nefarious purposes depending on the perpetrator. Eavesdropping can also be used to get information about which devices, such as medical or other appliances, are being used at what time (Aouini & Azzouz, 2015). This poses privacy concerns because the attacker can also follow and determine when someone is at home, which can lead to tragedies such as theft or burglary.

Industry 5.0 and the IoT have numerous benefits, but security and privacy problems have arisen. Connected devices and systems create more data, which must be safeguarded from cyber attacks and unlawful access. Smart locks, cameras, and sensors can increase hack risk in smart homes. These gadgets save personal information like home addresses and timetables, which cybercriminals may use. Smart home security solutions must be developed to guard against cyber threats and illegal access to personal data to meet these issues. Smart health gadgets and telemedicine services raise issues about medical data security and privacy. Personal and sensitive data must be safeguarded against cyberattacks and illegal access. Smart health systems must be built with strong security to secure medical data (Fraga-Lamas et al., 2021).

Figure 7. Smart energy

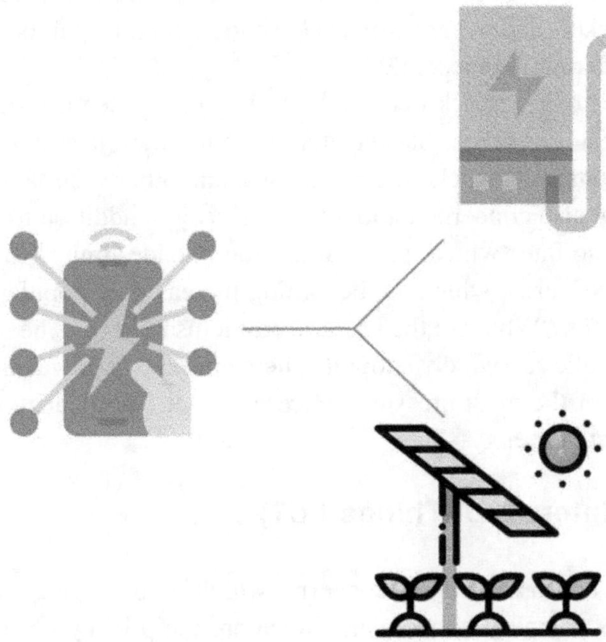

Table 2. IOT device and locations in different forms

sector of service	Locations	Devices
Smart Home	HVAC, Entertainment, Lighting, power, Network	CCTV, E-readers, Washing appliance, Alarms, Lights, etc.
Smart city	Tracking, Traffic, detectors, Management, Quality monitors	Voice assistants, IOT Radars, 360 degree cameras, sensors, IAQ(Indoor air quality) etc.
Smart health	Home, Hospitals, Public areas	Protection masks, wearables, AI bikes, Smart mats, Body scanners
Smart vehicles	Consumer, commercial, personal	Smart cars, Tolls, Navigation
Smart energy	Vehicle, Home, Security	Thermostats, Ev charging stations, Home sensors, Smart speakers, portable solar

IOT PRIVACY ISSUES TAXONOMY (PRIVATE AND PERSONAL, BUSINESS, PUBLIC SECTOR AND SERVICES, SOCIAL APPLICATION SECURITY IN CITIES)

There will be 64 billion IoT devices in the world by 2025 as more and more gadgets are connected to the Internet of Things. People's daily routines will be altered, and the planet may be transformed due to this expansion. Your guests will be impressed by your smart house, but smart lighting can save you money in the long run by reducing your overall energy consumption and lowering your electric bill. Connected automobiles and smart city infrastructure might create a new ecology for the driver, who is merely used to the standard method of travelling from Point A to Point B. People may now get a complete picture of their own health or lack thereof more than ever before because of the proliferation of Internet-connected medical equipment. However, hackers and cybercriminals have greater entry points because of the proliferation of linked gadgets. (insiderintelligence, 2022)

The first blackout caused by a cyber-attack occurred late last year when a group of hackers shut down a power grid in western Ukraine. As these hackers hunt for other ways to attack key infrastructure, such as electricity grids, hydroelectric dams, chemical factories, and other such facilities, this is likely just the beginning. Consumers are also concerned about their privacy in addition to security concerns. The consumer's life has become so intertwined, so what are the outside limits? IoT security worries are common, but so are privacy concerns, which are becoming increasingly popular as the Internet of Things expands. People also wonder, "What are the privacy problems in IoT?" The answers could help improve IoT so that the general public can widely adopt it. There are several prevalent privacy concerns in IoT nowadays. Here are some of the most pressing concerns about IoT security and privacy as we move closer to a fully interconnected society.

Privacy Concerns on the Internet of Things (IoT)

IoT security worries are common, but so are privacy concerns, which are becoming increasingly popular as the Internet of Things expands. People also wonder, "What are the privacy problems in IoT?" The answers could help improve IoT so that the general public can widely adopt it. There are several prevalent privacy concerns in IoT nowadays, so let's look at a few.

A Plethora of Information

Data created by the Internet of Things (IoT) devices is staggering, and this is a good thing. According to the FTC, fewer than 10,000 households may generate approximately 150 million distinct data points per day. As a result, it's easy to see how IoT poses a greater risk of data leakage. Hackers have more access points to your IoT devices and sensitive data, which makes them more vulnerable.

Eavesdropping

One of the gloomy answers to the question "What are the privacy risks in IoT?" that IoT users would have to find is eavesdropping. Consider the possibility that a hacker could infiltrate your private life through one of your smart home devices. Indeed, linked devices can be used by hackers and even manufacturers to invade the privacy of a person's house.

Researchers have successfully intercepted unencrypted data from a smart metre gadget to eavesdrop on the Internet of Things. An individual's television show of choice could be discovered thanks to the available unencrypted data (Langkjaer-Bain, 2011).

Unnecessary Exposure in public

As far as IoT privacy concerns go, unwanted public exposure is the next and most crucial one. The terms of service documents provided by IoT device makers are frequently lengthy, and few people really take the time to read them.

Figure 8. Data privacy and threats

A linked car, for example, might be used by an insurance company to gather information about an individual's driving patterns. Like health and life insurance companies, wearable fitness trackers might be used to figure out how much an individual would pay for insurance.

The right of individuals or users who cooperate with one another to protect the secrecy of their information and retain control over it even after it has been shared with a third party is known as privacy. Regarding Internet of Things applications, privacy issues can mostly be detected from the users' point of view and the datasets they maintain. Both communication service providers (CSPs) and internet service providers (ISPs) have access to the personal information of their customers, which means that they could potentially launch attacks or threats against users' privacy.

The Internet of Things (IoT) can include anywhere from tens to millions of devices, each of which can have unique qualities such as resource restrictions, mobility, scalability, degree of autonomy, and interoperability, among other things.(Porambage et al., 2016) Therefore, concerns around privacy in the Internet of Things can vary greatly depending on the applications in play.

Table 3. IOT privacy issues

sector of service	Attack type	Consequences/ Breach
Smart Home Smart city Smart health Smart vehicles Smart Energy	Access control Dos attack Skill Squatting Eavesdropping Spear phishing Rube Goldberg attack Bluebugging Signal Jamming Bluesnarfing GPS spoofing ZED sabotage	Data Confidentiality Data Availability Data Privacy and confidentiality Data confidentiality Privacy and data confidentiality Privacy and data availability Privacy and data confidentiality Data Availability Data Privacy and confidentiality Data Availability Data Availability

User Confidentiality

Identifying personally identifiable information as it is being transmitted over the internet presents a significant challenge to user privacy. Consider the scenario in which a customer by the name of John uses his credit card to purchase an item that contains an RFID tag. The CSP might be aware of John's personal information in certain instances since it is automatically linked to the object in question. The disclosure of such user information can put users at risk of having their privacy invaded through tracking, localisation, and personalisation. User tracking and profiling are both possible in these kinds of situations. Smartphones and other mobile devices connected to the internet could reveal the geographic location of the user, which would be a breach of privacy. In practice, users have varying degrees of awareness and worry regarding their privacy, and as a result, their willingness to provide information varies (Porambage et al., 2016).

Policies Regarding Safety and Confidentiality

The use of cloud-based services, which provide support for data storage, processing, and sharing, is considered an essential component of the infrastructure required for the Internet of Things (IoT). As IoT devices and nodes store or transmit sensitive information, they become targets for hackers and attackers. This is particularly true in the healthcare industry, where the reliance on computerised medical records and patient information makes it a prime target for cybercriminals. However, each layer of the IoT architecture also presents new opportunities to implement privacy and security protocols and standards (Razzaq et al., 2017). For example, in the device layer, the data from sensors are transmitted to the edge, fog, and cloud. To reduce the risk of attacks, certificates and permissions that trust specific servers are required, but this comes at the cost of increased power consumption for battery-run devices like wearables. Other security features, such as firmware security and hardware address authentication, also play a role. Finding a balance between security and power consumption is a critical challenge in this layer (Sicari et al., 2015).

In the cloud layer, network protocols between edge nodes, fog nodes, and even sensors must be protected with appropriate safety measures, such as certificates, point-to-point encryption, and message transfer protocols. This helps reduce the amount of data snooping and logging that can occur. Long-term data storage and real-time data processing must also be protected from SQL injections, sniffing, and phishing scripting attacks at both the end-user and data processing levels, provided the service certificate complies with HIPAA standards in health systems. Data fusion can also provide another entry point for hackers to breach privacy.

The fact that IoT devices can join and leave networks of sensors and data sources at will makes standard security measures more complicated. As a result, there is a pressing need for new security measures that are intelligent and adaptive in nature to address this challenge. (Tawalbeh et al., 2020).

Policies and laws must address safety and secrecy concerns raised by Industry 5.0 and the IoT. These regulations safeguard person's and organisations' privacy and security by assuring safe and secure IoT use. Industry 5.0 requires safety and confidentiality standards for linked devices and systems in production. Policies must protect sensitive production data and guarantee the safe and secure usage of robots and autonomous systems in the manufacturing process. Policies must also protect linked devices and system data. Personal and sensitive data must be safeguarded against cyberattacks and illegal access. Policies must guarantee data is gathered, processed, and kept in accordance with privacy rules and utilised for its intended purpose (Coelho et al., 2023).

Threats and Challenges / Developer and Society-End User Approach

Due to the lack of security policies and procedures, IOT applications and devices are easy prey for hackers. The high-priority research interest in IoT security stems from its evolution from the unsecured Internet model, where communications in the digital world meet the physical world. For the Internet of Things to become as pervasive and connected as expected, the IoT's security mechanisms must address the security flaws that have plagued traditional networks and the security standards that will be established for communication between people and machines. Traditional network security mechanisms will not be adequate for IoT systems. Such systems will need functionalities that support both human-to-machine and machine-to-machine interactions.(Radoglou Grammatikis et al., 2019).

Table 4. IOT threats

sector of service	Attack type
Home	Dos attacks MITM attacks Phishing attacks Formjacking
Industries	Evedropping Dos attacks Control hijacking attacks Rube golberg attacks Bluebugging
Transportation	Access control Dos attacks Zigbee attacks Black hole attack Worm hole attack GPS spoofing attack Sybil attack
Networks	DOS attacks Brute force attacks TLS level attacks Fragmentation attack
Healthcare	Signal jamming Ransomware MITM Sinkhole attack
Energy	Rube Goldberg attack Spear phishing Bluebugging Eavesdropping

Ethical and Sociological Issues and Concerns

Researchers in the social sciences have shown that discourses on the Internet of Things in industry, developer, and government discussions frequently present techno-utopian imaginaries. In these discussions, IoT technologies are portrayed as offering innovative solutions and ways to optimise the economy, industrial production, and transportation systems and improve citizens' everyday lives. In addition, these technologies are portrayed as generating useful data that can be used for commercial, developmental, or policy purposes. An increased sense of optimism is frequently put forward in these discussions, which is obvious from other promotional portrayals of emerging digital technologies such as artificial intelligence and big data (M. C. Elish & danah boyd, 2017). The capabilities of IoT technologies, as well as their potential to be "disruptive" and "revolutionary," are frequently presented as almost magical (Lupton, 2020).

CHARACTERISTICS OF THE INTERNET OF THINGS THAT MAY CAUSE ETHICAL ISSUES

The Internet of Things (IoT) is ubiquitous and omnipresent. The consumer is enthralled with IoT, and there appears to be no way out of it.

In the future, computers and equipment will shrink and become invisible, preventing any inspections, audits, quality control, and accounting procedures.

Confusion: it will become increasingly difficult to distinguish between natural objects, artefacts, and human beings due to the ease with which tags can be used to switch between categories.

Objects and things must have a unique identifier to be connected to the Internet of Things (IoT). Security and control in the IoT ecosystem may be threatened by the ability to access and manipulate these items' identities.

Because of the sheer number of things and people who are now connected, vast amounts of data (known as "big data") are being transmitted, which poses a security risk.

Autonomous and Unpredicted Behaviour: the networked objects may intervene in human activities autonomously and unpredictably for the users or design team. Hybrid systems, including people, things, and devices, will emerge due to all three's Internet of Things integration. It's possible that IoT's progressive evolution will lead to new behaviours that people will not comprehend.

Objects with built-in intelligence will serve as stand-ins for human interaction. The dynamic and emergent behaviour of the intelligent objects will be demonstrated. Problems will arise if certain gadgets are unavailable (e.g., teenagers without Google, smartphones or social media might feel themselves cognitively or socially handicapped).

A high number of hubs, switches and data makes it impossible for IoT control and governance to be centralised. Data transfers will be faster and more cost-effective, making them difficult to monitor. As new features and phenomena emerge that necessitates ongoing monitoring and regulation, accounting and control will be impacted further.

Data and Information Ownership Rights: IoT sensors and devices cannot identify who owns the data they collect because of the difficulties in specifying the identity of objects and humans.

Their omnipresence makes it impossible to distinguish between public and private areas. There is no way for people to know where their information goes.

Data Accessibility: a computer attack may result in the loss of important data. An attack on the Internet of Things (IoT) could significantly impact human existence (e.g., on the life of the driver of a car connected to IoT). The Internet of Things (IoT) has a long list of potential security flaws. It includes home appliances, traffic lights, food delivery networks, and transportation systems.

The generation gap in the Internet of Things has grown. Experts are the only ones who can understand IoT operations. It is impossible to forecast or imagine how IoT devices' communication impacts human life. It is only possible to narrow the digital divide when the legal and democratic frameworks for this process are properly defined (Tzafestas, 2018).

Many socialists have investigated objects having social qualities. In his book, L. Winner investigated the relationship between autonomous technology and political difficulties. Using the door closer as an example, J. Johnson explored the social role of nonhuman objects (J. Johnson, 1988). Sociability is not a human trait but rather a human trait accompanied by a group of delegated traits, according to that paper. To put it another way, devices having delegation (such as smartphones that send tweets on behalf of their users) can have sociability property as well.

COMPLEXITY PROBLEMS AND ETHICAL CONCERNS

Challenges

There's No Getting Around It

The user is completely enmeshed in the Internet of Things (IoT). The Internet of Things (IoT) network has a high level of user dependability, particularly in healthcare applications.

Internet of Things (IoT) Globalisation

Since medical applications, in particular, use the Internet of Things, it is impossible to restrict its use to a single country. Managing this new notion is difficult for nations, as it may be possible that nearly every whisper in a country is gathered and forwarded to the country offering the service.

Innovative Business Models

New business models that consider the wide variety of data accessible and the high stream will be required for medical service providers who use IoT. In the near future, virtual hospitals will be established. The service will therefore be provided over the internet.

Lack of Clarity

It will be more difficult to distinguish between physical and virtual devices and human beings because of the ease with which they can be transformed.

Identifying Issues

Each device must have a unique identifier to join the network. Problems with proving one's identity, such as identifying oneself, are bound to arise.

Availability at All Times

Hundreds of millions of devices will be always-on. Massive amounts of data (also known as "big data") will be generated, increasing the risk of cyberattacks.

Behaviour that Is Independent and Unanticipated

The Internet of Things (IoT) will include humans, gadgets, and sensors, creating a hybrid network. There is a risk that connected gadgets may interfere with human behaviour at any time. Uncertainty is inevitable as the Internet of Things (IoT) grows.

Governance

IoT control and governance will be difficult because of the large number of routers, switches, and information. We should expect speedier, less expensive, yet difficult-to-monitor data flows in the future. As a result, there is an additional challenge to deal with.

Concerns About Morality

According to (Caron et al., 2016), ethical conduct necessitates the enforcement of the following principles:

- The ability to obtain knowledge.
- The accuracy and reliability of the data.

As a result, new ethical concerns about the Internet of Things have emerged.

Identifying the source of the data collected in a typical Internet of Things (IoT) system will be difficult. Concerns have also been raised concerning the data being used without the patient's consent. Eliminating the distinction between private and public life, IoT omnipresence will make the boundary lines between these two realms virtually undetectable.

Attacks on People's Lives: Both data loss and computer system destruction can result from hacking or virus attacks on ordinary computer systems. Losses will not be limited to this stage in IoT assaults; they will eventually damage people's lives. In the case of a typical IoT medical application, an attacker's ability to log in could lead to the wrong drug being prescribed to a patient, which could have serious consequences for their health.

Laws

If they are not legally enforceable, smart contracts won't be useful even as their applications continue to proliferate, and that's a problem. Due to the frequent occurrence of disagreements regarding the definitions of terms, the subject of contract law is particularly complex. The origins of the fundamental concepts underlying contract law can be traced back to mediaeval England. In light of the present day, rules such as UETA and ESIGN make allowances for using smart contracts in situations where they are permitted. Therefore, blockchain-based smart contracts should be regarded as a legally binding declarations in accordance with the UETA and ESIGN rules. Consequently, they should be open to novelty and development (Alan Cohn & Chelsea Parker, 2017).

At the moment, there is no international framework that has been developed specifically with smart contracts in mind. It might be argued that the absence of clear standards for smart contracts does not suggest that the existing legislation does not apply to smart contracts or that they are unregulated. This is because smart contracts are not unregulated in any way. When it comes to deciding legality, smart contracts suffer the same challenges as traditional contracts do. This is because the contract would be considered voidable if it were to be executed illegally, just like traditional contracts. As a result, the frameworks of contract law now in place are suitable enough to accommodate the incorporation of smart contracts without creating new legal divisions (Riccardo De Caria, 2018).

Legislative and Regulatory Frameworks

This section will overview the guidelines issued through prominent legislative and regulatory frameworks in recent years.

In 2018 the UK Government issued a 'Code of Practice for Consumer IoT Security' developed by the Department for Digital, Culture, Media, and Sport (DCMS) with the National Cyber Security Centre (NCSC) to provide guidance on IoT security issues for manufacturers and consumers and help organisations adhere to data protection laws such as GDPR. The guide impresses on the importance of security by design and regular re-assessment of risks. To make products easy to use securely without compromising privacy and resilient against Distributed Denial of Service (DDoS) attacks (DCMS, 2018).

This guidance went on to influence the European Telecommunications Standards Institute (ETSI) 1029 standard 'ETSI TS 103 645 CYBER; Cyber Security for Consumer Internet of Things ' (ETSI, 2019) and 2020 'ETSI EN 303 645: CYBER; Cyber Security for Consumer Internet of Things: Baseline Requirements' which provides advice on standard recommendations for IoT security detailing provisions in the areas covered by the 'Code of Practice for Consumer IoT Security' using examples of application. To assist organisations with developing assurance strategies (ETSI, 2020). In 2021 ETSI also published the 'ETSI TS 103 701: CYBER; Cyber Security for Consumer Internet of Things: Conformance Assessment of Baseline Requirements', which provides vendor-neutral advice for various stakeholders involved with IoT. Such as manufacturers, implementers, user organisations, testers and bodies creating conformance declaration schemes. It is not a conformance declaration definition (ETSI, 2021).

In 2022, the UK Government introduced the 'Product Security and Telecommunications Infrastructure Bill', which would allow the government to create legislation enforcing security requirements for IoT devices. This was partly in response to the parse adoption of the 2018 Code of Practice. The top three guidelines to be enforced would be banning default passwords, enforcing vulnerability disclosure policies for all devices, and transparent product support periods in which manufacturers would continue to provide security updates. Which would help improve security and place more responsibilities on IoT manufacturers and distributors (Barber & Hutton, 2022).

The International Organization for Standardization (ISO) and International Electrotechnical Commission (IEC) have released several IoT standards. ISO/IEC 21823 1 (ISO, 2019) and 2 (ISO, 2020), provide a framework for IoT and transport interoperability. ISO/IEC TR 30164 (ISO, 2020), covers aspects of edge computing, including heterogeneity, security, and optimisation. Plus, ISO/IEC TR 30166 (ISO, 2020) focuses on standardising Industrial IoT (IIoT) systems. NIST has published the NISTIR 8259 Series (NIST, 2020-2021) providing manufacturers with guidelines for IoT development and testing. NIST also released the SP 800-213 series (NIST, 2021) for federal agencies deploying IoT systems and has led an initiate under Executive Order 14028 for clear labelling of IoT consumer devices (NIST, 2021).

Current Approaches To Addressing Iot Privacy And Security Issues, Methods Of Detection And Prevention To Enhance Privacy Iot

The UK Government's and ETSI's recommendations include are generally accepted as good practice for IoT (Burton, Tanczer, Vasudevan, Hailes, & Carr, 2021). The advice includes not releasing devices with default passwords, securely storing, and transmitting sensitive data and credentials, minimising attack surfaces (E.g., closing unused ports), and outage resiliency against DDoS attacks of failures, validating data input to protect from attacks, monitoring and disclosing known vulnerabilities (with a Coordinated Vulnerability Disclosure (CVD)), and providing regular software updates or setting specific end-of-life dates. Furthermore, alerting the consumer to unauthorised software changes protects the consumer's data, ensuring they are informed of how it is being used and allowing them to delete their PII. Telemetry data should be monitored for anomalies, but any PII should be kept to a minimum. Consumers should also be guided on securely configuring their devices from setup (DCMS, 2018). The British Toy and Hobby Association (BTHA) encourages its members to self-regulate and follow these recommended practices and proactively consult cyber security experts on manufacturing secure devices which are secure by design (Burton Et al., 2021).

PII collected and stored in the cloud is vulnerable to attack, and misuse, so abstracting data models can help conceal privacy (Yang, 2022). It is possible to enhance privacy through various anonymisation techniques. For example, raw data is aggregated and obfuscated to detach the data from its source to achieve k-anonymity. It can also be encrypted with the authorisation granted to a trusted party to access it. Locational data can be replaced with 'dummy' locations algorithmically. There is also a privacy-protecting technique called multi-party computation which encrypts, divides, and distributes data among multiple trusted parties for processing anonymously. Homomorphic encryption could also be used to allow companies to process encrypted data, and the individual could control the key as the data source (Andrew & Karthikeyan, 2019).

Figure 9. Privacy-preserving IoT model

The limited resources of IoT devices mean that traditional security methods must be tailored specifically for IoT to address security issues (Hussain, Hussain, Hassan, & Hossain, 2020). Internet Engineering Task Force (IETF) has developed various lightweight protocol stacks to protect communication and work with the architectural IoT layers of perception, network, and application, which sense, transmit and process data. They have also released solutions for secure authentication and cryptographic key management. Devices should be authenticated before joining an IoT network, and keys should be distributed with effective key management. Furthermore, users should be authenticated, and user data should be protected on the application layer (Yang, 2022).

Encryption between devices for data-in-transit is another method to protect privacy and prevent eavesdropping and man-in-the-middle attacks (Thales, 2022). The Cloud Security Alliance notes that the increase in 'machine-to-machine negotiation' in IoT networks lessen human involvement in the decision-making process thus increasing the importance of products and services interconnection points are secured by design (CSA, 2016). IoT architecture (devices, cloud, connected we and mobile applications and their APIs) can be pen tested to detect security issues. E.g., Firmware can be tested for backdoors that could allow unauthorised access to the IoT network (Deloitte, 2019).

Hussain et al. (2020) highlight Machine Learning (ML) and Deep Learning (DL) as useful for addressing current IoT limitations- dynamically adapting for detecting and mitigating security and privacy issues of IoT. Used for malware analysis, DDoS attacks, intrusion, anomaly detection and mitigation. However, challenges to consider would be resource constraints, heterogeneity of IoT networks, data classification and minimising data collection.

Currently Unresolved Issues

Burton et al., (2021) identified three concerning areas of IoT that they advised should be researched further and promptly addressed. Including the issue of domestic abusers using IoT devices to aide their abusive activity, like monitoring and humiliating victims, utilising the normal functionality of the devices. One issue is that usual threat models do not account for the abuse of IoT devices internally to the systems, as there is an assumption of trust and consent between 'internal' users. An issue not addressed in current guidelines. Plus, fitness devices, like medical devices, collect a great deal of PII but are not regulated like medical devices are and are easy to attack. The interconnectedness of such devices can increase the attack surface and reach of an attack, providing a way to access other connected networks. Furthermore, the insecurity of IoT children's toys can house cameras and microphones with the 'potential for misuse'. These issues highlight manufacturers' lack of commitment to baseline security requirements like encryption, regular assessments, Multi-Factor Authentication (MFA) and password protection. The manufacturer's need to introduce products to the market quickly is at odds with the need for cyber security measures in the interest of public protection. There is also a dearth of coordinated standards across IoT sectors. Hussain et al. (2020) also raise the heterogeneity of IoT networks, and the high volume of data sources creates issues related to security dependency and ML/DL data analysis for security and suggests that fresh big data techniques must be developed to address this. Furthermore, the systems are not working with false data to detect when IoT data has 'health' been compromised.

Song et al. have also noted that the pressure for manufacturers to launch devices on the market quickly and the heterogeneity of networks leads to issues with malware spreading easily on multiple devices with different processor architectures. They developed a cross-architecture solution that analyses binary similarity to detect malware (Song, Zhang, Wang, & Chen, 2022).

Burton et al., (2021) recommend that basic manufacturing codes be applied to all IoT sectors to underpin and support stakeholders in applying additional security measures. Additionally, devices functdevicey should not only undergo traditional cyber-security testing but also be assessed for 'unintended negative consequences' that could occur from everyday use by malicious users. Establishing a 'Zero Trust Architecture' (ZTA), which limits communication between devices, could restrict the attack surface. Regulation of unregulated IoT devices is required, especially when they incorporate technology that could be used for surveillance.

THE FUTURE OF IOT / FUTURE OF PRIVACY IN IOT

Following the discussion presented earlier, the increase in the use of IoT devices is exponential due to their usefulness in solving daily life problems. From home automation to healthcare and in smart cities, IoT devices are everywhere. On the hand, the privacy and confidentiality of the data collected using IoT devices are at greater risk. The future of IoT is tightly coupled with privacy-enhanced IoT devices of the future. It involves securing the device first (Tawalbeh, L.A. et al., 2020) and then ensuring the network's security. In our work, we explored five different sectors where IoT devices are becoming one of the major sources of information gathering. Those sectors deal with different types of critical data and follow different communication protocols and security firewalls while making the overall communication mechanism heterogeneous. Based upon the analysis performed for IoT devices in different application sectors, it is evident that privacy has become the biggest problem while using IoT devices. It is necessary to investigate other methods to secure this heterogenous network of devices. Like in (Butt, T.A., et al., 2019), the architecture presented for the Internet of Vehicles introduces seven different aspects related to privacy, and they are not just limited to the privacy of data. They include parameters for preserving privacy of human behaviors, communications, associations, thoughts and images etc. In simple words, ensuring data privacy through IoT devices has become the highest-level goal to achieve. However, the scope of privacy mechanisms is not similar for each sector where IoT devices are applicable. To provide an explicit definition of the privacy mechanism, we explored benchmark literature and presented future action points for improving IoT devices and their network.

Proposals In Security & Privacy Enhancements Based On Literature And Personal Observations

An earlier discussion on maintaining the highest level of privacy and security of data through IoT devices mainly depends upon the application sector of IoT, and we studied five different sectors smart homes, smart cities, smart health, smart vehicles and smart energy. To identify the areas for enhanced privacy using IoT devices, we will summarise very specific action points in each domain. Like in (Zheng, S., et al., 2018), it was identified that users maintain trust in the manufacturer of a particular IoT device in home automation, allowing them to track and manage their data by the device. However, the impact of various machine learning algorithms applied by the manufacturer to analyse the generated data is a big issue while preserving the privacy of the data, and it should be addressed by the manufacturer separately. Another source of compromising data privacy may be during packet transfer, and in (Anthi, E., et al., 2019), it was suggested to perform feature engineering and deep learning-based predictions to identify any malicious activity while using IoT devices as part of the network. As a future course of action, associating contextual information with sensory data may be useful for maintaining the integrity of the data (Almusaylim, Z.A. & Zaman, N., 2019). However, data breaches may occur at one of the many different states of the data (Zaidan, A.A. & Zaidan, B.B., 2020) in IoT-based smart home automation.

In terms of smart cities, IoT devices' infrastructure is heterogenous compared to smart homes. Like in (Gheisari, M., et al., 2021), it was suggested to identify vulnerabilities using several different operating systems. The idea is to avoid traditional network security methods and devise a focused policy framework for a heterogenous smart city network of IoT devices. The use of blockchain may be a good idea for smart cities' data management. In addition, smart cities are considered complex infrastructures, and it is of utmost importance to define the protocols for institutions and the environment in a particular context (Ismagilova, E., et al., 2020). Moreover, introducing user-centric privacy methods and data protection mechanisms may be useful for lightweight security solutions (Cui, L., et al., 2018).

Healthcare is one of the most important sectors using IoT devices for the generation and processing of data. This is personalised health information of the individual, and it is very important to secure it from unauthorised access. As in (Khan, J., et al., 2020), it was proposed to use a dynamic, secure key generation method to enhance healthcare data security. In another work (Alshehri, F. & Muhammad, G., 2020), it was recommended not to store all the healthcare data in the public domain but rather only statistics about the data. More importantly, personalised encryption methods were highly recommended in health care (Karunarathne, S.M., et al., 2021), along with a definition of trust management policy. It is important to mention that healthcare is one of the main areas for cyber-criminals to attack, and in the first attempt, they go for IoT devices. Usually, they use password-guessing methods to get access to personal healthcare portfolios, which is why it is critical to introduce features like multifactor authentication etc., to secure the personal healthcare portfolio (Gheisari, M., et al., 2021).

Generally, smart cities are a big domain, including smart vehicles too. However, smart vehicles have their privacy protocols. Defining the location access rights of smart vehicles is very important to save it from unauthorised access (Campanile, L., et al., 2022). There are many different types of vehicles always on the roads and rail tracks etc., and they communicate with each other at the same time. However, not all of them with each other all the time. This is only possible if one peer intends to establish the connection, and at the same time anyone else should not be able to get unauthorised access. One of the key improvements required in terms of privacy enhanced smart vehicles is use of reliable data transmission (Adhikari, M., et al., 2021).

Another important sector where IoT is contributing a lot is smart energy e.g., the use of smart devices like in the domestic and commercial energy meters. There is a huge amount of data generated by smart energy devices every day and transmitted over the network. Later on, companies and third parties use this data for different analytics. It was reported that smart energy devices are more vulnerable to cyber-attacks, and it becomes the responsibility of the manufacturers to ensure privacy in the development, deployment and operations of smart energy devices (Ahmed, G., 2021). On the other hand, it should be defined more whether the generated data will be shared with third parties in its original form or the metadata because the data is linked with the users, and they have privileges over it. Like in (Shouran, Z., et al., 2019), a blockchain-based method called Privacy Sharing is proposed to preserve the privacy and security of the data following the GDPR.

CONCLUSION

This chapter includes a comprehensive discussion on IoT, its increasing number of applications in five major sectors e.g., smart homes, healthcare and smart cities, smart vehicles and smart energy. More specifically, many different types of IoT devices including their purpose and operational location are covered to identify the privacy and security risks associated with those devices. The IoT devices deals directly with the personal data, or the data related to personal activities in daily life and they are at higher level of risk and pose greater challenge for the end-user and at the same time creating many opportunities for the researchers working for IoT development and IT infrastructure security. The IoT network is heterogenous, where devices from many different manufacturers are in use by many different public or private entities and they are connected through the network for sending and receiving data all the time, using the heterogenous web, mobile and cloud interfaces (Tawalbeh, L.A., et al., 2020). To this end, securing the IoT device first and, later, the communication mechanism is critical. In our work, we identified an explicit list of cyber-attacks directly associated with major IoT application sectors, from home automation to healthcare and urban management. These attacks are very common on the web and mobile. However, IoT devices are becoming one of the major reasons for exploiting these cyber-attack types to make the IT infrastructure vulnerable. It is equally important to secure IoT devices and their connection mechanism like web, mobile and cloud platforms (Sookhak, M., et al., 2018).

One of the biggest challenges due to vulnerability created by IoT devices is data privacy, whether it is home automation or healthcare. The data generated, processed or transferred through IoT devices have several social, ethical and legal constraints (Shouran, Z., et al., 2019). In our work, we identified several factors like data governance, lifecycle ownership of the data and ensuring the integrity of the data. In our opinion, there should be an appropriate standardisation framework to include any new type of IoT device in the existing IT infrastructure. On the other hand, the increasing number of cyber-attacks motivated institutions and state bodies to develop a legislative framework to counter cyber-attacks (Butt, T.A., et al., 2019). The NCSC has already developed a code of practice for Consumer IoT security by following the GDPR. In this regard, the UK govt is already introducing many new legislations to maintain the minimum standard for the operational qualification of IoT devices. However, there are several other security challenges still open.

Industry 5.0 and the Internet of Things (IoT) will likely have a big effect on privacy and data protection in the future. With increasingly connected devices and systems being used in manufacturing, it is becoming more and more important to protect personal and sensitive data from unauthorised access and cyberattacks. The future of IoT and privacy will be shaped by changes in technology, how people feel about privacy, and the development of new applications and use cases sensitive to privacy (Coelho et al., 2023). This will require developing more secure and privacy-friendly technologies and stronger policies and laws that protect personal data and promote privacy. As Industry 5.0 continues to develop, it will be important to ensure privacy and data protection are at the centre of the process and to design and deploy connected devices and systems to protect the privacy and security of both individuals and organisations. This will help ensure that Industry 5.0 is developed in a responsible, sustainable way and that it helps all stakeholders (Özdemir & Hekim, 2018).

REFERENCES

Abdulrahman, L. M., Zeebaree, S. R., Kak, S. F., Sadeeq, M. A., Adel, A. Z., Salim, B. W., & Sharif, K. H. (2021). A state of art for smart gateways issues and modification. *Asian Journal of Research in Computer Science*, 1-13.

Adhikari, M., Munusamy, A., Hazra, A., Menon, V. G., Anavangot, V., & Puthal, D. (2021). Security in Edge-Centric Intelligent Internet of Vehicles: Issues and Remedies. *IEEE Consumer Electronics Magazine*, *11*(6), 24–31. doi:10.1109/MCE.2021.3116415

Ahmed, G. (2021). Improving IoT Privacy, Data Protection and Security Concerns. *International Journal of Technology, Innovation and Management (IJTIM)*, *1*(1).

Akundi, A., Euresti, D., Luna, S., Ankobiah, W., Lopes, A., & Edinbarough, I. (2022). State of Industry 5.0—Analysis and identification of current research trends. *Applied System Innovation*, *5*(1), 27.

Alan Cohn, T. W. & Parker, C. (2017). *Smart After All: Blockchain, Smart Contracts, Parametric Insurance, And Smart Energy Grids.*

Alferidah, D. K., & Jhanjhi, N. Z. (2020). Cybersecurity impact over bigdata and iot growth. *2020 International Conference on Computational Intelligence (ICCI)* (pp. 103-108). IEEE. 10.1109/ICCI51257.2020.9247722

Ali, A. I., Partal, S. Z., Kepke, S., & Partal, H. P. (2019). ZigBee and LoRa based wireless sensors for smart environment and IoT applications. *2019 1st Global Power, Energy and Communication Conference (GPECOM)* (pp. 19-23). IEEE.

Almusaylim, Z. A., & Zaman, N. (2019). A review on smart home present state and challenges: Linked to context-awareness internet of things (IoT). *Wireless Networks*, *25*(6), 3193–3204. doi:10.100711276-018-1712-5

Alshehri, F., & Muhammad, G. (2020). A comprehensive survey of the Internet of Things (IoT) and AI-based smart healthcare. *IEEE Access: Practical Innovations, Open Solutions*, *9*, 3660–3678. doi:10.1109/ACCESS.2020.3047960

Andrew, J., & Karthikeyan, J. (2019). Privacy-preserving internet of things: Techniques and applications. [IJEAT]. *International Journal of Engineering and Advanced Technology*, *8*(6), 3229–3234. doi:10.35940/ijeat.F8830.088619

Anthi, E., Williams, L., Słowińska, M., Theodorakopoulos, G., & Burnap, P. (2019). A supervised intrusion detection system for smart home IoT devices. *IEEE Internet of Things Journal*, *6*(5), 9042–9053. doi:10.1109/JIOT.2019.2926365

Aouini, I., & Azzouz, L. ben. (2015). *Smart Meter: Applications, Security Issues And Challenges*. http://www.uum.edu.my

Aslam, F., Aimin, W., Li, M., & Ur Rehman, K. (2020). Innovation in the era of IoT and industry 5.0: Absolute innovation management (AIM) framework. *Information*, *11*(2), 124.

Babun, L., Denney, K., Celik, Z. B., McDaniel, P., & Uluagac, A. S. (2021). A survey on IoT platforms: Communication, security, and privacy perspectives. *Computer Networks*, *192*, 108040. doi:10.1016/j.comnet.2021.108040

Barber, S., & Hutton, G. (2022). *The Product Security and Telecommunications Infrastructure Bill.* House of Commons Library.

Bennati, S., & Pournaras, E. (2018). Privacy-enhancing aggregation of Internet of Things data via sensors grouping. *Sustainable Cities and Society*, *39*, 387–400. https://doi.org/10.1016/j.scs.2018.02.013

Burton, S. D., Tanczer, L. M., Vasudevan, S., Hailes, S., & Carr, M. (2021). *The UK Code of Practice for Consumer IoT Security: Where we are and what next.* The PETRAS National Centre of Excellence for IoT Systems Cybersecurity.

Butt, S. A., Diaz-Martinez, J. L., Jamal, T., Ali, A., De-La-Hoz-Franco, E., & Shoaib, M. (2019). IoT Smart Health Security Threats. *Proceedings - 2019 19th International Conference on Computational Science and Its Applications, ICCSA 2019*, (pp. 26–31). IEEE. doi:10.1109/ICCSA.2019.000-8

Butt, T. A., Iqbal, R., Salah, K., Aloqaily, M., & Jararweh, Y. (2019). Privacy management in social internet of vehicles: Review, challenges and blockchain based solutions. *IEEE Access: Practical Innovations, Open Solutions*, *7*, 79694–79713. doi:10.1109/ACCESS.2019.2922236

Campanile, L., Iacono, M., Marulli, F., & Mastroianni, M. (2020, May). Privacy regulations challenges on data-centric and iot systems: A case study for smart vehicles. In IoTBDS (pp. 507-518). doi:10.5220/0009839305070518

Caron, X., Bosua, R., Maynard, S. B., & Ahmad, A. (2016). The Internet of Things (IoT) and its impact on individual privacy: An Australian perspective. *Computer Law & Security Review*, *32*(1), 4–15. https://doi.org/10.1016/j.clsr.2015.12.001

Coelho, P., Bessa, C., Landeck, J., & Silva, C. (2023). Industry 5.0: The Arising of a Concept. *Procedia Computer Science*, *217*, 1137–1144. https://doi.org/10.1016/J.PROCS.2022.12.312

CSA. (2016). *Future-proofing the Connected World: 13 Steps to Developing Secure IoT Products*. Cloud Security Alliance.

Cui, L., Xie, G., Qu, Y., Gao, L., & Yang, Y. (2018). Security and privacy in smart cities: Challenges and opportunities. *IEEE Access: Practical Innovations, Open Solutions*, *6*, 46134–46145. doi:10.1109/ACCESS.2018.2853985

Danbatta, S. J., & Varol, A. (2019). Comparison of Zigbee, Z-Wave, Wi-Fi, and bluetooth wireless technologies used in home automation. *2019 7th International Symposium on Digital Forensics and Security (ISDFS)* (pp. 1-5). IEEE.

DCMS. (2018). *Code of Practice for Consumer IoT Security*. Department for Digital, Culture, Media and Sport.

De Caria, R. (2018). The Legal Meaning of Smart Contracts. *Kluwerlawonline*, *26*(6), 731–751.

Deloitte. (2019). *IoT Security Testing*. Deloitte.

M. C. Elish, & Boyd, D. (2017). Situating methods in the magic of Big Data and AI. *Tandfonline.*

Espinoza, H. G., McGroarty, F., O'Mahony, M., & Ziouvelou, X. (2020). Estimating the impact of the Internet of Things on productivity in Europe. *Heliyon*, *6*(5), e03935. doi:10.1016/j.heliyon.2020.e03935 PMID:32435711

ETSI. (2019). [CYBER; Cyber Security for Consumer Internet of Things.]. *ETSI TS*, *103*, 645.

ETSI. (2020). [CYBER; Cyber Security for Consumer Internet of Things: Baseline Requirements.]. *ETSI EN*, *303*, 645.

ETSI. (2021). [CYBER; Cyber Security for Consumer Internet of Things: Conformance Assessment of Baseline Requirements.]. *ETSI TS*, *103*, 701.

Fatima, Z., Tanveer, M. H., Zardari, S., Naz, L. F., Khadim, H., Ahmed, N., & Tahir, M. (2022). Production plant and warehouse automation with IoT and industry 5.0. *Applied Sciences (Basel, Switzerland)*, *12*(4), 2053.

Fraga-Lamas, P., Lopes, S. I., & Fernández-Caramés, T. M. (2021). Green IoT and edge AI as key technological enablers for a sustainable digital transition towards a smart circular economy: An industry 5.0 use case. *Sensors (Basel)*, *21*(17), 5745.

Francis, T. (2018). A Comparison of Cloud Execution Mechanisms Fog, Edge, and Clone Cloud Computing. *Iranian Journal of Electrical and Computer Engineering*, *8*(6), 2088–8708. doi:10.11591/ijece.v8i6.pp4646-4653

Gheisari, M., Najafabadi, H. E., Alzubi, J. A., Gao, J., Wang, G., Abbasi, A. A., & Castiglione, A. (2021). OBPP: An ontology-based framework for privacy-preserving in IoT-based smart city. *Future Generation Computer Systems*, *123*, 1–13. doi:10.1016/j.future.2021.01.028

Hajjaji, Y., Boulila, W., Farah, I. R., Romdhani, I., & Hussain, A. (2021). Big data and IoT-based applications in smart environments: A systematic review. *Computer Science Review*, *39*, 100318. doi:10.1016/j.cosrev.2020.100318

Hussain, F., Hussain, R., Hassan, S. A., & Hossain, E. (2020). Machine learning in IoT security: Current solutions and future challenges. *IEEE Communications Surveys and Tutorials*, *22*(3), 1686–1721. doi:10.1109/COMST.2020.2986444

Insights, F. B. (2022, January). *Home Automation Market Industry Reports*. FB Insights.

IoT Analytics. (2018). *State of the IoT 2018: Number of IoT devices now at 7B - Market accelerating*. https://iot-analytics.com/state-of-the-iot-update-q1-q2-2018-number-of-iot-devices-now-7b/

Ismagilova, E., Hughes, L., Rana, N. P., & Dwivedi, Y. K. (2020). Security, privacy and risks within smart cities: Literature review and development of a smart city interaction framework. *Information Systems Frontiers*, 1–22. PMID:32837262

ISO. (2019). *ISO/IEC 21823-1:2019*. https://www.iso.org: https://www.iso.org/standard/71885.html

ISO. (2020). *ISO/IEC 21823-2:2020*. https://www.iso.org: https://www.iso.org/standard/80986.html

ISO. (2020). *ISO/IEC TR 30164:2020*. https://www.iso.org: https://www.iso.org/standard/53284.html

ISO. (2020). *ISO/IEC TR 30166:2020*. https://www.iso.org: https://www.iso.org/standard/53286.html

J. Johnson. (1988). Mixing humans and nonhumans together: The sociology of a door-closer. *Jstor*, 298–310.

Karunarathne, S. M., Saxena, N., & Khan, M. K. (2021). Security and privacy in IoT smart healthcare. *IEEE Internet Computing*, *25*(4), 37–48. doi:10.1109/MIC.2021.3051675

Kaur, H., & Kushwaha, A. S. (2018). A review on integration of big data and IoT. *2018 4th International Conference on Computing Sciences (ICCS)* (pp. 200-203). IEEE.

Khan, J., Li, J. P., Ahamad, B., Parveen, S., Haq, A. U., Khan, G. A., & Sangaiah, A. K. (2020). SMSH: Secure surveillance mechanism on smart healthcare IoT system with probabilistic image encryption. *IEEE Access: Practical Innovations, Open Solutions*, *8*, 15747–15767. doi:10.1109/ACCESS.2020.2966656

Kimani, K., Oduol, V., & Langat, K. (2019). Cyber security challenges for IoT-based smart grid networks. *International Journal of Critical Infrastructure Protection*, *25*, 36–49. https://doi.org/10.1016/j.ijcip.2019.01.001

Langkjaer-Bain, R. (2011). *Smart Meters Could Be Used To Spy On Tv Viewing, Say Researchers.*

Lanka, S., & Bajracharya, S. (2018). Incorporating big data with iot in data center analytics. *2018 International Conference on Smart Systems and Inventive Technology (ICSSIT)* (pp. 240-245). IEEE. 10.1109/ICSSIT.2018.8748507

Li, Y., Chi, Z., Liu, X., & Zhu, T. (2018). Passive-zigbee: Enabling zigbee communication in iot networks with 1000x+ less power consumption. *Proceedings of the 16th ACM conference on embedded networked sensor systems*, (pp. 159-171). 10.1145/3274783.3274846

Lin, M., Huang, C., Xu, Z., & Chen, R. (2020). Evaluating IoT platforms using integrated probabilistic linguistic MCDM method. *IEEE Internet of Things Journal*, *7*(11), 11195–11208. doi:10.1109/JIOT.2020.2997133

Lippett, M. (2022, May). *Privacy-Intelligence-Agency-Security-In-The-Smart-Home.*

Lupton, D. (2020). The Internet of Things: Social dimensions. *Sociology Compass*, *14*(4). https://doi.org/10.1111/soc4.12770

Muller, H. (2022, May 20). *Smart-Home-Data-Privacy.*

NIST. (2021). *IoT Product Criteria*. https://www.nist.gov: https://www.nist.gov/itl/executive-order-14028-improving-nations-cybersecurity/iot-product-criteria

NIST. (2021). *SP 800-213 Series*. https://www.nist.gov: https://www.nist.gov/itl/applied-cybersecurity/nist-cybersecurity-iot-program/sp-800-213-series

NIST. (2020-2021). *NISTIR 8259 Series*. Retrieved from https://www.nist.gov: https://www.nist.gov/itl/applied-cybersecurity/nist-cybersecurity-iot-program/nistir-8259-series

Özdemir, V., & Hekim, N. (2018). Birth of industry 5.0: Making sense of big data with artificial intelligence,"the internet of things" and next-generation technology policy. *OMICS: A Journal of Integrative Biology*, *22*(1), 65–76.

Patrik Salmela, T. A. (2021, January 8). *Ericsson Blog*.

Porambage, P., Ylianttila, M., Schmitt, C., Kumar, P., Gurtov, A., & Vasilakos, A. v. (2016). The Quest for Privacy in the Internet of Things. *IEEE Cloud Computing, 3*(2), 36–45. doi:10.1109/MCC.2016.28

Radoglou Grammatikis, P. I., Sarigiannidis, P. G., & Moscholios, I. D. (2019). Securing the Internet of Things: Challenges, threats and solutions. In *Internet of Things (Netherlands)* (*Vol. 5*, pp. 41–70). Elsevier B.V. doi:10.1016/j.iot.2018.11.003

Razzaq, M. A., Gill, S. H., Qureshi, M. A., & Ullah, S. (2017). Security issues in the Internet of Things (IoT): A comprehensive study. *International Journal of Advanced Computer Science and Applications*, *8*(6).

Rehman, S. U., Khan, I. U., & Moiz, M. -Ur-Rehman, A., & Hasan, S. (2016). Security and privacy issues in IoT. In *International Journal of Communication Networks and Information Security*. https://www.researchgate.net/publication/313574376

Sean O'Kane. (2019, August 1). *Tesla hit with another lawsuit over a fatal Autopilot crash*.

Sedrati, A., Abdellatif, M., & Aafaf, O. (2022). IoT Governance: A state of the Art and a Comparative analysis. *2022 13th International Conference on Information and Communication Systems (ICICS)* (pp. 76-81). IEEE.

Shamayleh, A., Mahmoud, A., & Jumana, F. (2020). IoT based predictive maintenance management of medical equipment. *Journal of Medical Systems*, *44*(4), 1–12. doi:10.100710916-020-1534-8 PMID:32078712

Sharma, C., & Gondhi, N. K. (2018). Communication protocol stack for constrained IoT systems. *2018 3rd International Conference On Internet of Things: Smart Innovation and Usages (IoT-SIU)* (pp. 1-6). IEEE.

Shouran, Z., Ashari, A., & Priyambodo, T. (2019). Internet of things (IoT) of smart home: Privacy and security. *International Journal of Computers and Applications*, *182*(39), 3–8.

Sicari, S., Rizzardi, A., Grieco, L. A., & Coen-Porisini, A. (2015). Security, privacy and trust in Internet of Things: The road ahead. *Computer Networks*, *76*, 146–164.

Siqin, T., Choi, T.-M., Chung, S.-H., & Wen, X. (2022). Platform operations in the industry 4.0 era: Recent advances and the 3As framework. *IEEE Transactions on Engineering Management*, 1–18. doi:10.1109/TEM.2021.3138745

Sobin, C. C. (2020). A survey on architecture, protocols and challenges in IoT. *Wireless Personal Communications*, *112*(3), 1383–1429. doi:10.100711277-020-07108-5

Song, Q., Zhang, Y., Wang, B., & Chen, Y. (2022). Inter-BIN: Interaction-based Cross-architecture IoT Binary Similarity Comparison. *IEEE Internet of Things Journal*, *9*(20), 20018–20033. doi:10.1109/JIOT.2022.3170927

Sookhak, M., Tang, H., He, Y., & Yu, F. R. (2018). Security and privacy of smart cities: A survey, research issues and challenges. *IEEE Communications Surveys and Tutorials, 21*(2), 1718–1743.

Statista. (2022). *Number of Internet of Things (IoT) connected devices worldwide from 2019 to 2030.* Statista. https://www.statista.com/statistics/1183457/iot-connected-devices-worldwide/

Syed, A. S., Sierra-Sosa, D., Kumar, A., & Elmaghraby, A. (2021). Iot in smart cities: A survey of technologies, practices and challenges. *Smart Cities, 4*(2), 429–475. doi:10.3390/smartcities4020024

Tawalbeh, L., Muheidat, F., Tawalbeh, M., & Quwaider, M. (2020). IoT privacy and security: Challenges and solutions. *Applied Sciences (Switzerland), 10*(12). doi:10.3390/APP10124102

Tawalbeh, L. A., Muheidat, F., Tawalbeh, M., & Quwaider, M. (2020). IoT Privacy and security: Challenges and solutions. *Applied Sciences (Basel, Switzerland), 10*(12), 4102. doi:10.3390/app10124102

Thales. (2022). 07 24). *IoT Security* [Retrieved from thalesgroup.com: https://www.thalesgroup.com/en/markets/digital-identity-and-security/iot/magazine/internet-threats]. *Issues (Chicago, Ill.), 2022.*

Tzafestas, S. G. (2018). Ethics and law in the internet of things world. In *Smart Cities, 1*(1), 98–120). MDPI. doi:10.3390/smartcities1010006

Yang, Y., Wu, L., Yin, G., Li, L., & Zhao, H. (2017). A Survey on Security and Privacy Issues in Internet-of-Things. *IEEE Internet of Things Journal, 4*(5), 1250–1258. doi:10.1109/JIOT.2017.2694844

Yang, G. (2022). An Overview of Current Solutions for Privacy in the Internet of Things. *Frontiers in Artificial Intelligence, 5.*

Zaidan, A. A., & Zaidan, B. B. (2020). A review on intelligent process for smart home applications based on IoT: Coherent taxonomy, motivation, open challenges, and recommendations. *Artificial Intelligence Review, 53*(1), 141–165. doi:10.100710462-018-9648-9

Zheng, S., Apthorpe, N., Chetty, M., & Feamster, N. (2018). User perceptions of smart home IoT privacy. *Proceedings of the ACM on human-computer interaction, 2*(CSCW), (pp. 1-20). ACM. 10.1145/3274469

Compilation of References

Aamer, A., Sahara, C. R., & Al-Awlaqi, M. A. (2022). Digitalization of the supply chain: transformation factors. *Journal of Science and Technology Policy Management*. doi:10.1108/JSTPM-01-2021-0001

Abdulrahman, L. M., Zeebaree, S. R., Kak, S. F., Sadeeq, M. A., Adel, A. Z., Salim, B. W., & Sharif, K. H. (2021). A state of art for smart gateways issues and modification. *Asian Journal of Research in Computer Science*, 1-13.

Abou-Shouk, M., Gad, H. E., & Abdelhakim, A. (2021, September). Exploring customers' attitudes to the adoption of robots in tourism and hospitality. *Journal of Hospitality and Tourism Technology*, *12*(4), 762–776. doi:10.1108/JHTT-09-2020-0215

Acs, Z. J., Stam, E., Audretsch, D. B., & O'Connor, A. (2017). The lineages of the entrepreneurial ecosystem approach. *Small Business Economics*, *49*(1), 1–10. doi:10.100711187-017-9864-8

Ada, N., Kazancoglu, Y., Sezer, M. D., Ede-Senturk, C., Ozer, I., & Ram, M. (2021). Analyzing Barriers of Circular Food Supply Chains and Proposing Industry 4.0 Solutions. *Sustainability*, *13*(12), 6812. doi:10.3390u13126812

Aday, S., & Aday, M. S. (2020). Impacts of COVID-19 on Food Supply Chain. *Food Quality and Safety*, *4*(4), 167–180. doi:10.1093/fqsafe/fyaa024

Adel, A. (2022). Future of industry 5.0 in society: human-centric solutions, challenges and prospective research areas. *Journal of Cloud Computing: Advances, Systems and Applications*.

Adel, A. (2022). Future of industry 5.0 in society: Human-centric solutions, challenges and prospective research areas. *Journal of Cloud Computing*, *11*(1), 1–15. PMID:36101900

Adhikari, M., Munusamy, A., Hazra, A., Menon, V. G., Anavangot, V., & Puthal, D. (2021). Security in Edge-Centric Intelligent Internet of Vehicles: Issues and Remedies. *IEEE Consumer Electronics Magazine*, *11*(6), 24–31. doi:10.1109/MCE.2021.3116415

Agarwal, N., & Chauhan, S. (2022). Amplifying Employability Skills to Create Co-Working Space for Human and Cobots in the E-Commerce Industry. *Procedia Computer Science*, *214*, 1040–1048. doi:10.1016/j.procs.2022.11.275

Agarwal, U., Rishiwal, V., Tanwar, S., Chaudhary, R., Sharma, G., Bokoro, P. N., & Sharma, R. (2022). Blockchain Technology for Secure Supply Chain Management: A Comprehensive Review. *IEEE Access: Practical Innovations, Open Solutions*, *10*, 85493–85517. doi:10.1109/ACCESS.2022.3194319

Ageron, B., Bentahar, O., & Gunasekaran, A. (2020). Digital supply chain: challenges and future directions. *Supply Chain Forum: An International Journal*, *21*(3), 133–138. Tandfonline. 10.1080/16258312.2020.1816361

Ahmad, F., Draz, M. U., & Yang, S. C. (2018). Causality nexus of exports, FDI and economic growth of the ASEAN5 economies: Evidence from panel data analysis. *The Journal of International Trade & Economic Development, 28*(6), 685–700. doi:10.1080/09638199.2018.1426035

Ahmed, A. (2012). India – ASEAN relations in 21st century: strategic implications for India. *Eurasia Review.* https://www.eurasiareview.com/

Ahmed, G. (2021). Improving IoT Privacy, Data Protection and Security Concerns. *International Journal of Technology, Innovation and Management (IJTIM), 1*(1).

Ahmed, S. (2012). *Sectoral and gender implications for India–ASEAN FTA: A CGE analysis for India.* Centre for Development Studies. http://www.cds.edu/wp-content/uploads/2012/09/Sahid-Ahmed-Paper.pdf

Aisyah, F. (2020). Malaysian manufacturing sector declines at slower pace. *Malysian Reserve.* https://themalaysianreserve.com/2018/07/03/malaysian-manufacturing-sector-declines-at-slower-pace/

Ajmal, F., Yasin, N. M., & Norman, A. A. (2017). Critical success factors influencing e-commerce adoption in SMEs: A review and model. *International Journal of Advanced and Applied Sciences, 4*(7), 159–172. doi:10.21833/ijaas.2017.07.023

Ajouz, M., Abdullah, A., & Kassim, S. (2020). Acceptance of Sharīʿah-compliant precious metal-backed cryptocurrency as an alternative currency: An empirical validation of adoption of innovation theory. *Thunderbird International Business Review, 62*(2), 171–181. doi:10.1002/tie.22106

Ajzen, I. (1985). From Intentions to Actions: A Theory of Planned Behavior. In J. Kuhl & J. Beckmann (Eds.), *Action Control: From Cognition to Behavior* (pp. 11–39). Springer. doi:10.1007/978-3-642-69746-3_2

Ajzen, I. (1991). The theory of planned behavior. *Organizational Behavior and Human Decision Processes, 50*(2), 179–211. doi:10.1016/0749-5978(91)90020-T

Ajzen, I. (2020). The theory of planned behavior: Frequently asked questions. *Human Behavior and Emerging Technologies, 2*(4), 314–324. doi:10.1002/hbe2.195

Akundi, A., Euresti, D., Luna, S., Ankobiah, W., Lopes, A. & Edinbarough, I. (2022). *State of Industry 5.0—Analysis and Identification of Current Research Trends.* Applied system innovation MDPI

Akundi, A., Euresti, D., Luna, S., Ankobiah, W., Lopes, A., & Edinbarough, I. (2022). State of Industry 5.0—Analysis and identification of current research trends. *Applied System Innovation, 5*(1), 27.

Alaklabi, S., & Kang, K. (2021). Perceptions towards cryptocurrency adoption: A case of Saudi Arabian citizens. *IBIMA Business Review, 2021*, 1–17. doi:10.5171/2021.110411

Alaloul, L., Zawawi, & Mohammed. (2018). Industry revolution IR 4.0: future opportunities and challenges in construction industry. Paper presented at the *MATEC web of conferences.* EDP Sciences. 10.1051/matecconf/201820302010

Alaloul, W. S., Liew, M. S., Zawawi, N. A. W. A., & Kennedy, I. B. (2020). Industrial Revolution 4.0 in the construction industry: Challenges and opportunities for stakeholders. *Ain Shams Engineering Journal, 11*(1), 225–230. doi:10.1016/j.asej.2019.08.010

Alan Cohn, T. W. & Parker, C. (2017). *Smart After All: Blockchain, Smart Contracts, Parametric Insurance, And Smart Energy Grids.*

Al-Dmour, H. H. (2018). A Conceptual Framework for Determinants of E-Exporting (Marketing Applications) Practices and the Business Performance: Empirical Study. *Modern Applied Science, 12*(11), 358. doi:10.5539/mas.v12n11p358

Alexander, J. G. (2009). *Daily Life in Immigrant America, 1870–1920: How the Second Great Wave of Immigrants Made Their Way in America* (2nd ed.). Ivan R. Dee.

Alferidah, D. K., & Jhanjhi, N. Z. (2020). Cybersecurity impact over bigdata and iot growth. *2020 International Conference on Computational Intelligence (ICCI)* (pp. 103-108). IEEE. 10.1109/ICCI51257.2020.9247722

Ali, A. I., Partal, S. Z., Kepke, S., & Partal, H. P. (2019). ZigBee and LoRa based wireless sensors for smart environment and IoT applications. *2019 1st Global Power, Energy and Communication Conference (GPECOM)* (pp. 19-23). IEEE.

Aljawazneh, B. (2016). The Prospects of Cloud Computing in Supply Chain Management (A Theoretical Perspective). *Journal of Management Research, 8*(4), 145. doi:10.5296/jmr.v8i4.9998

Almusaylim, Z. A., & Zaman, N. (2019). A review on smart home present state and challenges: Linked to context-awareness internet of things (IoT). *Wireless Networks, 25*(6), 3193–3204. doi:10.100711276-018-1712-5

Alqahtani, N., & Uslay, C. (2020). Entrepreneurial marketing and firm performance: Synthesis and conceptual development. *Journal of Business Research, 113*, 62–71. doi:10.1016/j.jbusres.2018.12.035

Al-Refaie, A., & Ramadna, A. M. (2020). Barriers to E-Government Adoption in Jordanian Organizations from Users' and Employees' Perspectives. In Open Government: Concepts, Methodologies, Tools, and Applications (pp. 2190-2210): IGI Global.

Alshehri, F., & Muhammad, G. (2020). A comprehensive survey of the Internet of Things (IoT) and AI-based smart healthcare. *IEEE Access: Practical Innovations, Open Solutions, 9*, 3660–3678. doi:10.1109/ACCESS.2020.3047960

Alsmadi, A. A., Alrawashdeh, N., Al-Dweik, A. F., & Al-Assaf, M. (2022). Cryptocurrencies: A bibliometric analysis. *International Journal of Data and Network Science, 6*(3), 619–628. doi:10.5267/j.ijdns.2022.4.011

Alsultanny, Y., & AlZuhair, S. (2018). Evaluating influence of technology readiness factors on the Saudi cement companies market and financial based performance. *Journal of Science and Technology Policy Management.*

Altunışık, R., Coşkun, R., Bayraktaroğlu, S., & Yıldırım, E. (2012). Sosyal Bilimlerde Araştırma Yöntemleri [Research Methods in Social Sciences]. *Sakarya Yayıncılık, Sakarya, 126.*

Ambad, Andrew, & Amit. (2020). Growth Challenges of SMEs: Empirical Evidence in Sabah, Malaysia. *ASEAN Entrepreneurship Journal, 6*(1), 8-14.

Amin, N. A. N., Almunawar, M. N., Hasnan, A. S., & Besar, N. N. (2020). The Utilization of Web 2.0 for Knowledge Sharing: The Case of Tertiary Education in Brunei Darussalam. In *Handbook of Research on Managerial Practices and Disruptive Innovation in Asia* (pp. 1–25). IGI Global. doi:10.4018/978-1-7998-0357-7.ch001

Anbumozhi, V., & Kalirajan, K. (2020). South Asia's Economic Integration with East Asia: An Exploratory Analysis with a Focus on India. *Journal of Economic Integration, 35*(1), 91–110. doi:10.11130/jei.2020.35.1.91

Anderson, E. (2022, November 22). FMCG Packaging Market size to hit US$ 901.2 billion by 2027 according to a new research report. *WhaTech.* https://www.whatech.com/og/markets-research/industrial/735396-fmcg-packaging-market-size-to-hit-us-901-2-billion-by-2027-according-to-a-new-research-report

Andrew, J., & Karthikeyan, J. (2019). Privacy-preserving internet of things: Techniques and applications. [IJEAT]. *International Journal of Engineering and Advanced Technology, 8*(6), 3229–3234. doi:10.35940/ijeat.F8830.088619

Angelina, N. H. L., Khoi, N. H., & Nguyen, D. P. (2021). Unravelling the dynamic and contingency mechanism between service experience and customer engagement with luxury hotel brands. *International Journal of Hospitality Management.*

Angelis, J., & Da Silva, E. R. (2019). Blockchain adoption: A value driver perspective. *Business Horizons*, *62*(3), 307–314. doi:10.1016/j.bushor.2018.12.001

Anouk, A., and Bos-nehles, A. (n.d.). *What is Industry 4 . 0 and what are its implications on HRM Practices ?* Graduation Committee members :

Anthi, E., Williams, L., Słowińska, M., Theodorakopoulos, G., & Burnap, P. (2019). A supervised intrusion detection system for smart home IoT devices. *IEEE Internet of Things Journal*, *6*(5), 9042–9053. doi:10.1109/JIOT.2019.2926365

Aouini, I., & Azzouz, L. ben. (2015). *Smart Meter: Applications, Security Issues And Challenges*. http://www.uum.edu.my

ARC. (2021). *ARC Advisory Group: Key Technology Trends for 2021 Rockwell Automation India*. Rockwell Automation. https://www.rockwellautomation.com/en-us/company/news/blogs/technology-trends-report-2021.html

Arenkov, I., Tsenzharik, M., & Vetrova, M. (2019). *Digital technologies in supply chain management*, 448–453. Atlantis Press. doi:10.2991/icdtli-19.2019.78

Aria, M., & Cuccurullo, C. (2017). bibliometrix: An R-tool for comprehensive science mapping analysis. *Journal of Informetrics*, *11*(4), 959–975. doi:10.1016/j.joi.2017.08.007

ARIC. (n.d.). Asian Development Bank database. ARIC. https://aric.adb.org/integrationindicators

Arjun, R., & Suprabha, K. R. (2020). Innovation and Challenges of Blockchain in Banking: A Scientometric View. *International Journal of Interactive Multimedia & Artificial Intelligence*, *6*(3), 7. doi:10.9781/ijimai.2020.03.004

Arpacı, Ö. Y., & Gülel, F. E. (2023). Are European Union Member and Candidate Countries Ready for Industry 5.0?: Spatial Clustering Analysis in the Context of Industry 4.0 Performance. In Implications of Industry 5.0 on Environmental Sustainability (pp. 52-66). IGI Global.

Arrigo, E. (2020). Global sourcing in fast fashion retailers: Sourcing locations and sustainability considerations. *Sustainability*, *12*(2), 508. doi:10.3390u12020508

Aslam, F., Aimin, W., Li, M., & Ur Rehman, K. (2020). Innovation in the era of IoT and industry 5.0: Absolute innovation management (AIM) framework. *Information*, *11*(2), 124.

ASTM International. (2019). *Additive Manufacturing: An Overview*. ASTM International. https://www.astm.org/DIGITAL_LIBRARY/MNL/SOURCE_PAGES/MNL119-70_foreword.pdf

Åström, J., Reim, W., & Parida, V. (2022). Value creation and value capture for AI business model innovation: A three-phase process framework. *Review of Managerial Science*, *16*(7), 2111–2133. doi:10.100711846-022-00521-z

Atkeson, A., & Kehoe, P. J. (2001). *The Transition to a New Economy after the Second Industrial Revolution. Working Paper No. 606*. Federal Reserve Bank of Minneapolis, Research Department.

Audretsch, D. B., Keilbach, S. R. F. M. C., Keilbach, M. C., Lehmann, E. E., & Lehmann, P. of M. and O. and D. E. E. (2006). Entrepreneurship and Economic Growth. Oxford University Press, USA.

Avlonitis, G. J., & Salavou, H. E. (2007). Entrepreneurial orientation of SMEs, product innovativeness, and performance. *Journal of Business Research*, *60*(5), 566–575. doi:10.1016/j.jbusres.2007.01.001

Avramov, D., Cheng, S., Lioui, A., & Tarelli, A. (2022). Sustainable investing with ESG rating uncertainty. *Journal of Financial Economics*, *145*(2), 642–664. doi:10.1016/j.jfineco.2021.09.009

Ayedh, A. M., Omar, M. M. S., & Echchabi, A. (2020). Factors Influencing Bitcoin Investment Intention: The case of Oman. *International Journal of Internet Technology and Secured Transactions*, *1*(1), 1. doi:10.1504/IJITST.2021.112867

Ayedh, A., Echchabi, A., Battour, M., & Omar, M. (2020). Malaysian Muslim investors' behaviour towards the blockchain-based Bitcoin cryptocurrency market. *Journal of Islamic Marketing*, *12*(4), 690–704. doi:10.1108/JIMA-04-2019-0081

Ayre, C., & Scally, A. J. (2014). Critical values for Lawshe's content validity ratio: revisiting the original methods of calculation. *Measurement and Evaluation in Counseling and Development, 47*(1), 79–86. doi: . doi:10.1177/0748175613513808

Azaria, C. (2010). *Export commerce and export marketing with the use of internet by Greek SMEs,* [Doctoral Dissertation, University of Macedonia, Greece].

Azzi, R., Chamoun, R. K., & Sokhn, M. (2019). The power of a blockchain-based supply chain. *Computers & Industrial Engineering*, *135*, 582–592. doi:10.1016/j.cie.2019.06.042

Babakhani, M., & Haji, H. (2011). An empirical study to determine the critical success factors of export industry. *Management science letters*, *1*(1), 23-28.

Babun, L., Denney, K., Celik, Z. B., McDaniel, P., & Uluagac, A. S. (2021). A survey on IoT platforms: Communication, security, and privacy perspectives. *Computer Networks*, *192*, 108040. doi:10.1016/j.comnet.2021.108040

Bacon, K. (2007). *The Dark Side of the Gilded Age*. The Atlantic.

Bain & Company. (2020). *BAIN_REPORT_Changing_Gears_2020.pdf.* Bain & Company. https://media.bain.com/bainweb/PDFs/BAIN_REPORT_Changing_Gears_2020.pdf

Bakar, N. A. A., Deraman, Z., Tarmiji, M. F., Yusoff, R., & Kama, N. (2020). Workplace Digitalization in Public Sector Organization Towards Operational Effectiveness: Current Landscape, Issues and Challenges. *International Journal of Innovation in Enterprise System*, *4*(01), 78–83. doi:10.25124/ijies.v4i01.50

Baker, W. E., & Sinkula, J. M. (2009). The Complementary Effects of Market Orientation and Entrepreneurial Orientation on Profitability in Small Businesses*. *Journal of Small Business Management*, *47*(4), 443–464. doi:10.1111/j.1540-627X.2009.00278.x

Bak, R. (2003). *Henry and Edsel: The Creation of the Ford Empire*. John Wiley and Sons.

Baldauf, A., Cravens, D. W., & Wagner, U. (2000). Examining determinants of export performance in small open economies. *Journal of World Business*, *35*(1), 61–79. doi:10.1016/S1090-9516(99)00034-6

Ballis, A., & Drakos, K. (2021). The explosion in cryptocurrencies: A black hole analogy. *Financial Innovation*, *7*(1), 8. doi:10.118640854-020-00222-0

Ballis, A., & Verousis, T. (2022). Behavioural finance and cryptocurrencies. In *Review of Behavioral Finance*. Emerald Group Holdings Ltd., doi:10.1108/RBF-11-2021-0256

Banik, N. (2014). India-ASEAN Free Trade Agreement: The Untapped Potential. *MPRA Paper No.57954*. https://mpra.ub.uni-muenchen.de/57954/

Barber, S., & Hutton, G. (2022). *The Product Security and Telecommunications Infrastructure Bill.* House of Commons Library.

Basile, V., Giacalone, M., & Cozzucoli, P. C. (2022). The Impacts of Bibliometrics Measurement in the Scientific Community A Statistical Analysis of Multiple Case Studies. *Review of European Studies*, *14*(3), 10. doi:10.5539/res.v14n3p10

Battisti, S., & Brem, A. (2020). Digital entrepreneurs in technology-based spinoffs: An analysis of hybrid value creation in retail public–private partnerships to tackle showrooming. *Journal of Business and Industrial Marketing*, *36*(10), 1780–1792. doi:10.1108/JBIM-01-2020-0051

Baur, A. W., Bühler, J., Bick, M., & Bonorden, C. S. (2015). Cryptocurrencies as a disruption? empirical findings on user adoption and future potential of Bitcoin and Co. Lecture Notes in Computer Science (Including Subseries Lecture Notes in Artificial Intelligence and Lecture Notes in Bioinformatics), 9373, 63–80. doi:10.1007/978-3-319-25013-7_6

Baur, D. G., Hong, K. H., & Lee, A. D. (2018). Bitcoin: Medium of exchange or speculative assets? *Journal of International Financial Markets, Institutions and Money*, *54*, 177–189. doi:10.1016/j.intfin.2017.12.004

Bawack, R. E., Wamba, S. F., Carillo, K. D. A., & Akter, S. (2022). Artificial intelligence in E-Commerce: A bibliometric study and literature review. *Electronic Markets*, *32*(1), 297–338. doi:10.100712525-022-00537-z PMID:35600916

Baxter, M. (2018). Business Analytics Intelligence. *Information-age*. www. information-age. com/business-analytics-intelligence-123477004/

Bayo-Moriones, A., & Lera-López, F. (2007). A firm-level analysis of determinants of ICT adoption in Spain. *Technovation*, *27*(6-7), 352–366. doi:10.1016/j.technovation.2007.01.003

Bayraktar, O. (2019). *Globalization, Institutions and Socio-Economic Performance Macro and Micro Perspectives..*

BBC. (2022). European Union reveals fast fashion crackdown. *BBC News*. https://www.bbc.com/news/science-environment-60913226#:~:text=Fast%20fashion%3A%20European%20Union%20reveals%20fast%20fashion%20crackdown,-Publishedandtext=Manufacturers%20will%20have%20to%20ensure,repair%20and%20recycle%20their%20clothes

BCR. (2022a, May 27). *AI in Supply Chain Market to Extend to USD 20 Billion & Growing at a CAGR of 20.5% by 2028*. GlobeNewswire News Room. https://www.globenewswire.com/en/news-release/2022/05/27/2452056/0/en/AI-in-Supply-Chain-Market-to-Extend-to-USD-20-Billion-Growing-at-a-CAGR-of-20-5-by-2028-BlueWeave-Consulting.html

BCR. (2022b, October 6). *Internet of Things (IoT) in Logistics Market to Grow at a CAGR of 14.0%, during Forecast Period*. GlobeNewswire News Room. https://www.globenewswire.com/en/news-release/2022/10/06/2529734/0/en/Internet-of-Things-IoT-in-Logistics-Market-to-Grow-at-a-CAGR-of-14-0-during-Forecast-Period-BlueWeave-Consulting.html

Beck, E. (2022). Working Conditions in the Industrial Revolution. *History Crunch*. https://www.historycrunch.com/working-conditions-in-the-industrial-revolution.html#/

Behera, R. K., & Dhal, S. K. (2020). A Meta-Analysis of Impact of ERP Implementation. In *Advances in Data Science and Management* (pp. 123–135). Springer. doi:10.1007/978-981-15-0978-0_12

Belanche, D., Casaló, L. V., & Flavián, C. (2020). Frontline robots in tourism and hospitality: Service enhancement or cost reduction? *Journal of Electronic Markets*, *31*(3), 477–492. doi:10.100712525-020-00432-5

Ben-Daya, M., Hassini, E., & Bahroun, Z. (2017). Internet of things and supply chain management: A literature review. *International Journal of Production Research*, *57*(15-16), 1–24. doi:10.1080/00207543.2017.1402140

Bennati, S., & Pournaras, E. (2018). Privacy-enhancing aggregation of Internet of Things data via sensors grouping. *Sustainable Cities and Society*, *39*, 387–400. https://doi.org/10.1016/j.scs.2018.02.013

Berentsen, A., & Schär, F. (2018). The case for central bank electronic money and the non-case for central bank cryptocurrencies. *Review - Federal Reserve Bank of St. Louis*, *100*(2), 97–106. doi:10.20955/r.2018.97-106

Berger, I. W. (2011, March 7). *The co-evolution of humans and our tools*. Irving Wladawsky-Berger. https://blog.irvingwb.com/blog/2011/03/the-co-evolution-of-humans-and-our-tools.html

Bernama. (2019). Many SMEs Unaware of Industry 4WRD Readiness Assessment Programme. *Bernama*. https://www.bernama.com/en/news.php?id=1774994

Bertolozzi-Caredio, D., Bardají, I., Garrido, A., Berry, R., Bijttebier, J., Gavrilescu, C., Harizanova, H., Jendrzejewski, B., Meuwissen, M. M. P., Ollendorf, F., Pinsard, C., Rommel, J., Severini, S., & Soriano, B. (2021). Stakeholder perspectives to improve risk management in European farming systems. *Journal of Rural Studies*, *84*, 147–161. doi:10.1016/j.jrurstud.2021.04.004

Bharadwaj, S., & Deka, S. (2021). Behavioural intention towards investment in cryptocurrency: An integration of rogers' diffusion of innovation theory and the technology acceptance model. *Forum Scientiae Oeconomia*, *9*(4), 137–159. doi:10.23762/FSO_VOL9_NO4_7

Bhat, K. S., & Singh, S. P. (2016). 3D printing in supply chain management: A review. *International Journal of Production Research*, *54*(7), 2037–2050. doi:10.1080/00207543.2015.1114053

Bhattacharyya, R., & Mandal, A. (2010). Estimating the Impact of the Indo-ASEAN Free Trade Agreement on India's Balance of Trade. *Journal of Global Analysis*, *1*(1), 9–25.

Bhattacharyya, R., & Mandal, A. (2014). Estimating the impact of the India-ASEAN Free trade agreement on Indian Industries. *South Asia Economic Journal*, *15*(1), 93–114. doi:10.1177/1391561414527050

Bianchi, C., & Mathews, S. (2013). The role of the internet on export market growth: An empirical study in Latin America. In Strategic Management in Latin America, Mexico City, Mexico.

Bill, E. (2020). Journal of Self-Governance and Management Economics. *Cognitive Automation, Business Process Optimization, and Sustainable Industrial Value Creation in Artificial Intelligence Data-Driven Internet of Things Systems.*, *8*(3), 9–15.

Birda, R. K. & Dadhich, M. (2022). Industry 5.0 Revolution towards an Imminent Future Driven Society. *International Research Journal of Engineering and Technology, 9*(5), 3709-3714.

Bjerke, B., & Hultman, C. (2004). *Entrepreneurial Marketing: The Growth of Small Firms in the New Economic Era*. Edward Elgar Publishing.

Blohm, I., Riedl, C., Füller, J., & Leimeister, J. M. (2016). Rate or trade? Identifying winning ideas in open idea sourcing. *Information Systems Research*, *27*(1), 27–48. doi:10.1287/isre.2015.0605

Blondel, V. D., Guillaume, J. L., Lambiotte, R., & Lefebvre, E. (2008). Journal of statistical mechanics: Theory and experiment. *Fast Unfolding of Communities in Large Networks*, *10*, P10008.

Bock, J. (2018). Blockchain logistics: A case study of the potential benefits and challenges of distributed ledger technology in the supply chain. *Journal of Business Logistics*, *39*(4), 324–334. doi:10.1111/jbl.12203

Bogicevic, V., Liu, S. Q., Seo, S., Kandampully, J., & Rudd, N. A. (2021). Virtual reality is so cool! How technology innovativeness shapes consumer responses to service preview modes. *International Journal of Hospitality Management*, *93*, 102806. doi:10.1016/j.ijhm.2020.102806

Boilard, M., & Roucolle, G. (2020). *Will 3D Printing "Vaporize" the Supply Chain?* Oliver Wyman. https://www.oliverwyman.com/our-expertise/insights/2017/feb/will-3D-printing-vaporize-the-supply-chain.html

Borges, A. F., Laurindo, F. J., Spínola, M. M., Gonçalves, R. F., & Mattos, C. A. (2021). The strategic use of artificial intelligence in the digital era: Systematic literature review and future research directions. *International Journal of Information Management*, *57*, 102225. doi:10.1016/j.ijinfomgt.2020.102225

Börold, A., Teucke, M., Rust, J., & Freitag, M. (2020). Recognition of car parts in automotive supply chains by combining synthetically generated training data with classical and deep learning based image processing. *Procedia CIRP*, *93*, 377–382. doi:10.1016/j.procir.2020.03.142

Bosovska, M., Boiko, M., Bovsh, L., & Okhrimenko, A. (2022, October). Models of the Industrial Revolution 5.0. In *2022 IEEE 4th International Conference on Modern Electrical and Energy System (MEES)* (pp. 1-4). IEEE.

Bostrom, N. (2014). *Superintelligence: Paths, dangers, strategies* (1st ed.). Oxford University Press.

Bouazza, A. B., & Ardjouman, D. (2015).. . *Establishing the Factors Affecting the Growth of Small and Medium-sized Enterprises in Algeria.*, *4*(2), 15.

Bowman, T. (2020). Library Guides: Literature Review: Systematic literature reviews. *Libguides.* https://libguides.csu.edu.au/review/Systematic

Boyd, N. G., & Vozikis, G. S. (1994). The influence of self-efficacy on the development of entrepreneurial intentions and actions. *Entrepreneurship Theory and Practice*, *18*(4), 63–77. doi:10.1177/104225879401800404

Bozarth, C. C., & Handfield, R. B. (2019). *Introduction to operations and supply chain management* (5th ed.). Pearson Education Limited.

Browne, M. (2021). Artificial intelligence data-driven internet of things systems, real-time process monitoring, and sustainable industrial value creation in smart networked factories. *Journal of Self-Governance and Management Economics*, *9*(2), 21–31. doi:10.22381/jsme9220212

Brylska, P., Cobanoglu, C., & Dogan, S. (2022). Users Versus Non-users: The Impact of Experience on Hotel Guests' Attitudes Towards Service Robots in Hotels. *Journal of Information and Communication Technologies in Tourism, 2022*, 55–66. doi:10.1007/978-3-030-94751-4_5

Buolamwini, J., & Gebru, T. (2018). Gender shades: Intersectional accuracy disparities in commercial gender classification. *Proceedings of Machine Learning Research*, *81*(1), 1–15.

Burström, T., Parida, V., Lahti, T., & Wincent, J. (2021). AI-enabled business-model innovation and transformation in industrial ecosystems: A framework, model and outline for further research. *Journal of Business Research*, *127*, 85095. doi:10.1016/j.jbusres.2021.01.016

Burton, S. D., Tanczer, L. M., Vasudevan, S., Hailes, S., & Carr, M. (2021). *The UK Code of Practice for Consumer IoT Security: Where we are and what next.* The PETRAS National Centre of Excellence for IoT Systems Cybersecurity.

Butt, S. A., Diaz-Martinez, J. L., Jamal, T., Ali, A., De-La-Hoz-Franco, E., & Shoaib, M. (2019). IoT Smart Health Security Threats. *Proceedings - 2019 19th International Conference on Computational Science and Its Applications, ICCSA 2019*, (pp. 26–31). IEEE. doi:10.1109/ICCSA.2019.000-8

Butt, J. (2020). A Strategic Roadmap for the Manufacturing Industry to Implement Industry 4.0. *Designs*, *4*(2), 11. doi:10.3390/designs4020011

Butt, T. A., Iqbal, R., Salah, K., Aloqaily, M., & Jararweh, Y. (2019). Privacy management in social internet of vehicles: Review, challenges and blockchain based solutions. *IEEE Access: Practical Innovations, Open Solutions*, *7*, 79694–79713. doi:10.1109/ACCESS.2019.2922236

Büyüközkan, G., & Göçer, F. (2018). Digital Supply Chain: Literature review and a proposed framework for future research. *Computers in Industry*, *97*, 157–177. doi:10.1016/j.compind.2018.02.010

Cai, Y. J., & Choi, T. M. (2020). A United Nations' Sustainable Development Goals perspective for sustainable textile and apparel supply chain management. *Transportation Research Part E, Logistics and Transportation Review*, *141*, 102010. doi:10.1016/j.tre.2020.102010 PMID:32834741

Calleo, D., & Rowland, B. (1973). *America and the World Political Economy.* Indiana University Press.

Camargo, L. R., Pereira, S. C. F., & Scarpin, M. R. S. (2020). Fast and ultra-fast fashion supply chain management: An exploratory research. *International Journal of Retail & Distribution Management*, *48*(6), 537–553. doi:10.1108/IJRDM-04-2019-0133

Campanile, L., Iacono, M., Marulli, F., & Mastroianni, M. (2020, May). Privacy regulations challenges on data-centric and iot systems: A case study for smart vehicles. In IoTBDS (pp. 507-518). doi:10.5220/0009839305070518

Canhoto, A. I., & Clear, F. (2020). Artificial intelligence and machine learning as business tools: A framework for diagnosing value destruction potential. *Business Horizons*, *63*(2), 183–193. doi:10.1016/j.bushor.2019.11.003

Cao, L. (2021). Artificial intelligence in retail: Applications and value creation logics. *International Journal of Retail & Distribution Management*, *49*(7), 958–976. doi:10.1108/IJRDM-09-2020-0350

Capgemini Consulting. (2018). *AR-VR-in-Operations1.pdf.* Capgemini. https://www.capgemini.com/wp-content/uploads/2018/09/AR-VR-in-Operations1.pdf

Car, T., & Stifanich, L. P. (2020). Mobile technology: a tool to increase hotel sales and revenue. Journal of economics, business and organization research, 454-465.

Caron, X., Bosua, R., Maynard, S. B., & Ahmad, A. (2016). The Internet of Things (IoT) and its impact on individual privacy: An Australian perspective. *Computer Law & Security Review*, *32*(1), 4–15. https://doi.org/10.1016/j.clsr.2015.12.001

Carree, M. A., & Thurik, A. R. (2010). The Impact of Entrepreneurship on Economic Growth. In Z. J. Acs & D. B. Audretsch (Eds.), *Handbook of Entrepreneurship Research: An Interdisciplinary Survey and Introduction* (pp. 557–594). Springer., doi:10.1007/978-1-4419-1191-9_20

Carrère, C., & Strauss-Kahn, V. (2017). Export survival and the dynamics of experience. *Review of World Economics*, *153*(2), 271–300. doi:10.100710290-017-0277-1

Carter, S. B., Gartner, S. S., Haines, M. R., Olmstead, A. L., Sutch, R., & Wright, G. (Eds.). (2006). *Historical Statistics of the United States: Earliest Times to the Present. Millennial Edition* (Vol. 5). Cambridge University Press.

Carver, J. C., Hassler, E., Hernandes, E., & Kraft, N. A. (2013). Identifying Barriers to the Systematic Literature Review Process. *2013 ACM / IEEE International Symposium on Empirical Software Engineering and Measurement.* ACM, IEEE. 10.1109/ESEM.2013.28

Cath, C. (2018). Governing artificial intelligence: Ethical, legal and technical opportunities and challenges. *Philosophical Transactions - Royal Society. Mathematical, Physical, and Engineering Sciences*, *376*(2133), 20180080. doi:10.1098/rsta.2018.0080 PMID:30322996

Centobelli, P., Abbate, S., Nadeem, S. P., & Garza-Reyes, J. A. (2022). Slowing the fast fashion industry: An all-round perspective. *Current Opinion in Green and Sustainable Chemistry*, *100684*, 100684. doi:10.1016/j.cogsc.2022.100684

Çetinsöz, B. C., Doğan, S., & Duran, A. (2022). Perceptions about the applicability of robot technology in the tourism industry. *Journal of multidisciplinary academic tourism.*

Chander, B., Pal, S., De, D., & Buyya, R. (2022). Artificial intelligence-based internet of things for industry 5.0. *Artificial intelligence-based internet of things systems*, 3-45.

Chandler, A. D. (1993). *The Visible Hand: The Management Revolution in American Business.* Belknap Press of Harvard University Press. doi:10.2307/j.ctvjghwrj

Chandler, G. N., & Hanks, S. H. (1994). Market attractiveness, resource-based capabilities, venture strategies, and venture performance. *Journal of Business Venturing*, *9*(4), 331–349. doi:10.1016/0883-9026(94)90011-6

Chandran, B. P. S., & Sudarsan, P. K. (2012). India-ASEAN free trade agreement implications for fisheries. *Economic and Political Weekly*, *47*(16), 65–70.

Chang, R., Kaltani, L., & Loayza, N. V. (2009). Openness can be good for growth: The role of policy complementarities. *Journal of Development Economics*, *90*(1), 33–49. doi:10.1016/j.jdeveco.2008.06.011

Chapman, J., Power, A., Netzel, M. E., Sultanbawa, Y., Smyth, H. E., Truong, V. K., & Cozzolino, D. (2021). Challenges and opportunities of the fourth revolution: A brief insight into the future of food. *Critical Reviews in Food Science and Nutrition*, 1–9. doi:10.1080/10408398.2020.1863328 PMID:33401934

Charlesworth, A. (2014). *Digital Marketing: A Practical Approach* (2nd ed.). Routledge. doi:10.4324/9780203493717

Chatfield, T. (2019, February 8). Technology in Deep time: How it evolves alongside Us. *BBC Future.* https://www.bbc.com/future/article/20190207-technology-in-deep-time-how-it-evolves-alongside-us

Chatzoglou, P., & Chatzoudes, D. (2016). Factors affecting e-business adoption in SMEs: An empirical research. *Journal of Enterprise Information Management*, *29*(3), 327–358. doi:10.1108/JEIM-03-2014-0033

Chauhan, C., & Singh, A. (2019). A review of Industry 4.0 in supply chain management studies. *Journal of Manufacturing Technology Management*, *31*(5), 863–886. doi:10.1108/JMTM-04-2018-0105

Chen, K. P., Dai, A., Yang, C., & Ge, Y. (2022). Exploring factors affecting customer trust in social distancing technology and impact on hotel booking intentions. *Cogent Social Sciences Leisure and Tourism.*

Chen, C. C., Greene, P. G., & Crick, A. (1998). Does entrepreneurial self-efficacy distinguish entrepreneurs from managers? *Journal of Business Venturing*, *13*(4), 295–316. doi:10.1016/S0883-9026(97)00029-3

Chen, J., Sousa, C. M., & He, X. (2016). The determinants of export performance: A review of the literature 2006-2014. *International Marketing Review*, *33*(5), 626–670. doi:10.1108/IMR-10-2015-0212

Chen, Y., Visnjic, I., Parida, V., & Zhang, Z. (2021). On the road to digital servitization–The (dis) continuous interplay between business model and digital technology. *International Journal of Operations & Production Management*, *41*(5), 694–722. doi:10.1108/IJOPM-08-2020-0544

Chen, Z., & Xie, G. (2022). ESG disclosure and financial performance: Moderating role of ESG investors. *International Review of Financial Analysis*, *83*(1), 102291. doi:10.1016/j.irfa.2022.102291

Chiarello, F., Trivelli, L., Bonaccorsi, A., & Fantoni, G. (2018). Extracting and mapping industry 4.0 technologies using wikipedia. *Computers in Industry*, *100*, 244–257. doi:10.1016/j.compind.2018.04.006

Chimienti, M. T. (2019). *ECB Internal Crypto-Assets Task Force (ICA-TF) Stablecoins: Implications for monetary policy, financial stability, market infrastructure and payments, and banking supervision in the euro area.* POEU. doi:10.2866/822388

Chin, A., Juhn, C., & Thompson, P. (2004). Technical Change and the Wage Structure during the Second Industrial Revolution: Evidence from the Merchant Marine, 1865–1912. *Discussion Paper No. 1285.* The Institute for the Study of Labor (IZA), Germany.

Chitadze. (2022). *Which are the most expensive and largest employer companies in the world?* The Center for International Studies. https://centerforis.blogspot.com/

Chittithaworn, C., Islam, M., Keawchana, T., & Muhd Yusuf, D. H. (2011). Factors Affecting Business Success of Small & Medium Enterprises (SMEs) in Thailand. *Asian Social Science*, *7*(5), 180. doi:10.5539/ass.v7n5p180

Choi, Y.-H., & Choi, S.-H. (2018). A Study of Crossing the Chasm in applying Smart Factory System for SMEs. *International Journal of Pure and Applied Mathematics, 118*(19), 469–487. https://acadpubl.eu/jsi/2018-118-19/articles/19a/32.pdf

Chopra, S., & Meindl, P. (2017). *Supply chain management: Strategy, planning, and operation* (6th ed.). Pearson Education.

Christopher, M., Payne, A., & Ballantyne, D. (2002). *Relationship Marketing: Creating Stakeholder Value*. Routledge., doi:10.4324/9780080516042

Cobo, M. J., López-Herrera, A. G., Herrera-Viedma, E., & Herrera, F. (2012). SciMAT: A new science mapping analysis software tool. *Ournal of the American Society for Information Science and Technology, 63*(8), 1609–1630. doi:10.1002/asi.22688

Coelho, P., Bessa, C., Landeck, J., & Silva, C. (2023). Industry 5.0: The Arising of a Concept. *Procedia Computer Science, 217*, 1137–1144. https://doi.org/10.1016/J.PROCS.2022.12.312

Cohen, R., Smith Philip, Arulchandran Vic, & Sehra Avtar. (2018). Automation and blockchain in securities issuances. *Butterworths Journal of International Banking and Financial Law Automation And Blockchain In Securities Issuances Feature*.

Cojocariu, O. (n.d.). Industry 5.0 opportunities and challenges: bring your factory into the future. *Digitalya*. https://digitalya.co/blog/industry-5-opportunities-and-challenges/

Collinson, E., & Shaw, E. (2001). Entrepreneurial marketing – a historical perspective on development and practice. *Management Decision, 39*(9), 761–766. doi:10.1108/EUM0000000006221

Concetta, A. (2014). *DePaolo, & Kelly Wilkinson*. Assessing the Use of Key Words in Student Responses.

Cook, P., Schmiege, S., Reeder, B., Horton-Deutsch, S., Lowe, N., & Meek, P. (2018). Temporal immediacy: A two-system theory of mind for understanding and changing health behaviors. *Nursing Research, 67*(2), 108–121. doi:10.1097/NNR.0000000000000265 PMID:29489632

Cova, B. (1996). ENTREPRENEURIAL VISION: Making Enthusiasm and Opportunity Coincide into Design. [Former Series]. *Design Management Journal, 7*(4), 32–39. doi:10.1111/j.1948-7169.1996.tb00626.x

Covin, J. G., Green, K. M., & Slevin, D. P. (2006). Strategic Process Effects on the Entrepreneurial Orientation–Sales Growth Rate Relationship. *Entrepreneurship Theory and Practice, 30*(1), 57–81. doi:10.1111/j.1540-6520.2006.00110.x

Covin, J. G., & Slevin, D. P. (1989). Strategic management of small firms in hostile and benign environments. *Strategic Management Journal, 10*(1), 75–87. doi:10.1002mj.4250100107

Covin, J. G., & Wales, W. J. (2012). The Measurement of Entrepreneurial Orientation. *Entrepreneurship Theory and Practice, 36*(4), 677–702. doi:10.1111/j.1540-6520.2010.00432.x

Crafts, N., & Mills, T. C. (1994). Trends in real wages in Britain, 1750-1913¢. *Explorations in Economic History, 31*(2), 176–181. doi:10.1006/exeh.1994.1007

Crane, A. (2021, October 6). 4 reasons why technology makes us vulnerable and how to fix it. *Untamed Science*. https://untamedscience.com/blog/4-reasons-why-technology-makes-us-vulnerable-and-how-to-fix-it/

Cronin, J. E. (1987). Strikes and Power in Britain, 1870–1920. *International Review of Social History, 32*(2), 144–167. doi:10.1017/S0020859000008403

CSA. (2016). *Future-proofing the Connected World: 13 Steps to Developing Secure IoT Products*. Cloud Security Alliance.

Cui, L., Xie, G., Qu, Y., Gao, L., & Yang, Y. (2018). Security and privacy in smart cities: Challenges and opportunities. *IEEE Access: Practical Innovations, Open Solutions*, *6*, 46134–46145. doi:10.1109/ACCESS.2018.2853985

Czakó, E., & Könczöl, E. (2014). Critical success factors of export excellence and policy implications: the case of Hungarian small and medium-sized enterprises. *International Entrepreneurship and Corporate Growth in Visegrad Countries*, 69-84.

Dadi, V., Nikhil, S. R., Mor, R. S., Agarwal, T., & Arora, S. (2021). Agri-Food 4.0 and Innovations: Revamping the Supply Chain Operations. *Production Engineering Archives*, *27*(2), 75–89. doi:10.30657/pea.2021.27.10

Dalenogare, B., Benitez, G. B., Ayala, N. F., & Frank, A. G. (2018). The expected contribution of Industry 4.0 technologies for industrial performance. *International Journal of Production Economics*, *204*, 383–394. doi:10.1016/j.ijpe.2018.08.019

Danbatta, S. J., & Varol, A. (2019). Comparison of Zigbee, Z-Wave, Wi-Fi, and bluetooth wireless technologies used in home automation. *2019 7th International Symposium on Digital Forensics and Security (ISDFS)* (pp. 1-5). IEEE.

Daneshvar Kakhki, M., & Gargeya, V. B. (2019). Information systems for supply chain management: A systematic literature analysis. *International Journal of Production Research*, *57*(15–16), 5318–5339. doi:10.1080/00207543.2019.1570376

Dania, W. A. P., Xing, K., & Amer, Y. (2018). Collaboration behavioural factors for sustainable agri-food supply chains: A systematic review. *Journal of Cleaner Production*, *186*, 851–864. doi:10.1016/j.jclepro.2018.03.148

Dashottar, S., & Srivastava, V. (2021). Corporate banking—risk management, regulatory and reporting framework in India: A Blockchain application-based approach. *Journal of Banking Regulation*, *22*(1), 39–51. doi:10.105741261-020-00127-z

Davari, A., & Najmabadi, A. D. (2018). Entrepreneurial Ecosystem and Performance in Iran. In N. Faghih & M. R. Zali (Eds.), *Entrepreneurship Ecosystem in the Middle East and North Africa (MENA): Dynamics in Trends, Policy and Business Environment* (pp. 265–282). Springer International Publishing., doi:10.1007/978-3-319-75913-5_8

Davenport, T. H. (1998, July 1). Putting the Enterprise into the Enterprise System. *Harvard Business Review*. https://hbr.org/1998/07/putting-the-enterprise-into-the-enterprise-system

Davenport, T. H., & Mahidhar, V. (2018). What's your cognitive strategy. *MIT Sloan Management Review*, *59*(4), 19–23.

DCMS. (2018). *Code of Practice for Consumer IoT Security*. Department for Digital, Culture, Media and Sport.

De Caria, R. (2018). The Legal Meaning of Smart Contracts. *Kluwerlawonline*, *26*(6), 731–751.

de Kervenoael, R., Hasan, R., Schwob, A., & Goh, E. (2020). Leveraging human-robot interaction in hospitality services: Incorporating the role of perceived value, empathy, and information sharing into visitors' intentions to use social robots. *Tourism Management*, *78*, 104042. doi:10.1016/j.tourman.2019.104042

Dekimpe, M. G. (2020). Retailing and retailing research in the age of big data analytics. *International Journal of Research in Marketing*, *37*(1), 3–14. doi:10.1016/j.ijresmar.2019.09.001

Delgado-garcía, J. B., Rodríguez-escudero, A. I., & Martín-cruz, N. (2012). Influence of Affective Traits on Entrepreneur's Goals and Satisfaction. *Journal of Small Business Management*, *50*(3), 408–428. doi:10.1111/j.1540-627X.2012.00359.x

Deloitte. (2014). *Industry 4.0: Challenges and solutions for the digital transformation and use of exponential technologies*. Deloitte. https://www2.deloitte.com/content/dam/Deloitte/ch/Documents/ manufacturing/chenmanufacturing-industry-4-0-24102014.pdf

Deloitte. (2017). *Deloitte-robots-are-ready.pdf*. Deloitte. https://www2.deloitte.com/content/dam/Deloitte/tr/Documents/technology/deloitte-robots-are-ready.pdf

Deloitte. (2018). *Deloitte-uk-deloitte-insight-implementing-advanced-analytics.pdf*. Deloitte. https://www2.deloitte.com/content/dam/Deloitte/uk/Documents/ConsumerIndustrialProducts/deloitte-uk-deloitte-insight-implementing-advanced-analytics.pdf

Deloitte. (2019). *IoT Security Testing*. Deloitte.

Deloitte. (2020). *DI_Automotive-News-Supplement.pdf*. Deloitte. https://www2.deloitte.com/content/dam/insights/us/articles/automotive-news_industry-4-0-in-automotive/DI_Automotive-News-Supplement.pdf

Deloitte. (2022). *2022 manufacturing industry outlook*. Deloitte. https://www2.deloitte.com/content/dam/Deloitte/us/Documents/energy-resources/us-2022-manufacturing-industry-outlook.pdf

Demir, K. A., and Cicibaş, H. (2019). The next industrial revolution: Industry 5.0 and discussions on industry 4.0. *Industry 4.0 from the MIS Perspective,* 247–260.

Demir, S., Yilmaz, I., & Paksoy, T. (2020). *Augmented Reality in Supply Chain Management* (pp. 136–145). CRC Press. doi:10.1201/9780429327636-14

Demir, K. A., & Cicibaş, H. (2018). *"The Next Industrial Revolution: Industry 5.0 and Discussions on Industry 4.0." Industry 4.0 From the Management Information Systems Perspectives*. Peter Lang Publishing House.

Demir, K. A., Döven, G., & Sezen, B. (2019). Industry 5.0 and Human-Robot Co-working. *Procedia Computer Science, 158*(January), 688–695. doi:10.1016/j.procs.2019.09.104

Depietro, R., Wiarda, E., & Fleischer, M. (1990). The context for change: Organization, technology and environment. *The processes of technological innovation, 199*(0), 151-175.

Despoudi, S., Papaioannou, G., Saridakis, G., & Dani, S. (2018). Does collaboration pay in agricultural supply chain? An empirical approach. *International Journal of Production Research, 56*(13), 4396–4417. doi:10.1080/00207543.2018.1440654

DeVries, P. D. (2016). An analysis of cryptocurrency, bitcoin, and the future. *International Journal of Business Management and Commerce, 1*(2), 1–9.

Dillard, J. P., & Pfau, M. (2002). *The Persuasion Handbook: Developments in Theory and Practice*. SAGE Publications. doi:10.4135/9781412976046

Dimson, E., Marsh, P., & Staunton, M. (2020). Divergent ESG ratings. *Journal of Portfolio Management, 47*(1), 75–87. doi:10.3905/jpm.2020.1.175

Ding, Y., & Cronin, B. (2011). Popular and/or prestigious? Measures of scholarly esteem. *Information Processing & Management, 47*(1), 80–96. doi:10.1016/j.ipm.2010.01.002

District, T. (2018). *Impact of fourth industrial revolution in human resource management. 3*(2), 59–61.

Dogru, T., Mody, M., & Leonardi, C. (2018). *Blockchain Technology & its Implications for the Hospitality Industry*. Boston Hospitality Review.

Donaldson, D. A. (2021). Digital from farm to fork: Infrastructures of quality and control in food supply chains. *Journal of Rural Studies*. doi:10.1016/j.jrurstud.2021.10.004

Donthu, N., Kumar, S., Mukherjee, D., Pandey, N., & Lim, W. M. (2021). How to conduct a bibliometric analysis: An overview and guidelines. *Journal of Business Research, 133*, 285–296. doi:10.1016/j.jbusres.2021.04.070

Dorofeyev, M. A., Kosov, M., Ponkratov, V., Masterov, A., Karaev, A., & Vasyunina, M. (2018). Trends and prospects for the development of blockchain and cryptocurrencies in the digital economy. *European Research Studies, 21*(3), 429–445. doi:10.35808/ersj/1073

Douglass, M. E. (2017). *Entrepreneurial Education Level Related to Business Performance.* Academy of Management Proceedings., doi:10.5465/ambpp.1976.4975936

Dragomir, V. D., & Dumitru, M. (2022). Practical solutions for circular business models in the fashion industry. *Cleaner Logistics and Supply Chain, 4*, 100040. doi:10.1016/j.clscn.2022.100040

Duan, X., Deng, H., & Corbitt, B. (2012). Evaluating the critical determinants for adopting e-market in Australian small-and-medium sized enterprises. *Management Research Review, 35*(3/4), 289–308. doi:10.1108/01409171211210172

Dubey, R., Gunasekaran, A., Childe, S. J., Papadopoulos, T., Luo, Z., Wamba, S. F., & Roubaud, D. (2019). Can big data and predictive analytics improve social and environmental sustainability? *Technological Forecasting and Social Change, 144*, 534–545. doi:10.1016/j.techfore.2017.06.020

Dubofsky, M., & Dulles, F. R. (2010). *Labor in America: A History.* WileyBlackwell.

Duginets, G. (2020). Global imperatives for development of international production networks: Case of Ukraine. *Problems and Perspectives in Management, 18*(1), 57–69. doi:10.21511/ppm.18(1).2020.06

DW. (2022). *EU proposes new rules to tackle 'fast fashion.'* DW. https://www.dw.com/en/eu-proposes-new-rules-to-tackle-fast-fashion/a-61308009

Earth. (2022). *10 Stunning Fast Fashion Waste Statistics.* Earth.Org. https://earth.org/statistics-about-fast-fashion-waste/

Eaton, J., Eslava, M., Kugler, M., & Tybout, J. (2008). *The margins of entry into export markets: evidence from Colombia.*

Echegaray, N., Hassoun, A., Jagtap, S., Tetteh-Caesar, M., Kumar, M., Tomasevic, I., Goksen, G., & Lorenzo, J. M. (2022). Meat 4.0: Principles and Applications of Industry 4.0 Technologies in the Meat Industry. *Applied Sciences (Basel, Switzerland), 12*(14), 6986. doi:10.3390/app12146986

Economy. (2019). Malaysia's business condition in manufacturing sector remains challenging. *The Star.* https://www.thestar.com.my/business/business-news/2019/10/01/malaysia039s-business-condition-in-manufacturing-sector-remains-challenging

EIBIS. (2022). *Digitalisation in Europe 2021-2022.* EIB.org. https://www.eib.org/en/publications-research/economics/digitalisation-in-european-union.htm

Ekanayake, E. M. A. C., Shen, G. Q. P., Kumaraswamy, M. M., & Owusu, E. K. (2022). Identifying supply chain vulnerabilities in industrialized construction: An overview. *International Journal of Construction Management, 22*(8), 1464–1477. doi:10.1080/15623599.2020.1728487

Ellitan, L. (2020). *Competing in the Era of Industrial Revolution 4 . 0 and Society 5 . 0. 10*(1), 1–12.

Engle, R. F., & Granger, C. W. J. (1987). Cointegration and error correction representation: Estimation and testing. *Econometrica, 55*(2), 251–276. doi:10.2307/1913236

Eskandari, S. (2015). *Real-world Deployability and Usability of Bitcoin.*

Espinoza, H. G., McGroarty, F., O'Mahony, M., & Ziouvelou, X. (2020). Estimating the impact of the Internet of Things on productivity in Europe. *Heliyon, 6*(5), e03935. doi:10.1016/j.heliyon.2020.e03935 PMID:32435711

Esteve-Pérez, S., Mánez-Castillejo, J. A., Rochina-Barrachina, M. E., & Sanchis-Llopis, J. A. (2007). A survival analysis of manufacturing firms in export markets. *Entrepreneurship, industrial location, and economic growth. Cheltenham etc.: Elgar*, 313-332

ETSI. (2019). [CYBER; Cyber Security for Consumer Internet of Things.]. *ETSI TS, 103*, 645.

ETSI. (2020). [CYBER; Cyber Security for Consumer Internet of Things: Baseline Requirements.]. *ETSI EN, 303*, 645.

Euronews. (2022). Is this the beginning of the end for fast fashion? *Euronews*. https://www.euronews.com/green/2022/03/31/is-this-the-beginning-of-the-end-for-fast-fashion-the-eu-is-moving-to-clean-up-the-dirty-i

Europa. (2022). Climate change: what the EU is doing. *Consilium*. https://www.consilium.europa.eu/en/policies/climate-change/#:~:text=By%20the%20European%20climate%20law,EU%20climate%20neutral%20by%202050

Europa. (2022). *Textiles and clothing legislation*. Eurpoa. https://single-market-economy.ec.europa.eu/sectors/fashion/textiles-and-clothing-industries/legislation_en#:~:text=The%20EU%20has%20aligned%20laws,functioning%20of%20the%20internal%20market

European Commission Report (2021). *Industry 5.0*. EC. https://op.europa.eu/en/publication-detail/-/publication/468a892a-5097-11eb-b59f-01aa75ed71a1/

European Commission. (2021) *Industry 5.0: Towards more sustainable, resilient and human-centric industry*. EC. https://research-and-innovation.ec.europa.eu/news/all-research-and-innovation-news/industry-50-towards-more-sustainable-resilient-and-human-centric-industry-2021-01-07_en

European Commission. (2022). *Human Capital and Digital Skills in the Digital Economy and Society Index | Shaping Europe's digital future*. Digital-Strategy. https://digital-strategy.ec.europa.eu/en/policies/desi-human-capital

European Commission. Directorate-General for Research and Innovation, Breque, M., De Nul, L., & Petridis, A. (2021). Industry 5.0: towards a sustainable, human-centric and resilient European industry. Publications Office.

Eurostat. (2022). *Government budget allocations for R&D (GBARD)*. Ec.europa.eu. https://ec.europa.eu/eurostat/statistics-explained/index.php?title=Government_budget_allocations_for_R%26D_(GBARD)&oldid=552767

FAO. (2022). *The State of Food and Agriculture 2022. Leveraging agricultural automation for transforming agrifood systems*. FAO. doi:10.4060/cb9479en

Fatima, Z., Tanveer, M. H., Zardari, S., Naz, L. F., Khadim, H., Ahmed, N., & Tahir, M. (2022). Production plant and warehouse automation with IoT and industry 5.0. *Applied Sciences (Basel, Switzerland)*, *12*(4), 2053.

Fayolle, A., Basso, O., & Tornikoski, E. T. (2011). Entrepreneurial Commitment and New Venture Creation: A Conceptual Exploration. *Handbook of Research on New Venture Creation*. https://www.elgaronline.com/view/edcoll/9781847200952/9781847200952.00016.xml

Felsberger, A., Qaiser, F. H., Choudhary, A., & Reiner, G. (2020). The impact of Industry 4.0 on the reconciliation of dynamic capabilities: Evidence from the European manufacturing industries. *Production Planning and Control*, *33*(2-3), 1–24. doi:10.1080/09537287.2020.1810765

Feng, H., Wang, X., Duan, Y., Zhang, J., & Zhang, X. (2020). Applying blockchain technology to improve agri-food traceability: A review of development methods, benefits and challenges. *Journal of Cleaner Production*, *260*, 121031. doi:10.1016/j.jclepro.2020.121031

Fernández-Salinero, C., & de la Riva, B. (2014). Entrepreneurial Mentality and Culture of Entrepreneurship. *Procedia: Social and Behavioral Sciences*, *139*, 137–143. doi:10.1016/j.sbspro.2014.08.044

Ferreira, M. P., Santos, J. C., de Almeida, M. I. R., & Reis, N. R. (2014). Mergers & acquisitions research: A bibliometric study of top strategy and international business journals, 1980-2010. *Journal of Business Research*, *67*(12), 2550–2558. doi:10.1016/j.jbusres.2014.03.015

Financial Times. (2022). Interest in European ESG ETFs holds up despite headwinds. *Financial Times*. https://www.ft.com/content/07f01ade-ed62-4fa0-a805-f92c61f391d3

Fink, L. (1988). The New Labor History and the Powers of Historical Pessimism: Consensus, Hegemony, and the Case of the Knights of Labor. *The Journal of American History*, *75*(1), 115–136. doi:10.2307/1889657

Fishbein, M. (1979). A theory of reasoned action: Some applications and implications. *Nebraska Symposium on Motivation*, *27*, 65–116. PMID:7242751

Foner, P. S. (1978). History of the Labor Movement in the United States.: Vol. 1. *From Colonial Times to the Founding of the American Federation of Labor*. International Publishers.

Food and Agriculture Organization of the United Nations (FAO). (2020). *Status of Digital Agriculture in 18 countries of Europe and Central Asia International Telecommunication Union Development Sector*. ITUPublications. https://www.itu.int/en/ITU-D/Regional-Presence/Europe/Documents/Events/2020/Series%20of%20Webinars/20-00244_Status_digital_Agriculture-revFAOV4.0-MASTER-FILE-20-JUNE_REVIEW-FAO_PL_print%20%28002%29.pdf

Fraga-Lamas, P., Lopes, S. I., & Fernández-Caramés, T. M. (2021). Green IoT and edge AI as key technological enablers for a sustainable digital transition towards a smart circular economy: An industry 5.0 use case. *Sensors (Basel)*, *21*(17), 5745.

Francis, S. (2011). A sectoral impact analysis of the ASEAN–India Free Trade Agreement. *Economic and Political Weekly*, *46*(2), 46–55.

Francis, T. (2018). A Comparison of Cloud Execution Mechanisms Fog, Edge, and Clone Cloud Computing. *Iranian Journal of Electrical and Computer Engineering*, *8*(6), 2088–8708. doi:10.11591/ijece.v8i6.pp4646-4653

Franco-Leal, N., Camelo-Ordaz, C., Fernandez-Alles, M., & Sousa-Ginel, E. (2020). The Entrepreneurial Ecosystem: Actors and Performance in Different Stages of Evolution of Academic Spinoffs. *Entrepreneurship Research Journal*, *10*(2). doi:10.1515/erj-2018-0228

Freeman, C., & Soete, L. (2008). *A Economia da Inovação Industrial*. Psychology Press.

Frey, T. (2021, December 16). What happens when we lose control of ai? *Futurist Speaker*. https://futuristspeaker.com/artificial-intelligence/what-happens-when-we-lose-control-of-ai/#:~:text=Yes%2C%20AI%20will%20eventually%20break,and%20specific%2C%20limited%20process%20improvement

Fujiki, H. (2020). Who adopts crypto assets in Japan? Evidence from the 2019 financial literacy survey. *Journal of the Japanese and International Economies*, *58*, 101107. doi:10.1016/j.jjie.2020.101107

Fusté-Forné, F. & Jamal, T. (2021). Co-Creating New Directions for Service Robots in Hospitality and Tourism. *Journal of Tourism and Hospitality*, *2*, 43-61.

Gale, J., & Abraham, D. (2005). Introduction: Toward understanding e-business transformation. *Journal of Organizational Change Management*, *18*(2), 113–116. doi:10.1108/09534810510589543

Gambhir, P., Bevan, P., Davenport, F., & Thirion, J. (2018). *Unlocking supply chain benefits through blockchain technology*. https://assets.kpmg/content/dam/kpmg/ca/pdf/2018/10/digital-disruption-blockchain.pdf

Gamoura, S., Derrouiche, R., Damand, D., & Barth, M. (2019). Insights from big Data Analytics in supply chain management: An all-inclusive literature review using the SCOR model. *Production Planning and Control*, 1–27. doi:10.1080/09537287.2019.1639839

Gan, J. L., and Yusof, H. M. (2019). *Industrial Revolution 4 . 0 : the Human Resource Practices. 3*, 620–624. doi:10.35940/ijrte.C1203.1083S219

Gans, J., & Ryall, M. D. (2017). Value capture theory: A strategic management review. *Strategic Management Journal*, *38*(1), 17–41. doi:10.1002mj.2592

Garbuio, M., & Lin, N. (2018). Artificial Intelligence as a Growth Engine for Health Care Startups: Emerging Business Models. *California Management Review*, *61*(2), 59–83. doi:10.1177/0008125618811931

Garg, P., Gupta, B., Chauhan, A. K., Sivarajah, U., Gupta, S., & Modgil, S. (2021). Measuring the perceived benefits of implementing blockchain technology in the banking sector. *Technological Forecasting and Social Change*, *163*, 120407. doi:10.1016/j.techfore.2020.120407

Garten, J. (1992). *A Cold peace: America, Japan, Germany and the struggle for Supremacy*. Times Books.

Gartner. (2022). *Supply Chain Cybersecurity | Cyber Protection*. Gartner. https://www.gartner.com/en/supply-chain/trends/supply-chain-cybersecurity

Gay, D., Ng, L., Cheng, H. W., Vergara, S., Ernst, E., Tobin, S., Milasi, S., Pin-Heiro, V., Kraft, C., Women, U. N., Fernandez, A., Renner, S., Roig, M., Jimenez, M., Perry, J., Mukherjee, S., Roehrl, R. A., and Freire, C. (2017). *Substantive contributions in the form of draft text for sections and boxes and research assistance were made by of the Division of Social Policy and Develop-ment (DESA/DSPD); and. July.*

Gebauer, H., Arzt, A., Kohtamäki, M., Lamprecht, C., Parida, V., Witell, L., & Wortmann, F. (2020). How to convert digital offerings into revenue enhancement – Conceptualizing business model dynamics through explorative case studies. *Industrial Marketing Management*, *91*, 429–441. doi:10.1016/j.indmarman.2020.10.006

Geissbauer, R., Lübben, E., Schrauf, S., & Pillsbury, S. (2018). *How industry leaders build integrated operations ecosystems to deliver end-to-end customer solutions*. Digital Champions. https://www.strategyand.pwc.com/gx/en/insights/industry4-0/global-digital-operations-study-digital-champions.pdf

George, A. S., & George, A. S. H. (2020). Industrial Revolution 5.0: The Transformation of the Modern Manufacturing Process To Enable Man and Machine To Work Hand in Hand. *Journal of Seybold Report*, *15*(9), 214–234. doi:10.5281/zenodo.6548092

Gerschewski, S., Scott-Kennel, J., & Rose, E. L. (2020). Ready to export? The role of export readiness for superior export performance of small and medium-sized enterprises. *World Economy*, *43*(5), 1253–1276. doi:10.1111/twec.12928

Gerwin, D., & Tarondeau, J. C. (1982). Case studies of computer integrated manufacturing systems: A view of uncertainty and innovation processes. *Journal of Operations Management*, *2*(2), 87–99. doi:10.1016/0272-6963(82)90025-0

Gheisari, M., Najafabadi, H. E., Alzubi, J. A., Gao, J., Wang, G., Abbasi, A. A., & Castiglione, A. (2021). OBPP: An ontology-based framework for privacy-preserving in IoT-based smart city. *Future Generation Computer Systems*, *123*, 1–13. doi:10.1016/j.future.2021.01.028

Ghirmay, T., Grabowski, R., & Sharma, S. (2001). Exports, investment, efficiency, and economic growth in LDCs: An empirical investigation. *Applied Economics*, *33*(6), 689–700. doi:10.1080/00036840122027

Gilchrist, A. (2016). *Industry 4.0: The Industrial Internet of Things*. Apress. doi:10.1007/978-1-4842-2047-4

Gillan, S., Koch, A., & Starks, L. (2021). Firms and social responsibility: A review of ESG and CSR research in corporate finance. *Journal of Corporate Finance*, *66*(1), 101889. doi:10.1016/j.jcorpfin.2021.101889

Gill, S. S., Xu, M., Ottaviani, C., Patros, P., Bahsoon, R., Shaghaghi, A., Golec, M., Stankovski, V., Wu, H., Abraham, A., Singh, M., Mehta, H., Ghosh, S. K., Baker, T., Parlikad, A. K., Lutfiyya, H., Kanhere, S. S., Sakellariou, R., Dustdar, S., & Uhlig, S. (2022). AI for next generation computing: Emerging trends and future directions. *Internet of Things*, *19*, 100514. doi:10.1016/j.iot.2022.100514

Gilpin. (1992). Three Models of the future. In: *International politics. Enduring Concepts and Contemporary issues.* Harper and Collins Publishers.

Gilpin, R. (1987). *The Political Economy of International Relations*. Princeton University Press. doi:10.1515/9781400882779

Gilpin, R. (1989). *War and Change in World Politics*. Cambridge University Press.

Giones, F., & Brem, A. (2017). *Digital Technology Entrepreneurship: A Definition and Research Agenda* (SSRN Scholarly Paper No. 2984542). https://papers.ssrn.com/abstract=2984542 doi:10.22215/timreview/1076

Global damage costs from natural disasters. (2022). Our World in Data. https://ourworldindata.org/grapher/damage-costs-from-natural-disasters

Global Reporting Initiative. (2022). *GRI - Home*. GRI. https://www.globalreporting.org/

Gorbach, G. (2017, September 1). *Technology Spotlight: The Great Digitization of Industry*. SCMR. https://www.scmr.com/article/technology_spotlight_the_great_digitization_of_industry

Gordon, R. J. (2000). Does the "New Economy" Measure up to the Great Inventions of the Past? *The Journal of Economic Perspectives*, *14*(2), 49–74. doi:10.1257/jep.14.4.49

Gordon, R. J. (2012). *Is US Economic Growth Over? Faltering Innovation Confronts the Six Headwinds. The Centre for Economic Policy Research, Policy Insight No. 63*. Northwestern University.

Gowda, N., & Chakravorty, C. (2021). Comparative study on cryptocurrency transaction and banking transaction. *Global Transitions Proceedings*, *2*(2), 530–534. doi:10.1016/j.gltp.2021.08.064

Güğerçin, S. (2021). How Employees Survive in the Industry 5.0 Era: in-Demand Skills of the Near Future. [IDEAstudies]. *International Journal of Disciplines In Economics and Administrative Sciences Studies*, *7*(31), 524–533. doi:10.26728/ideas.452

Guleria, D., & Kaur, G. (2021). Bibliometric analysis of ecopreneurship using VOSviewer and RStudio Bibliometrix, 1989–2019. *Library Hi Tech*, *39*(4), 1001–1024. doi:10.1108/LHT-09-2020-0218

Guo, Y. M., Huang, Z. L., Guo, J., Guo, X. R., Li, H., Liu, M. Y., Ezzeddine, S., & Nkeli, M. J. (2021). A bibliometric analysis and visualization of blockchain. *Future Generation Computer Systems*, *116*, 316–332. doi:10.1016/j.future.2020.10.023

Gupta, P., Guha, S., & Krishnaswami, S. (2013). Firm growth and its determinants. *Journal of Innovation and Entrepreneurship*, *2*(1), 15. doi:10.1186/2192-5372-2-15

Gupta, R., Rathore, B., & Biswas, B. (2021). Impact of COVID-19 on supply chains: lessons learned and future research directions. In *International Journal of Quality and Reliability Management*. Emerald Group Holdings Ltd., doi:10.1108/IJQRM-06-2021-0161

Gupta, S., Drave, V. A., Bag, S., & Luo, Z. (2019). Leveraging Smart Supply Chain and Information System Agility for Supply Chain Flexibility. *Information Systems Frontiers*, *21*(3), 547–564. doi:10.100710796-019-09901-5

Gupta, S., Gupta, S., Mathew, M., & Sama, H. R. (2020). Prioritizing intentions behind investment in cryptocurrency: A fuzzy analytical framework. *Journal of Economic Studies (Glasgow, Scotland)*. doi:10.1108/JES-06-2020-0285

Gurusamy, V., Akbari, D., & Pipaliya, J. (2018). *Bitcoin: A cryptocurrency.*

Gusakov, A. (2020). The Role of Design Thinking for Achieving Leadership in the Digital Transformation of Business. Paper presented at the 6th International Conference on Social, economic, and academic leadership (ICSEAL-6-2019). 10.2991/assehr.k.200526.052

H&M Group. (2022). *Sustainability.* H&M Group. https://hmgroup.com/sustainability/

H.R. Asia. (2021). E-commerce Boom Driving Rapid Adoption of Cobots. *HR Asia.* https://hr.asia/featured/e-commerce-boom-driving-rapid-adoption-of-cobots/

Haftor, D. M., Climent, R. C., & Lundström, J. E. (2021). How machine learning activates data network effects in business models: Theory advancement through an industrial case of promoting ecological sustainability. *Journal of Business Research, 131*, 196–205. doi:10.1016/j.jbusres.2021.04.015

Hair, J. F. (2009). *Multivariate data analysis.*

Hajjaji, Y., Boulila, W., Farah, I. R., Romdhani, I., & Hussain, A. (2021). Big data and IoT-based applications in smart environments: A systematic review. *Computer Science Review, 39*, 100318. doi:10.1016/j.cosrev.2020.100318

Haleem, A., & Javaid, M. (2019). *Industry 5.0 and its expected applications in medical field.* Current Medicine Research and Practice. doi:10.1016/j.cmrp.2019.07.002

Haleem, A., Javaid, M., Singh, R. P., Rab, S., & Suman, R. (2022). Perspectives of cybersecurity for ameliorative Industry 4.0 era: A review-based framework. Industrial Robot. *The International Journal of Robotics Research and Application, 49*(3), 582–597. doi:10.1108/IR-10-2021-0243

Hallbäck, J., & Gabrielsson, P. (2011). Entrepreneurial Marketing Strategies During the Growth of International New Ventures. In E. Hutson, R. R. Sinkovics, & J. Berrill (Eds.), Firm-Level Internationalization, Regionalism and Globalization: Strategy, Performance and Institutional Change (pp. 177–197). Palgrave Macmillan UK. doi:10.1057/9780230305106_12

Hamel, G., & Prahalad, C. K. (1991). Corporate imagination and expeditionary marketing. *Harvard Business Review, 69*(4), 81–92. PMID:10112922

Harahap, N. J., and Rafika, M. (n.d.). *Industrial revolution 4 . 0 : and the impact on human*, 89–96.

Harris, L. A. (2021). Artificial Intelligence: Background, Selected Issues, and Policy Considerations. *Artificial Intelligence.*

Hartwell, R. M. (1963). The rising standards of living in England, 1800-1850. *The Economic History Review, 13*(3), 397–416. doi:10.2307/2599511

Hartwell, R. M. (1971). *The industrial revolution and economic growth.* Methuen and Co.

Hasbullah, N., Mahajar, A., & Ithnin, M. (2014). *A Conceptual Framework of Extending the Theory of Planned Behavior: The Role of Service Quality and Trust in the Consumer Cooperatives. 5.*

Hasbullah, N., & Mahajar, D. A. J. (2014). A Conceptual Framework of Extending the Theory of Planned Behavior. *The Role of Service Quality and Trust in the Consumer Cooperatives., 5*(12), 8.

Hashemi, H., Rajabi, R., & Brashear-Alejandro, T. G. (2022). COVID-19 research in management: An updated bibliometric analysis. *Journal of Business Research, 149*, 795–810. doi:10.1016/j.jbusres.2022.05.082 PMID:35669095

Hassoun, A., Aït-Kaddour, A., Abu-Mahfouz, A. M., Rathod, N. B., Bader, F., Barba, F. J., Biancolillo, A., Cropotova, J., Galanakis, C. M., Jambrak, A. R., Lorenzo, J. M., Måge, I., Ozogul, F., & Regenstein, J. (2022). The fourth industrial revolution in the food industry—Part I: Industry 4.0 technologies. *Critical Reviews in Food Science and Nutrition*, 1–17. doi:10.1080/10408398.2022.2034735 PMID:35114860

Hatton, T. J., & Williamson, J. G. (2005). *Global Migration and the World Economy: Two Centuries of Policy and Performance*. MIT Press. doi:10.7551/mitpress/3303.001.0001

Heartland (2022) *Industry 5.0: The Bridge Between Capitalism And Sustainability*. Heartland. https://www.heartland.io/sustainability-news/industry-5-0-the-bridge-between-capitalism-and-sustainability/

Heartland (2022) *Industry 5.0: The Bridge Between Capitalism And Sustainability*. Heartland. https://www.heartland.io/sustainability-news/industry-5-0-the-bridge-between-capitalism-and-sustainability/ (Accessed: 28 January 2023).

Heeks, R., & Nicholson, B. (2004). Software export success factors and strategies in 'follower nations. *Competition & Change*, *8*(3), 267–303. doi:10.1080/1024529042000301962

Helo, P., & Hao, Y. (2021). Artificial intelligence in operations management and supply chain management: An exploratory case study. *Production Planning and Control*, *33*(16), 1573–1590. doi:10.1080/09537287.2021.1882690

Henisz, W., Koller, T. and Nuttall, R. (2019) *Five ways that ESG creates value Getting your environmental, social, and governance (ESG) proposition right links to higher value creation. Here's why*. McKinsey.

Henisz, W., Koller, T. and Nuttall, R. (2019). Five ways that ESG creates value.

Herath, H. M. A., & Mahmood, R. (2014). Dimensions of Entrepreneurial Self-Efficacy and Firm Performance. *Global Journal of Management and Business Research, ((A) Volume XIV*, 21–28).

Hidayatno, A., Rahman, I., & Irminanda, K. R. (2019). A Conceptualization of Industry 4.0 Adoption on Textile and Clothing Sector in Indonesia. Paper presented at the *Proceedings of the 2019 5th International Conference on Industrial and Business Engineering*. ACM. 10.1145/3364335.3364351

Hidayatullah, S., Firdiansjah, A., Patalo, R. G., & Waris, A. (2019).. . *The Effect Of Entrepreneurial Marketing And Competitive Advantage On Marketing Performance.*, *8*(10), 5.

Higgins, J., & Green, S. (2011). Cochrane Handbook for Systematic Reviews of Interventions. *Handbook*. https://handbook-5-1.cochrane.org/

Higgins, D., & Elliott, C. (2011). Learning to make sense: What works in entrepreneurial education? *Journal of European Industrial Training*, *35*(4), 345–367. doi:10.1108/03090591111128324

Hills, G. E., Hultman, C. M., & Miles, M. P. (2008). The Evolution and Development of Entrepreneurial Marketing. *Journal of Small Business Management*, *46*(1), 99–112. doi:10.1111/j.1540-627X.2007.00234.x

Hirsch, J. E. (2007). Does the h index have predictive power? *Proceedings of the National Academy of Sciences of the United States of America*, *104*(49), 19193–19198. doi:10.1073/pnas.0707962104 PMID:18040045

Hirsch-Kreinsen, H., Weyer, J., & Wilkesmann, J. D. M. (2016). *"Industry 4.0" as Promising Technology: Emergence.* Semantics and Ambivlent Character.

Holimchayachotikul, P., Derrouiche, R., Damand, D., & Leksakul, K. (2014). Value creation through collaborative supply chain: Holistic performance enhancement road map. *Production Planning and Control*, *25*(11), 912–922. doi:10.1080/09537287.2013.780313

Holub, M., & Johnson, J. (2018). Bitcoin research across disciplines. *The Information Society*, *34*(2), 114–126. doi:10.1080/01972243.2017.1414094

Horváth, D., & Szabó, R. Z. (2019). Driving forces and barriers of Industry 4.0: Do multinational and small and medium-sized companies have equal opportunities? *Technological Forecasting and Social Change*, *146*, 119–132. doi:10.1016/j.techfore.2019.05.021

Hossain, S. T. (2020). Impacts of COVID-19 on the Agri-food Sector: Food Security Policies of Asian Productivity Organization Members. *Journal of Agricultural Sciences – Sri Lanka, 15*(2), 116. doi:10.4038/jas.v15i2.8794

Hossein Ronaghi, M. (2020). A Blockchain Maturity Model in Agricultural Supply chain. *Information Processing in Agriculture*. doi:10.1016/j.inpa.2020.10.004

Houdeloudi, Z., & Hajidimitriou, Y. A. (2014). *Success factors of internet use for exporting by Greek companies during the period of the financial crisis*. MIBES Transactions International Journal.

Houston, R. A. (1982). The development of literacy: Northern England, 1640-1750¢. *The Economic History Review*, *35*(2), 199–216.

Hoyer, C., Gunawan, I., & Reaiche, C. H. (2020). The Implementation of Industry 4.0 - A Systematic Literature Review of the Key Factors. *Systems Research and Behavioral Science*, *37*(4), 557–578. doi:10.1002res.2701

Huang, J. Z., Huang, W., & Ni, J. (2019). Predicting bitcoin returns using high-dimensional technical indicators. *Journal of Finance and Data Science*, *5*(3), 140–155. doi:10.1016/j.jfds.2018.10.001

Huang, M. H., & Rust, R. T. (2018). Artificial intelligence in service. *Journal of Service Research*, *21*(2), 155–172. doi:10.1177/1094670517752459

Hull, J. O. (1996). From Rostow to Chander to You: How revolutionary was the second industrial revolution? *The Journal of European Economic History*, *25*(1), 191–208.

Humphrey, J., & Memedovic, O. (2003). The Global Automotive Industry Value Chain: What Prospects for Upgrading by Developing Countries (SSRN Scholarly Paper No. 424560). doi:10.2139/ssrn.424560

Hunt, E.K. & Lautzenheiser, M. (2014), History of economic thought: a critical perspective. *PHI Learning*.

Hussain, F., Hussain, R., Hassan, S. A., & Hossain, E. (2020). Machine learning in IoT security: Current solutions and future challenges. *IEEE Communications Surveys and Tutorials*, *22*(3), 1686–1721. doi:10.1109/COMST.2020.2986444

Huynh, K. P., Henry, C. S., Nicholls, G., & Nicholson, M. W. (2020). Benchmarking bitcoin adoption in canada: Awareness, ownership and usage in 2018. *Ledger*, *5*, 74–88. doi:10.5195/ledger.2020.206

Hye, Q. M. A., & Lau, W. Y. (2015). Trade openness and economic growth: Empirical evidence from India. *Journal of Business Economics and Management*, *16*(1), 188–205. doi:10.3846/16111699.2012.720587

Hye, Q. M. A., Wizarat, S., & Lau, W. Y. (2013). Trade-led growth hypothesis: An empirical analysis of South Asian countries. *Economic Modelling*, *35*, 654–660. doi:10.1016/j.econmod.2013.07.040

IBISWorld—Industry Market Research, Reports, and Statistics. (2022, November 1). *Homepage*. IBIS World. https://www.ibisworld.com/default.aspx

IMF. (2019). *The world economic outlook*. IMF. https://www.imf.org/external/datamapper/datasets/WEO

Inci, A. C., & Lagasse, R. (2019). Cryptocurrencies: Applications and investment opportunities. *Journal of Capital Markets Studies*, *3*(2), 98–112. doi:10.1108/JCMS-05-2019-0032

Inditex. (2022). *Corporate governance.* Inditex. https://static.inditex.com/annual_report_2016/en/our-priorities/corporate-governance/

Ing, Lee, & Chan, Alipal, & Hamid. (2019). An Overview of the Rising Challenges in Implementing Industry 4.0. Int. J Sup. Chain. *Mgt*, *8*(6), 1181.

Innovation PEI report. (n.d.). E-exporting. http://www.gov.pe.ca/photos/original/IPEI_ebiz_exprt.pdf

Insights, F. B. (2022, January). *Home Automation Market Industry Reports*. FB Insights.

IoT Analytics. (2018). *State of the IoT 2018: Number of IoT devices now at 7B - Market accelerating*. https://iot-analytics.com/state-of-the-iot-update-q1-q2-2018-number-of-iot-devices-now-7b/

Irani, Z., Sharif, A. M., Lee, H., Aktas, E., Topaloğlu, Z., Van't Wout, T., & Huda, S. (2018). Managing food security through food waste and loss: Small data to big data. *Computers & Operations Research*, *98*, 367–383. doi:10.1016/j.cor.2017.10.007

Irem Onder University of Massachusetts Amherst. (2020). Blockchain: Is it the future for the tourism and hospitality industry? Tourism Economics Business and Finance of Tourism & Recreation, pp 1-7

Irianto, D. (2017). Традиційний Банкінг В Умовах Industry 4.0: Переваги Та Ризики Нових Технологій [Traditional Banking in the Conditions of Industry 4.0: Advantages and Risks of New Technologies]. *Ukrainian Society, 4 (63)*, 114–122. http://nbuv.gov.ua/UJRN/Usoc_2017_4_11%0Ahttps://doi.org/10.15407/socium2017.04.114

Ismagilova, E., Hughes, L., Rana, N. P., & Dwivedi, Y. K. (2020). Security, privacy and risks within smart cities: Literature review and development of a smart city interaction framework. *Information Systems Frontiers*, 1–22. PMID:32837262

Ismail, F., Kadir, A. A., Khan, M. A., and Yih, Y. P. (2019). *The Challenges and Role Played among Workers of Department Human Resources Management towards Industry 4 . 0 in SMEs. 2019*, 90–107. doi:10.18502/kss.v3i22.5046

ISO. (2019). *ISO/IEC 21823-1:2019*. https://www.iso.org: https://www.iso.org/standard/71885.html

ISO. (2020). *ISO/IEC 21823-2:2020*. https://www.iso.org: https://www.iso.org/standard/80986.html

ISO. (2020). *ISO/IEC TR 30164:2020*. https://www.iso.org: https://www.iso.org/standard/53284.html

ISO. (2020). *ISO/IEC TR 30166:2020*. https://www.iso.org: https://www.iso.org/standard/53286.html

ITRISA (International Trade Institute of South Africa). (2002). *Export Training and Education Needs Analysis and Recommendations Report*. Compiled for Trade and Investment South Africa.

ITU. (2020). How 5 technologies are changing global trade. *ITU*. https://www.itu.int/hub/2020/04/how-5-technologies-are-changing-global-trade/

Ivanov, D., Dolgui, A., & Sokolov, B. (2018). The impact of digital technology and Industry 4.0 on the ripple effect and supply chain risk analytics. *International Journal of Production Research*, *57*(3), 829–846. doi:10.1080/00207543.2018.1488086

Ivkov, M., Bleši, I., Dudi, B., Bartáková, G., & Dudi, Z. (2020). Are Future Professionals Willing to Implement Service Robots? Attitudes of Hospitality and Tourism Students towards Service Robotization. *Journal of Electronics, 9*, 1-16.

IyidoganE.AllenF.BoltonP.ChuprininO.IbragimovR.KacperczykM.KilicM.KirilenkoA.KosowskiR.SundaresanS.TinnK. (2020). *An Equilibrium Model of Proof-of-Work Cryptocurrencies **. https://ssrn.com/abstract=3152803

J. Johnson. (1988). Mixing humans and nonhumans together: The sociology of a door-closer. *Jstor*, 298–310.

Jacobs, F. R., & Chase, R. B. (2020). *Operations and Supply Chain Management* (16th ed.). Mcgraw-Hill Education.

Jacobs, F., Berry, W., Whybark, D., & Vollmann, T. (2019). *Manufacturing planning and control for supply chain management: APICS/CPIM Certification Edition* (2nd ed.). McGraw-Hill Education.

Jagtap, S., Saxena, P., & Salonitis, K. (2021). Food 4.0: Implementation of the Augmented Reality Systems in the Food Industry. *Procedia CIRP*, *104*, 1137–1142. doi:10.1016/j.procir.2021.11.191

Jalal, R. N. U. D., Alon, I., & Paltrinieri, A. (2021). A bibliometric review of cryptocurrencies as a financial asset. *Technology Analysis and Strategic Management*, 1–16. doi:10.1080/09537325.2021.1939001

Jaworski, B. J., & Kohli, A. K. (1993). Market orientation: Antecedents and consequences. *Journal of Marketing*, *57*(3), 53–70. doi:10.1177/002224299305700304

Jeevan, O, Saharuddin, P, & Do. (2018). An Evolution of a Nexus Between Malaysian Seaport Centric Logistic and Industrial Revolution 4.0: Current Status and Future Strategies. *International Journal of e-Navigation and Maritime Economy, 10*, 001-015.

Jennings, D. E., & Zeithaml, C. P. (1983). Locus of Control: A Review and Directions for Entrepreneurial Research. *Academy of Management Proceedings*, *1983*(1), 417–421. doi:10.5465/ambpp.1983.4976387

Jian, M. L., Vu, H. Q., Li, G., & Law, R. (2021). Understanding service attributes of robot hotels: A sentiment analysis of customer online reviews. *International Journal of Hospitality Management*.

Johansen, S., & Juselius, K. (1990). Maximum likelihood estimation and inference on cointegration with application to money demand. *Oxford Bulletin of Economics and Statistics*, *52*(2), 169–210. doi:10.1111/j.1468-0084.1990.mp52002003.x

Jolia, G. (2015). *International Economic Relations*. Georgian Technical University.

Jones, G., & Wadhwani, R. D. (2006). *Entrepreneurship and Business History: Renewing the Research Agenda. Working Paper No. 07-007.* Harvard Business School, Boston MA.

Jonker, N. (2019). What drives the adoption of crypto-payments by online retailers? *Electronic Commerce Research and Applications*, *35*, 100848. doi:10.1016/j.elerap.2019.100848

Joubert, R.-L., & Jokonya, O. (2021). A systematic literature review of factors affecting the adoption of technologies in food waste management. *Procedia Computer Science*, *181*, 1034–1040. doi:10.1016/j.procs.2021.01.298

JuhaniS. (2022). The Role Of Information Technology In Influencing Digitalization Of Contemporary Businesses. A Conceptual Review Of Literature. Https://Doi.Org/10.5281/Zenodo.6553360

Kagermann, H., Helbig, J., Hellinger, A., & Wahlster, W. (2013). *Recommendations for implementing the strategic initiative industrie 4.0: Securing the future of German manufacturing industry; final report of the Industrie 4.0 Working Group*. Forschungsunion.

Kamble, S. S., Gunasekaran, A., & Gawankar, S. A. (2020). Achieving sustainable performance in a data-driven agriculture supply chain: A review for research and applications. *International Journal of Production Economics*, *219*, 179–194. doi:10.1016/j.ijpe.2019.05.022

Kamble, S. S., Gunasekaran, A., & Sharma, R. (2018). Analysis of the driving and dependence power of barriers to adopt industry 4.0 in Indian manufacturing industry. *Computers in Industry*, *101*, 107–119. doi:10.1016/j.compind.2018.06.004

Kapil, S., & Kapil, K. N. (2021). Blockchain in hospitality and tourism industry way forward. *International Journal of Business and Economics*, *6*(2), 289–298.

Kariv, D., Cisneros, L., & Ibanescu, M. (2019). The role of entrepreneurial education and support in business growth intentions: The case of Canadian entrepreneurs. *Journal of Small Business and Entrepreneurship*, *31*(5), 433–460. doi:10.1080/08276331.2018.1468974

Karunarathne, S. M., Saxena, N., & Khan, M. K. (2021). Security and privacy in IoT smart healthcare. *IEEE Internet Computing*, *25*(4), 37–48. doi:10.1109/MIC.2021.3051675

Kaur, H., & Kushwaha, A. S. (2018). A review on integration of big data and IoT. *2018 4th International Conference on Computing Sciences (ICCS)* (pp. 200-203). IEEE.

Kearns, K. P. (1995). Accountability and Entrepreneurial Public Management: The Case of the Orange County Investment Fund. *Public Budgeting & Finance*, *15*(3), 3–21. doi:10.1111/1540-5850.01043

Kelly, C. D., & Jennions, M. D. (2006). The h index and career assessment by numbers. *Trends in Ecology & Evolution*, *21*(4), 167–170. doi:10.1016/j.tree.2006.01.005 PMID:16701079

Kennedy, P. (1987). Rise and fall of the great powers, (p. 149) based on Paul Bairoch's International Industrialization levels from 1970 to 1980.' *Journal of Economic History 1982, Vol. 11*(2), pp. 269-333.

Kennedy, R. (1987). *The rise and fall of the Great powers*. Random House.

Keohane, R. (1984). *After hegemony. Cooperation and Discord in the World Political Economy*. Princeton University Press.

Kessler, M. M. (1963). Bibliographic Coupling Between Scientific Papers. *American Documentation*, *14*(1), 10–25. doi:10.1002/asi.5090140103

Khan, J., Li, J. P., Ahamad, B., Parveen, S., Haq, A. U., Khan, G. A., & Sangaiah, A. K. (2020). SMSH: Secure surveillance mechanism on smart healthcare IoT system with probabilistic image encryption. *IEEE Access: Practical Innovations, Open Solutions*, *8*, 15747–15767. doi:10.1109/ACCESS.2020.2966656

Khin, S., & Kee, D. M. H. (2022). Factors influencing Industry 4.0 adoption. *Journal of Manufacturing Technology Management*. doi:10.1108/JMTM-03-2021-0111

Kholaif, M. M. N. H. K., & Ming, X. (2022). COVID-19's fear-uncertainty effect on green supply chain management and sustainability performances: The moderate effect of corporate social responsibility. *Environmental Science and Pollution Research International*, 1–22. doi:10.100711356-022-21304-9

Khozrevanidze, A. (2021). *Globalization, De-Globalization, and Tendencies of the International Business Development*. Caucasus International University.

Kim, S. (2007). Immigration, Industrial Revolution and Urban Growth in the United States, 1820–1920: Factor Endowments, Technology and Geography. *NBER Working Paper Series, Working Paper 12900,* Washington, DC.

Kim, S. K., & Huh, J. H. (2021). Artificial intelligence based electronic healthcare solution. *Advances in Computer Science and Ubiquitous Computing*, 575–581.

Kim, S., Kim, J., Badu-Baiden, F., Giroux M., & Choi, Y. (2021). Preference for robot service or human service in hotels? Impacts of the COVID-19 pandemic. *International Journal of Hospitality Management*.

Kimani, K., Oduol, V., & Langat, K. (2019). Cyber security challenges for IoT-based smart grid networks. *International Journal of Critical Infrastructure Protection*, *25*, 36–49. https://doi.org/10.1016/j.ijcip.2019.01.001

Kim, J. J., & Han, H. (2020, November). Hotel of the future: Exploring the attributes of a smart hotel adopting a mixed-methods approach. *Journal of Travel & Tourism Marketing*, *37*(7), 804–822. doi:10.1080/10548408.2020.1835788

Kitchenham, B., Pearl Brereton, O., Budgen, D., Turner, M., Bailey, J., & Linkman, S. (2009). Systematic literature reviews in software engineering – A systematic literature review. *Information and Software Technology*, *51*(1), 7–15. doi:10.1016/j.infsof.2008.09.009

Kittipanya-ngam, P., & Tan, K. H. (2019). A framework for food supply chain digitalization: Lessons from Thailand. *Production Planning and Control*, *31*(2-3), 158–172. doi:10.1080/09537287.2019.1631462

Knight, E., Daymond, J., & Paroutis, S. (2020). Design-led strategy: How to bring design thinking into the art of strategic management. *California Management Review*, *62*(2), 30–52. doi:10.1177/0008125619897594

Koberg, E., & Longoni, A. (2019). A systematic review of sustainable supply chain management in global supply chains. *Journal of Cleaner Production*, *207*, 1084–1098.

Koroma, J., Rongting, Z., Muhideen, S., Akintunde, T. Y., Amosun, T. S., Dauda, S. J., & Sawaneh, I. A. (2022a). Assessing citizens' behavior towards blockchain cryptocurrency adoption in the Mano River Union States: Mediation, moderation role of trust and ethical issues. *Technology in Society*, *68*, 101885. doi:10.1016/j.techsoc.2022.101885

Kotsantonis, S., & Serafeim, G. (2019). Four things no one will tell you about ESG data. *Journal of Applied Corporate Finance*, *31*(2), 50–58. https://dash.harvard.edu/bitstream/handle/1/37369828/kotsantonis%2Cserafeim_four-things-no-one-will.pdf?sequence=1&isAllowed=y

KPMG. (2016). *Global Manufacturing Outlook*. KPMG. https://assets.kpmg/content/dam/kpmg/pdf/2016/06/Global-Manufacturing-Outlook-2016.pdf

KPMG. (2017). *201706-CGF-KPMG-Top-of-Mind-Think-Like-a-Start-Up.pdf*. KPMG. https://www.theconsumergoodsforum.com/wp-content/uploads/2017/12/201706-CGF-KPMG-Top-of-Mind-Think-Like-a-Start-Up.pdf

KPMG. (2018). *A reality check for today's C-suite on Industry 4.0*. KPMG. https://assets.kpmg/content/dam/kpmg/xx/pdf/2018/11/a-reality-check-for-todays-c-suite-on-industry-4-0.pdf

KPMG. (2018). *Augmented Reality in the Automotive Sector: Opportunities and Challenges*. KPMG.

KPMG. (2018). *Digital Supply Chain – the hype and the risks*. KPMG. https://assets.kpmg/content/dam/kpmg/co/pdf/2019/01/Digital%20Supply%20Chain%20Hype%20And%20Risks.pdf

KPMG. (2018). *Supply Chain Big Data Series – Part 4*. KPMG. https://assets.kpmg/content/dam/kpmg/au/pdf/2017/disruptive-technologies-supply-chain-future.pdf

Kreiser, P. M., & Davis, J. (2010). Entrepreneurial Orientation and Firm Performance: The Unique Impact of Innovativeness, Proactiveness, and Risk-taking. *Journal of Small Business and Entrepreneurship*, *23*(1), 39–51. doi:10.1080/08276331.2010.10593472

Krumholz, A. (2017). Ethical considerations for augmented reality. *IEEE Consumer Electronics Magazine*, *6*(2), 25–30. doi:10.1109/MCE.2017.2693601

Kuan, K. K., & Chau, P. Y. (2001). A perception-based model for EDI adoption in small businesses using a technology–organization–environment framework. *Information & Management*, *38*(8), 507–521. doi:10.1016/S0378-7206(01)00073-8

Kudriashov, N., Prostav, I, Markov, S, Yadgarova, Y., & Taratukhin, V. (2016). Implementation of cloud services for advance management of steel transport for continuous casting production. *Annals of DAAAM & Proceedings, 27*. Gale Academic.

Kumar, R. (2019). India-China: Changing bilateral trade and its effect on economic growth. *The Singapore Economic Review*. doi:10.1142/S021759081950005X

Kumar, R. (2020). India & South Asia: Geopolitics, regional trade and economic growth spillovers. *The Journal of International Trade & Economic Development*, *29*(1), 69–88. doi:10.1080/09638199.2019.1636121

Kumar, S., Pandey, N., & Mukherjee, D. (2022). Cross Cultural and Strategic Management: A retrospective overview using bibliometric analysis. *Cross Cultural & Strategic Management*, *29*(1), 171–194. doi:10.1108/CCSM-08-2021-0147

Kumar, S., Sharma, D., Rao, S., Lim, W. M., & Mangla, S. K. (2022). Past, present, and future of sustainable finance: Insights from big data analytics through machine learning of scholarly research. *Annals of Operations Research*. doi:10.100710479-021-04410-8 PMID:35002001

Kumar, V., Shankar, R., & Vrat, P. (2021). An analysis of Industry 4.0 implementation-variables by using SAP-LAP and e-IRP approach. *Benchmarking*. doi:10.1108/BIJ-03-2021-0153

Kuznetsova, O., Kuznetsov, A., & Mcdonald, F. (2000). Entrepreneurial Qualities: A Case from Russia. *Journal of Small Business Management*, 38.

Labuschagne, C., Brent, A. C., & Van Erck, R. P. (2005). Assessing the sustainability performances of industries. *Journal of Cleaner Production*, *13*(4), 373–385. doi:10.1016/j.jclepro.2003.10.007

Lad, K. & Zade, A. (2020). *Role of Artificial Intelligence in Hotel Industry.*

Ladzani, W. M., & van Vuuren, J. J. (2002). Entrepreneurship Training for Emerging SMEs in South Africa. *Journal of Small Business Management*, *40*(2), 154–161. doi:10.1111/1540-627X.00047

Lakshmi. (2021, February 1). *Negative effects of technology & how to overcome them.* Mobicip. https://www.mobicip.com/blog/negative-effects-of-technology

Lambert, D. M., & Cooper, M. C. (2020). Issues in supply chain management. *Industrial Marketing Management*, *29*(1), 65–83.

Landes, D. S. (2003). *The unbound Prometheus: technological change and industrial development in Western Europe from 1750 to the present.* Cambridge University Press. doi:10.1017/CBO9780511819957

Lane, A. (2019, March 1). What is technology? *Open Learn.* https://www.open.edu/openlearn/science-maths-technology/engineering-technology/what-technology

Langkjaer-Bain, R. (2011). *Smart Meters Could Be Used To Spy On Tv Viewing, Say Researchers.*

Langley, D. J., Van Doorn, J., Ng, I. C., Stieglitz, S., Lazovik, A., & Boonstra, A. (2021). The Internet of Everything: Smart things and their impact on business models. *Journal of Business Research*, *122*, 853–863. doi:10.1016/j.jbusres.2019.12.035

Lanka, S., & Bajracharya, S. (2018). Incorporating big data with iot in data center analytics. *2018 International Conference on Smart Systems and Inventive Technology (ICSSIT)* (pp. 240-245). IEEE. 10.1109/ICSSIT.2018.8748507

Lankton, N., McKnight, D. H., & Thatcher, J. B. (2014). Incorporating trust-in-technology into Expectation Disconfirmation Theory. *The Journal of Strategic Information Systems*, *23*(2), 128–145. doi:10.1016/j.jsis.2013.09.001

Laosethakul, K., & Boulton, W. (2007). Critical Success Factors for E-commerce in Thailand: Cultural and Infrastructural Influences. *The Electronic Journal on Information Systems in Developing Countries*, *30*(1), 1–22. doi:10.1002/j.1681-4835.2007.tb00205.x

Laudon, K. C., & Traver, C. G. (2016). *E-commerce 2018: Business, technology, society* (14th ed.). Pearson. https://www.pearsonhighered.com/assets/preface/0/1/3/4/0134868064.pdf

Lawshe, C. H. (1975). A quantitative approach to content validity. *Personnel Psychology, 28*(4), 563–575. doi:10.1111/j.1744-6570.1975.tb01393.x

Le Roux, I., & Bengesi, K. M. K. (2014). Dimensions of entrepreneurial orientation and small and medium enterprise performance in emerging economies. *Development Southern Africa, 31*(4), 606–624. doi:10.1080/0376835X.2014.913474

LeCun, Y., Bengio, Y., & Hinton, G. (2015). Deep learning. *Nature, 521*(7553), 436–444. doi:10.1038/nature14539 PMID:26017442

Lee, E. (2017). Coevolution of human and Artificial Intelligences. *The Berkeley Blog.* https://blogs.berkeley.edu/2017/09/18/coevolution-of-human-and-artificial-intelligences/

Lee, S., Lee, M., & Jeong¸M. (2021). The role of virtual reality on information sharing and seeking behaviours. *Journal of Hospitality and Tourism Management*, 215-223.

Lee, H., Ahmed, U., Zhussupova, B., & Khalid, N. (2019). Impact of innovation capability and competitiveness on entrepreneurial orientation regarding to the entrepreneurial education in business performance among South Korean firms. *Polish Journal of Management Studies, 20*(2), 358–367. Advance online publication. doi:10.17512/pjms.2019.20.2.30

Lee, J., Bagheri, B., & Kao, H.-A. (2015). A cyber-physical systems architecture for industry 4.0-based manufacturing systems. *Manufacturing Letters, 3*, 18–23. doi:10.1016/j.mfglet.2014.12.001

Lee, K. P., Wu, B. H., & Peng, S. L. (2019). Deep-learning-based fault detection and diagnosis of air-handling units. *Building and Environment, 157*, 24–33. doi:10.1016/j.buildenv.2019.04.029

Lee, Y., Lee, S., & Kim, D.-Y. (2021). Exploring hotel guests' perceptions of using robot assistants. *Tourism Management Perspectives, 37*, 100781. doi:10.1016/j.tmp.2020.100781

Leipras, A. (2019). Determinants of export performance: Differences between service and manufacturing SMEs. *Service Business, 13*(1), 171–198. doi:10.100711628-018-0376-7

Leng, J., Sha, W., Wang, B., Zheng, P., Zhuang, C., Liu, Q., Wuest, T., Mourtzis, D., & Wang, L. (2022). Industry 5.0: Prospect and retrospect. *Journal of Manufacturing Systems, 65*, 279–295. doi:10.1016/j.jmsy.2022.09.017

Leone, D., Schiavone, F., Appio, F. P., & Chiao, B. (2021). How does artificial intelligence enable and enhance value co-creation in industrial markets? An exploratory case study in the healthcare ecosystem. *Journal of Business Research, 129*, 849–859. doi:10.1016/j.jbusres.2020.11.008

Leskovec, J., Adamic, L. A., & Huberman, B. A. (2007). The dynamics of viral marketing. *ACM Transactions on the Web, 1*(1), 5-es. doi:10.1145/1232722.1232727

Lezoche, M., Hernandez, J. E., Alemany Díaz, M., Panetto, H., & Kacprzyk, J. (2020). Agri-food 4.0: A survey of the supply chains and technologies for the future agriculture. *Computers in Industry, 117*, 103187. doi:10.1016/j.compind.2020.103187

Li, F. F., Jr., & Fu, K. (2009). *Factors Influencing the Growth of Small and Medium Sized Firms in Different Growth Stages. A Study of Four Chinese SMEs.* https://scholar.googleusercontent.com/scholar?q=cache:6ZhdI8kvYWAJ:scholar.google.com/+Factors+Influencing+the+Growth+of+Small+and+Medium+Sized+Firms+in+Different+Growth+Stages+&hl=en&as_sdt=0,5

Liang, K., & Dunn, P. (2008). ARE ENTREPRENEURS OPTIMISTIC, REALISTIC, BOTH OR FUZZY? RELATIONSHIP BETWEEN ENTREPRENEURIAL TRAITS AND ENTREPRENEURIAL LEARNING. *Academy of Entrepreneurship Journal, 14*, 51–76.

Liang, T.-P., You, J.-J., & Liu, C.-C. (2010). A resource-based perspective on information technology and firm performance: A meta analysis. *Industrial Management & Data Systems, 110*, 1138–1158. https://doi.org/10.1108/02635571011077807

Li, M., Yin, D., Qiu, H., & Bai, B. (2021, June). Examining the effects of AI contactless services on customer psychological safety, perceived value, and hospitality service quality during the COVID-19 pandemic. *Journal of Hospitality Marketing & Management.*

Limna, P. (2022). Artificial Intelligence (AI) in the Hospitality Industry: A Review Article. *International Journal of Computing Sciences Research.*

Lin, M., Huang, C., Xu, Z., & Chen, R. (2020). Evaluating IoT platforms using integrated probabilistic linguistic MCDM method. *IEEE Internet of Things Journal*, *7*(11), 11195–11208. doi:10.1109/JIOT.2020.2997133

Lippett, M. (2022, May). *Privacy-Intelligence-Agency-Security-In-The-Smart-Home.*

Li, T., Wang, K., Sueyoshi, T., & Wang, D. (2021). ESG: Research progress and future prospects. *Sustainability*, *13*(21), 11663. doi:10.3390u132111663

Liu, H., Hu, Z., & Hu, J. (2022). E-Commerce Logistics Intelligent Warehousing System Solution Based on Multimedia Technology. *Journal of Electrical and Computer Engineering*, *2022*, 2022. doi:10.1155/2022/1754797

Liu, Y., Ma, X., Shu, L., Hancke, G. P., & Abu-Mahfouz, A. M. (2021). From Industry 4.0 to Agriculture 4.0: Current Status, Enabling Technologies, and Research Challenges. *IEEE Transactions on Industrial Informatics*, *17*(6), 4322–4334. doi:10.1109/TII.2020.3003910

Liu, Z., Hu, B., Huang, B., Lang, L., Guo, H., & Zhao, Y. (2020). Decision Optimization of Low-Carbon Dual-Channel Supply Chain of Auto Parts Based on Smart City Architecture. *Complexity*, *2020*, e2145951. https://doi.org/10.1155/2020/2145951

Li, Y., Chi, Z., Liu, X., & Zhu, T. (2018). Passive-zigbee: Enabling zigbee communication in iot networks with 1000x+ less power consumption. *Proceedings of the 16th ACM conference on embedded networked sensor systems*, (pp. 159-171). 10.1145/3274783.3274846

Longley, R. (2019). *Glorious Revolution: Definition, History, and Significance.* ThoughtCo. https://www.thoughtco.com/glorious-revolution-definition-4692528

Looi, H. C. (2005). E-commerce adoption in Brunei Darussalam: A quantitative analysis of factors influencing its adoption. *Communications of the Association for Information Systems*, *15*(1), 3. doi:10.17705/1CAIS.01503

Lopez-Martin, C. (2022). Ramadan effect in the cryptocurrency markets. *Review of Behavioral Finance*. doi:10.1108/RBF-09-2021-0173

Love, J., & Chandra, R. (2005). Testing export-led growth in South Asia. *Journal of Economic Studies (Glasgow, Scotland)*, *32*(2), 132–145. doi:10.1108/01443580510600913

Love, P. E., & Irani, Z. (2004). An exploratory study of information technology evaluation and benefits management practices of SMEs in the construction industry. *Information & Management*, *42*(1), 227–242. doi:10.1016/j.im.2003.12.011

LSE. (2019). *Careers in Fast Moving Consumer Goods (FMCG).* LSE.https://info.lse.ac.uk/current-students/careers/information-and-resources/employment-sectors/consumer-goods

Lua, L., Caib, R., & Gursoy, D. (2019). Developing and validating a service robot integration willingness scale. *International Journal of Hospitality Management*, *80*, 36–51. doi:10.1016/j.ijhm.2019.01.005

Lu, H.-P., & Weng, C.-I. (2018). Smart manufacturing technology, market maturity analysis and technology roadmap in the computer and electronic product manufacturing industry. *Technological Forecasting and Social Change*, *133*, 85–94. doi:10.1016/j.techfore.2018.03.005

Lumpkin, G. T., Cogliser, C. C., & Schneider, D. R. (2009). Understanding and Measuring Autonomy: An Entrepreneurial Orientation Perspective. *Entrepreneurship Theory and Practice*, *33*(1), 47–69. doi:10.1111/j.1540-6520.2008.00280.x

Lumpkin, G. T., & Dess, G. G. (2001). Linking two dimensions of entrepreneurial orientation to firm performance: The moderating role of environment and industry life cycle. *Journal of Business Venturing*, *16*(5), 429–451. doi:10.1016/S0883-9026(00)00048-3

Lumpkin, G. T., Wales, W. J., & Ensley, M. D. (2006). Entrepreneurial orientation effects on new venture performance: The moderating role of venture age. *Academy of Management Proceedings*, *2006*(1), N1–N6. doi:10.5465/ambpp.2006.22898263

Luong, N. A. M., & Wang, L. (2019). Factors Influencing E-commerce Usage within Internationalisation: A study of Swedish small and medium-sized fashion retailers. *Science Direct.*

Lupton, D. (2020). The Internet of Things: Social dimensions. *Sociology Compass*, *14*(4). https://doi.org/10.1111/soc4.12770

Luther, W. J. (2016). Bitcoin and the Future of Digital Payments. In *Source: The Independent Review, 20*(3). https://about.jstor.org/terms

Luthra, S., Mangla, S. K., Garg, D., & Kumar, A. (2018). Internet of Things (IoT) in Agriculture Supply Chain Management: A Developing Country Perspective. In Y. K. Dwivedi, N. P. Rana, E. L. Slade, M. A. Shareef, M. Clement, A. C. Simintiras, & B. Lal (Eds.), Emerging Markets from a Multidisciplinary Perspective: Challenges, Opportunities and Research Agenda (pp. 209–220). Springer International Publishing. https://doi.org/10.1007/978-3-319-75013-2_16.

Lu, Y., Zheng, H., Chand, S., Xia, W., Liu, Z., Xu, X., Wang, L., Qin, Z., & Bao, J. (2022). Outlook on human-centric manufacturing towards Industry 5.0. *Journal of Manufacturing Systems*, *62*, 612–627. doi:10.1016/j.jmsy.2022.02.001

M. C. Elish, & Boyd, D. (2017). Situating methods in the magic of Big Data and AI. *Tandfonline.*

MacGregor, R. C., & Vrazalic, L. (2005). A basic model of electronic commerce adoption barriers: A study of regional small businesses in Sweden and Australia. *Journal of Small Business and Enterprise Development*, *12*(4), 510–527. doi:10.1108/14626000510628199

Mahalingam, S. & Ashokkumar, B. (2020). An Overview of Digital Marketing Practices in India. *International Journal of Research in Engineering, Science and Management 3*(9), 66-70.

Majumdar, A., Garg, H., & Jain, R. (2020). Managing the barriers of Industry 4.0 adoption and implementation in textile and clothing industry: Interpretive structural model and triple helix framework. *Computers in Industry*, *103372*. doi:10.1016/j.compind.2020.103372

Makhdoom, I., Abolhasan, M., Abbas, H., & Ni, W. (2019). Blockchain's adoption in IoT: The challenges, and a way forward. *Journal of Network and Computer Applications*, *125*, 251–279. doi:10.1016/j.jnca.2018.10.019

Makori, E. O. (2023). Digital Innovations and Applications in Information Science and Humanistic Knowledge. In Handbook of Research on Technological Advances of Library and Information Science in Industry 5.0 (pp. 397-414). IGI Global.

Maldifassi, J. O., & Caorsi, J. C. (2014). Export success factors of small and medium-sized firms in Chile. *Journal of Small Business and Enterprise Development*, *21*(3), 450–469. doi:10.1108/JSBED-03-2014-0053

Malhotra, N., Hall, J., Shaw, M., & Oppenheim, P. (2006). *Marketing research: An applied orientation*. Pearson Education Australia. doi:10.1108/S1548-6435(2006)2

Malik, A., Ul Haq, M. I., Raina, A., & Gupta, K. (2022). 3D printing towards implementing Industry 4.0: Sustainability aspects, barriers and challenges. Industrial Robot. *The International Journal of Robotics Research and Application, 49*(3), 491–511. doi:10.1108/IR-10-2021-0247

Manavalan, E., & Jayakrishna, K. (2019). A review of Internet of Things (IoT) embedded sustainable supply chain for industry 4.0 requirements. *Computers & Industrial Engineering, 127*(1), 925–953. doi:10.1016/j.cie.2018.11.030

Manufacturing Leadership Council. (2017). *A Practical Guide to Scale Industry 4.0*. The Manufacturing Leadership Council. https://www.manufacturingleadershipcouncil.com/a-practical-guide-to-scale-industry-15158/

Margherita, A., Elia, G., & Klein, M. (2021). Managing the COVID-19 emergency: A coordination framework to enhance response practices and actions. *Technological Forecasting and Social Change, 166*, 120656. doi:10.1016/j.techfore.2021.120656 PMID:33551496

Mashayekhy, Y., Babaei, A., Yuan, X.-M., & Xue, A. (2022). Impact of Internet of Things (IoT) on Inventory Management: A Literature Survey. *Logistics, 6*(2), Article 2. doi:10.3390/logistics6020033

Mason, C., & Brown, R. (2014). *ENTREPRENEURIAL ECOSYSTEMS AND GROWTH ORIENTED ENTREPRENEURSHIP Background paper prepared for the workshop organised by the OECD LEED Programme and the Dutch Ministry of Economic Affairs on.*

Massaro, A., & Galiano, A. (2020). Re-engineering process in a food factory: An overview of technologies and approaches for the design of pasta production processes. *Production & Manufacturing Research, 8*(1), 80–100. doi:10.1080/21693277.2020.1749180

Massaro, M., Dal Mas, F., Jabbour, C. J. C., & Bagnoli, C. (2020). Crypto-economy and new sustainable business models: Reflections and projections using a case study analysis. *Corporate Social Responsibility and Environmental Management, 27*(5), 2150–2160. doi:10.1002/csr.1954

Mayer, B., Sorko, S. R., & Pessl, E. (2017). Roadmap Industry 4.0 – Implementation Guideline for Enterprises. International Journal of Science. *Technology in Society, 5*(6), 193. doi:10.11648/j.ijsts.20170506.14

Mazambani, L., & Mutambara, E. (2020). Predicting FinTech innovation adoption in South Africa: The case of cryptocurrency. *African Journal of Economic and Management Studies, 11*(1), 30–50. doi:10.1108/AJEMS-04-2019-0152

Mazzucato & Tancioni. (2008). Innovation and idiosyncratic risk: an industry-and firm-level analysis. *Industrial and Corporate Change, 17*(4), 779-811.

Mccain, K. W., Verner, J. M., Hislop, G. W., Evanco, W., & Cole, V. (2005). The use of bibliometric and knowledge elicitation techniques to map a knowledge domain: Software Engineering in the 1990s. In Budapest Scientometrics, and Springer, 65(1).

Mckenna, R. (1995). Real-time marketing. *Harvard Business Review, 73*(4). https://elibrary.ru/item.asp?id=2473650

McKinsey & Company. (2015). *Unlocking_the_potential_of_the_internet_of_things_executive_summary.pdf*. McKinsey. https://www.mckinsey.com/~/media/mckinsey/industries/technology%20media%20and%20telecommunications/high%20tech/our%20insights/the%20internet%20of%20things%20the%20value%20of%20digitizing%20the%20physical%20world/unlocking_the_potential_of_the_internet_of_things_executive_summary.pdf

McKinsey & Company. (2017). *Additive manufacturing: A long-term game changer for manufacturers.* McKinsey. https://www.mckinsey.com/capabilities/operations/our-insights/additive-manufacturing-a-long-term-game-changer-for-manufacturers

McKinsey & Company. (2019). *Perspectives-on-retail-and-consumer-goods_issue-8.pdf.* McKinsey. https://www.mckinsey.com/~/media/mckinsey/industries/retail/our%20insights/perspectives%20on%20retail%20and%20consumer%20goods%20number%208/perspectives-on-retail-and-consumer-goods_issue-8.pdf

McKinsey & Company. (2022). *The state of AI in 2022—And a half decade in review.* McKinsey & Company. https://www.mckinsey.com/capabilities/quantumblack/our-insights/the-state-of-ai-in-2022-and-a-half-decade-in-review

McKinsey Digital. (2016). *Industry 4.0 after the initial hype Where manufacturers are finding value and how they can best capture it.* McKinsey. https://www.mckinsey.com/~/media/mckinsey/business%20functions/mckinsey%20digital/our%20insights/getting%20the%20most%20out%20of%20industry%204%200/mckinsey_industry_40_2016.ashx

McMaster, M., Nettleton, C., Tom, C., Xu, B., Cao, C., & Qiao, P. (2020). Risk management: Rethinking fashion supply chain management for multinational corporations in light of the COVID-19 outbreak. *Journal of Risk and Financial Management, 13*(8), 173. doi:10.3390/jrfm13080173

Mcmullan, W. E., & Long, W. A. (1987). Entrepreneurship education in the nineties. *Journal of Business Venturing, 2*(3), 261–275. doi:10.1016/0883-9026(87)90013-9

Meghani, K. (2020). Use of Artificial Intelligence and Blockchain in Banking Sector: A Study of Scheduled Commercial Banks in India. *Indian Journal of Applied Research*, 10.

Meidute-Kavaliauskiene, I., Çi˘gdem, S., Yıldız, B., & Davidavicius, S. (2021). The Effect of Perceptions on Service Robot Usage Intention: A Survey Study in the Service Sector. *Journal of Sustainability.*

Melewar, T. C., & Smith, N. (2003). The internet revolution: Some global marketing implications. *Marketing Intelligence & Planning, 2*(6), 363–369. doi:10.1108/02634500310499220

Mell, P., & Grance, T. (2011). The NIST definition of cloud computing. *National Institute of Standards and Technology, Special Publication 800-145.*

Mendoza-Tello, J. C., Mora, H., Pujol-López, F. A., & Lytras, M. D. (2018). Social Commerce as a Driver to Enhance Trust and Intention to Use Cryptocurrencies for Electronic Payments. *IEEE Access: Practical Innovations, Open Solutions, 6*, 50737–50751. doi:10.1109/ACCESS.2018.2869359

Merig'O, J. M., Mas-Tur, A., Roig-Tierno, N., & Ribeiro-Soriano, D. (2015). A bibliometric overview of the journal of business research between 1973 and 2014. *Journal of Business Research, 68*(12), 2645–2653. doi:10.1016/j.jbusres.2015.04.006

Messersmith, J. G., & Wales, W. J. (2013). Entrepreneurial orientation and performance in young firms: The role of human resource management. *International Small Business Journal, 31*(2), 115–136. doi:10.1177/0266242611416141

Migdadi, M. M., Abu Zaid, M. K. S., Al-Hujran, O. S., & Aloudat, A. M. (2016). An empirical assessment of the antecedents of electronic-business implementation and the resulting organizational performance. *Internet Research, 26*(3), 661–688. doi:10.1108/IntR-08-2014-0203

Milohnić, I., & Madžar, D. (2017). Importance of creativity in entrepreneurship. *4th International Scientific Conference ToSEE - Tourism in Southern and Eastern Europe 2017 "Tourism and Creative Industries: Trends and Challenges,* (pp. 409–421). IEEE.

Ministry of Commerce and Industry. (n.d.). *India.* Ministry of Commerce and Industry. https://commerce.gov.in/

Mintzberg, H., & Waters, J. A. (1985). Of strategies, deliberate and emergent. *Strategic Management Journal*, *6*(3), 257–272. doi:10.1002mj.4250060306

Mithas, S., Chen, Z., Saldanha, T., & De Oliveira Silveira, A. (2022). How will artificial intelligence and industry 4.0 emerging technologies transform operations management? *Production and Operations Management*, *31*(12), 4475–4487. doi:10.1111/poms.13864

Mohajan, H. K. (2020). The Second Industrial Revolution has Brought Modern Social and Economic Developments. *Journal of Social Sciences and Humanities*, *6*(1), 1–14.

Mohamed, M. (2019). Challenges and Benefits of Industry 4.0: An overview. *International Journal of Supply and Operations Management*, *5*(3), 256–265. doi:10.22034/2018.3.7

Mohammadzadeh, M., Poloee, M., & Ghari, T. (2016). *Export readiness assessment of ten Iranian pharmaceutical companies and comparison with their export performance*. Research Gate.

Mohammadzadeh, M. (2012). An analysis of the relationship between staff qualification and export readiness of pharmaceutical companies: The case of Iran. *Iranian journal of pharmaceutical research. IJPR*, *11*(3), 985. PMID:24250528

Moktadir, M., Ali, S. M., Kusi-Sarpong, S., & Shaikh, M. A. A. (2018). Assessing challenges for implementing Industry 4.0: Implications for process safety and environmental protection. *Process Safety and Environmental Protection*, *117*, 730–741. doi:10.1016/j.psep.2018.04.020

Moodley, S. (2002). Connecting to global markets in the internet age: The case of South African wooden furniture producers. *Development Southern Africa*, *19*(5), 641–658. doi:10.1080/03768835022000019338

Moon, B. J., & Jain, S. (2007). Determinants and outcomes of internet marketing activities of exporting firms. *Journal of Global Marketing*, *20*(4), 55–71. doi:10.1300/J042v20n04_05

Morakanyane, R., Grace, A., & O'Reilly, P. (2017, January 1). Conceptualizing Digital Transformation in Business Organizations: A Systematic Review of Literature. *BLED 2017 Proceedings*. AIS eLibrary. https://aisel.aisnet.org/bled2017/21

Morris, M. H., Schindehutte, M., & LaForge, R. W. (2002). Entrepreneurial Marketing: A Construct for Integrating Emerging Entrepreneurship and Marketing Perspectives. *Journal of Marketing Theory and Practice*, *10*(4), 1–19. doi:10.1080/10696679.2002.11501922

Morse, J. M. (2010). Simultaneous and sequential qualitative mixed method designs. *Qualitative Inquiry*, *16*(6), 483–491. doi:10.1177/1077800410364741

Mourtzis, D., Angelopoulos, J., & Panopoulos, N. (2022). A Literature Review of the Challenges and Opportunities of the Transition from Industry 4.0 to Society 5.0. *Energies*, *15*(17), 6276. doi:10.3390/en15176276

Mueller, S. L., & Thomas, A. S. (2001). Culture and entrepreneurial potential: A nine country study of locus of control and innovativeness. *Journal of Business Venturing*, *16*(1), 51–75. doi:10.1016/S0883-9026(99)00039-7

Mujahid, S., Mubarik, S., & Naghavi, N. (2019). Prioritizing dimensions of entrepreneurial ecosystem: A proposed framework. *Journal of Global Entrepreneurship Research*, *9*(1), 51. doi:10.118640497-019-0176-0

Mukherjee, D., Kumar, S., Donthu, N., & Pandey, N. (2021). Research Published in Management International Review from 2006 to 2020: A Bibliometric Analysis and Future Directions. In Management International Review, 61(5), 599–642. Springer Science and Business Media Deutschland GmbH. doi:10.100711575-021-00454-x

Muller, H. (2022, May 20). *Smart-Home-Data-Privacy*.

Müßigmann, B., von der Gracht, H., & Hartmann, E. (2020). Blockchain Technology in Logistics and Supply Chain Management—A Bibliometric Literature Review From 2016 to January 2020. *IEEE Transactions on Engineering Management, 67*(4), 988–1007. https://doi.org/10.1109/TEM.2020.2980733

Nadeem, M. A., Liu, Z., Pitafi, A. H., Younis, A., & Xu, Y. (2021a). Investigating the Adoption Factors of Cryptocurrencies—A Case of Bitcoin: Empirical Evidence From China. *SAGE Open, 11*(1). doi:10.1177/2158244021998704

Nag, B., & Sikdar, C. (2011). Welfare implication of India–ASEAN FTA: An analysis using GTAP model. *Working paper no. EC-11-06*, Indian Institute of Foreign Trade, New Delhi

Nagoor, B. H., & Kumar, C. N. (2010). Assessing the impact of the ASEAN-India FTA on the tea industry. *Economic and Political Weekly, 45*(44), 112–116.

Nahavandi, S. (2019). INDUSTRY 5. 0 definition. *Sustainability, 11*, 43–71.

Nahavandi, S. (2019). Industry 5.0—A Human-Centric Solution. *Multidisciplinary Digital Publishing Institute, 11*(16), 4371. doi:10.3390/SU11164371

Nahavandi, S. (2019). Industry 5.0—A human-centric solution. *Sustainability, 11*(16), 4371. doi:10.3390u11164371

Nahodil, P., & Vítků, J. (2013). How to Design an Autonomous Creature Based on Original Artificial Life Approaches. *Beyond. Artificial Intelligence*, 161–180.

Nair, S., Sundar, S., & Mangadu Paramasivam, G. (2020). Role of entrepreneurial education in nurturing entrepreneurial orientation among engineering students. *Asia Pacific Journal of Innovation and Entrepreneurship, 14*(2), 139–149. doi:10.1108/APJIE-05-2019-0031

Naldi, L., Nordqvist, M., Sjöberg, K., & Wiklund, J. (2007). Entrepreneurial Orientation, Risk Taking, and Performance in Family Firms. *Family Business Review, 20*(1), 33–47. doi:10.1111/j.1741-6248.2007.00082.x

Narayanan, A. (2016). *Bitcoin and cryptocurrency technologies : a comprehensive introduction.*

Narayanasamy, K. (2008). The Role of Centralized Knowledge Development Centre for Success of SME Sector. *Communications of the IBIMA, 2*, 16.

Naumann, C. (2017). Entrepreneurial Mindset: A Synthetic Literature Review. *Entrepreneurial Business and Economics Review, 5*(3), 149–172. doi:10.15678/EBER.2017.050308

Naveen, B. R. (2023). Industry 5.0 has the potential to make India a smarter hub. *Industry 5.0 Implementation: Opportunities and Challenges India Chapter book.*

Naveen, B. R. (2023). Industry 5.0 Implementation: Opportunities and Challenges. *IndiaChapter.in.* https://indiachapter.in/index.php?/user/article/2/2/121

NC State University. (2004) *The SCOR Model for Supply Chain Strategic Decisions | SCM | Supply Chain Resource Cooperative (SCRC).* North Carolina State University. https://scm.ncsu.edu/scm-articles/article/the-scor-model-for-supply-chain-strategic-decisions

Nestle. (2020, July 24). *Nestlé speeds up factory support with augmented reality.* Nestlé Global. https://www.nestle.com/media/news/nestle-factory-support-augmented-reality

Nica, E., Stan, C. I., Luțan, A. G., & Oașa, R. S. (2021). Internet of things-based real-time production logistics, sustainable industrial value creation, and artificial intelligence-driven big data analytics in cyber-physical smart manufacturing systems. *Economics, Management, and Financial Markets, 16*(1), 52. doi:10.22381/emfm16120215

Niinimäki, K., Peters, G., Dahlbo, H., Perry, P., Rissanen, T., & Gwilt, A. (2020). The environmental price of fast fashion. *Nature Reviews Earth & Environment*, *1*(4), 189–200. doi:10.103843017-020-0039-9

Niller, E. (2019). How the second industrial revolution changed Americans lives. *History.com.*

Nilsson, N. J. (2010). *The quest for artificial intelligence: A history of ideas and achievements.* Cambridge University Press.

Nimawat, D., & Gidwani, B. D. (2021). Identification of cause and effect relationships among barriers of Industry 4.0 using decision-making trial and evaluation laboratory method. *Benchmarking*, *28*(8), 2407–2431. doi:10.1108/BIJ-08-2020-0429

Niranjan, K., Narayana, K. S., & Rao, M. V. A. L. N. (2021). Role of Artifical Intelligence in Logistics and Supply Chain. *2021 International Conference on Computer Communication and Informatics (ICCCI)*, 1–3. doi:10.1109/ICCCI50826.2021.9402625

NIST. (2020-2021). *NISTIR 8259 Series.* Retrieved from https://www.nist.gov: https://www.nist.gov/itl/applied-cybersecurity/nist-cybersecurity-iot-program/nistir-8259-series

NIST. (2021). *IoT Product Criteria.* https://www.nist.gov: https://www.nist.gov/itl/executive-order-14028-improving-nations-cybersecurity/iot-product-criteria

NIST. (2021). *SP 800-213 Series.* https://www.nist.gov: https://www.nist.gov/itl/applied-cybersecurity/nist-cybersecurity-iot-program/sp-800-213-series

Njoroge, C. W. (2013). *The Effect Of Entrepreneurial Educationandtraining On Development Of Small And Medium Size Enterprises In Githunguri District- Kenya. 1*(8), 22.

Noyons, E. C., Moed, H. F., & Luwel, M. (1999). Combining mapping and citation analysis for evaluative bibliometric purposes: A bibliometric study. *Journal of the American Society for Information Science*, *50*(2), 115–131. doi:10.1002/(SICI)1097-4571(1999)50:2<115::AID-ASI3>3.0.CO;2-J

Obeidat, B., Tarhini, A., Masa'deh, R., & Aqqad, N. (2017). The impact of intellectual capital on innovation via the mediating role of knowledge management: A structural equation modeling approach. *International Journal of Knowledge Management Studies*, *8*(4), 273–298. doi:10.1504/IJKMS.2017.087071

Obschonka, M., Silbereisen, R. K., & Schmitt-Rodermund, E. (2010). Entrepreneurial intention as developmental outcome. *Journal of Vocational Behavior*, *77*(1), 63–72. doi:10.1016/j.jvb.2010.02.008

Oliveira-Dias, D., Maqueira-Marín, J. M., & Moyano-Fuentes, J. (2022). The link between information and digital technologies of industry 4.0 and agile supply chain: Mapping current research and establishing new research avenues. *Computers & Industrial Engineering*, *167*, 108000. doi:10.1016/j.cie.2022.108000

Oliveira, T., & Martins, M. F. (2010). Understanding e-business adoption across industries in European countries. *Industrial Management & Data Systems*, *110*(9), 1337–1354. doi:10.1108/02635571011087428

Ontario. (2021). *E-exporting*. Ontario. https://www.ontario.ca/page/e-exporting

Ooi, S. K., Ooi, C. A., Yeap, J. A. L., & Goh, T. H. (2021). Embracing Bitcoin: Users' perceived security and trust. *Quality & Quantity*, *55*(4), 1219–1237. doi:10.100711135-020-01055-w

Orús, C., Iba'nez-Sanchez, S., & Flavian, C. (2021). Enhancing the customer experience with virtual and augmented reality: The impact of content and device type. *International Journal of Hospitality Management*, *98*, 103019. doi:10.1016/j.ijhm.2021.103019

Owen, & Darkwa. (2000). *Role of multipurpose community telecentres in accelerating national development in Ghana.* First Monday.

Oyewola, D. O., & Dada, E. G. (2022). Exploring machine learning: A scientometrics approach using bibliometrix and VOSviewer. *SN Applied Sciences*, *4*(5), 143. doi:10.100742452-022-05027-7 PMID:35434524

Özdemir, V., & Hekim, N. (2018). Birth of industry 5.0: Making sense of big data with artificial intelligence,"the internet of things" and next-generation technology policy. *OMICS: A Journal of Integrative Biology*, *22*(1), 65–76. doi:10.1089/omi.2017.0194 PMID:29293405

Palombarini, J. A., & Martínez, E. C. (2021). End-to-end on-line rescheduling from Gantt chart images using deep reinforcement learning. *International Journal of Production Research*, 1–30.

Pal, P., & Dasgupta, M. (2008). Does a Free Trade Agreement with ASEAN make sense? *Economic and Political Weekly*, *43*(46), 8–12.

Pal, P., & Dasgupta, M. (2009). The ASEAN-India Free Trade Agreement: An Assessment. *Economic and Political Weekly*, *44*(38), 11–15.

Pal, R., Shen, B., & Sandberg, E. (2019). Circular fashion supply chain management: Exploring impediments and prescribing future research agenda. *Journal of Fashion Marketing and Management*. doi:10 doi:.1108/JFMM-07-2019-166

Pant, H. V., & Deb, A. (2017). India-ASEAN Partnership at 25. Observer Research Foundation (ORF) Issue Brief, 189.

Parente, R., & Feola, R. (2013). Entrepreneurial intent and entrepreneurial commitment of young researchers. *International Journal of Technology Management & Sustainable Development*, *12*(2), 155–166. doi:10.1386/tmsd.12.2.155_1 PMID:28057083

Parhi, S., Joshi, K., Wuest, T., & Akarte, M. (2022). Factors Affecting Industry 4.0 Adoption - A Hybrid SEM-ANN Approach. *Computers & Industrial Engineering*, *108062*, 108062. doi:10.1016/j.cie.2022.108062

Partida, B. (2019, January 7). *Technology benefits sales and operations planning*. SCMR. https://www.scmr.com/article/technology_benefits_sales_and_operations_planning

Patki, A., & Sople, V. (2020). Indian banking sector: Blockchain implementation, challenges and way forward. *Journal of Banking and Financial Technology*, *4*(1), 65–73. doi:10.100742786-020-00019-w

Patrik Salmela, T. A. (2021, January 8). *Ericsson Blog*.

Paul, J., & Barari, M. (2022). Meta-analysis and traditional systematic literature reviews—What, why, when, where, and how? *Psychology and Marketing*, *39*(6), 1099–1115. https://doi.org/10.1002/mar.21657

Paul, J., & Bhukya, R. (2021). Forty-five years of International Journal of Consumer Studies: A bibliometric review and directions for future research. *International Journal of Consumer Studies*, *45*(5), 937–963. doi:10.1111/ijcs.12727

Payton, F. C. (2000). Lessons learned from three interorganizational health care information systems. *Information & Management*, *37*(6), 311–321. doi:10.1016/S0378-7206(99)00057-9

Pedersen, L., Fitzgibbons, S., & Pomorski, L. (2021). Responsible investing: The ESG-efficient frontier. *Journal of Financial Economics*, *142*(2), 572–597. doi:10.1016/j.jfineco.2020.11.001

Pelet, J.-E., Lick, E., & Taieb, B. (2019). *Internet of Things and Artificial Intelligence in the Hotel Industry: Which Opportunities and Threats for Sensory Marketing?* Springer Nature.

Pereira, A. C., & Romero, F. (2017). A review of the meanings and the implications of the Industry 4.0 concept. *Procedia Manufacturing*, *13*, 1206–1214. doi:10.1016/j.promfg.2017.09.032

Pesaran, M. H., Shin, Y., & Smith, R. J. (2001). Bounds testing approaches to the analysis of level relationships. *Journal of Applied Econometrics*, *16*(3), 289–326. doi:10.1002/jae.616

Peters, G., Li, M., & Lenzen, M. (2021). The need to decelerate fast fashion in a hot climate-A global sustainability perspective on the garment industry. *Journal of Cleaner Production*, *295*, 126390. doi:10.1016/j.jclepro.2021.126390

Phase, A., & Mhetre, N. (2018). *Using IoT in Supply Chain Management. 4*(2). https://d1wqtxts1xzle7.cloudfront.net/56617116/IJET-V4I2P148-libre.pdf

PHDCCI. (n.d.). *PHD Chamber of Commerce and Industry*. PHDCCI. www.phdcci.in

Phillips, S., Thai, V. V., & Halim, Z. (2019). Airline value chain capabilities and CSR performance: The connection between CSR leadership and CSR culture with CSR performance, customer satisfaction and financial performance. *The Asian Journal of Shipping and Logistics*, *35*(1), 30–40. doi:10.1016/j.ajsl.2019.03.005

Philosophy, L. (2022). *DigitalCommons @ University of Nebraska - Lincoln Challenges of The Industrial Revolution Era 1 . 0 to 5 . 0* . University Digital Library In Indoensia.

Pillai, S. G., Haldorai, K., Seo, W. S., & Kim, W. G. (2021,). COVID-19 and hospitality 5.0: Redefining hospitality operations. *International Journal of Hospitality Management*, *94*, 102869. doi:10.1016/j.ijhm.2021.102869 PMID:34785847

Pitardi, V., Wirtz, J., Paluch S., &. Kunz, W. (2021) Service robots, agency and embarrassing service encounters. *Journal of Service Management Emerald Publishing Limited.*

Pittaway, L., & Cope, J. (2007). Entrepreneurship Education: A Systematic Review of the Evidence. *International Small Business Journal*, *25*(5), 479–510. doi:10.1177/0266242607080656

Poon, J. M. L., Ainuddin, R. A., & Junit, S. H. (2006). Effects of Self-concept Traits and Entrepreneurial Orientation on Firm Performance. *International Small Business Journal*, *24*(1), 61–82. doi:10.1177/0266242606059779

Poon, S., & Swatman, P. M. C. (1997). Internet-based small business communications: Seven Australian case. *The PACIS Conference*, Brisbane, Australia. 10.1080/10196789700000019

Porambage, P., Ylianttila, M., Schmitt, C., Kumar, P., Gurtov, A., & Vasilakos, A. v. (2016). The Quest for Privacy in the Internet of Things. *IEEE Cloud Computing, 3*(2), 36–45. doi:10.1109/MCC.2016.28

Porter, M. E., & Heppelmann, J. E. (2017, March 17). How Smart, Connected Products Are Transforming Competition. *Harvard Business Review*. https://hbr.org/2014/11/how-smart-connected-products-are-transforming-competition

PR. (2022). *Artificial Intelligence in Transportation Market Size, Report 2030* [Independent Research Agency]. Precedence Research. https://www.precedenceresearch.com/artificial-intelligence-in-transportation-market

Prakash GiriO.ShahiP. B.BhaumikA.PoddarS. (2022). *A Bibliometric Analysis on Road Traffic Safety, 2009 to 2022.* https://ssrn.com/abstract=4148189

Premkumar, G., & Roberts, M. (1999). Adoption of new information technologies in rural small businesses. *Omega*, *27*(4), 467–484. doi:10.1016/S0305-0483(98)00071-1

PRG. (2022). *Peerless Media Custom Reports Supply Chain Software Page 21*. PRG. https://bt.e-ditionsbyfry.com/publication/?i=562391&p=21&view=issueViewer&pp=1

Puhovichova, D., and Jan, N. (2020). *Changes of human resource management in the context of impact of the fourth industrial revolution. 141*(3), 138–141.

PwC. (2017). *3D Printing comes of age in US industrial manufacturing*. PwC. https://www.pwc.com/us/en/industrial-products/publications/assets/pwc-next-manufacturing-3d-printing-comes-of-age.pdf

PwC. (2018). *Industry 4.0: Global digital operations study 2018*. PwC. https://www.pwc.com/gx/en/industries/industry-4-0.html

PwC. (2019). *Partner, PwC Strategy& Germany*. PwC. https://www.strategyand.pwc.com/gx/en/insights/2017/the-future-spare-parts-3d/the-future-of-spare-parts-is-3d.pdf

PwC. (2020). *PwC's Global Artificial Intelligence Study: Sizing the prize*. PwC. https://www.pwc.com/gx/en/issues/data-and-analytics/publications/artificial-intelligence-study.html

Racheal. (2020). Cover Story: IR4.0 in Malaysia: The challenges. *The Edge Markets*. https://www.theedgemarkets.com/article/cover-story-ir40-malaysia-challenges

Rada, M. (2018, January 21). Industry 5.0 definition. *Medium*. https://michael- rada.medium.com/industry-5-0-definition-6a2f9922dc48

Radnor, Z. J., & Barnes, D. (2007). Historical analysis of performance measurement and management in operations management. *International Journal of Productivity and Performance Management*, *56*(5/6), 384–396. doi:10.1108/17410400710757105

Radoglou Grammatikis, P. I., Sarigiannidis, P. G., & Moscholios, I. D. (2019). Securing the Internet of Things: Challenges, threats and solutions. In *Internet of Things (Netherlands)* (*Vol. 5*, pp. 41–70). Elsevier B.V. doi:10.1016/j.iot.2018.11.003

Rafique, M., Asim, M., and Manzoor, S. (2021). *Human Resource Management in Industrial Revolution 4 . O. 5*(I), 564–580.

Raj, A., Dwivedi, G., Sharma, A., Lopes de Sousa Jabbour, A. B., & Rajak, S. (2020). Barriers to the adoption of industry 4.0 technologies in the manufacturing sector: An inter-country comparative perspective. *International Journal of Production Economics*, *224*(1), 107546. doi:10.1016/j.ijpe.2019.107546

Rajagopal, A. (2019, February 7). *Cyber Attacks Top List Of Risks Impacting Supply Chain*. Cyber Security Hub. https://www.cshub.com/attacks/articles/cyber-attacks-top-list-of-risks-impacting-supply-chain

Ramaciotti, L., & Rizzo, U. (2015). The determinants of academic spin-off creation by Italian universities. *R & D Management*, *45*(5), 501–514. doi:10.1111/radm.12105

Rashid, A., & Tjahjono, B. (2016). Achieving manufacturing excellence through the integration of enterprise systems and simulation. *Production Planning and Control*, *27*(10), 837–852. doi:10.1080/09537287.2016.1143132

Rauch, E., Linder, C., & Dallasega, P. (2020). Anthropocentric perspective of production before and within Industry 4.0. *Computers & Industrial Engineering*, *139*, 105644. doi:10.1016/j.cie.2019.01.018

Razzaq, M. A., Gill, S. H., Qureshi, M. A., & Ullah, S. (2017). Security issues in the Internet of Things (IoT): A comprehensive study. *International Journal of Advanced Computer Science and Applications*, *8*(6).

Rehman, S. U., Khan, I. U., & Moiz, M. -Ur-Rehman, A., & Hasan, S. (2016). Security and privacy issues in IoT. In *International Journal of Communication Networks and Information Security*. https://www.researchgate.net/publication/313574376

Rejeb, A., Rejeb, K., & Zailani, S. (2021). Big data for sustainable agri-food supply chains: A review and future research perspectives. Journal of Data. *Information & Management*, *3*(3), 167–182. doi:10.100742488-021-00045-3

Remondino, M. (2020). Augmented reality in logistics: Qualitative analysis for a managerial perspective. *International Journal of Logistics Systems and Management*, *36*(1), 1–15. https://doi.org/10.1504/IJLSM.2020.107218

Rezaee, Z. (2018). Supply chain management and business sustainability synergy: A theoretical and integrated perspective. *Sustainability*, *10*(1), 275.

Rhaiem, K., & Amara, N. (2021). Learning from innovation failures: A systematic review of the literature and research agenda. *Review of Managerial Science*, *15*(2), 189–234. doi:10.100711846-019-00339-2

Richard, J. (2010). *Network Nation: Inventing American Telecommunications*. Belknap Press of Harvard University Press.

Ridaryanto, R. & Kartono, A. M. S. (2015). E3S Web of Conferences. *International Journal of Advanced Trends in Computer Science and Engineering*. *4*(2), 15–21.

Rimol, M. (2022). Infrastructure Automation and Predictions for 2022. *Gartner*. https://www.gartner.com/en/articles/4-predictions-for-i-o-leaders-on-the-path-to-digital-infrastructure

Rodríguez-Gutiérrez, M. J., Moreno, P., & Tejada, P. (2015). Entrepreneurial orientation and performance of SMEs in the services industry. *Journal of Organizational Change Management*, *28*(2), 194–212. doi:10.1108/JOCM-01-2015-0020

Rodríguez, M. Á., Alemany, M. M. E., Boza, A., Cuenca, L., & Ortiz, Á. (2020). Artificial Intelligence in Supply Chain Operations Planning: Collaboration and Digital Perspectives. *Boosting Collaborative Networks*, *4*(0), 365–378. doi:10.1007/978-3-030-62412-5_30

Rogers, E. (2003). *Diffusions of Innovations* (5th ed.). Free Press.

Rondeli. (2003). *International Relations*. Nekeri.

Rossi, B. (2018). Manufacturing Gets Personal in Industry 5.0. *Reconteur*. . https:// www.raconteur.net/technology/manufacturing-gets-personal-industry-5-0

Rosson, P. (2004 in press). The internet and SME exporting: Canadian success stories. In H. Etemad (Ed.), *International Entrepreneurship in Small and Medium Size Enterprises: Orientation, Environment, and Strategy*. Edward Elgar Publishing.

Rugman, A.M. & Verbeke, A. (2004). A Perspective on Regional and Global Strategies of Multinational Enterprises. *Journal of International Business Studies, 35*.

Rüßmann, M., Lorenz, M., Gerbert, P., Waldner, M., Justus, J., Engel, P., & Harnisch, M. (2015). Industry 4.0: The future of productivity and growth in manufacturing industries. *Boston consulting group, 9*(1), 54-89.

Rüßmann, M., Lorenz, M., Gerbert, P., Waldner, M., Justus, J., Engel, P., & Harnisch, M. (2015). *Industry 4.0: The Future of Productivity and Growth in Manufacturing Industries*. Inovasyon. https://inovasyon.org/images/Haberler/bcgperspectives_Industry40_2015.pdf

Rüßmann, M., Lorenz, M., Gerbert, P., Waldner, M., Justus, J., Engel, P., & Harnisch, M. J. (2016). *Industry 4. 0: The Future of Productivity and Growth in Manufacturing Industries April 09*. https://www.semanticscholar.org/paper/Industry-4-.-0-%3A-The-Future-of-Productivity-and-in-R%C3%BC%C3%9Fmann-Lorenz/42b15ae5e1aa17638fac89b026680d9361fa7c7a

Ryan, Y., Khoo-Lattimore, C., & Potter, L. (2021). VR the world: Experimenting with emotion and presence for tourism marketing. *Journal of Hospitality and Tourism Management*, 160-171.

Sachin, N., & Rajesh, R. (2022). An empirical study of supply chain sustainability with financial performances of Indian firms. *Environment, Development and Sustainability, 24*(5), 6577–6601.

Sadiku-Dushi, N., Dana, L.-P., & Ramadani, V. (2019). Entrepreneurial marketing dimensions and SMEs performance. *Journal of Business Research, 100*, 86–99. doi:10.1016/j.jbusres.2019.03.025

Safari, A., & Saleh, A. S. (2020). Key determinants of SMEs' export performance: A resource-based view and contingency theory approach using potential mediators. *Journal of Business and Industrial Marketing, 35*(4), 635–654. doi:10.1108/JBIM-11-2018-0324

Sagi, V., & Gokarn, S. (2022). Determinants of reduction of food loss and waste in Indian agri-food supply chains for ensuring food security: A multi-stakeholder perspective. *Waste Management & Research: The Journal for a Sustainable Circular Economy*, 0734242X2211264. doi:10.1177/0734242X221126421

Sahoo, S., & Lo, C.-Y. (2022). Smart manufacturing powered by recent technological advancements: A review. *Journal of Manufacturing Systems, 64*, 236–250. doi:10.1016/j.jmsy.2022.06.008

Saiedi, E., Broström, A., & Ruiz, F. (2021). Global drivers of cryptocurrency infrastructure adoption. *Small Business Economics, 57*(1), 353–406. doi:10.100711187-019-00309-8

Saini, A., & Bhalla, R. (2022). Artificial Intelligence and Automation: Transforming the Hospitality or threat to human touch. Handbook of Research on Innovative Management Using AI in Industry 5.0

Samiee, S. (1998). Exporting and the internet: A conceptual perspective. *International Marketing Review, 15*(5), 413–426. doi:10.1108/02651339810236452

Samiullah, S., Sami, A., & Ahmad, T. (2021). Entrepreneurial Ecosystem and Performance of SMEs in Pakistan. *International Journal of Economics and Business Administration, IX*(2), 192–204. doi:10.35808/ijeba/697

Saniuk, S., Grabowska, S., & Straka, M. (2022). Identification of Social and Economic Expectations: Contextual Reasons for the Transformation Process of Industry 4.0 into the Industry 5.0 Concept. *Sustainability, 14*(3), 1391. doi:10.3390u14031391

Saptono, A., Wibowo, A., Narmaditya, B. S., Karyaningsih, R. P. D., & Yanto, H. (2020). Does entrepreneurial education matter for Indonesian students' entrepreneurial preparation: The mediating role of entrepreneurial mindset and knowledge. *Cogent Education, 7*(1), 1836728. doi:10.1080/2331186X.2020.1836728

Sas, C., & Khairuddin, I. E. (2015). Exploring trust in bitcoin technology: A framework for HCI research. *OzCHI 2015: Being Human - Conference Proceedings*, (pp. 338–342). 10.1145/2838739.2838821

Sayem, A., Biswas, P. K., Khan, M. M. A., Romoli, L., & Dalle Mura, M. (2022). Critical Barriers to Industry 4.0 Adoption in Manufacturing Organizations and Their Mitigation Strategies. *Journal of Manufacturing and Materials Processing, 6*(6), 136. doi:10.3390/jmmp6060136

Schuetz, S., & Venkatesh, V. (2020). Blockchain, adoption, and financial inclusion in India: Research opportunities. *International Journal of Information Management, 52*, 101936. doi:10.1016/j.ijinfomgt.2019.04.009

Schuh, G., Anderl, R., Gausemeier, J., ten Hompel, M., & Wahlster, W. (2017). *Industrie 4.0 maturity index. Managing the digital transformation of companies*. Herbert Utz.

Sean O'Kane. (2019, August 1). *Tesla hit with another lawsuit over a fatal Autopilot crash.*

Sebora, T. C., Lee, S. M., & Sukasame, N. (2009). Critical success factors for e-commerce entrepreneurship: An empirical study of Thailand. *Small Business Economics, 32*(3), 303–316. doi:10.100711187-007-9091-9

Secinaro, S., Brescia, V., Calandra, D., & Biancone, P. (2020a). Employing bibliometric analysis to identify suitable business models for electric cars. In *Journal of Cleaner Production* (Vol. 264). Elsevier Ltd., doi:10.1016/j.jclepro.2020.121503

Sedrati, A., Abdellatif, M., & Aafaf, O. (2022). IoT Governance: A state of the Art and a Comparative analysis. *2022 13th International Conference on Information and Communication Systems (ICICS)* (pp. 76-81). IEEE.

Sen, R., Asher, M. G., & Rajan, R. S. (2004). ASEAN-India Economic Relations: Current Status and Future Prospects. *Economic and Political Weekly*, *39*(29), 3297–3308.

Shahzad, F., Xiu, G. Y., Wang, J., & Shahbaz, M. (2018). An empirical investigation on the adoption of cryptocurrencies among the people of mainland China. *Technology in Society*, *55*, 33–40. doi:10.1016/j.techsoc.2018.05.006

Shamayleh, A., Mahmoud, A., & Jumana, F. (2020). IoT based predictive maintenance management of medical equipment. *Journal of Medical Systems*, *44*(4), 1–12. doi:10.100710916-020-1534-8 PMID:32078712

Sharma, C., & Gondhi, N. K. (2018). Communication protocol stack for constrained IoT systems. *2018 3rd International Conference On Internet of Things: Smart Innovation and Usages (IoT-SIU)* (pp. 1-6). IEEE.

Sharma, A., & Singh, B. J. (2020). Evolution of Industrial Revolutions: A Review. *International Journal of Innovative Technology and Exploring Engineering*, *9*(11), 66–73. doi:10.35940/ijitee.I7144.0991120

Shengelia, T. (2008). *Basics of Business Administration.* Georgian Technical University.

Shepherd, D. A., & Krueger, N. F. (2002). An Intentions–Based Model of Entrepreneurial Teams' Social Cognition*. *Entrepreneurship Theory and Practice*, *27*(2), 167–185. doi:10.1111/1540-8520.00005

Shiller Robert, J. (2019). Narratives about Technology-Induced Job Degradations Then and Now. *NBER Working Paper*.

Shouran, Z., Ashari, A., & Priyambodo, T. (2019). Internet of things (IoT) of smart home: Privacy and security. *International Journal of Computers and Applications*, *182*(39), 3–8.

Shwetzer Herrera, C., Maritz, A., & Nguyen, Q. (2021). *Entrepreneurial ecosystems: A holistic and dynamic approach.* doi:10.26181/600506b67b4d5

Sicari, S., Rizzardi, A., Grieco, L. A., & Coen-Porisini, A. (2015). Security, privacy and trust in Internet of Things: The road ahead. *Computer Networks*, *76*, 146–164.

Sikdar, C., & Nag, B. (2011). Impact of India-ASEAN Free Trade Agreement: A Cross Country Analysis Using Applied General Equilibrium Modeling. *Asia Pacific Research and Network on Trade, Working Paper Series, No. 107.*

Sila, I. (2013). Factors affecting the adoption of B2B e-commerce technologies. *Electronic Commerce Research*, *13*(2), 199–236. doi:10.100710660-013-9110-7

Silk, L. (1993). Dangers of Slow Growth. *Foreign Affairs*, *72*.

Simons, R. (2013). *The Entrepreneurial Gap: How Managers Adjust Span of Accountability and Span of Control to Implement Business Strategy* (SSRN Scholarly Paper No. 2280355). Social Science Research Network. doi:10.2139/ssrn.2280355

Sin, K. Y., Osman, A., Salahuddin, S. N., Abdullah, S., Lim, Y. J., & Sim, C. L. (2016). Relative advantage and competitive pressure towards implementation of e-commerce: Overview of small and medium enterprises (SMEs). *Procedia Economics and Finance*, *35*, 434–443. doi:10.1016/S2212-5671(16)00054-X

Siqin, T., Choi, T.-M., Chung, S.-H., & Wen, X. (2022). Platform operations in the industry 4.0 era: Recent advances and the 3As framework. *IEEE Transactions on Engineering Management*, 1–18. doi:10.1109/TEM.2021.3138745

Sivarajah, U., Irani, Z., Gupta, S., & Mahroof, K. (2020). Role of big data and social media analytics for business to business sustainability: A participatory web context. *Industrial Marketing Management*, *86*, 163–179. doi:10.1016/j.indmarman.2019.04.005

Slack, N., Jones, A. B., & Burgess, N. (2022). *SLACK: operations management* (10th ed.). Pearson Education Limited.

Sobin, C. C. (2020). A survey on architecture, protocols and challenges in IoT. *Wireless Personal Communications*, *112*(3), 1383–1429. doi:10.100711277-020-07108-5

Soini, E., & Veseli, L. (2011). Factors Influencing Smes Growth In Kosovo. *International Business Management*, 76.

Soliman, K. S., & Janz, B. D. (2004). An exploratory study to identify the critical factors affecting the decision to establish Internet-based interorganizational information systems. *Information & Management*, *41*(6), 697–706. doi:10.1016/j.im.2003.06.001

Sonar, H., Khanzode, V., & Akarte, M. (2022). Additive Manufacturing Enabled Supply Chain Management: A Review and Research Directions. *Vision (Basel)*, *26*(2), 147–162. https://doi.org/10.1177/09722629221087308

Song, Q., Zhang, Y., Wang, B., & Chen, Y. (2022). Inter-BIN: Interaction-based Cross-architecture IoT Binary Similarity Comparison. *IEEE Internet of Things Journal*, *9*(20), 20018–20033. doi:10.1109/JIOT.2022.3170927

Song, X., Cong, Y., Song, Y., Chen, Y., & Liang, P. (2021). A bearing fault diagnosis model based on CNN with wide convolution kernels. *Journal of Ambient Intelligence and Humanized Computing*. doi:10.100712652-021-03177-x

Sony, M. (2020). Pros and cons of implementing Industry 4.0 for the organizations: a review and synthesis of evidence. *Production & Manufacturing Research*, *8*(1), 244–272. Tandfonline. doi:10.1080/21693277.2020.1781705

Sony, M., & Naik, S. (2019a). Key ingredients for evaluating Industry 4.0 readiness for organizations: A literature review. *Benchmarking*, *27*(7), 2213–2232. doi:10.1108/BIJ-09-2018-0284

Sookhak, M., Tang, H., He, Y., & Yu, F. R. (2018). Security and privacy of smart cities: A survey, research issues and challenges. *IEEE Communications Surveys and Tutorials*, *21*(2), 1718–1743.

Souiden, N., Ladhari, R., & Chaouali, W. (2021). Mobile banking adoption: A systematic review. *International Journal of Bank Marketing*, *39*(2), 214–241. doi:10.1108/IJBM-04-2020-0182

Souitaris, V., Zerbinati, S., & Al-Laham, A. (2007). Do entrepreneurship programmes raise entrepreneurial intention of science and engineering students? The effect of learning, inspiration and resources. *Journal of Business Venturing*, *22*(4), 566–591. doi:10.1016/j.jbusvent.2006.05.002

Sousa, A., Calçada, E., Rodrigues, P., & Pinto Borges, A. (2022). Cryptocurrency adoption: A systematic literature review and bibliometric analysis. *EuroMed Journal of Business*, *17*(3), 374–390. doi:10.1108/EMJB-01-2022-0003

Sousa, C. M., Martínez-López, F. J., & Coelho, F. (2008). The determinants of export performance: A review of the research in the literature between 1998 and 2005. *International Journal of Management Reviews*, *10*(4), 343–374. doi:10.1111/j.1468-2370.2008.00232.x

Spanaki, K., Karafili, E., & Despoudi, S. (2021). AI applications of data sharing in agriculture 4.0: A framework for role-based data access control. *International Journal of Information Management*, *59*, 102350. doi:10.1016/j.ijinfomgt.2021.102350

Stam, E. (2014). *The Dutch Entrepreneurial Ecosystem* (SSRN Scholarly Paper No. 2473475). Social Science Research Network. doi:10.2139/ssrn.2473475

Star, T. (2019). Malaysia falls behind in IR4.0 migration. *NST*. https://www.nst.com.my/news/%20nation/2019/08/514242/%20malaysia-falls-behind-ir40-migration

Statista. (2020a). *IoT: Supply chain management benefits by industry UK 2015-2020*. Statista. https://www.statista.com/statistics/608357/iot-supply-chain-management-efficiency-benefits-uk/

Statista. (2020b). *Sectors most disrupted by XR 2021*. Statista. https://www.statista.com/statistics/1185060/sectors-disrupted-immersive-technology-xr-ar-vr-mr/

Statista. (2022). *Fast fashion in Europe - statistics & facts*. Statista. https://www.statista.com/topics/6088/fast-fashion-in-europe/

Statista. (2022). *Number of Internet of Things (IoT) connected devices worldwide from 2019 to 2030*. Statista. https://www.statista.com/statistics/1183457/iot-connected-devices-worldwide/

Steinmetz, F., von Meduna, M., Ante, L., & Fiedler, I. (2021). *Ownership, uses and perceptions of cryptocurrency: Results from a population survey*.

Stewart, R., & Niero, M. (2018). Circular economy in corporate sustainability strategies: A review of corporate sustainability reports in the fast-moving consumer goods sector. *Business Strategy and the Environment*, *27*(7), 1005–1022. https://doi.org/10.1002/bse.2048

Stjepić, A.-M., Pejić Bach, M., & Bosilj Vukšić, V. (2021). Exploring Risks in the Adoption of Business Intelligence in SMEs Using the TOE Framework. *Journal of Risk and Financial Management*, *14*(2), 58. doi:10.3390/jrfm14020058

Stokes, D. (2000). Putting Entrepreneurship into Marketing: The Processes of Entrepreneurial Marketing. *Journal of Research in Marketing and Entrepreneurship*, *2*(1), 1–16. doi:10.1108/14715200080001536

Strange, S. (1987). The persistent myth of lost hegemony. *International Organization*, *14*.

Stranieri, S., Orsi, L., Banterle, A., & Ricci, E. C. (2019). Sustainable development and supply chain coordination: The impact of corporate social responsibility rules in the European Union food industry. *Corporate Social Responsibility and Environmental Management*, *26*(2), 481–491.

Sundarakani, B., Abdul Razzak, H., & Manikandan, S. (2018). Creating a competitive advantage in the global flight catering supply chain: A case study using SCOR model. *International Journal of Logistics Research and Applications*, *21*(5), 481–501. doi:10.1080/13675567.2018.1448767

Sundblad, W. (2018, September 11). Human-technology symbiosis in manufacturing: Changing the discussion about automation and workforce. *Forbes*. https://www.forbes.com/sites/willemsundbladeurope/2018/09/11/human-technology-symbiosis-in-manufacturing-changing-the-discussion-about-automation-and-workforce/?sh=7f42454b2176

Sung, T. K. (2006). E-commerce critical success factors: East vs. West. *Technological Forecasting and Social Change*, *73*(9), 1161–1177. doi:10.1016/j.techfore.2004.09.002

Supply Chain Collaborative Robot Market Report. (2022). Global Market Estimates. https://www.globalmarketestimates.com/market-report/supply-chain-collaborative-robots-market-3427

Sussan, F., & Acs, Z. J. (2017). The digital entrepreneurial ecosystem. *Small Business Economics*, *49*(1), 55–73. doi:10.100711187-017-9867-5

Suwannarat, P. (2016). The study of export intermediary performance determinants. *Multinational Business Review*, *24*(2), 123–143. doi:10.1108/MBR-10-2015-0050

Swan, D., Lund, S., & Alicke, K. (2020). *Is your supply chain risk blind—Or risk resilient?* McKinsey. https://www.mckinsey.com/capabilities/operations/our-insights/is-your-supply-chain-risk-blind-or-risk-resilient

Syed, A. S., Sierra-Sosa, D., Kumar, A., & Elmaghraby, A. (2021). Iot in smart cities: A survey of technologies, practices and challenges. *Smart Cities, 4*(2), 429–475. doi:10.3390/smartcities4020024

Syngenta. (2021). *Syngenta Crop Protection and Insilico Medicine to harness artificial intelligence to transform sustainable product innovation.* Syngenta. https://www.syngenta.com/en/company/media/syngenta-news/year/2021/syngenta-crop-protection-and-insilico-medicine-harness

Szabo, R. Z., Vuksanović Herceg, I., Hanák, R., Hortovanyi, L., Romanová, A., Mocan, M., & Djuričin, D. (2020). Industry 4.0 Implementation in B2B Companies: Cross-Country Empirical Evidence on Digital Transformation in the CEE Region. *Sustainability, 12*(22), 9538. doi:10.3390u12229538

Szerb, L., Lafuente, E., Horváth, K., & Páger, B. (2019). The relevance of quantity and quality entrepreneurship for regional performance: The moderating role of the entrepreneurial ecosystem. *Regional Studies, 53*(9), 1308–1320. doi:10.1080/00343404.2018.1510481

Tabim, V. M., Ayala, N. F., & Frank, A. G. (2021). Implementing Vertical Integration in the Industry 4.0 Journey: Which Factors Influence the Process of Information Systems Adoption? *Information Systems Frontiers*, (0123456789). doi:10.100710796-021-10220-x PMID:34776762

Tajpour, M., & Hosseini, E. (2021). Entrepreneurial Intention and the Performance of Digital Startups. *The Mediating Role of Social Media., 13*(7), 2456–9011. doi:10.31620/JCCC.06.21/02

Tambe, P., Cappelli, P., & Yakubovich, V. (2019). Artificial intelligence in human resources management: Challenges and a path forward. *California Management Review, 61*(4), 15–42. doi:10.1177/0008125619867910

Tarigan, Z., Jiputra, J., & Siagian, H. (2021). The effect of supply chain practices on retailer performance with information technology as moderating variable. *International Journal of Data and Network Science, 5*(1), 47–54.

Tavitiyaman, P., Qu, H., Wing-sze, L. T., & Chin-wah, R. L. (2021). The influence of smart tourism applications on perceived destination image and behavioral intention: The moderating role of information search behaviour. *Journal of Hospitality and Tourism Management, 46*, 476–487. doi:10.1016/j.jhtm.2021.02.003

Tavitiyaman, P., Zhang, X., & Tsang, W. Y. (2020, August). How Tourists Perceive the Usefulness of Technology Adoption in Hotels: Interaction Effect of Past Experience and Education Level. *Journal of China Tourism Research.*

Tawalbeh, L., Muheidat, F., Tawalbeh, M., & Quwaider, M. (2020). IoT privacy and security: Challenges and solutions. *Applied Sciences (Switzerland), 10*(12). doi:10.3390/APP10124102

Tawalbeh, L. A., Muheidat, F., Tawalbeh, M., & Quwaider, M. (2020). IoT Privacy and security: Challenges and solutions. *Applied Sciences (Basel, Switzerland), 10*(12), 4102. doi:10.3390/app10124102

Tawalbeh, L., Muheidat, F., Tawalbeh, M., & Quwaider, M. (2020). IoT Privacy and Security: Challenges and Solutions. *Applied Sciences (Basel, Switzerland), 10*(12), 12. https://doi.org/10.3390/app10124102

Teh, & Kee. (2019). The Readiness of Small and Medium Enterprises for the Industrial Revolution 4.0. *Global J. Bus. Soc. Sci. Review, 7*(4), 217-223.

Teo, E. G. S. (2015). Emergence, Growth, and Sustainability of Bitcoin: The Network Economics Perspective. In Handbook of Digital Currency: Bitcoin, Innovation, Financial Instruments, and Big Data (pp. 191–200). Elsevier Inc. doi:10.1016/B978-0-12-802117-0.00009-6

Teo, T. S., Lin, S., & Lai, K. (2009). Adopters and non-adopters of e-procurement in Singapore: An empirical study. *Omega*, *37*(5), 972–987. doi:10.1016/j.omega.2008.11.001

Teo, T. S., Tan, M., & Buk, W. K. (1997). A contingency model of Internet adoption in Singapore. *International Journal of Electronic Commerce*, *2*(2), 95–118. doi:10.1080/10864415.1997.11518310

Thales. (2022). 07 24). *IoT Security* [Retrieved from thalesgroup.com: https://www.thalesgroup.com/en/markets/digital-identity-and-security/iot/magazine/internet-threats]. *Issues (Chicago, Ill.)*, *2022*.

The Economist (2014). The G20 e-Trade Readiness Index. *The Economist.* https://eiuperspectives.economist.com/economic-development/g20-e-trade-readiness-index/white-paper/g20-e-trade-readiness-index

The Guardian. (2022). EU wants to force fashion firms to make clothes more durable. *The Guardian.* https://www.theguardian.com/environment/2022/mar/30/eu-wants-to-force-fashion-firms-to-make-clothes-more-durable-and-recyclable

The Guardian. (2022). Racism is at the heart of fast fashion – it's time for change. *The Guardian.* https://www.theguardian.com/global-development/2020/jun/11/racism-is-at-the-heart-of-fast-fashion-its-time-for-change

The world bank. (2021, July 1). *Digital Agricultural Profiles for Argentina, Kenya, Turkey, and Vietnam.* World Bank. https://www.worldbank.org/en/topic/agriculture/publication/digital-agricultural-profiles-for-argentina-kenya-turkey-and-viet-nam

Theodore, S. H. (1989). *The birth of a new Europe: state and society in the nineteenth century.* University of North Carolina Press.

Theodosiou, M., & Katsikea, E. (2012). Antecedents and performance of electronic business adoption in the hotel industry. *European Journal of Marketing*, *46*(1/2), 258–283. doi:10.1108/03090561211189329

Thoben, K. D., Wiesner, S., & Wuest, T. (2017). "Industrie 4.0" and smart manufacturing-a review of research issues and application examples. *International Journal of Automotive Technology*, *11*(1), 4–16. doi:10.20965/ijat.2017.p0004

Tiwari, S., Bahuguna, P. C., & Walker, J. (2022). Industry 5.0: A macroperspective approach. In Handbook of Research on Innovative Management Using AI in Industry 5.0 (pp. 59-73). IGI Global.

Tornatzky, L. G., Fleischer, M., & Chakrabarti, A. K. (1990). *Processes of technological innovation.* Lexington books.

Torrens, E. W., Amal, M., & Tontini, G. (2014). Determinants of export performance of small and medium-sized manufacturing Brazilian enterprises from the perspective of resource-based view and Uppsala model. *Revista Brasileira de Gestão de Negócios-RBGN*, *16*(53), 511–539.

Treiblmaier, H., Leung, D., Kwok, A. O. J., & Tham, A. (2021). Cryptocurrency adoption in travel and tourism–an exploratory study of Asia Pacific travellers. *Current Issues in Tourism*, *24*(22), 3165–3181. doi:10.1080/13683500.2020.1863928

Trevelyan, R. (2008). Optimism, overconfidence and entrepreneurial activity. *Management Decision*, *46*(7), 986–1001. doi:10.1108/00251740810890177

Tsanidis, C., Nerantzaki, M., Karavasilis, G., Vrana, V., & Paschaloudis, D. (2015). Greek consumers and the use of Bitcoin. In The Business & Management Review, 6.

Tuomi, A., Tussyadiah, I., & Stienmetz, J. (2021). Applications and Implications of Service Robots in Hospitality. *Cornell Hospitality Quarterly*, *62*(2), 232–247

Tuomi, A., Tussyadiah, I., & Stienmetz, J. (2022). Applications and Implications of Service Robots in Hospitality. *Cornell Hospitality Quarterly 2021*, *62*(2), 232–247.

TWI. (2023). What is Industry 5.0? *TWI Global.* https://www.twi-global.com/technical-knowledge/faqs/industry-5-0#WhatisIndustry50

Tzafestas, S. G. (2018). Ethics and law in the internet of things world. In *Smart Cities*, *1*(1), 98–120). MDPI. doi:10.3390/smartcities1010006

Uddin, M. R., & Bose, T. K. (2013). Factors Affect the Success of SME in Bangladesh: Evidence from Khulna City. *Journal of Management and Sustainability*, *3*(3), 166. doi:10.5539/jms.v3n3p166

UNCTAD. (2022). Global foreign direct investment rebounded strongly in 2021, but the recovery is highly uneven. *UNCTAD.* https://unctad.org/news/global-foreign-direct-investment-rebounded-strongly-2021-recovery-highly-uneven

UNCTAD. (2022). Global Investment Trend Monitor, No. 40. *UNCTAD.* https://unctad.org/webflyer/global-investment-trend-monitor-no-40

UNCTAD. (2022). Global trade hits record high of $28.5 trillion in 2021, but likely to be subdued in 2022. *UNCTAD.* https://unctad.org/news/global-trade-hits-record-high-285-trillion-2021-likely-be-subdued-2022

UNEP. (2022). *Emissions Gap Report 2022.* UNEP. https://www.unep.org/resources/emissions-gap-report-2022

Van Eck, N., & Waltman, L. (2010). Software survey: VOSviewer, a computer program for bibliometric mapping. *Scientometricsc*, *84*(2), 523–538. doi:10.100711192-009-0146-3 PMID:20585380

Van Gelderen, M., Kautonen, T., & Fink, M. (2015). From entrepreneurial intentions to actions: Self-control and action-related doubt, fear, and aversion. *Journal of Business Venturing*, *30*(5), 655–673. doi:10.1016/j.jbusvent.2015.01.003

Van Vuuren, J. J., & Nieman, G. (1997). Entrepreneurship education and training: A prospective content model. *Unpublished Paper.*

van Vuuren, J., & Botha, M. (2010). The practical application of an entrepreneurial performance training model in South Africa. *Journal of Small Business and Enterprise Development*, *17*(4), 607–625. doi:10.1108/14626001011088750

Vanclay, J. K. (2007). On the robustness of the h-index. *Journal of the American Society for Information Science and Technology*, *58*(10), 1547–1550. doi:10.1002/asi.20616

Vantage Market. (2021). *Digital Agriculture Market Size USD 22.1 Billion by 2028.* Vantage Market Research. https://www.vantagemarketresearch.com/industry-report/digital-agriculture-market-1751

Varela, M. L. R., Araújo, A. F., Vieira, G. G., Manupati, V. K., & Manoj, K. (2017). Integrated framework based on critical success factors for e-Commerce. *Journal of Information Systems Engineering & Management*, *2*(1), 4. doi:10.20897/jisem.201704

Verma, Bhattacharya, P., Madhani, N., Trivedi, C., Bhushan, B., Tanwar, S., Sharma, G., Bokoro, P. N., & Sharma, R. (2022). Blockchain for Industry 5.0: Vision, Opportunities, Key Enablers, and Future Directions. *IEEE Access: Practical Innovations, Open Solutions*, *10*, 69160–69199. doi:10.1109/ACCESS.2022.3186892

Viviers, W., & Van Eldik, S. (2005). The measurement of export readiness of companies in South Africa. *Southern African Business Review*, *9*(2), 1–11.

Wagire, R., Rathore, A. P. S., & Jain, R. (2019). Analysis and synthesis of Industry 4.0 research landscape. *Journal of Manufacturing Technology Management*, *31*(1), 31–51. doi:10.1108/JMTM-10-2018-0349

Wang, X., Kumar, V., Kumari, A., & Kuzmin, E. (2022). Impact of Digital Technology on Supply Chain Efficiency in Manufacturing Industry. Springer. https://doi.org/10.1007/978-3-030-94617-3_25.

Wang, C., Teo, T. S., & Janssen, M. (2021). Public and private value creation using artificial intelligence: An empirical study of AI voice robot users in Chinese public sector. *International Journal of Information Management*, *61*, 102401. doi:10.1016/j.ijinfomgt.2021.102401

Wang, Z., Pham, T. L. H., Sun, K., Wang, B., Bui, Q., & Hashemizadeh, A. (2022). The moderating role of financial development in the renewable energy consumption-CO2 emissions linkage: The case study of Next-11 countries. *Energy*, *254*, 124386. doi:10.1016/j.energy.2022.124386

Wardynski, D. J. (2019, November 7). Different effects of technology on human interaction. *Brain Spire*. https://www.brainspire.com/blog/what-are-the-effects-of-technology-on-human-interaction

Wathanakom, N., Khlaisang, J., & Songkram, N. (2020). The study of the causal relationship between innovativeness and entrepreneurial intention among undergraduate students. *Journal of Innovation and Entrepreneurship*, *9*(1), 15. doi:10.118613731-020-00125-5

WEF. (2021). *This is how COVID-19 has disrupted global supply chains*. World Economic Forum. https://www.weforum.org/agenda/2021/10/this-is-the-state-of-supply-chain-disruptions/

Wennekers, S., & Thurik, R. (1999). Linking Entrepreneurship and Economic Growth. *Small Business Economics*, *13*(1), 27–56. doi:10.1023/A:1008063200484

White, R. (2011). *Railroaded: The Transcontinentals and the Making of Modern America*. W. W. Norton and Company.

Whysall, Z., Owtram, M., & Brittain, S. (2019). The new talent management challenges of Industry 4.0. *Journal of Management Development*, *38*(2), 118–129. doi:10.1108/JMD-06-2018-0181

Wilson, F., Kickul, J., & Marlino, D. (2007). Gender, Entrepreneurial Self–Efficacy, and Entrepreneurial Career Intentions: Implications for Entrepreneurship Education. *Entrepreneurship Theory and Practice*, *31*(3), 387–406. doi:10.1111/j.1540-6520.2007.00179.x

Wirtz, B. W., Weyerer, J. C., & Geyer, C. (2018). Artificial Intelligence and the Public Sector—Applications and Challenges. *International Journal of Public Administration*, *42*(7), 596–615. doi:10.1080/01900692.2018.1498103

Wolcott, K., Kamal, M., & Qureshi, S. (2008). Meeting the challenges of ICT adoption by micro-enterprises. *Journal of Enterprise Information Management*, *21*(6), 616–632. doi:10.1108/17410390810911212

Wong, L., & Hew, T. (2020). Time to seize the digital evolution: Adoption of blockchain in operations and supply chain management among Malaysian SMEs. *International Journal of Information Management*, *52*, 101997. doi:10.1016/j.ijinfomgt.2019.08.005

World development indicators (2020). Databank, World Bank.s https://databank.worldbank.org/data/source/world-development-indicators

World Economic Forum. (2018). The Future of Supply Chains: A Roadmap for the Fourth Industrial Revolution. WEF.

Wu, R., Ishfaq, K., Hussain, S., Asmi, F., Siddiquei, A. N., & Anwar, M. A. (2022). Investigating e-Retailers' Intentions to Adopt Cryptocurrency Considering the Mediation of Technostress and Technology Involvement. *Sustainability (Switzerland)*, *14*(2), 641. doi:10.3390u14020641

Wu, Y., & Zhou, Z. (2006). Changing bilateral trade between China and India. *Journal of Asian Economics*, *17*(3), 509–518. doi:10.1016/j.asieco.2006.04.007

Xie, L., Chen, Z., Wang, H., Zheng, C., & Jiang, J. (2020). Bibliometric and Visualized Analysis of Scientific Publications on Atlantoaxial Spine Surgery Based on Web of Science and VOSviewer. In *World Neurosurgery* (Vol. 137, pp. 435–442.e4). Elsevier Inc., doi:10.1016/j.wneu.2020.01.171

Xu, X., Rahman, F., Shakya, B., Vassilev, A., Forte, D., & Tehranipoor, M. (2019). Electronics Supply Chain Integrity Enabled by Blockchain. *ACM Transactions on Design Automation of Electronic Systems, 24*(3), 31:1-31:25. doi:10.1145/3315571

Xu, L. D., Xu, E. L., & Li, L. (2018). Industry 4.0: State of the art and future trends. *International Journal of Production Research, 56*(8), 2941–2962. doi:10.1080/00207543.2018.1444806

Xu, X., Lu, Y., Vogel-Heuser, B., & Wang, L. (2021). Industry 4.0 and Industry 5.0—Inception, conception and perception. *Journal of Manufacturing Systems, 61*(October), 530–535. doi:10.1016/j.jmsy.2021.10.006

Yadav, V. S., Singh, A. R., Raut, R. D., Kumar Mangla, S., Luthra, S., & Kumar, A. (2022). Exploring the application of Industry 4.0 technologies in the agricultural food supply chain: A systematic literature review. *Computers & Industrial Engineering, 108304*, 108304. doi:10.1016/j.cie.2022.108304

Yalcin, H., & Daim, T. U. (2022). Logistics, supply chain management and technology research: An analysis on the axis of technology mining. *Transportation Research Part E, Logistics and Transportation Review, 168*, 102943. https://doi.org/10.1016/j.tre.2022.102943

Yang, G. (2022). An Overview of Current Solutions for Privacy in the Internet of Things. *Frontiers in Artificial Intelligence, 5.*

Yang, Y., Wu, L., Yin, G., Li, L., & Zhao, H. (2017). A Survey on Security and Privacy Issues in Internet-of-Things. *IEEE Internet of Things Journal, 4*(5), 1250–1258. doi:10.1109/JIOT.2017.2694844

Yang, X. (2019). How perceived social distance and trust influence reciprocity expectations and eWOM sharing intention in social commerce. *Industrial Management & Data Systems, 119*(4), 867–880. doi:10.1108/IMDS-04-2018-0139

Ye, H., Sun, S. & Law, R. (2022). A Review of Robotic Applications in Hospitality and Tourism Research. *Journal of Sustainability.*

Yeh, C.-H., Lin, H.-H., Wang, Y.-M., Wang, Y.-S., & Lo, C.-W. (2021). Investigating the relationships between entrepreneurial education and self-efficacy and performance in the context of internet entrepreneurship. *International Journal of Management Education, 19*(3), 100565. doi:10.1016/j.ijme.2021.100565

Yelowitz, A., & Wilson, M. (2015). Characteristics of Bitcoin users: an analysis of Google search data. *Applied Economics Letters, 22*(13), 1030–1036. doi:10.1080/13504851.2014.995359

Yin, Y., Stecke, K. E., & Li, D. (2018). *The Evolution of Production Systems from Industry 2.0 through Industry 4.0. DBS Discussion Paper*. Series supported by the OMRON Foundation. DBS.

Yin, S., & Yu, Y. (2022). An adoption-implementation framework of digital green knowledge to improve the performance of digital green innovation practices for industry 5.0. *Journal of Cleaner Production, 363*, 132608. doi:10.1016/j.jclepro.2022.132608

Yunda, N.R. (2019). Dampak Revolusi Industri 4.0 dan Society 5.0 Mencipatakan Kesempatan Baru Bagi Indonesia [The Impact of the Industrial Revolution 4.0 and Society 5.0 Created New Opportunities for Indonesia]. *SERSC.*

Yuneline, M. H. (2019). Analysis of cryptocurrency's characteristics in four perspectives. *Journal of Asian Business and Economic Studies, 26*(2), 206–219. doi:10.1108/JABES-12-2018-0107

Yu, W., Jacobs, M., Chavez, R., & Yang, J. (2019). Dynamism, disruption orientation, and resilience in the supply chain and the impacts on financial performance A dynamic capabilities perspective. *International Journal of Production Economics*, *218*(1), 352–362.

Zaidan, A. A., & Zaidan, B. B. (2020). A review on intelligent process for smart home applications based on IoT: Coherent taxonomy, motivation, open challenges, and recommendations. *Artificial Intelligence Review*, *53*(1), 141–165. doi:10.100710462-018-9648-9

Zhang, F., Wang, H., Bai, Y., & Zhang, H. (2022). A Bibliometric Analysis of the Landscape of Problem-Based Learning Research (1981–2021). *Frontiers in Psychology*, *13*, 828390. Advance online publication. doi:10.3389/fpsyg.2022.828390 PMID:35369264

Zhang, J. Y., Pandya, J. K., McClements, D. J., Lu, J., & Kinchla, A. J. (2021). Advancements in 3D food printing: A comprehensive overview of properties and opportunities. *Critical Reviews in Food Science and Nutrition*, 1–18. doi:10.1080/10408398.2021.1878103 PMID:33533641

Zhao, J. (2022). Do economic crises cause trading in Bitcoin? *Review of Behavioral Finance*. doi:10.1108/RBF-02-2022-0048

Zhao, G., Liu, S., Wang, Y., Lopez, C., Zubairu, N., Chen, X., Xie, X., & Zhang, J. (2022). Modelling enablers for building agri-food supply chain resilience: Insights from a comparative analysis of Argentina and France. *Production Planning and Control*, 1–25. doi:10.1080/09537287.2022.2078246

Zheng, S., Apthorpe, N., Chetty, M., & Feamster, N. (2018). User perceptions of smart home IoT privacy. *Proceedings of the ACM on human-computer interaction, 2*(CSCW), (pp. 1-20). ACM. 10.1145/3274469

Zhou, K., Liu, T., & Zhou, L. (2015). Industry 4.0: Towards future industrial opportunities and challenges. *2015 12th International Conference on Fuzzy Systems and Knowledge Discovery (FSKD)*. FSKD. 10.1109/FSKD.2015.7382284

Zhuang, T., Qian, Q., Visscher, H. E., & Wu, W. (2019). The role of stakeholders and their participation network in decision-making of urban renewal in China: The case of Chongqing. *Cities (London, England)*, *92*(1), 47–58. doi:10.1016/j.cities.2019.03.014

Zhu, K., & Kraemer, K. L. (2002). E-commerce metrics for net-enhanced organizations: Assessing the value of e-commerce to firm performance in the manufacturing sector. *Information Systems Research*, *13*(3), 275–295. doi:10.1287/isre.13.3.275.82

Zhu, K., Kraemer, K., & Xu, S. (2003). Electronic business adoption by European firms: A cross-country assessment of the facilitators and inhibitors. *European Journal of Information Systems*, *12*(4), 251–268. doi:10.1057/palgrave.ejis.3000475

Zion Market Research. (2022, June 24). *At 4.68% CAGR, Global FMCG Packaging Market Size & Share to Surpass USD 955.6 Billion by 2028 | Industry Trends, Growth, Value, Opportunities, Statistics, Analysis & Forecast Report by Zion Market Research.* Yahoo Finance. https://finance.yahoo.com/news/4-68-cagr-global-fmcg-160000325.html

Župič, I. & Čater, T. (2015). *Bibliometric Methods in Management and Organization.* https://research.gold.ac.uk/id/eprint/26859/

About the Contributors

Sumesh S. Dadwal is a Senior Lecturer and Programme Leader at the University of Northumbria, London Campus, London, UK .; Email: sumesh.dadwal@northumbria.ac.uk. Dr. Dadwal has 20 years of experience in business academic research, teaching, e-Learning, quality assurances and in a wide range of business, tourism and Healthcare subjects. He is actively engaged in postgraduate and Ph.D. research supervision. His core areas include International Marketing & Globalisation, contemporary and technological trends in the marketing, Strategic & technological innovation Management. Besides this, he is also a freelance consultant (business analysis) for emerging markets and also Member of Advisory and Editorial Board of Academics at some journals of repute.

Pawan Kumar is working as a Professor in the Department of Marketing at Mittal School of Business, Lovely Professional University, Punjab, India. He has 15 years of experience in business academic research .His areas of interest in research include entrepreneurship, marketing, e-commerce, consumer behaviour, marketing research, etc. He is an avid researcher. He is active in Ph.D research supervision and has good number of publications in Q1 and Q2 Journals to his credit in various research papers published Scopus indexed journals namely: The TQM Journal from Emerald, Visions: Journal of Business Perspectives from Sage, International Journal of Business and Globalization, International Journal of Business Information Systems from Inderscience and other national/international journals of repute.

Rajesh Verma is Sr. Dean & Professor of Strategy at Mittal School of Business, LPU, Punjab. His research & teaching interests entails areas like Business Models, Market Orientation & Political Marketing. He is recipient of Junior Research Fellowship from University Grant Commission of India and other research grants from bodies like UK-India Education and Research Initiative (UKIERI); European Commission; and Department of Science & Technology (DST), Government of India. He is a Wiley Certified Design Thinking Practitioner and has conducted several training programmes on design thinking, selling skills, changing business models, brand building and customer orientation etc. for corporates like India Oil, Radington etc.

Gursimranjit Singh is working as an Assistant Professor in the Department of Humanities and Management, Dr. B.R. Ambedkar National Institute of Technology Jalandhar, Punjab, India. He received his Doctoral in Management from the I.K. Gujral Punjab Technical University, Kapurthala, Jalandhar, India. He has published several research articles in international journals of repute. He has also published several book chapters published with IGI Global and Taylor and Francis. Further, he has presented research papers in various international conferences.

Alpana Agarwal is an Assistant Professor at Symbiosis Centre for Management Studies, NOIDA, Uttar Pradesh. She has over 12 years of experience in teaching and research. She has several research publications to her credit with journals of repute. Her interest areas include human resource management, performance management, behavioural science, HR analytics, system analysis, etc.

Abdul Ali is a Lecturer of Operations and Supply Chain Management and the Programme Director of MA Logistics in Supply Chain Management at the University of Greenwich. He has a PhD in Supply Chain Management from the University of Bedfordshire. He was a full-time faculty member at the University of Northumbria-London Campus (QA) for around three years. Before that Dr Abdul was with the University of Bedfordshire where he was a Visiting Lecturer & a Researcher at the Business and Management Research Institute from. He was also a visiting Lecturer & Dissertation Supervisor with QA at the University of Ulster London Campus, London Metropolitan University & Roehampton University London. Abdul's primary research interests are in the areas of sustainability, green/environmental supply chain management & logistics, circular economy, supply chain collaboration, lean six sigma & industry 4.0 in supply chain management and Halal Logistics and Supply Chain Management as well. He published peer-reviewed journal articles & book chapters and presented his works at national and international refereed conferences. Abdul is also a reviewer of many prestigious journals. He is a Fellow of the UK Higher Education Academy (Advance HE) and a member of various professional bodies.

Abdul Ali is a Lecturer of Operations and Supply Chain Management and the Programme Director of MA Logistics in Supply Chain Management at the University of Greenwich. He has a PhD in Supply Chain Management from the University of Bedfordshire. He was a full-time faculty member at the University of Northumbria-London Campus (QA) for around three years. Before that Dr Abdul was with the University of Bedfordshire where he was a Visiting Lecturer & a Researcher at the Business and Management Research Institute from. He was also a visiting Lecturer & Dissertation Supervisor with QA at the University of Ulster London Campus, London Metropolitan University & Roehampton University London. Abdul's primary research interests are in the areas of sustainability, green/environmental supply chain management & logistics, circular economy, supply chain collaboration, lean six sigma & industry 4.0 in supply chain management and Halal Logistics and Supply Chain Management as well. He published peer-reviewed journal articles & book chapters and presented his works at national and international refereed conferences. Abdul is also a reviewer of many prestigious journals. He is a Fellow of the UK Higher Education Academy (Advance HE) and a member of various professional bodies.

Anil Angrish At Present: - Associate Professor in the Department of Pharmaceutical Management. In Past, I was Associate Dean (Student Affairs), NIPER S.A.S. Nagar and Member of almost Seventy (70) different Committees (of NIPER S.A.S. Nagar as well as other organizations such as National Pharmaceutical Pricing Authority/Department of Pharmaceuticals, Punjab Biotechnology Incubator, Punjab Technical University (Jalandhar), Confederation of Indian Industry, (Northern Region, Chandigarh) in last 20 years.

Hafiz Waqas Ahmed Ansari Ph.D. Scholar at Universiti Utara Malaysia. Field of interests are Green Marketing, Marketing 5.0, Consumer Behavior, IR 4.0.

Muhammad Waleed Butt Butt Aspiring researcher whose passionate about furthering research and exploring career opportunities in academia. In addition to research, reading and writing, I am usually exploring PhD opportunities. You may reach me at m.waleed710@gmail.com

Usman Javed Butt received a Bachelor of Computer Science (Hons) degree in 2003, MSc. Degree in Computer Networks and Systems Security from the University of Greenwich in 2010, and currently doing PhD in Cyber Security from Brunel University. He is a certified Ethical Hacker, Certified CISMP and Certified ISO27001 Practitioner. He is also trained in GCHQ CyberFirst initiative. Along with his academic experience, he also possesses the commercial experience and has worked as a Systems Administrator and Network Engineer. He is currently Associated Dean & Head of Department Computing with Northumbria University London and holds an External Examiner position for UK HEI. He has also authored several book chapters on Ransomware, Cyberwarfare and Smart Homes Security, and his current research interests include Game-based learning, cyber resilience, Role of AI in cybersecurity.

Ajay Chandel is working as an Assistant Professor at Mittal School of Business, Lovely Professional University, Punjab. He has 12 years of teaching experience. He has 12 years of teaching and research experience. He has published papers in SCOPUS, WOS and UGC listed Journals in areas like Social Media marketing, E-Commerce and Consumer Behaviour. He has published cases on SMEs and Social Entrepreneurship in The Case Centre, UK. He is also a reviewer of The Case Journal, Emerald Group Publishing and International Journal of Business and Globalisation, Inderscience. He has authored and developed MOOCs on Tourism and Hospitality Marketing under Epg-Pathshala- A gateway to all Post Graduate courses (an UGC-MHRD project under its National Mission on Education Through ICT (NME-ICT).

Manne Neelima Chaudhary, MBA, Assistant Professor is presently working as HOD, UG Department of Commerce, SCS, JAIN (Deemed to be University), Bangalore. Her area of specialization is Management and Finance. With more than 20 years of academic experience, she contributes extensively towards academic excellence and has published many research papers in national and international journals. She has been a part of organizing committee of national and international conferences. She has been presented with the Award of Excellence for achievement of excellence in enabling students to be Industry ready at the IMA-Wiley-Miles University Excellence Awards 2019.

Sonia Chawla Dr. Sonia received her Ph.D. from Guru Nanak Dev University, Amritsar in 2008. She is also a Fellow of Cost & Management Accountants of India. Her primary research interests are in the areas of Financial Economics, Portfolio Management, Fintech, Entrepreneurship, and Cost Accounting.

Aristeidis Davelis completed his B.Sc. in Computer Science with the Athens University of Economics and Business in Greece, and his M.Sc. in Web and Mobile Development with distinction, from the Northumbria University in the UK. He is a member of QAHE UK, a Fellow of Higher Education (FHEA) and works as a lecturer at Northumbria University and other academic institutions. Alongside his academic career, he has strong professional experience in ERP Systems Development, Web Engineering and Integrated Systems, areas in which he is actively engaged. He has also had extensive experience in IT Management roles in senior positions, as well as Operational & Strategic Business Administration. His research interests include Software Engineering, the Internet of Things, Machine Learning and emerging technologies.

Srinivas G, MCOM, Assistant Professor is presently working as Co-coordinator, UG Department of Commerce, SCS, JAIN (Deemed to be University), Bangalore. His area of specialization is Accounting & Taxation. With more than 13 years of academic experience, he contributes extensively towards academic excellence and has published many research papers in national and international journals. He has been a part of organizing committee of national and international conferences; he has Authored *Income Tax, Advanced Corporate Accounting, Business Taxation, Indirect Taxes*, for BCOM & BBA students from Kalyani Publishers.

Büşra Garip has been a research assistant at Sakarya University, Department of International Trade and Finance since 2016, completed her undergraduate education in business administration and graduate education in international trade. She is PhD candidate and expert in the fields of supply chain, logistics, international trade and e-commerce. The researcher also gave e-commerce courses in projects realized jointly by Sakarya Chamber of Commerce and Industry and Sakarya University.

Baba shaheer Gutappa Northumbria University London.

Bilal Hassan is an established academician in Computer Science and an active researcher in the field of Biometrics and Human Centred Computing. Currently, he is leading MSc Computing and Technology program at Northumbria University London campus, with an additional lecturing role. His academic and research experience spans over a decade in multiple universities of UK and across the world. Bilal is an author of more than 20 publications at several recognized venues in the field including journal articles, conference papers, book chapters, and technical reports for EU funded research projects. Bilal is also associated with several journals and conferences on computer vision and deep learning in different capacities like member of technical committees and reviewer. He is also member of different professional organization like IEEE, BMVA, ACM and IET. He is currently working towards following projects, i) ENGAGE (funded): Establishing continuous engagement in virtual classrooms, ii) SMS (submitted for funding): A multi-modality soft biometrics data grid using crowdsourced annotation for surveillance, iii) Smart Borders: Forming Transformation 3, under 2025 UK Border Strategy, and iv) HighCrowd: Privacy-enabled Covert Surveillance and analytics under GDPR and 2000 Act of the UK.

Arsalan Hussain has completed his PhD in Business Management from Universiti Utara Malaysia. He holds an M.Phil degree in Business Management from the Institute of Business Management (IoBM) and MBA from Quaid-i-Azam University, Islamabad. His research interests are in the areas of capital structure, financial performance, innovation, entrepreneurship, and corporate finance. He has published more than 15 articles in international peer-reviewed and indexed journals of Scopus and ISI. He has also presented research papers in International & National conferences. He has been the assistant manager at alshieba trading in the Sultanate of Oman. Currently, Dr Arsalan is engaged in teaching Business Management courses.

Shivali Sunil Kankekar has been a student of MSC GLOSCM at Northumbria University London.

Pooja Kansra is working as Professor of Economics in the Mittal School of Business, Lovely Professional University, Jalandhar. She has over 11 years of teaching experience and seven years of research experience. Her areas of interest include econometrics methods, microeconomics, macroeconomics, managerial economics, quantitative techniques and economics of health and education. She is a member of Indian Economic Association. Her research interests include health economics, insurance and service operation management. She is an avid researcher and presented papers in various national and international conferences. She has to her credit various research papers published in refereed national and international journals of repute.

Pawan Kumar is working as a Professor in the Department of Marketing at Mittal School of Business, Lovely Professional University, Punjab, India. He has 13 years of experience in teaching, research and administration. His areas of interest in research include contemporary issue in business, entrepreneurship, marketing, e-commerce, consumer behavior, marketing research, etc. He is an avid researcher and e has good number of publications in Q1 and Q2 Journals to his credit in various research papers published Scopus indexed journals namely: The TQM Journal from Emerald, Visions: Journal of Business Perspectives from Sage, International Journal of Business and Globalization, International Journal of Business Information Systems from Inderscience and other national/international journals of repute.

Rakesh Kumar Lecturer at Deen Dayal Upadhyaya College, University of Delhi, New Delhi.

M. Nirmala, an academic professional with more than 14 years of experience in academics and industry. She has vast experience in curriculum development and designed a range of learning interventions, including behavioural and leadership programmes for various universities and institutions. She has published research papers in reputed journals and presented research papers in various national and international conferences.

Muhammad Qasim Maqbool I am working as Assistant Professor in the department of management sciences at University of Okara. Recently I Completed One million Startup Research Grant Project which was granted by National Academy higher education commission Pakistan.

Poornima Mathur is an Associate Professor of Human Resource Management in International School of Informatics and Management (ISIM), Jaipur. She has more than 11 years of teaching experience and 2 years of industry experience. Her area of research includes strategic human resource management, competitive advantage, HR analytics and innovation. She has published numerous research articles in national and international journals.

Haji Mohammad Izzuddin Bin Haji Mohammed Jamil is a PhD Candidate in Management at School of Business and Economics, Universiti Brunei Darussalam, conducting research in the field of Entrepreneurship. He received his Bachelor's Degree in Business Administration (Hons) at Coventry University, United Kingdom, and Master's Degree in Management at Universiti Brunei Darussalam. Prior to academia, his industry experiences started when he first became a salesman and distributor, and has since worked in various professions including becoming a Tutor/Teacher, Website and Application

Developer, Business Administrative Officer and has experiences starting-up enterprises. His research areas include Entrepreneurship, Growth, MSMEs and Emerging Technologies. He is also a research assistant and has taught classes at Universiti Brunei Darussalam for Management, Accounting and Economics.

Vipin Nadda As a competent, conscientious, and motivated academic professional driven with well-organized team spirit and goal-oriented approach; I am currently serving as Senior Lecturer and Programme Manager (Tourism, hospitality, and Events) with University of Sunderland in London. A science graduate with MBA (Marketing), MTA (Tourism) and PhD (Tourism Management), I have more than twenty years of experience in academics and Industry. As an active researcher, I have authored and edited eight books, published more than thirty research articles, presented papers in various international conferences and published scores of book chapters. As an experienced academician, I have been Lecturing a variety of courses ranging from Sustainable tourism development, Service Marketing, International business environment to Service quality, International Tourism and Hospitality Management in the UK as well as overseas which echo my research interests as well. I am co-editor in chief for International Journal of Entrepreneurship, Management, Innovation and Development and have organised many international conferences.

Hafiz Nasir PhD Scholar.

Parth Harshad Patel has been a student of MSc GLOSCM at Northumbria university London.

Gemma Pendlebury received her M.S. (Distinction) in Cyber Security Technology from Northumbria University. An IT professional with extensive experience in the IT industry and digital transformation projects. Experienced in business process consulting, solutions architecture, implementation, project management, information security and governance. She is also certified in networking technology and project management. Her research interests include blockchain, ransomware and IoT.

Deepika Reddy Research Scholar at Lovely Professional University Punjab. Deepika has a teaching experience of over 20 years in the field of education. Presently she is a Senior Lecturer at the Institute of Hotel Management, Mumbai.

Anguselvam Sekaran has completed his MSc in Global Logistics Operations and Supply chain management from Northumbria University London.

Rahul Sharma is an educator specialising in consultation of Business Management. He has completed his PhD in the area of Marketing. With more than 14 years of academic career producing learning opportunities for advanced level postgraduate courses, he is recognised for teaching excellence based on research fundamentals. He is currently working as a Professor at the Mittal School of Business, Lovely Professional University. He has published papers in SCOPUS and UGC listed Journals in areas like Digital Marketing, Advertising and Consumer Behaviour.

Hakan Tunahan has been a professor at Sakarya University, Department of International Trade and Finance He is expert in the fields of supply chain, logistics, international trade, e-commerce and finance.

Diksha Verma She is Assistant Professor at Chandigarh Group of Colleges in Punjab State.

Sandeep K. Walia is presently working as Professor and Associate Dean in School of Hotel Management and Tourism at Lovely Professional University, Jalandhar, Punjab, India. He is an alumnus of Himachal Pradesh University Shimla and IGNOU, New Delhi. Dr. Sandeep is associated as Visiting Faculty to School of Tourism, Hospitality and Event Management, Universiti Utara Malaysia Kedah (A QS ranked University), Malaysia and Himalayan Institutes of Alternative Learning.

Index

www.ingramcontent.com/pod-product-compliance
Lightning Source LLC
LaVergne TN
LVHW062121300926
849161LV00010B/2513